ORACLE® 11*g*: PL/SQL PROGRAMMING

ORACLE® 11*g*: PL/SQL PROGRAMMING

Second Edition

Joan Casteel

Australia • Brazil • Japan • Korea • Mexico • Singapore • Spain • United Kingdom • United States

COURSE TECHNOLOGY
CENGAGE Learning

Oracle® 11*g*: PL/SQL Programming, Second Edition, International Edition
by Joan Casteel

Editor-in-Chief: Joe Sabatino

Senior Acquisitions Editor: Charles McCormick, Jr.

Senior Product Manager: Kate Mason

Development Editor: Lisa M. Lord

Editorial Assistant: Anne Merrill

Media Editor: Chris Valentine

Manufacturing Coordinator: Julio Esperas

Sr. Brand Manager: Robin LeFevre

Market Development Manager: Jon Monahan

Marketing Coordinator: Mike Saver

Art and Cover Direction, Production Management, and Composition: PreMediaGlobal

Cover Credit: © kentoh/Shutterstock

Library of Congress Control Number: 2012942665

International Edition:
ISBN-13: 978-1-285-08501-2
ISBN-10: 1-285-08501-9

Cengage Learning International Offices

Asia
www.cengageasia.com
tel: (65) 6410 1200

Australia/New Zealand
www.cengage.com.au
tel: (61) 3 9685 4111

Brazil
www.cengage.com.br
tel: (55) 11 3665 9900

India
www.cengage.co.in
tel: (91) 11 4364 1111

Latin America
www.cengage.com.mx
tel: (52) 55 1500 6000

UK/Europe/Middle East/Africa
www.cengage.co.uk
tel: (44) 0 1264 332 424

Represented in Canada by Nelson Education, Ltd.
www.nelson.com
tel: (416) 752 9100 / (800) 668 0671

Cengage Learning is a leading provider of customized learning solutions with office locations around the globe, including Singapore, the United Kingdom, Australia, Mexico, Brazil, and Japan. Locate your local office at: **www.cengage.com/global**

For product information and free companion resources: **www.cengage.com/international**

Visit your local office: **www.cengage.com/global**

Visit our corporate website: **www.cengage.com**

Printed in the United States of America
1 2 3 4 5 23 22 21 20 19

TABLE OF CONTENTS

PREFACE

Almost every organization depends on a relational database to meet its information system needs. One important challenge these organizations face is providing user-friendly application interfaces that enable users to work efficiently. To facilitate logical processing and user interaction with the Oracle 11*g* database, Oracle offers a robust procedural language extension, PL/SQL, to complement the industry-standard SQL. PL/SQL is an integral part of the Oracle 11*g* database, and the PL/SQL compiler and interpreter are embedded in the Oracle 11*g* Developer Suite of tools. This arrangement results in a consistent development environment on both the client and server sides. PL/SQL knowledge leads to opportunities not only in developing applications with Oracle Developer tools, but also in supporting existing Oracle applications that are developed and marketed by Oracle in many industries. In addition to database software and application development tools, Oracle is one of the world's leading suppliers of application software.

The purpose of this book is to introduce you to using the PL/SQL language to interact with an Oracle 11*g* database and to support applications in a business environment. In addition, concepts related to objectives of the Oracle 11*g* PL/SQL certification exams have been incorporated for those wanting to pursue certification.

The Intended Audience

This book has been designed for students in technical two-year or four-year programs who need to learn how to develop application code with Oracle 11*g* databases. It's assumed you already understand relational database design and SQL commands.

Oracle Certification Program (OCP)

This book covers objectives of Exam 1Z0-147, Oracle 11*g*: Program with PL/SQL, the second exam in the Oracle PL/SQL Developer Certified Associate track. You can find information about exams, including registration and other reference material, at *www.oracle.com/education/certification*. In addition, grids showing the Oracle exam objectives and chapters of this book that address them are available for download at *cengagebrain.com* via the Student Downloads link on this book's Web page.

The Approach

The concepts introduced in this book are explained in the context of a hypothetical real-world business—Brewbean's, an online coffee goods retailer. First, the business operation and database structure are introduced and analyzed. Each chapter begins with a description of the current application challenge Brewbean's needs to address. Then PL/SQL statements are introduced and used throughout the chapter to solve the Brewbean's application challenge. This organization enables you to learn the syntax of PL/SQL statements and apply them in a real-world environment. A script file that generates the necessary database objects is included in each chapter's student data files so that you get hands-on practice in re-creating the examples and practicing variations of PL/SQL statements to enhance your understanding.

The core PL/SQL language elements are covered in Chapters 5 through 10, including procedures, functions, packages, and database triggers. Chapters 2 through 4 introduce the basic PL/SQL language elements and processing techniques. Later chapters cover more advanced topics, including dynamic SQL, compiler parameters, and code obfuscation. These topics go beyond certification objectives, but they help you appreciate Oracle's many development features.

To reinforce the material, there are topic summaries, review questions, hands-on assignments, and case projects at the end of each chapter. They test your knowledge and challenge you to apply it to solving business problems. In addition, to expand your knowledge of PL/SQL, the appendixes have tutorials on using software utilities, such as SQL*Loader, to assist in PL/SQL code development.

Overview of This Book

The examples, assignments, and cases in this book help you learn how to do the following:

- Create PL/SQL blocks.
- Use a variety of variable types to handle data in a block.
- Process statements conditionally with control structures.
- Reuse lines of code with looping structures.
- Manage errors with exception handlers.
- Create and use procedures and functions.
- Bundle program units with packages.
- Develop database triggers.
- Use the features of Oracle-supplied packages.
- Identify program unit dependencies.
- Use dynamic SQL.

The chapter contents build in complexity and reinforce previous concepts. **Chapter 1** introduces PL/SQL, explains how it fits into application programming, and describes the Brewbean's database used throughout this book. **Chapter 2** shows you how to retrieve and handle data in a block by using scalar variables and how to manipulate data with decision and looping structures. **Chapter 3** explains embedding SQL statements in blocks and using composite variable types. **Chapter 4** covers using cursors and managing exceptions. **Chapter 5** explains how to create a procedure and pass values by using parameters. **Chapter 6** shows you how to create functions and how to return values with functions. **Chapter 7** covers creating packages, including the package specification and body. **Chapter 8** describes methods of identifying program unit dependencies and compiler parameters. **Chapter 9** shows you how to create DML, `INSTEAD OF`, system, and compound triggers. **Chapter 10** describes a sampling of Oracle-supplied packages and covers dynamic SQL and code obfuscation. The appendixes support and expand on chapter materials. **Appendix A** is a printed version of the tables and data in the Brewbean's database. This database serves as a running example from chapter to chapter. **Appendix B** guides you through Oracle and SQL Developer installation and includes a tutorial on using

SQL Developer, a free utility from Oracle. **Appendix C** has a tutorial on using a third-party development utility, TOAD. **Appendix D** gives you an overview of SQL and PL/SQL statement tuning. **Appendix E** is an overview of using the SQL*Loader utility. **Appendix F** introduces object technology. (*Note*: Appendixes C through F are available on this book's Web page.)

Features

To enhance your learning experience, each chapter in this book includes the following elements:

- **Chapter objectives:** Each chapter begins with a list of the concepts to be mastered by the chapter's conclusion. It gives you a quick overview of chapter contents as well as a useful study aid.
- **Running case:** An application development challenge for the Brewbean's online coffee retail company is described at the beginning of each chapter.
- **Methodology:** New concepts are introduced in the context of solving the Brewbean's application challenge in that chapter. Step-by-step exercises illustrate the concepts, and many screenshots and code examples are included to help you understand the concepts better. As you work through the chapters, less detailed instructions are given for familiar tasks, and detailed instructions are reserved for new tasks.
- **Tips:** This feature, designated by the Tip icon, offers practical advice or information. In some instances, tips explain how a concept applies in the workplace.
- **Notes:** These explanations, designated by the Note icon, give you more information on the files and operations being discussed.
- **Cautions:** This feature, designated by the Caution icon, warns you of potential pitfalls.
- **Chapter summaries:** Each chapter's text is followed by a summary of the important concepts. These summaries are a helpful recap of chapter material.
- **Review questions:** End-of-chapter assessment begins with 15 review questions (10 multiple choice and 5 short answer) that reinforce the chapter's main ideas. These questions ensure that you have mastered the concepts and understand the information.
- **Advanced review questions:** Chapters 2 through 9 have an additional five multiple-choice questions covering the chapter material. They're similar to Oracle certification exam questions and are included to prepare you for the types of questions you can expect on a certification exam and to measure your level of understanding. (Chapter 10 has no advanced questions because its material goes beyond the certification objectives.)
- **Hands-on assignments:** Each chapter has 8 to 15 hands-on assignments related to the chapter's contents to give you practical experience. Many assignments are based on the Brewbean's database application to continue the examples given in the chapter; others are based on the DoGood Donor organization, a hypothetical company that tracks donors' pledges and payments.

- **Case projects:** Each chapter has case projects designed to help you apply what you have learned to real-world situations. These cases give you the opportunity to synthesize and evaluate information, examine potential solutions, and make recommendations, much as you would in an actual business setting. One case expands on the Brewbean's database application, and a second case involves developing database application code to support business processes for More Movies, a movie rental company.

Teaching Tools

The following supplemental materials are available when this book is used in a classroom setting. All teaching tools available with this book are provided on a single CD or at *login.cengage.com/sso*, accessible with your Single Sign-On username and password.

Electronic Instructor's Manual: The Instructor's Manual accompanying this book includes the following:

- Additional instructional material to assist in class preparation, including suggestions for lecture topics.
- Solutions to all in-chapter exercises and end-of-chapter projects, including review questions, hands-on assignments, and case projects.

ExamView®: This objective-based test generator lets the instructor create paper, LAN, or Web-based tests from testbanks designed specifically for this Course Technology book. Instructors can use the QuickTest Wizard to create tests in fewer than five minutes by taking advantage of Course Technology's question banks, or they can create customized exams.

PowerPoint presentations: Microsoft PowerPoint slides are included for each chapter. Instructors can use the slides in three ways: as teaching aids during classroom presentations, as printed handouts for classroom distribution, or as network-accessible resources for chapter review. Instructors can add their own slides for additional topics introduced to the class.

Data files: The script files for creating all necessary database objects are available through the Cengage Learning Web site (*login.cengage.com/sso*) and on the Instructor Resource CD.

Solution files: Solutions to chapter examples, review questions, hands-on assignments, and case projects are given on the Instructor Resource CD or can be downloaded from the Cengage Learning Web site at *login.cengage.com/sso*. The solutions are password protected.

ACKNOWLEDGMENTS

First and foremost, I need to thank my best friend, Scott, for the endless support and encouragement I needed to accomplish this goal. I am also grateful to my family, friends, and colleagues who continue to put up with me and to Tidewater Community College for giving me many opportunities to grow and learn.

As many of my students know, I am entirely too excited about PL/SQL to be completely human. However, my experience in producing this book has proved just how human I am. The usefulness of this book is due to the many efforts from Course Technology employees to entertain my ideas, mold my writing into a comprehensible learning style, and test the many code examples used throughout the book. Many people have made hands-on contributions in creating this book, and I will never be able to repay their incredible efforts.

I would like to express my appreciation to Senior Product Manager Kate Mason, who always respected and entertained my ideas, and Development Editor Lisa Lord, who had the gigantic challenge of managing my writing. Also, hats off to Nicole Ashton and her team at GreenPen for working through the examples and material in each chapter during the quality assurance stage. Many other people were involved who I didn't get the opportunity to work with directly. I would like to thank Senior Acquisitions Editor Charles McCormick, Jr., Production Site Lead Jen Feltri-George, and Senior Project Manager Divya Divakaran.

In addition to a number of my students who have offered valuable feedback in my classes, the following reviewers also provided helpful suggestions and insight into the development of this book: Jason C. H. Chen, Gonzaga University; Dean Jefferson, Madison Area Technical College; Eli Weissman, DeVry Institute of Technology; and David Welch, Nashville State Technical Community College.

READ THIS BEFORE YOU BEGIN

To the User

Data Files

To work through the examples and projects, you need to load the data files created for this book. Your instructor will supply these data files, or you can download them by going to the Cengage Learning Web site (*www.cengagebrain.com*) and searching for this book's title. Each chapter has its own set of data files; some are provided for in-chapter exercises, and others are used for end-of-chapter hands-on assignments or case projects. For example, you'll find script files to run for hands-on assignments involving the DoGood Donor database and case projects for the More Movies database.

The database objects used in projects are created with script files named in the format `c#_BBcreate.sql` (with the # representing the chapter number). These scripts are in the folder for each chapter's data files. Steps at the beginning of each chapter give you instructions on running the scripts. Each chapter folder also contains other files referenced in the chapter, including end-of-chapter projects. If the computer in your school lab—or your own computer—has Oracle 11*g* database software installed, you can work through the in-chapter exercises, hands-on assignments, and case projects. At a minimum, you need Oracle Database 11*g* Release 2 (Enterprise or Standard Edition) or Oracle 11*g* Express Edition Release 2.

Using Your Own Computer

To use your own computer to work through the in-chapter exercises, hands-on assignments, and case projects, you need the following to support Oracle Database 11*g* Enterprise or Standard Edition. See Appendix B for details and instructions for Oracle Database and SQL Developer installation. You can also use the free Oracle Express, which has fewer hardware requirements and might be more suitable for a desktop or laptop system.

Hardware: A computer capable of using Microsoft Windows Server 2003, XP Professional, Vista (Business, Enterprise, or Ultimate), Server 2008 (Server Core option not supported), or Windows 7 (Professional, Enterprise, or Ultimate) and with at least 1 GB of RAM and 5.35 GB of available drive space

Software: Oracle 11*g* Database Release 2, Standard or Enterprise Edition. You can find Oracle software downloads at the Oracle Technology Networks (OTN) site (*www.oracle.com/technetwork/database/enterprise-edition/downloads/index.html*).

When you install Oracle 11*g*, you're prompted to change the password for some default administrative user accounts. Make sure you record the names and passwords of these accounts because you might need to log on to the database with one of them in later chapters.

Data files: You can't use your own computer to work through examples and projects in this book unless you have the data files. You can get the data files from your instructor, or you can download them by going to the Cengage Learning Web site (*www.cengagebrain.com*) and then searching for the Student Downloads link under this book's title.

When you download the data files, they should be stored in a directory separate from other files on your hard drive. For example, create a directory named "plsql class" to contain this book's data files. You need to remember the path or folder because you use it to run or retrieve files in SQL Developer, the interface tool you use to interact with the database.

Naming Conventions

Every programming shop should follow variable-naming conventions to make code easier to read. The following tables outline the naming conventions used in this book. They include variable type prefixes, scalar variable data type suffixes, and program unit type suffixes.

Variable Type Prefixes

Variable Type	Prefix
PL/SQL block local scalar	`lv_`
Package	`pv_`
Packaged variable	`pvg_`
Parameter (program unit)	`p_`
Cursor	`cur_`
User-defined data type	`type_`
Record	`rec_`

Scalar Variable Data Type Suffixes

Data Type	Suffix
Character	`_txt`
Number	`_num`
Date	`_date`
Boolean	`_bln`

Program Unit Type Suffixes

Program Unit Type	Suffix
Stored procedure	_sp
Stored function	_sf
Stored package	_pkg
Packaged procedure	_pp
Packaged function	_pf
Database trigger	_trg

Visit Our World Wide Web Site

Additional materials designed for you are available on the World Wide Web. Go to *www.cengagebrain.com* periodically and search for more details. Appendixes C through F are also available online.

To the Instructor

To complete the chapters in this book, your students must have access to the data files. They're included in the Instructor's Resource Kit and can also be downloaded from the Cengage Learning Web site (*login.cengage.com/sso*).

The database objects used in the book are created with a script file supplied for each chapter. The files are named in the format `c#_BBcreate.sql` (with the # representing the chapter number) and stored in the folder for each chapter's data files. Steps at the beginning of each chapter give instructions on running these scripts. Each chapter folder also contains other files referenced in the chapter, including end-of-chapter projects. If your students are connecting to a shared server running the Standard or Enterprise Edition of Oracle (instead of Oracle Express), a separate account or schema should be created for each student. This book uses a fading strategy for describing SQL Developer steps, meaning that only the first few chapters give specific details on using this tool. Beyond this point, it's assumed students are comfortable with SQL Developer and don't need explicit directions.

Chapter concepts are explained by using a client SQL Developer installation. To expose students to other interface tools, Appendix D describes the TOAD utility.

The Oracle Server and Client Software

This book was written and tested with the following software:

- Oracle 11*g* Enterprise Edition Server, Release 2, installed on a Windows 2003 Server workstation, and Personal Oracle 11*g*, Release 2, installed on a Windows XP Professional workstation.
- SQL Developer is used throughout the book to provide a consistent interface to the Oracle database, regardless of the client tool or software edition used.

CHAPTER 1

INTRODUCTION TO PL/SQL

LEARNING OBJECTIVES

After completing this chapter, you should be able to understand:

- PL/SQL and application programming
- Application models
- How to locate Oracle resources
- SQL and PL/SQL tools
- The databases used in this book
- SQL `SELECT` and data manipulation syntax

INTRODUCTION

In this chapter, you learn the definition of programming and procedural languages, what PL/SQL is and why you need it, basic application models, locating documentation, SQL and PL/SQL tools, and the sample databases used throughout this book. A brief review of SQL statement syntax is included at the end of the chapter to make sure you're prepared to use SQL statements in the PL/SQL coding throughout this book. It's only a brief review to serve as a refresher; it doesn't cover all the facets of SQL you should already be familiar with, including queries, table creation, data manipulation, and transaction control. If you aren't well versed in these topics, be sure to review them before moving on to Chapter 2. After this chapter, you begin programming with PL/SQL.

APPLICATION PROGRAMMING AND PL/SQL

At its simplest, a **programming language** converts users' actions into instructions a computer can understand. All programming languages share some basic capabilities, such as manipulating data, using variables to hold data for processing, and making code reusable.

Structured Query Language (SQL) is a programming language that enables you to perform actions in a database, such as querying, adding, deleting, and changing data. However, it isn't a **procedural language** that programmers use to code a logical sequence of steps for making decisions and instructing a computer to perform tasks. For that purpose, you need a procedural language, such as Oracle PL/SQL. Oracle considers PL/SQL to be a procedural language extension of SQL, hence the "PL" in the name.

So what is PL/SQL? What role does it play in application programming? Why does a programmer need to learn it? These are probably some of the questions you have right now, and they need to be answered before you dive into Oracle programming. These answers should give you some insight into what you can accomplish with PL/SQL. The following section starts you off by covering general application programming concepts.

Application Programming

To clarify what's meant by "application programming," say you're an employee of a company named Brewbean's that retails coffee products on the Internet, and it needs to develop a software application to support the business. One part of the application consists of the user interface that customers use to access the product catalog and place an order. Figure 1-1 shows an example of this type of interface.

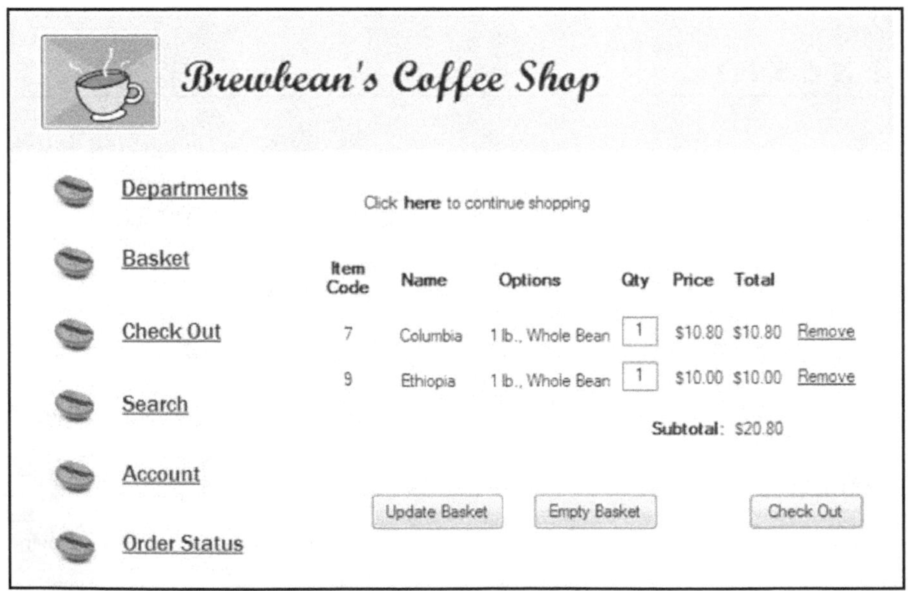

FIGURE 1-1 Brewbean's Coffee Shop shopping basket

This window displays the shopping basket containing the items a shopper has selected so far. The shopper has a number of choices at this point, such as continue shopping, change item quantities, remove items from the basket, or check out and complete the order.

Think of the potential processing this application might require. If, for example, the Check Out button is clicked, what should happen in the application? Possible processing activities include the following:

- Verify that the quantity ordered is greater than zero for each item.
- Calculate taxes.
- Calculate shipping charges.
- Check and/or update product inventory.
- Determine whether the shopper already has credit card information stored.

Behind the user interface in Figure 1-1 is where a programming language instructs the computer on what to do in response to a user's action, such as clicking the Check Out button. When the user clicks this button, several things might need to happen. First, the application needs to check the completeness of (or validate) the user's information. For example, you might need to verify that every line item has a quantity entered onscreen. You might also want to check the database to make sure all items are in stock. This is where PL/SQL enters the scene.

A procedural language makes it possible for developers to perform decision-making logic, such as `IF-THEN` conditions, in their applications. One example might be conditional statements that determine the shipping cost based on the total number of items ordered. If the total number of items is from three to five, the shipping cost equals $6; if the total number of items is more than five, the shipping cost equals $10; and so on.

PL/SQL Advantages

PL/SQL was modeled after Ada, a programming language built for the U.S. Department of Defense, and was considered conceptually advanced for the time. In the late 1980s, Oracle recognized a need for not only expanding functionality in its database system, but also for improving application portability and database security. At that point, PL/SQL was born and has been improved with every Oracle database release. PL/SQL is a proprietary language of Oracle, and a PL/SQL processing engine is built into the Oracle database and some developer tools. The following list summarizes a few advantages PL/SQL offers when working with an Oracle database:

- *Tight integration with SQL*—You can use your existing knowledge of SQL because PL/SQL supports SQL data manipulation, transaction control, functions, retrieving data with cursors, operators, and pseudocolumns. In addition, PL/SQL fully supports SQL data types, which reduces the need to convert data passed between your applications and the database.
- *Improved performance*—First, PL/SQL allows sending blocks of statements to Oracle in a single transmission. This is important in reducing network communication between your application and Oracle, especially if your application performs numerous database transactions. PL/SQL blocks can be used to group SQL statements before sending them to Oracle for execution. Otherwise, each SQL statement must be transmitted separately. Second, PL/SQL code modules (stored program units, described later in this section) are stored in executable form, which makes procedure calls efficient. Third, executable code is automatically cached in memory and shared among users. This can speed processing tremendously with a multiuser application that has repeated calls to modules of code. Fourth, a PL/SQL engine is embedded in

Oracle developer tools so that PL/SQL code can be processed on the client machine. This feature reduces network traffic.

- *Increased productivity*—PL/SQL can be used in many Oracle tools, and the coding is the same in all. Therefore, you can use your PL/SQL knowledge with many development tools, and the code you create can be shared across applications. Because a PL/SQL engine is part of the server, these code modules can also be used or called from almost any application development language. You can use Visual Basic or Java to develop an application but still harness the power of PL/SQL with Oracle.
- *Portability*—PL/SQL can run on any platform that Oracle can run. This feature is important so that developers can deploy applications on different platforms easily.
- *Tighter security*—Database security can be increased with application processing supported by PL/SQL stored program units, which give users access to database objects without having to be granted specific privileges. Therefore, users can access these objects only via PL/SQL stored program units.

NOTE

A database administrator (DBA) can automate and handle some tasks more easily by using the power of PL/SQL. Many PL/SQL scripts developed to handle DBA-type tasks are available free in books, Web sites, and user groups, so being familiar with the PL/SQL language is quite beneficial for DBAs.

One key advantage is that program units can be stored in the Oracle database and called from your development tool. Processing SQL statements stored in the database can be more efficient than processing those stored in application code. Statements stored in application code must be transmitted to the database server to be processed. PL/SQL program modules stored in the database are referred to as **stored program units**.

NOTE

If you have a piece of code that might be used by a variety of applications, saving it on the server allows several applications to share it. In addition, Oracle has built a PL/SQL engine into a number of its developer tools, such as Oracle Forms, so Oracle developers can code an entire application—from client screen logic to database manipulation—with PL/SQL.

APPLICATION MODELS

An application model is a general framework or design that describes the structure of an application's components in terms of where the supporting software is located. An application model has three main components:

- *User interface*—The windows displayed to users to enter information or take actions, such as clicking a button. The user interface component can be developed with tools such as Visual Basic, Java, or Oracle Forms.

- *Program logic*—The programming code that provides the logic of what the application does. PL/SQL handles this component, which can be considered the "brains" of an application.
- *Database*—The database management system providing the physical storage structure for data and mechanisms to retrieve, add, change, and remove data. The Oracle server provides this component.

To see more clearly where PL/SQL is used in an application, take a closer look at basic two-tier and three-tier application models, in which each tier manages different application components.

NOTE

The traditional two-tier application model is also called a "client/server application." Both terms are used throughout this book.

Two-Tier or Client/Server Application Model

In a client/server model, shown in Figure 1-2, an executable program or application is loaded on the user's computer. The application contains the user interface and some programming logic. Some processing can take place on the client side (the user's computer). For instance, the processing might be verifying that information has been entered in required fields. Other processing might require transmitting requests, such as an SQL statement to query requested data, to the database server.

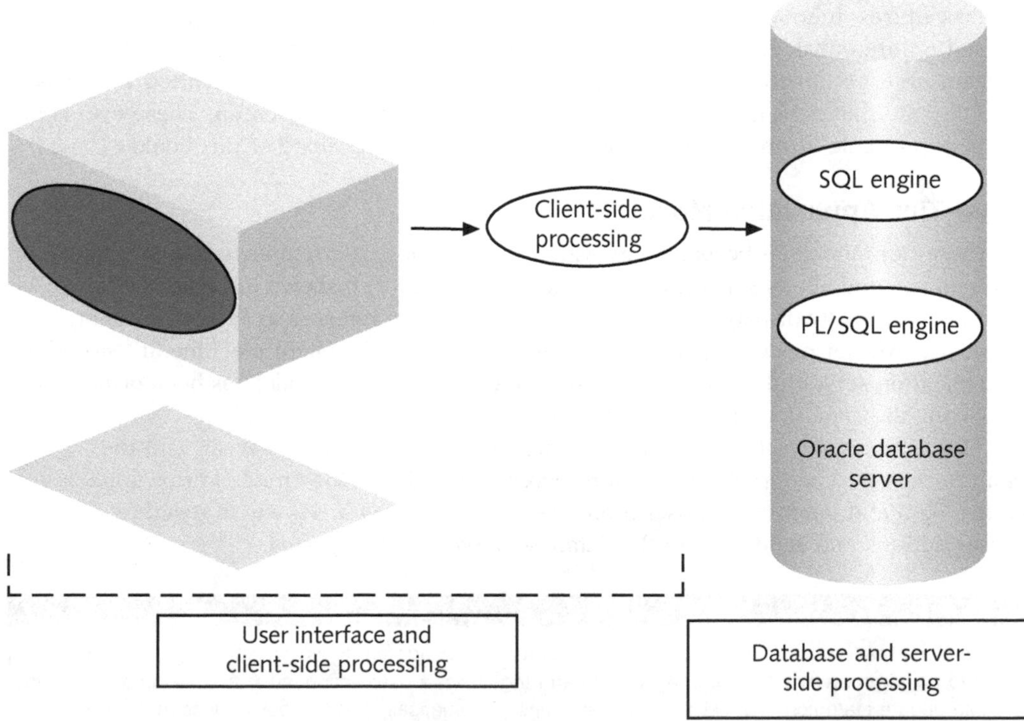

FIGURE 1-2 The client/server application model

If you're using non-Oracle developer tools, such as Visual Basic, client-side code can be VBScript that includes calls to PL/SQL program units stored on the Oracle server. However, if you're using Oracle development tools, such as Oracle Forms, a PL/SQL engine exists on the client as well as on the database server, so all application coding is done with PL/SQL.

With Oracle development tools, PL/SQL code resides on both the client side and server side. That is, PL/SQL is saved as part of the Oracle Forms application logic on the client side and stored as named program units on the database server. A **named program unit** is simply a block of PL/SQL code that has been named so that it can be saved (stored) and reused. The term "stored" indicates that the program unit is saved in the database and, therefore, can be used or shared by different applications. Table 1-1 describes each type of program unit briefly. You create all these program units in this book.

TABLE 1-1 Stored Program Unit Types

Stored Program Unit Type	Description
Procedure	Performs a task. Can receive and return multiple values.
Function	Performs a task and typically returns only one value. Within certain parameters, it can be used in SQL statements.
Database trigger	Performs a task automatically when a data manipulation language (DML) action occurs on the associated table or system event.
Package	Groups related procedures and functions, which makes additional programming features available.

Procedures, functions, triggers, and packages integrated in an Oracle Forms application are considered client-side program units. They're referred to as application program units rather than stored program units. An example of an application trigger is PL/SQL code that runs automatically when a button is clicked onscreen. These events are handled in Oracle Forms development, which is beyond the scope of this book.

Three-Tier Application Model

The three-tier model has become more widely used because it attempts to reduce application maintenance and allows supporting more users. In this model, shown in Figure 1-3, the user interface is typically displayed in a Web browser and often referred to as a "thin client." Unlike the two-tier model, application code isn't loaded on the client machine; it's stored on an application server, also referred to as the "middle tier." This model has been critical in supporting the explosion of mobile applications.

This model's three tiers are the user interface, the application server, and the database server. The Oracle application server allows deploying Oracle Forms applications via the Web and contains the user interface and processing logic, which together respond to user actions and send code to the database server for processing.

NOTE

In either application model, PL/SQL's role is the same: to provide the logic for instructing the computer what to do when an event occurs. (An **event** can range from a user action, such as clicking a button, to a table update statement that calls a database trigger automatically.) In this book, all code is placed server side as stored program units.

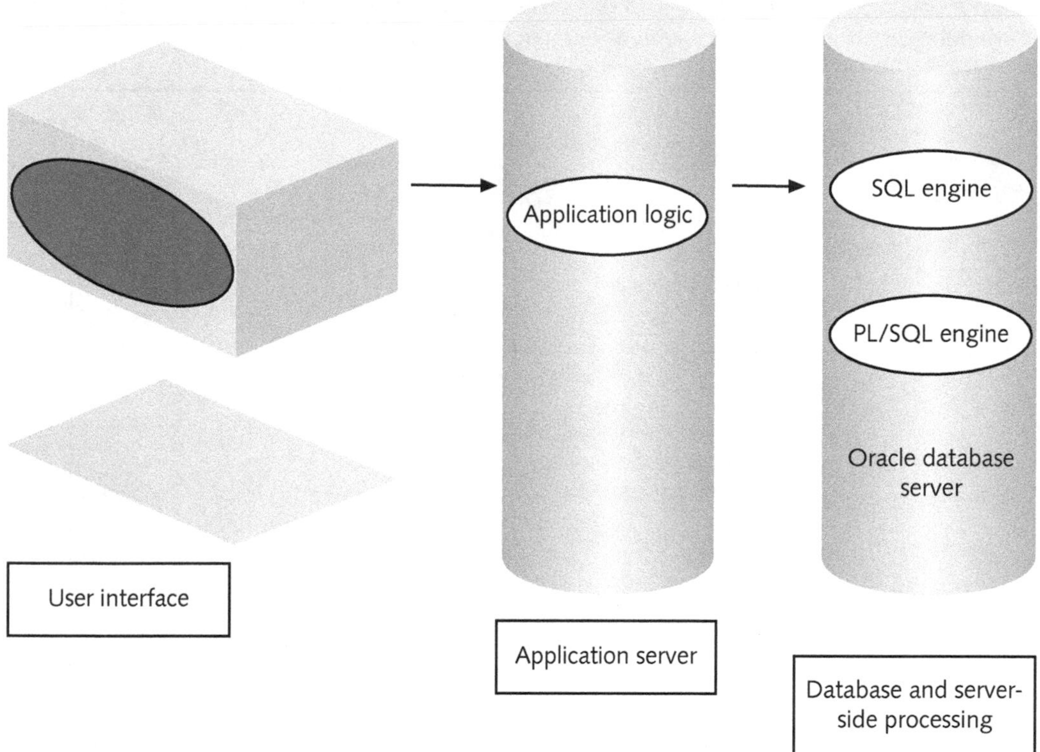

FIGURE 1-3 A three-tier application model

ORACLE RESOURCES

As you have probably discovered, numerous books are available on Oracle system topics—including PL/SQL. This section gives you information on Web resources for learning the PL/SQL language to complement the information in this book.

Web Resources

Oracle's Web site is called the Oracle Technology Network (OTN) and offers a variety of useful resources, including documentation, white papers, downloads, and discussion forums. You can access it from Oracle's home page (*www.oracle.com*) or by going directly to *http://otn.oracle.com*. You must log in to access certain areas of this Web site, but membership is free.

The OTN site is updated often, but the home page always lists categories of information to help you find what you're looking for. For example, the home page includes Documentation, Discussion Forums, Sample Code, and Learning Library links. You can click the Documentation link and follow the links to arrive at the Database Library page for the Oracle version you're interested in (for this book, Oracle Database 11g Release 2 [11.2]). Then use the Master Book List link to view all online books, including PL/SQL Language Reference (useful for the topics in this book) and PL/SQL Packages and Types Reference. A SQL Language Reference is also available.

The OTN Web site also has pages on specific technology topics, such as Oracle Database 11g XE, Database Focus Areas, and Application Development. After selecting a database version, click Database Focus Areas and then Application Development to arrive at a page with many useful developer resources. In the Languages section, click the link for PL/SQL to find the page shown in Figure 1-4. In the Tools section, click the SQL Developer link to find more detailed information on the development tool used in this book.

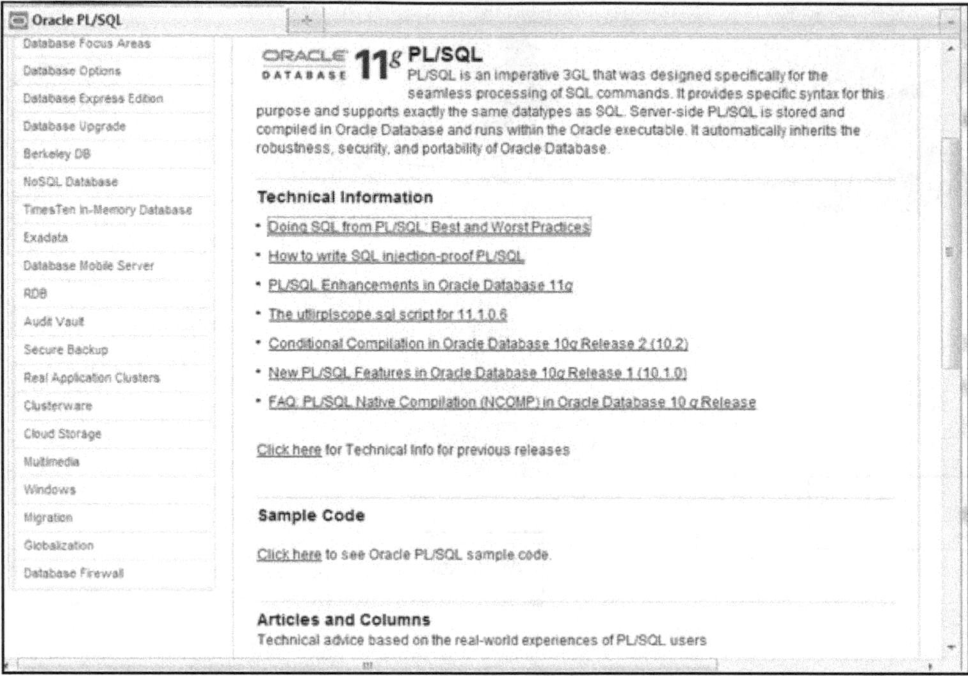

FIGURE 1-4 The PL/SQL page on the OTN site

Doing an Internet search on PL/SQL leads to a variety of Web pages with helpful information, such as PL/SQL Obsession (*www.toadworld.com/SF/*) by Steven Feuerstein, a leading expert in PL/SQL. Although these pages are useful, being familiar with the language basics first is usually better.

SQL AND PL/SQL TOOLS

Wading through the many software tools that Oracle offers can get confusing. In addition, you'll soon learn that many third-party software companies offer tools for Oracle developers. This section introduces the Oracle tools used in this book for PL/SQL development and lists some third-party tools that are popular in the Oracle development community. Note that this list isn't exhaustive, nor does it give recommendations. It merely attempts to acquaint you with some options for selecting tools.

NOTE

Your instructor is a valuable resource in helping you decide which tools are best for you.

Software Tools for This Book

This book covers the newest version of the Oracle database: Oracle 11*g*. However, this book can also be used with Oracle 10*g*. PL/SQL version numbering has matched the database version numbering starting with Oracle 8, so PL/SQL 11*g* is used in this book to complement the Oracle 11g database. Note, however, that the major enhancements in PL/SQL versions were mainly internal database engine changes made to improve the performance of PL/SQL processing. Any features that are new in Oracle 11g are noted as such. The following sections describe the two free PL/SQL developer tools from Oracle, SQL*Plus and SQL Developer.

SQL*Plus

Starting with Oracle 11g, only the console or command-line SQL*Plus interface is shipped with the database product. SQL*Plus is a basic tool included with the Oracle server that allows users to send SQL and PL/SQL statements directly to the Oracle database server for processing. Figure 1-5 shows the command-line SQL*Plus interface with a simple query entered. Many users don't find this interface as easy to use as SQL Developer, but Oracle users should be familiar with it because it's available with all Oracle installations.

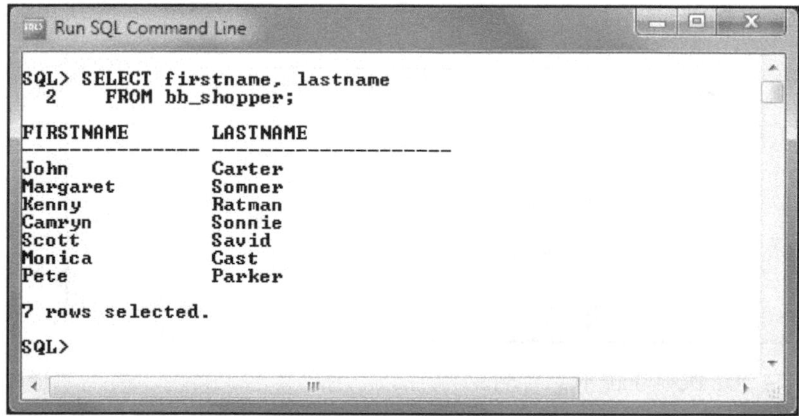
Run SQL Command Line
SQL> SELECT firstname, lastname
2 FROM bb_shopper;
FIRSTNAME LASTNAME
John Carter
Margaret Somner
Kenny Ratman
Camryn Sonnie
Scott Savid
Monica Cast
Pete Parker
7 rows selected.
SQL>

FIGURE 1-5 The SQL*Plus interface

> **NOTE**
>
> This book uses SQL Developer for examples and screenshots. However, you can run all the sample code in SQL*Plus. See Appendix B for more details on SQL*Plus and Oracle database installation.

Oracle SQL Developer

Oracle SQL Developer is available free on the Oracle Web site. This utility has a graphical user interface (GUI), which makes it easier for developers to explore database objects, review and edit code quickly, and create and debug program units. Figure 1-6 shows the main window of Oracle SQL Developer.

Even though you can run PL/SQL code in SQL*Plus, Oracle SQL Developer offers features that simplify development tasks, such as color-coding syntax and using breakpoints to assist in debugging code. (Breakpoints are stopping points during execution that enable programmers to evaluate variable values while code is running.)

In practice, SQL*Plus, Oracle SQL Developer, and third-party tools are used to test and debug stand-alone PL/SQL program units. Examples in this book are shown in the SQL Developer interface.

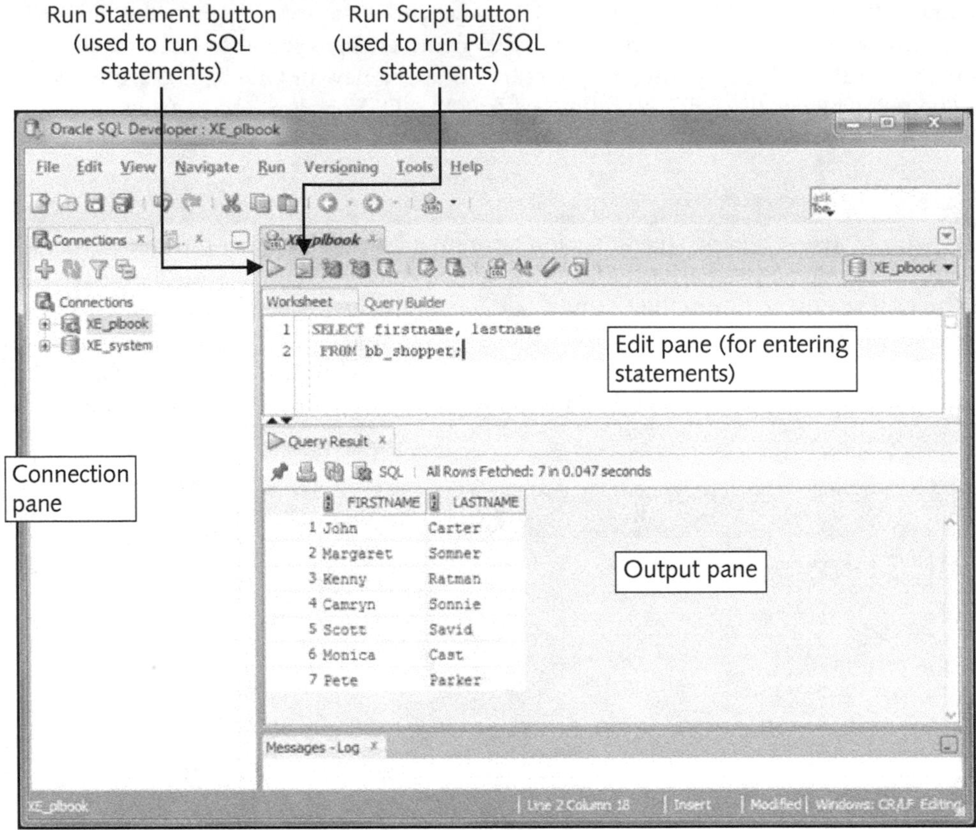

FIGURE 1-6 The Oracle SQL Developer main window

NOTE

Appendix B has instructions for Oracle SQL Developer installation.

Working with the Tools

To do the coding activities in this book, you need access to the Oracle 11*g* database and SQL Developer. In addition, the appendixes use SQL*Plus and Tool for Oracle Application Developers (TOAD), which is a third-party tool. If you're working in a computer lab setting, the correct software should already be installed for you.

If you want to install Oracle 11*g* on your own computer, follow the installation instructions for Oracle Database 11*g* Express Edition in Appendix B. For learning purposes, many programmers install Oracle Express, which is more suitable for desktop installations and is available free for learning and testing. It's offered on the disc accompanying this book, too.

Third-Party PL/SQL Development Tools

Many other companies have developed software for PL/SQL developers. As you progress through this book and become familiar with creating PL/SQL program units, you might want to take some time to experiment and compare some tools from third parties. Table 1-2 lists some popular tools and their Web sites for your reference. Many companies offer a free trial download for testing products.

TABLE 1-2 Third-Party PL/SQL Development Tools

Tool Name	Web Site
TOAD	*www.quest.com*
SQL Navigator	*www.quest.com*
PL/SQL Developer	*www.allroundautomations.com*

NOTE

TOAD by Quest Software is one of the most popular third-party Oracle tools and is explained briefly in Appendix C.

DATABASES USED IN THIS BOOK

Programmers soon realize that to become successful application developers, they must understand databases thoroughly. Therefore, be sure to review this section carefully to gain a good understanding of the design of databases used in this book. The SQL review in the next section also helps you become familiar with this book's databases.

The main database used in this book supports a company retailing coffee via the Internet, over the phone, and in one walk-in store. The company, Brewbean's, has two main product categories: coffee consumables and brewing equipment. It also hopes to add a coffee club feature to entice return shoppers. The Brewbean's database is referenced throughout chapter material and used in Hands-On Assignments at the end of each chapter. Two additional databases are used in end-of chapter exercises. A donor database that tracks donation pledges and payments is used in Hands-On Assignments, and a database involving a movie rental company is used in Case Projects. The next sections introduce these three databases.

The Brewbean's Database

Figure 1-7 shows the basic entity-relationship diagram (ERD) for the Brewbean's database pertaining to customer orders. An ERD serves as a visual representation of a database.

Note that all table names for the Brewbean's database start with the prefix BB_. The BB_DEPARTMENT table lists the two main business areas in the company (coffee sales and equipment sales), and the BB_PRODUCT table contains information on all products, including name, description, price, and sales pricing.

Three tables are used to manage product options. The BB_PRODUCTOPTION CATEGORY table lists main categories for products, such as size and form. The BB_PRODUCTOPTIONDETAIL table identifies choices in each category (for example, whole bean or ground for form). The BB_PRODUCTOPTION table links each product to its applicable options. Each product can be associated with many options, so there's a one-to-many relationship between the BB_PRODUCT and the BB_PRODUCTOPTION tables.

The BB_SHOPPER table serves as the focal point for identifying customers and contains customers' names, addresses, e-mail addresses, and logon information. When a

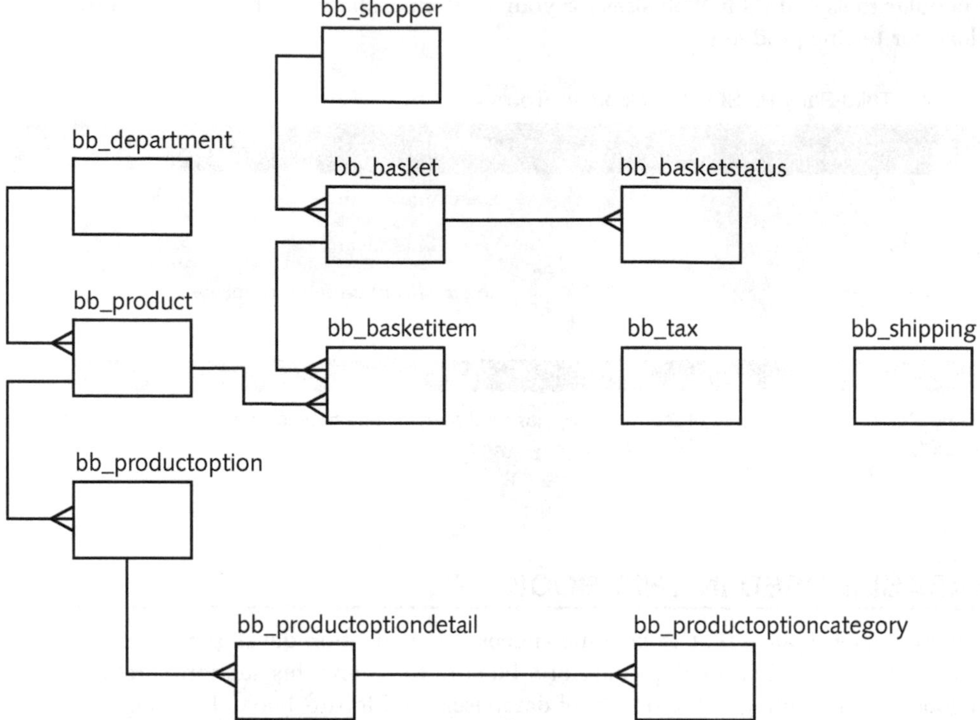

FIGURE 1-7 The Brewbean's database ERD

customer begins shopping, a new basket is created in the BB_BASKET table. This table is one of the largest in the database; it holds order summary, shipping, and billing information. As the shopper selects items, they're inserted in the BB_BASKETITEM table, which holds shopper selections by basket number.

The BB_BASKETSTATUS table stores data related to order status. Each status update is recorded as a new row in this table. Possible statuses include order placed, order verified and sent to shipping, order shipped, order canceled, and order on back-order. The other tables associated with completing an order include BB_TAX and BB_SHIPPING. The company currently calculates shipping based on the quantity of items ordered.

Appendix A lists data by table for your reference. Take some time now to review this information and become familiar with the database.

Creating the Database

To create the Brewbean's database, you need to run a script file containing a series of SQL statements that build all the necessary objects and insert data. Follow these steps to run the script:

1. Make sure you have the `c1_BBcreate.sql` file in the Chapter01 folder. This file contains the script for creating the database.
2. Start SQL Developer and connect to the Oracle database.
3. Click **File**, **Open** from the menu.

4. Click the **`c1_BBcreate.sql`** file, and then click **Open**. The code in this script is displayed in the Edit pane of SQL Developer. Scroll through the SQL statements; they should look familiar.
5. Run the script by clicking the **Run Script** button on the Edit pane toolbar. If necessary, click **OK** in the Select Connection dialog box. Figure 1-8 shows the results.

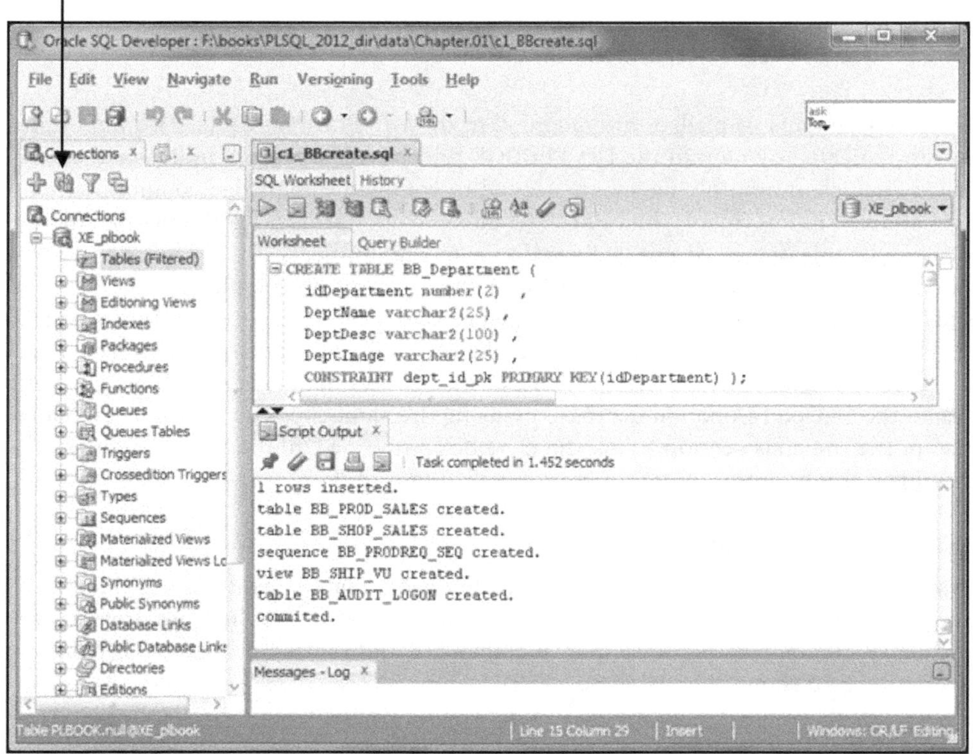

FIGURE 1-8 Creating the Brewbean's database

6. Scroll through the Script Output pane at the bottom to review results of the statements. If you have any errors caused by insufficient privileges, ask your instructor for assistance.
7. In the Connections pane on the left, expand the **Tables** node to view the tables that were created. You might need to click the **Refresh** button at the top of the Connections pane to see these objects.

The DoGood Donor Database

The DoGood Donor database, used in Hands-On Assignments at the end of each chapter, is used to track donors, donation pledges, and pledge payments. Figure 1-9 shows a basic ERD for this database.

The DD_DONOR table is the core of this database because all other data depends on the donor, who represents a person or company that has committed to make a donation to the DoGood organization. Donor identification data is stored in the DD_DONOR table, and

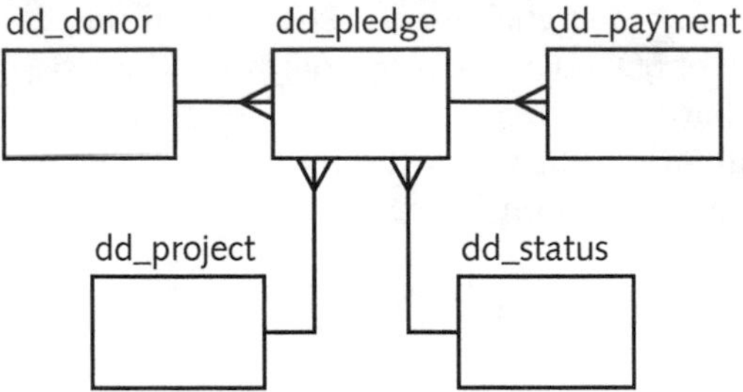

FIGURE 1-9 The DoGood Donor database ERD

donation commitments or pledges are recorded in the DD_PLEDGE table. Two important options are indicated by data in the DD_PLEDGE table: PAY_MONTHS indicates the number of equivalent monthly payments needed to complete the pledge commitment (a 0 indicates a lump sum payment), and PROJ_ID indicates the project for the pledge amount. A pledge can be unassigned or not dedicated to a specific project.

The DD_PROJECT table is the master list of all projects to which pledges can be dedicated. The DD_STATUS table defines the pledge status values assigned to each pledge in the DD_PLEDGE table, indicating whether the pledge is still active, complete, overdue, or closed without full collection. The DD_PAYMENT table stores data for each pledge payment.

Create the DoGood Donation database by using the same steps as for the Brewbean's database in the previous section. Click the `c1_DDcreate.sql` file in the Chapter01 folder and run this script.

The More Movies Database

To work with the second Case Project at the end of each chapter, you need to build a database that supports a movie rental company named More Movies. In these projects, you create application components to support membership and renting processes for More Movies. Figure 1-10 shows this database's ERD.

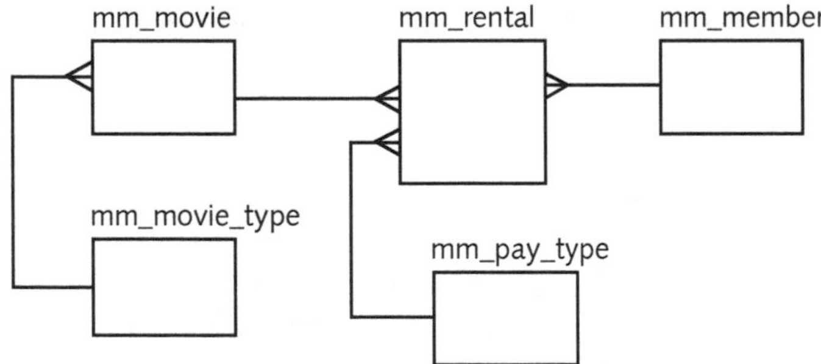

FIGURE 1-10 The More Movies database ERD

The MM_MEMBER table is the master customer list, and the MM_MOVIE table holds information for the movie inventory. All movie rental transactions are tracked with the MM_RENTAL table. The MM_MOVIE_TYPE table is a list of movie genres, and the MM_PAY_TYPE is a list of payment methods used for rentals.

To create the More Movies database, follow the same steps used to create the Brewbean's database, but click the `c1_MMcreate.sql` file in the Chapter01 folder and run this script.

SQL QUERY REVIEW

Before you begin learning PL/SQL coding, it's important to be familiar with SQL syntax. As mentioned, SQL statements are embedded in PL/SQL modules to perform database interaction tasks. This section includes examples of SQL queries, table creation, data manipulation, and transaction control statements.

The following brief review helps you recall the syntax of SQL statements. If you find you don't understand certain concepts, go back to what you learned about SQL statements in previous courses. You need to be familiar with queries (`SELECT`), DML statements (`INSERT`, `UPDATE`, `DELETE`), data definition language (DDL) statements (`CREATE`, `ALTER`, `DROP`), and transaction control statements (`COMMIT`, `ROLLBACK`).

First, review the basic syntax of a `SELECT` statement:

```
SELECT <columns>
FROM <tables, views>
WHERE <conditions>
GROUP BY <columns>
HAVING <aggregation conditions>
ORDER BY <columns>;
```

Try working through a few examples to make sure you're familiar with the coding techniques. Using the Brewbean's database built earlier in this chapter, what statement could be used to produce a list of all products displaying the product name, active status, and department name? Notice that both the BB_PRODUCT and BB_DEPARTMENT tables are needed to retrieve the required information. You need to join these two tables by using a traditional join in the `WHERE` clause (see Figure 1-11) or an ANSI join in the `FROM` clause (see Figure 1-12). Note that the `ON` keyword could be used instead of the `USING` clause. In addition, the `INNER` keyword could be left out.

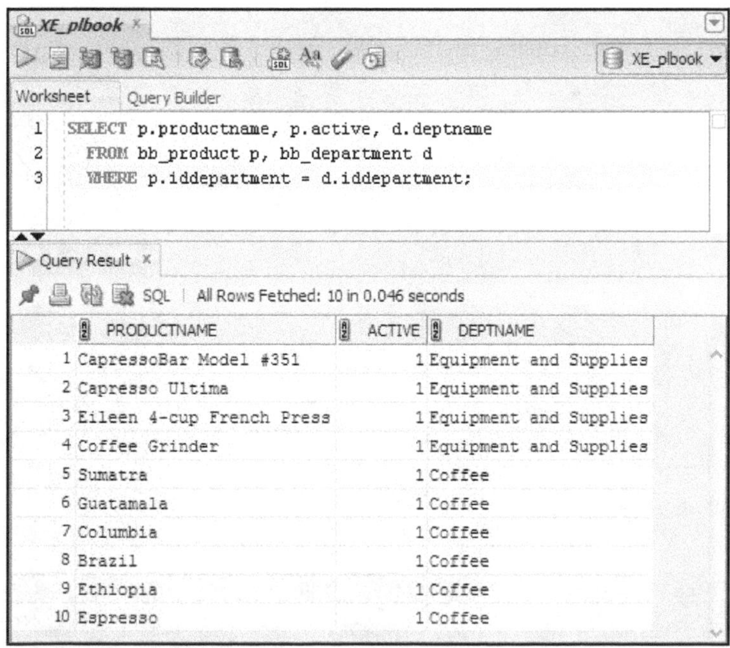

FIGURE 1-11 A query with a traditional join

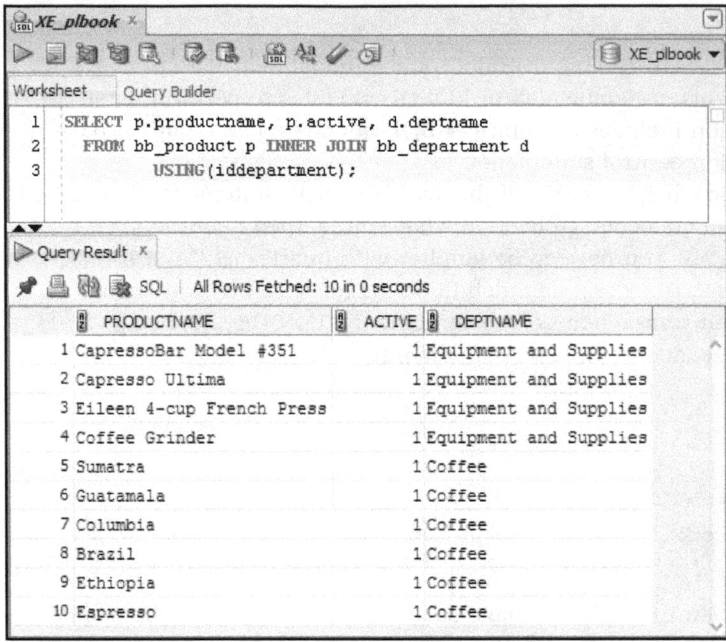

FIGURE 1-12 A query with an ANSI join

Notice the use of table aliases assigned in the `FROM` clause. An alias serves as a nickname to reference a table when qualifying columns.

Next, try a query with an aggregate function. What statement is needed to produce a list showing the number of products in the database by department name? Figure 1-13 displays the statement using the aggregate `COUNT` function.

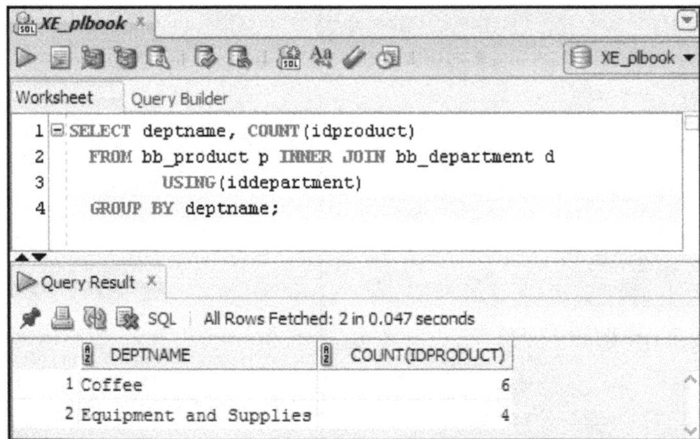

FIGURE 1-13 A query with an aggregate function

TIP

What if you want only departments with five or more products listed? A `HAVING` clause must be added to check whether the count is five or more. Try it!

Now try data-filtering techniques. Write a statement that produces the average price of coffee products. Review the BB_PRODUCT table data, and be sure to look at the data in the TYPE column. Figure 1-14 shows the statement using the aggregate AVG function and a WHERE clause to include only coffee products.

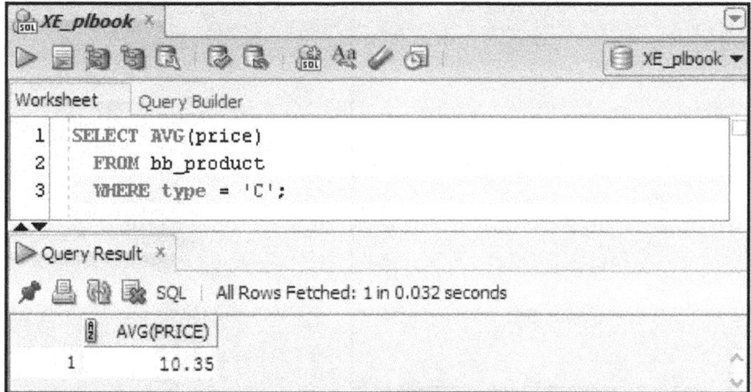

FIGURE 1-14 A query with a WHERE clause

TIP

What if the TYPE value could be stored in uppercase or lowercase characters? You can use the UPPER or LOWER function in the WHERE clause to eliminate the question of case sensitivity.

The preceding examples focus on querying data from an existing database. Next, you review commands used to create tables and manipulate table data. You create a table that holds information for automobiles available at a car rental agency. Build and run the statement shown in Figure 1-15 to create the table. Notice that a primary key constraint is included. Assigning constraint names is helpful because they're referenced if a constraint error occurs in a data manipulation operation.

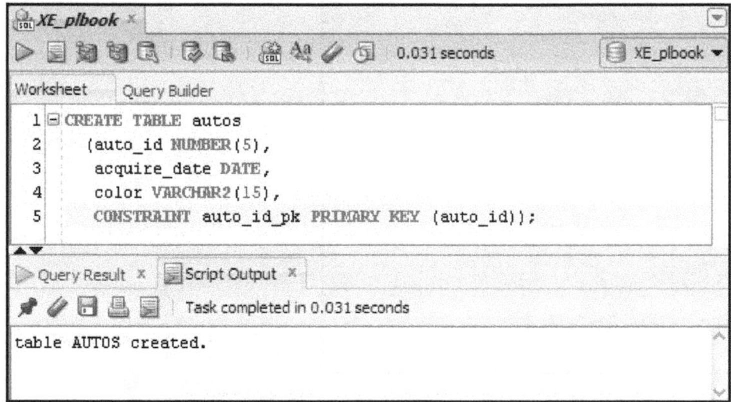

FIGURE 1-15 Creating a table

How can you verify what tables exist in your schema? In SQL Developer, you can simply expand the Tables node in the Connections pane and select the AUTOS table to view its structure. (Keep in mind that you might need to refresh the Connections pane.) However, you can also query the data dictionary view of USER_TABLES to list the tables in your schema. How can you check a table's structure with a command? Figure 1-16 shows the command for this task.

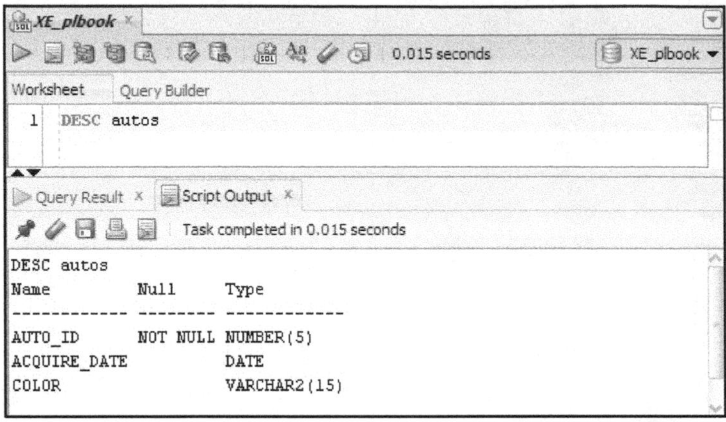

FIGURE 1-16 Listing the structure of a table

Now that you have a table, you can use DML statements to add, modify, and delete data in the table. You can also use transaction control statements to save or undo DML actions. First, issue the two INSERT statements shown in Figure 1-17 to add two rows to the table. The COMMIT statement that follows saves the data rows permanently. Finally, issue the SELECT query on the last line to verify that the data has been inserted.

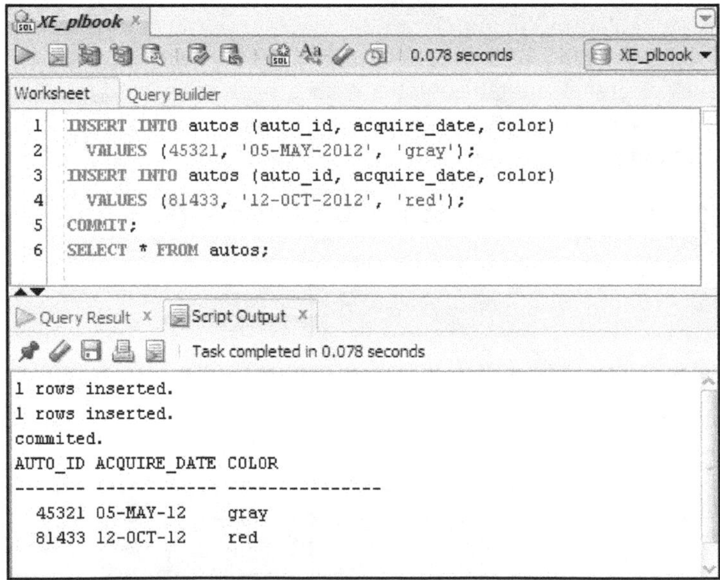

FIGURE 1-17 Adding rows of data

TIP

Four separate SQL statements are used in Figure 1-17. Select each statement, and click the Run Statement button on the Worksheet pane's toolbar to run each statement separately and view the results. If you use the Run Script button, all statements run at once.

NOTE

A sequence is typically used to provide primary key column values. A call of *sequence_name* NEXTVAL is used in an INSERT statement to retrieve a value from a sequence.

The UPDATE statement can be used to modify existing data in the database. Write and run a statement to change the color of the auto with the ID 45321 to silver. Be sure to include a WHERE clause, as shown in Figure 1-18, to ensure that only one row is updated. Keep in mind that omitting a WHERE clause means all rows are updated. Finally, issue a query to verify the modification.

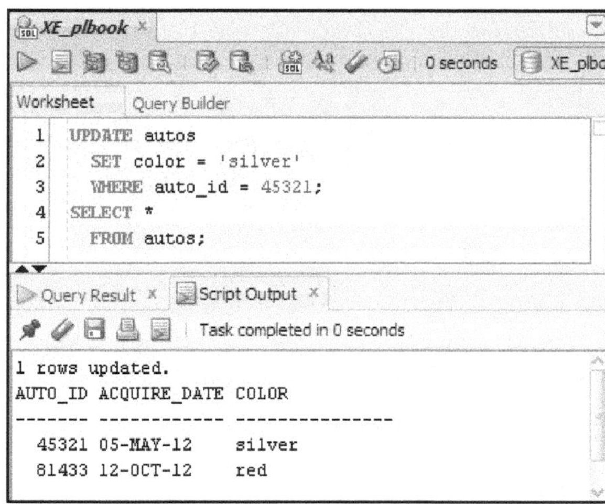

FIGURE 1-18 Modifying a row

Say the previous change was in error, and you want to undo the UPDATE. Because this action hasn't been saved permanently with a COMMIT statement, a ROLLBACK action can be issued to undo the UPDATE statement. Issue a ROLLBACK statement, and query the data to verify that the change has been reversed (see Figure 1-19).

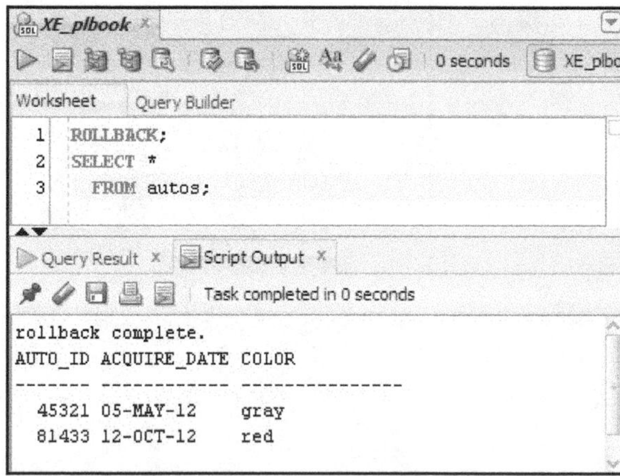

FIGURE 1-19 Using ROLLBACK to undo a DML action

To remove a row, you use the DELETE command. Issue a statement to remove the row of data for the auto with the ID 45321 (see Figure 1-20). Again, notice that the WHERE clause determines which rows are affected by the statement. To save this change permanently, you would need to issue a COMMIT statement.

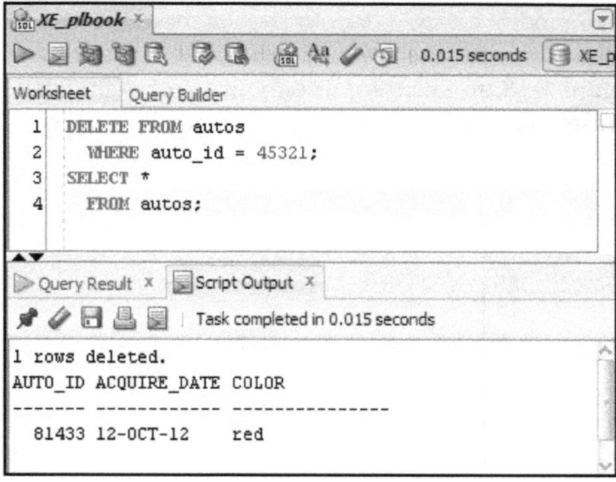

FIGURE 1-20 Using DELETE to remove a row

Remove the table from the database by using the DROP TABLE statement shown in Figure 1-21. Notice that a query attempt on the table after it's been removed displays an error stating that the object doesn't exist.

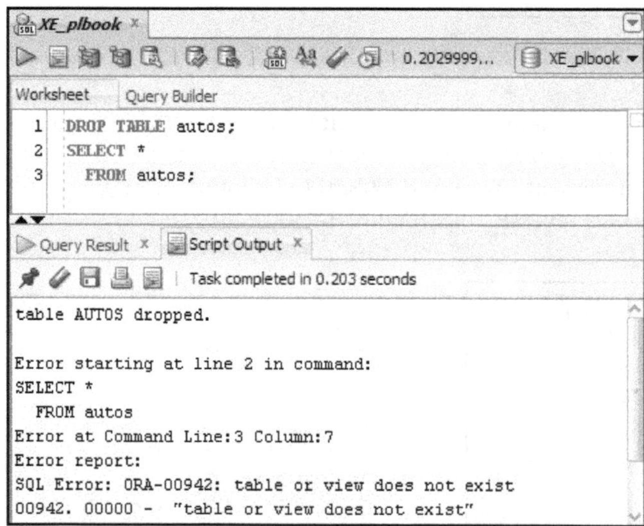

FIGURE 1-21 Removing a table

These examples should help you review the SQL statement syntax you have learned previously. Before you venture into PL/SQL coding, make sure you're thoroughly familiar with the following SQL query topics:

- Joins (traditional and ANSI)
- Restricting data with `WHERE` and `HAVING` clauses
- Single-row functions
- Group/aggregate functions
- Subqueries
- Views
- Sorting
- Tables (create, alter, drop, constraints)
- Sequences
- DML actions
- Transaction control

Chapter Summary

- Programmers can use a procedural language to code a logical sequence of steps for making decisions and instructing the computer on what tasks to perform.
- SQL is used for creating and manipulating a database, but it's not a procedural language.
- PL/SQL is a procedural language, and the Oracle database and software tools contain a PL/SQL processing engine.
- PL/SQL improves application portability because it can be processed on any platform Oracle runs on.
- Using PL/SQL can improve security because users don't need to be granted direct access to database objects.
- Applications contain three main components: a user interface, program logic, and a database.
- The two-tier or client/server application model splits programming logic between the client machine and the database server.
- The three-tier application model places much of the program code on an application server (the middle tier).
- Programming code on the client machine is referred to as client-side code, and code on the database server is referred to as server-side code.
- A named program unit is a block of PL/SQL code that has been saved and assigned a name so that it can be reused.
- A stored program unit is a named program unit that's saved in the database and can be shared by applications. Procedures and functions are named program units that are called to perform a specific task.
- A database trigger is PL/SQL code that's processed automatically when a particular DML action occurs. A package is a structure that allows grouping functions and procedures into one container.
- An application event is some activity that occurs, such as a user clicking an item onscreen, which causes some processing to occur.
- Documentation is available on the Oracle Technology Network (OTN) Web site.
- Both SQL*Plus and SQL Developer are Oracle software tools that allow submitting SQL and PL/SQL statements directly to the Oracle server. Oracle SQL Developer is a software tool for creating and testing program units.
- Many third-party software tools are available for developing PL/SQL program units.
- You need to review a database's ERD before you can work with the data effectively.
- You need to be familiar with SQL statement syntax before learning PL/SQL.

Review Questions

1. What application model typically displays the user interface in a Web browser?
   a. client/server
   b. two-tier
   c. three-tier
   d. thin-tier
2. Which of the following is *not* a type of stored program unit in PL/SQL?
   a. procedure
   b. application trigger
   c. package
   d. database trigger
3. The term "named program unit" indicates which of the following?
   a. The PL/SQL block is assigned a name so that it can be saved and reused.
   b. The PL/SQL block is of a certain type.
   c. The PL/SQL block is executable as an anonymous block.
   d. The PL/SQL block is saved client side.
4. Any application model usually represents which of the following basic components? (Choose all that apply.)
   a. user interface
   b. program logic
   c. coding style
   d. database
5. When working with an Oracle database, which of the following is considered an advantage of PL/SQL? (Choose all that apply.)
   a. tight integration with SQL
   b. easier naming conventions
   c. tighter security
   d. improved performance
6. Which of the following is a free GUI tool from Oracle for editing PL/SQL?
   a. SQL*Plus
   b. Oracle Developer
   c. Oracle SQL Developer
   d. Only third-party tools are available.

7. Which of the following is an Oracle tool included with the Oracle database server that allows sending SQL and PL/SQL statements to the server?
   a. SQL*Plus
   b. PL/SQL Builder
   c. PL/SQL Creator
   d. Procedure Builder
8. A procedural programming language allows including which of the following?
   a. decision-making logic
   b. inserts
   c. DML statements
   d. table creation statements
9. "Application portability" refers to the capability to ______________ .
   a. upload and download
   b. create a small executable
   c. move to other computer platforms
   d. transmit data efficiently
10. A two-tier application model is commonly referred to as a(n) ______________ application model.
    a. *n*-tier
    b. client/server
    c. double-layered
    d. user-database
11. Name the four types of stored program unit structures and the basic differences between them.
12. If you aren't using Oracle development tools, such as Oracle Forms, should you pursue learning PL/SQL? Why or why not?
13. Describe the major difference between a two-tier and a three-tier application model.
14. Describe what a user interface is and the role a procedural language plays in user interfaces.

Hands-On Assignments Part I

Assignment 1-1: Reviewing SQL and Data in the Brewbean's Database

Becoming familiar with the Brewbean's database is important because it's used in examples and exercises throughout this book. For this assignment, you create a few queries to review the data.

First, you query the database by following these steps:

1. Start SQL Developer and connect to Oracle.
2. Enter the query shown in Figure 1-22 and check your data against the listing shown.

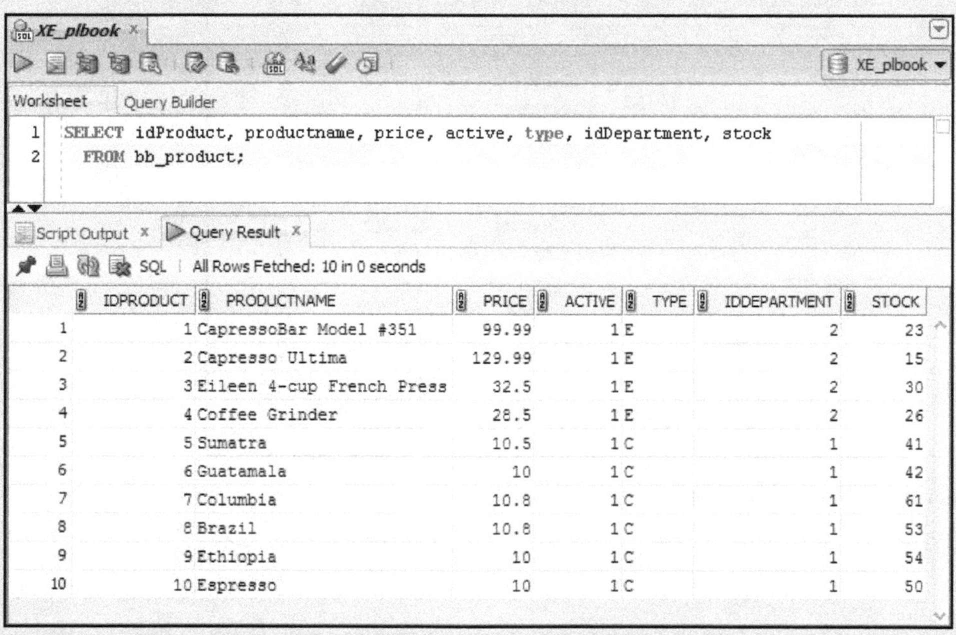


```
SELECT idProduct, productname, price, active, type, idDepartment, stock
  FROM bb_product;
```

	IDPRODUCT	PRODUCTNAME	PRICE	ACTIVE	TYPE	IDDEPARTMENT	STOCK
1	1	CapressoBar Model #351	99.99	1	E	2	23
2	2	Capresso Ultima	129.99	1	E	2	15
3	3	Eileen 4-cup French Press	32.5	1	E	2	30
4	4	Coffee Grinder	28.5	1	E	2	26
5	5	Sumatra	10.5	1	C	1	41
6	6	Guatamala	10	1	C	1	42
7	7	Columbia	10.8	1	C	1	61
8	8	Brazil	10.8	1	C	1	53
9	9	Ethiopia	10	1	C	1	54
10	10	Espresso	10	1	C	1	50

FIGURE 1-22 Querying Brewbean's product information

3. Enter the query shown in Figure 1-23 and check your data against the listing shown. Note that ANSI standard joins introduced in Oracle 9*i* are used.

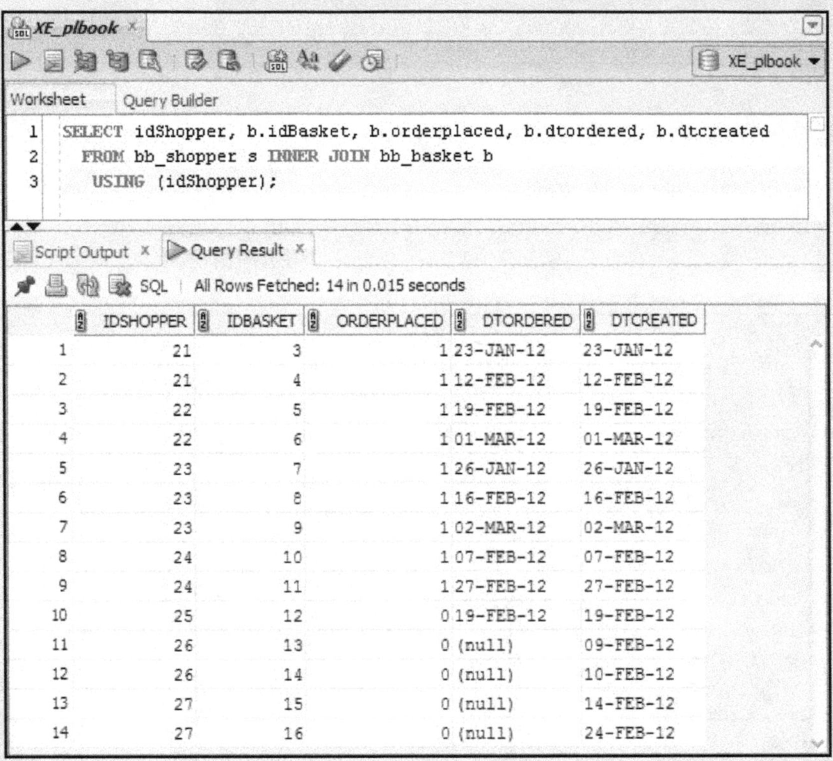


```
SELECT idShopper, b.idBasket, b.orderplaced, b.dtordered, b.dtcreated
  FROM bb_shopper s INNER JOIN bb_basket b
   USING (idShopper);
```

	IDSHOPPER	IDBASKET	ORDERPLACED	DTORDERED	DTCREATED
1	21	3	1	23-JAN-12	23-JAN-12
2	21	4	1	12-FEB-12	12-FEB-12
3	22	5	1	19-FEB-12	19-FEB-12
4	22	6	1	01-MAR-12	01-MAR-12
5	23	7	1	26-JAN-12	26-JAN-12
6	23	8	1	16-FEB-12	16-FEB-12
7	23	9	1	02-MAR-12	02-MAR-12
8	24	10	1	07-FEB-12	07-FEB-12
9	24	11	1	27-FEB-12	27-FEB-12
10	25	12	0	19-FEB-12	19-FEB-12
11	26	13	0	(null)	09-FEB-12
12	26	14	0	(null)	10-FEB-12
13	27	15	0	(null)	14-FEB-12
14	27	16	0	(null)	24-FEB-12

FIGURE 1-23 Querying Brewbean's order information

4. Enter the query shown in Figure 1-24 and check your data for idProduct 5 and idProduct 6 against the listing shown. The full results should contain 24 rows of output.

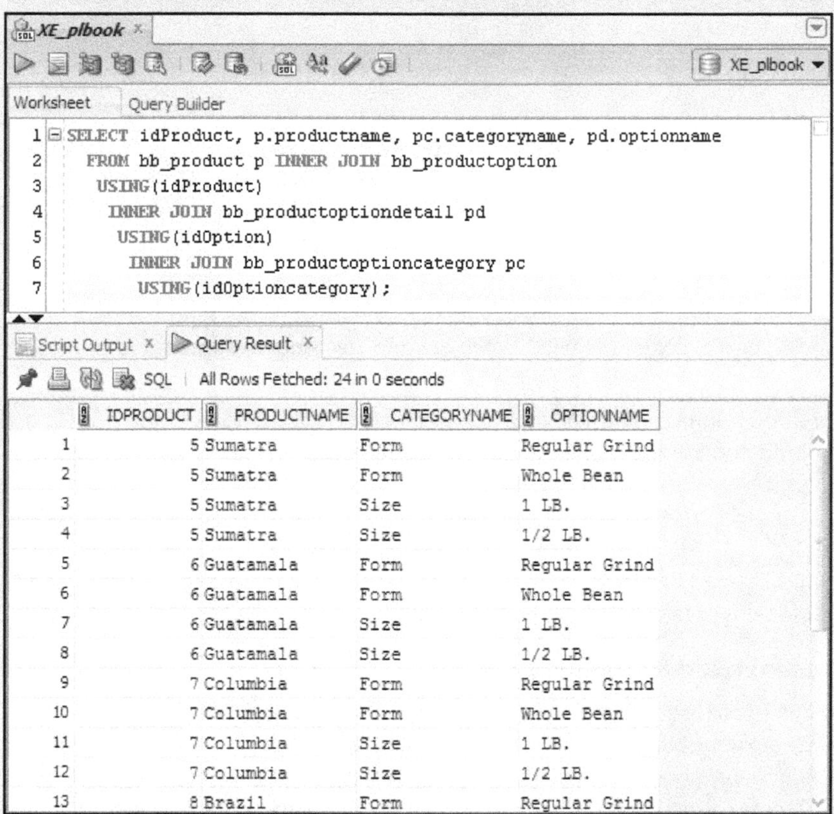

FIGURE 1-24 Querying Brewbean's product option information

Next, you write and run your own SQL statements:

1. Produce an unduplicated list of all product IDs for all products that have been sold. Sort the list.
2. Show the basket ID, product ID, product name, and description for all items ordered. (Do it two ways—one with an ANSI join and one with a traditional join.)
3. Modify the queries in Step 2 to include the customer's last name.
4. Display all orders (basket ID, shopper ID, and date ordered) placed in February 2012. The date should be displayed in this format: February 12, 2012.
5. Display the total quantity sold by product ID.
6. Modify the query in Step 5 to show only products that have sold less than a quantity of 3.
7. List all active coffee products (product ID, name, and price) for all coffee items priced above the overall average of coffee items.

8. Create a table named CONTACTS that includes the following columns:

Column Name	Data Type	Length	Constraint/Option
Con_id	NUMBER	4	Primary key
Company_name	VARCHAR2	30	Not null
E-mail	VARCHAR2	30	
Last_date	DATE	n/a	Default to current date
Con_cnt	NUMBER	3	Check constraint to ensure that value is greater than 0

9. Add two rows of data to the table, using data values you create. Make sure the default option on the LAST_DATE column is used in the second row added. Also, issue a command to save the data in the table permanently.
10. Issue a command to change the e-mail value for the first row added to the table. Show a query on the table to confirm that the change was completed. Then issue a command to undo the change.

Assignment 1-2: Reviewing Third-Party Software Tools

Table 1-2 lists several third-party PL/SQL software tools. Go to the Web site for one of these tools and describe at least two features that can help in developing PL/SQL code.

Assignment 1-3: Identifying Processing Steps

Review the Brewbean's application page in Figure 1-25. List the logical processing steps that need to occur if the Check Out button is clicked for the next page to display the order subtotal, shipping amount, tax amount, and final total. The shipping costs are stored in a database table by number of items. The tax percentage, stored by state in a database table, is based on the customer's billing state.

FIGURE 1-25 Brewbean's application page

Assignment 1-4: Using OTN Documentation

Go to the Oracle 11*g* database documentation section on the OTN Web site. Find PL/SQL Language Reference in the list of available resources, and then find the chapter covering control structures. Explain briefly what a control structure is and give an example of a PL/SQL statement that's considered a control structure statement.

Hands-On Assignments Part II

Assignment 1-5: Querying the DoGood Donor Database

Review the DoGood Donor data by writing and running SQL statements to perform the following tasks:

1. List each donor who has made a pledge and indicated a single lump sum payment. Include first name, last name, pledge date, and pledge amount.
2. List each donor who has made a pledge and indicated monthly payments over one year. Include first name, last name, pledge date, and pledge amount. Also, display the monthly payment amount. (Equal monthly payments are made for all pledges paid in monthly payments.)
3. Display an unduplicated list of projects (ID and name) that have pledges committed. Don't display all projects defined; list only those that have pledges assigned.
4. Display the number of pledges made by each donor. Include the donor ID, first name, last name, and number of pledges.
5. Display all pledges made before March 8, 2012. Include all column data from the DD_PLEDGE table.

Case Projects

Case 1-1: Reviewing Oracle SQL Developer Documentation

Locate and review the getting started guide for Oracle SQL Developer on the OTN Web site and describe at least two features you believe will be helpful in creating PL/SQL code.

Case 1-2: Understanding the More Movies Database

In this chapter, you saw the ERD and steps for creating the More Movies database, which is used for the second case project in every chapter. In this project, you perform several queries on the data to become familiar with it and to verify the content. Perform the queries listed in Table 1-3 and compare them with Figures 1-26 to 1-28 to verify your results.

TABLE 1-3 Query tasks for the More Movies database

Query #	What to Query	Results Figure
1	List the ID, title, category ID, and category name for every movie in the database. What five categories are used for movies?	Figure 1-26
2	List the member ID, last name, and suspension code for every member. Are any members suspended at this point?	Figure 1-27
3	List the member last name, rental checkout date, and movie title for all rentals. What checkout data applies to all recorded rentals?	Figure 1-28

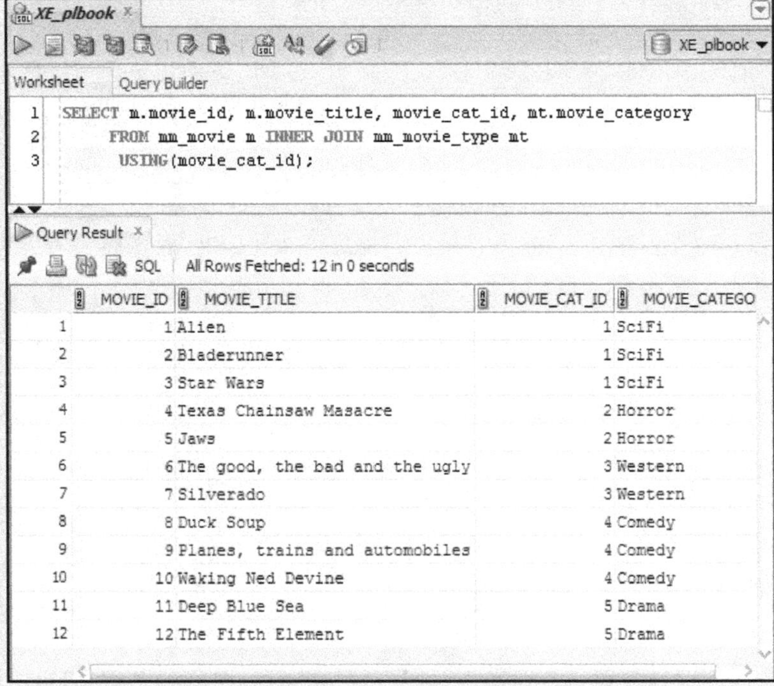

	MOVIE_ID	MOVIE_TITLE	MOVIE_CAT_ID	MOVIE_CATEGO
1	1	Alien	1	SciFi
2	2	Bladerunner	1	SciFi
3	3	Star Wars	1	SciFi
4	4	Texas Chainsaw Masacre	2	Horror
5	5	Jaws	2	Horror
6	6	The good, the bad and the ugly	3	Western
7	7	Silverado	3	Western
8	8	Duck Soup	4	Comedy
9	9	Planes, trains and automobiles	4	Comedy
10	10	Waking Ned Devine	4	Comedy
11	11	Deep Blue Sea	5	Drama
12	12	The Fifth Element	5	Drama

FIGURE 1-26 Results for Query 1

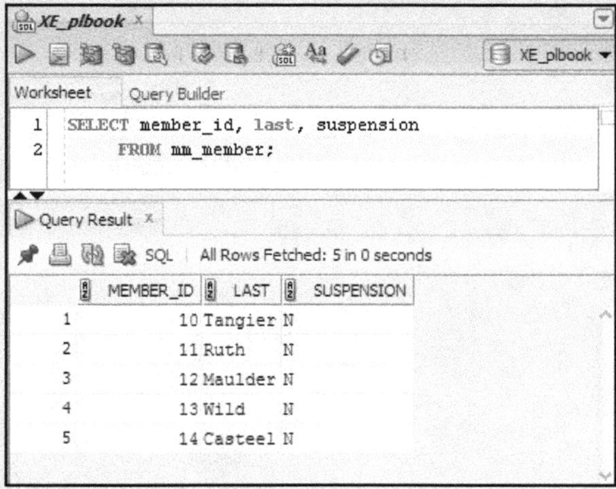

FIGURE 1-27 Results for Query 2

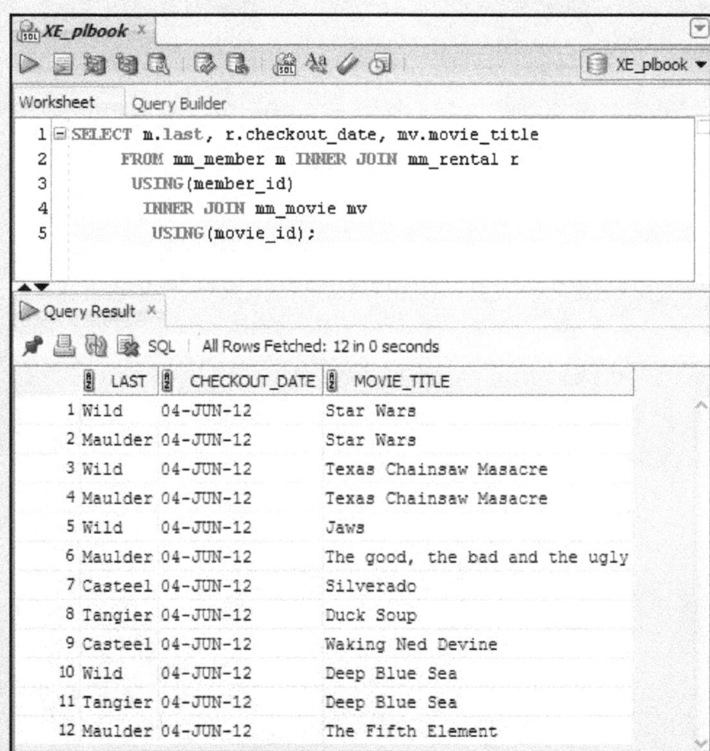

FIGURE 1-28 Results for Query 3

CHAPTER 2

BASIC PL/SQL BLOCK STRUCTURES

LEARNING OBJECTIVES

After completing this chapter, you should be able to understand:

- Programming fundamentals
- PL/SQL blocks
- How to define and declare variables
- How to initialize and manage variable values
- The `NOT NULL` and `CONSTANT` variable options
- How to perform calculations with variables
- The use of SQL single-row functions in PL/SQL statements
- Decision structures: `IF/THEN` and `CASE`
- Looping actions: basic, `FOR`, and `WHILE`
- `CONTINUE` statements
- Nested statements

INTRODUCTION

If you're new to programming, you should learn some basic principles of program design first. A **program** is a set of instructions requesting the computer to perform specific actions, and it might be used to support a system or application. For example, say you're purchasing a book from an online retailer. To begin the purchase, you enter a search for all books containing the term "PL/SQL" in the title. You type this term in a text entry box, and then click a search button. To support this action, a program is started (triggered) when the search button is clicked. It causes another program to run that reads your text input of "PL/SQL," searches the book database, and displays the results.

A program is also used for activities such as database monitoring. Many database administrators need to monitor system activity, such as the number of active users. A program could be developed to check the number of active users and record the information in the database so that it could be analyzed over time. This program could be scheduled to run automatically at specified periods so the database administrator doesn't need to monitor and record this information manually.

The first section of this chapter gives you an overview of programming fundamentals. Then you begin learning and using the basic PL/SQL block structure.

PROGRAMMING FUNDAMENTALS

Regardless of a program's purpose, all programs have similar basic structures. First, every program has a sequence of actions. Identifying the required actions before coding is essential; therefore, the initial layout of program steps doesn't involve any coding. To illustrate this structure, the Brewbean's application is used. It allows users to enter a term to search for coffee products and then click a search button. Coffee products with the search term in their name or description are then displayed. Figure 2-1 is a flowchart showing a simple layout of the sequence of events that happen after the search button is clicked. Notice that actions are described with text, not code.

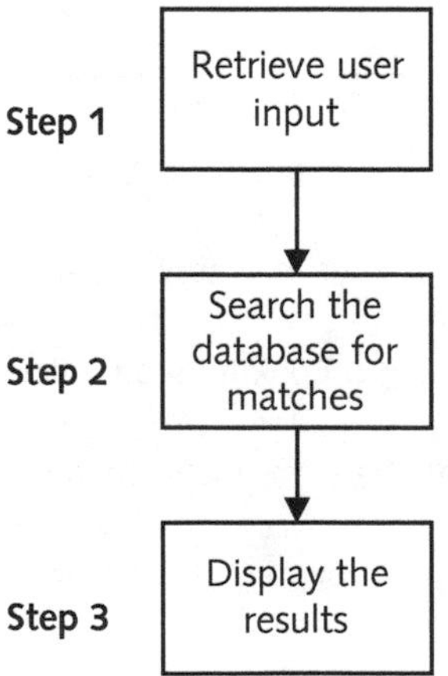

FIGURE 2-1 Flowchart with a sequence structure

NOTE

Some developers prefer to use pseudocode (English-like statements) instead of a flowchart's symbols to describe actions needed for a program.

Second, programs typically include decision structures that outline different sequences of events depending on a question determined at runtime. Take a look at another example involving the Brewbean's application. A customer clicks an order button in the shopping basket screen to place an order online. When this button is clicked, a summary of information, including the total cost, should be displayed. The total cost needs to reflect a 10% discount if the customer is a member of the company's coffee club. Figure 2-2 is a flowchart including a decision structure to determine the sequence of events based on club membership.

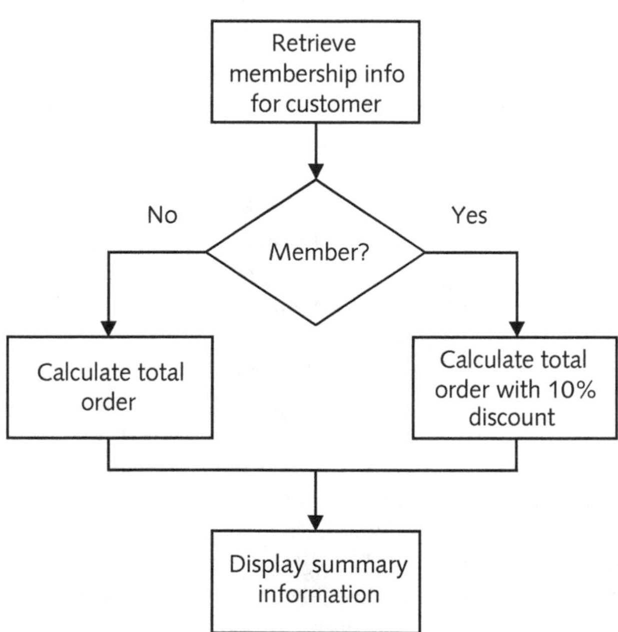

FIGURE 2-2 Flowchart including a decision structure

Third, many programs use a looping structure to repeat actions. For example, Brewbean's might need to calculate new sales prices for all products and store this information in the product database. Say that Brewbean's wants to set all product sale prices to reflect a 10% discount. Figure 2-3's flowchart includes the looping action to repeat the sales price calculation and update for each product in the database. Because the same actions need to occur for each product retrieved from the database, the calculation and update coding can be written once and repeated for each product.

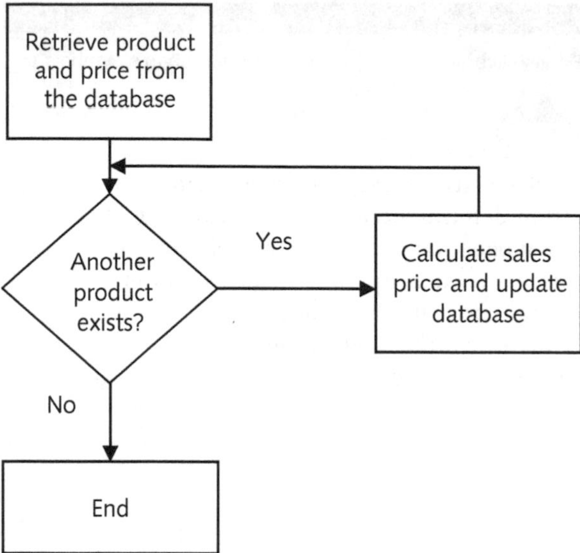

FIGURE 2-3 Flowchart including a looping structure

Now that you have an idea of the basic logic structure involved in programs, you need to translate these actions into PL/SQL code. Chapters 2 through 4 focus on showing PL/SQL coding to address data handling, making decisions, looping, and handling errors. As coding tasks get more complex, you can return to these flowcharting concepts to help you determine the code steps you need for your programs.

The flowcharts shown in this book are basic, using a diamond shape to indicate decision processes and a square shape for all other actions. Formal flowcharting includes a wider variety of symbols and standardized formatting, but this book's intent isn't to teach you formal flowcharting. Flowcharts are included solely as a simple way to organize the processing steps required for a block of code. If you're new to programming, laying out the sequence of processing steps before coding is important. This book uses flowcharts only in the first few chapters to show how they might be used in developing your PL/SQL programs; however, programmers use several other methods to outline program logic flow, including simply writing numbered steps. Don't underestimate the importance of determining program steps before writing code. Even advanced programmers emphasize the importance of this preparation to increase programming productivity and reduce the time spent debugging coding problems.

TIP

Those new to programming should practice using flowcharts or writing coding steps in pseudocode when attempting assignment problems. Determine the method you find most helpful, and use it throughout this book to assist in solving coding problems.

THE CURRENT CHALLENGE IN THE BREWBEAN'S APPLICATION

Before jumping into coding, there's another data-handling challenge in the Brewbean's application you should consider. In the rest of this chapter, you learn PL/SQL coding techniques to address some requirements for this challenge.

The Brewbean's application already has certain functions. As you can see in Figure 2-4, a shopping basket screen shows shoppers all the items and quantities selected so far. A number of processing tasks could be required when the shopper clicks the Check Out button. These tasks include calculating taxes, calculating shipping charges, checking and/or updating product inventory, and determining whether the shopper already has credit card information stored.

FIGURE 2-4 The Brewbean's shopping basket

So how do you approach programming the required tasks? Typically, a block is written to perform a particular task. For example, for the Brewbean's shopping basket, a PL/SQL block might be written to handle calculating shipping costs based on the number of items in the order and the type of shipping method that's selected. In addition, separate blocks can be developed to calculate applicable taxes and handle inventory issues. Using this modular approach makes developing an application and maintaining and reusing code more manageable than having large, more complex blocks of code.

Keep reusability in mind as you construct blocks or modules of code. Look at the shipping calculation as an example. This block could accept input, such as a basket number, from the shopping basket. The program then might use this input to query the database for the number of items in the basket. By accepting input values, the same PL/SQL block is made dynamic, meaning it can calculate the shipping costs for any order because it queries the database for the total number of items based on the basket number.

PL/SQL BLOCK STRUCTURE

In this section, you start with the basic structure of a PL/SQL block. To learn the syntax of a block, you begin working with **anonymous blocks**, which are blocks of code that aren't stored for reuse and, as far as the Oracle server is concerned, no longer exist after they run. The block code is entered in SQL Developer, just as you would enter an SQL statement.

As outlined in Table 2-1, PL/SQL code is created in a block structure containing four main sections: DECLARE, BEGIN, EXCEPTION, and END. A block is always closed with an `END;` statement. The only required sections of a PL/SQL block are the BEGIN and END sections; however, most blocks use all four sections.

TABLE 2-1 PL/SQL Block Sections

Block Section	Section Content
DECLARE	Creates variables, cursors, and types
BEGIN	Contains SQL statements, conditional logic processing, loops, and assignment statements
EXCEPTION	Contains error handlers
END	Closes the block

The following sections discuss the first three sections in Table 2-1 in detail.

DECLARE Section

The DECLARE section contains code that creates variables, cursors, and data types, used to hold data for processing and manipulation. For example, if a shopper on the Brewbean's Web site clicks the Check Out button, the code needs to retrieve all the item quantities in the shopper's basket to calculate shipping costs. In addition, the code needs to calculate the actual shipping cost. Variables store this data to be used while the block runs.

TIP

As you progress in your studies, you'll discover that a number of different variable types exist, and they serve different purposes. For example, a scalar variable can hold only a single value, whereas a composite variable can hold multiple values.

BEGIN Section

The BEGIN section, the heart of the PL/SQL block, contains all the processing action or programming logic. SQL is used for database queries and data manipulation. Conditional logic, such as `IF` statements (explained later in this chapter), is used to make decisions on what action to take. Loops are used to repeat code, and assignment statements are used to put or change values in variables. In the shipping cost example, you can use `IF` statements to check the quantity of items and apply the correct shipping cost.

EXCEPTION Section

One job of a developer is to anticipate possible errors and include exception handlers to show users understandable messages for corrections that are needed or system problems that must be addressed. The EXCEPTION section contains handlers that enable you to control what the application does if an error occurs during executable statements in the BEGIN section. For example, if your code attempts to retrieve all the items in a basket, but there are no items, an Oracle error occurs. You can use exception handlers so that shoppers don't see Oracle system error messages and the application doesn't halt operation. Instead, you can display easy-to-understand messages to users and allow the application to continue via exception handlers.

NOTE

As you work through the next sections, keep in mind that PL/SQL isn't a case-sensitive language. However, to improve readability, the code examples in this book use uppercase letters for keywords such as `DECLARE` and `BEGIN`.

WORKING WITH VARIABLES

In most PL/SQL blocks, variables are needed to hold values for use in the program logic. **Variables** are named memory areas that hold values so that they can be retrieved and manipulated in programs. For example, if a `SELECT` statement is included in a block, variables are needed to hold data retrieved from the database. In addition, if the block contains a calculation, a variable is needed to hold the resulting value.

The type of data to be stored determines the type of variable needed. For example, if only a single value needs to be stored, scalar variables are used. However, if multiple values need to be stored, such as an entire row from a database table, a record (which is a composite variable) is needed. Finally, if you intend to process a number of rows retrieved with a `SELECT` statement, you might create a cursor, which is a structure specifically suited to processing a group of rows.

Don't feel overwhelmed by these different data types at this point. They're discussed in more detail in subsequent chapters. For now, just remember that a variable is used to hold data, and no matter what type of variable is needed, the variable must be declared in the DECLARE section of the block before you can use it in the BEGIN section.

To declare a variable, you must supply a variable name and data type. Variable names follow the same naming conventions as Oracle database objects:

- Begin with an alpha character
- Contain up to 30 characters
- Can include uppercase and lowercase letters, numbers, and special characters (_, $, and #)
- Exclude PL/SQL reserved words and keywords

TIP

You can find a list of PL/SQL reserved words and keywords in the Oracle PL/SQL User's Guide and Reference, available on the OTN Web site.

Naming conventions are rules used in assigning variable names, and you learn some in the following sections. These rules are helpful to programmers because variable names indicate information about the variable, such as what type of data it stores (a date or a number, for example).

Working with Scalar Variables

Scalar variables, as mentioned, can hold a single value. The common data types for scalar variables include character, numeric, date, and Boolean. Table 2-2 describes them briefly.

TABLE 2-2 Scalar Variable Data Types

Type	Written in PL/SQL Code	Description
Character	CHAR(*n*)	Stores alphanumeric data, with *n* representing the number of characters. The variable always stores *n* number of characters, regardless of the actual length of the value it's storing because it pads the data with blanks. If *n* isn't provided, the length defaults to 1. The maximum length is 32,767 characters. Use CHAR for items that always contain the same number of characters. Otherwise, it's more efficient (in terms of system resources) to use VARCHAR2.
	VARCHAR2(*l*)	Stores alphanumeric data, with *l* representing the number of characters. The variable stores only the number of characters needed to hold the value placed in this variable, regardless of the actual variable length (hence "VAR" for variable). The *l* value is required. The maximum length is 32,767 characters.
Numeric	NUMBER(*p*, *s*)	Stores numeric data, with *p* representing the size or precision and *s* representing the scale. The size includes the total number of digits, and the scale is the number of digits to the right of the decimal point. For example, a variable declared as NUMBER(2,1) can hold the number 9.9 but is too small for 19.9. If *s* isn't provided, the variable can't store decimal amounts. If both *p* and *s* are omitted, the variable defaults to a size of 40.
Date	DATE	Stores date and time values. The default format for Oracle to identify a string value as a date is *DD-MON-YY*. For example, 15-NOV-12 is recognized as a date. This setting is in the init.ora file and can be changed by the DBA.
Boolean	BOOLEAN	Stores a value of TRUE, FALSE, or NULL. Typically used to indicate the result of checking a condition or group of conditions. In other words, it provides a variable that represents a logical condition's state in terms of true or false. A nonexistent value or NULL is more accurately referenced as UNKNOWN in terms of a Boolean variable.

Other data types are available that you can use after you're comfortable with basic PL/SQL programming. For example, date data types of INTERVAL and TIMESTAMP can be used. Also, the numeric data type SIMPLE_INTEGER, introduced in Oracle 11*g*, can be useful for arithmetic-heavy operations.

You're already familiar with most of these data types, as they're used as column data types in tables. The Boolean data type might be new to you, however, as it's not a column data type. This data type holds a TRUE or FALSE value and is used quite a bit with logic that checks for the existence of some condition in a program. For example, a Boolean variable might be set to TRUE if the shipping address should be the same as the shopper's address. In your program logic, you can check this flag easily to determine which database fields to use to retrieve the shipping address.

TIP

Many database developers use a CHAR column containing Y/N or a NUMBER column containing 0/1 to mimic a Boolean data type.

In the following sections, you learn how to use scalar variables, starting with their declarations.

Variable Declarations in Code

To give you a picture of what variable declarations look like, the following code snippet displays four scalar variable declarations in the DECLARE section of a PL/SQL block. Notice that only one variable declaration per line is allowed, and each ends with a semicolon.

```
DECLARE
  lv_ord_date DATE;
  lv_last_txt VARCHAR2(25);
  lv_qty_num NUMBER(2);
  lv_shipflag_bln BOOLEAN;
BEGIN
---- PL/SQL executable statements ----
END;
```

Each line of code declares a variable by supplying a variable name and data type, which is the minimum information necessary to declare a variable. The `lv_` prefix indicates scalar variables that are local to (created in) the block. The suffixes, such as DATE and NUMBER, indicate the data type for the variable. As you create and modify blocks of code, this information helps you identify the types of values each variable holds. Each variable in the preceding code example contains a NULL value (empty) when the BEGIN section starts execution.

Try the first block, which creates the four variables, assigns a value to each variable, and displays each variable to verify the contents. First, you need to know how to assign values to variables and display variable values. These actions occur in a block's executable or BEGIN section. PL/SQL assignment statements are constructed as follows:

```
variable_name := value or expression;
```

Notice that a colon is used with an equals sign to assign a value. One simple way to display values onscreen in SQL Developer is to use the `DBMS_OUTPUT.PUT_LINE` procedure. To display the contents or value of a variable named `lv_ord_date`, you use the following statement:

```
DBMS_OUTPUT.PUT_LINE(lv_ord_date);
```

NOTE

The PUT_LINE procedure is available in the DBMS_OUTPUT Oracle-supplied package.

Be aware that the PUT_LINE procedure displays string values by default and can't display the value for a Boolean variable; if you try to do so, it causes an error. Later in this section, you see an example that includes declaring and assigning a value to a Boolean variable to work around this display limitation.

SQL Developer has an output pane for displaying the output of the PUT_LINE procedure. To prepare for running some code examples, follow these steps:

1. Start SQL Developer and connect to the database.
2. If the Dbms Output pane isn't displayed under the Worksheet, click **View**, **Dbms Output** from the main menu to display it (see Figure 2-5). Notice that the Script Output pane is closed in this figure.
3. Click the green plus symbol on the Dbms Output toolbar to enable this display feature. You need to confirm for which connection this feature is to be activated.

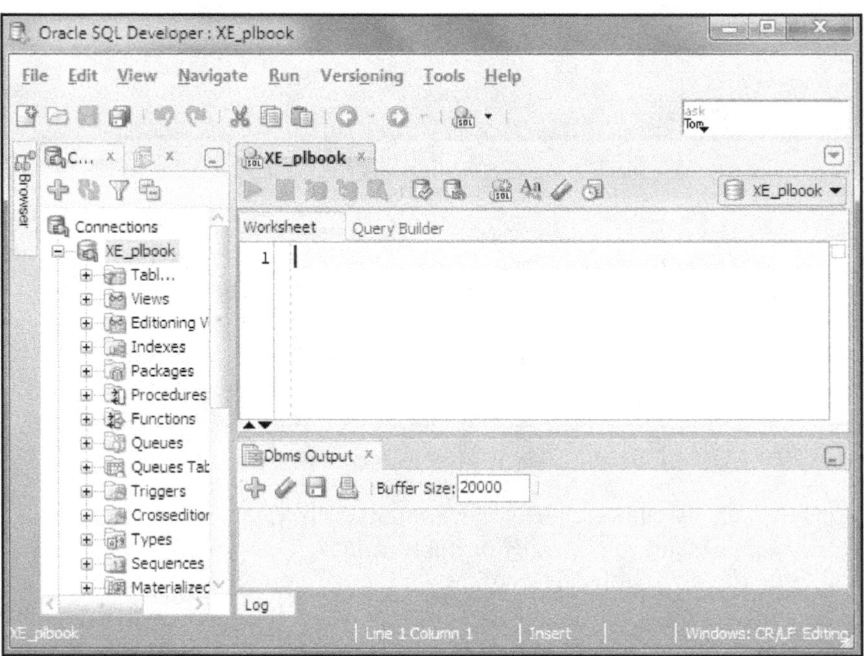

FIGURE 2-5 The SQL Developer Dbms Output pane

NOTE

In subsequent coding examples, it's assumed you have completed the preceding steps.

Now you have all the pieces to build and run the first block. Enter the block of code shown in Figure 2-6 and run it by clicking the Run Script button on the Worksheet toolbar. Verify the execution results in four output lines (see Figure 2-7).

Run Script button

XE_plbook

0 seconds

Worksheet Query Builder

```
DECLARE
  lv_ord_date DATE;
  lv_last_txt VARCHAR2(25);
  lv_qty_num NUMBER(2);
  lv_shipflag_bln BOOLEAN;
  lv_bln_txt VARCHAR2(5);
BEGIN
   lv_ord_date := '12-JUL-2012';
   lv_last_txt := 'Brown';
   lv_qty_num := 3;
   lv_shipflag_bln := TRUE;
   DBMS_OUTPUT.PUT_LINE(lv_ord_date);
   DBMS_OUTPUT.PUT_LINE(lv_last_txt);
   DBMS_OUTPUT.PUT_LINE(lv_qty_num);
   IF lv_shipflag_bln THEN
      lv_bln_txt := 'OK';
   END IF;
   DBMS_OUTPUT.PUT_LINE(lv_bln_txt);
END;
```

FIGURE 2-6 The block to declare and display variables

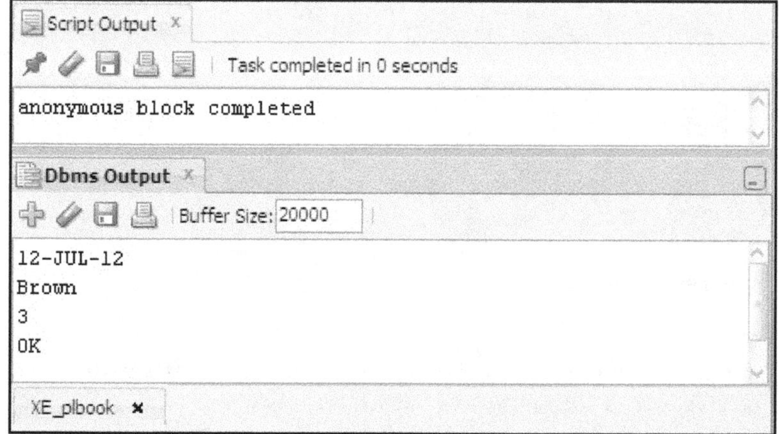

FIGURE 2-7 Results of running the code block

TIP

In the SQL*Plus client tool, a forward slash on the line after the block of code instructs the system to run the code.

PL/SQL programmers should be aware that it's possible to break the rules for variable names, but it's considered a poor practice because it can cause difficulties in reading and debugging code someone else has developed. Using double quotes around an identifier or a variable name is one way to circumvent naming rules, as when you want to begin a variable name with a number or include whitespace in a name. However, doing so makes the variable name case sensitive, which can cause some confusion. Figure 2-8 shows some examples.

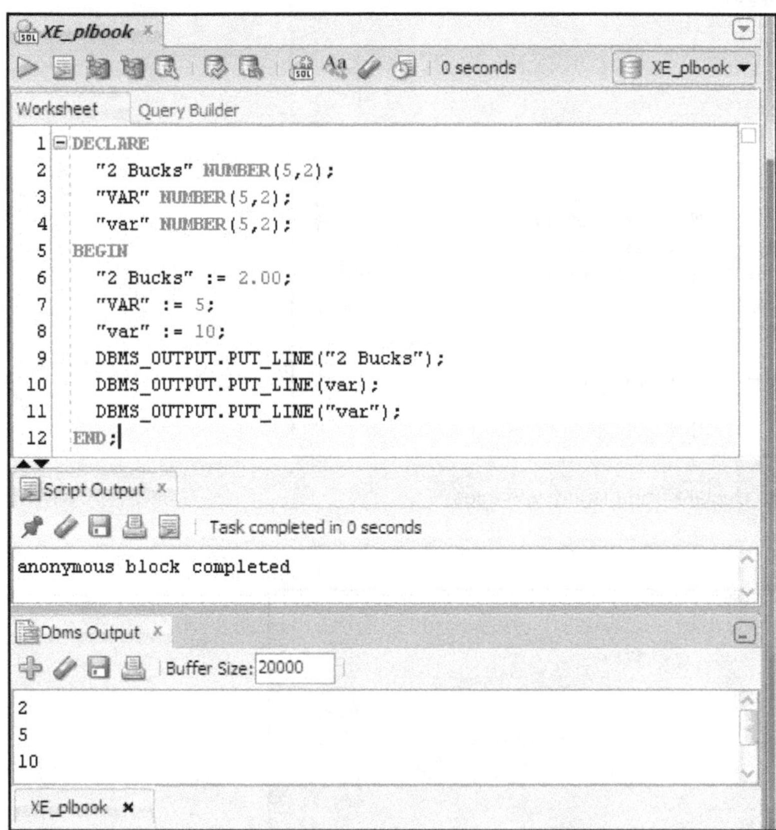

FIGURE 2-8 Using double quotes with variable names

Notice that the `"2 Bucks"` variable name is allowed, even though it starts with a number and includes whitespace. The second line of output returns a 5 for the `var` variable. You might expect a 10 to be returned because the lowercase `var` variable is assigned the value 10. However, the output statement didn't use double quotes around the variable name, so the system defaults to interpreting it as the uppercase `VAR`. The last line of output returns the 10 you expect for `var` because double quotes are used around the variable name. As you can observe with this simple block, using double quotes in variable naming can become confusing quite quickly.

Managing Variable Values

Now that you're familiar with assignment statements and displaying values in PL/SQL, it's time to examine some common hurdles with handling data values. This section describes common problems in using formatting characters in number values, string conversions on numbers, and including quotes in variable values.

A typical issue with numeric assignment statement is attempting to include formatting characters. For example, when working with monetary amounts, you might accidentally include a dollar sign or commas. Review the code block and error shown in Figure 2-9. An attempt is made to assign the value $5,246.22 to a number variable. Notice that the error references encountering a $ symbol. In SQL Developer, you can detect errors before execution by the color coding in the Worksheet pane; the editor detects a possible issue with the syntax before execution.

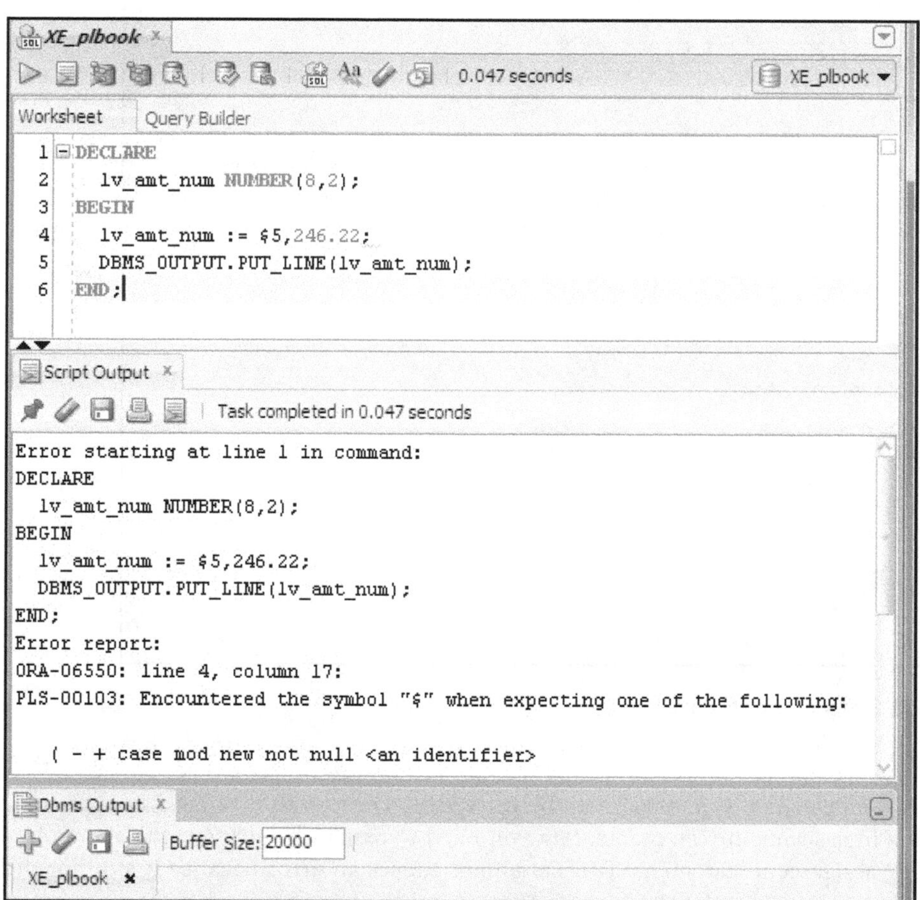

FIGURE 2-9 An error with a number value

String conversion on number values using TO_CHAR can also cause problems in rounding and insufficient display length. At times, you need to convert a number value to include formatting for display, such as the dollar symbol and commas shown in the previous example. The TO_CHAR function enables you to perform this task; however, you need to be aware of some typical problems associated with format arguments. Review the three output statements and results in Figure 2-10. In the first output, the ####### display indicates that the format argument is too small to hold the value. This format argument '$99.99' allows only two whole numbers, but the value contains three. The second output of $257.85 is displayed accurately because the format argument provides enough length for the value. The third output of $258 is often the most unexpected and can be misleading to users. A format argument with no decimal places automatically rounds a value containing decimal values. Notice that the amount was rounded up to the next whole dollar value.

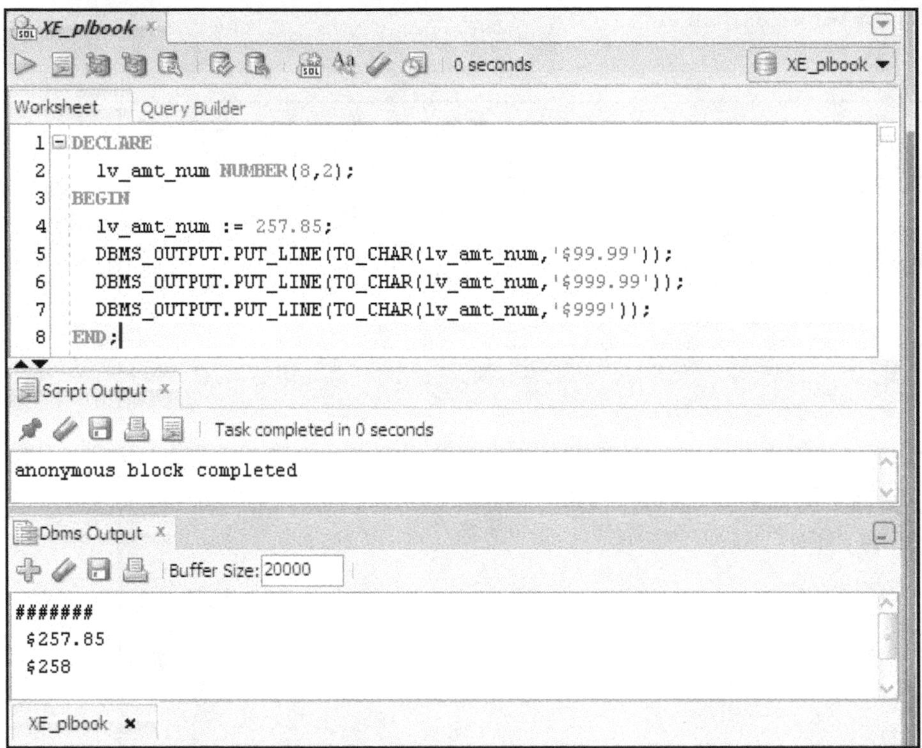

FIGURE 2-10 String conversion issues

Including single quotes in strings can be frustrating because they're used to surround string values in assignment statements. Say you need to assign the string value shown in the following assignment statement. This statement causes an error because it stops at the second single quote to end the string value `Donor` and then can't interpret the remainder of the line: `s Best'`.

```
lv_title_txt := 'Donor's Best';
```

You have two options for including single quotes in string values: Use two single quotes together to represent a single quote in the string or, starting with Oracle 10*g*, use the user-defined delimiters option. Figure 2-11 shows both options. In the first example, note that the string includes two single quotes in succession to represent a single quote in the value; using a double quote doesn't work. The second and third examples use the user-defined delimiter, which begins with the `q` character. Notice the difference in the two examples. The last one actually includes quotes surrounding the string value as part of the variable value. All text inside the parentheses becomes part of the resulting string value.

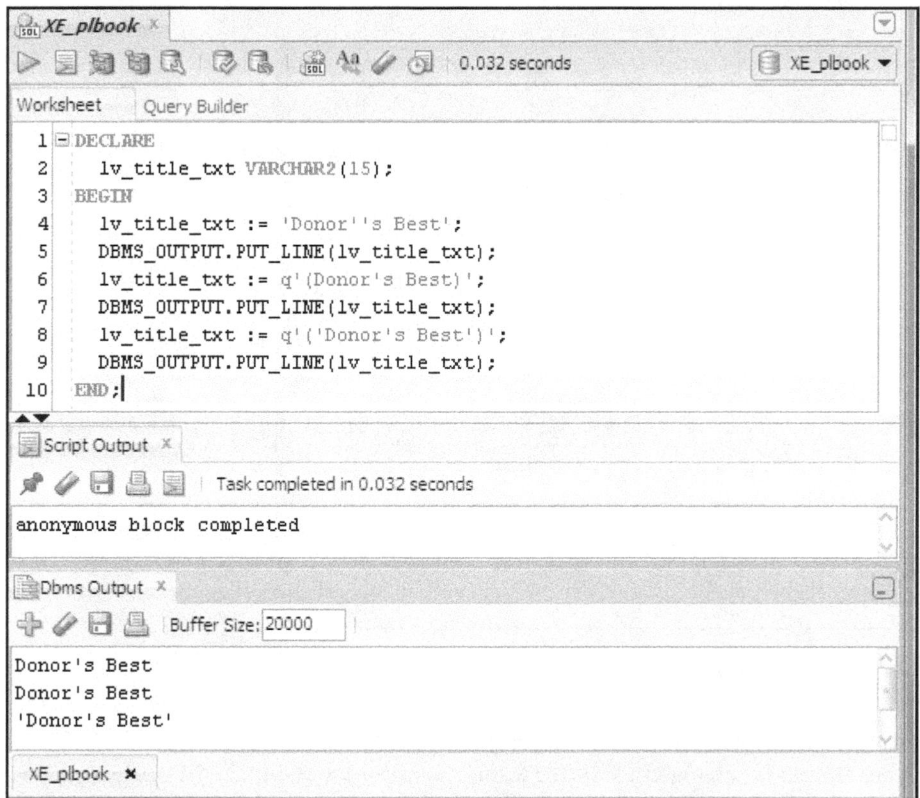

FIGURE 2-11 Including quotes in string values

In the previous examples, the variables don't contain a value until the assignment statements in the BEGIN section run. What if you need a variable to contain a beginning or default value? For example, you might have a date variable that needs to contain the current date. You can set a default value in a variable when it's declared. This technique, called variable initializing, is covered next.

Variable Initialization

Sometimes you need to set a starting value in a variable. You can do this with initialization in the variable declaration so that the variable already contains a value when the block's BEGIN section starts running. To see how to initialize variables in the earlier example, review Figure 2-12 and the changes in the DECLARE section.

The := followed by a value is used to assign initial values to variables in declaration statements. The `DEFAULT` keyword can be used in place of the := symbol to achieve the same result. Typically, a Boolean variable is initialized to `FALSE`, and executable

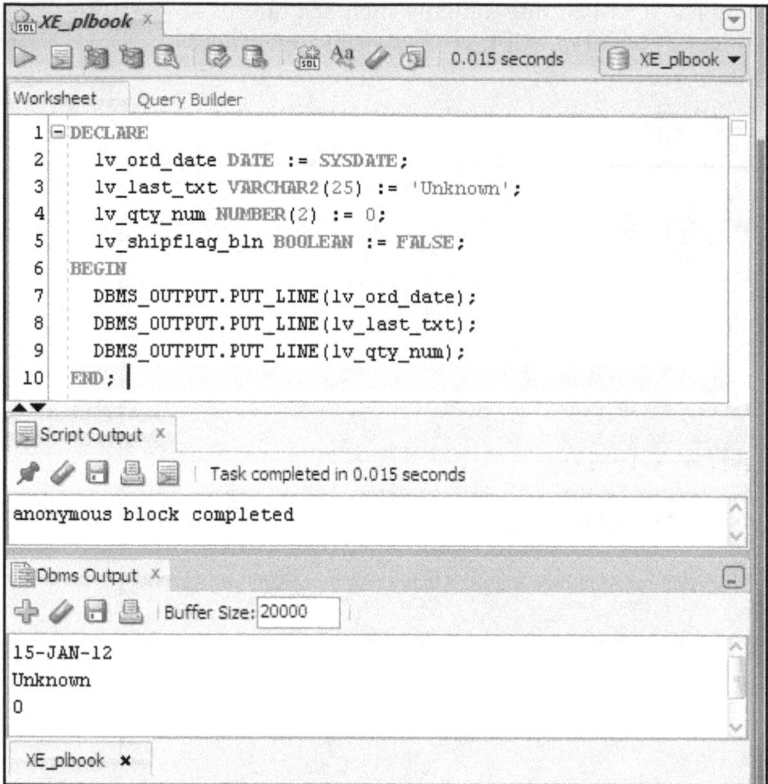

FIGURE 2-12 Variable initialization

statements in the BEGIN section check for conditions and determine whether the variable's value should be changed to TRUE. Numeric variables to be used in calculations are usually initialized to 0 to prevent performing calculations on a NULL value, which isn't the same as a 0 value.

> **TIP**
>
> The DEFAULT keyword can be used in place of the := to get the same result. In practice, the := symbol is more widely used.

Build and run the block in Figure 2-12 with the variable initializations and display all variable values to confirm that the variables contain values as the block begins execution. No assignment statements are performed in the block's executable section. Notice that a display statement isn't included for the Boolean variable. Add the statements needed to confirm that the Boolean variable contains a value from initialization (as explained earlier in "Working with Scalar Variables").

NOT NULL and CONSTANT

In addition to assigning initial values, you can set other controls on variable values with the NOT NULL and CONSTANT options. The NOT NULL option requires that the variable always contains a value. This value can change during the block execution, but the variable must always contain a value. The CONSTANT option can be added to the variable declaration to ensure that the variable always contains a particular value in the block. That is, it prevents the variable's value from being changed in the block. Take a look at how the NOT NULL and CONSTANT options are included in the variable declaration:

```
DECLARE
  lv_shipcntry_txt VARCHAR2(15) NOT NULL := 'US';
  lv_taxrate_num CONSTANT NUMBER(2,2) := .06;
BEGIN
---- PL/SQL executable statements ----
END;
```

In both declarations, the variable is initialized with a value, using the := assignment symbol. This assignment is required because both options require that the variable always contains a value. In the Brewbean's application, assume the same tax rate applies to all sales; therefore, the lv_taxrate_num variable is declared as a constant to make sure this value isn't modified mistakenly in the block's executable section. The lv_shipcntry_txt variable contains 'US' because at this point, all shoppers are from the United States. Also, note that the CONSTANT keyword is listed before the variable data type, whereas the NOT NULL keywords are listed after the data type.

Try experimenting with these two options in the following steps:

1. Type and run the block shown in Figure 2-13. The errors indicate that both variables require an initialization assignment.

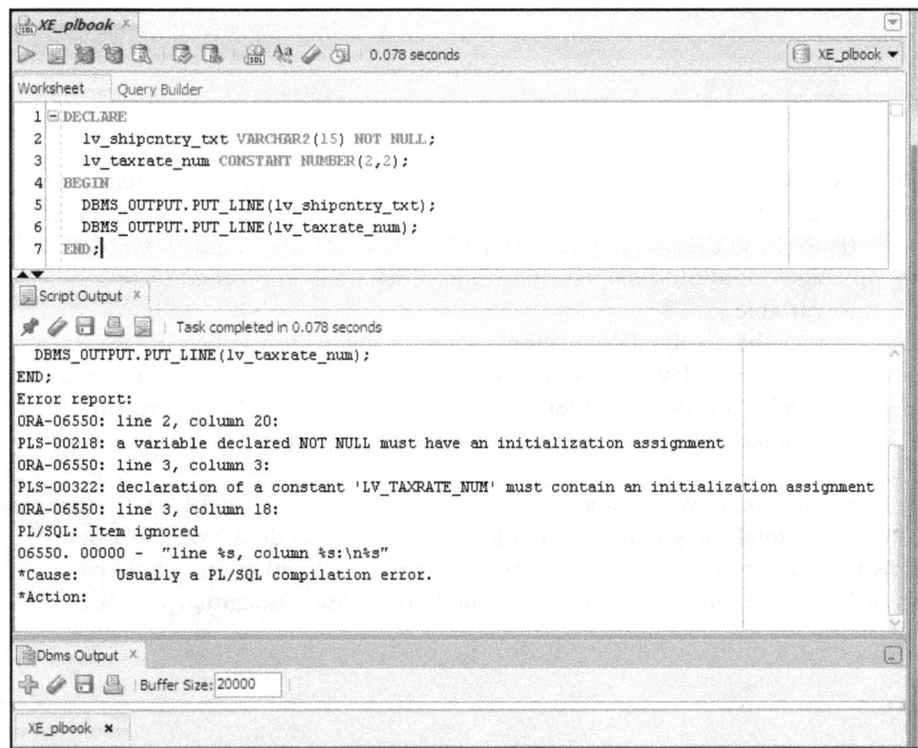

FIGURE 2-13 Error caused by not initializing variables

2. Modify the block to match the following code and run the code. It should run correctly and display the variable values now that the variables are initialized.

```
DECLARE
  lv_shipcntry_txt VARCHAR2(15) NOT NULL := 'US';
  lv_taxrate_num CONSTANT NUMBER(2,2) := .06;
BEGIN
  DBMS_OUTPUT.PUT_LINE(lv_shipcntry_txt);
  DBMS_OUTPUT.PUT_LINE(lv_taxrate_num);
END;
```

3. Modify the block to add the following assignment statement, which changes the tax rate variable's value, and run the code again. An error should be raised stating that the CONSTANT variable can't be used as a target for an assignment statement; it can't be changed in the block.

```
lv_taxrate_num := .08;
```

Calculations with Scalar Variables

You can perform calculations with scalar variables. The following example includes a calculation to determine the tax amount for an order:

```
DECLARE
  lv_taxrate_num CONSTANT NUMBER(2,2) := .06;
  lv_total_num NUMBER(6,2) := 50;
  lv_taxamt_num NUMBER(4,2);
BEGIN
  lv_taxamt_num := lv_total_num * lv_taxrate_num;
  DBMS_OUTPUT.PUT_LINE(lv_taxamt_num);
END;
```

The BEGIN section in the preceding block contains one assignment statement that involves a calculation. All variables declared are used in this statement. The multiplication needed is 50 * .06, or 3, so the `lv_taxamt_num` variable holds this value. Try creating and running this block. It should display the value 3, which is contained in the `lv_taxamt_num` variable.

Again, notice that the `:=` symbol (beginning with a colon) is used to create the assignment statement. Many developers become accustomed to using an equals sign in SQL and forget the colon needed in PL/SQL—don't be one of them! Remove the colon from the assignment statement and run the block again to review the error, shown in Figure 2-14.

Keep in mind that you have hard-coded values for the first two variables to indicate a tax rate and an order total. As you advance in learning PL/SQL coding, you'll see that values such as the order total are typically supplied by the application and could be different for each shopper. For now, you'll continue hard-coding (assigning) values to variables for testing.

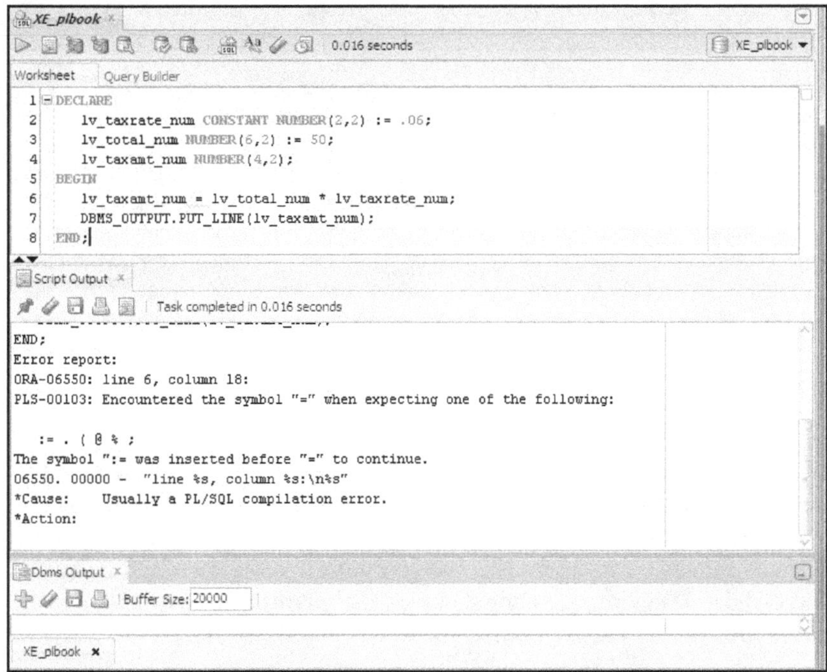

FIGURE 2-14 Error caused by a missing colon in the assignment operator

TIP

The Oracle error messages in the previous examples display both an ORA error number and a PLS error number. You should be familiar with ORA errors from your SQL experience. PLS errors are specific to PL/SQL and can be looked up in Oracle documentation or with an Internet search. Keep in mind that specific errors can involve many different coding problems, so some messages might not seem clear. Always start your investigation on both the coding line referenced in the error and the line before.

Because a number of concepts involving variables have now been covered, try a couple of blocks on your own as practice. Challenge problems, such as those following this section, are sprinkled throughout chapters to give you the opportunity to apply the concepts you're learning. You can find solutions for challenges in this book's student data files. Try these problems on your own before reviewing the solutions to help ensure that you have learned and can apply the skills. Keep in mind that you might have variable names that are different from those in the solutions, which is fine. For these challenges, compare the number of variables, the data types assigned, use of initialization, options applied, and assignment statements in the block's executable section.

CHALLENGE 2-1

Create a block containing a variable that can hold a date value (for a billing date), a variable that can hold a character string (for a last name), and a variable that can hold a numeric value (for a credit balance). For variable names, follow the naming conventions introduced in this chapter. Initialize the date variable to the value October 21, 2012 and the numeric variable to 1,000. In the executable (BEGIN) section of the block, assign the character variable's value as Brown, and include statements to display the value of each variable.

CHALLENGE 2-2

Create a block containing a variable that can hold a Y or an N to indicate whether a newsletter should be mailed, a variable that can hold a balance owed for a customer (initialize to $1,200), a variable that can hold a two-digit decimal value representing the minimum payment rate (initialize to .05), and a variable to hold the minimum payment amount to be calculated. Make sure the value in the variable for the minimum payment rate can't be modified in the block. The newsletter variable should always contain a value, and the default value should be set to Y. In the executable section of the block, calculate the minimum balance owed (balance times the minimum payment rate), set the newsletter variable to N, and display the value of each variable. After you have finished these tasks, add a statement at the top of the executable section to assign a value of .07 to the minimum payment rate. When you run the code, this statement produces an error. Why?

Using SQL Functions with Scalar Variables

SQL single-row functions can be used in PL/SQL statements to manipulate data. You might recall the `ROUND` function, the `SUBSTR` function, and the `UPPER` function, for example. These functions can provide a variety of data manipulation tasks with scalar variables. For example, say you have a block containing two date variables, and you want to calculate the number of months between these two dates. Figure 2-15 shows a block that performs this calculation and displays the result, using the dates September 20, 2010, and October 20, 2012.

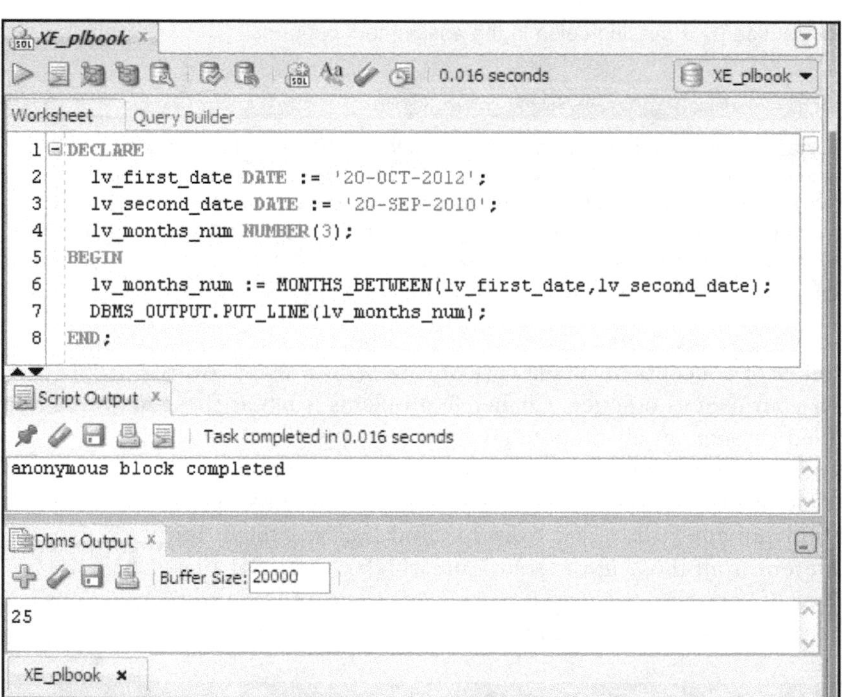

FIGURE 2-15 Using single-row functions in an assignment statement

Notice that two date variables are declared and initialized with the date values indicated. Then a numeric variable is declared to hold the number of months between the two dates. The assignment statement in the executable section uses the `MONTHS_BETWEEN` function to determine the difference in months. The result of the function is held in the lv_months_num variable. This variable is declared with a number data type because the MONTHS_BETWEEN function returns a numeric value.

CHALLENGE 2-3

Create a block containing a variable for a promotion code that's initialized to the value A0807X. The second and third characters of the promotion code value indicate the month the promotion is applied. The fourth and fifth characters of the promotion code indicate the year the promotion is applied. The code in the block needs to extract these characters. Extract the month and year values separately, and display the values.

Now that you have declared and used scalar variables, you need to look at statements for performing decision making and looping. The statements used to control the flow of logic processing in programs are commonly called **control structures**. They provide the capability to use conditional logic that determines which statements should run, how many times statements should run, and the overall sequence of events. The PL/SQL coding techniques for these tasks are covered next.

DECISION STRUCTURES

Decision structures determine which statements in a block are executed. For example, if the tax amount is assigned based on the state the customer lives in, the code needs to assign a different tax rate based on the state value. There are different types of decision control structures; the following sections cover the condition-processing capabilities of IF-THEN and CASE statements.

Simple IF Statements

An IF statement is a mechanism for checking a condition to determine whether statements should or shouldn't be processed. These statements are often used to check values of variables and direct the processing flow to the particular statements that need to be processed based on the values checked. Review the syntax of an IF statement:

```
IF condition THEN statement END IF;
```

The IF portion of the statement lists the condition to check, and the THEN portion specifies the action to take if the IF portion is true.

Take a look at IF statements in the context of the Brewbean's application. The PL/SQL block that calculates taxes for online orders might need to determine whether the order is from a state requiring taxes. This situation starts with the following assumptions:

- Taxes should be applied only in the company's home state of Virginia.
- You need to check for only one condition: whether the shipping state is Virginia. If it is, the tax amount is calculated by using the order subtotal.
- If the shipping state isn't Virginia, no calculation is performed. The tax amount is then 0.

When an IF statement checks only one condition and performs actions only if the condition is TRUE, it's referred to as a simple IF condition. In the example, the condition that needs to be checked is whether the state is Virginia. The action needed if the condition is true is performing a calculation to determine the tax amount. The tax amount should be set to 0 if the condition is FALSE.

The block in Figure 2-16 includes variables for the state and subtotal values. Notice that the state is set to 'VA'; therefore, the condition in the IF statement is true, and the tax amount is calculated by using 6%. What if the shipping state isn't VA? The IF condition resolves to FALSE, and the tax calculation doesn't take place.

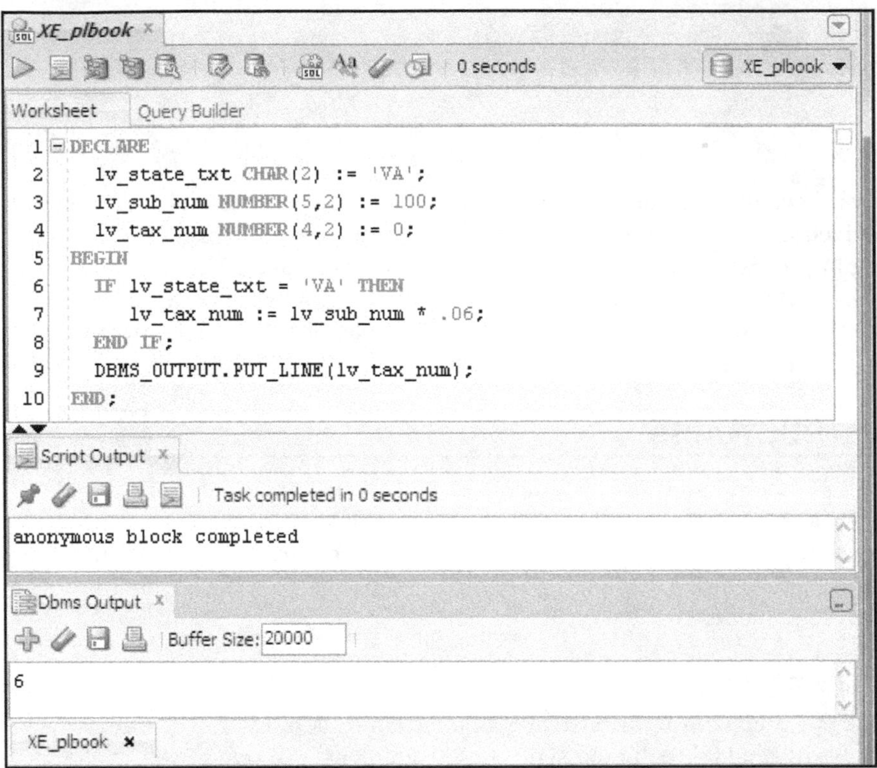

FIGURE 2-16 A basic IF statement

> **TIP**
>
> The = symbol is used in the IF statement to check for a value of VA. It's not an assignment statement, so the := symbol isn't used.

As an application developer, your testing must include a variety of data situations, so try testing the same block, using a shipping state of NC (North Carolina). Modify the block in Figure 2-16 to initialize the state variable to NC, and run the code. The output should confirm that the tax amount is 0 because the shipping state isn't VA, and the tax amount variable is initialized to 0. In this case, the IF condition resolves to FALSE, so the lv_tax_num assignment statement isn't processed. If the tax amount variable hadn't been initialized to 0, it would contain a NULL value.

IF/THEN/ELSE Statements

A simple IF statement performs an action only if the condition is TRUE. What if you need to perform one action if the condition is TRUE and a different action if the condition is FALSE? Say that if the shipping state is VA, a tax rate of 6% is applied, and if the shipping state is anything other than VA, a tax rate of 4% is applied. An ELSE clause is added to indicate actions to perform if the condition is FALSE. The following example shows the syntax for this statement:

```
IF condition THEN statement
ELSE statement
END IF;
```

CHALLENGE 2-4

Because blocks are beginning to include more execution steps, return to the flowcharts introduced at the beginning of the chapter to help you lay out the sequence of actions needed before you begin coding. Create a flowchart for the tax rate calculation covered in this section.

The block in Figure 2-17 reflects adding an ELSE clause to the IF statement, which uses a 6% tax if the condition checking the shipping state resolves to TRUE. If the condition resolves to FALSE, a 4% tax rate is used. In this example, the state is NC; therefore, a tax rate of 4% is applied. Note that by using an IF/THEN/ELSE statement, one tax amount calculation always occurs, regardless of the shipping state's value. Build the block and test with different state values.

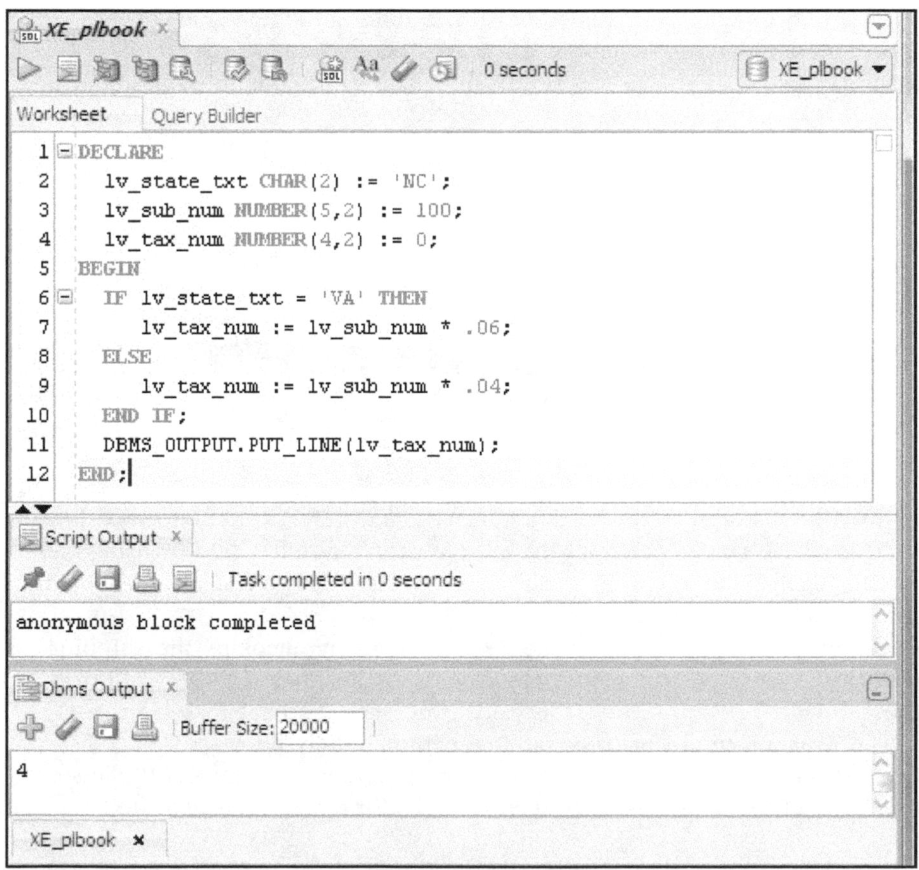

FIGURE 2-17 Adding an ELSE clause to an IF statement

IF/THEN Versus IF

Instead of using the ELSE clause, what if you create the IF tax condition with two simple IF statements, as shown in the following code?

```
IF lv_state_txt = 'VA' THEN
  lv_tax_num := lv_sub_num * .06;
END IF;
IF lv_state_txt <> 'VA' THEN
  lv_tax_num := lv_sub_num * .04;
END IF;
```

This code produces the same result as the IF/THEN/ELSE statement. Which method should be used? One method operates more efficiently than the other. In the preceding code, each IF clause is processed regardless of the shipping state value. On the other hand, the ELSE clause in Figure 2-17 processes only one IF clause (checking the value of the shipping state). This is an important difference in processing efficiency: The less code to process, the faster the program runs.

IF/THEN/ELSIF/ELSE

Now go a step further with this tax calculation example. What if it changes so that a tax rate of 6% should be applied to VA, 5% to ME, 7% to NY, and 4% to all other states? Then you need to check for the existence of several different state values because you no longer have an either/or situation. An ELSIF clause is added to handle checking a variety of conditions for the state value. The syntax for this statement is as follows:

```
IF condition THEN statement
ELSIF condition THEN statement
ELSE statement
END IF;
```

CHALLENGE 2-5

Create a flowchart for the condition described in this section.

Next, convert the flowchart to code, using the IF/THEN/ELSIF/ELSE syntax. Review the code in Figure 2-18, which checks for the existence of different values by using ELSIF clauses. Note that each condition in the ELSIF clauses is mutually exclusive, meaning that only one of the ELSIF conditions can evaluate to TRUE.

The processing begins at the top of the IF statement by checking the shipping state value until it finds a condition that resolves to TRUE. After a TRUE condition is found, the associated program statements are processed, and the IF statement is finished. The program then runs the statement immediately after the END IF; line. If no condition resolves to TRUE, the program statements in the ELSE clause are processed. An ELSE clause isn't required, and if none had been provided

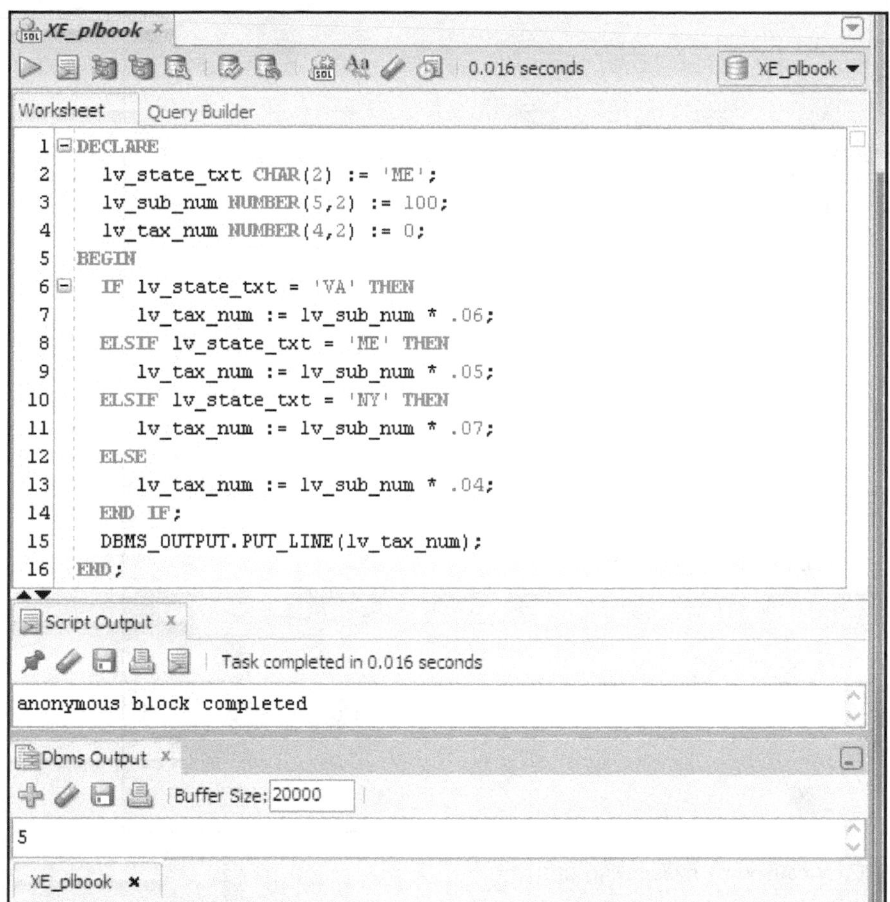

FIGURE 2-18 Adding more conditions with `ELSIF` clauses

in this example, the `IF` statement could be completed without processing a tax calculation.

NOTE

Because `IF` clauses are evaluated from the top down, knowing the nature of your data can make the code more efficient. If much of the data processed matches a particular value, for example, list this value in the first `IF` condition so that only one `IF` clause typically has to run.

You might be tempted to put an "E" in the `ELSIF` keyword, but this is one of the most common mistakes PL/SQL programmers make. Figure 2-19 shows the error caused by using `ELSEIF` rather than `ELSIF`. The error is raised on the term that follows the `ELSEIF`. Because this spelling doesn't represent a keyword, the system thinks the `ELSEIF` is something else, such as a variable.

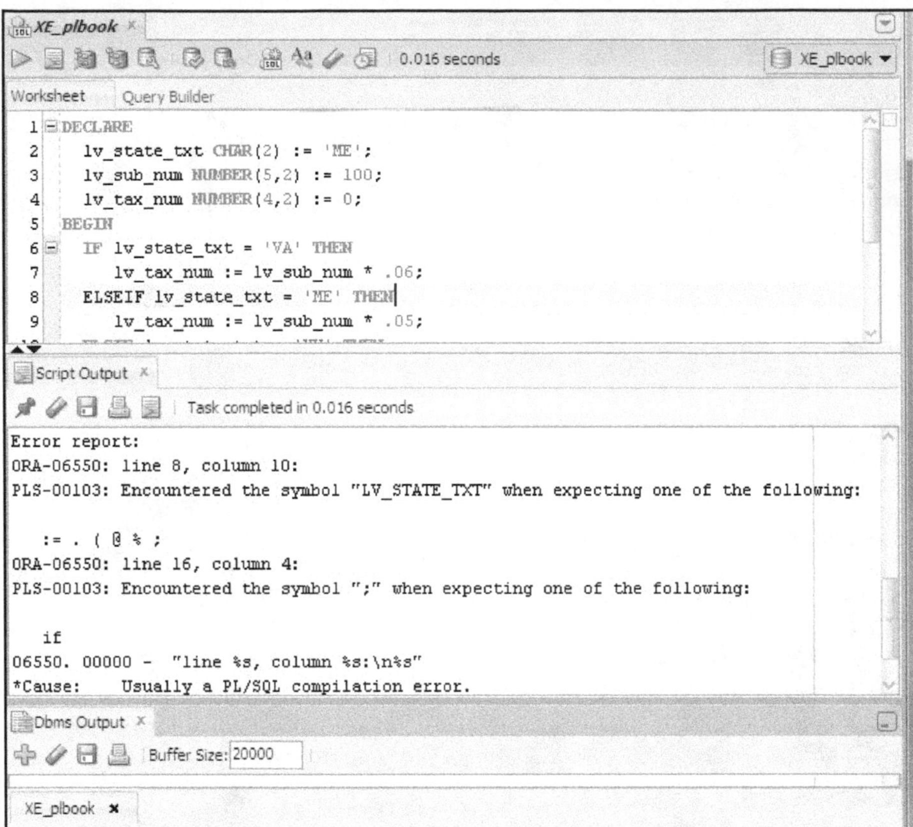

FIGURE 2-19 Error caused by misspelling `ELSIF`

`IF` Statement Evaluations

Now that you understand the `IF` statement structure, it's time to look at factors involved in `IF` statement evaluations, such as `NULL` values, Boolean testing, and order of conditions. When writing an `IF` statement, you need to determine how a `NULL` value in conditions should be handled. For example, Brewbean's needs a block of code to display "Whole Bean" (option value 3) or "Ground" (option value 4) based on the option selected on a coffee product order. Review the following code for performing this task:

```
DECLARE
  lv_option_num NUMBER(2) := 3;
BEGIN
  IF lv_option_num = 3 THEN
    DBMS_OUTPUT.PUT_LINE('Whole Bean');
  ELSE
    DBMS_OUTPUT.PUT_LINE('Ground');
  END IF;
END;
```

What results if the option variable is empty or NULL? Figure 2-20 confirms that the ELSE clause runs if the option variable value is anything except 3, including NULL. This result might not be what you intend, however.

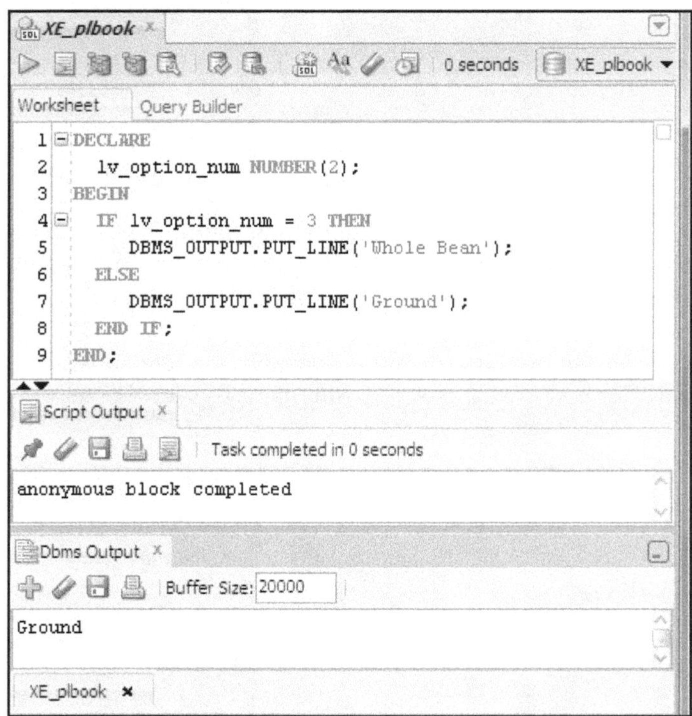

FIGURE 2-20 NULL values with IF conditions

If you know the option variable has possible values of 3, 4, and NULL, and you want to display N/A if a NULL value is detected, you could edit the IF statement several different ways. You can address each possible value with an IF condition and allow the ELSE clause to handle the NULL values, as shown:

```
IF lv_option_num = 3 THEN
  DBMS_OUTPUT.PUT_LINE('Whole Bean');
ELSIF lv_option_num = 4 THEN
  DBMS_OUTPUT.PUT_LINE('Ground');
ELSE
  DBMS_OUTPUT.PUT_LINE('N/A');
END IF;
```

Another alternative is addressing all possible values with IF conditions, including the NULL value, by using the IS NULL comparison operation shown in the following example. The ELSE clause is added to handle any unexpected values for the option selection.

```
IF lv_option_num = 3 THEN
  DBMS_OUTPUT.PUT_LINE('Whole Bean');
ELSIF lv_option_num = 4 THEN
  DBMS_OUTPUT.PUT_LINE('Ground');
ELSIF lv_option_num IS NULL THEN
  DBMS_OUTPUT.PUT_LINE('N/A');
ELSE
  DBMS_OUTPUT.PUT_LINE('Unknown');
END IF;
```

Recall that the functions to check for or convert `NULL` values for easier handling are `IS NULL`, `IS NOT NULL`, `NVL`, and `NVL2`.

In terms of Boolean values, an `IF` statement can be used to determine the value of a Boolean variable; however, it might be possible to eliminate the `IF` statement and simply use an expression to set the Boolean value. For example, Brewbean's needs a block of code using a Boolean variable to indicate whether an order is considered a delayed shipment. Any order taking more than three days to ship is considered a late shipment. The following block accomplishes this task by using an `IF` statement to set a Boolean variable value:

```
DECLARE
  lv_ord_date DATE := '15-SEP-2012';
  lv_ship_date DATE := '19-SEP-2012';
  lv_shipflag_bln BOOLEAN;
BEGIN
  IF (lv_ship_date - lv_ord_date) > 3 THEN
    lv_shipflag_bln := TRUE;
  ELSE
    lv_shipflag_bln := FALSE;
  END IF;
  --- Additional PL/SQL statements ---
END;
```

Even though the preceding code works fine, there's a better alternative. A Boolean value can be set with an assignment statement, which requires evaluating an expression. The following statement replaces the entire `IF` statement and sets the value of the Boolean variable:

```
lv_shipflag_bln := (lv_ship_date - lv_ord_date) > 3;
```

Last, because `IF` statements always evaluate from top to bottom and execute the first `TRUE` clause encountered, considering the order of `IF` conditions is critical. Review the block of code and execution results shown in Figure 2-21. Even though the `lv_amt_num` variable value is 30, the block executed the first `IF` clause rather than the second because 30 is greater than 20, resulting in a `TRUE` condition. This seems obvious with a short statement, as in this example, but it can be overlooked easily when statements become more complex. An `IF` statement should be tested by invoking every conditional clause to ensure correct operation. Notice that the block example in Figure 2-21 embeds an output statement in each clause to verify which clause is executed.

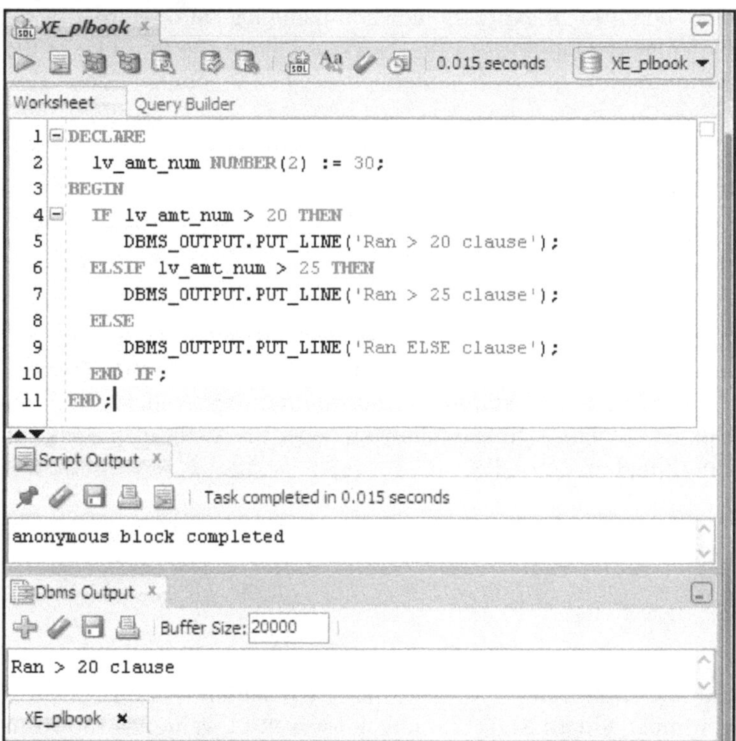

FIGURE 2-21 Testing the order of `IF` conditions

CHALLENGE 2-6

Create a flowchart and block for the following requirements: The block should calculate the discount amount based on a promotion code value. Discounts assigned by a promotion code are A=5%, B=10%, and C=15%. A discount of 2% should be applied if no promotion code is used. Create a variable to hold the promotion code value. Use an order total variable containing a value of $100 to test the block and a variable to hold the discount amount calculated. Run the code block for each possible promotion code value and display the discount amount to test your conditional processing. Next, modify the block so that no discount is applied if a promotion code isn't used. (In other words, the discount should be 0.)

Operators in an `IF` Clause

Keep in mind that more than one condition can be checked in each `IF` clause. The logical operators of `OR` and `AND` used in SQL are also available in PL/SQL. For example, the `IF` clause using an `OR` operator in the following code uses a tax rate of 6% if the shipping state is VA or PA:

```
IF lv_state_txt = 'VA' OR lv_state_txt = 'PA' THEN
  lv_tax_num := lv_sub_num * .06;
ELSE
  lv_tax_num := lv_sub_num * .04;
END IF;
```

Be careful to use complete conditional expressions when using logical operators. A common mistake is using incomplete conditions in the IF clause, as in the first line of the following code. (Notice that the first line of the IF statement uses an incomplete condition with the OR.)

```
IF lv_state_txt = 'VA' OR 'PA' THEN
  lv_tax_num := lv_sub_num * .06;
ELSE
  lv_tax_num := lv_sub_num * .04;
END IF;
```

As part of being familiar with your data, you need to consider whether the values being checked in the IF clauses could be NULL. If an action must occur when the value being checked contains a NULL value, the IF statement must contain an explicit check for a NULL value (IS NULL) or an ELSE clause. In the following code, the ELSE clause runs if the state value is NULL or anything but VA or PA:

```
IF lv_state_txt = 'VA' OR lv_state_txt = 'PA' THEN
  lv_tax_num := lv_sub_num * .06;
ELSE
  lv_tax_num := lv_sub_num * .04;
END IF;
```

However, if you eliminate the ELSE clause but still want a particular action to occur if the state is a NULL value, you must add an ELSIF to check for a NULL value, as shown in the following code:

```
IF lv_state_txt = 'VA' OR lv_state_txt = 'PA' THEN
  lv_tax_num := lv_sub_num * .06;
ELSIF lv_state_txt IS NULL THEN
  lv_tax_num := lv_sub_num * .04;
END IF;
```

This IF statement calculates a 6% tax amount for states of VA or PA and 4% if the state is a NULL value. No activity occurs if the state is any other value.

The IN operator is another method to check several conditions in one IF clause by providing a list of values. The following example uses the IN operator to check for three state values in the first IF clause:

```
IF lv_state_txt IN ('VA','PA','ME') THEN
  lv_tax_num := lv_sub_num * .06;
ELSE
  lv_tax_num := lv_sub_num * .04;
END IF;
```

CHALLENGE 2-7

Create a block to calculate the discount amount based on a promotion code value. A variety of promotion codes are used to identify the source of the promotion, so some of the codes might apply the same percentage discount. Discounts assigned by a promotion code are A=5%, B=10%, C=10%, D=15%, and E=5%. If no promotion code value is indicated, the discount should be 0. Create a variable to hold the promotion code. Use an order total variable containing a value of $100 to test the block and a variable to hold the discount amount calculated. Run the code block for each possible promotion code value, and display the discount amount calculated to test your conditional processing.

Nested IF Statements

As conditional checking becomes more complex in a program, you might need to nest IF statements, which means embedding a complete IF statement inside another IF statement. For example, Brewbean's might want to apply product price discounts based on both the type of product (Equipment or Coffee) and the price of an item. The following example shows the outer IF statement in bold, which checks for the type of product. The inner or nested IF statement runs only when the product type is E (equipment) and checks the price to determine the discount percent to assign. For the product type C (coffee), a discount of .05 is assigned regardless of the product price.

```
IF lv_type_txt = 'E' THEN
  IF lv_price_num > 85 THEN        <-- Inner or nested IF begins
    lv_disc_num = .20;
  ELSIF lv_price_num > 45 THEN
    lv_disc_num = .15;
  ELSE
    lv_disc_num = .10;
  END IF;                          <-- Inner or nested IF ends
ELSIF lv_type_txt = 'C' THEN
  lv_disc_num = .05;
END IF;
```

An alternative approach to the nested IF example is using compound conditions with logical operators, as in the following example. However, this method can lead to inefficient execution. Using this approach, the type variable might need to be checked a number of times before hitting the price level condition that matches. In addition, most programmers find it easier to read and interpret nested statements.

```
IF lv_type_txt = 'E' AND lv_price_num > 85 THEN
  lv_disc_num = .20;
```

CASE Statements

CASE statements are another method for checking conditions. Oracle 9*i* introduced CASE statements to process conditional logic in a manner similar to how IF statements work. CASE statements are available in most programming languages, and many developers are familiar with this type of code. Most programmers choose one method to code decision processing: IF/THEN or CASE statements.

TIP

The addition of the CASE statement doesn't really add functionality in PL/SQL programming; however, advocates of the CASE statement claim it leads to more compact, understandable coding. The choice between IF statements and CASE statements is more a preference of the programming shop, which should establish standard practices to maintain consistency of coding.

The CASE statement begins with the keyword CASE followed by a selector that indicates the value to be checked; typically, it's a variable name. This selector is followed by WHEN clauses to determine which statements should run based on the selector's value.

An ELSE clause can be included at the end, as in the IF statements. The following example shows the syntax for this statement:

```
CASE variable
  WHEN condition THEN statement;
  WHEN condition THEN statement;
  ELSE statement;
END CASE;
```

Review the tax calculation in Figure 2-18. The code in Figure 2-22 performs the same task, except it uses a CASE statement. The CASE statement evaluates the same way the IF statement does, in that it works from the top down until finding a condition that's TRUE. However, the evaluation of the state variable is included only once at the top of the CASE statement instead of with every condition clause in the IF statement.

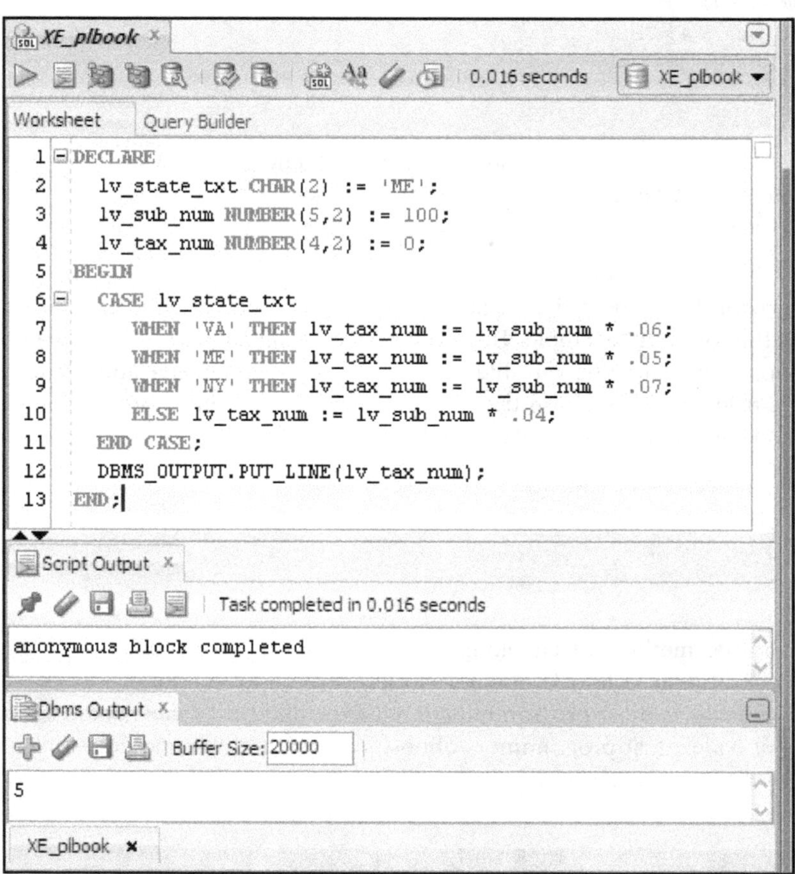

FIGURE 2-22 A basic CASE statement

Refer to Figure 2-18 again. If the ELSE clause is omitted in an IF statement, the IF statement can run and potentially not execute any code. If no matches are found in the IF/ELSIF clauses, the IF statement ends successfully without running any code. This isn't what happens, however, when the ELSE clause is omitted from the CASE statement in Figure 2-22. If no TRUE conditions are found in the WHEN clauses, and an ELSE clause isn't included, the CASE statement includes an implicit ELSE clause that raises an Oracle error. Follow these steps to generate a "CASE not found" error:

1. Enter the PL/SQL block shown in Figure 2-22 and run it.
2. Remove the ELSE clause from the block.
3. Initialize the state variable to the value TX. Notice that the WHEN clauses in the CASE statement don't execute for this state value.
4. Run the modified block. You should get a "CASE not found" error, as shown in Figure 2-23, because no statement is executed by the CASE statement. None of the WHEN clauses address the state value of TX, and the ELSE clause has been removed.

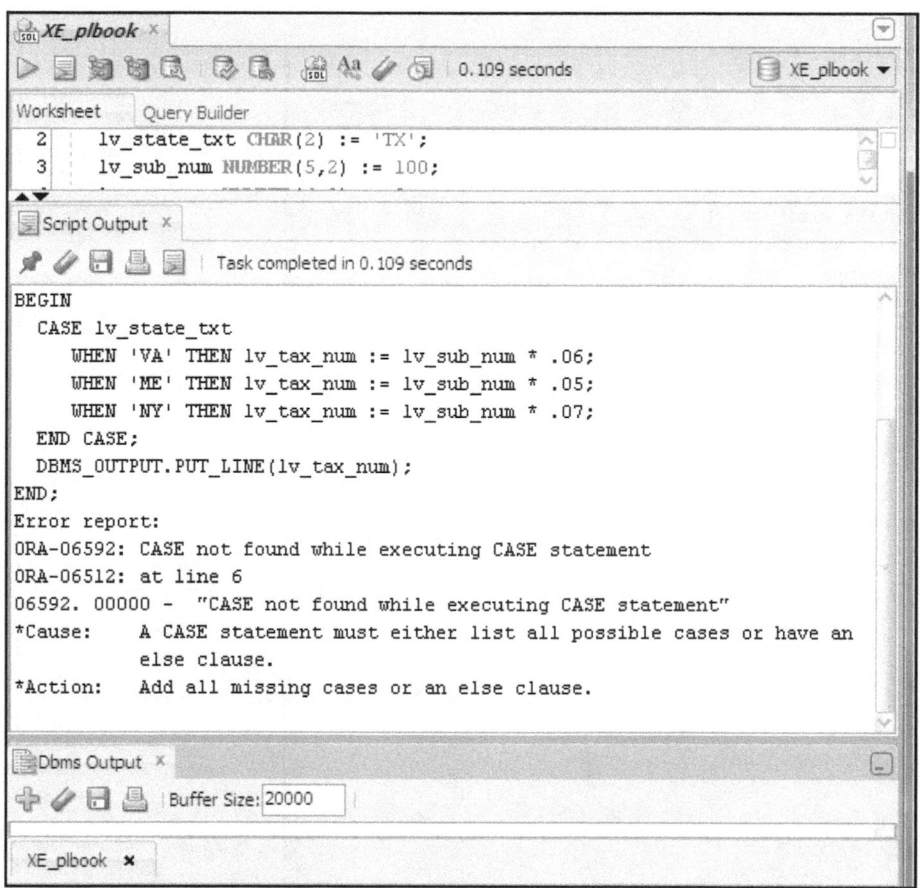

FIGURE 2-23 Error caused when a basic CASE statement doesn't find a WHEN clause match

CHALLENGE 2-8

Create a block that uses a CASE statement to determine the discount amount based on a promotion code value. Discounts assigned by a promotion code are A=5%, B=10%, and C=15%. A discount of 2% should be applied if no promotion code is used. Create a variable to hold the promotion code value. Use an order total variable containing a value of $100 to test the block and a variable to hold the discount amount calculated. Run the code block for each possible promotion code value, and display the discount amount to test your conditional processing.

Searched CASE Statements

Another form of the CASE statement, called a **searched CASE statement**, is available. It doesn't use a selector but evaluates conditions placed in WHEN clauses separately. The structure of a searched CASE statement is quite similar to an IF statement. The conditions checked in WHEN clauses must evaluate to a Boolean value of TRUE or FALSE to allow different items, such as shipping state and zip code, to be checked in the same CASE statement.

To see how a searched CASE statement is used, assume that Brewbean's tax calculation must consider not only the state, but also special rates applied by some localities that can be identified via zip codes. Figure 2-24 shows using a CASE statement to apply a 6% tax rate to all VA residents except those in zip code 23321, which uses a rate of 2%.

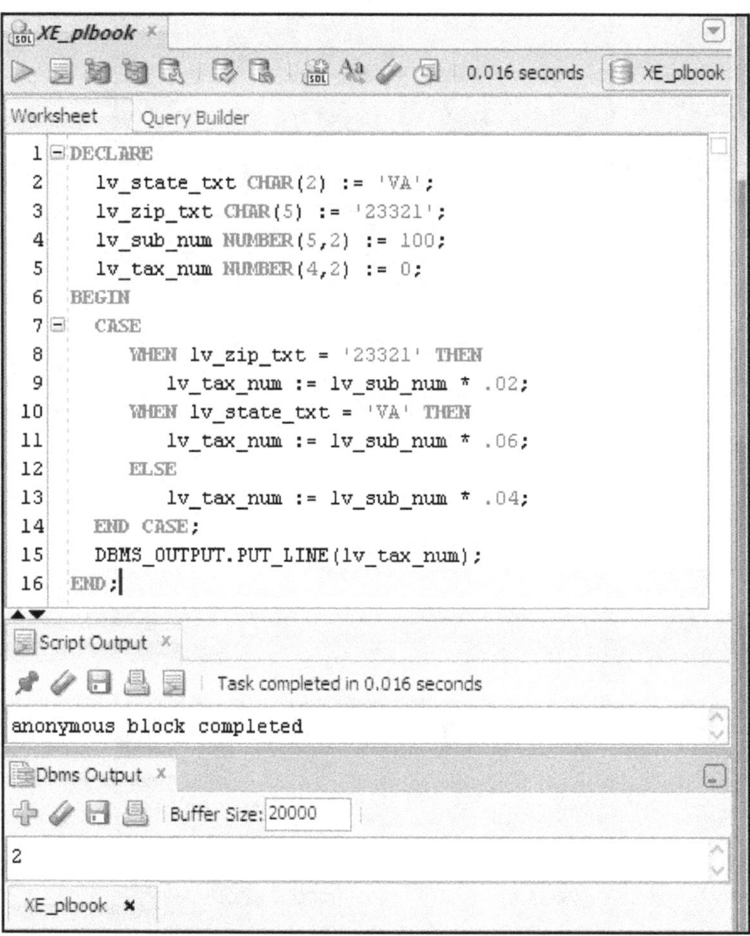

FIGURE 2-24 A searched CASE statement checking different variable values

This block processes with a state of VA and a zip code of 23321. Keep in mind that conditional statements are evaluated from the top down and end when a TRUE condition is discovered. Therefore, processing finds a TRUE condition with the first WHEN clause and uses a tax rate of 2%.

This structure allows checking multiple conditions in each WHEN clause, such as the following example checking price ranges. The conditions checked in the WHEN clause can involve different variables.

```
CASE
  WHEN lv_price_num >= 10 AND lv_price_num < 20 THEN
    lv_disc_num := .05;
  WHEN lv_price_num >= 20 AND lv_price_num < 40 THEN
    lv_disc_num := .10;
  ELSE
    lv_disc_num := 0;
END CASE;
```

Using a CASE Expression

The CASE keyword can also be used as an expression rather than a statement. A **CASE expression** evaluates conditions and returns a value in an assignment statement. For example, in the tax calculation, the end result has been putting a value for the calculated tax amount in a variable. You can also use a CASE expression for this task, as shown in Figure 2-25.

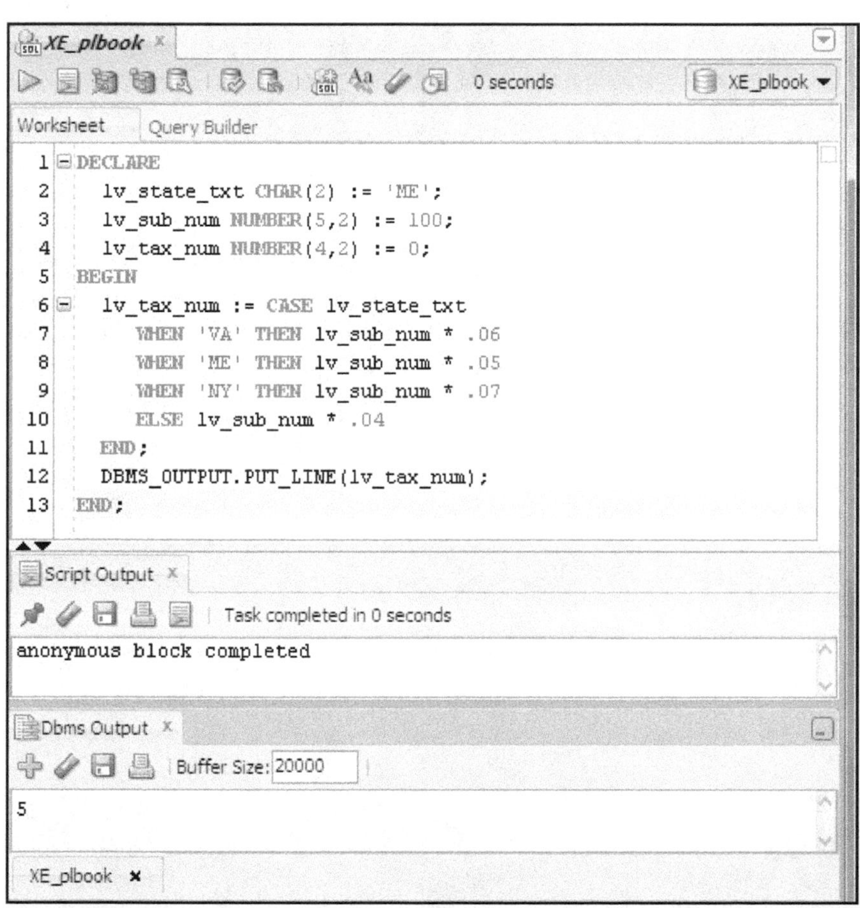

FIGURE 2-25 Using a CASE expression to determine the applicable tax rate

The CASE clause in this figure actually serves as the value expression of an assignment statement. If the goal of your conditional checking is to assign a value to a variable, this format makes this intention clear because it begins with the assignment statement. A CASE expression, even though constructed much the same as a basic CASE statement, has some subtle syntax differences. The WHEN clauses don't end with semicolons, and the statement doesn't end with END CASE;. (Instead, it ends with END;.) Also, unlike a CASE statement, if a CASE expression has no ELSE clause and no WHEN conditions are matched, the result is a NULL value rather than a "CASE not found" error.

A CASE expression can be structured with more flexibility, as shown in the following code, that allows checking multiple conditions in the WHEN clauses with logical operators. Also, notice that the WHEN clauses assign a specific discount amount, which is then used in the calculation included in the END statement (* lv_sub_num).

```
DECLARE
  lv_state_txt CHAR(2) := 'ME';
  lv_sub_num NUMBER(5,2) := 100;
  lv_tax_num NUMBER(4,2) := 0;
BEGIN
  lv_tax_num :=
    CASE
      WHEN lv_state_txt = 'VA' OR lv_state_txt = 'TX' THEN .06
      WHEN lv_state_txt = 'ME' OR lv_state_txt = 'WY' THEN .05
      ELSE 0
  END * lv_sub_num;
  DBMS_OUTPUT.PUT_LINE(lv_tax_num);
END;
```

Nested CASE Statements

Just as IF statements can be nested, CASE statements can be embedded in each other. As an example, return to the earlier nested IF statement that checked for product type and then checked product price for equipment products. In the following code, the outer CASE statement checks the product type, and the inner CASE statement is executed only if the product type is E. The inner CASE statement checks the price value to set the discount amount. If the product type is C, the inner CASE statement doesn't execute.

```
CASE
  WHEN lv_type_txt = 'E' THEN
    CASE
      WHEN lv_price_num >= 85 THEN
        lv_disc_num := .20;
      WHEN lv_price_num >= 45 THEN
        lv_disc_num := .15;
      ELSE
        lv_disc_num := .10;
    END CASE;
  WHEN lv_type_txt = 'C' THEN
    lv_disc_num := 0;
END CASE;
```

CHALLENGE 2-9

Create a block using a CASE expression to determine the discount amount based on a promotion code value. Discounts assigned by a promotion code are A=5%, B=10%, and C=15%. A discount of 2% should be applied if no promotion code is used. Create a variable to hold the promotion code value. Use an order total variable containing a value of $100 to test the block and a variable to hold the discount amount calculated. Run the code block for each possible promotion code value, and display the discount amount to test your conditional processing.

Conditional IF/THEN and CASE statements are invaluable in creating programming logic; however, additional constructs are needed. The next section introduces looping structures that allow running portions of code more than once.

LOOPING CONSTRUCTS

What if you need to calculate the total tax amount for an order and apply different tax rates on coffee (as a food item) and equipment items? You would need to look at each detailed item (products purchased in an order) to determine the correct tax amount and apply the same logic to each item. If an order contains five items, the same logic that determines the tax amount for each item needs to be processed five times—once for each item. To handle this type of situation more efficiently, you can use **looping constructs**, which make it possible to repeat processing a portion of code. The flowchart in Figure 2-26 illustrates the processing described in this example.

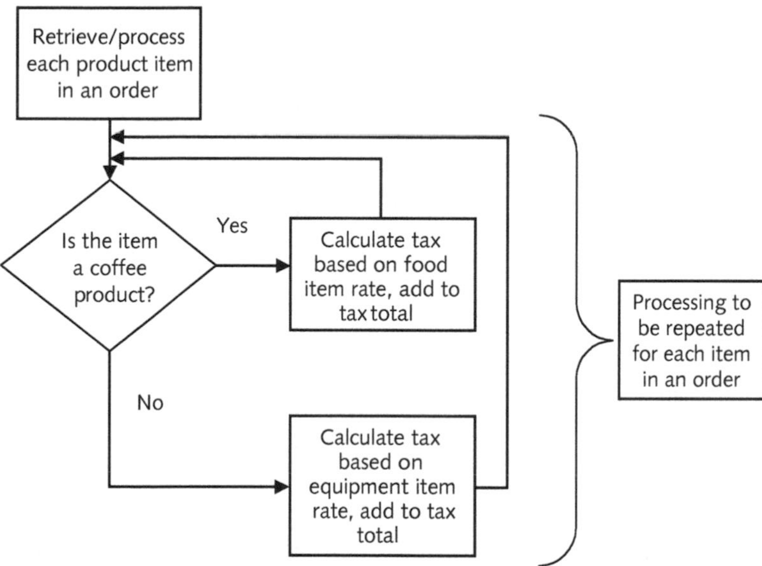

FIGURE 2-26 Flowchart including the tax calculation looping structure

Loops are used when you need to repeat a line or lines of code in a block. In every loop, the system must be instructed on which statements should be repeated and when to end the repeating action or stop the loop. Three types of PL/SQL loops are covered in the following sections: basic, WHILE, and FOR.

Basic Loops

A **basic loop** uses the LOOP and END LOOP markers to begin and end the loop code, which includes any statements to be repeated. One of the most important parts of a loop is making sure something stops the loop iteration. The EXIT WHEN clause must include a condition that evaluates to TRUE at some point, which serves as the instruction to stop the loop. The following code shows the syntax of a basic loop:

```
LOOP
    -- Statements --
    EXIT WHEN condition;
END LOOP;
```

The code in Figure 2-27 contains a basic loop that loops five times. The only statement that runs is the `DBMS_OUTPUT` action, which displays the counter's value onscreen. The counter is established as a mechanism to instruct the loop when to stop repeating. The `lv_cnt_num` variable holds the value 1 on the loop's first iteration. The numbers 1 to 5 are displayed onscreen, and then the loop stops because the `lv_cnt_num` variable holds a value of 5, and the `EXIT WHEN` condition evaluates to `TRUE`.

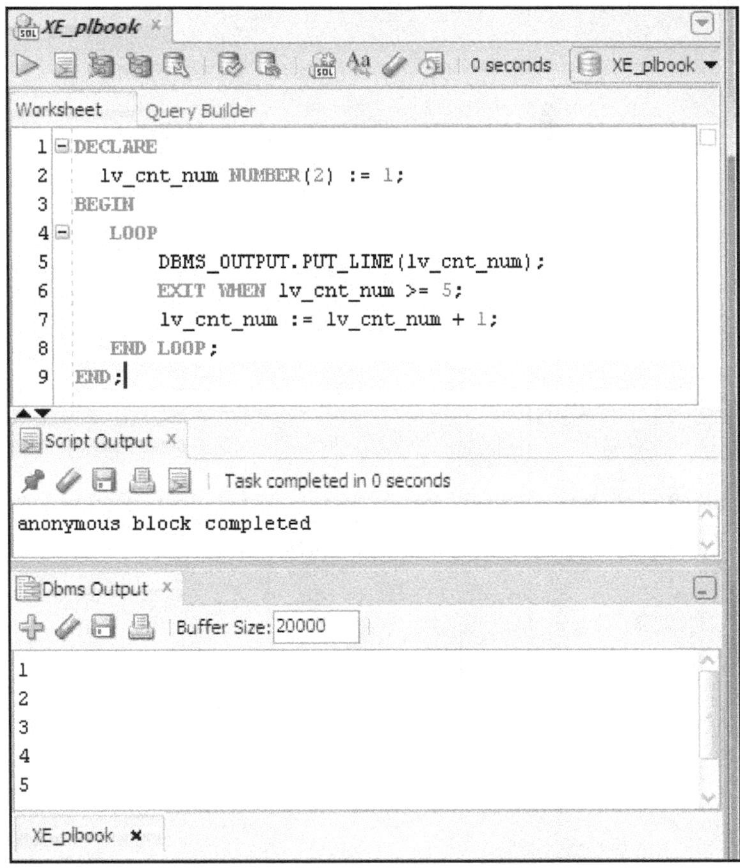

FIGURE 2-27 Using a basic loop

TIP

If the `EXIT WHEN` clause isn't included in the code in Figure 2-27, the result is the programmer's nightmare of an **infinite loop**, a loop that's never instructed to stop and continues looping indefinitely. When this happens, the code can't continue with any processing beyond the loop.

NOTE

Because you haven't processed rows of data from a database yet, the looping examples use scalar variables to show the flow of processing. Retrieving rows of data from a database is covered in subsequent chapters, and looping constructs are used to process multiple rows returned from a database.

To see the effect of the order of loop statements on processing, follow these steps:

1. Enter the PL/SQL block shown in Figure 2-27 with one modification. Move the `EXIT WHEN` line of code to the top of the loop so that it's the first statement in the loop to execute.
2. Run the block and review the output. How did the results change? Only values 1 through 4 are displayed because the loop ends before displaying the value 5.

CHALLENGE 2-10

Create a block that initializes a variable to the value 11. Include a loop to display the variable value and subtract 2 from the variable. End the loop processing when the variable value is less than 2.

Other languages offer variations on loop statements, such as a `LOOP UNTIL`, which evaluates a condition at the bottom of the loop. This bottom-of-the-loop evaluation guarantees that the loop always iterates at least once. PL/SQL doesn't include this type of loop statement, but you can use a basic loop with an `EXIT WHEN` clause at the end of the loop to make sure the loop runs at least one time, as shown in the following code:

```
DECLARE
  lv_cnt_num NUMBER(2) :=1;
BEGIN
  LOOP
    DBMS_OUTPUT.PUT_LINE(lv_cnt_num);
    lv_cnt_num := lv_cnt_num + 1;
    EXIT WHEN lv_cnt_num >= 5;
  END LOOP;
END;
```

An `EXIT` statement rather than an `EXIT WHEN` condition statement can also be used to end a loop. In the following loop, an `IF` statement is used to check the state of the `lv_cnt_num` value and executes an `EXIT` (ends the loop) if the value is greater than or equal to 5:

```
LOOP
  DBMS_OUTPUT.PUT_LINE(lv_cnt_num);
  IF lv_cnt_num >= 5 THEN
    EXIT;
  ELSE
    lv_cnt_num := lv_cnt_num + 1;
END LOOP;
```

TIP

Multiple `EXIT` statements can be included in a loop as needed. Keep in mind that after any `EXIT` instruction is carried out, processing leaves the loop and continues with the next statement in the block.

WHILE Loops

A **WHILE loop** differs from other types of loops, in that it includes a condition to check at the top of the loop in the LOOP clause. For each iteration of the loop, this condition is checked, and if it's TRUE, the loop continues. If the condition is FALSE, the looping action stops. Ensure that whatever is checked in the loop condition actually changes value as the loop iterates so that at some point, the condition resolves to FALSE and, therefore, ends the looping action. The following example shows the WHILE loop syntax:

```
WHILE condition LOOP
   -- Statements --
END LOOP;
```

Figure 2-28 shows a rewrite of the basic loop example shown in Figure 2-27, except that it uses the WHILE loop format. Notice that this loop iterates only five times, at which time the lv_cnt_num variable holds the value 6. At this point, the WHILE clause runs and determines that the condition evaluates to FALSE (in other words, that 6 isn't <= 5); therefore, the looping action stops. Keep in mind that the condition is evaluated at the top of the loop, which means there's no guarantee the code inside the loop will run at all. If lv_cnt_num has a value of 11 before reaching the loop statement, for example, the WHILE condition evaluates to FALSE, and the looping action never runs.

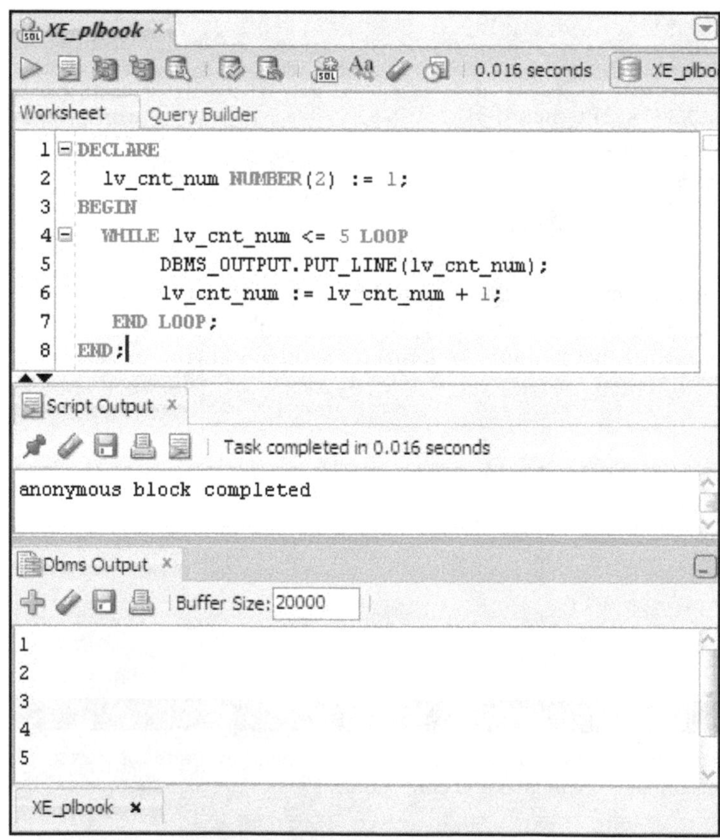

FIGURE 2-28 Using WHILE loop processing

CHALLENGE 2-11

Create the same block described in Challenge 2-10, but use a `WHILE` loop instead of a basic loop.

`FOR` Loops

A **`FOR` loop** performs the same job of iterating; however, this type of loop indicates how many times to loop by including a range in the statement. The following example shows the syntax of the `FOR` loop:

```
FOR counter IN lower_bound..upper_bound LOOP
  -- Statements --
END LOOP;
```

The counter is a variable that holds the value of the current iteration number and is automatically incremented by 1 each time the loop iterates. It begins with the value supplied for the *`lower_bound`*, and the iterations continue until the counter reaches the value supplied for the *upper_bound*. Even though any name can be used for the counter, using `i` is typical. The lower and upper bounds can be numbers or variables containing numeric values.

By indicating a numeric range, the `FOR` loop specifies how many times the loop in the opening `LOOP` clause should run. Figure 2-29 shows a `FOR` loop, which produces the same results as the counter examples used with the basic and `WHILE` loops. The range is indicated in the `FOR` clause on Line 2.

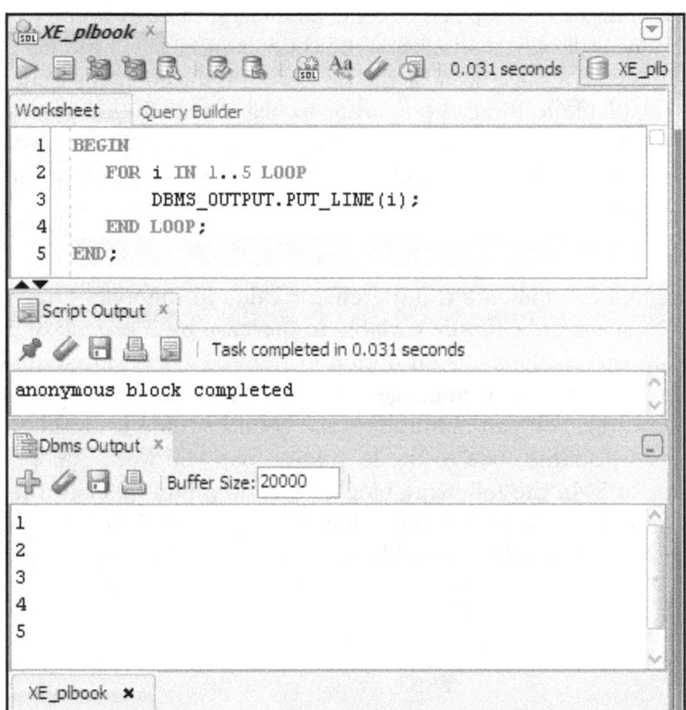

FIGURE 2-29 Using a `FOR` loop

Several tasks are performed in the `FOR` clause that starts the loop in Figure 2-29. First, the `FOR` clause sets up a counter variable automatically. In this example, the counter is named `i`. The second task is setting up a range of values for the counter variable that control the number of times the loop runs (1..5). In this example, the counter (i) holds the value 1 in the loop's first iteration. Each iteration increments the counter by 1 automatically, and the loop stops after running five repetitions.

The loop range must indicate a lower bound and upper bound value that determines the number of times the loop iterates. The values can be provided in the form of numbers, variables, or expressions evaluating to numeric values. By default, the counter starts at the lower bound value and is incremented by 1 for each loop iteration. The loop in this example always iterates five times because the range is indicated with numeric values. However, a variable could be used in the range to make the number of iterations more dynamic. That is, each time the block containing the loop is run, the loop might iterate a different number of times. For example, the number of iterations of the FOR loop in the following block is determined by the value of lv_upper_num:

```
DECLARE
  lv_upper_num NUMBER(3) := 3;
BEGIN
  FOR i IN 1..lv_upper_num LOOP
    DBMS_OUTPUT.PUT_LINE(i);
  END LOOP;
END;
```

Instead of being initialized to a value, the lv_upper_num variable could be populated with a value at runtime (which you do in Chapters 3 and 4), which could be different for each execution. The counter's value can be referenced inside the loop and become an integral value in your processing. In this example, the i value is displayed onscreen. The counter variable (i) can be referenced in the loop but can't be assigned a value because the loop controls the counter's value.

The REVERSE option is also available to force the counter to begin with the range's upper bound and increment by -1 in each loop iteration until the lower bound is reached. The REVERSE keyword should be included in the FOR LOOP clause immediately before the range, as shown in the following code:

```
FOR i IN REVERSE 1..5 LOOP
```

In many languages, programmers can indicate the increment value in the loop. For example, an increment value of 2 causes the counter variable to increase by 2 instead of 1 in each loop iteration. This feature isn't available as an option in the FOR LOOP statement, which forces the increment value to be 1. Other languages have a STEP option for specifying an increment value. However, you can manipulate the counter value to simulate an increment value greater than 1 by adding code to the loop logic. Say you want a loop that simulates an increment value of 5. In the following block, you add a multiplier in the loop statements. The loop runs only twice; however, the values displayed are 5 and 10 because a multiplier of 5 is used with the counter variable in Line 3:

```
BEGIN
  FOR i IN 1..2 LOOP
    DBMS_OUTPUT.PUT_LINE (i*5);
  END LOOP;
END;
```

CHALLENGE 2-12

Create a block that initializes a variable to the value 11. Use a FOR loop to display the variable value and subtract 2 from the variable. Set the loop to iterate five times.

CONTINUE Statements

The CONTINUE statement introduced in Oracle 11*g* provides a mechanism for exiting a loop's current iteration. It doesn't end loop processing, as the EXIT statement does; it simply moves loop processing to the next iteration. This statement has two forms: CONTINUE and CONTINUE WHEN. Try using this feature to create a loop that executes only every fifth iteration. The output in Figure 2-30 confirms that the CONTINUE WHEN statement at the beginning of the loop instructs the loop to move to the next iteration if the counter value can't be evenly divided by 5 (determined with the MOD function). If the loop counter can be evenly divided by 5, the remaining statements in the loop run.

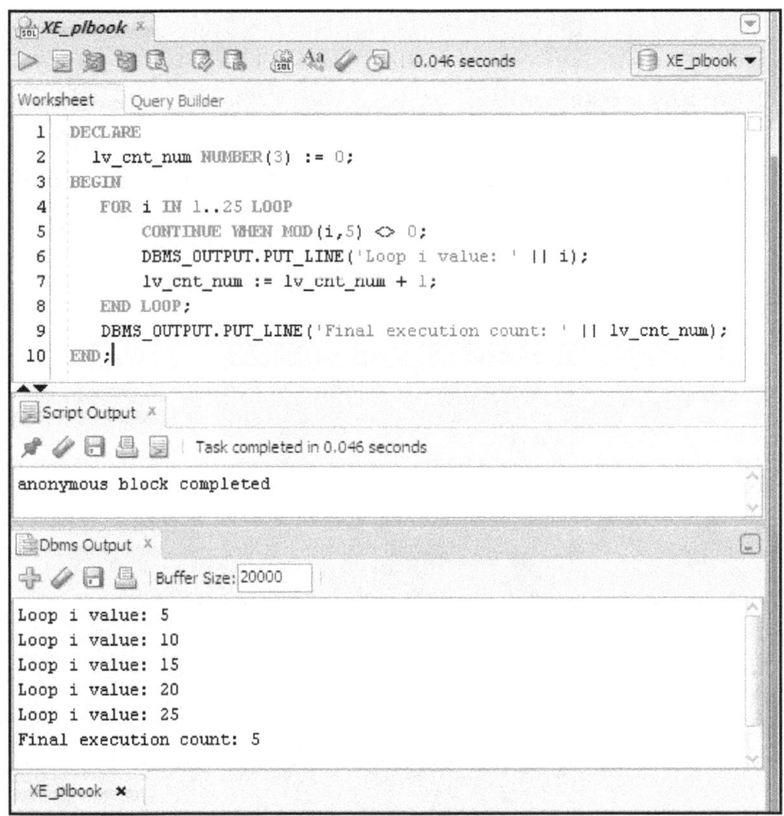

FIGURE 2-30 Using a CONTINUE WHEN statement

Common Errors in Using Looping Statements

Now that you have looked at all three loop types, it's time to discuss a couple of factors to consider when creating loops.

EXIT Clause in Loops

One caution concerns using the EXIT clause in loops. Even though it can be used in any type of loop to stop the looping action, it's considered good form to use it only in basic loops. The WHILE and FOR loops are constructed with conditions in the LOOP statement to determine when the looping action begins and ends. Using an EXIT clause can circumvent these conditions and stop the looping at a different point in the processing. This type of loop is both hard to read and debug.

Static Statements

A second caution is to remember that loops execute all the statements they contain in each iteration. To keep code efficient and minimize statement processing, any statements that are static in nature should be placed outside a loop. For example, say you have a loop containing a calculation that tallies up values, as shown in the following code:

```
DECLARE
  lv_upper_num NUMBER(3) := 3;
  lv_total_num NUMBER(3);
BEGIN
  FOR i IN 1..lv_upper_num LOOP
    lv_total_num := lv_total_num + i;
  END LOOP;
  DBMS_OUTPUT.PUT_LINE(lv_total_num);
END;
```

The loop calculates the total, which is stored in the `lv_total_num` variable. If only the final total needs to be displayed, the `DBMS_OUTPUT` statement is moved outside the loop so that it processes only once, after the loop, as shown in the preceding code.

Nested Loops

Similar to `IF` and `CASE` statements, loops can be nested, too. Figure 2-31 shows a `FOR` loop nested inside another `FOR` loop. The output confirms that for each iteration of the outer loop, the inner loop iterates twice.

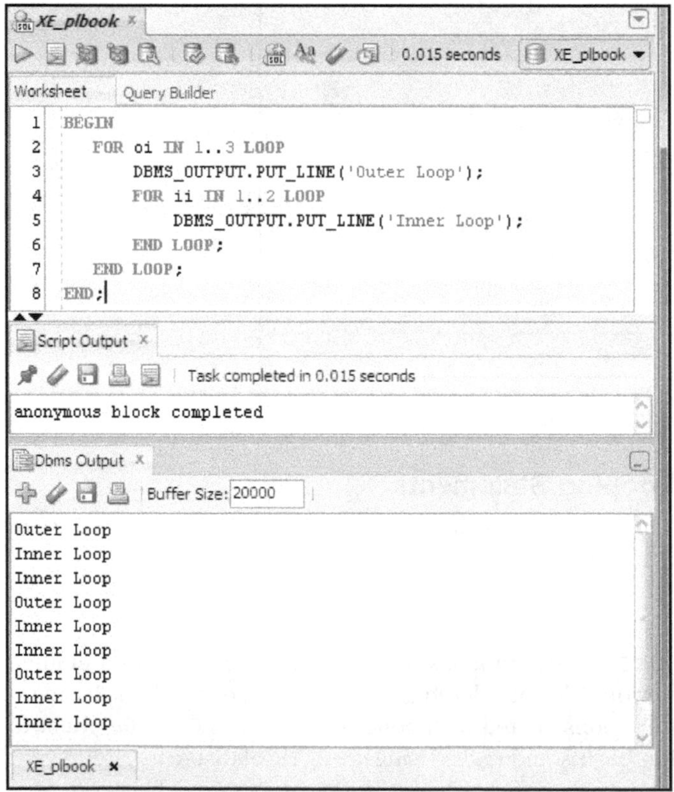

FIGURE 2-31 Nesting `FOR` loops

Nesting loops can be controlled by adding labels to each loop. The following block assigns labels to each loop (such as `<<outer>>`). The `IF` statement in the inner loop is checking the counter value for the outer loop (`oi`) and instructs the inner loop to execute only if it's 2. Otherwise, return to the outer loop as instructed with the `CONTINUE` statement referring to the outer loop's label. Labels can be referenced to control processing flow, and they also make code more readable.

```
BEGIN
  <<outer>>
  FOR oi IN 1..3 LOOP
    DBMS_OUTPUT.PUT_LINE('Outer Loop');
    <<inner>>
    FOR ii IN 1..2 LOOP
      IF oi <> 2 THEN CONTINUE outer; END IF;
      DBMS_OUTPUT.PUT_LINE('Inner Loop');
    END LOOP;
  END LOOP;
END;
```

The output for this block is as follows:

```
Outer Loop
Outer Loop
Inner Loop
Inner Loop
Outer Loop
```

Chapter Summary

- Flowcharts help developers map out the sequence of events to be coded.
- A decision structure identifies different actions that occur during execution, depending on values at runtime.
- Looping structures allow repeating code execution.
- A PL/SQL block can contain DECLARE, BEGIN, EXCEPTION, and END sections. The BEGIN and END sections are required.
- Variables are named memory areas that hold values to allow retrieving and manipulating values in your programs.
- Variables to store and manipulate values in a block are created in the DECLARE section.
- Scalar variables can hold a single value. Common data types are `VARCHAR2`, `CHAR`, `NUMBER`, `DATE`, and `BOOLEAN`.
- Variable-naming rules are the same as those for database objects, including beginning with an alpha character, and can contain up to 30 characters.
- At a minimum, variable declarations must include a name and data type.
- Variables can be initialized with a value in the DECLARE section, using the PL/SQL assignment operator.
- A `NOT NULL` option can be used in a variable declaration to require that the variable always contains a value. These variables must be initialized.
- A `CONSTANT` option can be used in a variable declaration to enforce that the value can't be changed in the block. These variables must be initialized.
- The `DBMS_OUTPUT.PUT_LINE` statement is used to display values onscreen.
- Calculations can be performed with scalar variables.
- SQL single-row functions can be used in PL/SQL statements.
- `IF` statements are a decision-making structure to control program execution based on runtime values. They use the structure of `IF/THEN/ELSIF/ELSE`.
- `CASE` statements are another method for performing decision making in PL/SQL. A searched `CASE` statement allows evaluating different values in an operation.
- A basic loop structure needs an `EXIT WHEN` statement to instruct the system when to stop repeating the code.
- A `WHILE` loop includes a condition in its opening statement that determines whether the loop executes.
- A `FOR` loop includes a range in its opening statement to control how many times the loop repeats.
- A `CONTINUE` statement can be used to move to the next iteration of a loop.
- Use caution when incorporating an `EXIT` clause and placing static statements in looping constructs because doing so can lead to unexpected or inefficient results.
- `IF`, `CASE`, and looping constructs can be nested.

Review Questions

1. Which of the following variable declarations is illegal?
   a. `lv_junk NUMBER(3);`
   b. `lv_junk NUMBER(3) NOT NULL;`
   c. `lv_junk NUMBER(3) := 11;`
   d. `lv_junk NUMBER(3) CONSTANT := 11;`
2. Which of the following is *not* a possible value for a Boolean variable?
   a. `TRUE`
   b. `FALSE`
   c. `BLANK`
   d. `NULL`
3. What type of variable can store only one value?
   a. local
   b. scalar
   c. simple
   d. declared
4. What keyword is used to check multiple conditions with an `IF` statement?
   a. `ELSE IF`
   b. `ELSEIF`
   c. `ELSIF`
   d. `ELSIFS`
5. What type of loop can be used if the loop might not need to execute under certain circumstances?
   a. `FOR`
   b. `WHILE`
   c. basic
   d. All of the above
6. How is the looping action of a basic loop stopped?
   a. It's stopped when the condition in the `LOOP` statement is `FALSE`.
   b. This type of loop has a predetermined number of loops to complete.
   c. The condition in an `EXIT WHEN` statement is `FALSE`.
   d. The condition in an `EXIT WHEN` statement is `TRUE`.
7. When does a `WHILE` loop evaluate the condition that determines whether the looping action continues?
   a. at the beginning of the loop
   b. somewhere inside the loop
   c. at the end of the loop
   d. all of the above

8. If you know the number of loop iterations ahead of time, what type of loop should be used?
   a. `FOR`
   b. `WHILE`
   c. basic
   d. none of the above
9. What commands can be used to end loop execution? (Choose all that apply.)
   a. `CONTINUE`
   b. `EXIT`
   c. `EXIT WHEN`
   d. `STOP`
10. Which programming constructs can use a `CONTINUE` statement?
    a. `IF/THEN` statements
    b. loops
    c. `CASE` statements
    d. all of the above
11. What are variables, and why are they needed?
12. Name the three main types of loop structures in PL/SQL, and explain the difference in how each determines how many times a loop iterates.
13. What are the two types of decision structures in PL/SQL?
14. How can flowcharts assist developers?
15. What happens when a `CONSTANT` option is set in a variable declaration?

Advanced Review Questions

1. Review the following block. What value is displayed by the `DBMS_OUTPUT` statement?

```
DECLARE
  lv_junk1 CHAR(1) := 'N';
  lv_junk2 CHAR(1) := 'N';
BEGIN
  lv_junk1 := 'Y';
  DBMS_OUTPUT.PUT_LINE(lv_junk2);
END;
```

   a. Y
   b. N
   c. NULL
   d. This block raises an error.
2. Review the following `IF` statement. What is the resulting value of `lv_ship_num` if `lv_amt_num` has the value 1200?

```
IF lv_amt_num > 500 THEN
  lv_ship_num := 5;
```

```
ELSIF lv_amt_num > 1000 THEN
  lv_ship_num := 8;
ELSIF lv_amt_num > 1700 THEN
  lv_ship_num := 10;
ELSE
  lv_ship_num := 13;
END IF;
```

a. 5
b. 8
c. 10
d. 13

3. Review the following block. How many times does the FOR loop process?

```
DECLARE
  lv_cnt_num NUMBER(3);
BEGIN
  FOR i IN 1..7 LOOP
    lv_cnt_num := lv_cnt_num + 2;
  END LOOP;
END;
```

a. 3
b. 4
c. 6
d. 7

4. What does the following code produce?

```
DECLARE
  lv_flag_txt CHAR(1) := 'X';
  lv_amt_num NUMBER(4,2);
BEGIN
  CASE lv_state_txt
    WHEN 'A' THEN lv_amt_num := .10;
    WHEN 'E' THEN lv_amt_num := .05;
  END CASE;
  DBMS_OUTPUT.PUT_LINE(lv_amt_num);
END;
```

a. X
b. A
c. E
d. an error

5. Which of the following assignment statements contains an error (assuming all variables have been declared)?
   a. `lv_test_num := (lv_one_num * 3)/2;`
   b. `lv_test_num := ROUND(lv_one_num,1);`
   c. `lv_test_num = lv_one_num - 100;`
   d. None have errors.

Hands-On Assignments Part I

Document all coding and results of testing.

Assignment 2-1: Using Scalar Variables

Create a PL/SQL block containing the following variables:

Name	Data Type	Option	Initial Value
lv_test_date	DATE		December 10, 2012
lv_test_num	NUMBER(3)	CONSTANT	10
lv_test_txt	VARCHAR2(10)		

Assign your last name as the value of the text variable in the executable section of the block. Include statements in the block to display each variable's value onscreen.

Assignment 2-2: Creating a Flowchart

The Brewbean's application needs a block that determines whether a customer is rated high, mid, or low based on his or her total purchases. The block needs to determine the rating and then display the results onscreen. The code rates the customer high if total purchases are greater than $200, mid if greater than $100, and low if $100 or lower. Develop a flowchart to outline the conditional processing steps needed for this block.

Assignment 2-3: Using `IF` Statements

Create a block using an `IF` statement to perform the actions described in Assignment 2-2. Use a scalar variable for the total purchase amount, and initialize this variable to different values to test your block.

Assignment 2-4: Using `CASE` Statements

Create a block using a `CASE` statement to perform the actions described in Assignment 2-2. Use a scalar variable for the total purchase amount, and initialize this variable to different values to test your block.

Assignment 2-5: Using a Boolean Variable

Brewbean's needs program code to indicate whether an amount is still due on an account when a payment is received. Create a PL/SQL block using a Boolean variable to indicate whether an amount is still due. Declare and initialize two variables to provide input for the account balance and the payment amount received. A `TRUE` Boolean value should indicate an amount is still owed, and a `FALSE` value should indicate the account is paid in full. Use output statements to confirm that the Boolean variable is working correctly.

Assignment 2-6: Using Looping Statements

Create a block using a loop that determines the number of items that can be purchased based on the item prices and the total available to spend. Include one initialized variable to represent the price and another to represent the total available to spend. (You could solve it with division, but you need to practice using loop structures.) The block should include statements to display the total number of items that can be purchased and the total amount spent.

Assignment 2-7: Creating a Flowchart

Brewbean's determines shipping costs based on the number of items ordered and club membership status. The applicable rates are shown in the following chart. Develop a flowchart to outline the condition-processing steps needed to handle this calculation.

Quantity of Items	Nonmember Shipping Cost	Member Shipping Cost
Up to 3	\$5.00	\$3.00
4–6	\$7.50	\$5.00
7–10	\$10.00	\$7.00
More than 10	\$12.00	\$9.00

Assignment 2-8: Using `IF` Statements

Create a block to accomplish the task outlined in Assignment 2-7. Include a variable containing a Y or N to indicate membership status and a variable to represent the number of items purchased. Test with a variety of values.

Hands-On Assignments Part II

Assignment 2-9: Using a `FOR` Loop

Create a PL/SQL block using a `FOR` loop to generate a payment schedule for a donor's pledge, which is to be paid monthly in equal increments. Values available for the block are starting payment due date, monthly payment amount, and number of total monthly payments for the pledge. The list that's generated should display a line for each monthly payment showing payment number, date due, payment amount, and donation balance (remaining amount of pledge owed).

Assignment 2-10: Using a Basic Loop

Accomplish the task in Assignment 2-9 by using a basic loop structure.

Assignment 2-11: Using a `WHILE` Loop

Accomplish the task in Assignment 2-9 by using a `WHILE` loop structure. Instead of displaying the donation balance (remaining amount of pledge owed) on each line of output, display the total paid to date.

Assignment 2-12: Using a `CASE` Expression

Donors can select one of three payment plans for a pledge indicated by the following codes: 0 = one-time (lump sum) payment, 1 = monthly payments over one year, and 2 = monthly payments over two years. A local business has agreed to pay matching amounts on pledge payments during the current month. A PL/SQL block is needed to identify the matching amount for a pledge payment. Create a block using input values of a payment plan code and a payment amount. Use a `CASE` expression to calculate the matching amount, based on the payment plan codes 0 = 25%, 1 = 50%, 2 = 100%, and other = 0. Display the calculated amount.

Assignment 2-13: Using Nested `IF` Statements

An organization has committed to matching pledge amounts based on the donor type and pledge amount. Donor types include I = Individual, B = Business organization, and G = Grant funds. The matching percents are to be applied as follows:

Donor Type	Pledge Amount	Matching %
I	$100–$249	50%
I	$250–$499	30%
I	$500 or more	20%
B	$100–$499	20%
B	$500–$999	10%
B	$1,000 or more	5%
G	$100 or more	5%

Create a PL/SQL block using nested `IF` statements to accomplish the task. Input values for the block are the donor type code and the pledge amount.

Case Projects

Case 2-1: Flowcharting

Find a Web site with basic information on flowcharting. Describe at least two interesting aspects of flowcharting discussed on the Web site.

Case 2-2: Working with More Movie Rentals

The More Movie Rentals Company wants to display a rating value for a movie based on the number of times the movie has been rented. The rating assignments are outlined in the following chart:

Number of Rentals	Rental Rating
Up to 5	Dump
5–20	Low
21–35	Mid
More than 35	High

Create a flowchart and then a PL/SQL block to address the processing needed. The block should determine and then display the correct rental rating. Test the block, using a variety of rental amounts.

CHAPTER 3

HANDLING DATA IN PL/SQL BLOCKS

LEARNING OBJECTIVES

After completing this chapter, you should be able to understand:

- SQL queries in PL/SQL
- The %TYPE attribute
- Expanding block processing to include queries and control structures
- Embedding DML statements in PL/SQL
- Using record variables
- Creating collections
- Bulk processing basics
- GOTO statements

INTRODUCTION

Many applications require database interaction tasks, such as querying or manipulating data. Your next step is integrating these data-handling tasks in a PL/SQL block. You begin by incorporating queries that return single values into scalar variables (explained in Chapter 2). DML statements are also addressed because data manipulation is often required in applications. To expand your data-handling capabilities, this chapter then introduces variable structures that can contain more than a single value; these structures are referred to as composite data types and collections. Next, you learn what bulk processing is and how it can affect performance. Last, you see how to control the flow of execution in a block by using GOTO statements. Data-handling challenges in with the Brewbean's application are included throughout the chapter to help you understand the concepts by applying them.

NOTE

The next chapter expands on data-handling capabilities by discussing the use of cursors.

THE CURRENT CHALLENGE IN THE BREWBEAN'S APPLICATION

To start, return to the Brewbean's application example introduced in Chapter 1. Figure 3-1 shows a basket displaying all the items and quantities selected so far. A number of processing tasks could be needed when a shopper clicks the Check Out button, such as calculating taxes, calculating shipping charges, checking and/or updating product inventory, and determining whether the shopper already has credit card information stored.

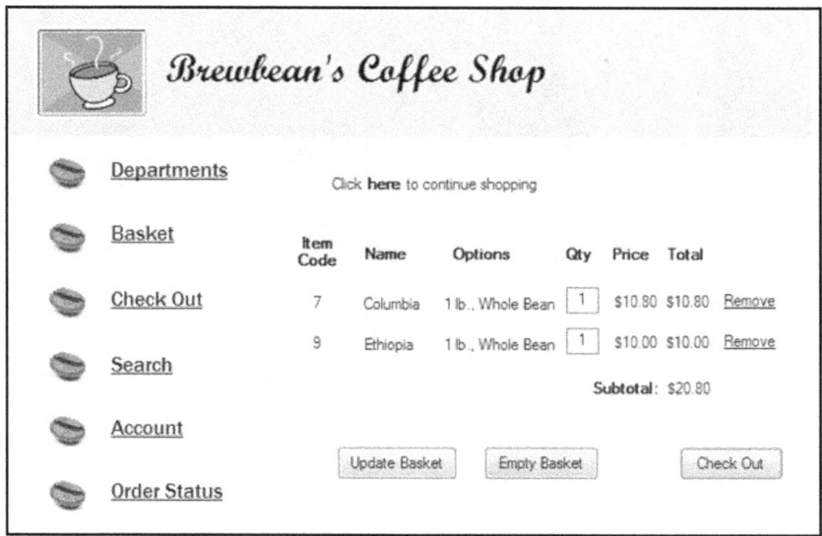

FIGURE 3-1 The Brewbean's application

What database interaction is needed to perform these tasks? For example, to determine whether the shopper's credit card information is already stored in the database, a query on the credit card information columns in the BB_SHOPPER table is needed. To calculate the shipping cost, assume shipping charges are based on the number of items in an order. The program can use the basket number to query the BB_BASKETITEM table and determine the quantity of items in the basket. By accepting input values, such as a basket number, the PL/SQL block is made dynamic, in that it can calculate shipping costs for any order because it queries the database for the total number of items based on the basket number.

Database interaction is also needed after an order is completed. The ORDERPLACED column of the BB_BASKET table is set to the value 1 to indicate that the order has been placed. An `UPDATE` statement is required to modify order data to reflect this change. Like queries, data manipulation statements are embedded in a PL/SQL block to perform these database tasks. This chapter explains these types of PL/SQL data-handling techniques.

NOTE

In this chapter, you continue providing input values to PL/SQL blocks by initializing variables. In Chapter 5, you begin creating stored program units that accept input values via parameters, which makes the PL/SQL blocks reusable. Therefore, no code modification is required.

Rebuilding the Database

From now on, before you start working through each chapter's examples, you need to run a script to rebuild the database. This step ensures that the database is in the correct state to achieve the coding results shown in the chapter and includes the new objects required for chapter examples. As you review the script supplied in your student data files, keep in mind that the first series of statements in the script deletes the existing objects in the database. If an object doesn't exist, these statements raise an error, but it's not a cause for concern. It just indicates that the object hadn't been created in your schema previously. To rebuild the Brewbean's database, follow these steps:

1. Make sure you have the `c3_BBcreate.sql` file in the Chapter03 folder. This file contains the script for creating the database.
2. Start SQL Developer and connect to the Oracle database.
3. Click **File**, **Open** from the menu.
4. Click the **`c3_BBcreate.sql`** file. The code in this script is displayed in the Edit pane. Scroll through the SQL statements; they should look familiar.
5. Run the script by clicking the **Run Script** button on the Edit pane toolbar. If necessary, click **OK** in the Select Connection dialog box.
6. Scroll through the Script Output pane at the bottom to review the results of the statements.
7. In the Connections pane on the left, expand the **Tables** node to view the tables that were created. While this node is selected, click the **Refresh** button at the top of the Connections pane to update the list of tables. The Brewbean's table list should match Figure 3-2.

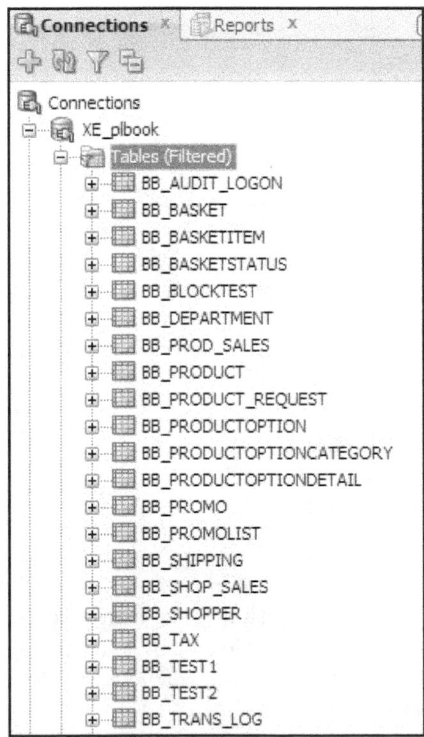

FIGURE 3-2 Brewbean's table list

INCLUDING A QUERY IN A PL/SQL BLOCK

SQL SELECT statements can be embedded in the executable section (BEGIN section) of a PL/SQL block to retrieve data from the database and use the data in the block. When included in a PL/SQL block, a SELECT statement is written much the same way as in SQL, with one major exception—an INTO clause must be used. This clause follows the SELECT clause and indicates which variables should hold the values retrieved from the database.

Adding an INTO Clause to a SELECT Statement

Chapter 2 explained how to declare scalar variables and check values stored in variables. Now take a look at a few blocks that show using declared variables to hold data retrieved from the database. The first example, shown in Figure 3-3, is a block containing a SELECT statement to retrieve the total number of items in a basket, which is used to calculate the shipping cost.

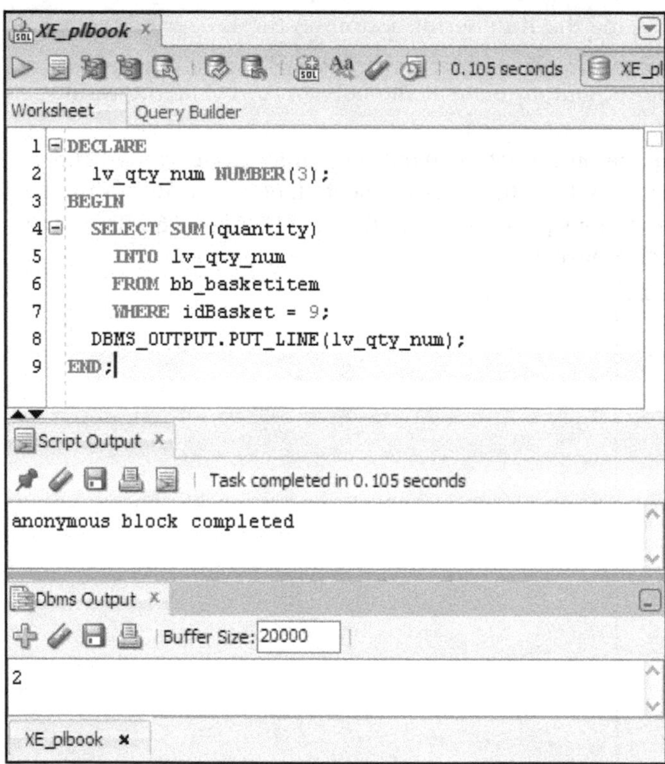

FIGURE 3-3 A SELECT statement

In this example, only a single value is retrieved from the database, so only one variable is needed. The WHERE clause ensures that only rows for basket 9 are retrieved, and the SUM operation makes sure only a single value is returned, which is all a scalar variable can hold. DBMS_OUTPUT.PUT_LINE is used to display the value retrieved, which you can check against the database table to ensure accuracy.

Next, look at a more complex SELECT statement. Figure 3-4 shows an application page that Brewbean's developed to notify a shopper logging on to the site if he or she already started a basket that hasn't been completed. Most online shopping sites allow saving a shopping cart or basket for completion later. For the Brewbean's application, assume a shopper can have only one saved, uncompleted basket.

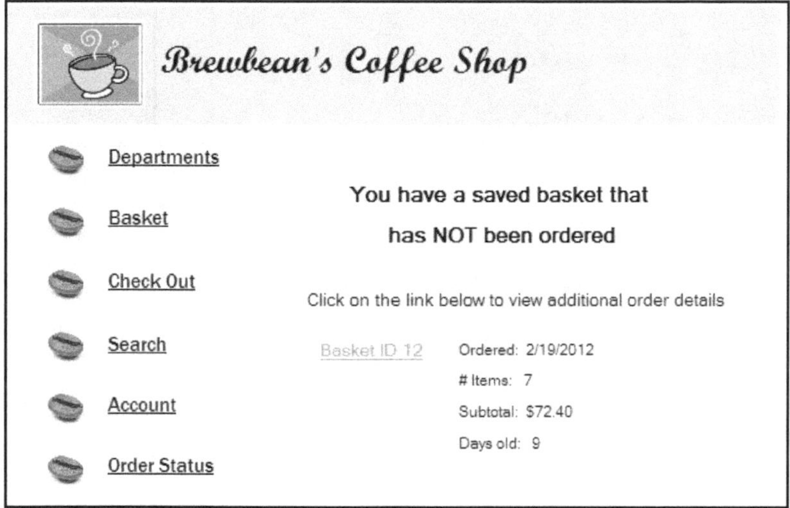

FIGURE 3-4 Brewbean's application page reminding shoppers of existing baskets

When a shopper logs on to the Brewbean's Web site, code is needed to determine whether the shopper has an existing uncompleted basket saved. If so, the ORDERPLACED column of the BB_BASKET table has a value of 0. If a saved basket is found, the basket date, amounts, and age (time since the basket was saved) need to be retrieved to display onscreen. For this task, data from the BB_BASKET table needs to be queried, and the age needs to be calculated by comparing the current date with the date the basket was created. Typically, you use SYSDATE to retrieve the current date; however, a specific date is used as input in this example so that you can get the same results for comparison. Figure 3-5 shows the PL/SQL block for performing these tasks.

The first action occurs at Line 9, which retrieves data with a SELECT statement that uses a WHERE clause to make sure only one row of data is returned. The WHERE clause specifies a shopper and indicates that only a saved basket should be retrieved. This clause is critical because only single values can be stored in the scalar variables declared. The first four variables declared are used in the INTO clause to hold the values retrieved in the SELECT statement. The column values retrieved are moved to variables based on their position. In other words, the value retrieved for the first column in the SELECT clause (which is IDBASKET) is placed in the first variable listed in the INTO clause (lv_basket_num). The same thing happens for the second column in the SELECT statement and the second variable in the INTO clause, and so forth. The SELECT statement retrieves only a single row from the table because of the WHERE clause, so scalar variables are fine in this block.

Line 14 has an assignment statement calculating the basket age with the date 2/28/2012 to represent the current day minus the lv_created_date variable. (lv_created_date contains the value retrieved from the DTCREATED column.) The result of this calculation is stored in the lv_days_num variable and represents the number of days between the two dates—that is, the basket age.

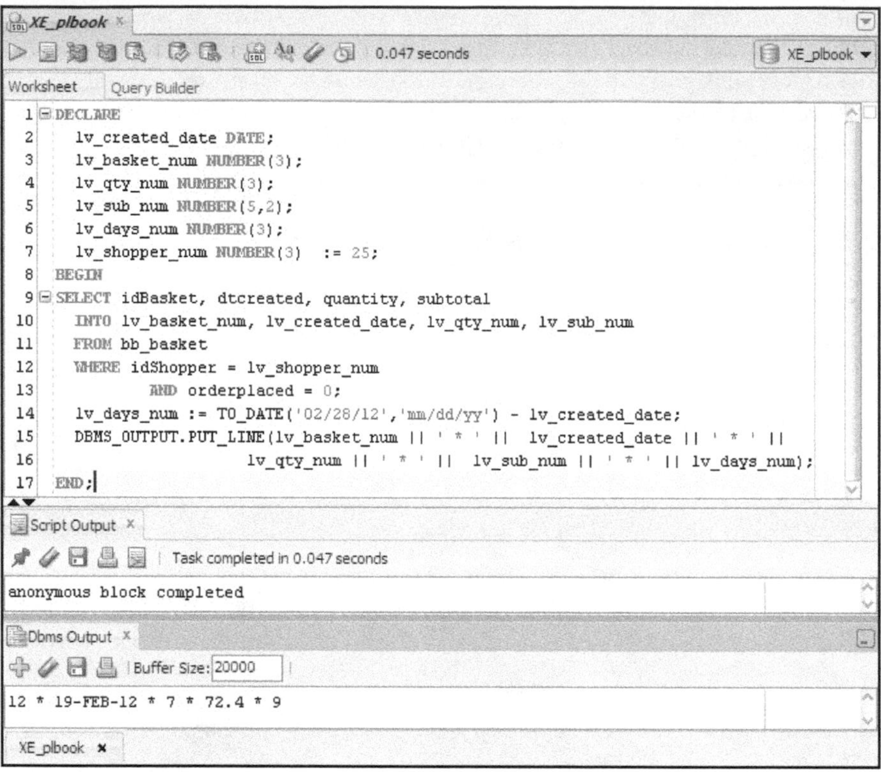

FIGURE 3-5 A block checking for an uncompleted basket

TIP

Leaving the colon off the assignment statement is probably one of the most common errors new PL/SQL programmers make. It takes a bit to adjust to using the `:=` symbol. However, don't get it mixed up with SQL syntax. The `WHERE` clause of the SQL query in Figure 3-5 uses a plain equals sign, just as you always have in SQL statements. The `:=` syntax applies only to PL/SQL statements.

The last statement in the block uses `DBMS_OUTPUT.PUT_LINE` to display values onscreen. Developers often use this method to check the values of variables during block execution. Each `DBMS_OUTPUT` statement can display only one item, so the concatenation operator is used in this example to display the values of all variables with a single statement. You can include multiple `DBMS_OUTPUT` statements throughout a block to test values at any point in the block.

NOTE

Managing queries when retrieving multiple rows of data in a block is covered later in "Introduction to Bulk Processing" and in Chapter 4.

CHALLENGE 3-1

Create a PL/SQL block to retrieve and display the credit card number and type used in purchasing the basket with an ID of 10.

Encountering PL/SQL Error Messages

Before exploring more data-handling techniques, you need to become familiar with some common PL/SQL errors you might encounter. Jump in and experiment with running several versions of the PL/SQL block in Figure 3-5. First, you run it as-is with no errors. Then you run the block to generate different errors so that you get accustomed to common PL/SQL error messages.

To run an anonymous block with scalar variables, follow these steps:

1. Start SQL Developer, if necessary.
2. Open the `scalarA03.sql` file from the Chapter03 folder by clicking **File**, **Open** from the menu.
3. Run the block. The results should be similar to Figure 3-5, which shows information for basket 12.
4. Next, open the `scalarB03.sql` file from the Chapter03 folder. Review the code. The same block is used, but the assignment statement for `lv_days_num` has been modified to contain an error: The colon is missing in the assignment statement operator. (Each File, Open menu action opens a new Edit pane. To close one, click the X on the corresponding tab so that you don't have too many panes open at once.)
5. Run the block. Review the error message, which should match Figure 3-6. It states that an = symbol was encountered when something else was expected; in this case, it's the PL/SQL assignment syntax of `:=`.

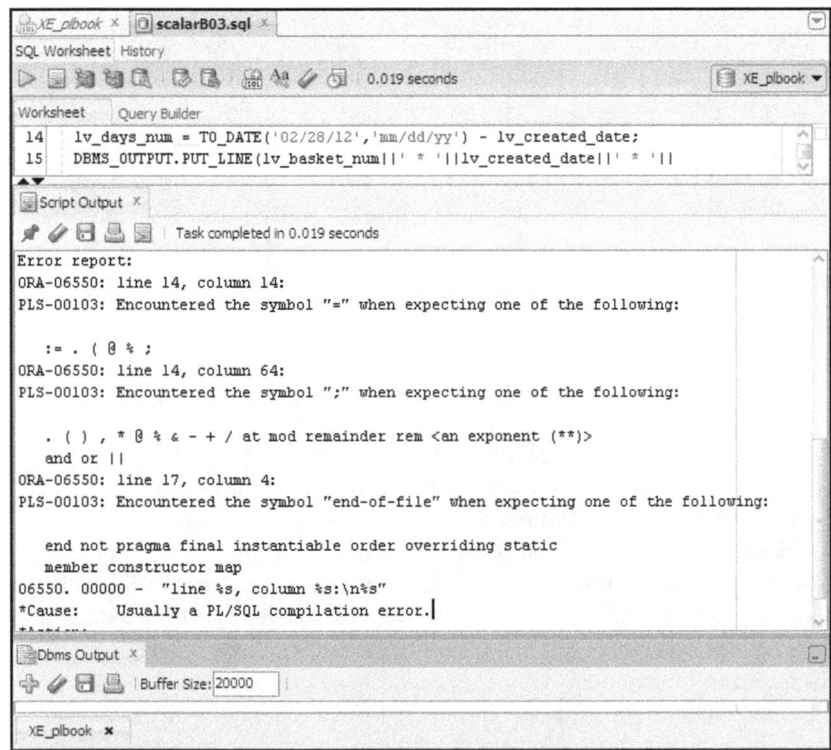

FIGURE 3-6 An assignment statement error message

TIP

When multiple errors are listed, you should correct the first one and then rerun the block. Many times, addressing the first error corrects the other errors, which usually result from the first error offsetting the statements in the block.

6. Next, open the **scalarC03.sql** file from the Chapter03 folder. The same block is used, except the `lv_basket_num` variable is misspelled in the `INTO` clause.
7. Run the block. You should see the error message "identifier 'LV_BASKET_NU' must be declared," shown in Figure 3-7. This message is common because forgetting to declare a variable or misspelling a variable name are easy mistakes to make.

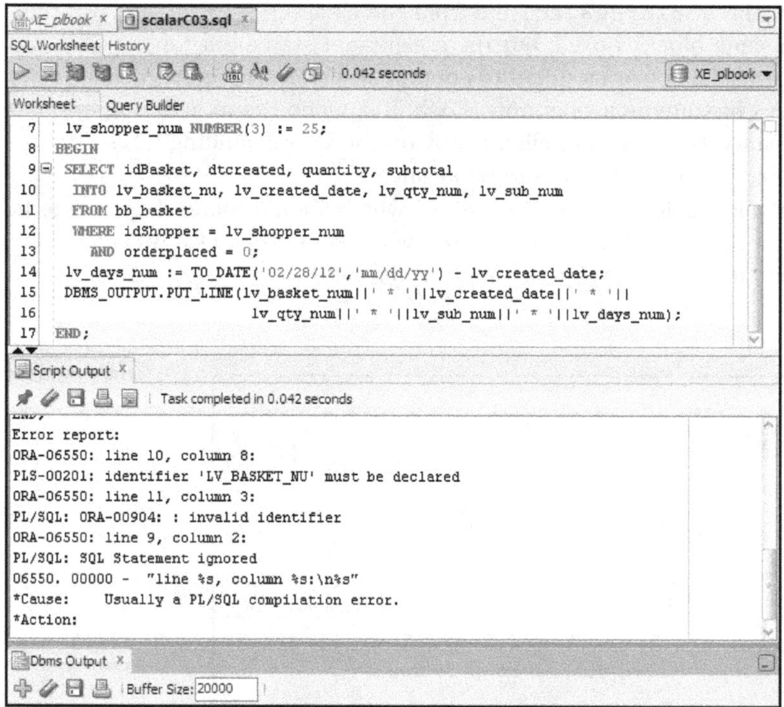

FIGURE 3-7 An error for a variable that's not declared

8. Next, open the **scalarD03.sql** file from the Chapter03 folder. The same block is used again, except the semicolon is left off the end of the `lv_days_num` assignment statement.
9. Run the block. The error message shown in Figure 3-8 is displayed. When an error occurs at the beginning of a line starting a new statement, the cause is often that the previous statement wasn't terminated correctly with a semicolon.
10. Next, open the **scalarE03.sql** file from the Chapter03 folder. Again, the same block is used, but the shopper ID is 33, which doesn't exist in the database.
11. Run the block. The error message shown in Figure 3-9 is displayed. Notice the reference to "no data found." A `SELECT` statement embedded in a PL/SQL block must return a row, or it generates this error.

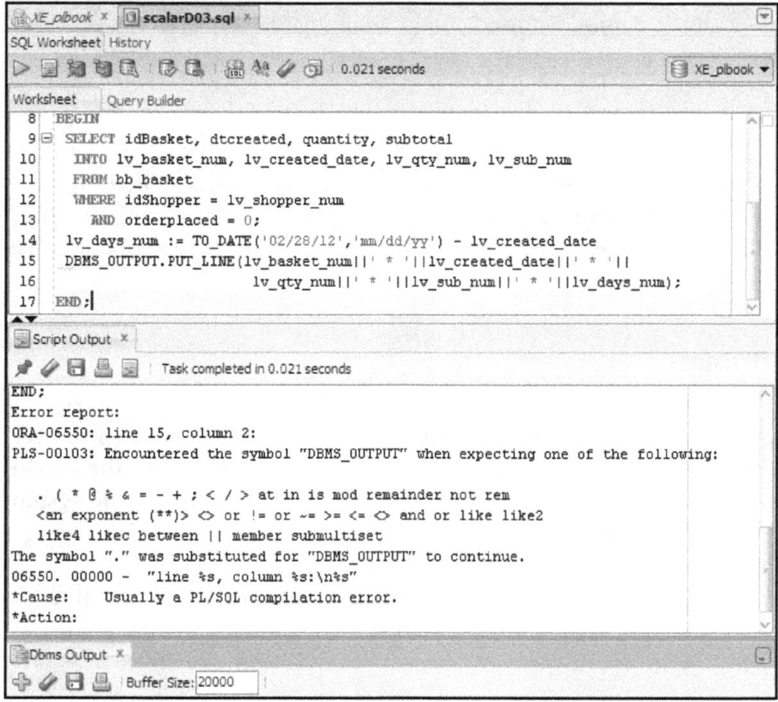

FIGURE 3-8 An error caused by not closing the previous statement

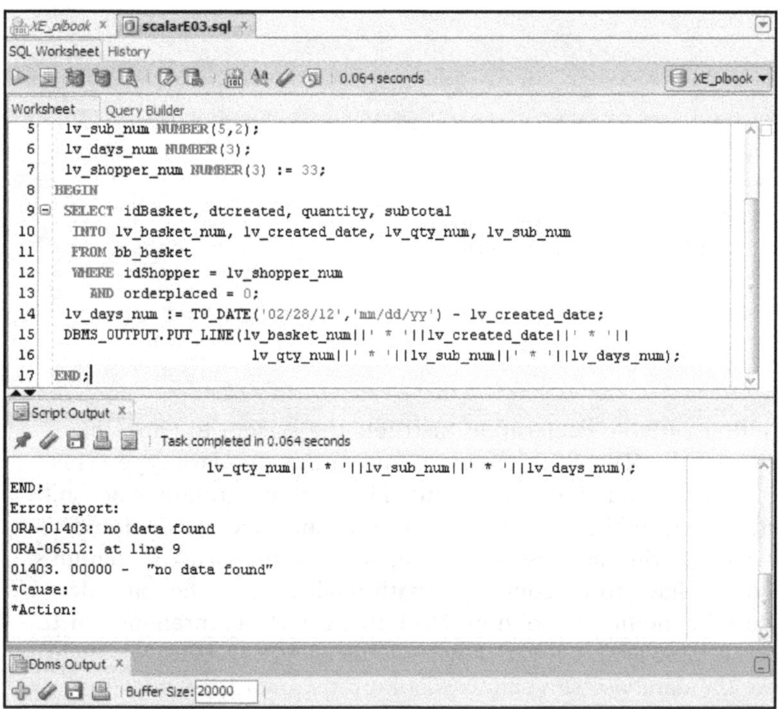

FIGURE 3-9 A "no data found" error from a `SELECT` statement

NOTE

The "no data found" error is a runtime error rather than a syntax error. In other words, the code syntax in the block is correct, but an error occurred during the code's execution.

Keep these common errors in mind when running PL/SQL blocks. Misspelled or undeclared variables are typical causes of errors. In addition, always check the code line immediately before the line referenced in the error to see whether a closing semicolon has been omitted.

Using the `%TYPE` Attribute

Another important point about the previous example is that all the variables declared, with the exception of `lv_days_num`, are created specifically for holding values retrieved from database columns. When creating variables to hold database column values, the `%TYPE` attribute can be used in the variable declaration to provide the data type. It tells the system to look up a database column's data type and use it for the declared variable. Specifying a data type this way is called using an **anchored data type**.

The modified block using the `%TYPE` attribute in variable declarations looks like the following:

```
DECLARE
  lv_basket_num bb_basket.idBasket%TYPE;
  lv_created_date bb_basket.dtcreated%TYPE;
  lv_qty_num bb_basket.quantity%TYPE;
  lv_sub_num bb_basket.subtotal%TYPE;
  lv_days_num NUMBER(3);
BEGIN
  SELECT idBasket, dtcreated, quantity, subtotal
    INTO lv_basket_num, lv_created_date, lv_qty_num, lv_sub_num
    FROM bb_basket
    WHERE idShopper = 25
      AND orderplaced = 0;
  lv_days_num := TO_DATE('02/28/12','mm/dd/yy') - lv_created_date;
  DBMS_OUTPUT.PUT_LINE(lv_basket_num || ' * ' ||
    lv_created_date || ' * ' || lv_qty_num || ' * ' ||
    lv_sub_num || ' * ' || lv_days_num);
END;
```

Using `%TYPE` in the first variable declaration instructs the system to go to the BB_BASKET TABLE, look up the IDBASKET column, and return the data type. This data type declaration is advantageous for two reasons. First, the programmer doesn't have to look up the data type to make sure the correct type and size are declared. Second, if changes are made to the database structure, such as increasing a column's size, the programmer doesn't have to be concerned with modifying all the variable declarations in any code referencing the column. Minimizing code maintenance in this fashion is always a programming goal. On the downside, using `%TYPE` causes a slight performance hit because the database server must look up the data type from the data dictionary.

CHALLENGE 3-2

Revise the PL/SQL block in Challenge 3-1 to use the `%TYPE` attribute where appropriate.

DATA RETRIEVAL WITH CONTROL STRUCTURES

Chapter 2 introduced `IF` and `CASE` control structures to incorporate decision-making processes into a block. Now you need to reconsider some processing needs when using condition statements to incorporate the required data-retrieval tasks. PL/SQL block processing is expanded in this section to combine decision-control structures and data-retrieval tasks.

Take another look at some tax-calculation examples from Chapter 2. The first example starts with the following assumptions:

- Taxes should be applied only in the company's home state of Virginia.
- You need to check for only one condition: whether the shipping state is Virginia. If it is, the tax amount is calculated by using the order subtotal retrieved from the database.
- If the shipping state isn't Virginia, no calculation is performed, and a tax amount of 0 should be applied.

To support the tax calculation, some processing steps are needed in a block. First, a query is needed to determine the state for the shopper who's completing an order. Second, an `IF` statement is needed to determine the correct tax amount based on the state value retrieved. Last, the tax amount should be displayed. The flowchart in Figure 3-10 illustrates these steps.

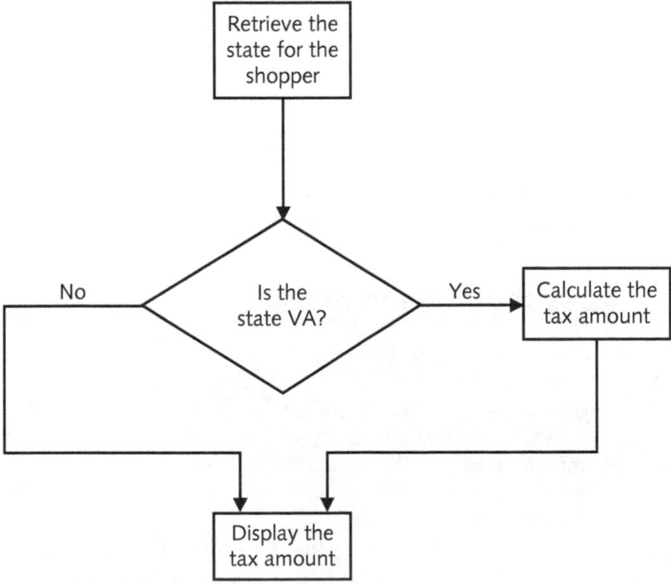

FIGURE 3-10 A flowchart for the tax calculation process

Review the block tested with the basket ID 6, which belongs to a Virginia customer. Figure 3-11 shows the results with the tax amount calculated by using a 6% rate. Notice that the `lv_tax_num` variable is initialized to 0, so running the block with a customer state other than Virginia results in a tax amount of 0. (Test it!)

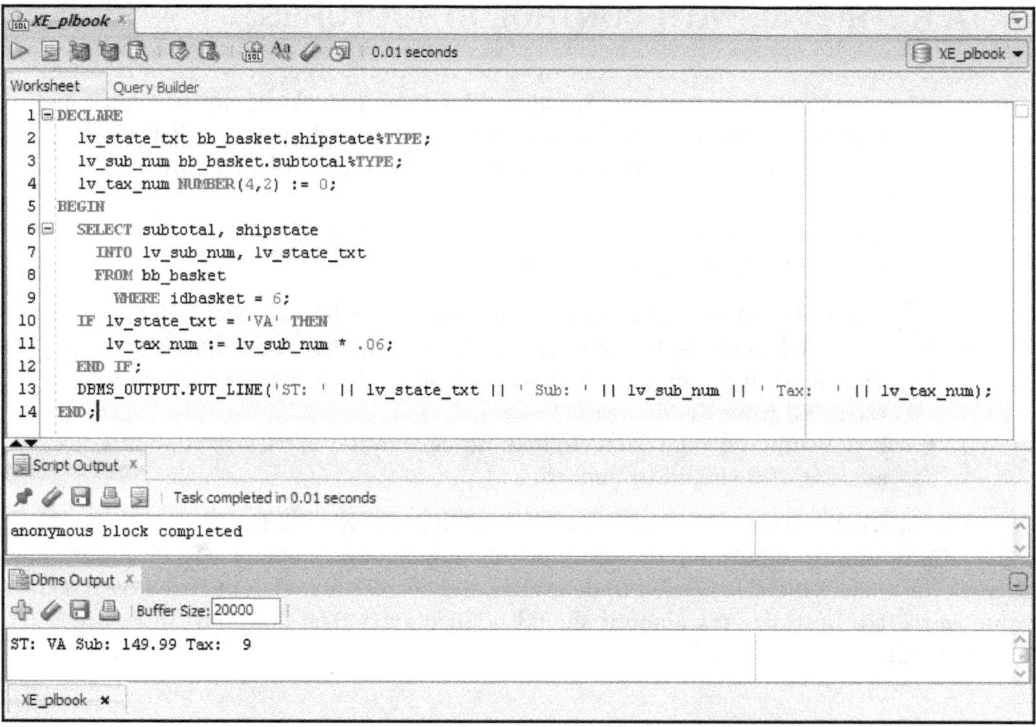

FIGURE 3-11 Retrieving state data to determine the tax amount

Next, review the more complex tax calculation explained in Chapter 2. What if the requirements change so that a tax rate of 6% is applied to VA, 5% to ME, 7% to NY, and 4% to all other states? Review the code in Figure 3-12, which checks for different values by using `ELSIF` clauses. The basic processing steps are the same: Query the state data, calculate the tax, and display the tax amount.

CHALLENGE 3-3

Revise the PL/SQL block in Challenge 3-2 to include an `IF` statement that determines the message to display. You want to display the message `Shopper used credit card type of xxxxxx`. The *xxxxxx* represents a card type, based on the following: V = Visa, X = American Express, and M = MasterCard. If no type is indicated, as for uncompleted baskets, the message `No credit card type indicated` should be displayed. Test the block with different baskets.

You have also used `CASE` statements for decision-making tasks in your blocks. Try redoing the tax-calculation block in Figure 3-12 to use a `CASE` statement rather than an `IF` statement to determine the tax amount. Figure 3-13 shows the results of using a `CASE` statement.

XE_plbook

0.013 seconds

Worksheet Query Builder

```
DECLARE
  lv_state_txt bb_basket.shipstate%TYPE;
  lv_sub_num bb_basket.subtotal%TYPE;
  lv_tax_num NUMBER(4,2) := 0;
BEGIN
  SELECT subtotal, shipstate
    INTO lv_sub_num, lv_state_txt
    FROM bb_basket
      WHERE idbasket = 4;
  IF lv_state_txt = 'VA' THEN
     lv_tax_num := lv_sub_num * .06;
  ELSIF lv_state_txt = 'ME' THEN
     lv_tax_num := lv_sub_num * .05;
  ELSIF lv_state_txt = 'NY' THEN
     lv_tax_num := lv_sub_num * .07;
  ELSE
     lv_tax_num := lv_sub_num * .04;
  END IF;
  DBMS_OUTPUT.PUT_LINE('ST: ' || lv_state_txt || ' Sub: ' || lv_sub_num || ' Tax:  ' || lv_tax_num);
END;
```

Script Output

Task completed in 0.013 seconds

```
anonymous block completed
```

Dbms Output

Buffer Size: 20000

```
ST: NC Sub: 28.5 Tax:  1.14
```

XE_plbook

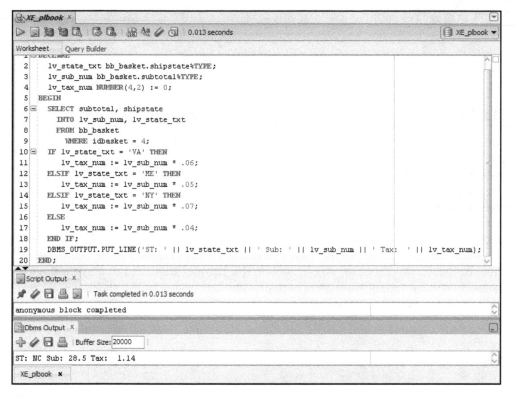

FIGURE 3-12 Including data retrieval and conditional `IF` processing in a block

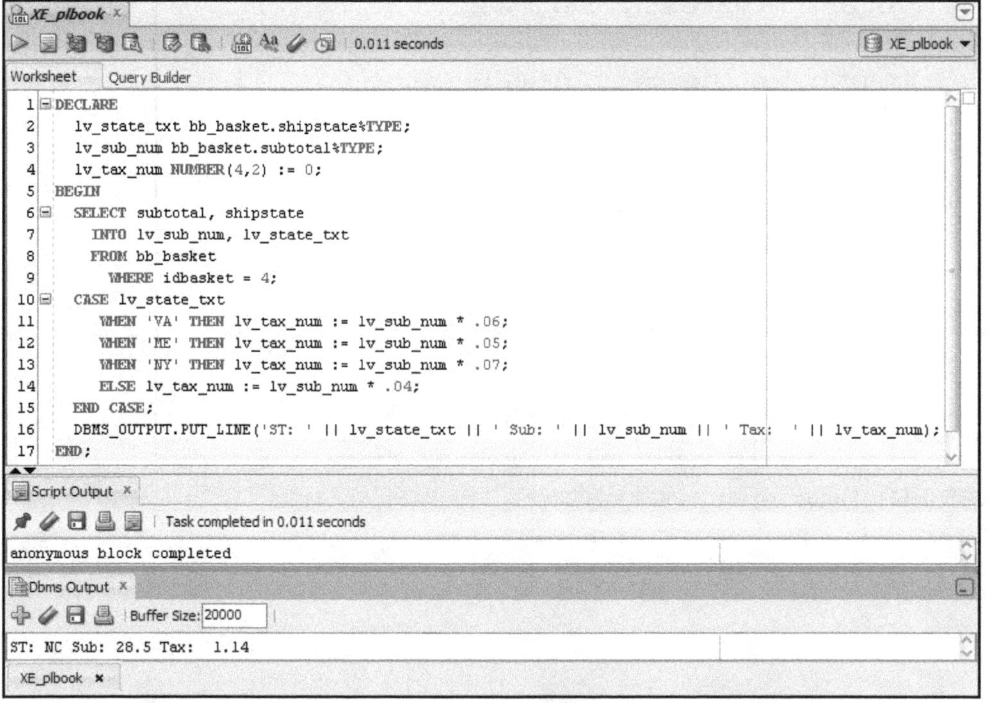

FIGURE 3-13 Including data retrieval and conditional `CASE` processing in a block

CHALLENGE 3-4

Revise the PL/SQL block in Challenge 3-3 to use a `CASE` statement rather than an `IF` statement to determine the message to display. Test the block with different baskets.

INCLUDING DML STATEMENTS IN A PL/SQL BLOCK

Data-manipulation tasks are commonly required in applications. For example, when a new customer enters information, such as name and address, a block must include an `INSERT` statement to add this new data to the database. DML and transaction control statements can be embedded in a PL/SQL block's executable section. No syntax modifications are required to include these statements.

Say you're adding a new customer who has provided only first name, last name, and e-mail information so far. You use an `INSERT` statement with a column list for these three columns and the ID column and a `COMMIT` to save the data permanently to the database. A sequence named `BB_SHOPPER_SEQ` is used in the `INSERT` statement to provide shopper ID values. Initialized variables are created to provide data values for the shopper columns. Figure 3-14 shows this `INSERT` statement.

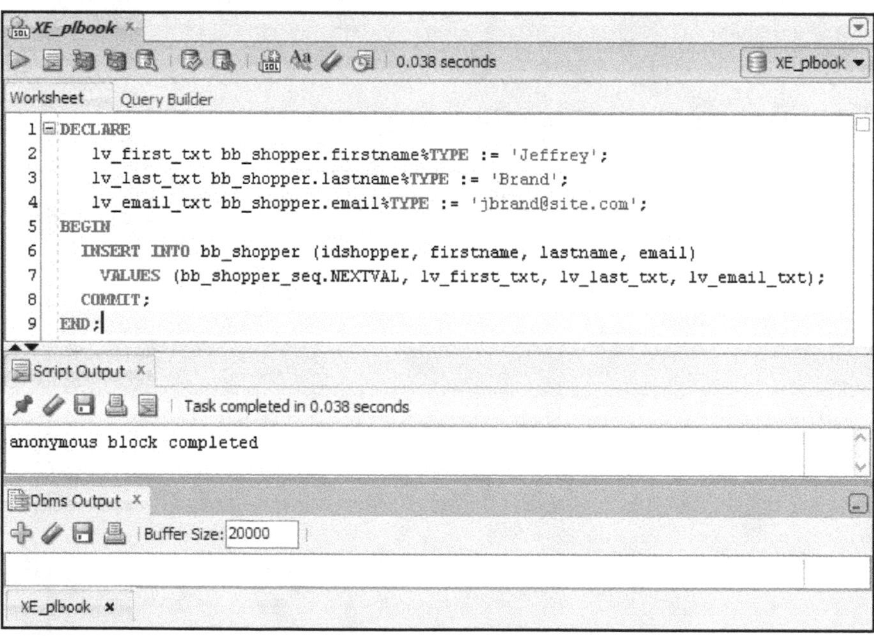

FIGURE 3-14 Performing an `INSERT` in a block

How do you verify that a block containing a DML statement has processed correctly? Query the database to confirm the data action, as shown in Figure 3-15.

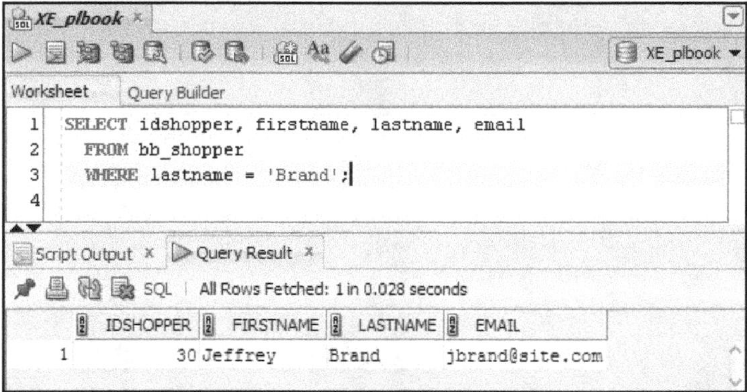

FIGURE 3-15 Verifying that a DML statement was processed correctly

> **TIP**
>
> To make experimenting with embedded DML statements easier, exclude the `COMMIT` statement and use `ROLLBACK` to return data to its original state (before the DML action was processed).

Another requirement of the Brewbean's application is that the ORDERPLACED column should be set to a value of 1 after the shopper completes the order. This action requires updating the existing basket row. To test an `UPDATE` action, you need to confirm the data's current state, perform the update, and then confirm the data's state again. Figures 3-16 to 3-18 show the SQL and PL/SQL statements for this process.

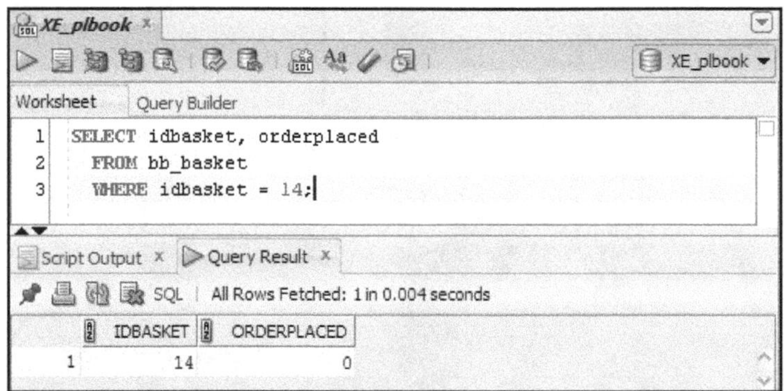

FIGURE 3-16 Verifying existing data

```
DECLARE
  lv_basket_num bb_basket.idbasket%TYPE :=14;
BEGIN
  UPDATE bb_basket
    SET orderplaced = 1
    WHERE idbasket = lv_basket_num;
  COMMIT;
END;
```

```
anonymous block completed
```

FIGURE 3-17 Performing an `UPDATE` in a block

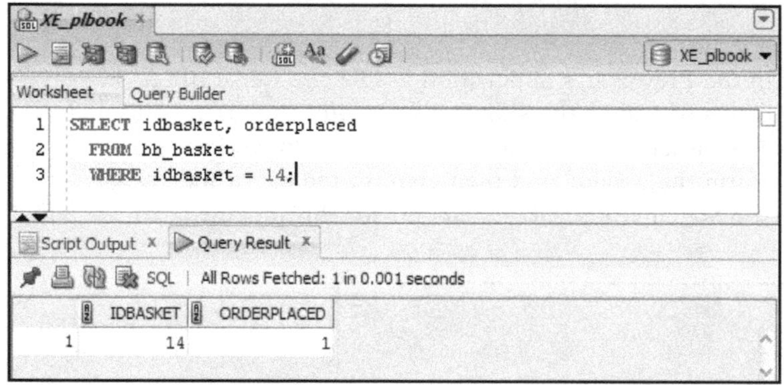

FIGURE 3-18 Verifying data after an `UPDATE`

CHALLENGE 3-5

Review the PL/SQL block in Figure 3-12, which calculates the tax amount for an order. Modify the block to store the tax amount value calculated in the TAX column of the BB_BASKET table instead of simply displaying this value. Test the block with a basket ID of 13.

CHALLENGE 3-6

If you didn't do so earlier, create and run the block shown in Figure 3-14 to add a new customer to the BB_SHOPPER table. Query the BB_SHOPPER table, and note the shopper ID assigned to the new customer. Then write a new block that removes a customer from the database. Use an initialized variable to provide the previously inserted customer's shopper ID to the block.

USING RECORD VARIABLES

Scalar variables are quite useful; however, programs often need to handle logical groups of data, such as an entire row from a database table or a number of rows entered from an application page. To make these tasks easier to manage, PL/SQL offers composite data types that allow creating a variable that can hold multiple values as a single unit. Two kinds of composite data types are covered in this chapter: records and collections.

A **record** can store and handle multiple values or fields, each having its own name and data type, as one unit. This structure is similar to a table row. A **collection** can store an ordered group of elements of the same type, with each element having a unique subscript or index. This structure is similar to arrays found in other languages. A striking difference between the two is that record variables hold a variety of data types, whereas a collection holds a group of elements of the same data type.

Record Data Type

A record data type is quite similar to the structure of a database table row, and a variable declared with a record data type can hold one row of data consisting of a number of column values. A row of data typically includes a number of different fields. For a record variable, you must construct your own data type, using a `TYPE` statement indicating the fields to include in the record and their associated data types. Then you can declare a variable with that data type.

Up to this point, you have declared only scalar variables that use data types already available in PL/SQL, such as `NUMBER` and `VARCHAR2`. Declaring a record variable is different from declaring a scalar variable because you must create your own data types to assign. Creating a record data type with the `TYPE` statement is often called "declaring a programmer-defined record." The syntax of the `TYPE` statement is as follows:

```
TYPE type_name IS RECORD (
field_1_name data type [NOT NULL] [:= default_value],
  ...
field_n_name data type [NOT NULL] [:= default_value]);
```

Return to the block you constructed for the Brewbean's application to retrieve an uncompleted basket that a shopper has saved (shown previously in Figure 3-5). Earlier, you created four scalar variables to hold values retrieved from the BB_BASKET table for a particular shopper. Figure 3-19 shows the modified code for using a record variable to handle data in the query. The new code is shown in bold to make it easy to identify.

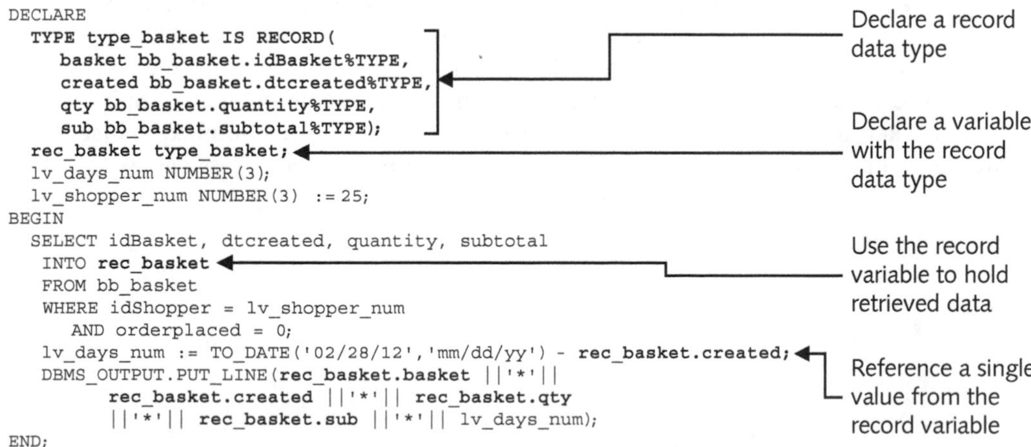
```
DECLARE
  TYPE type_basket IS RECORD(
     basket bb_basket.idBasket%TYPE,
     created bb_basket.dtcreated%TYPE,
     qty bb_basket.quantity%TYPE,
     sub bb_basket.subtotal%TYPE);
  rec_basket type_basket;
  lv_days_num NUMBER(3);
  lv_shopper_num NUMBER(3) := 25;
BEGIN
  SELECT idBasket, dtcreated, quantity, subtotal
   INTO rec_basket
   FROM bb_basket
   WHERE idShopper = lv_shopper_num
     AND orderplaced = 0;
   lv_days_num := TO_DATE('02/28/12','mm/dd/yy') - rec_basket.created;
   DBMS_OUTPUT.PUT_LINE(rec_basket.basket ||'*'||
         rec_basket.created ||'*'|| rec_basket.qty
         ||'*'|| rec_basket.sub ||'*'|| lv_days_num);
END;
```


FIGURE 3-19 Declaring a record variable

The TYPE statement (starting in the second line) creates a record data type named type_basket that can hold four values: one date and three numbers. Because the record variable is used to hold data from the database, the %TYPE attribute is used to declare the data type for each field in the TYPE statement. Any data type you have used for scalar variables could be used here, too. The rec_basket variable is then declared by using the type_basket data type you just created. rec_basket is a record variable, meaning it's a variable declared with a record data type.

Data handling for the query is now much simpler. The INTO clause of the SELECT statement contains only one variable, rec_basket, which stores all four values the query returns. The column data values are moved into the record fields based on their positions in the underlying structure. Keep in mind that you now have a single variable holding multiple values, so you must be careful to match the order of the query columns with the order of fields defined in the record data type. For example, the value of the first column, IDBASKET, is copied to the first field defined in the data type creation, which is the basket field. Make sure the order of columns in the SELECT statement matches the order of fields in the record variable.

Because you now have only one variable, how do you reference the four values it holds separately? Review the lv_days_num assignment statement that must reference the date created value the query returns to calculate the basket age in days, as shown in the following code:

```
lv_days_num := TO_DATE('02/28/12','mm/dd/yy') - rec_basket.created;
```

Using the *record_variable_name.field_name* notation, you can reference each field in the record variable separately. In this example, the date created value is referenced as rec_basket.created, with rec_basket being the record variable and created being a field defined in the record data type in the TYPE statement.

Follow these steps to try this example:

1. Start SQL Developer, if necessary.
2. Open the **record03.sql** file from the Chapter03 folder. Review the code.
3. Run the PL/SQL block. The results of the DBMS_OUTPUT statement should look like the following:

```
12 * 19-FEB-12 * 7 * 72.4 * 9
```

In the preceding example, all four fields in the record variable are displayed in the DBMS_OUTPUT statement to verify that the correct values were moved to the expected fields in the record. The record variable allows storing multiple values together, so you must be careful to populate record elements in the correct order. Typically, you use a record variable to store related values, such as data elements making up a specific basket, as shown in the example. As code becomes more complex, managing related data in a composite structure can simplify coding logic and debugging.

The Role of the %ROWTYPE Attribute

In the uncompleted basket example, only a few columns from the BB_BASKET table are retrieved. However, what if you want to retrieve most or all of the columns of a row from a table? To do so, you could create a data type with a TYPE statement. However, this method might become cumbersome if you need to retrieve many columns. You can accomplish this task more simply by using the %ROWTYPE attribute to declare a record data type. A %ROWTYPE attribute is similar to %TYPE in that it determines the needed data type by referencing a database table structure. This attribute goes a step further and reviews the table structure for all column names and data types and creates the record data type based on this information. In essence, PL/SQL creates the record data type to match the table structure information. The table column names are assigned as the record field names.

Take a look at a page in the Brewbean's application where you can use the %ROWTYPE attribute. Shoppers have profiles saved to avoid having to reenter their names, addresses, and contact information. A page displays user profile information and enables them to make edits (such as an address change). The profile information includes almost all the 17 columns in the BB_SHOPPER table. In this case, instead of using the TYPE attribute to build the record data type for including all these columns, you could use the %ROWTYPE attribute to simplify the code by creating a record variable to hold the row of data queried for a shopper. The following block performs this task:

```
DECLARE
  rec_shopper bb_shopper%ROWTYPE;
BEGIN
  SELECT *
    INTO rec_shopper
    FROM bb_shopper
    WHERE idshopper = 25;
  DBMS_OUTPUT.PUT_LINE(rec_shopper.lastname);
  DBMS_OUTPUT.PUT_LINE(rec_shopper.address);
  DBMS_OUTPUT.PUT_LINE(rec_shopper.email);
END;
```

NOTE

Only three columns of data are displayed from the record variable to verify that the data was retrieved; however, all the columns from the row could be displayed because the entire row of data is retrieved.

Now only one statement in the DECLARE section is needed to create a record variable. No TYPE statement is needed to create the data type because the %ROWTYPE attribute instructs the system to create the data type automatically based on the table structure. Notice that column names from the table are used as field names of the record variable, as shown in the DBMS_OUTPUT statements. A SELECT * statement is used to query all columns and move the entire row of data from the table to the record variable, ensuring that the order of column values being pushed into the record fields matches. The %ROWTYPE attribute can simplify code maintenance with database structure modifications. If table columns are altered, you don't need to modify data-handling variables because the columns and data types are retrieved automatically from the data dictionary and reflect the current table structure.

Why not use the %ROWTYPE attribute to declare all record variables? First, you need to consider processing efficiency. For example, say you have a table containing 100 columns but need to retrieve only 7 for the block. Retrieving and transmitting 100 values are inefficient when only 7 are needed. Therefore, the %ROWTYPE attribute is typically used when a large portion of data values from a row are needed. Second, keep in mind that you can use a record variable for purposes other than holding data retrieved from the database. You might have an application that calls for manipulating a group of related values not associated with a database table. For example, a user might input a variety of data to request a complex financial calculation that simply displays the result.

CHALLENGE 3-7

Review your code for Challenge 3-2, which retrieves credit card information. Modify this block to use a record variable. Use a TYPE statement to declare the record data type.

CHALLENGE 3-8

One Brewbean's application page is used to display all details for a particular item in a basket. Create a PL/SQL block to retrieve all data for a specific row from the BB_BASKETITEM table. Use an initialized variable to provide a basket item ID in the block, and use a record variable to hold the data retrieved from the table. Display at least the idproduct and price values.

Record Operations

Record variables are quite flexible and allow a variety of operations, such as assigning values and manipulating data. For example, you might need to create a variable to hold values a user enters to create a new department in Brewbean's. Using a record variable, you can store these values in a single unit and assign them as needed. The following block handles this task; assume the values being assigned are user input. A record variable based on the BB_DEPARTMENT table is declared, and then values are assigned to fields in the record variable.

```
DECLARE
  rec_dept bb_department%ROWTYPE;
BEGIN
  rec_dept.iddepartment := 4;
  rec_dept.deptname := 'Teas';
  rec_dept.deptdesc := 'Premium teas';
  DBMS_OUTPUT.PUT_LINE(rec_dept.deptname);
END;
```

Using DBMS_OUTPUT enables you to confirm that the assigned values have actually been stored in the record variable. What about the DEPTIMAGE column of the BB_DEPARMENT table? This column isn't assigned a value, so does it exist in the record variable? Yes. Because %ROWTYPE is used, the record variable has a field for every column in the table. In this case, a value isn't assigned to the DEPTIMAGE field, so it's NULL. You can test this by using an IF statement with an IS NULL check on the rec_dept.deptimage field.

Now that you have a record variable holding data that needs to be inserted into a table, you might wonder whether the record variable can be used to simplify data-manipulation tasks. Record variables can be used in INSERT and UPDATE statements. Follow these steps to explore using data manipulation with a record variable in several examples:

1. Start SQL Developer, if necessary.
2. Verify existing data rows in the BB_DEPARTMENT table. (Three rows should exist, and none reflect the new product department, Teas, introduced in the previous example.)
3. Enter the PL/SQL block shown in Figure 3-20. It adds an INSERT statement to the earlier example for adding a new department. The VALUES clause of the INSERT statement simply references the record variable. Also, the COMMIT statement is left out intentionally so that you can roll back any changes made in your experiments.

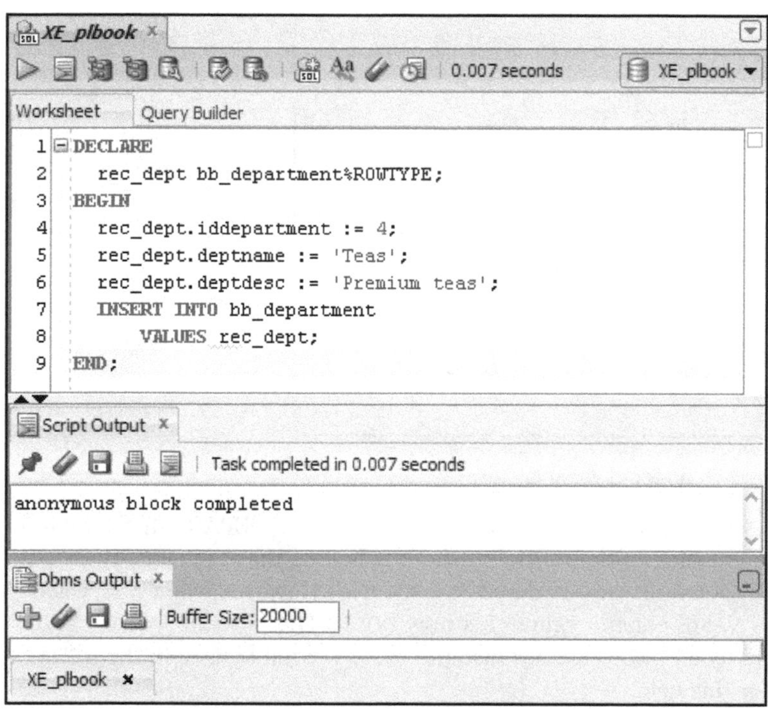

FIGURE 3-20 Adding an INSERT statement with a record variable

TIP

In SQL coding, values you're inserting in the VALUES clause of the INSERT statement are typically enclosed in parentheses, as in VALUES (rec_dept). Using parentheses with record variables in the VALUES clause causes an error, however.

4. Run the PL/SQL block. View the data rows in the BB_DEPARTMENT table to confirm that the new row for Teas has been added. Notice that a NULL value is assigned to the DEPTIMAGE column because it wasn't assigned a value in the record variable.

5. Next, try an UPDATE with a record variable. Enter the PL/SQL block shown in Figure 3-21. Notice three important items of coding in the block. A SET ROW command is used in the UPDATE statement to indicate that a record variable is being used. A WHERE clause is used to ensure that a single row is updated for this example. A value isn't set in the record for the DEPTNAME field; the value was set to 'Teas' in the previous INSERT and doesn't need to be changed.

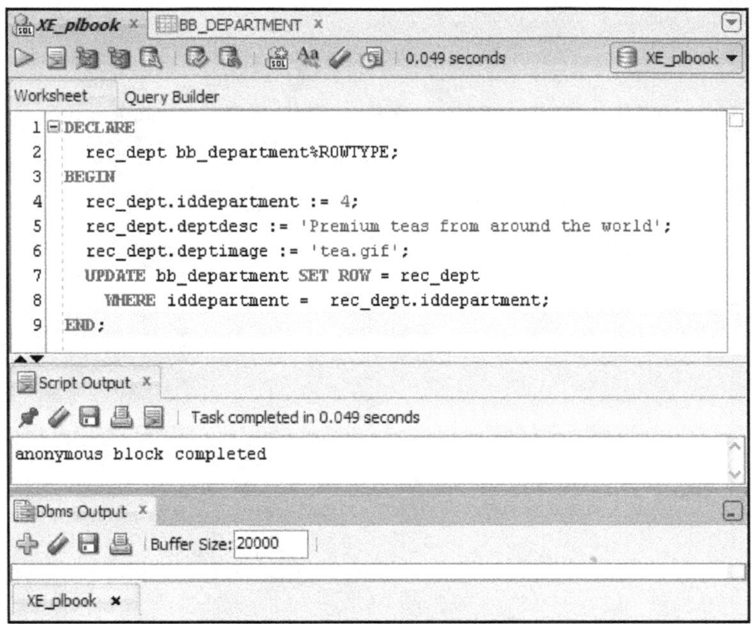

FIGURE 3-21 An UPDATE with a record variable

6. Run the PL/SQL block. View the data rows in the BB_DEPARTMENT table to confirm the changes as shown in Figure 3-22. Notice that the DEPTDESC and DEPTIMAGE columns were updated as expected. However, what happened to the DEPTNAME column value? It's now NULL. The previous value 'Teas' was replaced by a NULL value because the record variable used in the UPDATE was NULL for this field.

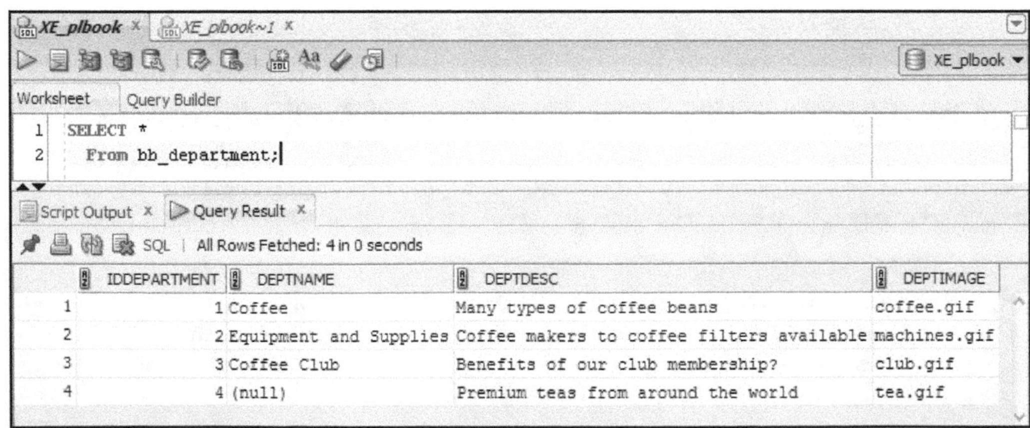

	IDDEPARTMENT	DEPTNAME	DEPTDESC	DEPTIMAGE
1	1	Coffee	Many types of coffee beans	coffee.gif
2	2	Equipment and Supplies	Coffee makers to coffee filters available	machines.gif
3	3	Coffee Club	Benefits of our club membership?	club.gif
4	4	(null)	Premium teas from around the world	tea.gif

FIGURE 3-22 Viewing results of the UPDATE statement

7. Next, a record variable is used in the RETURNING clause of an UPDATE statement. Sometimes you need to update a table row and return the row's values for more processing. Instead of doing the update and then performing a SELECT, a RETURNING clause in the UPDATE statement can consolidate these two tasks into one statement. Enter the PL/SQL block shown in Figure 3-23.

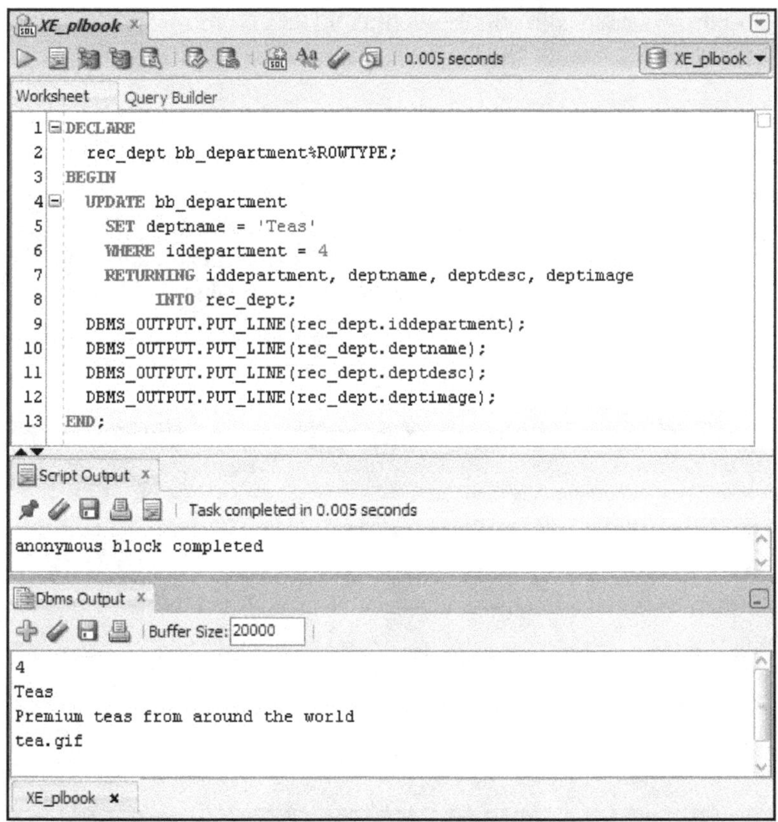

FIGURE 3-23 Using a record variable in a RETURNING clause

8. Run the PL/SQL block. The UPDATE restores the DEPTNAME value of 'Teas'. This UPDATE affects one row in the table, so the record variable is able to handle the RETURNING values.
9. Issue a ROLLBACK statement to undo the data manipulation performed in this example. Confirm that the BB_DEPARTMENT table has the original three rows of data and the Teas row has been removed.

The previous example shows using a record variable in INSERT and UPDATE statements. Keep in mind that all code examples exclude the COMMIT statement that's required in production to save DML activity permanently.

WORKING WITH COLLECTIONS

As mentioned, a collection is an ordered group of elements that allows handling multiple values of the same data type as a single unit. It can hold many rows of data but only a single field. This field, however, can be defined by a composite data type, such as a record. The values in each row of the collection must be of the same data type, and an index allows references to separate values or rows in the collection.

The following sections introduce two collection types: an associative array (index-by table) and a table of records. Other collections, such as VARRAYs and nested tables, are mentioned briefly at the end of this section but are beyond the scope of this book.

Associative Arrays

An **associative array** is still commonly referred to as a "PL/SQL table" or an "index-by table" from terminology in earlier Oracle versions. It's a variable that can handle many rows of data but only one field. This structure is a set of key-value pairs in which each key uniquely identifies a value in the array. The index can be an integer or a string value. Table 3-1 describes the main characteristics of an associative array.

TABLE 3-1 Associative Array Characteristics

Characteristic	Description
One-dimensional	Can have only one column.
Unconstrained	Rows added dynamically as needed.
Sparse	A row exists only when a value is assigned. Rows don't have to be assigned sequentially.
Homogeneous	All elements have the same data type.
Indexed	Integer index serves as the table's primary key.

NOTE

Recognize that associative arrays aren't physical tables in the database. They're variables used to hold and manipulate data in PL/SQL programs. Therefore, you can't perform SQL commands on these structures. Some composite data types might be used as column data types, but this topic is beyond the scope of this book.

To create an associative array, first use a TYPE statement to declare a data type defining a table structure consisting of one column and an index to reference the rows. Second, declare a variable, using the data type you created with the TYPE statement.

Table attributes or **table methods** are functions that can be used with table variables, and they give you more capability to manipulate table values. Table 3-2 describes available table attributes for associative arrays.

TABLE 3-2 PL/SQL Associative Array Attributes

Attribute Name	Description
COUNT	Number of rows in the table
DELETE	Removes a row from the table
EXISTS	TRUE if the specified row does exist
FIRST and LAST	Smallest and largest index value in the table
PRIOR and NEXT	Index for the previous and next row in the table, compared with the specified row

The FIRST, LAST, NEXT, and PRIOR attributes are used to allow moving through rows of data in an associative array variable. COUNT returns the total number of values in the array, which is quite useful when using a loop. EXISTS checks whether a value has been entered for the stated index number. These functions are referenced by using dot notation, as shown in the following assignment statement:

```
v_rows := tbl_orders.COUNT;
```

In this statement, tbl_orders represents an associative array variable, and the .COUNT attribute notation instructs the system to return the total count of rows in the associative array variable. This value is stored in a PL/SQL scalar variable named v_rows.

Take a look at an example. Brewbean's roasts its own coffee beans. As a quality assurance test to monitor the roasting equipment's performance, sample weight measurements are taken for each batch. Depending on the batch size, an employee records four or five one-cup measurements. Only the average of the measurements is saved to a database table that stores the average weight for each batch. Brewbean's has an application page that allows an employee to record all the sample measurements. The application then calculates the average and inserts the result in the correct table. The PL/SQL block to support this application page uses an associative array to hold all the sample measurements for processing.

The code in Figure 3-24 tackles this processing by using an associative array to manage the sample measurement data. The first statement in the DECLARE section creates an associative array data type that stores numeric values. The next statement declares the array variable using the data type. The remaining declaration statements establish scalar variables that represent user input and variables needed for calculations. Notice that only four measurement values are initialized.

The first statements in the executable section place the values of the sample measurement variables in the array variable. Because the number of measurements entered varies by batch size, the IF statements are used to add rows to the array variable only for measurement variables actually containing a value. Notice the syntax for identifying a row in the array tbl_roast(1). The array name is followed by parentheses enclosing a numeric value that serves as the index or key to identifying that array row. Only the row number or index value needs to be indicated when entering a value in an array variable because only a single column is available in the variable.

To perform the calculation, the FOR loop iterates through the array items to sum the values of all measurements. In addition, because the number of measurements entered can vary, the FOR loop iteration is controlled by using the array variable's COUNT attribute. At the end, the assignment statement for lv_avg_num calculates the average of the

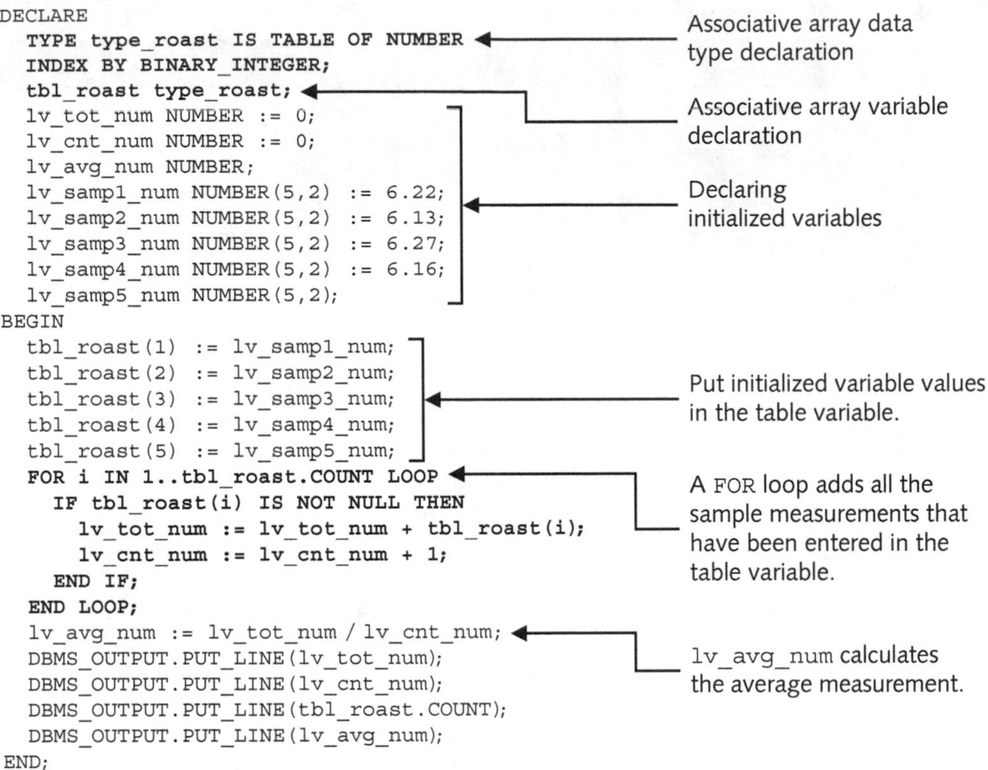

DECLARE
TYPE type_roast IS TABLE OF NUMBER
INDEX BY BINARY_INTEGER;
tbl_roast type_roast;
lv_tot_num NUMBER := 0;
lv_cnt_num NUMBER := 0;
lv_avg_num NUMBER;
lv_samp1_num NUMBER(5,2) := 6.22;
lv_samp2_num NUMBER(5,2) := 6.13;
lv_samp3_num NUMBER(5,2) := 6.27;
lv_samp4_num NUMBER(5,2) := 6.16;
lv_samp5_num NUMBER(5,2);
BEGIN
tbl_roast(1) := lv_samp1_num;
tbl_roast(2) := lv_samp2_num;
tbl_roast(3) := lv_samp3_num;
tbl_roast(4) := lv_samp4_num;
tbl_roast(5) := lv_samp5_num;
FOR i IN 1..tbl_roast.COUNT LOOP
IF tbl_roast(i) IS NOT NULL THEN
lv_tot_num := lv_tot_num + tbl_roast(i);
lv_cnt_num := lv_cnt_num + 1;
END IF;
END LOOP;
lv_avg_num := lv_tot_num / lv_cnt_num;
DBMS_OUTPUT.PUT_LINE(lv_tot_num);
DBMS_OUTPUT.PUT_LINE(lv_cnt_num);
DBMS_OUTPUT.PUT_LINE(tbl_roast.COUNT);
DBMS_OUTPUT.PUT_LINE(lv_avg_num);
END;
Associative array data type declaration
Associative array variable declaration
Declaring initialized variables
Put initialized variable values in the table variable.
A FOR loop adds all the sample measurements that have been entered in the table variable.
lv_avg_num calculates the average measurement.

FIGURE 3-24 Using an associative array

measurements by using the sum calculated in the `FOR` loop divided by the array variable's `COUNT` attribute. Using the `COUNT` attribute in this manner makes this block flexible enough to handle any number of measurements. Try the following example, and review the results:

1. Start SQL Developer, if necessary.
2. Open the **ibtable03.sql** file from the Chapter03 folder.
3. Run the PL/SQL block. The output shows that the array row count is 4, the sum of the measurement values is 24.78, and the average is 6.195.

This example shows an array data type declared with a `BINARY_INTEGER` as the index value. This declaration produces a numeric index value to identify the rows stored in the array. You aren't limited to using numeric index values, however. Say you want to store some product prices in an array for processing, and the product ID values are character strings. You can use the product ID as an indexing value because it has unique values. To do so, use an `INDEX BY` string method in the `TYPE` statement, as shown in this code:

```
TYPE type_prod IS TABLE OF NUMBER
  INDEX BY VARCHAR2(5);
```

NOTE

Cursors, introduced in Chapter 4, can be used to query data from the database and populate an associative array with data values.

Table of Records

A **table of records** is another type of collection. It's similar to a record data type except that it can handle more than one record or row of data. To see why you might need this data type, examine another part of the Brewbean's application. As a shopper is perusing the site and selecting items to purchase, the Brewbean's application needs a variable to hold information on all items selected so far in the basket until the shopper indicates saving the basket for completion later or finishing the purchase (at which time data is inserted in the database). You need a variable that holds data similar to a row of the BB_BASKETITEM table. In addition, the shopper might select more than one item, so the variable must be able to handle more than one row of data. A table of records can handle this requirement.

First, review the application page shown in Figure 3-25. If a user clicks the Add to Basket button to select a product, the application should add this selection to the table of records variable.

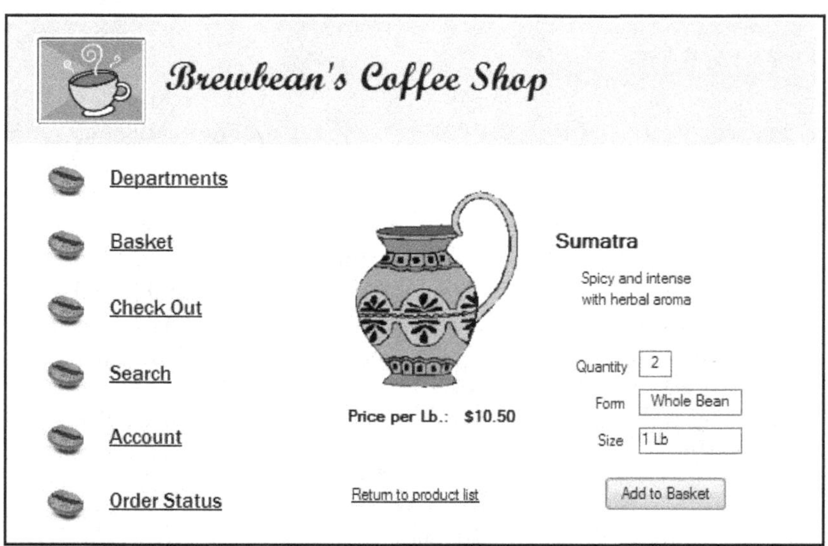

FIGURE 3-25 The application page in which shoppers can add an item

In constructing a block to handle this task, a group of initialized variables is declared to represent data from the application page and a number to indicate the row number or index of the table of records that should be added. Keep in mind that you now have a variable that can hold multiple rows and fields. Therefore, when placing data in the table of records variable, you must indicate not only which field, but also which row to insert the values into. Review the block shown in Figure 3-26.

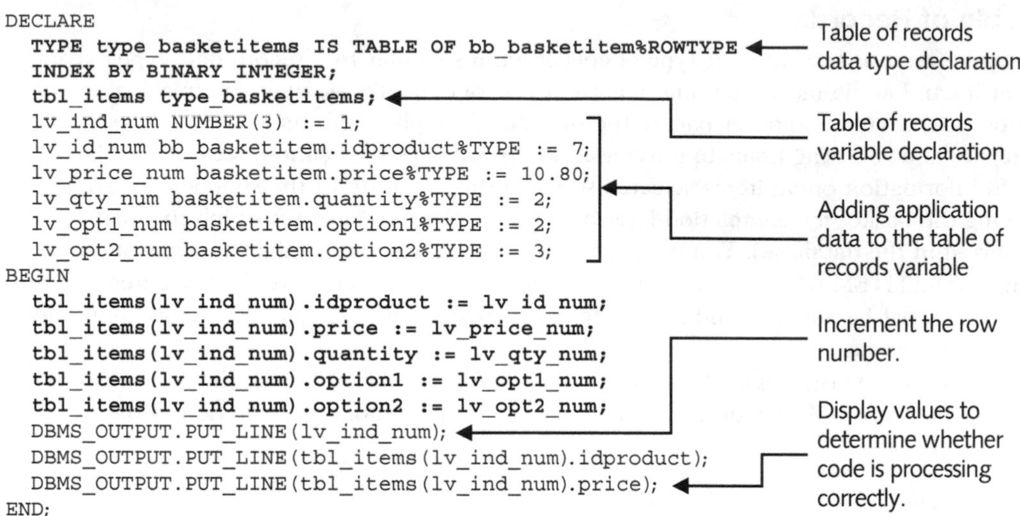

FIGURE 3-26 Using a table of records variable

First, a variable data type is created with the `TYPE` statement containing the keywords `IS TABLE OF bb_basketitem%ROWTYPE` to provide a record data type—just as you used in creating a record variable. You could also use a record data type you had created in this statement. The `INDEX BY BINARY_INTEGER` statement creates a primary key index for referencing the rows of the table of records variable. Again, keep in mind that the data type must set up not only different fields of data to handle, but also the capability to handle multiple rows. The table of records variable named `tbl_items` is then declared just as you would any variable—by indicating a variable name and data type. In this example, `type_basketitems` is used for the table of records data type.

The executable section of the block needs to place the variables in a row of the `tbl_items` table of records. In the following code, notice the assignment statements for this task:

```
tbl_items(lv_ind_num).idproduct := lv_id_num;
```

This statement follows the structure shown in this syntax:

```
variable(row index value).record field name := value;
```

The `lv_ind_num` scalar variable indicates which row of the table of records the data should be added in, and `.idproduct` indicates the field the value will be placed in. Enter this code and experiment with it to become familiar with the table of records data type. When you run the code shown in Figure 3-26, the output is as follows:

```
1
7
10.8
```

You might be asking, "Don't the variables in a PL/SQL block exist only during the block's execution? If so, what happens to the table of records variable in this example?" Good questions. It's true that variables declared in a block last only as long as the block is running. In other words, these variables don't persist beyond the block's execution.

So the question becomes "How can I solve the problem in this example so that the table of records variable persists for a user session?" To do this, you need to declare the table of records variable in a package specification; this declaration allows variables to persist for a user session. You learn how to create packages in Chapter 7.

NOTE

Discussing packages does raise the important issue of the persistence of variables. At times, applications need to have variables that persist across executing a number of PL/SQL blocks. This need is typical of a table of records variable.

Other Collections: `VARRAYs` and Nested Tables

With nested tables and `VARRAY`s, you can have database columns that hold more than one value. A major advantage of using collections as part of the physical database is being able to retrieve multiple values by querying a single column. For example, you might use a nested table with a column created to hold customer preference choices. A single column of the customer table could be created as a nested table and hold any number of preference values. The main differences between a nested table and a `VARRAY` are that a `VARRAY` has a set size when it's created, the order of elements is preserved, and the data is stored inline with the table data. These structures are considered collections but are beyond the scope of this book.

INTRODUCTION TO BULK PROCESSING

Now that you have begun to incorporate SQL statements into PL/SQL blocks, you need to learn the concept of bulk processing. Bulk processing options improve performance and add capabilities to a program. Performance tuning is an advanced topic, but you need to be aware of it in relation to incorporating SQL queries and DML statements into PL/SQL.

As mentioned in Chapter 1, PL/SQL is a procedural extension of SQL. When PL/SQL code containing SQL statements is processed, processing control must move back and forth between the PL/SQL and SQL engines. Moving control in this fashion is called a "context switch" and can decrease performance as the amount of switching increases. An example is performing DML actions in a loop that produces a context switch for each iteration. Imagine the effect on performance if you need to process thousands of rows. As you see in Chapter 4, this same issue comes up when querying data via cursors.

Bulk processing is a mechanism Oracle uses to reduce performance issues. When the `BULK COLLECT` clause and `FORALL` statements are used in PL/SQL programs, they provide instructions to the processing engine to group SQL actions for processing, which reduces context switching.

Bulk processing can add new capabilities, too. For example, you can expand the use of the table of records variable. Using `%ROWTYPE` to create this variable data type allows constructing a variable that matches a table's structure. Therefore, you might think that querying a set of rows from the table and pushing the query results to the table of records variable should be possible. Figure 3-27 shows the result of attempting this action: an error with using the table of records variable.

```
XE_plbook
0.033 seconds    XE_plbook
Worksheet    Query Builder

DECLARE
  TYPE type_product IS TABLE OF bb_product%ROWTYPE
     INDEX BY PLS_INTEGER;
  tbl_prod type_product;
BEGIN
 SELECT * INTO tbl_prod
    FROM bb_product
    WHERE type = 'E';
 FOR i IN 1..tbl_prod.COUNT LOOP
   DBMS_OUTPUT.PUT_LINE(tbl_prod(i).productname);
 END LOOP;
END;

Script Output
Task completed in 0.033 seconds
Error report:
ORA-06550: line 6, column 16:
PLS-00597: expression 'TBL_PROD' in the INTO list is of wrong type
ORA-06550: line 7, column 5:
PL/SQL: ORA-00904: : invalid identifier
ORA-06550: line 6, column 2:
PL/SQL: SQL Statement ignored
06550. 00000 -  "line %s, column %s:\n%s"
*Cause:    Usually a PL/SQL compilation error.

Dbms Output
Buffer Size: 20000
XE_plbook
```

FIGURE 3-27 An error in using a table of records

If you just add a BULK COLLECT option in the SELECT statement, Oracle can handle this process, as shown in Figure 3-28.

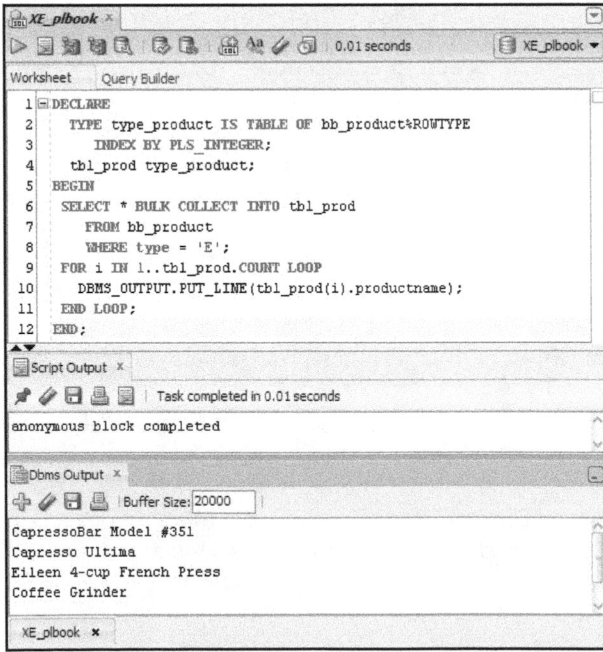

FIGURE 3-28 Using a BULK COLLECT option

NOTE

More information and examples of FORALL and BULK COLLECT are in Chapter 4.

GOTO STATEMENTS

A **GOTO statement** is sometimes called a "jumping control" because it instructs a program to "jump to" a specific area of the code. It's used to branch logic so that only certain portions of code are processed based on some condition. A GOTO statement can branch to a label marking a particular spot in the code that must precede an executable statement. The statement instructs the system to skip any executable statements until reaching the label referenced in the GOTO statement. Then the statements from that point on are processed. In PL/SQL, the << >> markers are used to identify a label.

The following code shows part of an executable section of a block with a GOTO statement that instructs processing to jump to the INSERT_ROW label:

```
BEGIN
  IF lv_rows_num = 0 THEN
    GOTO insert_row;
  END IF;
 ...
 ...
  <<insert_row>>
  INSERT INTO bb_basket (idBasket)
    VALUES (bb_basket_seq.NEXTVAL);
 ...
 ...
END;
```

Even though the GOTO statement is available, most developers believe it should be used sparingly and only if no other method can be used to accomplish a task. Why? The GOTO action interrupts the flow of execution, which makes understanding and maintaining code more difficult. However, you should know about this statement because you might need to support existing code that includes GOTO statements.

Chapter Summary

- SQL queries (SELECT) and DML statements (INSERT, UPDATE, DELETE) can be embedded in the executable section of a PL/SQL block.
- Transaction control statements (COMMIT, ROLLBACK) can be included in a PL/SQL block.
- A SELECT statement must include an INTO clause to indicate the variables to hold the database values being retrieved.
- A SELECT statement in a PL/SQL block must return at least one row of data, or a "no data found" error occurs.
- When variables are used to hold data from database tables, the %TYPE attribute can be used to retrieve the correct data type from the data dictionary based on the table and column indicated.
- Composite data types allow creating a variable that can hold multiple values as a single unit. Two composite data types are records and collections.
- A record can hold multiple fields, each having its own name and data type, as one unit. This structure is similar to a table row. A collection can store an ordered group of elements of the same type, with each element having a unique subscript or index. This structure is similar to an array.
- The %ROWTYPE attribute can be used to declare a record variable data type based on a table.
- An associative array is a collection that can handle many rows of data but only one field.
- A table of records is a collection that can hold many rows and many columns of data, a structure similar to a table in the database.
- Bulk processing can reduce context switching and improve performance when processing a large set of rows from a database.
- A GOTO statement is used to branch logic (by jumping to a specific area of code) so that only certain portions of code are processed based on some condition.

Review Questions

1. What clause must be added to a SELECT statement in a PL/SQL block?
   a. WHERE
   b. TO
   c. INTO
   d. STORE
2. Which of the following references the third row and the ID field of a table of records variable named emp_tbl?
   a. emp_tbl(3).id
   b. emp_tbl.id(3)
   c. id.emp_tbl(3)
   d. id(3).emp_tbl
3. What type of variable can store only one value?
   a. implicit cursor
   b. scalar
   c. %ROWTYPE
   d. explicit cursor

4. What does the %TYPE attribute instruct the system to do?
   a. retrieve the database column data type for the variable
   b. copy a variable
   c. retrieve data from the database
   d. use a Boolean data type
5. Which item is a valid reference to a value in a record variable named rec_junk?
   a. rec_junk(1)
   b. rec_junk(1).col
   c. rec_junk.col
   d. rec_junk.col(1)
6. A table of records variable can hold which of the following?
   a. only one row and many columns of data
   b. many columns and only one row of data
   c. many rows and many columns of data
   d. none of the above
7. If a record variable contains a NULL value for a field, how is it treated if it's used in an UPDATE statement?
   a. The associated column is unaffected.
   b. The UPDATE action fails.
   c. The associated column is set to NULL.
   d. A record variable can't hold a NULL value.
8. When should you use the %ROWTYPE attribute in creating a record variable?
   a. when using most of the columns from a table
   b. when using only a small portion of the columns from a table
   c. whenever a record variable is created
   d. none of the above
9. Which of the following isn't an associative array attribute?
   a. VALUE
   b. COUNT
   c. NEXT
   d. FIRST
10. Which of the following is a valid reference to a value in an associative array named tbl_junk?
    a. tbl_junk(1).col
    b. tbl_junk.col
    c. tbl_junk(1)
    d. tbl_junk.col(1)
11. What are variables, and why are they needed?
12. In what way is a SELECT statement different when issued in a PL/SQL block?
13. Describe how and why the %TYPE attribute is used.
14. Describe how and why the %ROWTYPE attribute is used.
15. Define a composite data type and name two available in PL/SQL.

Advanced Review Questions

1. Review the following DECLARE section of a block. How is the `id` value in the record variable referenced in the executable section?

```
DECLARE
  TYPE type_rec IS RECORD (
    id NUMBER(3),
    brand CHAR(3) );
  rec_one type_rec;
```

   a. `type_rec.id`
   b. `rec_one.id`
   c. `id`
   d. `type_rec.rec_one(id)`

2. In the following DECLARE section, what type of variable is `v_junk`?

```
DECLARE
  TYPE type_junk IS TABLE OF CHAR(1)
    INDEX BY BINARY_INTEGER;
  v_junk type_junk;
```

   a. scalar
   b. table of records
   c. associative array
   d. cursor

3. What must you do to an `UPDATE` statement to include it in a PL/SQL block?
   a. You must use a column list.
   b. The statement must contain a `WHERE` clause.
   c. An `UPDATE` can't be included in a block.
   d. No change is necessary.

4. In the following DECLARE section, the JOBS table contains a column named TITLE. How is the TITLE column's value referenced from the record variable?

```
DECLARE
  TYPE type_jobs IS TABLE OF jobs%ROWTYPE
    INDEX BY BINARY INTEGER;
  tbl_jobs type_jobs;
```

   a. `tbl_jobs(2).title`
   b. `type_jobs.tbl_jobs(2).title`
   c. `tbl_jobs.title(2)`
   d. `tbl_jobs.title.2`

5. What's used when creating a data type for a record variable that needs to hold all the column values from a table?
   a. `%TYPE`
   b. `%ROWTYPE`
   c. list of columns
   d. `%ROWCOUNT`

Hands-On Assignments Part I

Assignment 3-1: Querying Data in a Block

A Brewbean's application page is being developed for employees to enter a basket number and view shipping information for the order that includes date, shipper, and shipping number. An `IDSTAGE` value of 5 in the BB_BASKETSTATUS table indicates that the order has been shipped. In this assignment, you create a block using scalar variables to hold the data retrieved from the database. Follow these steps to create a block for checking shipping information:

1. Start SQL Developer, if necessary.
2. Open the **`assignment03-01.sql`** file in the Chapter03 folder.
3. Review the code, and note the use of scalar variables to hold the values retrieved in the `SELECT` statement.
4. Add data type assignments to the first three variables declared. These variables will be used to hold data retrieved from a query.
5. Run the block for basket ID **3**, and compare the results with Figure 3-29.

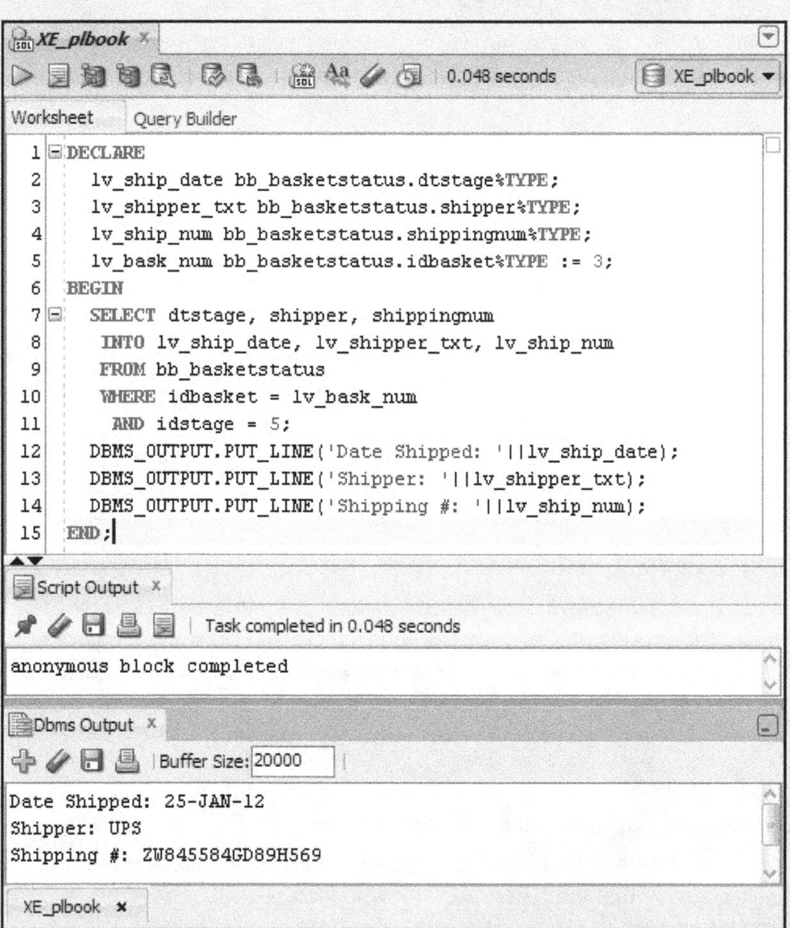

FIGURE 3-29 Running a block with an embedded query

6. Now try to run this same block with a basket ID that has no shipping information recorded. Edit the basket ID variable to be **7**.
7. Run the block again, and review the error shown in Figure 3-30.

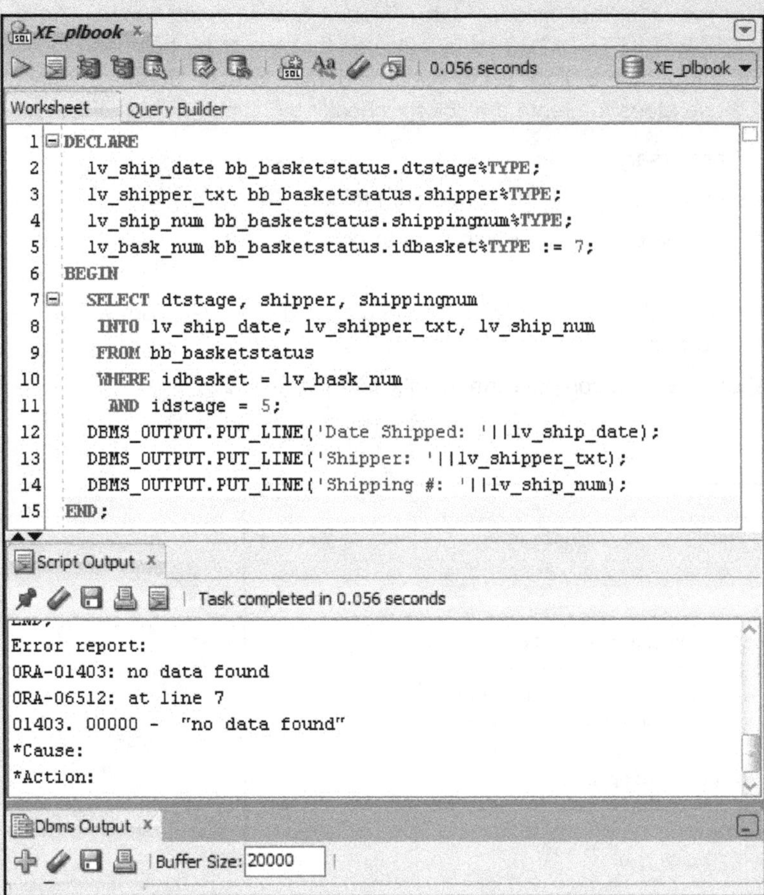

FIGURE 3-30 A "no data found" error

Assignment 3-2: Using a Record Variable

A Brewbean's application page is being developed for employees to enter a basket number and view shipping information for the order. The page needs to display all column values from the BB_BASKETSTATUS table. An `IDSTAGE` value of 5 in the BB_BASKETSTATUS table indicates that the order has been shipped. Follow these steps to create a block with a record variable:

1. Start SQL Developer, if necessary.
2. Open the **`assignment03-02.sql`** file in the Chapter03 folder.
3. Review the code, and note the use of a record variable to hold the values retrieved in the `SELECT` statement. Also, notice that the record variable's values are referenced separately in the `DBMS_OUTPUT` statements.
4. Run the block, and compare the results with Figure 3-31.

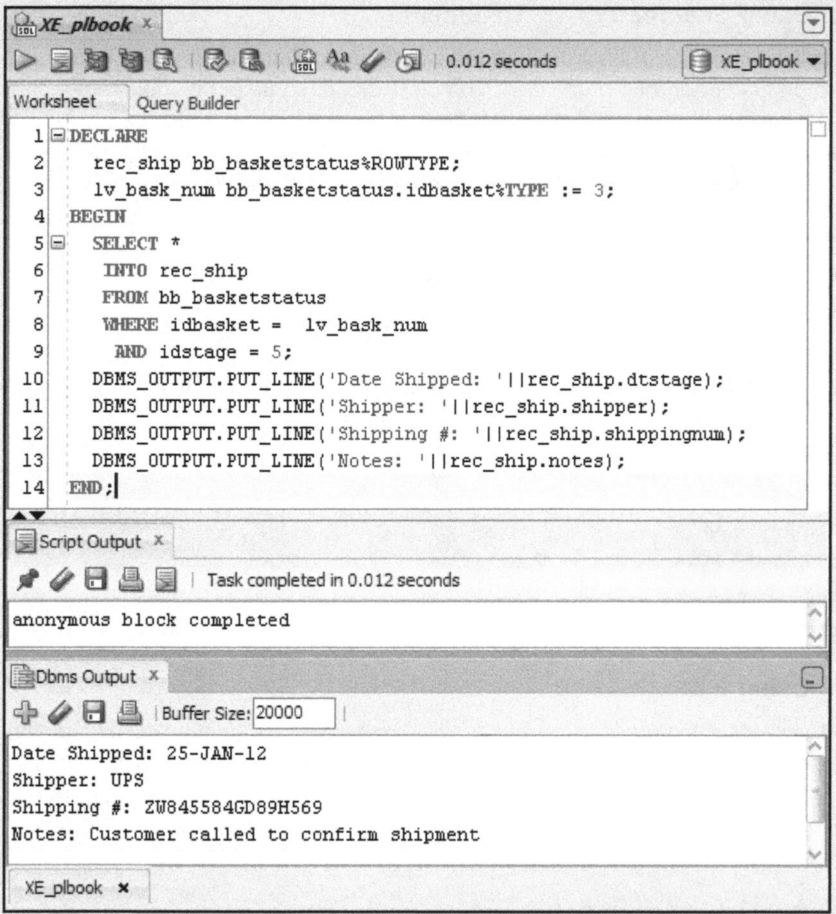

FIGURE 3-31 Using a record variable to retrieve shipping information

Assignment 3-3: Processing Database Data with `IF` Statements

The Brewbean's application needs a block to determine whether a customer is rated HIGH, MID, or LOW based on his or her total purchases. The block needs to select the total amount of orders for a specified customer, determine the rating, and then display the results onscreen. The code rates the customer HIGH if total purchases are greater than $200, MID if greater than $100, and LOW if $100 or lower. Use an initialized variable to provide the shopper ID.

1. Start SQL Developer, if necessary.
2. Open the **`assignment03-03.sql`** file from the Chapter03 folder. Review the partial block. Edit the block to perform the required task.
3. Run the block and verify the results. Enter and run the following SQL query to confirm that the total for this shopper is indeed greater than $200:

```
SELECT SUM(total)
  FROM bb_basket
  WHERE idShopper = 22
    AND orderplaced = 1
  GROUP BY idshopper;
```

4. Test other shoppers who have a completed order.

Assignment 3-4: Using Searched CASE Statements

The Brewbean's application needs a block to determine whether a customer is rated HIGH, MID, or LOW based on his or her total purchases. The block needs to select the total amount of orders for a specified customer, determine the rating, and then display the results onscreen. The code rates the customer HIGH if total purchases are greater than $200, MID if greater than $100, and LOW if $100 or lower. Use an initialized variable to provide the shopper ID.

1. Start SQL Developer, if necessary.
2. Modify the code used in Assignment 3-3 to use a searched CASE statement to check the shopper's total purchase amount and determine the correct rating.
3. Run the block, and verify the results.
4. Enter and run the following code to confirm that the total for this shopper is indeed greater than $200:

```
SELECT SUM(total)
  FROM bb_basket
  WHERE idShopper = 22
    AND orderplaced = 1
  GROUP BY idshopper;
```

5. Test other shoppers who have a completed order.

Assignment 3-5: Using a WHILE Loop

Brewbean's wants to include a feature in its application that calculates the total amount (quantity) of a specified item that can be purchased with a given amount of money. Create a block with a WHILE loop to increment the item's cost until the dollar value is met. Test first with a total spending amount of **$100** and product ID **4**. Then test with an amount and a product of your choice. Use initialized variables to provide the total spending amount and product ID.

Assignment 3-6: Working with IF Statements

Brewbean's calculates shipping cost based on the quantity of items in an order. Assume the quantity column in the BB_BASKET table contains the total number of items in a basket. A block is needed to check the quantity provided by an initialized variable and determine the shipping cost. Display the calculated shipping cost onscreen. Test using the basket IDs **5** and **12**, and apply the shipping rates listed in Table 3-3.

TABLE 3-3 Shipping Charges

Quantity of Items	Shipping Cost
Up to 3	$5.00
4–6	$7.50
7–10	$10.00
More than 10	$12.00

Assignment 3-7: Using Scalar Variables for Data Retrieval

The Brewbean's application contains a page displaying order summary information, including IDBASKET, SUBTOTAL, SHIPPING, TAX, and TOTAL columns from the BB_BASKET table. Create a PL/SQL block with scalar variables to retrieve this data and then display it onscreen. An initialized variable should provide the IDBASKET value. Test the block using the basket ID **12**.

Assignment 3-8: Using a Record Variable for Data Retrieval

The Brewbean's application contains a page displaying order summary information, including IDBASKET, SUBTOTAL, SHIPPING, TAX, and TOTAL columns from the BB_BASKET table. Create a PL/SQL block with a record variable to retrieve this data and display it onscreen. An initialized variable should provide the IDBASKET value. Test the block using the basket ID **12**.

Hands-On Assignments Part II

Assignment 3-9: Retrieving Pledge Totals

Create a PL/SQL block that retrieves and displays information for a specific project based on Project ID. Display the following on a single row of output: project ID, project name, number of pledges made, total dollars pledged, and the average pledge amount.

Assignment 3-10: Adding a Project

Create a PL/SQL block to handle adding a new project. Create and use a sequence named `DD_PROJID_SEQ` to handle generating and populating the project ID. The first number issued by this sequence should be 530, and no caching should be used. Use a record variable to handle the data to be added. Data for the new row should be the following: project name = HK Animal Shelter Extension, start = 1/1/2013, end = 5/31/2013, and fundraising goal = $65,000. Any columns not addressed in the data list are currently unknown.

Assignment 3-11: Retrieving and Displaying Pledge Data

Create a PL/SQL block to retrieve and display data for all pledges made in a specified month. One row of output should be displayed for each pledge. Include the following in each row of output:

- Pledge ID, donor ID, and pledge amount
- If the pledge is being paid in a lump sum, display "Lump Sum."
- If the pledge is being paid in monthly payments, display "Monthly - #" (with the # representing the number of months for payment).
- The list should be sorted to display all lump sum pledges first.

Assignment 3-12: Retrieving a Specific Pledge

Create a PL/SQL block to retrieve and display information for a specific pledge. Display the pledge ID, donor ID, pledge amount, total paid so far, and the difference between the pledged amount and total paid amount.

Assignment 3-13: Modifying Data

Create a PL/SQL block to modify the fundraising goal amount for a specific project. In addition, display the following information for the project being modified: project name, start date, previous fundraising goal amount, and new fundraising goal amount.

Case Projects

Case 3-1: Using Variable Types

The Brewbean's manager has just hired another programmer to help you develop application code for the online store. Explain the difference between scalar, record, and table variables to the new employee.

Case 3-2: Working with More Movie Rentals

The More Movie Rental Company is developing an application page that displays the total number of times a specified movie has been rented and the associated rental rating based on this count. Table 3-4 shows the rental ratings.

TABLE 3-4 Movie Rental Ratings

Number of Rentals	Rental Rating
Up to 5	Dump
5–20	Low
21–35	Mid
More than 35	High

Create a block that retrieves the movie title and rental count based on a movie ID provided via an initialized variable. The block should display the movie title, rental count, and rental rating onscreen. Add exception handlers for errors you can and can't anticipate. Run the block with movie IDs of **4** and **25**.

CHAPTER 4

CURSORS AND EXCEPTION HANDLING

LEARNING OBJECTIVES

After completing this chapter, you should be able to understand:

- Manipulating data with cursors
- Using bulk-processing features
- Managing errors with exception handlers
- Addressing exception-handling issues, such as RAISE_APPLICATION_ERROR and propagation
- Documenting code with comments

INTRODUCTION

PL/SQL programs often require the capability to process multiple rows in a block. This chapter introduces cursor processing, a common feature used to retrieve and process a group of rows in a block. Programmers also need to manage errors as they occur during execution to control an application's response to a variety of runtime issues, so this chapter also covers coding exception handlers. Finally, you learn how to include comments in your code to document programs, which makes later modification and maintenance easier.

The first step in this chapter is to identify the current data-handling challenge in the Brewbean's application. In the rest of the chapter, you learn what you need to do to address this challenge.

THE CURRENT CHALLENGE IN THE BREWBEAN'S APPLICATION

To begin, return to the Brewbean's shopping basket, which shows a shopper all the items and quantities selected so far (see Figure 4-1). As mentioned in previous chapters, one processing task is calculating taxes. You have seen what's involved in calculating taxes based on a shopper's state. What if different tax rates are applied to perishable items (coffee) and nonperishable items (equipment)?

FIGURE 4-1 Brewbean's shopping basket

The block to handle this task must retrieve all rows from the BB_BASKETITEM table for a specified basket. Then each row needs to be examined to calculate the applicable tax amount for each item. The item type, which can be coffee or equipment, should be checked to determine the correct tax rate to apply to each item.

Rebuilding the Database

To rebuild the Brewbean's database, perform the following steps. As you review the script supplied in your student data files, keep in mind that the first series of statements in the script deletes existing objects in the database. If an object doesn't exist, these statements raise an error, but it's not a cause for concern. It just indicates that the object hadn't been created in your schema previously.

1. Make sure you have the `c4_BBcreate.sql` file in the Chapter04 folder. This file contains the script for creating the database.
2. Start SQL Developer and connect to the Oracle database.
3. Click **File**, **Open** from the menu.
4. Click the **`c4_BBcreate.sql`** file. The code in this script is displayed in the Edit pane. Scroll through the SQL statements; they should look familiar.
5. Run the script by clicking the **Run Script** button on the Edit pane toolbar. If necessary, click **OK** in the Select Connection dialog box.
6. Scroll through the Script Output pane at the bottom to review the results of the statements.

7. In the Connections pane on the left, expand the **Tables** node to view the tables that were created. While this node is selected, click the **Refresh** button at the top of the Connections pane to update the list of tables. The Brewbean's table list should match Figure 4-2.

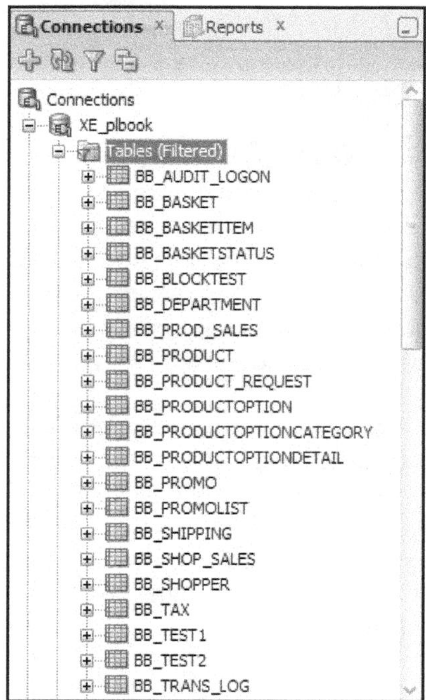

FIGURE 4-2 Brewbean's table list

WORKING WITH CURSORS

A **cursor** represents a work area or section of memory (also called the "context area") where an SQL statement is processed in the Oracle server; this area also contains the results of SQL statements. Cursors are a powerful mechanism for handling multiple rows of data retrieved with an SQL query.

Two types of cursors are available. **Implicit cursors** are declared automatically for all DML and `SELECT` statements issued in a PL/SQL block. **Explicit cursors** are declared and manipulated in PL/SQL code for handling rows returned by a `SELECT` statement. In addition, **cursor variables** are references or pointers to a work area. The following sections explain these cursor items in more detail.

Implicit Cursors

When an SQL statement is executed, the Oracle server creates an implicit cursor automatically. Cursor attributes, described in Table 4-1, can be used to check whether SQL statements affected any rows, and if so, how many.

TABLE 4-1 SQL Cursor Attributes

Attribute Name	Data Type	Description
SQL%ROWCOUNT	NUMBER	Number of rows affected by the SQL statement.
SQL%FOUND	BOOLEAN	TRUE if at least one row is affected by the SQL statement; otherwise, it's FALSE.
SQL%NOTFOUND	BOOLEAN	TRUE if no rows are affected by the SQL statement; otherwise, it's FALSE.

If an UPDATE statement is processed, for instance, you can check how many rows were affected by using SQL%ROWCOUNT or check whether any rows were affected by looking for a TRUE value in SQL%FOUND. You might need to check the results of an UPDATE statement with cursor attributes to confirm that at least one row was updated—if this is an application requirement. An update can affect no rows or many rows without raising an Oracle error. The SQL% preceding attribute names instructs the system to look at the implicit SQL cursor area, which contains information for the most recent SQL statement processed.

Take a look at an example in the Brewbean's application, which includes an inventory update page for employees who are recording product shipments received. An employee can enter a product ID and shipment quantity to add to stock data. The code block for this page includes an UPDATE statement on the BB_PRODUCT table that includes two cursor attributes (see Figure 4-3). SQL%ROWCOUNT returns the value 0 because no rows are updated; in other words, product ID 15 doesn't exist. SQL%NOTFOUND evaluates to TRUE, also indicating that no rows are affected by the UPDATE statement.

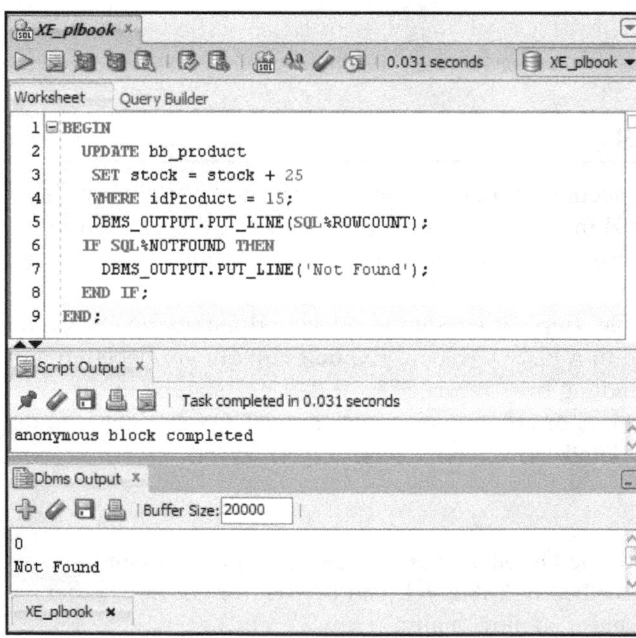

FIGURE 4-3 Using cursor attributes

NOTE

For example purposes, the product ID and quantity are coded as numeric values in the `UPDATE` statement. In reality, both values are supplied via the application.

The values returned from cursor attributes always reflect information from the most recent SQL statement processed. Therefore, when you have multiple SQL statements in a block, you need to consider where you check attribute values. To understand this point, expand the previous example by adding a `SELECT` statement. Then verify that the `%ROWCOUNT` attribute changes to reflect each SQL statement. The block in Figure 4-4 shows that the `%ROWCOUNT` is 1 after the `SELECT` and 0 after the `UPDATE`.

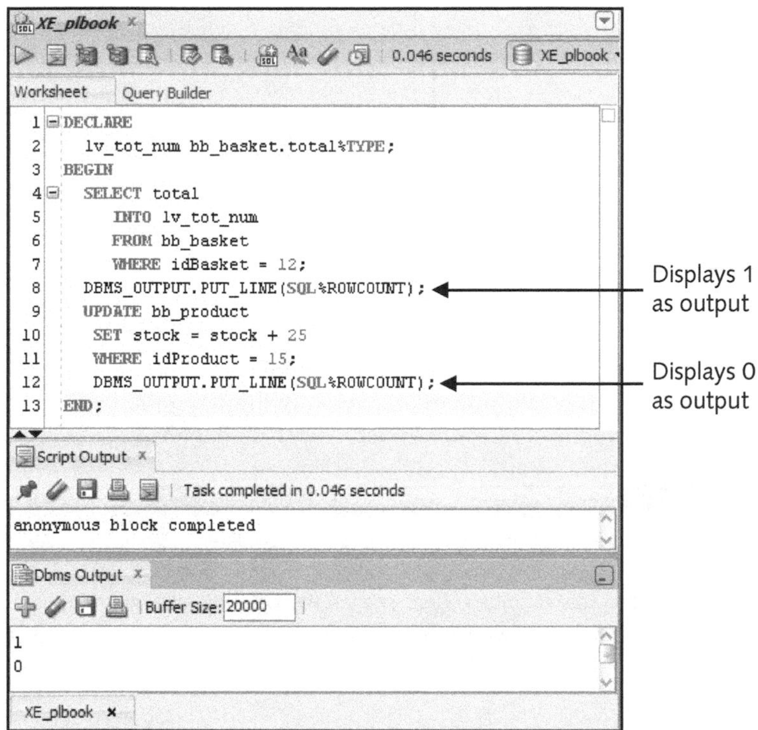

FIGURE 4-4 Cursor attributes reflecting the most recent SQL statement

Remember that a `SELECT` statement embedded in a PL/SQL block's executable section that returns no rows results in a "no data found" error. A common programming mistake is checking the `%NOTFOUND` cursor attribute immediately after a `SELECT` statement to determine whether rows were selected. This technique doesn't work. After the "no data found" error is raised, the remaining statements in the block aren't executed, as shown in Figure 4-5. The `IF` statement at the end of the block isn't executed, so the "no data found" message isn't displayed for this code line.

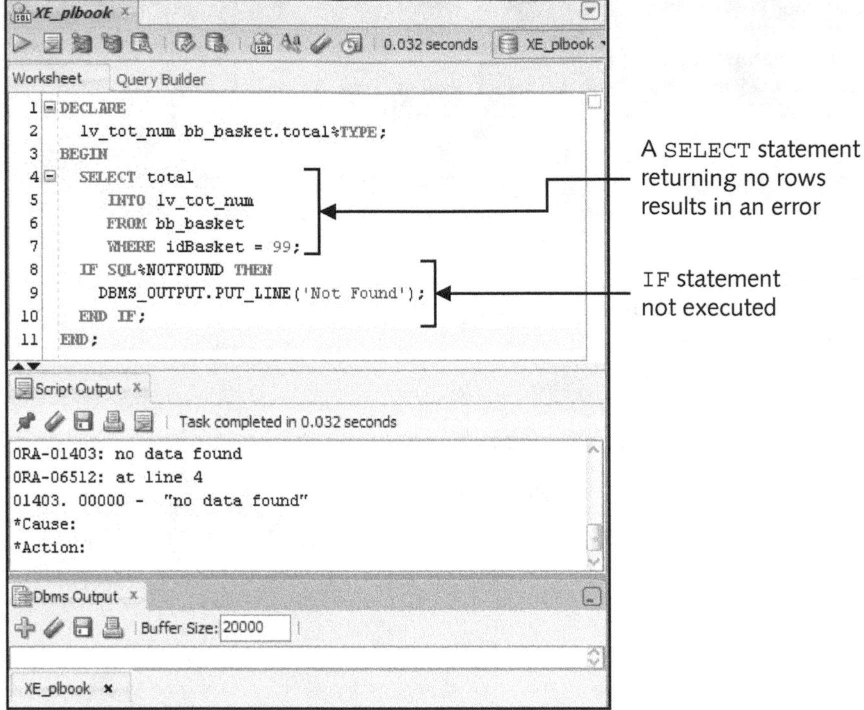

FIGURE 4-5 A "no data found" error

After an error is raised in a PL/SQL block, processing actually jumps to the last section—EXCEPTION. Exception handling is introduced later in this chapter.

CHALLENGE 4-1

Create a block that changes the zip code in the BB_SHOPPER table for a specific shopper. If any rows are updated, display the number of rows updated. If no rows are updated, display a message stating `No rows changed`. Test the block with two sets of values. First, change the zip code for shopper 27 to 67488. Second, attempt to change the zip code for shopper 37 to 67488.

Explicit Cursors

You can process a group of rows from a database by creating explicit cursors, which are declared with the declaration containing a `SELECT` statement. Examine the Brewbean's application page shown in Figure 4-6. A returning shopper logging in to the Web site should be notified if he or she has saved an uncompleted basket. A query is needed to retrieve the saved basket information. What if a shopper has more than one saved basket?

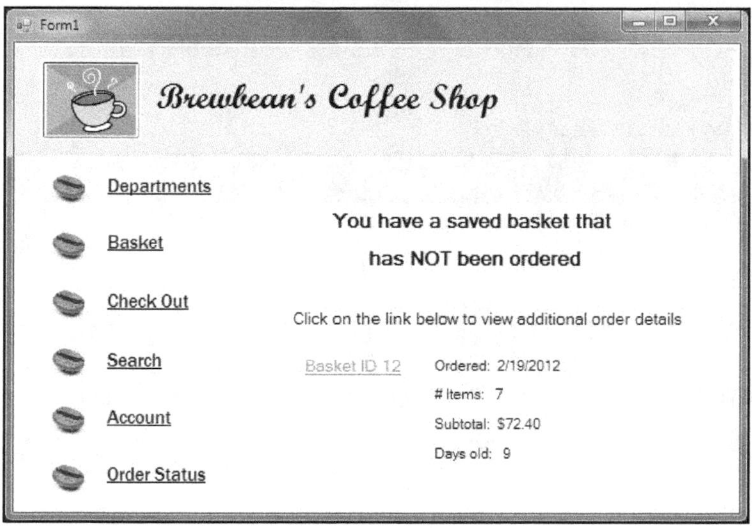

FIGURE 4-6 Brewbean's application page reminding shoppers of existing baskets

Review the code for this task and see what happens when a shopper has more than one uncompleted basket (see Figure 4-7). An error occurs because scalar variables can't handle more than one row being returned from a query. You can solve this problem by using an explicit cursor that makes handling multiple rows returned from a query easier.

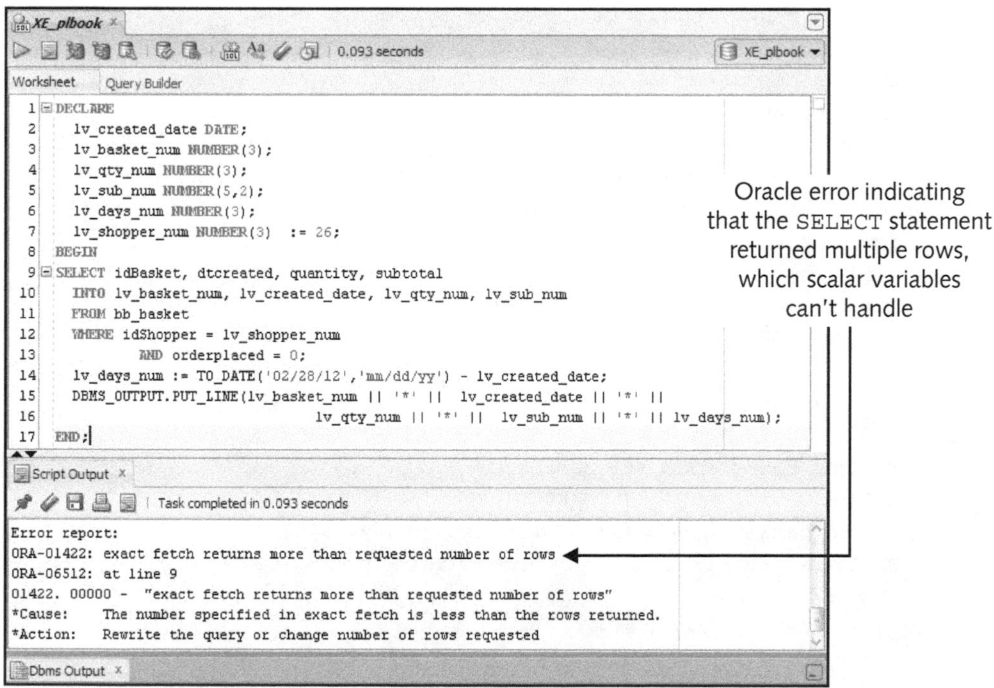

FIGURE 4-7 Scalar variables can't handle queries returning multiple rows

Using an explicit cursor involves several steps, listed in Table 4-2. Declaring the cursor takes place in a block's DECLARE section, and the remaining steps take place in the BEGIN (executable) section.

TABLE 4-2 Steps in Using an Explicit Cursor

Step	Step Activity	Activity Description
1	DECLARE	Creates a named cursor identified by a SELECT statement that doesn't include an INTO clause. Values in the cursor are moved to PL/SQL variables with the FETCH step.
2	OPEN	Processes the query and creates the active set of rows available in the cursor.
3	FETCH	Retrieves a row from the cursor into block variables. Each consecutive FETCH retrieves the next row in the cursor until all rows have been retrieved.
4	CLOSE	Clears the active set of rows and frees the memory area used for the cursor.

Try working through an example to see how an explicit cursor is set up and processed. Brewbean's sells both equipment and coffee, and all in-state orders must be taxed, with different tax rates applied to equipment and coffee items. Therefore, the product type for each item in the basket must be checked to calculate the correct tax amount. Review the following block, which uses a cursor to retrieve all the items in a basket and calculates the order's total tax by applying the correct rates to equipment and coffee items. Figure 4-8 shows the results.

```
DECLARE
  CURSOR cur_basket IS
    SELECT bi.idBasket, p.type, bi.price, bi.quantity
      FROM bb_basketitem bi INNER JOIN bb_product p
        USING (idProduct)
      WHERE bi.idBasket = 6;
  TYPE type_basket IS RECORD
    (basket bb_basketitem.idBasket%TYPE,
    type bb_product.type%TYPE,
    price bb_basketitem.price%TYPE,
    qty bb_basketitem.quantity%TYPE);
  rec_basket type_basket;
  lv_rate_num NUMBER(2,2);
  lv_tax_num NUMBER(4,2) := 0;
BEGIN
  OPEN cur_basket;
  LOOP
    FETCH cur_basket INTO rec_basket;
      EXIT WHEN cur_basket%NOTFOUND;
      IF rec_basket.type = 'E' THEN lv_rate_num := .05;
      ELSIF rec_basket.type = 'C' THEN lv_rate_num := .03;
      END IF;
    lv_tax_num := lv_tax_num +
      ((rec_basket.price * rec_basket.qty) * lv_rate_num);
  END LOOP;
  CLOSE cur_basket;
  DBMS_OUTPUT.PUT_LINE(lv_tax_num);
END;
```

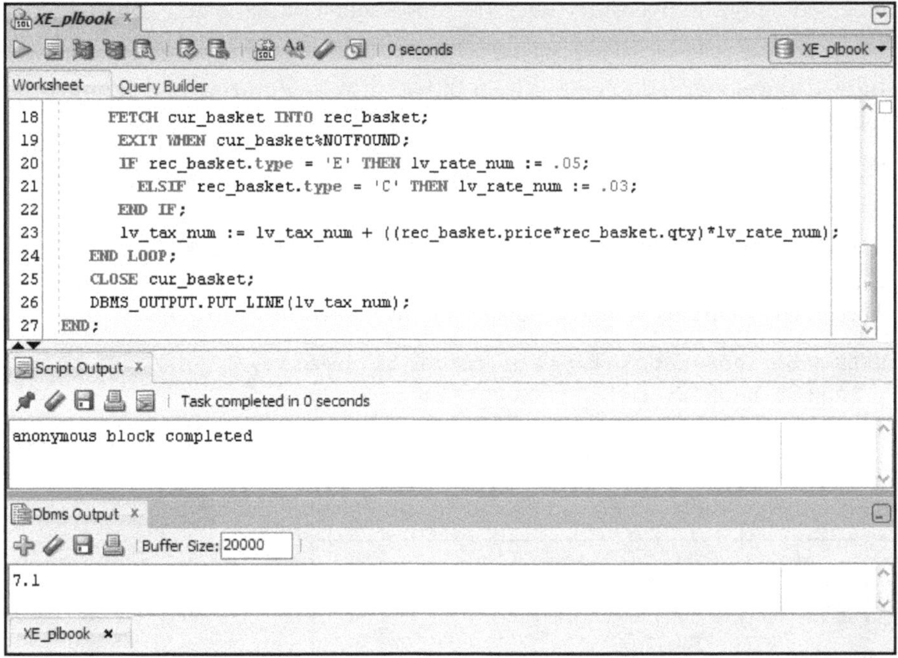

FIGURE 4-8 Using an explicit cursor to process rows from a query

In addition to declaring a cursor, a record variable was declared to hold values returned with the FETCH action. The declaration includes a SELECT statement, just as you would issue a stand-alone query in SQL Developer with no INTO clause. To make the cursor dynamic, a variable could be used in the cursor's WHERE clause to indicate which basket should be retrieved; in other words, a different set of rows might be retrieved each time the SELECT statement executes, depending on user input. The values of any variables used in the cursor at the time the OPEN is issued are used to create the active set of rows in the cursor.

The OPEN command prompts the cursor's SELECT statement to be processed and an active set of rows to be created in the cursor. The FETCH is used to move a row in the cursor into a record variable to become available for processing in the block. A list of scalar variables could be used instead of a record variable.

The cursor contains a pointer that automatically keeps track of the next row the FETCH returns, and it's initially set to the first row the query returns. The pointer moves to the next row in the active set with each consecutive FETCH statement. The FETCH is performed in a loop so that one row at a time is processed from the cursor, and the same processing logic is applied to each row. The EXIT WHEN clause instructs the loop to stop after all the cursor's rows have been fetched. This clause also checks the cursor attribute %NOTFOUND that would be TRUE if no more records remain in the cursor. So in this case, you're processing all the rows in the cursor. Then because you're finished with the cursor, the CLOSE command is issued to free associated resources.

Using explicit cursors gives you complete control over every aspect of cursor processing. For example, what if a maximum tax amount is used in the Brewbean's application? In this case, a statement could be added in the loop to exit after the lv_tax_num variable reaches this maximum. It might mean not all rows in the cursor need to be processed; only the necessary ones are processed. Try using an explicit cursor to calculate the tax amount and see whether the maximum limit of $5 has been reached:

1. In SQL Developer, add another item in basket 6 by entering and running the following `INSERT` statement:

```
INSERT INTO bb_basketitem
  VALUES (44, 8, 10.80, 1, 6, 2, 3);
```

2. Issue a `COMMIT` statement to save the added row permanently.
3. Check the items in basket 6 by entering and running the following query. Three rows or items should be displayed, as shown in Figure 4-9.

```
SELECT bi.idBasket, p.type, bi.price, bi.quantity
  FROM bb_basketitem bi INNER JOIN bb_product p
    USING (idProduct)
  WHERE bi.idBasket = 6;
```

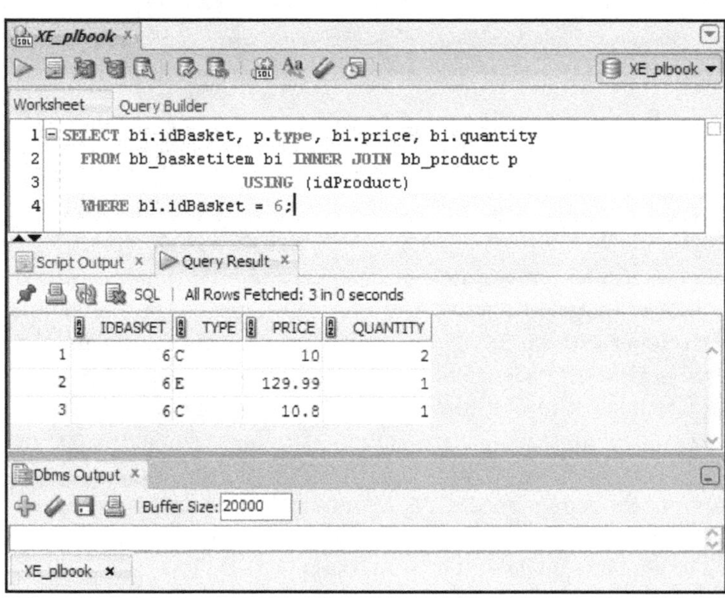

FIGURE 4-9 List of items in basket 6

4. In SQL Developer, click **File**, **Open** from the menu, and click the **`excurloop04.sql`** file in the Chapter04 folder. Notice that an `IF` statement is added to the bottom of the loop to check whether the maximum $5 limit has been reached. If so, exit the loop, as no further rows need to be processed.
5. When you run the block, two amounts are output. First, a 2 is displayed to indicate the cursor `ROWCOUNT`, which indicates that the cursor processed only two rows, even though three basket items exist. Second, a 5 is displayed to indicate that the maximum tax amount was reached.

To check the explicit cursor's ROWCOUNT attribute, a cursor name followed by a percent symbol is used instead of the SQL% used with implicit cursors: cur_basket%ROWCOUNT. This cursor attribute is checked with a DBMS_OUTPUT statement before the CLOSE statement is issued. If you attempt to check an explicit cursor attribute *after* the CLOSE, an Oracle error is raised stating that the cursor doesn't exist. In this case, the ROWCOUNT is 2, indicating it's the last row returned with a FETCH statement before closing the cursor. This confirms that only two of the three rows for basket 6 are processed because the $5 maximum tax amount was met after only two items. Therefore, keep in mind that ROWCOUNT with an implicit cursor always returns the total rows in the cursor, whereas ROWCOUNT with an explicit cursor reflects how many rows have been fetched.

Now that you know what implicit and explicit cursors are and how they work, take a look at a few more cursor considerations in the following sections, including CURSOR FOR loops and using parameters with cursors.

CHALLENGE 4-2

Review the block in Figure 4-7. Modify the block to use a cursor to read and display the information for the saved baskets of shopper 26.

CURSOR FOR Loops

A CURSOR FOR loop is another form of coding an explicit cursor that helps you avoid cursor errors in your programs. It simplifies coding because it handles many explicit cursor actions automatically, such as creating a record variable, opening a cursor, looping through one row at a time until the last row is retrieved from the cursor, and closing the cursor. Return to the first explicit cursor example from the previous section, in which you calculated the tax total by using different tax rates for each product type. Review the PL/SQL block in Figure 4-10 and compare it with the earlier example.

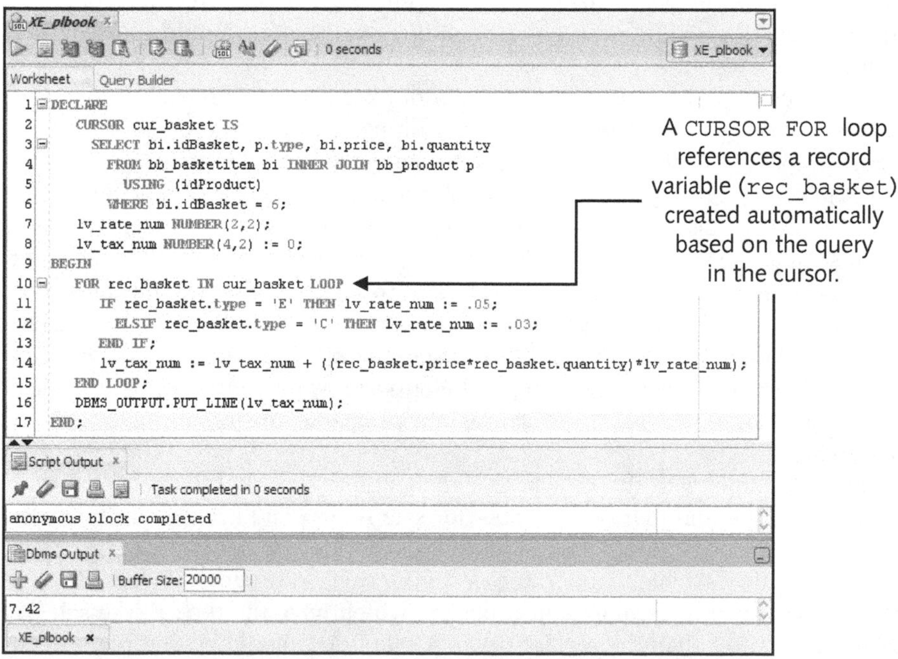

FIGURE 4-10 A CURSOR FOR loop

All the cursor handling in the block's executable section is done with a FOR loop statement. The OPEN, FETCH, EXIT WHEN EMPTY, and CLOSE actions are handled with the following two lines of code:

```
FOR rec_basket IN cur_basket LOOP
END LOOP;
```

The rec_basket variable in the FOR statement isn't declared in the block's declaration section. This record variable is constructed automatically based on the query in the declared cursor, cur_basket. Oracle constructs it by using table information from the database for the columns selected in the cursor. The record variable is created to hold one row of the cursor at a time through the loop.

Keep in mind that SQL statements in your cursor declaration can still use all the SQL features you're accustomed to, including column calculations, functions, and subqueries. However, be careful when including column aliases, which are typical in calculated columns. For example, say you have a cursor SELECT statement that multiplies product price by quantity ordered to retrieve an item total, as shown here:

```
SELECT bi.idBasket, p.type, bi.price*bi.quantity TOTAL
```

Any aliases in the SELECT statement must be used to reference values in the CURSOR FOR loop as part of the record variable. For example, if the total value calculated is to be used in the earlier tax calculation, the record item reference uses the alias total:

```
lv_tax_num := lv_tax_num + ((rec_basket.total)*lv_rate_num);
```

In many instances, you need to retrieve multiple rows from a database and perform processes on each row, including data manipulation commands. For example, say your application has a process for calculating new salaries, in which each row of an employee table is reviewed. In this case, the job class, years employed, and a performance rating might need to be reviewed for each employee to determine the correct percentage raise and then perform an update to store the new salary for each employee in the table. Explicit cursors offer two options to simplify this process: FOR UPDATE and WHERE CURRENT OF.

In this salary calculation process, you need to perform an update on each row to change the salary in the database. However, you're looking at rows from a cursor, so how do you perform an update on the database? Cursors have a feature that enable you to instruct the Oracle server to keep track of which physical database row corresponds to each row in the cursor. To use this feature, add a FOR UPDATE clause in the cursor declaration. It instructs the system to lock the rows retrieved with the SELECT statement because you intend to issue updates via the cursor and to keep track of the physical row in the database table that each row in the cursor corresponds to. In addition, the WHERE CURRENT OF cursor clause is added to the UPDATE statement to instruct the system to update the table's physical row corresponding to the cursor row currently being processed. The FOR UPDATE and WHERE CURRENT OF clauses work together to simplify update activity via a cursor.

Now look at an example with the Brewbean's application. The BB_PRODUCT table contains a SALEPRICE column that stores prices for sale items. The Brewbean's manager wants to analyze sale pricing and has requested that a sale price be loaded for every product. For coffee products, which have the type C, the sale price should be set 10% lower than the regular price. For equipment products, which have the type E, the sale price should be set 5% lower than the regular price. A sale price should be entered only for currently active products, which have the code 1 in the ACTIVE column. Review the following code (with new code in bold), which uses a CURSOR FOR loop to calculate and update the sale price:

```
DECLARE
  CURSOR cur_prod IS
    SELECT type, price
    FROM bb_product
    WHERE active = 1
FOR UPDATE NOWAIT;
  lv_sale bb_product.saleprice%TYPE;
BEGIN
FOR rec_prod IN cur_prod LOOP
  IF rec_prod.type = 'C' THEN lv_sale := rec_prod.price * .9;
  ELSIF rec_prod.type = 'E' THEN lv_sale := rec_prod.price * .95;
  END IF;
  UPDATE bb_product
    SET saleprice = lv_sale
WHERE CURRENT OF cur_prod;
  END LOOP;
  COMMIT;
END;
```

The first statement in the DECLARE section creates a cursor named cur_prod. The last line in the cursor declaration is a FOR UPDATE clause that instructs the system to track the physical database row (ROWID) related to each cursor row so that an UPDATE action can be performed with the cursor.

The FOR UPDATE clause ends with the NOWAIT option, which controls what occurs if another session has already locked the rows the cursor is retrieving. If you didn't use the NOWAIT option, the statement would wait indefinitely for the rows to unlock and become available. This option raises the following Oracle error if the rows are currently locked:

```
ORA-00054 resource busy and acquire with NOWAIT specified
```

NOWAIT makes it possible to let users know that the rows aren't currently available so that they can choose to continue with other tasks. Using this kind of error message is valuable when dealing with databases that have many users trying to perform DML activities on the same rows.

The first line of the executable section sets up the CURSOR FOR loop. Oracle automatically creates a record variable with the name supplied as the second item in this clause (rec_prod, in this example). The loop is exited automatically after all rows have been retrieved from the cursor. The UPDATE statement ends with the WHERE CURRENT OF cur_prod clause, which specifies that this update should occur on the physical database row corresponding to the current cursor row. After you finish the transaction, the last action is a COMMIT to save the DML actions permanently.

Try running the CURSOR FOR loop example and checking the results:

1. Verify the existing products' sale price data before doing the update by using the following query:

```
SELECT idProduct, type, saleprice, price
  FROM bb_product
  WHERE active = 1;
```

2. In SQL Developer, click **File**, **Open** from the menu, and click the **curloop04.sql** file in the Chapter04 folder.
3. Run the block. Verify the block execution by querying the BB_PRODUCT table, as shown in Figure 4-11, and reviewing the sale prices.

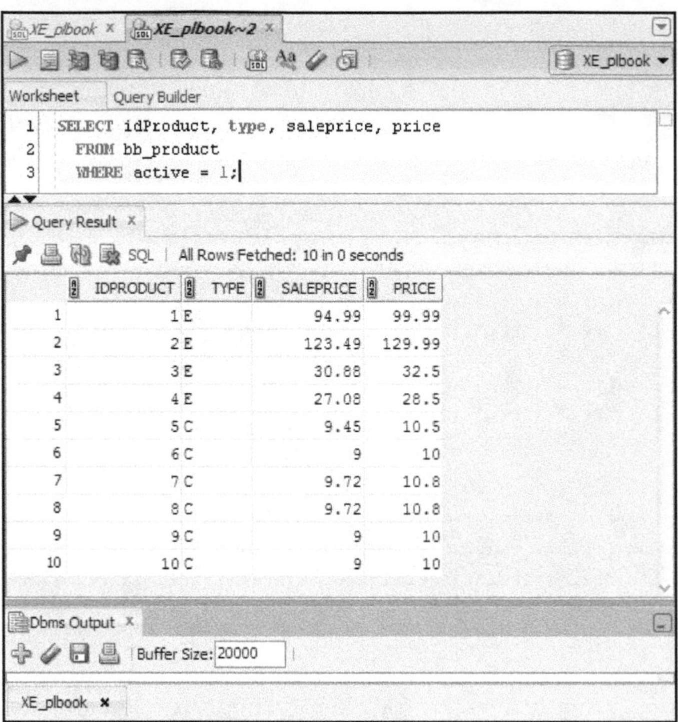

FIGURE 4-11 Checking `CURSOR FOR` loop results

You should always attempt to minimize row locking in an application to reduce the possibility of users having to wait for rows to be retrieved. Therefore, remember that a cursor's `FOR UPDATE` clause locks all table rows related to cursor rows when the cursor is opened. If the cursor involves multiple tables, but updates don't affect all the tables, an `OF` option can be used to minimize locked rows. For example, review the cursor declaration in the following code that includes an `OF` option in the `FOR UPDATE` clause:

```
CURSOR cur_prod IS
  SELECT s.idShopper, s.promo, b.total
  FROM bb_shopper s INNER JOIN bb_basket b
    USING (idShopper)
  FOR UPDATE OF s.promo NOWAIT;
```

The `OF s.promo` part of the `FOR UPDATE` clause specifies that only the PROMO column is needed for the `UPDATE` action, so only the BB_SHOPPER table rows need to be locked. The `OF` option prevents locking the BB_BASKET table rows, too, which aren't needed for the update. If more than one column is needed in the update, you can use a list of columns separated by commas in the `OF` option.

As you can see, the CURSOR FOR loop is much simpler to code because many of the cursor-processing steps occur automatically. Given this, should a CURSOR FOR loop always be used to process an explicit cursor? No, you should consider these factors when making this decision:

- Some advanced cursor features, such as bulk operations, might not be available with a CURSOR FOR loop.
- In Oracle versions before 10*g*, the CURSOR FOR loop typically results in inefficient or slow performance, particularly when thousands of rows are being processed. Oracle 10*g* and later optimize CURSOR FOR loop processing, much as bulk processing does (introduced in Chapter 3). This optimization applies to queries but not DML statements.
- Even in Oracle 10*g* and later, when many rows are being processed or the CURSOR FOR loop is being called by many users simultaneously, bulk processing might still result in more efficient processing. Performance testing should be done to compare the two approaches.

As a programmer, you might spend a lot of time editing existing application coding. Being familiar with both methods is an advantage when encountering different coding techniques in your editing tasks.

NOTE

Even though bulk processing is an advanced topic and beyond the scope of this book, it's still important for anyone learning PL/SQL to have at least some familiarity with it. For this reason, later in this chapter in "Bulk-Processing Features," you learn about the BULK COLLECT option and the FORALL statement to prepare you for coding issues you face as you advance in your PL/SQL skills.

TIP

Using a cursor for retrieving a single row from the database is considered a poor programming practice. A SELECT INTO statement should be used instead. Using a cursor indicates the intent to process a group of rows from the database and can be misleading if this isn't the case.

CHALLENGE 4-3

Review the block in Figure 4-7. Modify the block to use a CURSOR FOR loop to read and display the information for shopper 26's saved baskets.

Cursors with Parameters

Cursors can also use parameters to be more dynamic. Parameters are values passed to the cursor when it's opened and used in the cursor's SELECT statement to determine what data the cursor contains. With parameters, a single cursor can be used multiple times to return different sets of values. In the following block, a cursor uses a parameter, p_basket, to pass a basket number to the cursor's SELECT statement. The parameter is simply added in the cursor declaration inside parentheses after the cursor name. In the executable section, the cursor is called twice, and each call contains a different basket ID value to pass via the parameter.

```
DECLARE
  CURSOR cur_order (p_basket NUMBER) IS
    SELECT idBasket, idProduct, price, quantity
      FROM bb_basketitem
      WHERE idBasket = p_basket;
  lv_bask1_num bb_basket.idbasket%TYPE := 6;
  lv_bask2_num bb_basket.idbasket%TYPE := 10;
BEGIN
  FOR rec_order IN cur_order(lv_bask1_num) LOOP
  DBMS_OUTPUT.PUT_LINE(rec_order.idBasket || ' - ' ||
    rec_order.idProduct || ' - ' || rec_order.price);
  END LOOP;
  FOR rec_order IN cur_order(lv_bask2_num) LOOP
  DBMS_OUTPUT.PUT_LINE(rec_order.idBasket || ' - ' ||
    rec_order.idProduct || ' - ' || rec_order.price);
  END LOOP;
END;
```

The results in Figure 4-12 show that both calls were successful and return the correct rows based on the two basket IDs submitted.

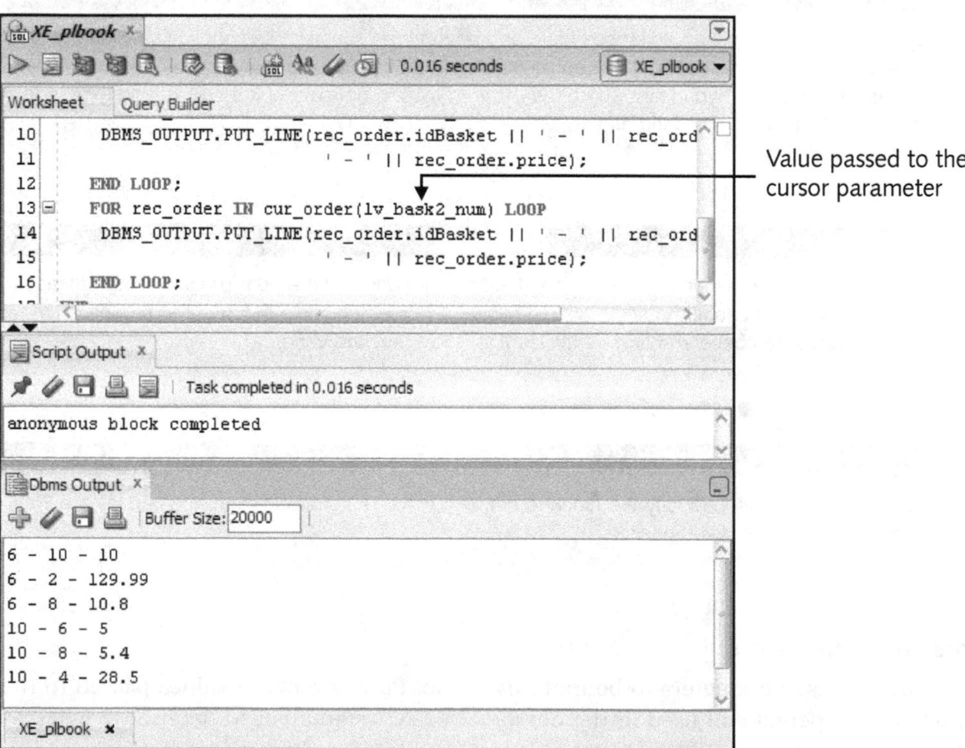

FIGURE 4-12 Using a cursor parameter

Only one parameter is used in this example; however, many parameters can be included by listing them separated by commas in the cursor declaration. If more than one parameter is used, the values passed when the cursor is opened work based on position. The first value in the open cursor command is placed in the first parameter in the cursor declaration, and so forth. Parameters can also be passed with an explicit cursor used without a CURSOR FOR loop by listing the values to pass to parameters in the OPEN statement, as shown:

```
OPEN cur_order(lv_bask1_num);
```

Cursor Variables

An explicit cursor assigns a name to a work area holding a specific result set, whereas a cursor variable is simply a pointer to a work area where a query can be processed. Implicit and explicit cursors are considered static because they're associated with specific queries. Because a cursor variable is just a pointer to a work area, this work area could be used for different queries. An important benefit of cursor variables is being able to pass the result sets of queries more efficiently. This method passes the pointer—rather than all the data—to the cursor.

Before Oracle 9*i*, creating a cursor variable required a TYPE statement for a REF CURSOR data type and a variable declaration using this data type, as shown:

```
TYPE type_curvar IS REF CURSOR;
```

Starting with Oracle 9*i*, a REF CURSOR type named SYS_REFCURSOR is defined. The processing is handled like an explicit cursor by using OPEN, FETCH, and CLOSE statements. However, the OPEN statement for a cursor variable provides the query to be processed.

Assume that Brewbean's has an application page that retrieves data from the BB_BASKETITEM or BB_BASKETSTATUS table, depending on user input. So based on the input, a different query needs to be processed in the cursor. The following code shows using a cursor variable for this task:

```
DECLARE
  cv_prod SYS_REFCURSOR;
  rec_item  bb_basketitem%ROWTYPE;
  rec_status  bb_basketstatus%ROWTYPE;
  lv_input1_num NUMBER(2) := 2;
  lv_input2_num NUMBER(2) := 3;
BEGIN
  IF lv_input1_num = 1 THEN
    OPEN cv_prod FOR SELECT * FROM bb_basketitem
      WHERE idBasket = lv_input2_num;
    LOOP
      FETCH cv_prod INTO rec_item;
      EXIT WHEN cv_prod%NOTFOUND;
      DBMS_OUTPUT.PUT_LINE(rec_item.idProduct);
    END LOOP;
  ELSIF lv_input1_num = 2 THEN
    OPEN cv_prod FOR SELECT * FROM bb_basketstatus
      WHERE idBasket = lv_input2_num;
    LOOP
      FETCH cv_prod INTO rec_status;
      EXIT WHEN cv_prod%NOTFOUND;
```

```
      DBMS_OUTPUT.PUT_LINE(rec_status.idStage || ' - '
       || rec_status.dtstage);
    END LOOP;
  END IF;
END;
```


In the declaration section, the `cv_prod` variable is declared with the `SYS_REFCURSOR` type. The other two declarations create record variables that can hold the rows fetched from the cursor. In the executable section, an `IF` statement determines (based on user input) what data is retrieved and placed in the cursor variable. The `OPEN` statement now indicates not only a cursor name, but also the query to process in the cursor. The same cursor is used in both `OPEN` statements; however, it holds different data, depending on which `OPEN` is executed, because the query is different in each.

BULK-PROCESSING FEATURES

Chapter 3 introduced using bulk processing to improve the performance of multirow queries and DML actions. In this section, you take another brief look at it and examine a few examples to understand additional features. The first example uses the `BULK COLLECT` clause in an explicit cursor's `FETCH` statement. Review the PL/SQL block in Figure 4-13, which retrieves all data rows from the BB_BASKETITEM table. The cursor's `FETCH` statement is no longer inside a loop. Instead, all data rows are retrieved with one `FETCH` because of the `BULK COLLECT` option, instead of fetching one row at a time, as in previous examples. The rows are placed in a table of records variable, and a loop is used to verify the data that's retrieved. Running this block displays data from all 29 rows of the BB_BASKETITEM table.

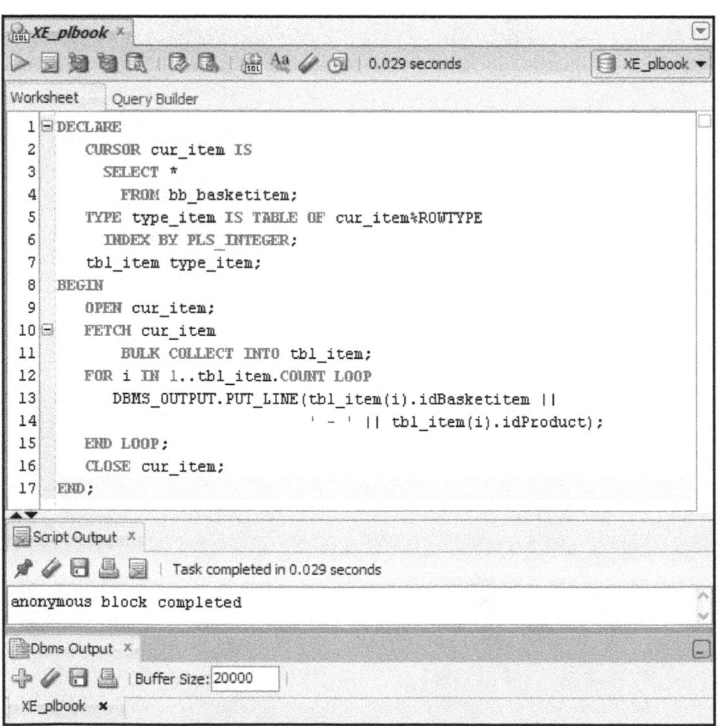

FIGURE 4-13 A `BULK COLLECT` option in a `FETCH` statement

The major advantage of using bulk processing is improving performance. If you're retrieving thousands of rows, you can also use a LIMIT clause to give you more control over the number of rows processed with each FETCH statement, thereby improving memory use on the database server. Say the BB_BASKETITEM table contains 20,000 rows of data, and you need to retrieve all rows. The bulk processing in Figure 4-13 would require using a lot of memory to retrieve all 20,000 rows with one FETCH. The following block adds the LIMIT clause to instruct each FETCH to retrieve only 1000 rows:

```
DECLARE
  CURSOR cur_item IS
    SELECT *
      FROM bb_basketitem;
  TYPE type_item IS TABLE OF cur_item%ROWTYPE
    INDEX BY PLS_INTEGER;
  tbl_item type_item;
BEGIN
  OPEN cur_item;
  LOOP
    FETCH cur_item BULK COLLECT INTO tbl_item LIMIT 1000;
      FOR i IN 1..tbl_item.COUNT LOOP
    DBMS_OUTPUT.PUT_LINE(tbl_item(i).idBasketitem || ' -'
     || tbl_item(i).idProduct);
      END LOOP;
    EXIT WHEN cur_item%NOTFOUND;
  END LOOP;
  CLOSE cur_item;
END;
```

The FETCH action must be inside a loop because each fetch is limited to 1000 rows, so multiple fetches are required to retrieve all rows. Also, the EXIT statement is included at the bottom of the loop to ensure that all rows fetched are processed before the loop ends. If a total of 20,500 rows were fetched and the EXIT statement were at the top of the loop, the DBMS_OUTPUT action wouldn't process the last 500 rows retrieved.

A FORALL statement provides bulk processing for DML activity. It must contain a single DML statement and reference collection elements by using an index that's declared automatically to iterate through the specified collection. Different collections can be referenced in the SET and WHERE clauses of an UPDATE statement. The following example processes UPDATE statements for all employees with the classtype 100. An array is created to hold all the employee IDs used in the WHERE clause of the UPDATE statement:

```
DECLARE
  TYPE emp_type IS TABLE OF NUMBER INDEX
    BY BINARY_INTEGER;
  emp_tbl emp_type;
BEGIN
  SELECT empID
    BULK COLLECT INTO emp_tbl
    FROM employees
    WHERE classtype = '100';
  FORALL i IN d_emp_tbl.FIRST .. emp_tbl.LAST
    UPDATE employees
```

```
      SET raise = salary * .06
        WHERE empID = emp_tbl(i);
    COMMIT;
  END;
```

The FORALL statement instructs the system to "bulk bind" all the collection elements together before sending SQL statements for processing. Again, the results of a group of DML statements are submitted at one time instead of each UPDATE statement being submitted separately.

EXCEPTION HANDLERS

An **exception handler** is a mechanism for trapping an error that occurs in processing. Its code handles the error in a user-friendly manner and allows the application to continue. The EXCEPTION section of a block begins with the EXCEPTION keyword and follows the BEGIN section.

The EXCEPTION section addresses two situations: An Oracle error has been raised, or a user-defined error has been raised. (In Oracle, "raised" means occurs.) The Oracle error happens automatically if there's a problem in the executable code—for example, a DELETE statement is issued but results in a foreign key error. Even if an Oracle error doesn't occur, you might want an error to be raised if something else happens. For example, suppose you issue an UPDATE statement, and no rows are updated. An Oracle error doesn't occur because it's legal for an UPDATE statement to affect no rows. However, you might recognize that this result means an invalid value has been supplied in the UPDATE statement's WHERE clause. In this case, you should create a user-defined error so that an error is raised if no rows are updated.

Some common Oracle errors already have exception names on the Oracle server. All other Oracle errors are considered undefined and must have a name assigned in code. The following sections explore three types of errors.

Predefined Exceptions in Oracle

Oracle supplies **predefined exceptions**, which are names associated with common errors. They're declared in the STANDARD package, which makes them globally available on the system. Table 4-3 lists some common predefined exceptions.

TABLE 4-3 Partial List of Predefined Exceptions

Exception Name	Description
NO_DATA_FOUND	A SELECT statement in a PL/SQL block retrieves no rows or a nonexistent row of an associative array that has been referenced.
TOO_MANY_ROWS	A SELECT statement in a PL/SQL block retrieves more than one row.
CASE_NOT_FOUND	No WHEN clause in the CASE statement is processed.
ZERO_DIVIDE	A division by zero is attempted.
DUP_VAL_ON_INDEX	A violation of a unique or primary key column constraint is attempted.

TIP

For a complete list of Oracle predefined exceptions, refer to the Oracle database documentation at *http://otn.oracle.com*.

A SELECT statement embedded in a PL/SQL block's executable section can raise the NO_DATA_FOUND or TOO_MANY_ROWS exception. If a SELECT statement returns no rows, the Oracle error associated with the NO_DATA_FOUND exception name is raised. It refers to a SELECT statement coded in a PL/SQL block's executable section, not one used in an explicit cursor. It's a departure from issuing SQL statements stand-alone, as in SQL Developer, when no error is raised if a SELECT statement returns no rows. This problem happens with a SELECT statement embedded in PL/SQL because you're moving data returned by the SELECT statement into variables. On the other hand, if a SELECT statement returns more than one row, but the variables in the INTO clause are scalar variables or a record variable, the TOO_MANY_ROWS exception occurs. The next section gives you some examples to explain these exceptions more clearly.

Error Examples

If a SELECT statement's INTO clause contains scalar or record variables, and more than one row is selected, the TOO_MANY_ROWS exception is raised because these variables can't handle multiple rows. Refer back to the Brewbean's application page in Figure 4-6, which displays information about a shopper's saved basket. The following example is one of the code blocks for this page. It uses a SELECT statement on the BB_BASKET table to display an uncompleted shopping basket if a user who logs in to the Web site has saved one:

```
DECLARE
  TYPE type_basket IS RECORD
    (basket bb_basket.idBasket%TYPE,
    created bb_basket.dtcreated%TYPE,
    qty bb_basket.quantity%TYPE,
    sub bb_basket.subtotal%TYPE);
  rec_basket type_basket;
  lv_days_num NUMBER(3);
  lv_shopper_num NUMBER(3) := 25;
BEGIN
  SELECT idBasket, dtcreated, quantity, subtotal
    INTO rec_basket
    FROM bb_basket
      WHERE idShopper = lv_shopper_num
      AND orderplaced = 0;
  lv_days_num := TO_DATE('02/28/12','mm/dd/yy') - rec_basket.created;
  DBMS_OUTPUT.PUT_LINE(rec_basket.basket);
  DBMS_OUTPUT.PUT_LINE(rec_basket.created);
  DBMS_OUTPUT.PUT_LINE(rec_basket.qty);
  DBMS_OUTPUT.PUT_LINE(rec_basket.sub);
  DBMS_OUTPUT.PUT_LINE(lv_days_num);
END;
```

If this SELECT statement could retrieve no rows or more than one row, you need to include exception handlers to manage these possibilities. Try running this block with different shoppers to see the types of errors that occur with a SELECT statement:

1. In SQL Developer, click **File**, **Open** from the menu, and click the **ex_select04.sql** file in the Chapter04 folder. Notice that the SELECT

statement is currently set to retrieve saved basket information for Shopper 22; the `lv_shopper_num` variable is initialized to this value.

2. Run the block. The results should match Figure 4-14, which shows a "no data found" error message because Shopper 22 has no saved baskets in the database.

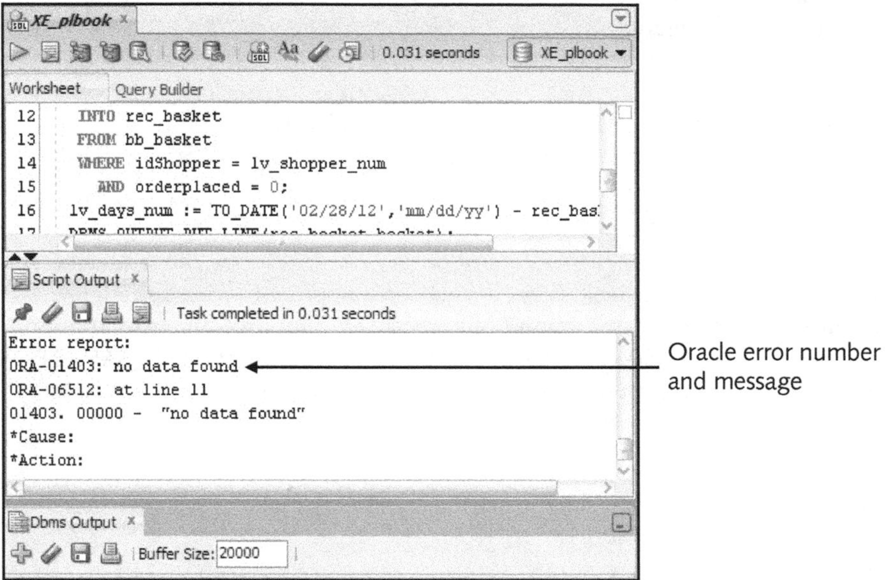

FIGURE 4-14 The "no data found" error is raised

TIP

Some Oracle error messages aren't as straightforward or easy to understand. The Oracle database documentation at *http://otn.oracle.com* contains a section listing all the Oracle errors in numerical order with brief descriptions.

3. Edit the block to change the `lv_shopper_num` variable declaration (in Line 9) to the initialized value **26**.
4. Run the block. The results should match Figure 4-15. The error message indicates that shopper 26 has more than one saved basket in the database.

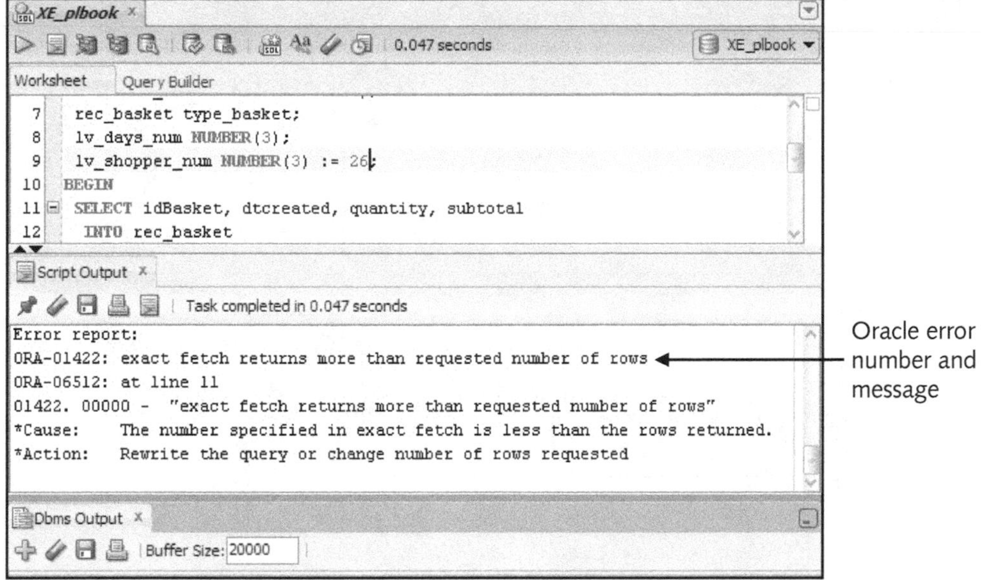

FIGURE 4-15 The "exact fetch returns more than requested number of rows" error

As you've seen, when an Oracle error occurs in the executable section of a PL/SQL block, processing stops, and an error message is displayed. This is definitely not what you want to happen in your applications! You need to anticipate and handle errors so that your application continues operating for users.

Exception Handler Coding

To create code that can anticipate and handle errors, modify the block you just ran to contain exception handlers for the two errors associated with the `SELECT` statement. This task is simplified because you're dealing with predefined Oracle exceptions. Exception names are already associated with these two errors, so you don't need to declare exceptions in the block's DECLARE section. In addition, both errors are raised automatically by the Oracle server, so you don't need to raise them in the block's executable section. You just need to add exception handlers in the block's EXCEPTION section containing instructions on what should be done if this error is raised. To test predefined exception handlers, follow these steps:

1. In SQL Developer, click **File**, **Open** from the menu, and click the **`ex_predef04.sql`** file in the Chapter04 folder. The `SELECT` statement is currently set to retrieve uncompleted basket information for shopper 22. Review the added EXCEPTION section (starting seven lines from the bottom). It contains two exception handlers to address the errors described previously.
2. Run the block. The results should match Figure 4-16: The block traps the "no data found" error and displays a message onscreen.

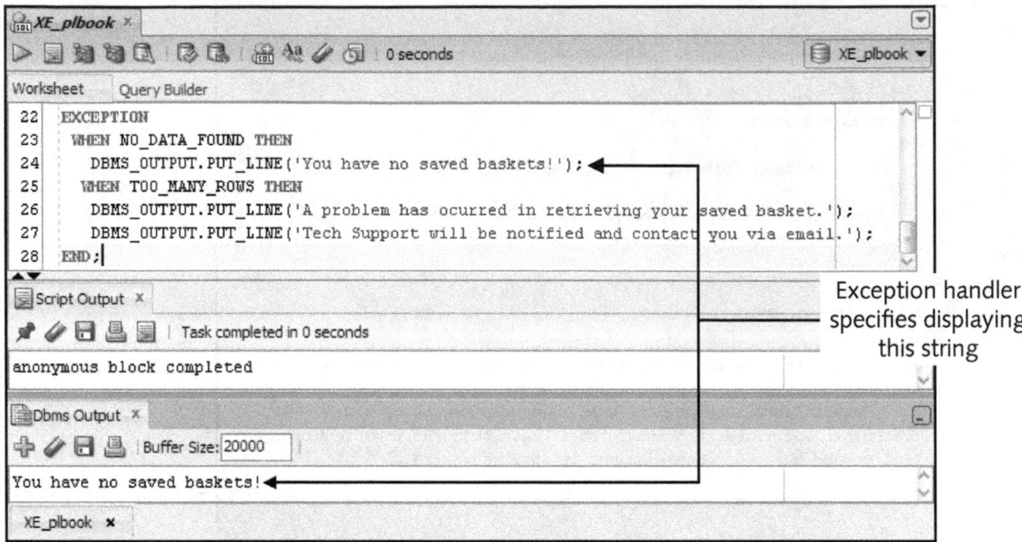

FIGURE 4-16 Code displaying an error message to users

3. Edit the block and change the `lv_shopper_num` variable declaration (on Line 9) to the initialized value **26**.
4. Run the block. The results should match Figure 4-17: The block traps the "too many rows" error and displays a message onscreen.

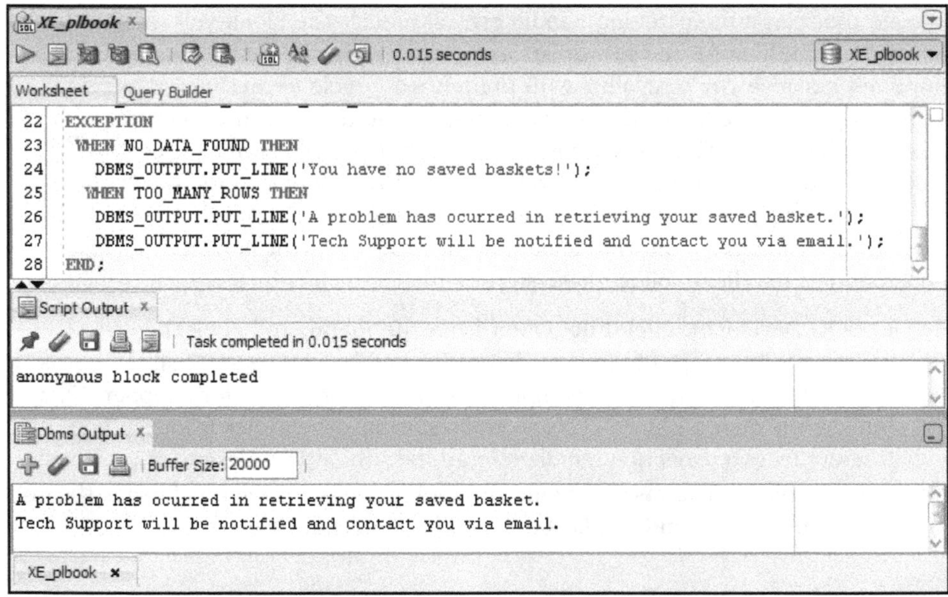

FIGURE 4-17 Exception handler trapping the `TOO_MANY_ROWS` exception

As soon as an error occurs in the block's executable section, processing moves to the EXCEPTION section and searches for a matching exception handler. If one is found, statements in the handler are executed, and this block is finished. Processing doesn't return to the next statement in the block's executable section. If this block is enclosed in another block (or called from another block, as you see in Chapter 5), control returns to the enclosing block.

In the preceding steps, notice that each handler displays a different message so that you can determine which handler executed when you test the block. Using `DBMS_OUTPUT` in this manner is quite useful for testing purposes. However, in an application, you would supply text to display to users onscreen or assign values to variables to be passed back to the application.

Undefined Exceptions in Oracle

What if an exception handler is needed for an Oracle error that doesn't have a predefined exception (an **undefined exception**, sometimes called an "unnamed Oracle error")? In this case, you need to declare an exception and associate an Oracle error number with it. These two tasks are done in the block's DECLARE section. Figure 4-18 shows a block including an error handler for a foreign key violation. The `DELETE` statement is attempting to eliminate a basket that still has item detail rows in the BB_BASKETITEM table.

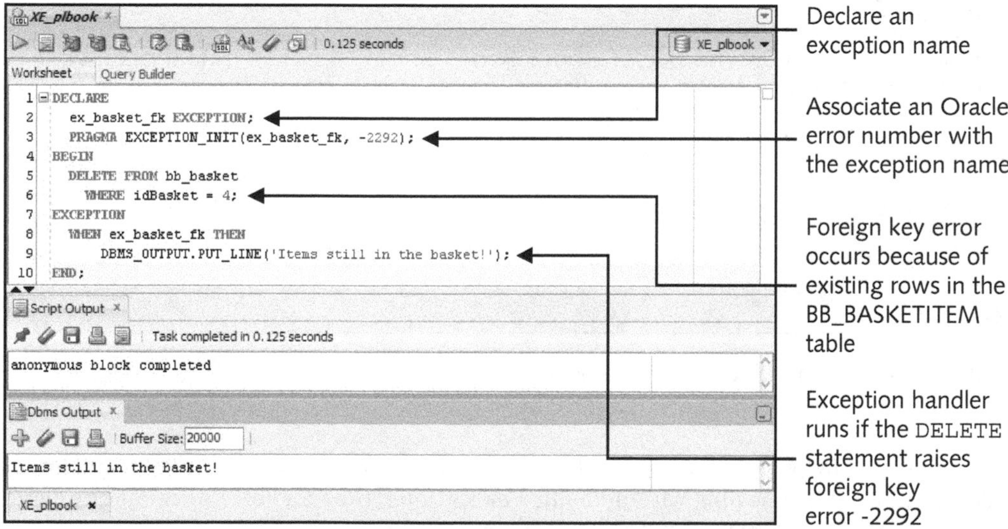

FIGURE 4-18 Exception handler for an undefined exception

First, the `EX_BASKET_FK` exception is declared, and then the `PRAGMA` statement associates Oracle error number -2292 with the exception. A **`PRAGMA` statement** specifies using additional information that's supplied when compiling and running the block.

Two arguments are required in a PRAGMA EXCEPTION_INIT statement: the exception name (declared in the previous line in this example) and the Oracle error number to associate with the exception name. In this example, the exception name EX_BASKET_FK is associated with Oracle error -2292 (displayed in the format ORA-02292 in error messages). After assigning an exception name, you just need to add an exception handler that references this error by exception name, in the same way you did to create a handler for a predefined exception.

To determine undefined Oracle error numbers, many developers use stand-alone SQL statements to test which Oracle errors might need to be handled in the block. For example, Figure 4-19 shows the DELETE statement from the block. This test confirms what kind of Oracle error can occur with this statement.

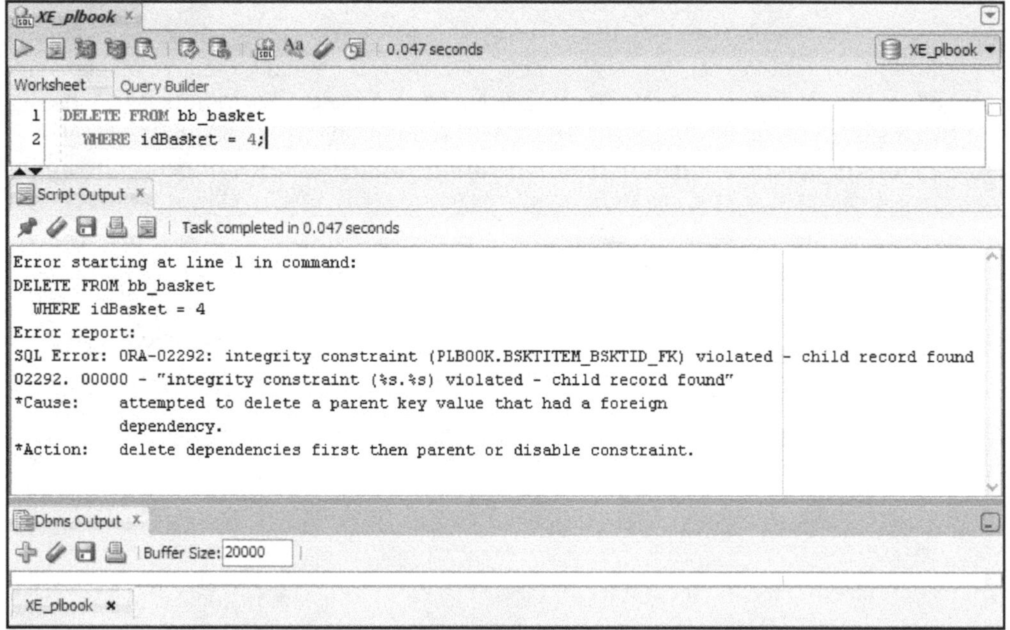

FIGURE 4-19 DELETE statement Oracle error

This testing helps you develop a list of potential Oracle errors that the SQL statement could generate. When dealing with undefined exceptions, the Oracle error number must be included in the PRAGMA EXCEPTION_INIT statement.

CHALLENGE 4-4

Create a block that includes the following UPDATE statement:

```
UPDATE bb_basketitem
  SET idbasket = 99
  WHERE idbasketitem = 38;
```

Determine the error the statement raises and add the correct exception handler to the block. The exception handler should display a brief message indicating the nature of the error.

User-Defined Exceptions

A **user-defined exception** is one that a developer raises in a block to enforce a business rule. For example, the Brewbean's application has a page for employees to update product descriptions. The list of products is growing, so employees wanted to be able to type the product ID instead of selecting it from a list. They think typing IDs is faster, but this method raises the possibility of entering an invalid product ID. How can this situation be handled? The first step is examining the code in Figure 4-20 to confirm that the `UPDATE` statement returning no rows doesn't raise an Oracle error.

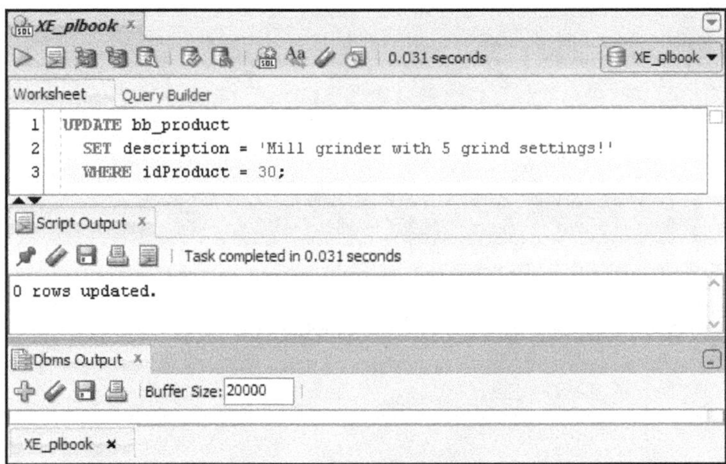

FIGURE 4-20 An `UPDATE` returning no rows doesn't raise an Oracle error

Because Oracle doesn't raise an error if an `UPDATE` statement doesn't affect any rows, you must include specific instructions to raise an error if no rows are updated. To do this, you need to add three items to the block, as shown in Figure 4-21. First, declare an exception. Second, specify when to raise this error in the executable section. Third, code an exception handler.

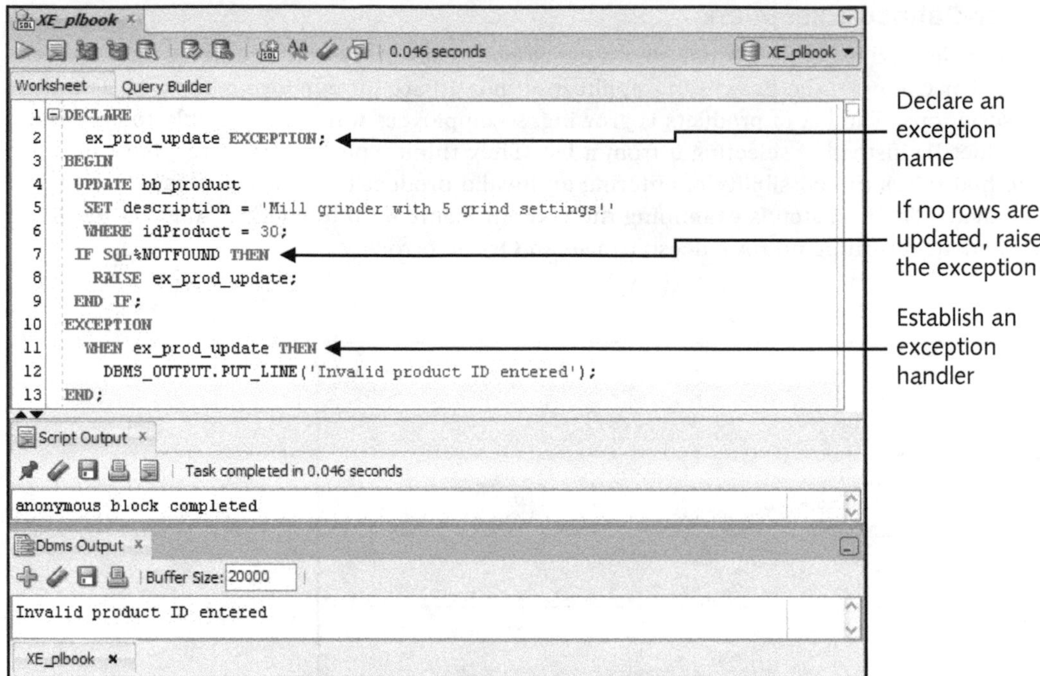

FIGURE 4-21 Coding a user-defined exception

The exception must be raised in the executable section by using the `RAISE` command. A declared exception must be referred to in the `RAISE` statement, or a PL/SQL error occurs. Do you remember the attributes for checking the results of an SQL statement, such as `SQL%ROWCOUNT` and `SQL%NOTFOUND`? In Figure 4-21, the cursor attribute `SQL%NOTFOUND` is used to test (behind the scenes) whether the `UPDATE` statement affected any rows and whether the exception needs to be raised.

Note that an exception doesn't have to be related to an SQL statement. Another business rule that might need to be enforced in the Brewbean's application is a check to ensure that the quantity ordered of an item doesn't exceed the quantity in stock, as shown in Figure 4-22. In this case, you simply compare the two amounts and raise a user-defined exception if the request exceeds the stock amount.

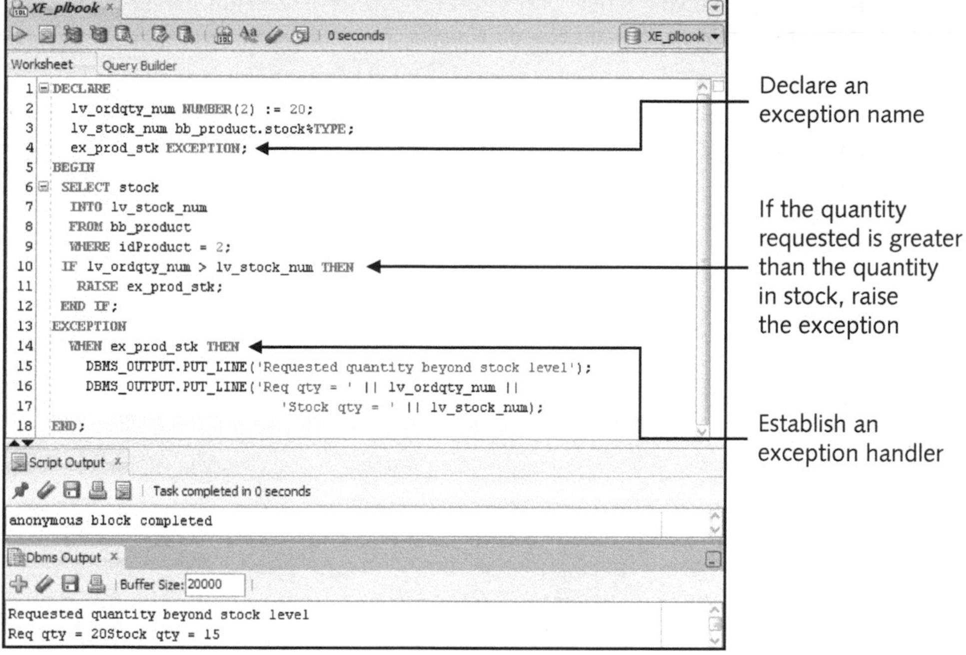

FIGURE 4-22 Checking the quantity of stock on hand

ADDITIONAL EXCEPTION CONCEPTS

The previous discussion of predefined, undefined, and user-defined exceptions are critical in handling anticipated errors. However, what if unexpected errors occur? You not only want to trap this error to handle it and allow the application to continue, but also want to document the error number to determine whether any code revisions are warranted. This task can be handled by using the `WHEN OTHERS` handler with the `SQLCODE` and `SQLERRM` functions, discussed in this section. This section also covers a mechanism to create your own Oracle error numbers with the `RAISE_APPLICATION_ERROR` procedure. Last, the flow of exception-handling propagation is introduced.

WHEN OTHERS, SQLCODE, and SQLERRM

Another feature available with exception handlers is the `WHEN OTHERS` clause in the EXCEPTION section, used to trap any errors not specifically addressed in other exception handlers. The `WHEN OTHERS` handler should always be the last one listed in the EXCEPTION section.

You can't always anticipate every error that might occur in an application, but if an unexpected error does occur, you need the application to handle it so that it doesn't end abruptly. If an error is raised in the block, processing jumps right to the EXCEPTION section and begins looking for a matching handler. If one isn't found, the error is then propagated to the application environment. In other words, an intimidating or confusing error message is likely to be displayed to users onscreen, and the application might lock up. To keep this from happening, the `WHEN OTHERS` handler offers a catchall handler that captures any errors that don't find a matching exception handler.

Return to the example of retrieving a saved basket for a shopper who logs in to the site, and assume you didn't anticipate the `TOO_MANY_ROWS` exception. Figure 4-23 shows the result of running the following block with a `WHEN OTHERS` exception handler added in the EXCEPTION section. Notice that there's no `WHEN TOO_MANY_ROWS` handler.

```
DECLARE
  TYPE type_basket IS RECORD
    (basket bb_basket.idBasket%TYPE,
    created bb_basket.dtcreated%TYPE,
    qty bb_basket.quantity%TYPE,
    sub bb_basket.subtotal%TYPE);
  rec_basket type_basket;
  lv_days_num NUMBER(3);
  lv_shopper_num NUMBER(3) := 26;
BEGIN
  SELECT idBasket, dtcreated, quantity, subtotal
    INTO rec_basket
    FROM bb_basket
      WHERE idShopper = lv_shopper_num
      AND orderplaced = 0;
  lv_days_num := TO_DATE('02/28/12','mm/dd/yy') - rec_basket.created;
  DBMS_OUTPUT.PUT_LINE(rec_basket.basket);
  DBMS_OUTPUT.PUT_LINE(rec_basket.created);
  DBMS_OUTPUT.PUT_LINE(rec_basket.qty);
  DBMS_OUTPUT.PUT_LINE(rec_basket.sub);
  DBMS_OUTPUT.PUT_LINE(lv_days_num);
EXCEPTION
  WHEN NO_DATA_FOUND THEN
    DBMS_OUTPUT.PUT_LINE('You have no saved baskets!');
  WHEN OTHERS THEN
    DBMS_OUTPUT.PUT_LINE('A problem has occurred');
    DBMS_OUTPUT.PUT_LINE('Tech support will be notified and contact you');
END;
```

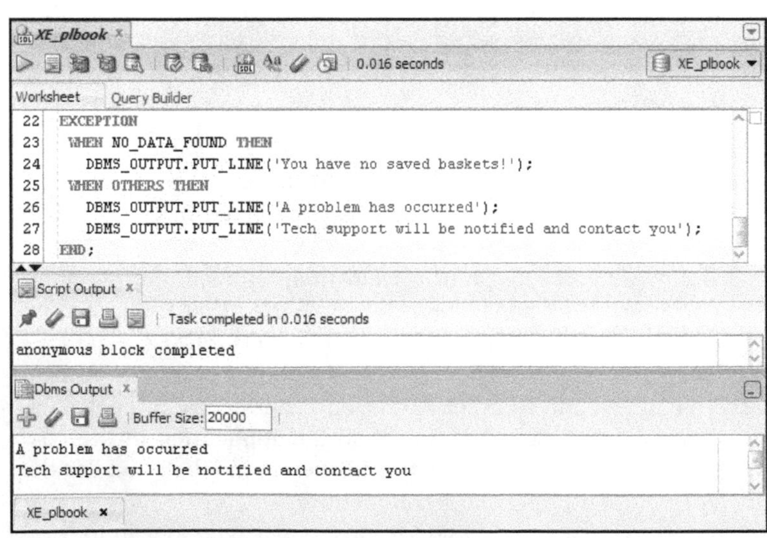

FIGURE 4-23 Using the `WHEN OTHERS` exception handler

In this block, the "exact fetch returns more than requested number of rows" error (or, more simply, "fetch too many rows" error) occurs, but no handler is included in the EXCEPTION section. Therefore, the last handler, `WHEN OTHERS`, is executed. If this handler is executed, it probably means an unexpected error occurred in the application, so as a developer, you should examine it to determine whether application modifications are needed. How do you capture information about the error so that you can research it?

Your research begins with two PL/SQL functions: The `SQLCODE` function returns the Oracle error number, and the `SQLERRM` function returns the Oracle error message. Using these functions to save error information in a transaction log table is quite useful for identifying errors that occur in a block but don't have an associated exception handler. This log file typically includes other types of information, such as user ID, date, and a description or name of the application page the user was on when the error happened. Figure 4-24 shows the same block with statements added in the `WHEN OTHERS` handler to capture error information with these functions and insert it in a table. A `COMMIT` should be included after the `INSERT` to save the data permanently; however, this statement has been left out to allow testing. Notice that two new scalar variables are declared as follows:

```
lv_errmsg_txt VARCHAR2(80);
lv_errnum_txt VARCHAR2(10);
```

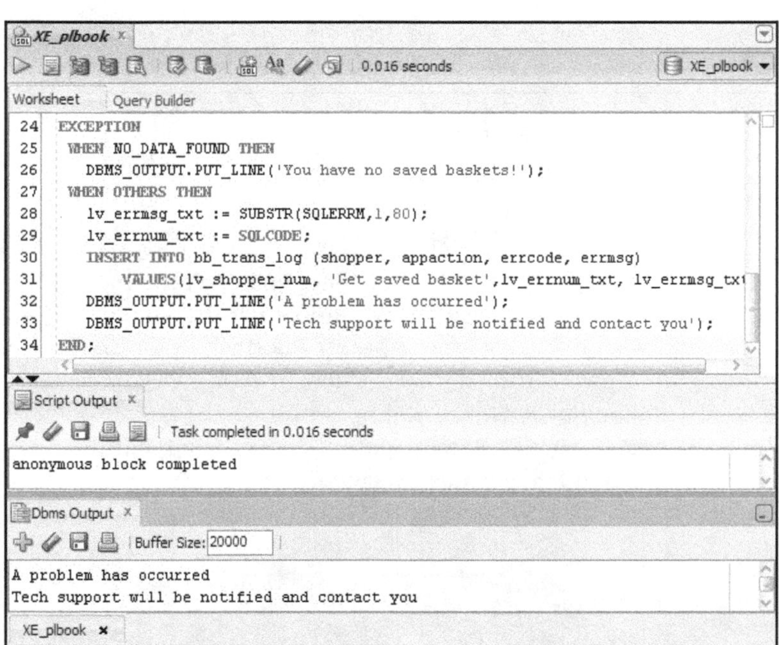

FIGURE 4-24 Using the `SQLCODE` and `SQLERRM` functions

Assignment statements are used to capture the values returned by the SQLCODE and SQLERRM functions. These functions must be used in a block's EXCEPTION section because they're associated with a raised error. They aren't SQL functions and can't be used directly in an SQL statement.

Notice that the SUBSTR function is used on the SQLERRM value. The error message can be up to 512 characters, but the column used in the BB_TRANS_LOG table to hold this data is only 80 characters. Therefore, the SUBSTR function is used to retrieve the first 80 characters of the error message.

Figure 4-25 shows the data inserted in the BB_TRANS_LOG table when the WHEN OTHERS handler executes. In this case, the TOO_MANY_ROWS exception is raised.

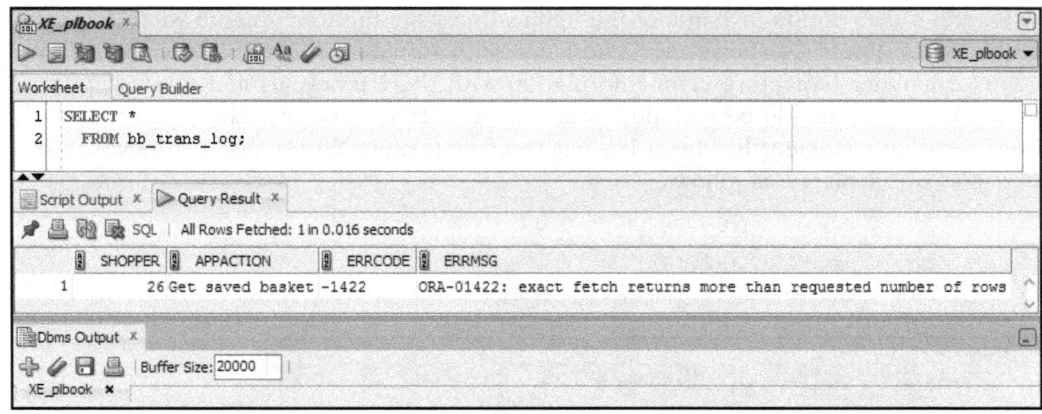

FIGURE 4-25 Results of the SQLCODE and SQLERRM functions

Follow these steps to test the exception-handling process:

1. In SQL Developer, click **File**, **Open** from the menu, and click the **ex_test04.sql** file in the Chapter04 folder. Notice that the SELECT statement is currently set to retrieve saved basket information for Shopper 22, which results in no rows returned. Also, review the EXCEPTION section containing two exception handlers.
2. Run the block. The results should match Figure 4-26, verifying that the NO_DATA_FOUND exception handler was executed.

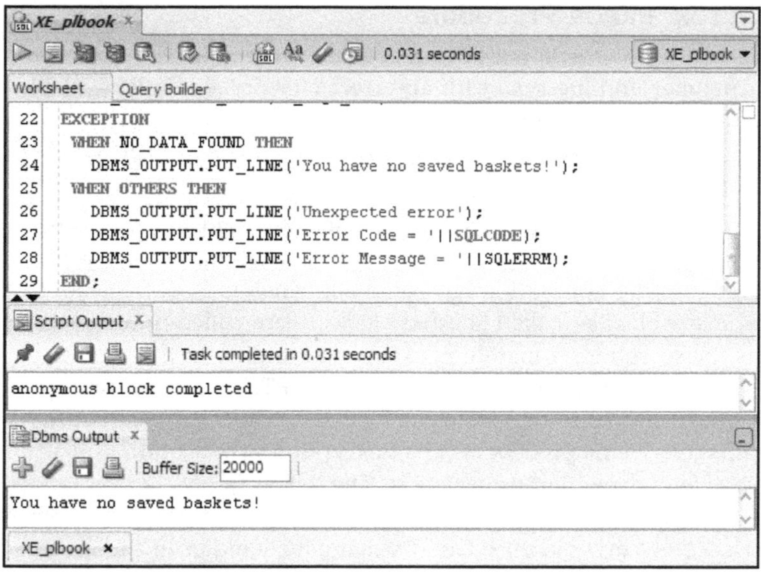

```
22 EXCEPTION
23   WHEN NO_DATA_FOUND THEN
24     DBMS_OUTPUT.PUT_LINE('You have no saved baskets!');
25   WHEN OTHERS THEN
26     DBMS_OUTPUT.PUT_LINE('Unexpected error');
27     DBMS_OUTPUT.PUT_LINE('Error Code = '||SQLCODE);
28     DBMS_OUTPUT.PUT_LINE('Error Message = '||SQLERRM);
29 END;
```


FIGURE 4-26 Processing the NO_DATA_FOUND handler

3. Modify the block and change the shopper number in the DECLARE section (on Line 9) to **26**.
4. Run the block. The results should match Figure 4-27, verifying that the WHEN OTHERS exception handler was executed. The DBMS_OUTPUT statements display the error number and message.

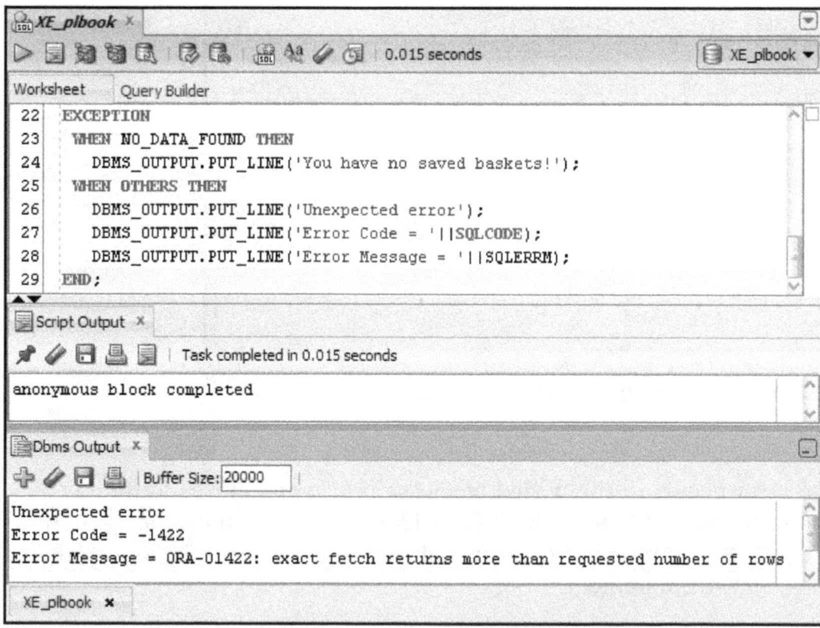

```
22 EXCEPTION
23   WHEN NO_DATA_FOUND THEN
24     DBMS_OUTPUT.PUT_LINE('You have no saved baskets!');
25   WHEN OTHERS THEN
26     DBMS_OUTPUT.PUT_LINE('Unexpected error');
27     DBMS_OUTPUT.PUT_LINE('Error Code = '||SQLCODE);
28     DBMS_OUTPUT.PUT_LINE('Error Message = '||SQLERRM);
29 END;
```


FIGURE 4-27 Processing the WHEN OTHERS handler

The RAISE_APPLICATION_ERROR Procedure

RAISE_APPLICATION_ERROR is an Oracle built-in procedure that enables developers to associate their own error number and message with an error. This procedure is available only in stored program units (covered in Chapter 5).

Exception Propagation

You know that an error raised in the executable section immediately moves processing to the EXCEPTION section in search of an exception handler. If a matching handler isn't found, the error is propagated to the application environment, which is SQL Developer in these examples. However, many blocks—called "nested blocks"—are called or enclosed by other blocks, which alters the search for a matching exception handler. In this situation, an exception raised in the executable section searches the EXCEPTION section first for a handler; if it doesn't find one, it moves to the enclosing block's EXCEPTION section to continue the search for a handler. This process is called **exception propagation**.

Take a look at an example of exception propagation. The following code shows nested blocks, each with its own EXCEPTION section. Figure 4-28 shows the results of the nested block in which a NO_DATA_FOUND error is raised, and a matching handler in the nested block is found and executed.

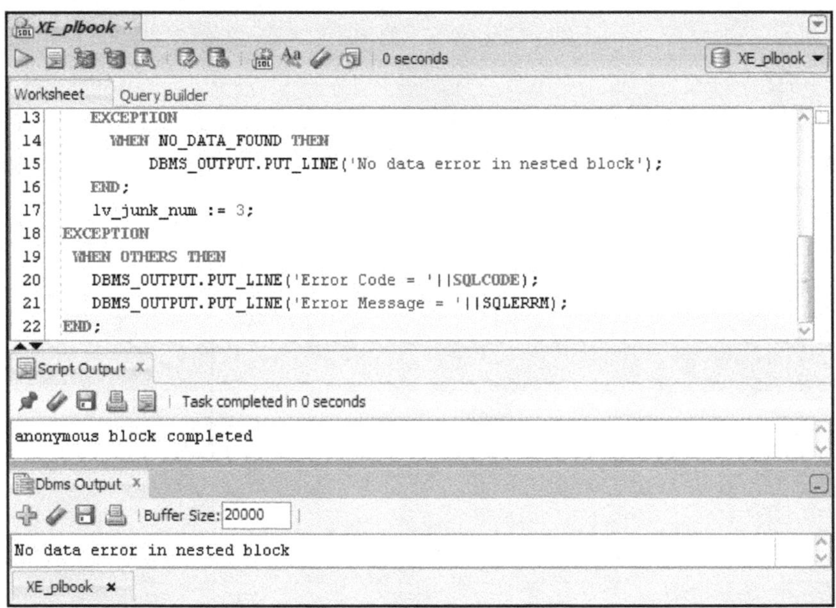

FIGURE 4-28 A nested block handling an error

In this case, the error occurs in the nested block, so processing moves to the EXCEPTION section of the nested block. The EXCEPTION section contains an exception handler (WHEN NO_DATA_FOUND) for this error, which runs and displays the associated message with a DBMS_OUTPUT statement.

What if a matching handler isn't found in the nested block? The exception then propagates to the enclosing block and searches for a handler in that block's EXCEPTION section. Figure 4-29 shows the same nested block with shopper 26 raising a `TOO_MANY_ROWS` error.

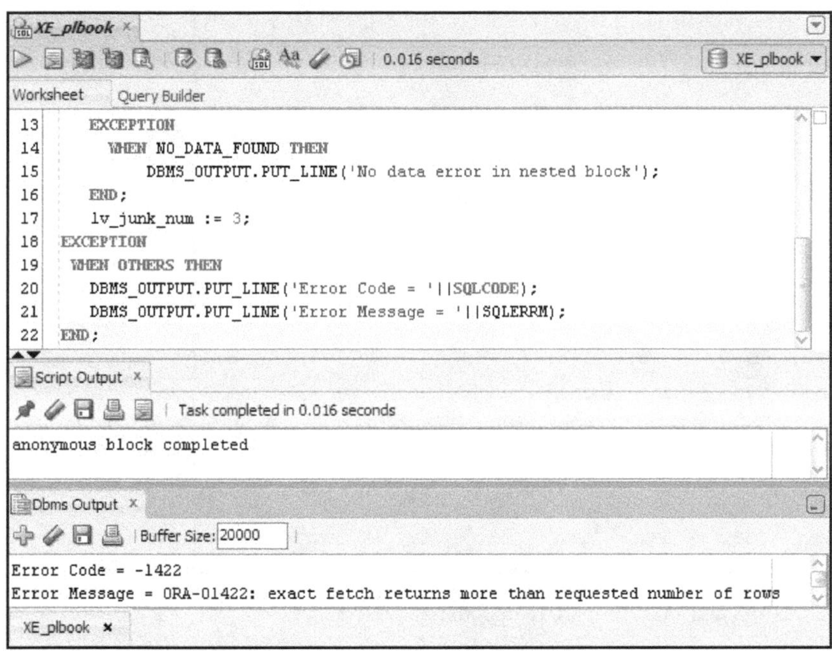

FIGURE 4-29 A nested block exception propagating to the enclosing block

Notice that the message verifies that the `WHEN OTHERS` handler in the enclosing block executed. The `SELECT` statement in the nested block retrieves more than one row, so an error is raised. The processing first moves to the nested block's EXCEPTION section; however, this section has no `TOO_MANY_ROWS` handler. Next, processing moves to the enclosing block's EXCEPTION section and processes the `WHEN OTHERS` handler.

If the error is raised in the nested block's DECLARE section, the exception is immediately propagated to the enclosing block. In this case, the nested block's EXCEPTION section isn't referenced. Figure 4-30 shows a nested block with this exception propagation.

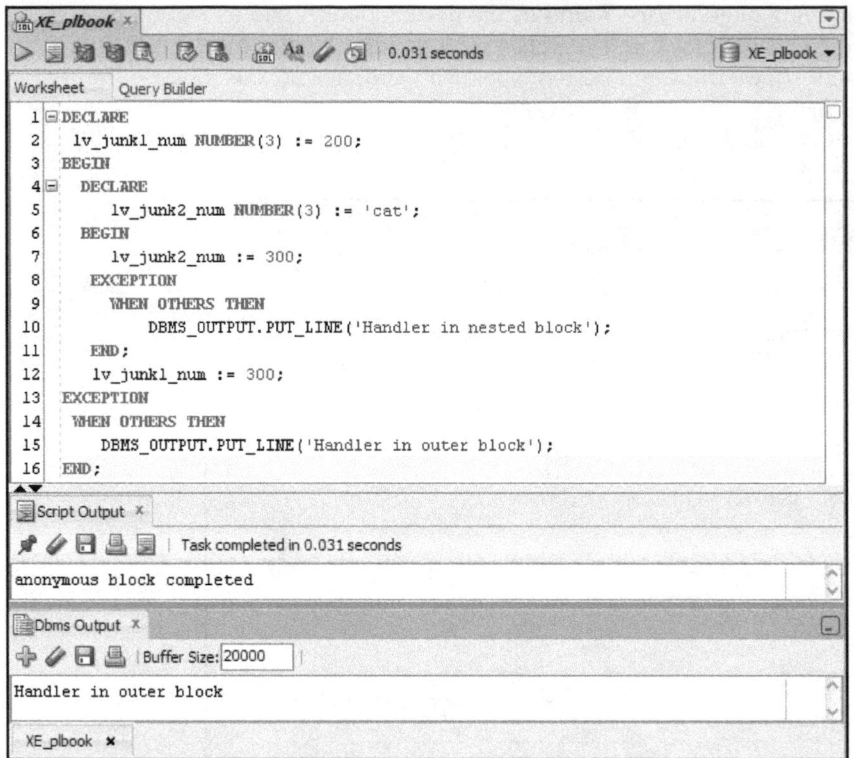

FIGURE 4-30 A DECLARE section error propagates immediately

The `lv_junk2_num` variable is declared in the nested block as a number, yet the code attempts to initialize it with a character string, which raises an error. Because the error occurs in the DECLARE section, the process moves immediately to the enclosing block's EXCEPTION section instead of the nested block's EXCEPTION section. The output confirms this process flow. Notice that both EXCEPTION sections include a `WHEN OTHERS` handler that processes any errors.

An error can also occur in the EXCEPTION section, which can be an Oracle error raised automatically or a user-defined error raised explicitly. In this case, the exception propagates to the enclosing block when the error occurs. Figure 4-31 shows a nested block with an error in the executable section and an error in the matching exception handler. The `WHEN OTHERS` exception handler in the enclosing block is now executed.

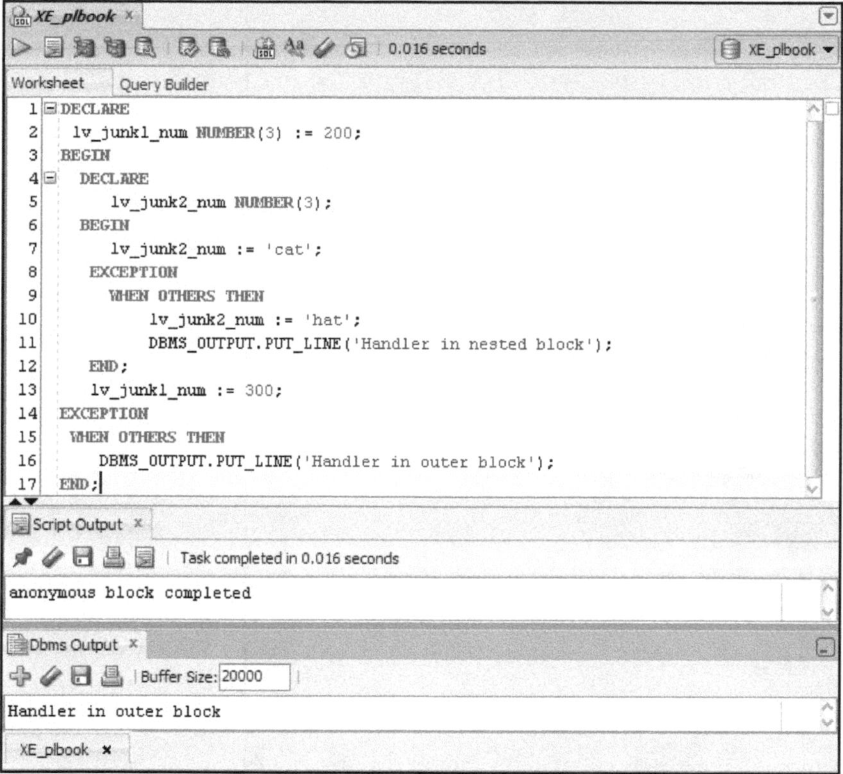

FIGURE 4-31 Error in an exception handler

In this example, the first error is raised in the nested block's BEGIN section by an attempt to assign a character value to a numeric variable. Processing then moves to the nested block's EXCEPTION section and runs the `WHEN OTHERS` handler. The first statement in the handler raises a second error with another attempt to assign character data to a numeric variable. Processing then moves to the enclosing block's EXCEPTION section, which displays the resulting message.

However, this propagation doesn't prevent statements in the first exception handler from executing. Look at the same example with the exception handler modified to contain a `DBMS_OUTPUT` statement before the error is raised in the exception handler. Figure 4-32 shows that lines from exception handlers in both the nested and enclosing blocks are processed.

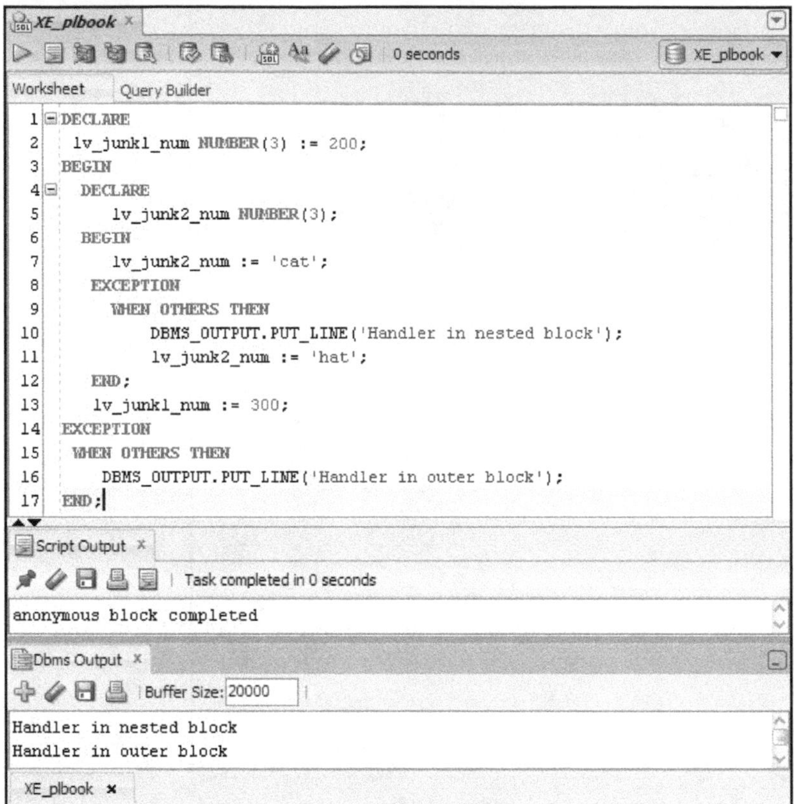

FIGURE 4-32 Timing of error propagation

In this case, the first statement in the nested block's `WHEN OTHERS` handler is a `DBMS_OUTPUT` that processes and displays the first message. However, the second statement in this handler raises an error so that the process moves to the enclosing block's EXCEPTION section and processes the `WHEN OTHERS` handler. At this stage, you might have trouble seeing the need to nest blocks, but it will become clearer in the next several chapters as you begin developing stored program units.

COMMENTING CODE

A good programming practice is including comments in your code to document what's happening in a program. Many developers also include comments with background information, such as the author, creation date, and date of the most recent change. Comment text isn't executed; it's included only for the benefit of developers working with the code.

In PL/SQL, you can include both single-line and multiline comments. A double hyphen (`--`) is used for single-line comments. Everything after the `--` is ignored, which means you can add a comment right after code on the same line or make an entire line a comment. Multiline comments start with the characters `/*` and end with `*/`. Comments for SQL statements embedded in a block are typically placed before the SQL statements, not inside the SQL statements. Placing comments in an SQL statement can make it hard to read. The following code shows using both types of comments in a block:

```
DECLARE
  ex_prod_update EXCEPTION;   --For UPDATE of no rows exception
BEGIN
 /* This block is used to update product descriptions
    Constructed to support the Prod_desc.frm app page
      Exception raised if no rows are updated */
  UPDATE bb_product
    SET description = 'Mill grinder with 5 grind settings!'
    WHERE idProduct = 30;
  --Check whether any rows were updated
    IF SQL%NOTFOUND THEN
      RAISE ex_prod_update;
    END IF;
EXCEPTION
  WHEN ex_prod_update THEN
    DBMS_OUTPUT.PUT_LINE('Invalid product ID entered');
END;
```

CHALLENGE 4-5

Add comments to the code in the `curloop04.sql` file that identify the processing steps.

Chapter Summary

- A cursor represents a work area or section of memory where an SQL statement is processed in the Oracle server.
- Implicit cursors are declared automatically for all DML and `SELECT` statements issued in a PL/SQL block.
- Explicit cursors are declared with the declaration containing a `SELECT` statement. Four processing steps are used: `DECLARE`, `OPEN`, `FETCH`, and `CLOSE`.
- `CURSOR FOR` loops simplify processing a set of rows from the database.
- If an `UPDATE` action is necessary, explicit cursors offer the `FOR UPDATE` and `WHERE CURRENT OF` clauses to assist.
- Parameters can make cursors more dynamic. Parameters are values passed to the cursor when it's opened and are used in the cursor's `SELECT` statement to determine what data the cursor contains.
- A cursor variable is a pointer to a work area where a query can be processed and is declared with the `REF CURSOR` clause.
- The bulk-processing features `BULK COLLECT` and `FORALL` can improve performance when querying or performing data manipulation on a large number of rows.
- Errors occurring in the PL/SQL block should be addressed with exception handlers. When handling an Oracle error, you can use predefined and undefined exceptions.
- Predefined exceptions in Oracle are names already declared in the system for common errors, such as `NO_ROWS_FOUND`, which occurs when a `SELECT` statement returns no rows.
- An exception must be declared for undefined Oracle errors. The `PRAGMA EXCEPTION_INIT` statement is used to associate an Oracle error number with a handler.
- A user-defined error is created when you want to raise an exception to enforce a business rule, even though the code doesn't raise an Oracle error. In this case, you must specify when the error occurs with the `RAISE` command.
- You can use the `WHEN OTHERS` handler with the `SQLCODE` and `SQLERRM` functions when you want to trap an error and allow the application to continue but also document the error number to determine whether any code revisions are warranted.
- In nested blocks, errors search for an exception handler in the local block; if it's not found, they propagate to the enclosing block.
- Commenting code helps developers document what's happening in a program. Comment text isn't executed; it's included only for the benefit of developers working with the code.

Review Questions

1. Which of the following do you use to check the number of rows affected by an `UPDATE` statement?
    a. `SQL%FOUND`
    b. `SQL%NOTFOUND`
    c. `SQL%COUNT`
    d. `SQL%ROWCOUNT`

2. The FOR UPDATE clause in a cursor declaration instructs the system to do which of the following?
   a. execute the cursor
   b. issue an SQL UPDATE statement
   c. keep track of the physical database row related to each cursor row
   d. allow transaction control statements
3. Which symbol is used to indicate a single-line comment in PL/SQL code?
4. The PRAGMA EXCEPTION_INIT statement performs what task?
   a. It associates an Oracle error number with an exception name.
   b. It associates a user-defined error with an exception name.
   c. It associates a predefined exception name with an Oracle error.
   d. It raises an error in a block's executable section.
5. Which type of exception must use a RAISE command?
6. What happens to program execution first when an error is raised in the executable section?
   a. It moves to the EXCEPTION section of that block.
   b. It moves to the enclosing block's EXCEPTION section.
   c. It propagates to the application environment.
   d. none of the above
7. Which characters indicate the start and end of a multiline comment in PL/SQL code?
8. Which of the following should be used to manage a query that returns multiple rows?
   a. implicit cursor
   b. explicit cursor
   c. record variable
   d. table variable
9. Which of the following is used to hold each row processed from a cursor?
   a. scalar variable
   b. record variable
   c. table variable
   d. none of the above
10. What cursor action retrieves the next row from a cursor?
    a. FETCH
    b. GET
    c. OPEN
    d. READ
11. Describe the differences between implicit and explicit cursors.
12. Describe how a CURSOR FOR loop makes cursor processing easier.
13. Explain the purpose of exception handlers.

14. Explain how to incorporate a user-defined exception in a block.
15. Describe the two types of exception handlers for managing Oracle errors.

Advanced Review Questions

1. In a CURSOR FOR loop, which command is used to open the cursor?
    a. FETCH
    b. OPEN
    c. FOR loop
    d. The cursor is opened automatically by a CURSOR FOR loop.
2. Which of the following is *not* true for CURSOR FOR loops?
    a. A record variable must be declared to hold a cursor row.
    b. Fetching rows is handled automatically by the loop.
    c. Opening the cursor is handled automatically by the loop.
    d. No exit condition is needed to end the looping action.
3. An Oracle PRAGMA statement does which of the following?
    a. associates an Oracle error with an exception name
    b. provides additional instructions to be used when the code runs
    c. forces the code to not compile until runtime
    d. creates Oracle predefined exceptions
4. Review the following block. What type of exception handler is ex_limit_hit?

```
DECLARE
  lv_amt_num NUMBER(7,2);
  ex_limit_hit EXCEPTION;
BEGIN
  SELECT amount
    INTO lv_amt_num
    FROM customer
    WHERE cust_no = :g_cust;
  IF lv_amt_num > 1000 THEN
    RAISE ex_limit_hit;
  END IF;
EXCEPTION
  WHEN ex_limit_hit THEN
    DBMS_OUTPUT.PUT_LINE('Limit Exceeded!');
END;
```

    a. predefined Oracle
    b. undefined Oracle
    c. user-defined
    d. PRAGMA

5. Which of the following is a valid predefined exception in Oracle?
   a. `DATA_NOT_FOUND`
   b. `TOO_MANY_ROWS`
   c. `NO_CASE_FOUND`
   d. `ZERO_DIVISION`

Hands-On Assignments Part I

Assignment 4-1: Using an Explicit Cursor

In the Brewbean's application, a customer can ask to check whether all items in his or her basket are in stock. In this assignment, you create a block that uses an explicit cursor to retrieve all items in the basket and determine whether all items are in stock by comparing the item quantity with the product stock amount. If all items are in stock, display the message "All items in stock!" onscreen. If not, display the message "All items NOT in stock!" onscreen. The basket number is provided with an initialized variable. Follow these steps:

1. In SQL Developer, open the **`assignment04-01.sql`** file in the Chapter04 folder.
2. Run the block. Notice that both a cursor and a record variable are created in the DECLARE section. The cursor must be manipulated with explicit actions of `OPEN`, `FETCH`, and `CLOSE`. A variable named `lv_flag_txt` is used to store the status of the stock check. The results should look like Figure 4-33.

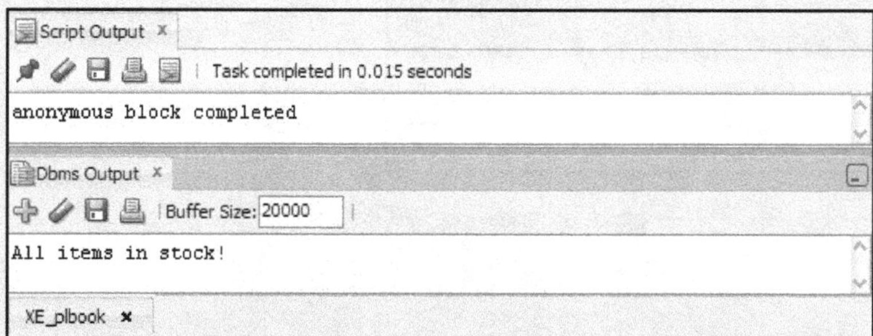

FIGURE 4-33 Using an explicit cursor to verify items in stock

Assignment 4-2: Using a `CURSOR FOR` Loop

Brewbean's wants to send a promotion via e-mail to shoppers. A shopper who has purchased more than $50 at the site receives a $5 coupon for his or her next purchase over $25. A shopper who has spent more than $100 receives a free shipping coupon.

The BB_SHOPPER table contains a column named PROMO for storing promotion codes. Follow the steps to create a block with a `CURSOR FOR` loop to check the total spent by each shopper and update the PROMO column in the BB_SHOPPER table accordingly. The cursor's `SELECT` statement contains a subquery in the `FROM` clause to retrieve the shopper totals because a cursor using a GROUP BY statement can't use the FOR UPDATE clause. Its results are summarized data rather than separate rows from the database.

1. In SQL Developer, open the **assignment04-02.sql** file in the Chapter04 folder.
2. Run the block. Notice the subquery in the SELECT statement. Also, because an UPDATE is performed, the FOR UPDATE and WHERE CURRENT OF clauses are used.
3. Run a query, as shown in Figure 4-34, to check the results.

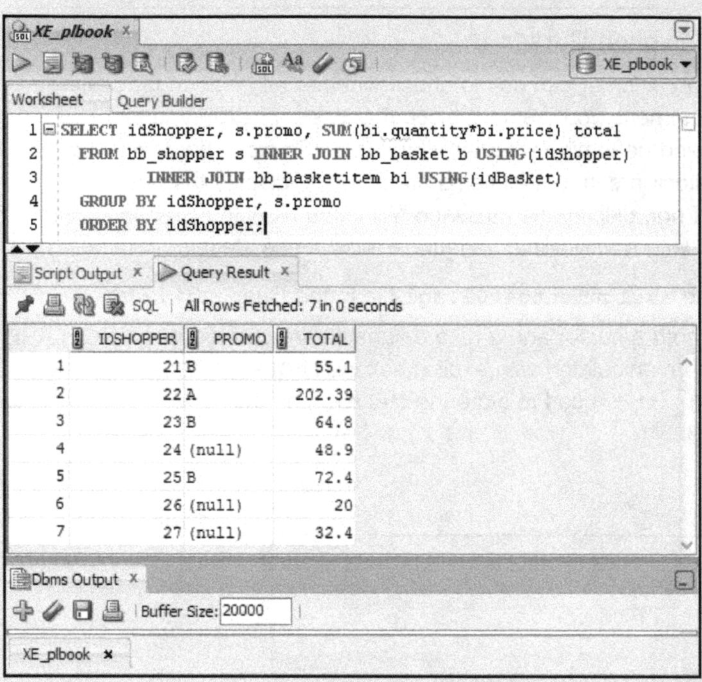

FIGURE 4-34 Querying the BB_SHOPPER table to check the PROMO column

Assignment 4-3: Using Implicit Cursors

The BB_SHOPPER table in the Brewbean's database contains a column named PROMO that specifies promotions to send to shoppers. This column needs to be cleared after the promotion has been sent. First, open the **assignment04-03.txt** file in the Chapter04 folder in a text editor (such as Notepad). Run the UPDATE and COMMIT statements at the top of this file (not the anonymous block at the end). Modify the anonymous block so that it displays the number of rows updated onscreen. Run the block.

Assignment 4-4: Using Exception Handling

In this assignment, you test a block containing a CASE statement for errors, and then add an exception handler for a predefined exception:

1. In Notepad, open the **assignment04-04.sql** file in the Chapter04 folder. Review the block, which contains a CASE statement and no exception handlers.
2. Copy and paste the block into SQL Developer, and run the block. Your results should look like Figure 4-35. An error is raised because the state of NJ isn't included in the CASE statement; recall that a CASE statement must find a matching case.

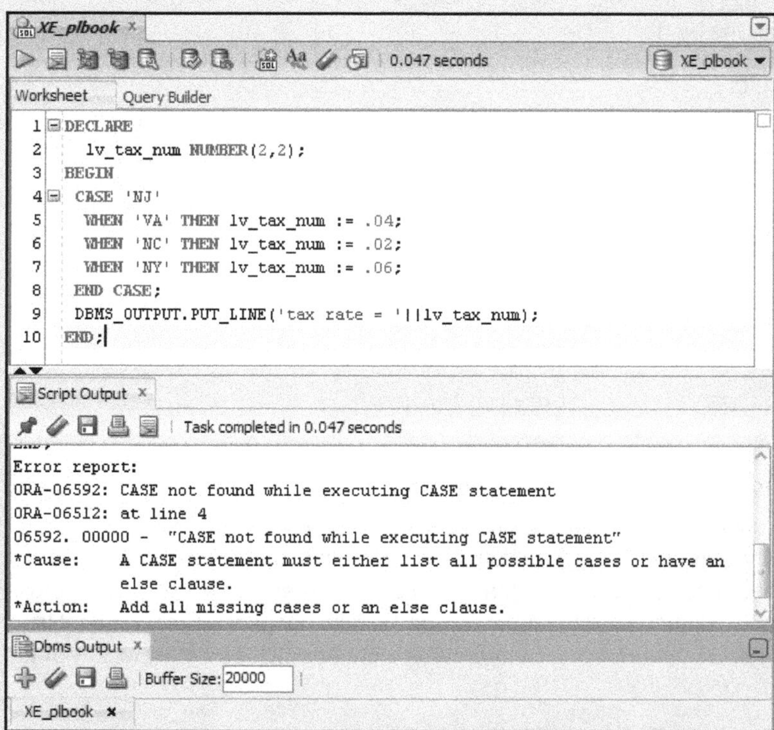

FIGURE 4-35 Raising an error with a CASE statement

3. To correct this problem, add a predefined EXCEPTION handler that addresses this error and displays "No tax" onscreen.
4. Run the block again. Your results should look like Figure 4-36. Now the error is handled in the block's EXCEPTION section.

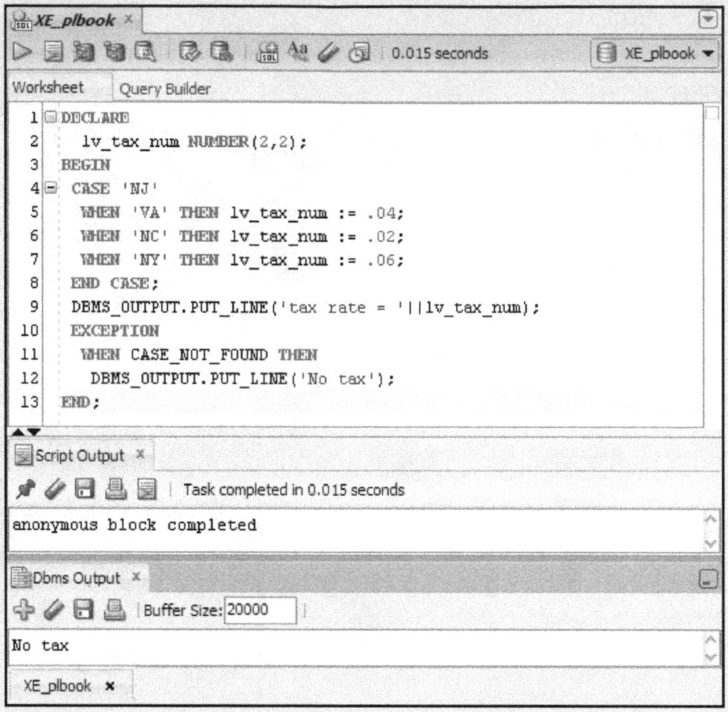

XE_plbook

0.015 seconds

Worksheet Query Builder

```
DECLARE
  lv_tax_num NUMBER(2,2);
BEGIN
 CASE 'NJ'
  WHEN 'VA' THEN lv_tax_num := .04;
  WHEN 'NC' THEN lv_tax_num := .02;
  WHEN 'NY' THEN lv_tax_num := .06;
 END CASE;
 DBMS_OUTPUT.PUT_LINE('tax rate = '||lv_tax_num);
 EXCEPTION
  WHEN CASE_NOT_FOUND THEN
   DBMS_OUTPUT.PUT_LINE('No tax');
END;
```

Script Output

Task completed in 0.015 seconds

```
anonymous block completed
```

Dbms Output

Buffer Size: 20000

```
No tax
```

XE_plbook

FIGURE 4-36 Using the `CASE_NOT_FOUND` exception handler

Assignment 4-5: Handling Predefined Exceptions

A block of code has been created to retrieve basic customer information (see the **`assignment04-05.sql`** file in the Chapter04 folder). The application page was modified so that an employee can enter a customer number that could cause an error. An exception handler needs to be added to the block that displays the message "Invalid shopper ID" onscreen. Use an initialized variable named `lv_shopper_num` to provide a shopper ID. Test the block with the shopper ID 99.

Assignment 4-6: Handling Exceptions with Undefined Errors

Brewbean's wants to add a check constraint on the QUANTITY column of the BB_BASKETITEM table. If a shopper enters a quantity value greater than 20 for an item, Brewbean's wants to display the message "Check Quantity" onscreen. Using a text editor, open the **`assignment04-06.txt`** file in the Chapter04 folder. The first statement, `ALTER TABLE`, must be executed to add the check constraint. The next item is a PL/SQL block containing an `INSERT` action that tests this check constraint. Add code to this block to trap the check constraint violation and display the message.

Assignment 4-7: Handling Exceptions with User-Defined Errors

Sometimes Brewbean's customers mistakenly leave an item out of a basket that's already been checked out, so they create a new basket containing the missing items. However, they request that the baskets be combined so that they aren't charged extra shipping. An application page has been developed that enables employees to change the basket ID of items in the BB_BASKETITEM table to another existing basket's ID to combine the baskets. A block has been constructed to support this page (see the **assignment04-07.sql** file in the Chapter04 folder). However, an exception handler needs to be added to trap the situation of an invalid basket ID being entered for the original basket. In this case, the `UPDATE` affects no rows but doesn't raise an Oracle error. The handler should display the message "Invalid original basket ID" onscreen. Use an initialized variable named `lv_old_num` with a value of 30 and another named `lv_new_num` with a value of 4 to provide values to the block. First, verify that no item rows with the basket ID 30 exist in the BB_BASKETITEM table.

Assignment 4-8: Processing and Updating a Group of Rows

To help track employee information, a new EMPLOYEE table was added to the Brewbean's database. Review the data in this table. A PL/SQL block is needed to calculate annual raises and update employee salary amounts in the table. Create a block that addresses all the requirements in the following list. All salaries in the EMPLOYEE table are recorded as monthly amounts. *Tip*: Display the calculated salaries for verification before including the update action.

- Calculate 6% annual raises for all employees except the president.
- If a 6% raise totals more than $2,000, cap the raise at $2,000.
- Update the salary for each employee in the table.
- For each employee number, display the current annual salary, raise, and proposed new annual salary.
- Finally, following the details for each employee, show the total cost of all employees' salary increases for Brewbean's.

Hands-On Assignments Part II

Assignment 4-9: Using an Explicit Cursor

Create a block to retrieve and display pledge and payment information for a specific donor. For each pledge payment from the donor, display the pledge ID, pledge amount, number of monthly payments, payment date, and payment amount. The list should be sorted by pledge ID and then by payment date. For the first payment made for each pledge, display "first payment" on that output row.

Assignment 4-10: Using a Different Form of Explicit Cursors

Redo Assignment 4-9, but use a different cursor form to perform the same task.

Assignment 4-11: Adding Cursor Flexibility

An administration page in the DoGood Donor application allows employees to enter multiple combinations of donor type and pledge amount to determine data to retrieve. Create a block with a single cursor that allows retrieving data and handling multiple combinations of donor type and pledge amount as input. The donor name and pledge amount should be retrieved and displayed for each pledge that matches the donor type and is greater than the pledge amount indicated. Use a collection to provide the input data. Test the block using the following input data. Keep in mind that these inputs should be processed with one execution of the block. The donor type code I represents Individual, and B represents Business.

```
Donor Type  <  Pledge Amount
    I              250
    B              500
```


Assignment 4-12: Using a Cursor Variable

Create a block with a single cursor that can perform a different query of pledge payment data based on user input. Input provided to the block includes a donor ID and an indicator value of D or S. The D represents details and indicates that each payment on all pledges the donor has made should be displayed. The S indicates displaying summary data of the pledge payment total for each pledge the donor has made.

Assignment 4-13: Exception Handling

The DoGood Donor application contains a page that allows administrators to change the ID assigned to a donor in the DD_DONOR table. Create a PL/SQL block to handle this task. Include exception-handling code to address an error raised by attempting to enter a duplicate donor ID. If this error occurs, display the message "This ID is already assigned." Test the code by changing donor ID **305**. (Don't include a `COMMIT` statement; roll back any DML actions used.)

Case Projects

Case 4-1: Using Exception Handlers in the Brewbean's Application

A new part-time programming employee has been reviewing some PL/SQL code you developed. The following two blocks contain a variety of exception handlers. Explain the different types for the new employee.

Block 1:

```
DECLARE
  ex_prod_update EXCEPTION;
BEGIN
  UPDATE bb_product
    SET description = 'Mill grinder with 5 grind settings!'
    WHERE idProduct = 30;
  IF SQL%NOTFOUND THEN
    RAISE ex_prod_update;
  END IF;
EXCEPTION
  WHEN ex_prod_update THEN
    DBMS_OUTPUT.PUT_LINE('Invalid product ID entered');
END;
```

Block 2:

```
DECLARE
  TYPE type_basket IS RECORD
    (basket bb_basket.idBasket%TYPE,
    created bb_basket.dtcreated%TYPE,
```

```
      qty bb_basket.quantity%TYPE,
      sub bb_basket.subtotal%TYPE);
   rec_basket type_basket;
   lv_days_num NUMBER(3);
   lv_shopper_num NUMBER(3) := 26;
BEGIN
   SELECT idBasket, dtcreated, quantity, subtotal
      INTO rec_basket
      FROM bb_basket
      WHERE idShopper = lv_shopper_num
         AND orderplaced = 0;
    lv_days_num := SYSDATE - rec_basket.created;
EXCEPTION
   WHEN NO_DATA_FOUND THEN
      DBMS_OUTPUT.PUT_LINE('You have no saved baskets!');
   WHEN OTHERS THEN
      DBMS_OUTPUT.PUT_LINE('A problem has occurred.');
      DBMS_OUTPUT.PUT_LINE('Tech Support will be notified and
will contact you via e-mail.');
END;
```

Case 4-2: Working with More Movie Rentals

Because business is growing and the movie stock is increasing at More Movie Rentals, the manager wants to do more inventory evaluations. One item of interest is any movie with a total stock value of $75 or more. The manager wants to focus on the revenue these movies are generating to make sure the stock level is warranted. To make these stock queries more efficient, the application team decides to add a column named STK_FLAG to the MM_MOVIE table that stores an asterisk (*) if the stock value is $75 or more. Otherwise, the value should be `NULL`. Add the column and create an anonymous block containing a `CURSOR FOR` loop to perform this task. The company plans to run this program monthly to update the STK_FLAG column before the inventory evaluation.

CHAPTER 5

PROCEDURES

LEARNING OBJECTIVES

After completing this chapter, you should be able to understand:

- Named program units
- Creating a procedure
- Calling procedures from another procedure
- Using the `DESCRIBE` command with procedures
- Debugging procedures with `DBMS_OUTPUT`
- Using subprograms
- The scope of variables, exception handling, and transaction control
- Using `RAISE_APPLICATION_ERROR` for error handling
- Removing procedures

INTRODUCTION

Naming a program unit or PL/SQL block makes it possible to store and reuse code, which saves programmers' time and computer resources. You can use SQL Developer to create and test these named code blocks. In this chapter, you see how to use them in the Brewbean's application and how to create and test them for other application needs.

THE CURRENT CHALLENGE IN THE BREWBEAN'S APPLICATION

The Brewbean's company owner wants to have a product catalog and ordering application. The application designer has already developed some screen layouts to support the coffee-ordering process, as shown in Figures 5-1 and 5-2.

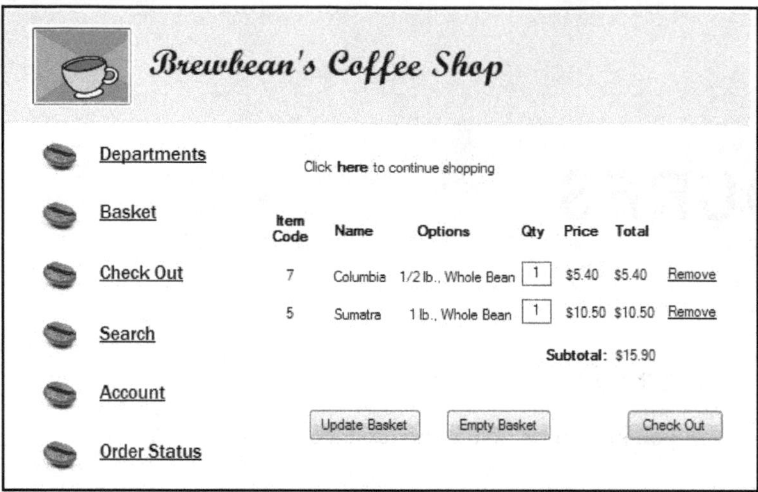

FIGURE 5-1 Order application page displaying basket items

Figure 5-1 is the shopping basket, which shows all the items a shopper has selected so far. When a shopper is ready to complete the order, the Check Out button is used. Checking out calls the page in Figure 5-2, which displays the order total summary, including shipping and tax, and allows the shopper to enter credit card information.

FIGURE 5-2 Order application page displaying the order total summary

You need to create PL/SQL blocks that provide the programming logic to support the tasks needed in this application page, such as calculating an order's shipping cost, which Brewbean's bases on the quantity of items ordered. These PL/SQL blocks need to be saved somewhere on the system so that they're always available and should be flexible enough to process any basket of items. For example, there might be two customers on the Web site ordering coffee, and one orders 10 items while the other orders 3 items. The shipping cost calculation must factor the quantity in each case and determine the correct shipping cost.

Rebuilding the Database

To rebuild the Brewbean's database, follow these steps:

1. Make sure you have the `c5_BBcreate.sql` file in the Chapter05 folder. This file contains the script for creating the database.
2. Start SQL Developer and connect to the Oracle database.
3. Click **File**, **Open** from the menu.
4. Click the **`c5_BBcreate.sql`** file. The code in this script is displayed in the Edit pane. Scroll through the SQL statements; they should look familiar.
5. Run the script by clicking the **Run Script** button on the Edit pane toolbar. If necessary, click **OK** in the Select Connection dialog box.
6. Scroll through the Script Output pane at the bottom to review the results of the statements.
7. In the Connections pane on the left, expand the **Tables** node to view the tables that were created. While this node is selected, click the **Refresh** button at the top of the Connections pane to update the list of tables.

INTRODUCTION TO NAMED PROGRAM UNITS

So far, you have created anonymous PL/SQL blocks and run the code in SQL Developer. The term "anonymous blocks" is used because the code isn't stored to be reused; as far as the Oracle server is concerned, the block no longer exists after it has run. Every time you run an anonymous block, it's compiled and then run.

However, often you want to save a PL/SQL block so that it can be reused, which means a name needs to be assigned so that the system can find the block when you refer to it—that is, call it by name. Therefore, you name your PL/SQL blocks so that they can be saved on the Oracle server and referenced when needed, just as you would with other database objects, such as tables and sequences.

As mentioned in Chapter 1, a PL/SQL block that's been named so that it can be saved is known as a "named program unit" or **subprogram**. The term "program unit" is used for a block of code created to perform a specific task that might be needed in a number of applications. This book focuses mainly on stored program units, which are saved in the database. Anyone connected to the database (and with the required rights) can use or call a stored program unit, so stored program units can be shared and used by many applications.

As an example of using stored program units, assume you have stored customer names in two columns called LAST and FIRST in the CUSTOMER table. If you have several application pages that display the customer name in the form "last name, first name," you'd have to program a concatenation operation for every page displaying customer names. Instead, you can create a stored program unit that performs this task and reuse it whenever it's needed. Sharing or reusing code in this way helps improve programming efficiency.

What happens when application users decide that names should be displayed in a different way, such as "first name, last name," on all application pages? The programmer needs to change only one stored program unit instead of changing the code on each application page using customer names. This method is a great time-saver.

As an application programmer, keep in mind that creating easy-to-maintain code is essential. PL/SQL program units are critical in Oracle 11g application development as a way to promote modularization and reusability of application code. In the shipping cost task you're tackling, for example, you need a program unit that's flexible enough to calculate the shipping cost for any order.

Types of Named Program Units

Named PL/SQL program units can be constructed in a variety of ways, based on where the code is stored, what type of task it performs, and how it's invoked (called). Table 5-1 describes these program unit types. Regardless of the type, all these program units consist of PL/SQL blocks. Program units can be stored as objects in a database or in an application library on the server. Typically, any PL/SQL block that might be used by multiple applications and involves heavy database activity can be saved to improve efficiency and allow sharing.

NOTE

Procedures and functions are quite similar in that they can accept input values and return values. However, a procedure is used to perform one or more tasks, can return no values or many values, and can be used only in PL/SQL statements. On the other hand, a function contains a `RETURN` clause and is used to manipulate data and return a single value. Functions you construct are similar to the Oracle-supplied functions, such as `ROUND`, that you have already used.

TABLE 5-1 Named Program Unit Types

Program Unit Type	Description
Stored procedure	Performs a task, such as calculating shipping costs, and can receive and input values as well as return values to the calling program. It's called explicitly from a program and is stored in the Oracle database.
Application procedure	Same as a stored procedure except it's saved in an Oracle application or library on the client side.
Package	Groups related procedures and functions. It's called from a program by name and is stored on the server side.
Database trigger	Performs a task automatically when a DML action occurs on the table it's associated with and is stored in the Oracle database.
Application trigger	Performs a task automatically when a particular event occurs, such as the user clicking a button; it's stored in an Oracle application.

Making Procedures Reusable: Parameters

When creating stored procedures, you should strive to make them flexible so that they can be reused. Keep in mind that these procedures provide an application's programming logic, and each user can enter different values to process in the application.

To make program units flexible, you use **parameters**, which are mechanisms for sending values in and out of a program unit. Procedures can accept and return no, one, or many parameters. So when formatting customer names for Brewbean's, a procedure could be written that accepts a customer number as a parameter, and the `SELECT` statement in the procedure could use this parameter to form the `WHERE` clause and return the customer name in the concatenated "last name, first name" format. Then every time this procedure runs, it could return the name of a different customer; however, it always performs the same task of retrieving a customer name based on customer number and concatenating the customer's first and last names.

A parameter must be assigned one of three modes, described in Table 5-2. The **mode** indicates which way the value supplied for the parameter flows: into the procedure, out of the procedure, or both. When creating a procedure, you list each parameter along with a mode and data type.

TABLE 5-2 Parameter Mode Types

Mode	Description
`IN`	Passes a value from the application environment to the procedure. This value is considered a constant because it can't be changed in the procedure. This mode is the default if no mode is indicated.
`OUT`	Passes a value from the procedure to the application environment. If values are calculated or retrieved from the database in the procedure, `OUT` parameters are used to return these values to the calling environment.
`IN OUT`	Allows passing a value in and out with the same parameter. The value sent out can be different from the value sent in.

Keep in mind that although using parameters in a procedure is typical, it isn't required. For example, you might create a procedure that inserts logon information, such as user ID and current date, that can be referenced from system variables, in a table that doesn't require any input values from the application or return any values. In this example, no parameters are needed in the procedure.

The `CREATE PROCEDURE` Statement

First, take a look at the syntax of the `CREATE PROCEDURE` command, shown in Figure 5-3.

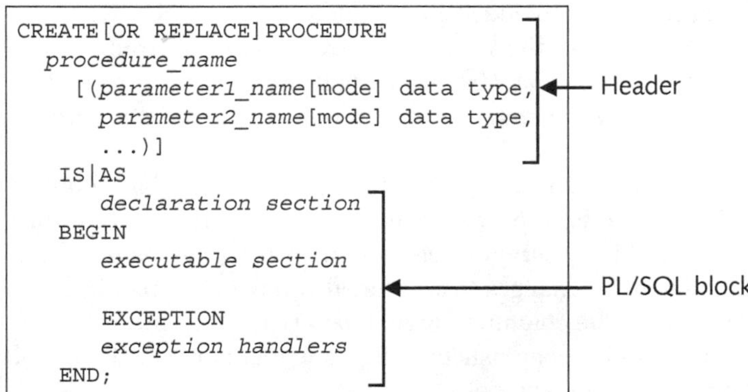

CREATE [OR REPLACE] PROCEDURE
procedure_name
[(parameter1_name [mode] data type,
parameter2_name [mode] data type,
...)]
IS|AS
declaration section
BEGIN
executable section
EXCEPTION
exception handlers
END;
Header
PL/SQL block

FIGURE 5-3 Syntax of the `CREATE PROCEDURE` command

The top portion is called the header section. It indicates what type of program unit is being created, an object name, parameter information, and the keyword `IS` or `AS` to indicate that a PL/SQL block follows. Below this keyword, the PL/SQL block looks the same as the anonymous blocks you have created, except that the `DECLARE` keyword is no longer needed. Why? The header section now marks the beginning of the PL/SQL block. You must supply three pieces of information (discussed in the following sections) for each parameter in the header: name, mode, and data type.

The Name

Programmers should choose a name that's useful in identifying what type of data the parameter represents. It must also conform to Oracle 11g naming standards, such as those that apply to table column names. Recall that names must begin with an alphabetic character and can contain up to 30 characters.

A naming convention strategy is an important survival tool to have in any programming shop. Some examples of naming conventions include using the prefix `p_` for a parameter name or the suffix `_num` in a numeric variable name. In both cases, the name tells you something about it, such as that it's a parameter or holds numeric data. When you're coding or reviewing existing code to make changes, clear naming conventions make the task much easier.

The Mode

Values are passed between program units and the application environment or user screens via parameters. You have three choices for parameter mode: `IN`, `OUT`, and `IN OUT`. If no mode is indicated, the default value `IN` is applied. However, specifying the mode is the preferred style to make reading code easier. If an `IN` or `IN OUT` parameter is used, the `IN` denotes that when the procedure is invoked or run, it expects a value to be provided for the parameter. If no value is provided, an error occurs. If an `OUT` or `IN OUT` parameter is used, the `OUT` means a variable must be created in the calling environment that can hold the value the procedure returns for this parameter.

The Data Type

The last required item for each parameter is an SQL data type, such as `CHAR`, `NUMBER`, or `DATE`. No size or precision information is included in parameters' data types. When a procedure is invoked, the size properties of the values supplied to pass to parameters control the parameters' size and precision. Values from the application that are passed to parameters are called **actual parameters**; parameters in a procedure declaration are called **formal parameters**.

The `%TYPE` and `%ROWTYPE` attributes can be used to provide a data type based on a table column, which is especially suitable for parameters holding data retrieved from the database. Using these attributes in variable declarations can minimize program maintenance. If a table column's data type is modified, no changes to associated variables are required because the `%TYPE` attribute always uses the column's current data type. A default value assignment on parameters is also legal and accomplished in the same manner as with PL/SQL variables—using the `DEFAULT` keyword or `:=` symbol.

The following code is a procedure's header section containing two parameter declarations. This procedure is intended to sum the total for all items in a basket with the basket number supplied as input with the `p_basket` parameter. The `p_total` parameter uses both the %TYPE and default value options and is used to return a total value:

```
CREATE OR REPLACE PROCEDURE total_calc_sp
  (p_basket IN bb_basket.idbasket%TYPE,
   p_total OUT bb_basket.total%TYPE := 0)
  IS
  -- PL/SQL block coded here --
```


CREATING A PROCEDURE

The Brewbean's application needs a procedure to calculate an order's shipping cost, so jump into creating your first procedure with parameters to meet this processing need. The company currently calculates shipping based on the number of items in an order. Figure 5-4 shows the data in the SHIPPING table that's in the company database.

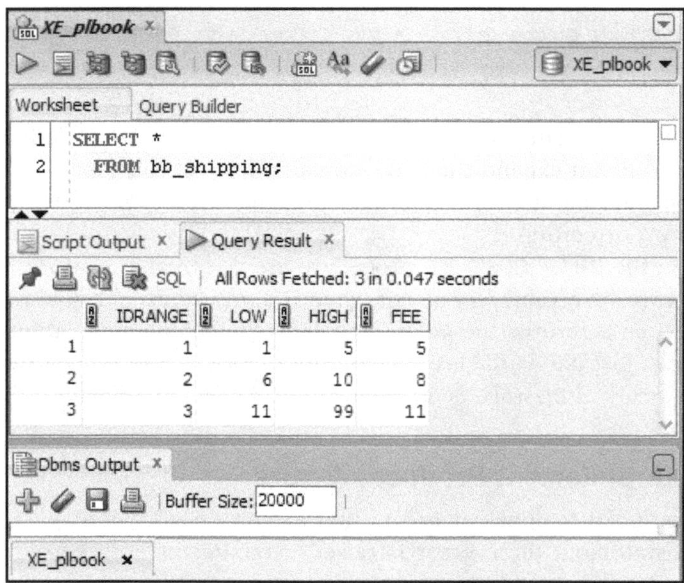

FIGURE 5-4 Data listing for the SHIPPING table

Notice that the SHIPPING table lists quantity ranges for determining shipping costs. For example, if a total of seven items is being ordered, the shipping cost is $8.00 because the quantity falls between the lower bound of 6 and the upper bound of 10. Assume the quantity is an amount passed to the procedure.

Figure 5-5 shows the CREATE statement to build the SHIP_COST_SP procedure for handling the shipping cost task. The SQL Developer pane for building program units is a bit different from the Worksheet pane you've been using; you examine it in more detail shortly when you go through the steps to create this procedure.

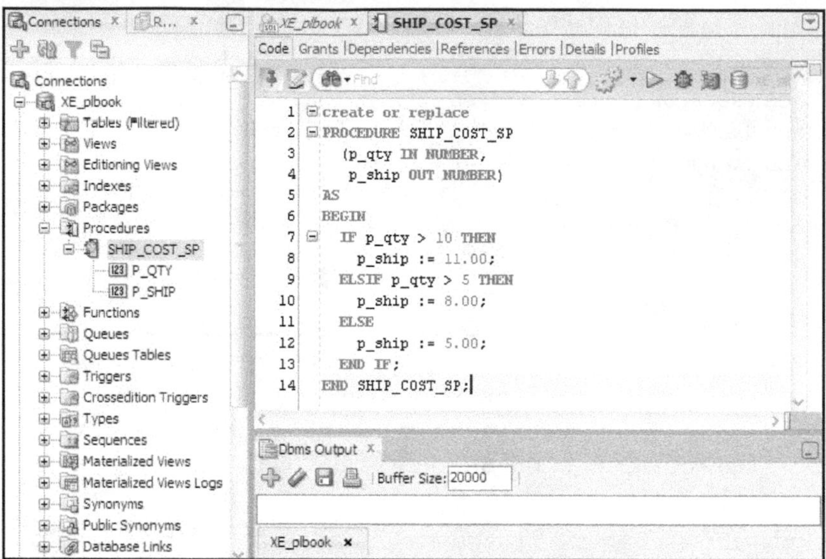

FIGURE 5-5 Creating the `SHIP_COST_SP` procedure

Notice in the Connections pane in Figure 5-5 that the `SHIP_COST_SP` program unit has been saved in the database. You can expand the Procedures node to check the parameter list. Clicking the procedure name in the Connections pane displays its code in a new pane on the right for review or editing.

The two parameters listed in the `SHIP_COST_SP` procedure are `p_qty` and `p_ship`. `p_qty` uses the `IN` mode, so it expects a value to be sent when the procedure is called or run. `p_ship` uses the `OUT` mode, so it returns the shipping cost to the calling application environment. Parameters are used just like variables declared in a block. If the procedure compiles and runs without any errors, a message is displayed stating that it compiled.

When a `CREATE PROCEDURE` Statement Produces Errors

Before creating a procedure, you need to consider errors that are produced when running a `CREATE PROCEDURE` statement. If an error is raised, compiler messages are displayed. Follow these steps to modify a procedure so that you can see how to view error details:

1. In SQL Developer, click **File**, **New** from the menu. In the Create a new dialog box, click **Procedure**, and then click **OK**.
2. Select your current connection.
3. In the Create PL/SQL Procedure dialog box, enter the name **`SHIP_COST_SP`** (see Figure 5-6). Other items, such as parameters, can be added here, but you enter all the code in the next steps.

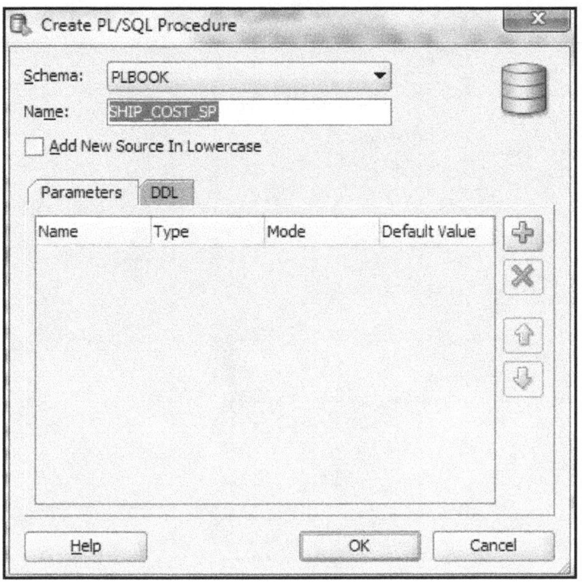

FIGURE 5-6 The Create PL/SQL Procedure dialog box

4. Click **OK** to display a tab with the procedure name, as shown in Figure 5-7. A basic template of code is filled in automatically, based on your previous input.

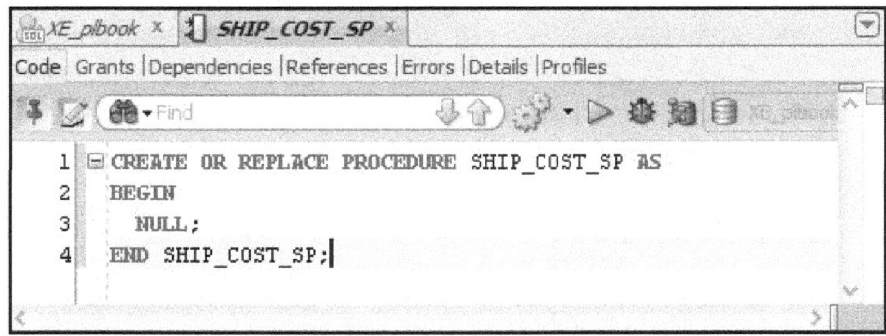

FIGURE 5-7 Viewing the procedure code template

5. Edit the `CREATE PROCEDURE` statement to match the code in Figure 5-5. Notice in comparing the code template with Figure 5-5 that the code template uses the keyword `AS` instead of `IS`. These keywords are interchangeable, so you can use either one.
6. Modify the data type for the `p_qty` parameter to **`NUMBER(3)`**. This change produces an error because size information can't be included with parameters' data types.
7. Click the **Compile** icon (which looks like gears) at the top of the procedure's tab to run the statement, and compare the results with Figure 5-8. The Compiler pane opens at the bottom, displaying an error message about the procedure code on Line 3 (where you added the size information to the parameter's data type). You might need to scroll to the right in the Compiler pane to see the entire error message. Note that the Compiler pane has two tabs: Messages, which provides general "success or fail" feedback, and Compiler, which displays details for compile errors.

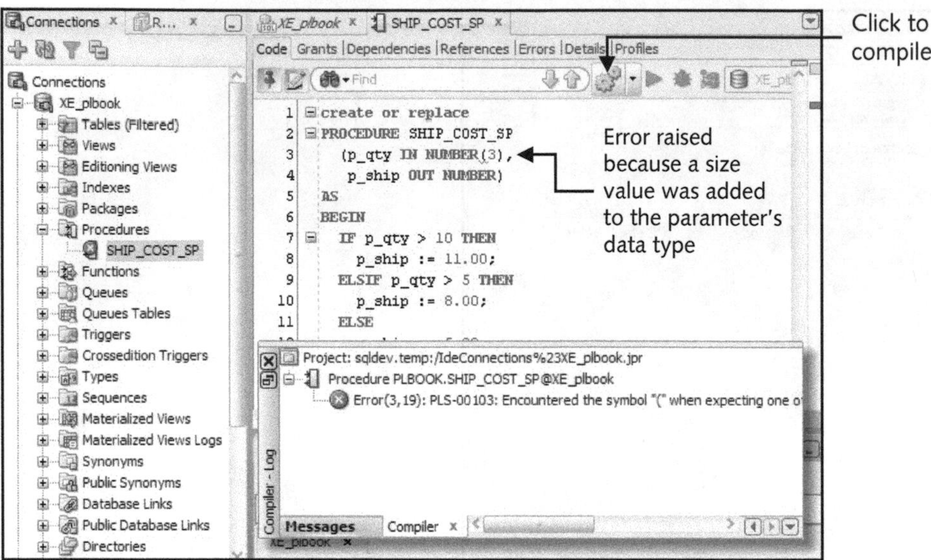

FIGURE 5-8 Compiling the procedure

8. Edit the procedure code to remove the data type size information so that the procedure can compile without errors.
9. Compile the procedure again, and notice the message shown in Figure 5-9. The Compiler pane shows a history of compile runs. To clear messages, right-click the **Compiler** pane tab you want to clear and click **Clear**.

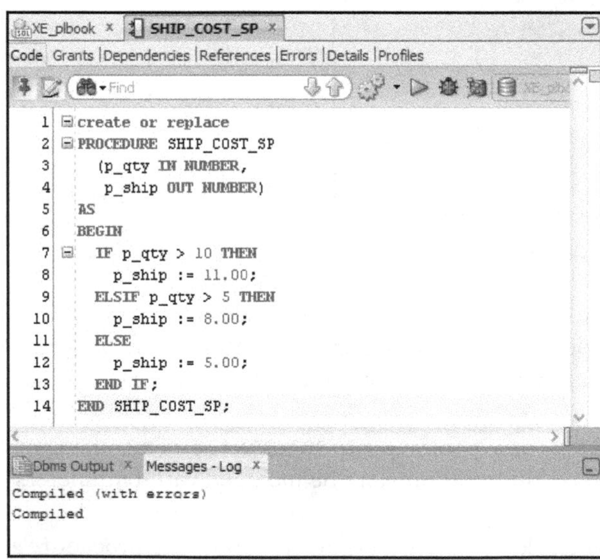

FIGURE 5-9 Successful compilation

In this example, the error message pointed right to the line with the error. However, not all error messages give you this information. A common error is forgetting a semicolon or comma at the end of a line in the procedure. In this case, the error points to the next line because an error isn't recognized until reaching the next line. Always check the line immediately before the one listed in the error message to help you identify the source of the error.

Testing a Procedure

Now you need to test the procedure to verify the execution and results. To do this, you use an anonymous block to call and run the procedure. Keep in mind that a procedure can be called from many sources, including application code, another procedure, or anonymous blocks. The call requires including an argument for each parameter in the procedure you're testing and listing any arguments in parentheses. The arguments' positions in the call match the positions of parameters listed in the procedure. In other words, the first argument in the call is sent to the first parameter, which is `p_qty`. However, the second parameter is an `OUT` parameter used to return the shipping cost, so you need to supply the name of a variable to hold the returned value. This variable could exist in an application environment, such as a field in an application page or a variable used in processing the page. In this example, you're testing the procedure in SQL Developer, so an anonymous block gives you a simple way to do this.

NOTE

In a complete application, program units provide the logic that runs behind all application pages.

To test the `SHIP_COST_SP` procedure, follow these steps:

1. Move to the Worksheet pane in SQL Developer. If it's not open, click **Tools**, **SQL Worksheet** from the menu.
2. Review the PL/SQL block in Figure 5-10. The call to the procedure is on Line 4; the procedure name is followed by arguments to match each parameter defined in the procedure. The first argument in Line 4, which is 7, is passed to the first parameter, which is `p_qty` (`IN` mode). A variable with a value assigned could be used instead of this literal value. However, because `p_qty` is an `IN` parameter, a literal value can be specified in the call for testing purposes. The second argument (`lv_ship_num` in Line 4) must be a variable because it must hold the value the `OUT` parameter returns for the shipping cost. The output statement displays the result for confirmation.

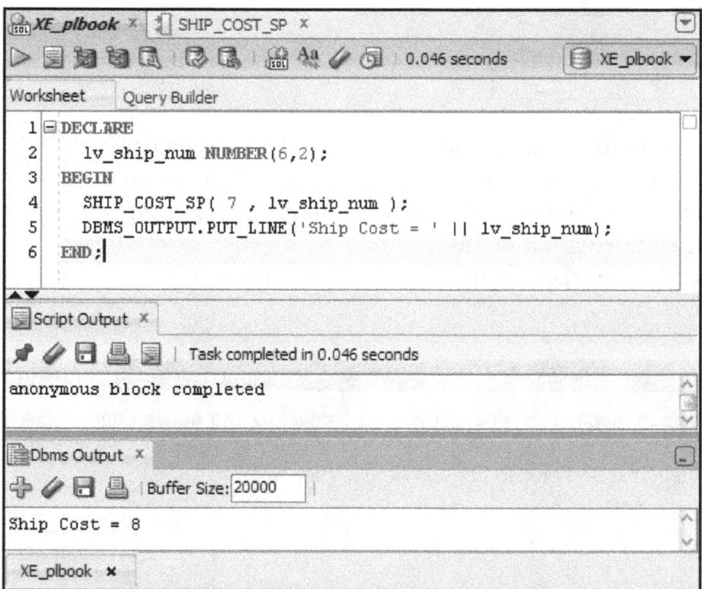

FIGURE 5-10 Testing a procedure

3. Enter and run the anonymous block shown in Figure 5-10.

The arguments used in the procedure call were passed with a **positional method**. That is, when invoking the procedure, the first argument value is matched up with the first parameter in the procedure, the second argument value is matched up with the second parameter in the procedure, and so on. In other words, when invoking a procedure, the values are listed in the order in which parameters are declared in the procedure.

Another method, **named association**, associates a value for each parameter by name in the calling statement. Take another look at the `SHIP_COST_SP` procedure, but this time, named association is used (see Figure 5-11).

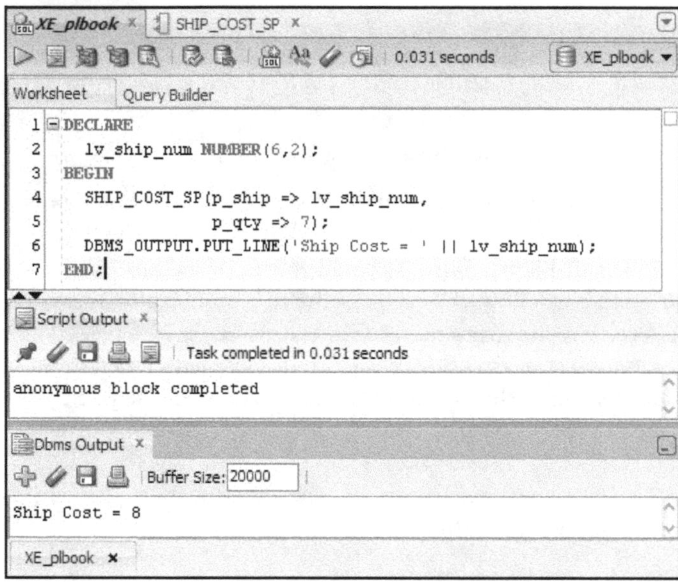

FIGURE 5-11 Using the named association method

The special symbol => is used for named association. In this case, values are passed to parameters starting with the last parameter in the procedure. A mixture of positional and named association methods can be used but tends to be confusing to most developers. An advantage of using named association is the ease of reading code and being able to identify the target easily for each value passed to the procedure.

CHALLENGE 5-1

Create a procedure that allows users to modify a product name. The product ID and new product name are values available onscreen. Test the procedure by using 1 for the product ID and CapressoBar Model #388 for the new product name. Verify that the procedure runs successfully when called from an anonymous block.

Using the `IN OUT` Parameter Mode

A parameter with only an `IN` mode can receive a value, but this value can't be changed in the procedure. With only an `OUT` mode, the parameter is empty when the procedure is called, and a value is assigned to the parameter during the procedure's execution and returned at completion.

Now take a look at using the third parameter mode: `IN OUT`. With this mode, the parameter can accept a value when the procedure is called, and this value can be changed in the procedure so that a different value could be returned to the calling environment. In other words, the `IN OUT` mode can achieve passing a value both in and out of a procedure with a single parameter. `IN OUT` parameters can't have a `DEFAULT` value, however, as other parameters can.

The Brewbean's application currently displays customers' phone numbers with no parentheses or dashes. The sales staff has requested that phone numbers be formatted to include parentheses and dashes so that they're easier to read. Follow these steps to build a procedure that formats a phone number with one `IN OUT` parameter:

1. In SQL Developer, click **File**, **New** from the menu. In the Create a new dialog box, click **Procedure**, and then click **OK**.
2. Select your current connection.
3. In the Create PL/SQL Procedure dialog box, enter the name **`PHONE_FMT_SP`**.
4. Click **OK** to display a tab with the procedure name and a basic template of code filled in.
5. Start Notepad, and open the **`phone05.txt`** file in the Chapter05 folder.
6. Copy the `CREATE PROCEDURE` code in the text file and paste it in SQL Developer to replace the template code.
7. Click the **Compile** icon at the top of the procedure's tab to run the statement and build the procedure. Refresh the Connections pane to confirm that the new procedure exists.
8. To test this procedure, enter and run the anonymous block shown in Figure 5-12 to call the procedure and view the value returned.

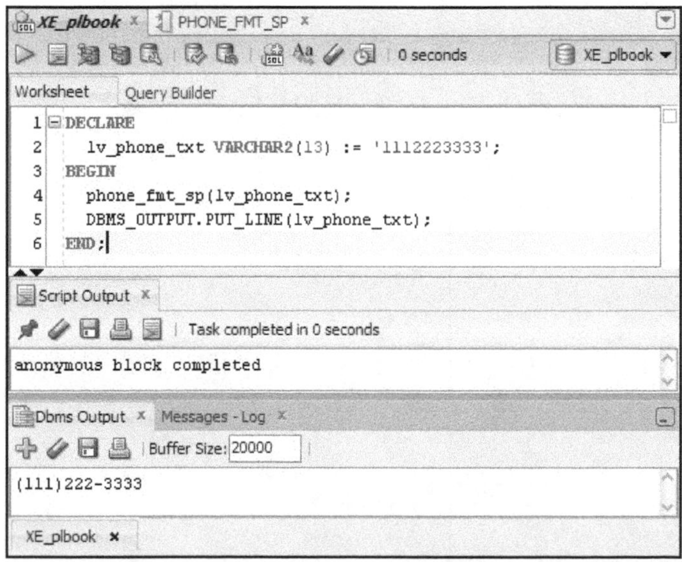

FIGURE 5-12 Testing an `IN OUT` parameter

9. Notice that the value placed in the p_phone parameter and sent to the procedure had no formatting. The same parameter was used to return a formatted value with parentheses and dashes.

This example passes a phone value in and out of the same parameter. Programmers can pass values in and out by using different IN OUT parameters; however, following the flow of value passing can be difficult when procedures become more complex.

CHALLENGE 5-2

Many of the pages in the Brewbean's application need to display the product type as coffee or equipment. The type value for these product categories is a C or an E. Create a procedure that accepts the type value C or E and returns the full description as "Coffee" or "Equipment." Use only one parameter in the procedure for this task.

CALLING A PROCEDURE FROM ANOTHER PROCEDURE

Recall that the Brewbean's shopping basket has a Check Out button that shoppers can click to calculate an order's subtotal and shipping costs. (The tax amount is also displayed in Figure 5-1, but you're tackling this application one step at a time, so ignore the tax part for now.) You need a procedure to perform this task and return the values to display to shoppers.

As a shopper selects items on the Web site, a basket ID number is assigned to the shopping basket and provided as input to the procedure. The procedure, named ORDER_TOTAL_SP, needs to retrieve basket items from the database and perform four tasks for the basket: Identify the total quantity of items ordered, calculate the subtotal for products ordered, check for the shipping cost, and calculate the overall order total, including products and shipping. You have already created a procedure to calculate the shipping cost, so you can recall this stored program unit from the new procedure.

Follow these steps to construct the ORDER_TOTAL_SP procedure, which uses or calls the SHIP_COST_SP procedure to calculate the shipping cost:

1. Review the code in Figure 5-13. Notice that Line 14 is calling the SHIP_COST_SP procedure you constructed previously. The ORDER_TOTAL_SP procedure includes one IN parameter to identify the basket and four OUT parameters to return all the values needed. The output statements in Lines 9 and 16 have been added just to help you identify the flow of execution in this example.

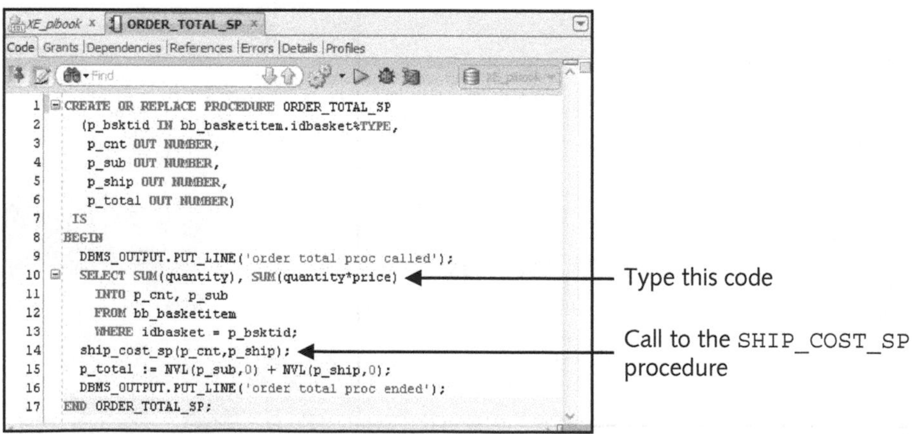

XE_plbook
ORDER_TOTAL_SP
Code Grants Dependencies References Errors Details Profiles
1 CREATE OR REPLACE PROCEDURE ORDER_TOTAL_SP
2 (p_bsktid IN bb_basketitem.idbasket%TYPE,
3 p_cnt OUT NUMBER,
4 p_sub OUT NUMBER,
5 p_ship OUT NUMBER,
6 p_total OUT NUMBER)
7 IS
8 BEGIN
9 DBMS_OUTPUT.PUT_LINE('order total proc called');
10 SELECT SUM(quantity), SUM(quantity*price)
11 INTO p_cnt, p_sub
12 FROM bb_basketitem
13 WHERE idbasket = p_bsktid;
14 ship_cost_sp(p_cnt,p_ship);
15 p_total := NVL(p_sub,0) + NVL(p_ship,0);
16 DBMS_OUTPUT.PUT_LINE('order total proc ended');
17 END ORDER_TOTAL_SP;
Type this code
Call to the SHIP_COST_SP procedure

FIGURE 5-13 A procedure calling another procedure

2. In SQL Developer, create and compile this new procedure.

The first task in the procedure's executable section is retrieving data from the BB_BASKETITEM table for the shopping basket identified with the `IN` parameter. The aggregate function `SUM` is used to total the number of items ordered and the cost of all items. The number of items ordered (`p_cnt`) becomes the `IN` parameter value for calling the `SHIP_COST_SP` procedure to calculate the shipping cost. The `SHIP_COST_SP` procedure is then called, passing variables for the `IN` and `OUT` parameters. It processes as though statements in the `SHIP_COST_SP` stored procedure were embedded where the call occurs. Finally, an assignment statement is used with a calculation to determine the overall order total.

As always, after completing a program unit, you should verify that it compiles correctly. To test the procedure, follow these steps:

1. In SQL Developer, click the **`SHIP_COST_SP`** procedure in the Connections pane so that you can edit it.
2. Edit the procedure to add the two output lines shown in Figure 5-14 on Lines 7 and 15. The output lines help you see the flow of execution.

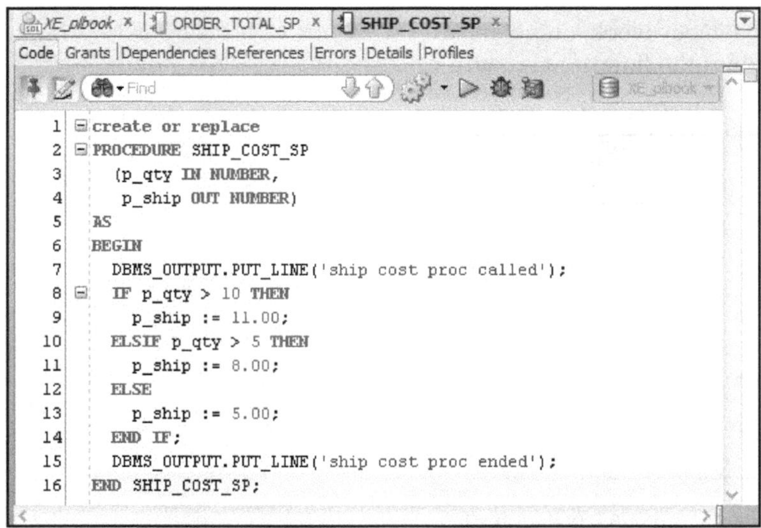

FIGURE 5-14 Editing the `SHIP_COST_SP` procedure

3. In SQL Developer, enter the anonymous block in Figure 5-15 to call the `ORDER_TOTAL_SP` procedure. A variable is created for each parameter. The basket ID variable is initialized and passed to the procedure's `IN` parameter, and the remaining variables hold the values returned from the `OUT` parameters. Output statements on Lines 8 and 15 show the execution flow, and output statements on Lines 11 through 14 display the returned values.

```
DECLARE
   lv_bask_num bb_basketitem.idbasket%TYPE := 12;
   lv_cnt_num NUMBER(3);
   lv_sub_num NUMBER(8,2);
   lv_ship_num NUMBER(8,2);
   lv_total_num NUMBER(8,2);
BEGIN
   DBMS_OUTPUT.PUT_LINE('Anonymous block started');
   order_total_sp(lv_bask_num, lv_cnt_num, lv_sub_num,
                       lv_ship_num, lv_total_num);
   DBMS_OUTPUT.PUT_LINE(lv_cnt_num);
   DBMS_OUTPUT.PUT_LINE(lv_sub_num);
   DBMS_OUTPUT.PUT_LINE(lv_ship_num);
   DBMS_OUTPUT.PUT_LINE(lv_total_num);
   DBMS_OUTPUT.PUT_LINE('Anonymous block ended');
END;
```

FIGURE 5-15 Running multiple procedures with a single call

4. Run the anonymous block, and compare the results with Figure 5-16. The output identifies the flow of procedure calls and the returned values.

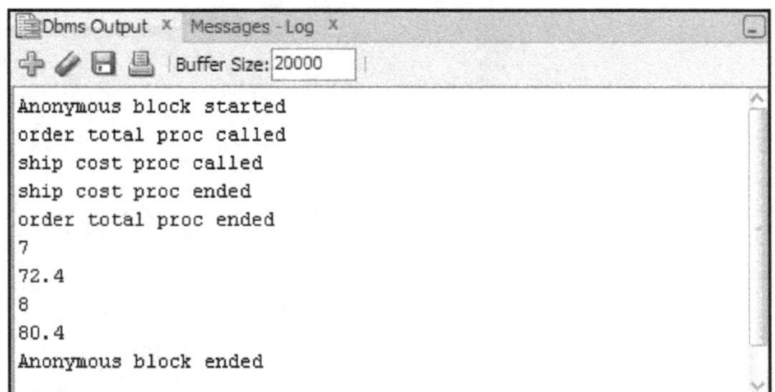

FIGURE 5-16 Output of the anonymous block for testing

5. To verify that the correct data was calculated, enter and run the following SELECT statement:

```
SELECT SUM(quantity), SUM(quantity*price)
  FROM bb_basketitem
  WHERE idbasket = 12;
```

USING THE DESCRIBE COMMAND

Just as you use the DESCRIBE command to list a table's structure, you can use it to list details about a procedure's structure, such as information on parameters. Figure 5-17 shows using the DESCRIBE command on the ORDER_TOTAL_SP procedure.

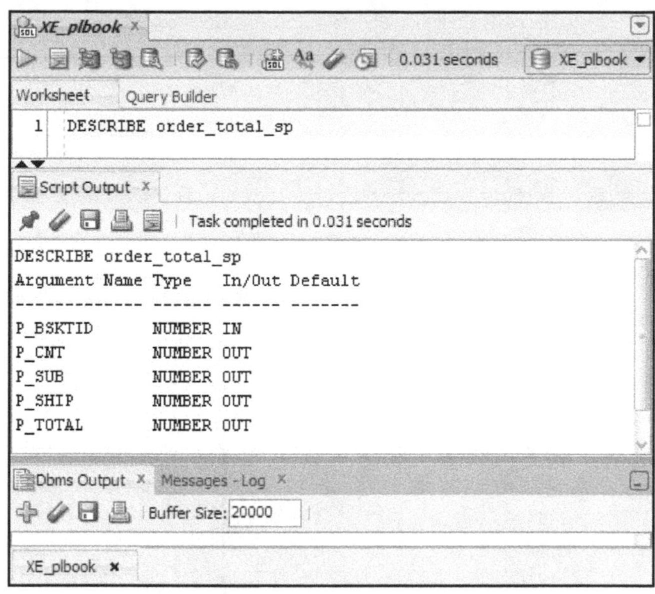

FIGURE 5-17 Results of using the `DESCRIBE` command on a procedure

NOTE

The listing displays parameters' (or arguments') names, data types, and modes. Depending on the development tool, this information can be quite useful when you're writing blocks that call a procedure to confirm that the procedure call returns the correct values to match the parameters.

USING DBMS_OUTPUT TO ASSIST IN DEBUGGING

An important step in debugging programs is displaying values onscreen to confirm logic processing or verify that statements have executed. You have used the DBMS_OUTPUT.PUT_LINE statement to confirm which procedure has run, verify that an exception handler executed, and display variable values. Now you can explore using DBMS_OUTPUT.PUT_LINE in a block's executable section to help debug your code. **Debugging** is the process of identifying errors in program code and removing them.

To see how this debugging method works, you use a new procedure, PROMO_TEST_SP, that calculates purchases for a free-shipping promotion. Brewbean's is experimenting with the idea of setting up purchase incentives to encourage repeat shoppers. If a shopper spends more than $25 in a month, a free shipping offer is extended for his or her next purchase over $25. If a shopper has spent more than $50 in a month, free shipping for his or her next purchase is offered regardless of the purchase total. The SUBTOTAL column is summed in the procedure to reflect actual purchase total. The procedure updates the BB_PROMOLIST table with shoppers' purchase information, which is used to e-mail the incentive offer to shoppers. The promo_flag variable is used to assign the correct promotion code.

Review the PROMO_TEST_SP procedure in Figure 5-18. It uses a CURSOR FOR loop to review total purchases by shopper for a given month and year. As described in Chapter 4, a CURSOR FOR loop automatically sets up the necessary record and counter variable for the looping action.

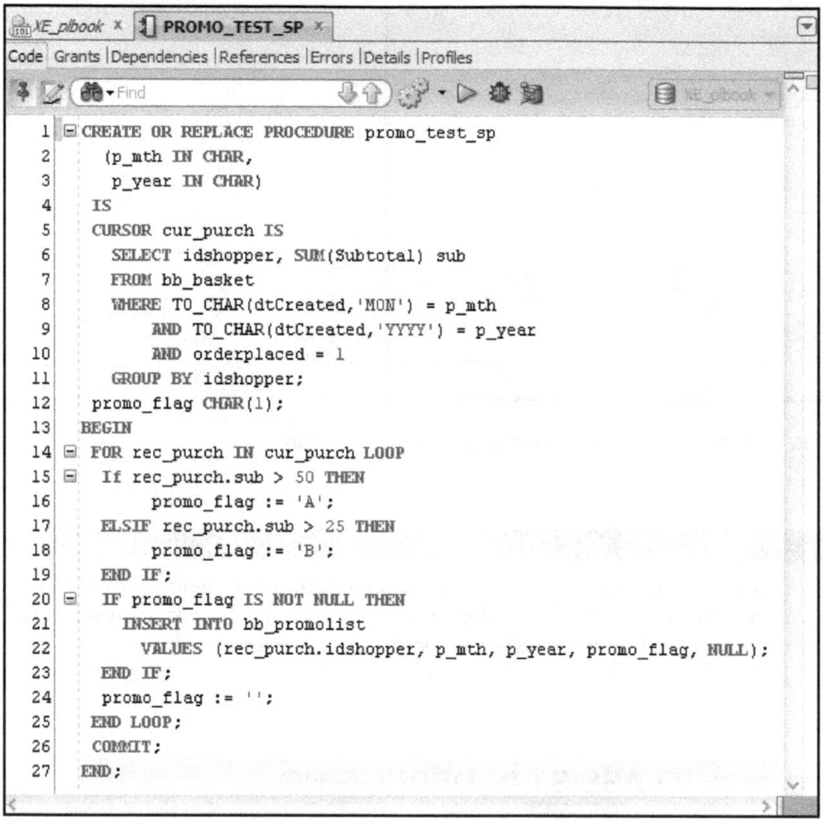

XE_plbook × PROMO_TEST_SP ×

Code | Grants | Dependencies | References | Errors | Details | Profiles

```
CREATE OR REPLACE PROCEDURE promo_test_sp
  (p_mth IN CHAR,
   p_year IN CHAR)
 IS
 CURSOR cur_purch IS
   SELECT idshopper, SUM(Subtotal) sub
   FROM bb_basket
   WHERE TO_CHAR(dtCreated,'MON') = p_mth
       AND TO_CHAR(dtCreated,'YYYY') = p_year
       AND orderplaced = 1
   GROUP BY idshopper;
 promo_flag CHAR(1);
BEGIN
 FOR rec_purch IN cur_purch LOOP
  If rec_purch.sub > 50 THEN
       promo_flag := 'A';
  ELSIF rec_purch.sub > 25 THEN
       promo_flag := 'B';
  END IF;
  IF promo_flag IS NOT NULL THEN
    INSERT INTO bb_promolist
      VALUES (rec_purch.idshopper, p_mth, p_year, promo_flag, NULL);
  END IF;
  promo_flag := '';
 END LOOP;
 COMMIT;
END;
```

FIGURE 5-18 The PROMO_TEST_SP procedure code

To use DBMS_OUTPUT.PUT_LINE for debugging, follow these steps:

1. Start Notepad, if necessary, and open the **promotest05.txt** file in the Chapter05 folder. Copy the code to SQL Developer to create the PROMO_TEST_SP procedure, and make sure you compile it.
2. Call the procedure by entering and running the following anonymous block:

```
BEGIN
  promo_test_sp('FEB','2012');
END;
```

3. Now it's time to run a query to check what the procedure inserted in the BB_PROMOLIST table. Type **SELECT * FROM bb_promolist;**, and run this statement. Five rows are inserted in the BB_PROMOLIST table. However, right off the bat, you can see that no promotion flag value has been inserted for Shopper 23 (see Figure 5-19).

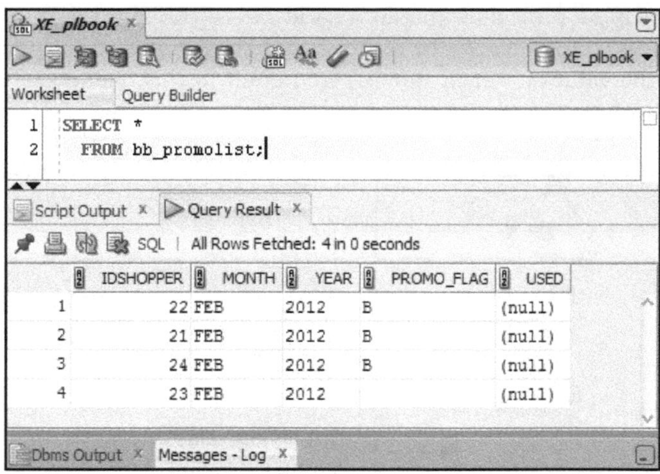

FIGURE 5-19 No flag value inserted for Shopper 23

4. To verify the results, you need to run a query on the BB_BASKET table to verify each shopper's order totals and who's eligible for the promotion. Type the **SELECT** statement shown in Figure 5-20. Notice that Shopper 23 has spent a total of only $21.60 and isn't eligible for the promotion.

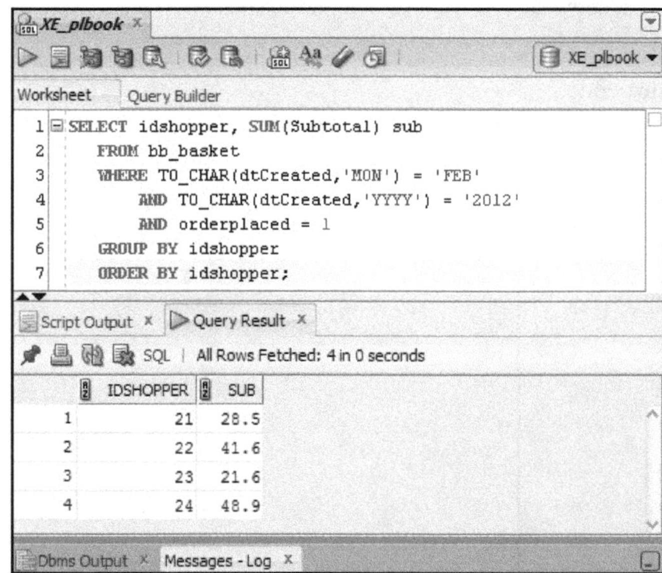

FIGURE 5-20 Verifying the results of the procedure

5. Now you have a problem. The procedure included Shopper 23 in the BB_PROMOLIST table; however, this shopper isn't eligible for the promotion and shouldn't be inserted in the table. How can you determine the problem with this procedure? In the next step, you add `DBMS_OUTPUT` statements to help.
6. First, undo the edits you made in the previous steps. Type and run **`DELETE FROM bb_promolist;`** to delete the rows you inserted earlier.
7. Type and run **`COMMIT;`** to save the `DELETE` action. Verify that the BB_PROMOLIST table is empty.

8. Open the **PROMO_TEST_SP** procedure to edit it. Add DBMS_OUTPUT lines inside the CURSOR FOR loop, as shown in Figure 5-21. They're placed inside the loop to confirm the values for each shopper and confirm that the insert is processed for each row.

```
BEGIN
 FOR rec_purch IN cur_purch LOOP
  If rec_purch.sub > 50 THEN
       promo_flag := 'A';
  ELSIF rec_purch.sub > 25 THEN
       promo_flag := 'B';
  END IF;
    DBMS_OUTPUT.PUT_LINE(rec_purch.idshopper || ' has sub ' ||
                         rec_purch.sub || ' and flag = ' ||
                         promo_flag);
  IF promo_flag IS NOT NULL THEN
    DBMS_OUTPUT.PUT_LINE('Insert processed for shopper ' ||
                            rec_purch.idshopper);
    INSERT INTO bb_promolist
      VALUES (rec_purch.idshopper, p_mth, p_year, promo_flag, NULL);
  END IF;
  promo_flag := '';
 END LOOP;
 COMMIT;
END;
```

Displaying values during execution

FIGURE 5-21 Adding DBMS_OUTPUT statements to confirm values and execution

9. Compile the procedure code.
10. Use the anonymous block from Step 2 to run the procedure. The DBMS_OUTPUT messages shown in Figure 5-22 should be displayed.

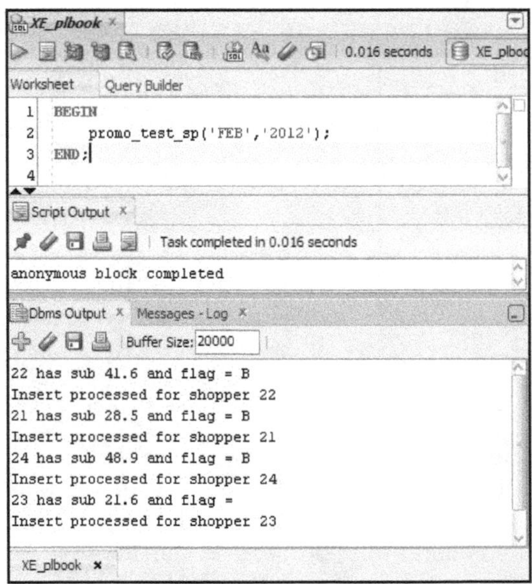
XE_plbook
0.016 seconds
Worksheet
Query Builder
BEGIN
promo_test_sp('FEB','2012');
END;
Script Output
Task completed in 0.016 seconds
anonymous block completed
Dbms Output
Messages - Log
Buffer Size: 20000
22 has sub 41.6 and flag = B
Insert processed for shopper 22
21 has sub 28.5 and flag = B
Insert processed for shopper 21
24 has sub 48.9 and flag = B
Insert processed for shopper 24
23 has sub 21.6 and flag =
Insert processed for shopper 23
XE_plbook

FIGURE 5-22 DBMS_OUTPUT messages

A review of the DBMS_OUTPUT messages confirms that the subtotal value for Shopper 23 is correct and the promotion flag is blank because this shopper shouldn't receive a promotion. However, the messages also confirm that the INSERT statement is processed for Shopper 23, which indicates the flag isn't NULL for this shopper. This message prompts you to review all the flag assignment statements in the procedure. Notice that the last line in the loop is the assignment statement promo_flag := ''. Is setting the flag to a blank the same as setting it to a NULL value? Follow these steps to correct the PROMO_TEST_SP procedure:

1. Type and run **DELETE FROM bb_promolist;** to delete the rows you inserted previously.
2. Type and run **COMMIT;** to save the DELETE action.
3. Open the **PROMO_TEST_SP** procedure to edit it. Modify the promo_flag assignment statement at the end of the loop to **promo_flag := NULL;**. Compile the procedure.
4. Use the anonymous block from Step 2 in the previous exercise to run the procedure.
5. Run a query to check what the procedure inserted in the BB_PROMOLIST table by typing **SELECT * FROM bb_promolist;**. Notice that a row for Shopper 23 is no longer inserted in the BB_PROMOLIST table.

SUBPROGRAMS

A subprogram is a program unit defined inside another program unit. If a code block is created to be used by only one procedure, it can be defined inside that procedure. For example, Figure 5-23 shows the ORDER_TOTAL_SP2 procedure with the SHIP_COST subprogram in the DECLARE section. In the previous example, you saved SHIP_COST_SP as a stand-alone procedure and called it from the ORDER_TOTAL procedure.

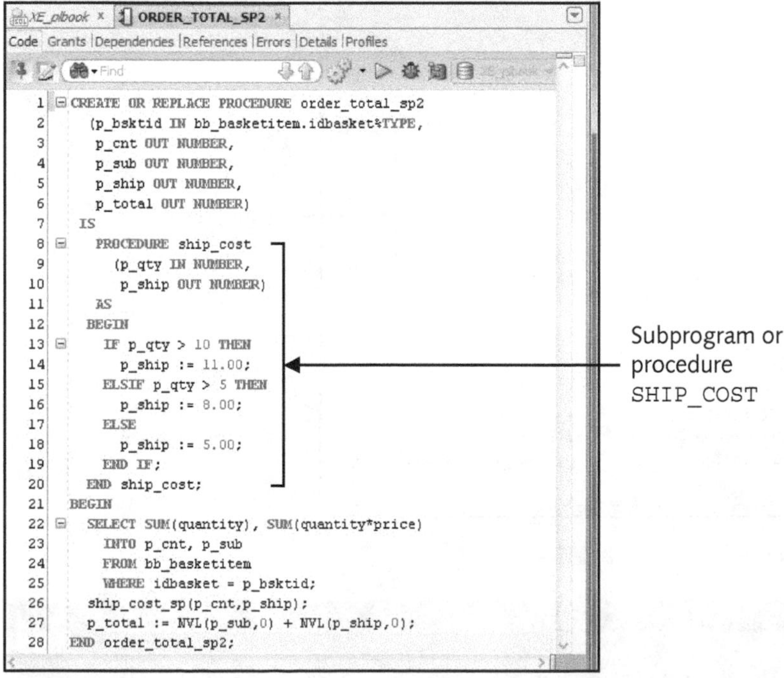
ORDER_TOTAL_SP2
Code Grants Dependencies References Errors Details Profiles
CREATE OR REPLACE PROCEDURE order_total_sp2
(p_bsktid IN bb_basketitem.idbasket%TYPE,
p_cnt OUT NUMBER,
p_sub OUT NUMBER,
p_ship OUT NUMBER,
p_total OUT NUMBER)
IS
PROCEDURE ship_cost
(p_qty IN NUMBER,
p_ship OUT NUMBER)
AS
BEGIN
IF p_qty > 10 THEN
p_ship := 11.00;
ELSIF p_qty > 5 THEN
p_ship := 8.00;
ELSE
p_ship := 5.00;
END IF;
END ship_cost;
BEGIN
SELECT SUM(quantity), SUM(quantity*price)
INTO p_cnt, p_sub
FROM bb_basketitem
WHERE idbasket = p_bsktid;
ship_cost_sp(p_cnt,p_ship);
p_total := NVL(p_sub,0) + NVL(p_ship,0);
END order_total_sp2;
Subprogram or procedure SHIP_COST

FIGURE 5-23 A subprogram in a procedure

Only the program unit where the subprogram is declared can use the subprogram. In this example, the `SHIP_COST` subprogram can be used only by `ORDER_TOTAL_SP2`. Therefore, you don't want to save a code block that a number of procedures can use as a subprogram. Instead, you should save it as a stand-alone procedure so that multiple program units can share it. A subprogram is created in the DECLARE section of the procedure block. If any variables are also declared in the procedure, they must be listed before the subprogram in the DECLARE section. Why create subprograms? A subprogram is typical in a procedure to include code blocks that could be reused numerous times in the same procedure.

SCOPE OF VARIABLES, EXCEPTION HANDLING, AND TRANSACTIONS

As you add complexity to your PL/SQL programs, including nested blocks and calling one program unit from another, you need to consider the impact on variable references, exception handling, and transaction control, explored in the following sections.

Working with Variable Scope

Nesting blocks raises a new issue with **variable scope**, which specifies the area of a block that can identify a particular variable. A nested block can be placed inside another block wherever an executable statement is allowed, which includes the BEGIN and EXCEPTION sections. A block first looks for a variable inside itself. If a nested block is searching for a variable and can't locate it, the block searches its enclosing block for the variable. Figure 5-24 shows a block containing a nested block.

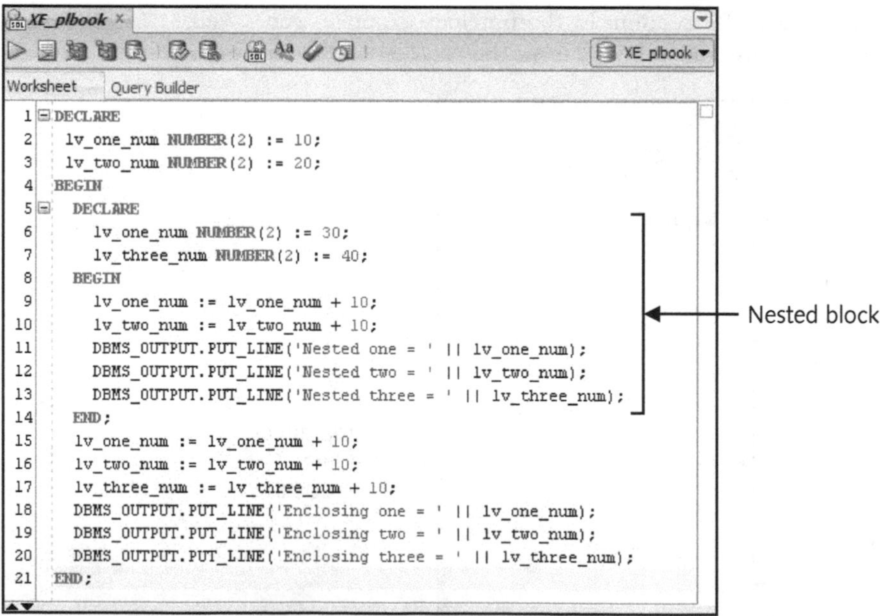

FIGURE 5-24 Nested blocks

> **TIP**
>
> A nested block can look "up" in its enclosing block; however, the reverse isn't true. The enclosing block can't look "down" into a nested block.

Try running the variable scope example in Figure 5-24 with `DBMS_OUTPUT` statements to check how assignment statements in the executable section resolve variable references. Notice that the `lv_one_num` variable is declared in both the enclosing and nested blocks. The `lv_two_num` variable is declared only in the enclosing block, and `lv_three_num` is declared only in the nested block. This first execution attempt produces an error (see Figure 5-25).

```
Script Output
Task completed in 0.062 seconds
Error report:
ORA-06550: line 17, column 3:
PLS-00201: identifier 'LV_THREE_NUM' must be declared
ORA-06550: line 17, column 3:
PL/SQL: Statement ignored
ORA-06550: line 20, column 48:
PLS-00201: identifier 'LV_THREE_NUM' must be declared
ORA-06550: line 20, column 3:
PL/SQL: Statement ignored
06550. 00000 -  "line %s, column %s:\n%s"
*Cause:    Usually a PL/SQL compilation error.
*Action:
```

FIGURE 5-25 Variable reference error

The error occurs in the enclosing block where the `lv_three_num` variable is referenced. Because this variable is declared only in the nested block, the enclosing block can't locate it, so it's considered undeclared. Comment out the `lv_three_num` variable references in Lines 17 and 20 of the enclosing block, and run the procedure again to examine the results of other variable references, shown in Figure 5-26.

> **TIP**
>
> You learned about commenting code in Chapter 4. "Commenting out" means adding the comment symbols `--` at the beginning of a code line so that it's not processed.

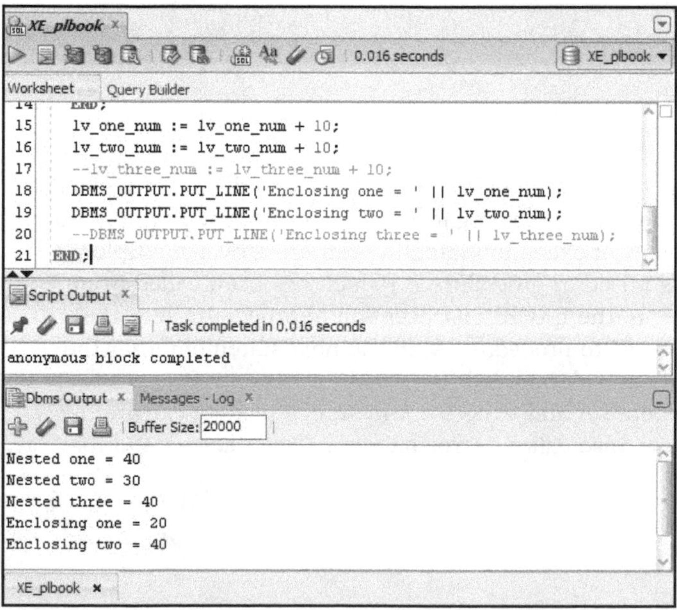

FIGURE 5-26 Results of modifying the variable references

Table 5-3 reviews the assignment statements in Figure 5-26 to explain how each instance of variable scope works.

TABLE 5-3 Variable Scope in Figure 5-26

Block	Assignment Statement	Result
Nested	`lv_one_num := lv_one_num + 10;`	The `lv_one_num` variable declared in the nested block is used and has a value of 40. `lv_one_num` in the enclosing block isn't affected.
Nested	`lv_two_num := lv_two_num + 10;`	The `lv_two_num` variable doesn't exist in the nested block. The nested block searches the enclosing block and does the calculation on the `lv_two_num` in the enclosing block. It doesn't move a copy of this variable to the nested block; it just uses the variable in the enclosing block. Therefore, both the enclosing block and the nested block see a value of 30 in the `lv_two_num` variable.
Enclosing	`lv_one_num := lv_one_num + 10;`	`lv_one_num` is declared in the enclosing block and has a value of 20.
Enclosing	`lv_two_num := lv_two_num + 10;`	`lv_two_num` exists in the enclosing block and has a value of 30 from the change the nested block made in the earlier assignment statement. This statement now results in the value 40.
Enclosing	`lv_three_num := lv_three_num + 10;`	`lv_three_num` doesn't exist in the enclosing block, which can't see variables in a nested block. Therefore, this statement raises an error.

Exception-Handling Flow

As you learned in Chapter 4, the exception-handling area of a block determines what happens if an error occurs. Developers must recognize when a procedure is called from another procedure because the flow of exception handling can cross over multiple program units. If an exception is raised in procedure B (which has been called from procedure A), control first moves to the EXCEPTION section of procedure B. If the exception is handled, control returns to procedure A, in the next statement after the call to procedure B. If the exception isn't handled in procedure B, control moves to the EXCEPTION section of procedure A and looks for a matching handler. Figure 5-27 shows the exception-handling flow (also called "error-handling flow") across multiple program units.

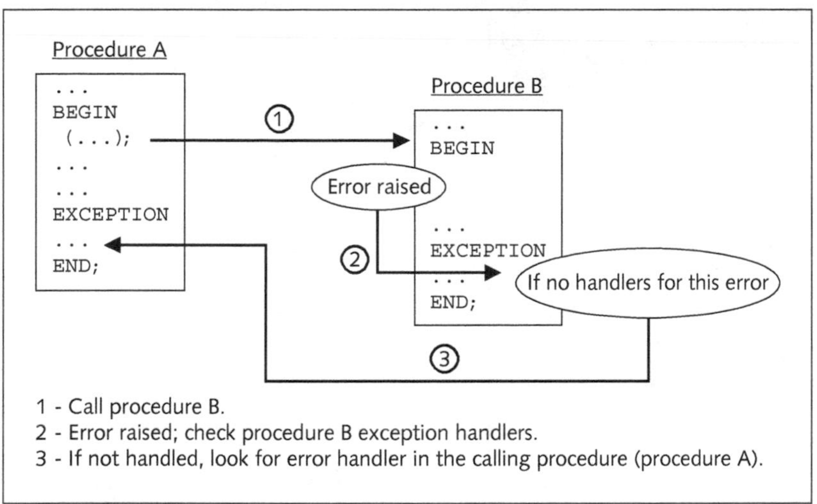

FIGURE 5-27 Exception-handling flow

Try working through an example to understand the effect of error handling on processing flow. Figure 5-28 shows two procedures, with one calling the other. Output statements have been included to help determine the processing flow.

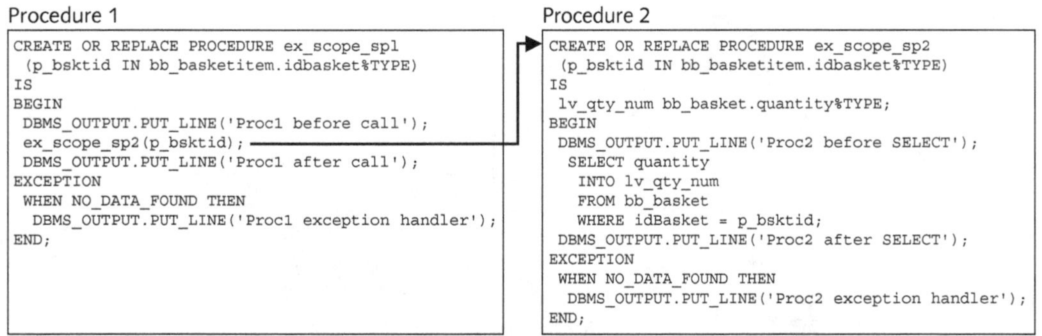

Procedure 1

```
CREATE OR REPLACE PROCEDURE ex_scope_sp1
 (p_bsktid IN bb_basketitem.idbasket%TYPE)
IS
BEGIN
 DBMS_OUTPUT.PUT_LINE('Proc1 before call');
 ex_scope_sp2(p_bsktid);
 DBMS_OUTPUT.PUT_LINE('Proc1 after call');
EXCEPTION
 WHEN NO_DATA_FOUND THEN
  DBMS_OUTPUT.PUT_LINE('Proc1 exception handler');
END;
```

Procedure 2

```
CREATE OR REPLACE PROCEDURE ex_scope_sp2
 (p_bsktid IN bb_basketitem.idbasket%TYPE)
IS
 lv_qty_num bb_basket.quantity%TYPE;
BEGIN
 DBMS_OUTPUT.PUT_LINE('Proc2 before SELECT');
  SELECT quantity
   INTO lv_qty_num
   FROM bb_basket
   WHERE idBasket = p_bsktid;
 DBMS_OUTPUT.PUT_LINE('Proc2 after SELECT');
EXCEPTION
 WHEN NO_DATA_FOUND THEN
  DBMS_OUTPUT.PUT_LINE('Proc2 exception handler');
END;
```

FIGURE 5-28 Procedures for determining processing flow

In Figure 5-29, the first run passes a valid basket ID and shows the processing flow without any exception handling needed. Procedure 1 calls procedure 2, and when procedure 2 finishes, processing returns to the next line in procedure 1 after the call to procedure 2.

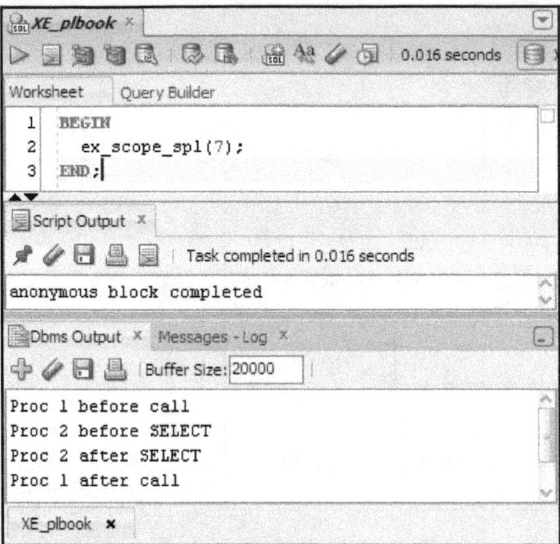

FIGURE 5-29 Successful run

Next, see what happens when the procedure runs with a basket ID that doesn't exist. It raises a "no data found" error in procedure 2 (see Figure 5-30). The processing flow in procedure 2 changes so that no lines following the `SELECT` run, and the error causes processing to move to the EXCEPTION section. However, because the error is handled in procedure 2, the processing flow returns normally to procedure 1 and continues.

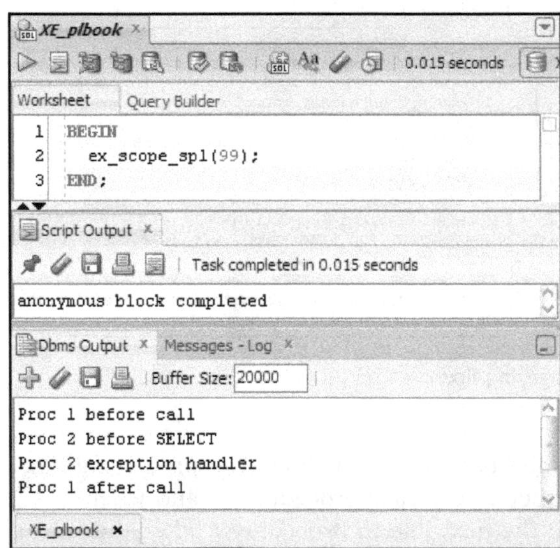

FIGURE 5-30 Exception handling in the called procedure

Finally, see what happens when procedure 2's EXCEPTION section is removed, and a call with an invalid basket ID is made again, as shown in Figure 5-31. The exception propagates to the calling procedure, procedure 1. The error is raised with the `SELECT` statement in procedure 2 and doesn't find an exception handler in that procedure, so processing moves to the calling procedure's EXCEPTION section. Note that no lines of code in procedure 1 run after the call to procedure 2 because the processing flow moves to procedure 1's EXCEPTION section. As a developer, you need to be cognizant of this processing flow when determining how you want to structure exception-handling activity.

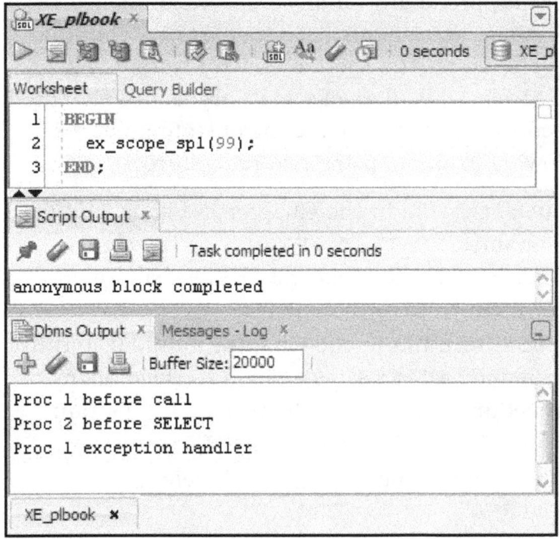

FIGURE 5-31 Exception handling passes to the calling procedure

What if you want to handle the exception in procedure 2 to perform some action but still propagate the error to the calling procedure (procedure 1) so that it's aware the error occurred? You can use a `RAISE` command for this task. To show how it works, procedure 2's EXCEPTION section is changed to the following:

```
EXCEPTION
  WHEN NO_DATA_FOUND THEN
    DBMS_OUTPUT.PUT_LINE('Proc 2 exception handler');
    RAISE;
```

Figure 5-32 shows the new results, which confirm that the processing flow moves from the exception handler in procedure 2 to the exception handler in procedure 1.

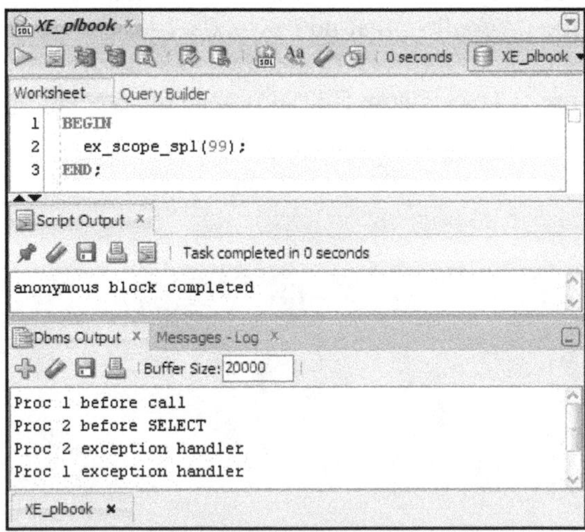

FIGURE 5-32 Using the `RAISE` command in exception handling

Transaction Control Scope

A procedure's transactions include not only DML actions in that procedure, but also DML actions in any procedures called from that procedure. If any DML action called from another procedure occurs in the procedure, these statements become part of a continuous transaction started in the main procedure. Therefore, transaction control statements affect any DML actions that have occurred so far, regardless of which procedure executed the DML actions and which procedure executes the transaction control statement.

To understand how this works, try the following example using two procedures:

1. In Notepad, open the **tctest05b.txt** file in the Chapter05 folder, and use the code to create a procedure named **TC_TEST_SP2** in SQL Developer. Make sure you compile the procedure. Notice that the INSERT statement isn't followed by a COMMIT statement to save the change.
2. In Notepad, open the **tctest05a.txt** file in the Chapter05 folder and use the code to create a procedure named **TC_TEST_SP1** in SQL Developer. Make sure you compile the procedure. Notice that the procedure contains an INSERT statement, a call to TC_TEST_SP2, and a COMMIT statement.
3. Now test these procedures with the following anonymous block:

```
BEGIN
  tc_test_sp1();
END;
```

4. To determine what data is actually committed to the database, start another SQL Developer session and log on.
5. In this second session, list all the data in the BB_TEST1 table by typing **SELECT * FROM bb_test1;**. Two rows should now be in the table: the value 1 from the procedure TC_TEST_SP1 and the value 2 from the procedure TC_TEST_SP2. Notice that COMMIT was the last statement to run, so the INSERT statements from both procedures were committed.
6. Return to the first SQL Developer session. Type and run the command **DELETE FROM bb_test1;** to delete the rows you inserted previously.
7. Enter and run a **COMMIT;** command to save the DELETE action. Verify that this action was saved by running the SELECT statement in Step 5 in the second SQL Developer session again, which should confirm that no rows exist in the table.
8. Edit the TC_TEST_SP1 procedure to move the COMMIT statement so that it's before the TC_TEST_SP2 procedure call (see Figure 5-33). Compile the procedure.

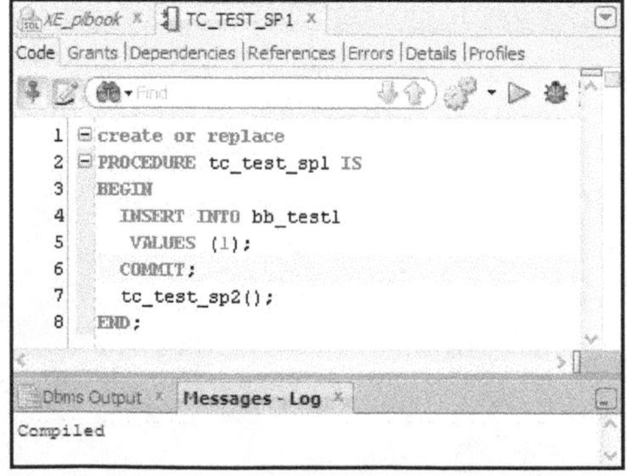

FIGURE 5-33 Moving the COMMIT statement

9. In the first session, test the procedures again with the anonymous block you used in Step 3.
10. List all the data in the BB_TEST1 table by entering and running **SELECT * FROM bb_test1;**. As expected, two rows are inserted.
11. Now move to the second SQL Developer session, and enter and run **SELECT * FROM bb_test1;**. Only one row is in the table: the value 1 from TC_TEST_SP1. The INSERT statement in the TC_TEST_SP2 procedure is executed after the COMMIT statement, so it's still in the transaction queue awaiting a COMMIT or ROLLBACK action. To verify this, issue a ROLLBACK statement in the first SQL Developer session, and then query the table again with the statement you used in Step 10. As you can see, only one row is saved.
12. Leave both sessions open to use in the next exercise.

At times, treating some SQL statements in a transaction separately from the rest is preferable. For example, what if you want to commit the INSERT action in the TC_TEST_SP2 procedure but don't want the COMMIT operation to affect the INSERT action in the TC_TEST_SP1 procedure? To do this, you use **autonomous transactions**, which are transactions created in another transaction called a "parent transaction." Autonomous transaction can be treated independently of the parent transaction.

To create these transactions, you use a PRAGMA statement (introduced in Chapter 4), which is a compiler directive—additional instructions for the PL/SQL compiler to use when compiling a program unit. Follow these steps to create an autonomous transaction:

1. In the first SQL Developer session you opened in the previous exercise, enter and run **DELETE FROM bb_test1;** and **COMMIT;** statements to delete the rows you inserted previously.
2. Edit the TC_TEST_SP2 procedure as follows: In the DECLARE section, add the **PRAGMA AUTONOMOUS_TRANSACTION;** statement shown in Figure 5-34, and add a **COMMIT;** statement after the INSERT action. The PRAGMA directive instructs the compiler to treat this program unit's transaction separately from the transaction in the calling block. Compile the procedure.

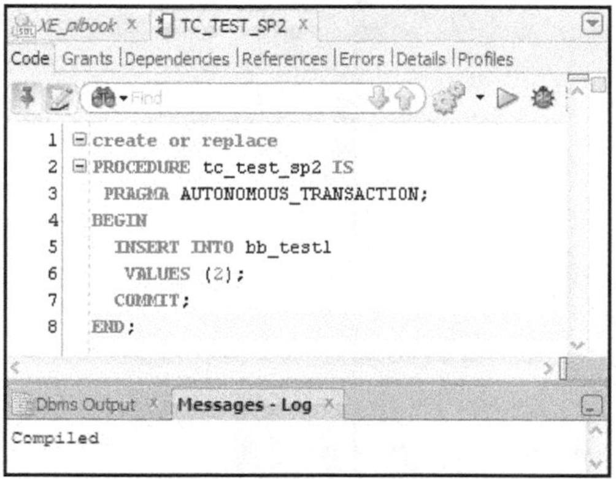

FIGURE 5-34 Making a procedure an autonomous transaction

3. In the first SQL Developer session, edit the TC_TEST_SP1 procedure by removing the COMMIT; statement. Compile the procedure.

4. Run the anonymous block used in Step 3 of the previous exercise to call the procedures. If you query the BB_TEST1 table in this session, you can see that both `INSERT`s executed, but which rows were committed?
5. Move to the second SQL Developer session to check the table data by typing and running **`SELECT * FROM bb_test1;`**. Only one row, with the value 2, is committed to the table because of the `INSERT` action in `TC_TEST_SP2`. Even though the `INSERT` action from the `TC_TEST_SP1` procedure executes before the `COMMIT` action, it wasn't committed. The `COMMIT` action affected only the `TC_TEST_SP2` procedure's `INSERT` action because it was declared as autonomous.
6. What happened with the `INSERT` action in the `TC_TEST_SP1` procedure? It's still in the transaction queue waiting for a transaction control statement. Return to the first SQL Developer session. Type and run **`COMMIT;`**.
7. Return to the second SQL Developer session, and type and run **`SELECT * FROM bb_test1;`**. Now the `INSERT` action in the `TC_TEST_SP1` procedure is committed, so both rows are displayed.

ERROR HANDLING WITH `RAISE_APPLICATION_ERROR`

In many exception-handling examples you've seen so far, `DBMS_OUTPUT` statements are used to display messages onscreen. When you're working with stored program units, you have another option for displaying error messages. `RAISE_APPLICATION_ERROR` is an Oracle built-in function for raising an error and creating your own error messages. This function accepts two arguments: an error number and an error message. The error number must be in the range -20,000 to -20,999; these error numbers are reserved for assignment by developers. The error message is a text string up to 512 characters.

Figure 5-35 shows a procedure that checks whether the an item's stock level is enough to fill an order. The `IF` statement checks whether the quantity requested is greater than the stock level.

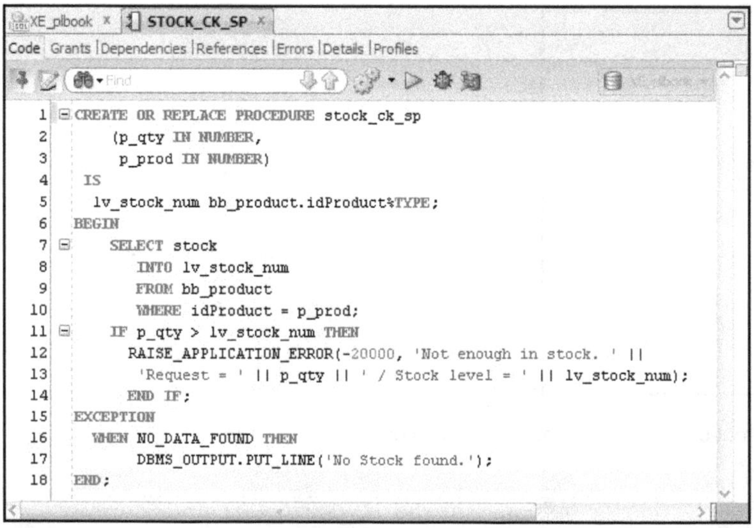
XE_plbook
STOCK_CK_SP
Code Grants Dependencies References Errors Details Profiles
CREATE OR REPLACE PROCEDURE stock_ck_sp
(p_qty IN NUMBER,
p_prod IN NUMBER)
IS
lv_stock_num bb_product.idProduct%TYPE;
BEGIN
SELECT stock
INTO lv_stock_num
FROM bb_product
WHERE idProduct = p_prod;
IF p_qty > lv_stock_num THEN
RAISE_APPLICATION_ERROR(-20000, 'Not enough in stock. ' ||
'Request = ' || p_qty || ' / Stock level = ' || lv_stock_num);
END IF;
EXCEPTION
WHEN NO_DATA_FOUND THEN
DBMS_OUTPUT.PUT_LINE('No Stock found.');
END;

FIGURE 5-35 Using the `RAISE_APPLICATION_ERROR` function

If the IF statement is TRUE, processing halts and the error message defined for error number -20000 is displayed. Figure 5-36 shows a procedure in which the quantity requested is greater than the stock level. Take a look to see what message the RAISE_APPLICATION_ERROR function returns.

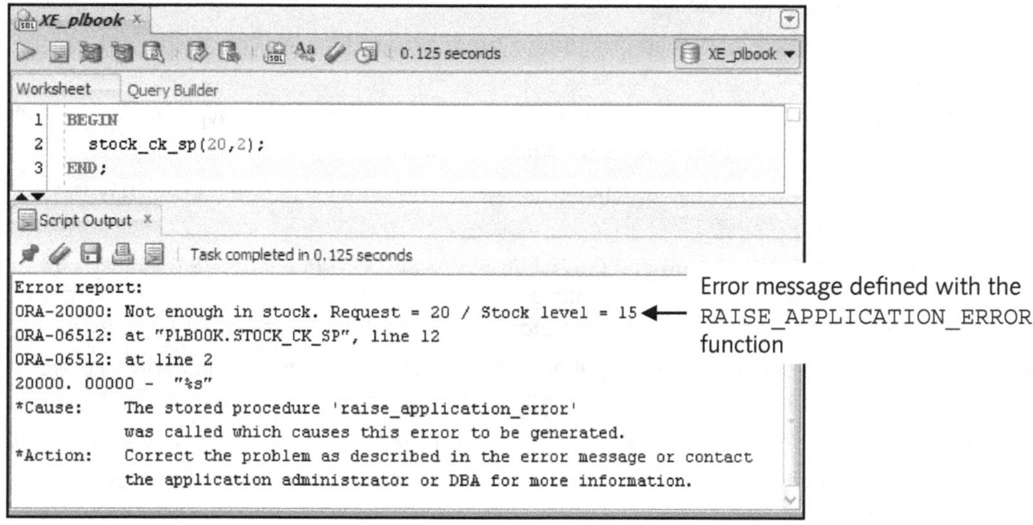

FIGURE 5-36 Message displayed by RAISE_APPLICATION_ERROR

REMOVING PROCEDURES

As with all database objects, you can use the DROP command to remove procedures, as shown:

```
DROP PROCEDURE procedure_name;
```

Chapter Summary

- Named program units are PL/SQL blocks that have been named and saved so that they can be reused. The term "program unit" is used for a block of code created to perform a specific task that might be needed in a number of applications. A stored program unit is one that's saved in the database.
- A procedure is a type of named program unit that can perform actions and accept parameters.
- The header is the section of a named program unit that indicates what type of program unit is being created, an object name, and parameter information.
- Parameters are mechanisms for sending values in and out of a program unit. They have three modes: `IN`, `OUT`, and `IN OUT`.
- The `IN` mode denotes that when a procedure is invoked or run, it expects a value to be provided for the parameter. The `OUT` mode means a variable must be created in the calling environment that can hold the value the procedure returns for this parameter.
- You can test procedures by invoking them with suitable arguments to match parameters in the procedure.
- Two methods can be used to pass values into parameters: positional and named association.
- The `IN OUT` parameter mode can achieve passing a value both in and out of a procedure with a single parameter.
- The `DESCRIBE` command is used to list a procedure's structure.
- The `DBMS_OUTPUT` package can be used for debugging by checking values and confirming which statements are executing.
- Subprograms are procedures declared inside another procedure. A subprogram can be used only by the containing procedure.
- Variable scope is involved with nested blocks. A block looks for a variable inside itself first. If a nested block is searching for a variable and can't locate it, the block searches its enclosing block for the variable.
- Exceptions raised in procedures called from another procedure can propagate to the calling procedure.
- Separate transactions aren't created for procedures called from other procedures unless a procedure is declared as autonomous by using a `PRAGMA` compiler directive.
- The `RAISE_APPLICATION_ERROR` function can be used in stored program units to return programmer-defined error messages.
- The `DROP PROCEDURE` command is used to remove a procedure from the system.

Review Questions

1. Which of the following explains the difference between an anonymous PL/SQL block and a named program unit?
   a. An anonymous block can't issue transaction control statements.
   b. A named program unit can't issue transaction control statements.
   c. An anonymous block has a header.
   d. A named program unit has a header.

2. Which of the following is a valid parameter mode in procedures? (Choose all that apply.)
   a. `IN`
   b. `IN OUT`
   c. `OUT`
   d. `OUT IN`
3. Which parameter mode must be used to have one value sent to a parameter and a different value returned by the same parameter?
   a. `IN`
   b. `OUT`
   c. `IN OUT`
   d. `OUT IN`
4. A stored program unit ______________.
   a. is created in SQL Developer
   b. can't be reused
   c. is saved as an object in the database
   d. must contain parameters
5. Which of the following methods can be used to pass values to parameters? (Choose all that apply.)
   a. positional
   b. ordered
   c. name association
   d. list
6. The section of a named program unit containing the name and parameters is called which of the following?
   a. named unit
   b. cap
   c. header
   d. title
7. Procedure C calls procedure D. If an error is raised in procedure D and no exception handler exists in procedure D, what happens?
   a. An error message is displayed to the user.
   b. An error is raised in procedure C.
   c. Program control moves to procedure C's EXCEPTION section.
   d. The results are unpredictable.
8. How many values can a procedure return to a calling environment?
   a. none
   b. the same as the number of parameters
   c. the same as the number of parameters that have the `OUT` mode
   d. at least one

9. Which built-in function is used to raise errors numbered in the range -20,000 to -20,999?
   a. `RAISE_ERROR`
   b. `RAISE_APPLICATION_ERROR`
   c. `WHEN EXCEPTION`
   d. `RAISE_EXCEPTION`

10. Which statement deletes the `SHIP_SP` procedure from the system?
    a. `DELETE ship_sp;`
    b. `DELETE PROCEDURE ship_sp;`
    c. `DROP PROCEDURE ship_sp;`
    d. `REMOVE PROCEDURE ship_sp;`
11. What is meant by the term "named program units"?
12. Describe how `DBMS_OUTPUT` can be used for debugging.
13. Describe the role of parameters in procedures.
14. Describe transaction handling across multiple procedures, as when procedure A calls procedure B. What can be used to override the default transaction scope?
15. What advantages are gained by storing a program unit in the database?

Advanced Review Questions

1. Review the following procedure header. Which of the following procedure calls is valid to include in another procedure?

```
PROCEDURE order_change_sp
  (p_prodid IN NUMBER, p_prodqty IN OUT NUMBER)
IS
```

   a. `order_change_sp(100, 362);`
   b. `EXECUTE order_change_sp(100, 362);`
   c. `order_change_sp(100, :g_qty);`
   d. `order_change_sp()`
2. Given this code, which of the following statements is correct?

```
CREATE OR REPLACE PROCEDURE test_sp
  (p_num IN NUMBER)
  IS
BEGIN
  UPDATE test_table
    SET range = v_range
    WHERE id = p_num;
END;
```

   a. The procedure compiles successfully.
   b. The procedure doesn't compile because a `COMMIT` statement isn't included in a block containing a DML action.
   c. The procedure doesn't compile because `v_range` isn't declared.
   d. The procedure doesn't compile because `p_num` isn't declared.

3. The `RESET_SP` procedure contains two parameters: The first is `p_num1` with the data type `NUMBER`, and the second is `p_num2` with the data type `CHAR`. Both parameters have the `IN` mode. Which of the following is a valid call of this procedure? (Choose all that apply.)
   a. `reset_sp(101, '33');`
   b. `reset_sp(p_num1 => lv_start_num, '33');`
   c. `reset_sp(p_num2 => '33', p_num1 => 101);`
   d. `reset_sp(101);`
4. Which of the following procedure parameter declarations isn't valid in a procedure?
   a. `p_test VARCHAR2;`
   b. `p_test IN OUT NUMBER :=1;`
   c. `p_test IN NUMBER(5);`
   d. `p_test OUT CHAR;`
5. If the following procedure is called from the `NEW_BASK_SP` procedure, what's the effect of the `COMMIT` statement in this procedure?

```
  CREATE OR REPLACE PROCEDURE new_shop_sp
    (p_last IN VARCHAR2(15),
     p_first IN VARCHAR2(10),
     p_id OUT NUMBER )
  IS
  PRAGMA_AUTONOMOUS_TRANSACTION;
BEGIN
  p_id := id_seq.NEXTVAL;
  INSERT INTO shopper (id, last, first)
    VALUES (p_id, p_last, p_first);
  COMMIT;
END;
```

   a. `INSERT`s in both the `NEW_BASK_SP` and `NEW_SHOP_SP` procedures are committed.
   b. Any DML statements in both the `NEW_BASK_SP` and `NEW_SHOP_SP` procedures are committed.
   c. Only the `INSERT` statement in `NEW_SHOP_SP` is committed.
   d. Only DML statements in `NEW_BASK_SP` are committed.

Hands-On Assignments Part I

Assignment 5-1: Creating a Procedure

Use these steps to create a procedure that allows a company employee to make corrections to a product's assigned name. Review the BB_PRODUCT table and identify the PRODUCT NAME and PRIMARY KEY columns. The procedure needs two `IN` parameters to identify the product ID and supply the new description. This procedure needs to perform only a DML action, so no `OUT` parameters are necessary.

1. In SQL Developer, create the following procedure:

```
CREATE OR REPLACE PROCEDURE prod_name_sp
  (p_prodid IN bb_product.idproduct%TYPE,
   p_descrip IN bb_product.description%TYPE)
```

```
  IS
BEGIN
  UPDATE bb_product
    SET description = p_descrip
    WHERE idproduct = p_prodid;
  COMMIT;
END;
```


2. Before testing the procedure, verify the current description value for product ID 1 with `SELECT * FROM bb_product;`.
3. Call the procedure with parameter values of `1` for the product ID and `CapressoBar Model #388` for the description.
4. Verify that the update was successful by querying the table with `SELECT * FROM bb_product;`.

Assignment 5-2: Using a Procedure with `IN` Parameters

Follow these steps to create a procedure that allows a company employee to add a new product to the database. This procedure needs only `IN` parameters.

1. In SQL Developer, create a procedure named **`PROD_ADD_SP`** that adds a row for a new product in the BB_PRODUCT table. Keep in mind that the user provides values for the product name, description, image filename, price, and active status. Address the input values or parameters in the same order as in the preceding sentence.
2. Call the procedure with these parameter values: `('Roasted Blend', 'Well-balanced mix of roasted beans, a medium body', 'roasted.jpg',9.50,1)`.
3. Check whether the update was successful by querying the BB_PRODUCT table.

Assignment 5-3: Calculating the Tax on an Order

Follow these steps to create a procedure for calculating the tax on an order. The BB_TAX table contains states that require submitting taxes for Internet sales. If the state isn't listed in the table, no tax should be assessed on the order. The shopper's state and basket subtotal are the inputs to the procedure, and the tax amount should be returned.

1. In SQL Developer, create a procedure named **`TAX_COST_SP`**. Remember that the state and subtotal values are inputs to the procedure, which should return the tax amount. Review the BB_TAX table, which contains the tax rate for each applicable state.
2. Call the procedure with the values **`VA`** for the state and `$100` for the subtotal. Display the tax amount the procedure returns. (It should be $4.50.)

Assignment 5-4: Updating Columns in a Table

After a shopper completes an order, a procedure is called to update the following columns in the BASKET table: ORDERPLACED, SUBTOTAL, SHIPPING, TAX, and TOTAL. The value 1 entered in the ORDERPLACED column indicates that the shopper has completed an order. Inputs to the procedure are the basket ID and amounts for the subtotal, shipping, tax, and total.

1. In SQL Developer, create a procedure named **`BASKET_CONFIRM_SP`** that accepts the input values specified in the preceding description. Keep in mind that you're modifying an existing row of the BB_BASKET table in this procedure.

2. Enter the following statements to create a new basket containing two items:

```
INSERT INTO BB_BASKET (IDBASKET, QUANTITY, IDSHOPPER,
                       ORDERPLACED, SUBTOTAL, TOTAL,
                       SHIPPING, TAX, DTCREATED, PROMO)
    VALUES (17, 2, 22, 0, 0, 0, 0, 0, '28-FEB-12', 0);
INSERT INTO BB_BASKETITEM (IDBASKETITEM, IDPRODUCT, PRICE,
                           QUANTITY, IDBASKET, OPTION1, OPTION2)
    VALUES (44, 7, 10.8, 3, 17, 2, 3);
INSERT INTO BB_BASKETITEM (IDBASKETITEM, IDPRODUCT, PRICE,
                           QUANTITY, IDBASKET, OPTION1, OPTION2)
    VALUES (45, 8, 10.8, 3, 17, 2, 3);
```

3. Type and run `COMMIT;` to save the data from these statements.
4. Call the procedure with the following parameter values: `17, 64.80, 8.00, 1.94, 74.74`. As mentioned, these values represent the basket ID and the amounts for the subtotal, shipping, tax, and total.
5. Query the BB_BASKET table to confirm that the procedure was successful:

```
SELECT subtotal, shipping, tax, total, orderplaced
  FROM bb_basket
  WHERE idbasket = 17;
```

Assignment 5-5: Updating Order Status

Create a procedure named `STATUS_SHIP_SP` that allows an employee in the Shipping Department to update an order status to add shipping information. The BB_BASKETSTATUS table lists events for each order so that a shopper can see the current status, date, and comments as each stage of the order process is finished. The IDSTAGE column of the BB_BASKETSTATUS table identifies each stage; the value 3 in this column indicates that an order has been shipped.

The procedure should allow adding a row with an IDSTAGE of 3, date shipped, tracking number, and shipper. The `BB_STATUS_SEQ` sequence is used to provide a value for the primary key column. Test the procedure with the following information:

```
Basket # = 3
Date shipped = 20-FEB-12
Shipper = UPS
Tracking # = ZW2384YXK4957
```

Assignment 5-6: Returning Order Status Information

Create a procedure that returns the most recent order status information for a specified basket. This procedure should determine the most recent ordering-stage entry in the BB_BASKETSTATUS table and return the data. Use an `IF` or `CASE` clause to return a stage description instead of an IDSTAGE number, which means little to shoppers. The IDSTAGE column of the BB_BASKETSTATUS table identifies each stage as follows:

- 1—Submitted and received
- 2—Confirmed, processed, sent to shipping
- 3—Shipped
- 4—Cancelled
- 5—Back-ordered

The procedure should accept a basket ID number and return the most recent status description and date the status was recorded. If no status is available for the specified basket ID, return a message stating that no status is available. Name the procedure **STATUS_SP**. Test the procedure twice with the basket ID **4** and then **6**.

Assignment 5-7: Identifying Customers

Brewbean's wants to offer an incentive of free shipping to customers who haven't returned to the site since a specified date. Create a procedure named **PROMO_SHIP_SP** that determines who these customers are and then updates the BB_PROMOLIST table accordingly. The procedure uses the following information:

- *Date cutoff*—Any customers who haven't shopped on the site since this date should be included as incentive participants. Use the basket creation date to reflect shopper activity dates.
- *Month*—A three-character month (such as APR) should be added to the promotion table to indicate which month free shipping is effective.
- *Year*—A four-digit year indicates the year the promotion is effective.
- `promo_flag`—1 represents free shipping.

The BB_PROMOLIST table also has a USED column, which contains the default value `N` and is updated to `Y` when the shopper uses the promotion. Test the procedure with the cutoff date 15-FEB-12. Assign free shipping for the month APR and the year 2012.

Assignment 5-8: Adding Items to a Basket

As a shopper selects products on the Brewbean's site, a procedure is needed to add a newly selected item to the current shopper's basket. Create a procedure named **BASKET_ADD_SP** that accepts a product ID, basket ID, price, quantity, size code option (1 or 2), and form code option (3 or 4) and uses this information to add a new item to the BB_BASKETITEM table. The table's PRIMARY KEY column is generated by `BB_IDBASKETITEM_SEQ`. Run the procedure with the following values:

- Basket ID—14
- Product ID—8
- Price—10.80
- Quantity—1
- Size code—2
- Form code—4

Assignment 5-9: Creating a Logon Procedure

The home page of the Brewbean's Web site has an option for members to log on with their IDs and passwords. Develop a procedure named **MEMBER_CK_SP** that accepts the ID and password as inputs, checks whether they make up a valid logon, and returns the member name and cookie value. The name should be returned as a single text string containing the first and last name.

The head developer wants the number of parameters minimized so that the same parameter is used to accept the password and return the name value. Also, if the user doesn't enter a valid username and password, return the value **INVALID** in a parameter named **p_check**. Test the procedure using a valid logon first, with the username **rat55** and password **kile**. Then try it with an invalid logon by changing the username to **rat**.

Hands-On Assignments Part II

Assignment 5-10: Returning a Record

Create a procedure named **DDPROJ_SP** that retrieves project information for a specific project based on a project ID. The procedure should have two parameters: one to accept a project ID value and another to return all data for the specified project. Use a record variable to have the procedure return all database column values for the selected project. Test the procedure with an anonymous block.

Assignment 5-11: Creating a Procedure

Create a procedure named **DDPAY_SP** that identifies whether a donor currently has an active pledge with monthly payments. A donor ID is the input to the procedure. Using the donor ID, the procedure needs to determine whether the donor has any currently active pledges based on the status field and is on a monthly payment plan. If so, the procedure is to return the Boolean value TRUE. Otherwise, the value FALSE should be returned. Test the procedure with an anonymous block.

Assignment 5-12: Creating a Procedure

Create a procedure named **DDCKPAY_SP** that confirms whether a monthly pledge payment is the correct amount. The procedure needs to accept two values as input: a payment amount and a pledge ID. Based on these inputs, the procedure should confirm that the payment is the correct monthly increment amount, based on pledge data in the database. If it isn't, a custom Oracle error using error number 20050 and the message "Incorrect payment amount - planned payment = ??" should be raised. The ?? should be replaced by the correct payment amount. The database query in the procedure should be formulated so that no rows are returned if the pledge isn't on a monthly payment plan or the pledge isn't found. If the query returns no rows, the procedure should display the message "No payment information." Test the procedure with the pledge ID **104** and the payment amount **$25**. Then test with the same pledge ID but the payment amount **$20**. Finally, test the procedure with a pledge ID for a pledge that doesn't have monthly payments associated with it.

Assignment 5-13: Creating a Procedure

Create a procedure named **DDCKBAL_SP** that verifies pledge payment information. The procedure should accept a pledge ID as input and return three values for the specified pledge: pledge amount, payment total to date, and remaining balance. Test the procedure with an anonymous block.

Case Projects

Case 5-1: Using Summary Tables

The Reporting and Analysis Department has a database containing tables that hold summarized data to make report generation simpler and more efficient. They want to schedule some jobs to run nightly to update summary tables. Create two procedures to update the following tables (assuming that existing data in the tables is deleted before these procedures run):

- Create the **PROD_SALES_SUM_SP** procedure to update the BB_PROD_SALES table, which holds total sales dollars and total sales quantity by product ID, month, and year. The order date should be used for the month and year information.
- Create the **SHOP_SALES_SUM_SP** procedure to update the BB_SHOP_SALES table, which holds total dollar sales by shopper ID. The total should include only product amounts—no shipping or tax amounts.

The BB_SHOP_SALES and BB_PROD_SALES tables have already been created. Use the `DESCRIBE` command to review their table structures.

Case 5-2: Working with the More Movie Rentals Rental Process

More Movie Rentals is experimenting with a new concept to make rentals more convenient. Members can request movies via the Internet, or they can check out at a store location. In either case, a small barcode sticker of the member ID and movie ID is printed at the time of rental. It's affixed to a paper slipcase for the movie, which can serve as an envelope. Members can return a movie by sending it via U.S. Mail or dropping it off at a store location. In either case, the clerk scans the member ID and movie ID from the slipcase barcodes.

Two procedures are needed to record rentals and returns in the database. Create a procedure named **`MOVIE_RENT_SP`** that adds a new record to the MM_RENTAL table and updates the movie inventory, which is the MOVIE_QTY column of the MM_MOVIE table. This procedure should accept a member ID, movie ID, and a payment method. The member ID is scanned in from a barcode on the membership card, and the movie ID is scanned in from a barcode on the movie case. The cashier selects the payment type. Test the procedure with member ID = **13**, movie ID = **12**, and payment method = **4**. Verify that the rental has been added and the movie inventory has been updated.

The second procedure needs to record the movie's return. Create a procedure named **`MOVIE_RETURN_SP`** that logs the current date in the CHECKIN_DATE column and updates the movie inventory. Inputs are the member ID and movie ID from the barcodes on the slipcase, so the procedure should determine the rental ID first. Test the procedure with member ID = **13** and movie ID = **12**.

CHAPTER 6

FUNCTIONS

LEARNING OBJECTIVES

After completing this chapter, you should be able to understand:

- Functions
- Creating a stored function
- Using OUT parameters in functions
- Including multiple RETURN statements in a function
- Using a RETURN statement in a procedure
- Using constraints of actual and formal parameters
- Understanding and controlling how parameter values are passed
- Working with function purity levels
- Additional program unit options
- Referencing the data dictionary for program units
- Deleting program units

INTRODUCTION

This chapter explores creating functions, using functions, differences between functions and procedures, parameter constraints, actual versus formal parameters, parameter value passing techniques, and function restrictions in SQL statements. In the process of working through this chapter, you learn that functions are similar to procedures but have several distinct qualities, such as using a RETURN statement and the capability to be used in both PL/SQL and SQL statements.

THE CURRENT CHALLENGE IN THE BREWBEAN'S APPLICATION

Development of the Brewbean's company catalog and ordering application is underway. Two application pages are being reviewed to determine what programming logic is required. First, repeat shoppers are encouraged to set up a member account consisting of a username and password. Having a member account simplifies ordering by saving information, such as the shopper's address, so that it doesn't have to be entered again for each shopping session. Figure 6-1 shows the page that's displayed after a successful member login.

FIGURE 6-1 Member login confirmation

Some application pages identify a shopper by displaying a string that includes the member ID and name. For this task, you need a program unit that retrieves the member ID and name in the format shown for all applicable pages.

The second page being reviewed is the checkout summary, shown in Figure 6-2. It displays order amounts, including the subtotal, shipping, tax, and total.

Brewbean's Coffee Shop

Departments
Basket
Check Out
Search
Account
Order Status

Billing Information

Order Recap:
Subtotal: $15.90
Shipping: $5.00
Tax: $ .64
Total: $21.54

Enter your credit card information:
Enter name on card:
Card number:
Card type: Visa Expire: January 2013

FIGURE 6-2 Order summary and checkout

The calculation of concern in this page is the shipping cost. Brewbean's calculates shipping cost based on the number of items in a basket, so it needs a program unit that counts the total number of items in the order and determines the correct shipping cost. Another goal is being able to use this program unit in SQL queries. In addition, some shoppers receive free shipping offers. To track the total cost of free shipping offers, the Brewbean's manager wants to calculate the shipping cost that would be charged if discounts aren't used.

Rebuilding the Database

To rebuild the Brewbean's database, follow these steps:

1. Make sure you have the `c6_BBcreate.sql` file in the Chapter06 folder. This file contains the script for creating the database.
2. Start SQL Developer and connect to the Oracle database.
3. Click **File**, **Open** from the menu.
4. Click the **`c6_BBcreate.sql`** file, and then click **Open**. The code in this script is displayed in the Edit pane. Scroll through the SQL statements; they should look familiar.
5. Run the script by clicking the **Run Script** button on the Edit pane toolbar. If necessary, click **OK** in the Select Connection dialog box.
6. Scroll through the Script Output pane at the bottom to review the results of the statements.
7. In the Connections pane on the left, expand the **Tables** node to view the tables that were created. While this node is selected, click the **Refresh** button at the top of the Connections pane to update the list of tables.

AN INTRODUCTION TO FUNCTIONS

As you know, a named program unit is a PL/SQL block saved with a name so that it can be reused. You also know a procedure is one type of program unit (used only in PL/SQL statements) used to perform tasks and can return no values or multiple values. In this section, you explore another type of program unit—a function.

Like a procedure, a **function** is a program unit that performs a task, can receive input values, and returns values to the calling environment. The main difference between functions and procedures is that a function is part of an expression. Unlike procedures, it can't serve as an entire statement. This difference is important because it means functions can be used in both SQL commands and PL/SQL statements. (Procedures can't be used in SQL statements.)

Take a look at some Oracle built-in functions you have already used in your SQL programming. The following listing shows an SQL query and its results. The query contains the Oracle built-in `ROUND` function that rounds a numeric value to a specified place:

```
SELECT idProduct, price, ROUND(price, 0)
  FROM bb_product
    WHERE idProduct < 4;
IDPRODUCT       PRICE  ROUND(PRICE,0)
---------- ---------- --------------
         1      99.99            100
         2     129.99            130
         3       32.5             33
```

The ROUND function is used as part of the entire SQL expression. Its task is to use the two arguments provided—a numeric value (the PRICE column) and the degree of rounding (0 for whole numbers)—and return the resulting value. In this case, the function looks at the value of PRICE in every row of the BB_PRODUCT table, performs the rounding action, and returns the result. This process is true of all the single-row functions you're familiar with from coding SQL statements that include Oracle built-in functions.

Oracle built-in functions can also be used in a PL/SQL statement, as shown in the following example, which displays the resulting value 33:


```
DECLARE
  v_amt1 number(5,2);
  v_amt2 number(3,0);
BEGIN
  v_amt1 := 32.50;
  v_amt2 := ROUND(v_amt1,0);
  DBMS_OUTPUT.PUT_LINE(v_amt2);
END;
```

Again, notice that the function is only part of the entire PL/SQL assignment statement for the v_amt2 variable. The function's job is to accept the values provided (the value to be rounded, or v_amt1, and the rounding level or whole dollars), manipulate them according to rounding rules, and return the result. Each time a function is used, a single value is returned. In this example, the function returned the single value 33, which is stored in the v_amt2 variable and displayed by using DBMS_OUTPUT.

Many Oracle-supplied functions are available, such as ROUND, SUBSTR, and TO_CHAR, but for some tasks, you need a function that isn't available in Oracle. In this case, you can create your own function. The functions you create are called "user-defined functions."

Creating a Stored Function

The syntax for creating a function is much like the syntax for creating a procedure with one important difference—a RETURN statement must be used to handle the value the function is to return. This statement is included in both the function header and body (executable sections of the block). Figure 6-3 shows the syntax for creating a function.

```
          ┌CREATE [OR REPLACE] FUNCTION function_name
          │  [ (parameter1_name [mode] data type,
Header  ──┤     parameter2_name [mode] data type,
          │      . . .) ]
          └  RETURN return_value_data type
           IS|AS
               declaration section
          ┌BEGIN
PL/SQL    │    executable section
 block  ──┤    RETURN variable_name;
          │EXCEPTION
          │    exception handlers
          └END;

   ---------------------------------------------------
   Notes on syntax:
        [ ] - indicates optional portions of the statement
        Key commands - in all uppercase
        User provided - in lowercase
        | - offers an OR option
        . . . - indicates continuation possible
```

FIGURE 6-3 The CREATE FUNCTION syntax

After the parameters listed in the header, a RETURN statement indicates the returned value's data type. This data type doesn't include any size information, as when declaring PL/SQL block variables. At least one RETURN statement must be included in the function body to specify which value to return.

Take a look at an example to see how to create a function to meet Brewbean's need for a shipping cost calculation. Figure 6-4 shows a CREATE FUNCTION statement in SQL Developer. The cost of shipping is calculated based on the quantity of items purchased. This task is handled with a function, as it should be, because you want the operation to return a single value.

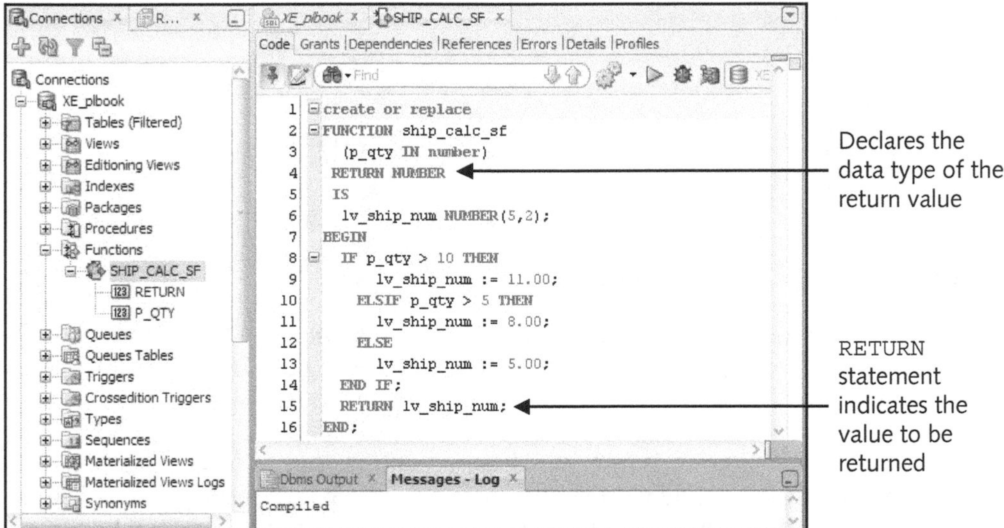

create or replace
FUNCTION ship_calc_sf
(p_qty IN number)
RETURN NUMBER
IS
lv_ship_num NUMBER(5,2);
BEGIN
IF p_qty > 10 THEN
lv_ship_num := 11.00;
ELSIF p_qty > 5 THEN
lv_ship_num := 8.00;
ELSE
lv_ship_num := 5.00;
END IF;
RETURN lv_ship_num;
END;
Compiled
Declares the data type of the return value
RETURN statement indicates the value to be returned

FIGURE 6-4 Creating a function

The function declares the returned value's data type in the header and then uses the RETURN statement in the function body to specify which value is to be returned. In this case, the RETURN statement instructs the system to return the value stored in the lv_ship_num variable.

NOTE

The RETURN statement can also return constant values, such as a text string, or use expressions to perform calculations in the statement.

Invoking and Testing a Created Function

Now that you have a function, how do you invoke (call) and test it? Figure 6-5 shows invoking a function from a PL/SQL block.

The SHIP_CALC_SF function is used as part of an assignment statement in an anonymous PL/SQL block. It accepts 12 as the input argument and feeds this value to the function's IN parameter. The function then checks which range the 12 falls in and assigns the correct shipping cost of $11 to the lv_ship_num variable. The last statement in the function (RETURN) returns the value in the lv_ship_num variable to the calling statement. After the value is returned to the calling block, the lv_cost_num variable then holds the value 11.

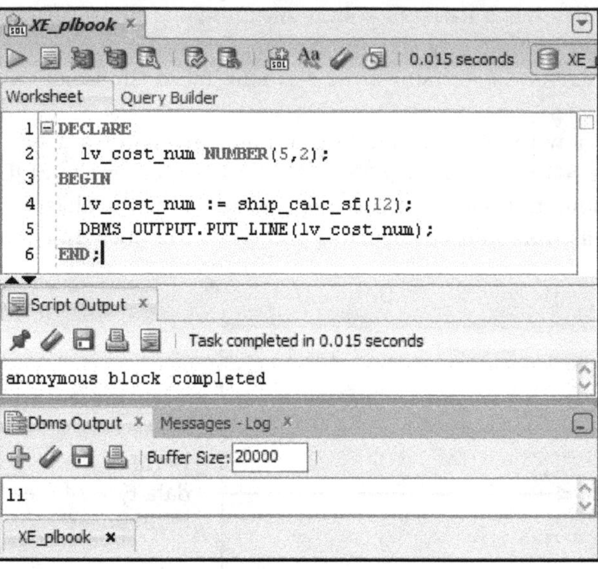

FIGURE 6-5 Invoking a function from a PL/SQL block

After the assignment statement in Figure 6-5 is carried out, the `DBMS_OUTPUT` statement is used in the anonymous block to simplify testing by displaying the value onscreen. The value 12 is hard-coded as the input to the function; however, the argument is usually a variable in the block.

After working with procedures, a common error is attempting to invoke functions by name only as a stand-alone call instead of as part of a statement. Figure 6-6 shows the `SHIP_CALC_SF` function being called by name only and the error that's raised. The error indicates that this type of program unit call is used for procedures, not functions.

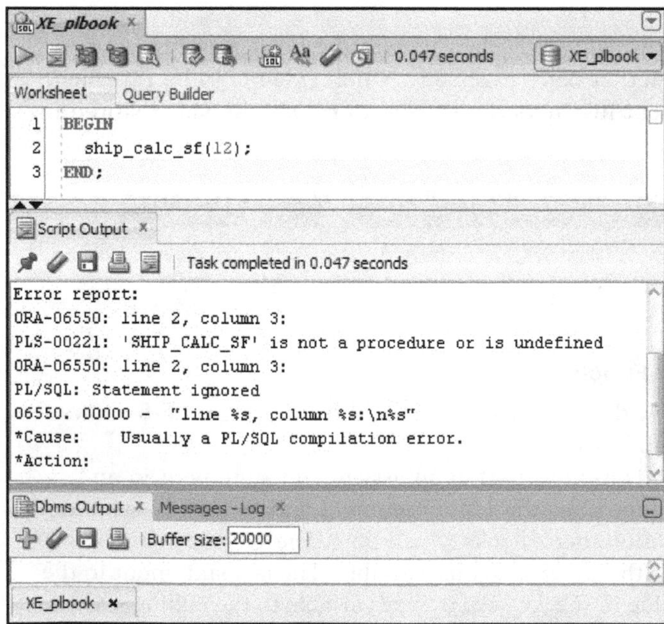

FIGURE 6-6 Invoking a function by name

TIP

Keep in mind that a function is part of an expression because the returned value needs to be held in a variable, so it can't be invoked in a stand-alone fashion, as with a procedure.

Using a Function in an SQL Statement

Unlike a procedure, a function you create can be used in SQL statements, just as you use Oracle built-in functions. This capability is useful when creating stored functions because the functionality can be available to both PL/SQL and SQL code.

Recall that the Brewbean's manager wants to be able to determine the cost of free shipping offers by comparing the actual shipping costs with what would have been charged without discounts. Figure 6-7 shows using the `SHIP_CALC_SF` function in an SQL statement to help with this analysis.

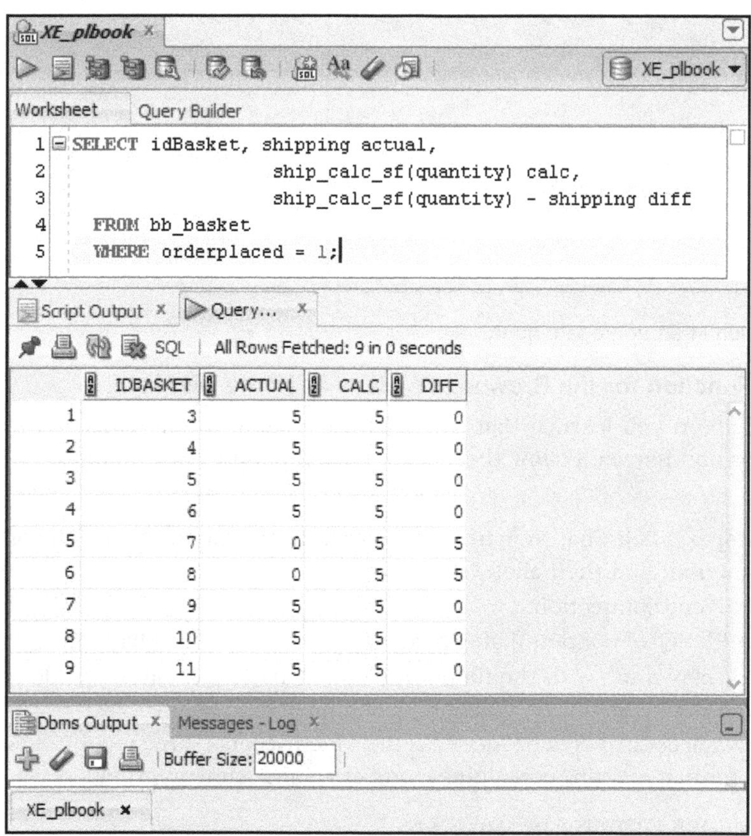

FIGURE 6-7 Using a function in an SQL statement

The SQL query displays details about each shopper basket in the database. The output shows the basket ID, actual shipping charges recorded, shipping cost without any discount, and the difference between these two shipping costs. The `SHIP_CALC_SF` function uses the QUANTITY column as the `IN` argument to determine what shipping cost would be charged without a discount. The function is applied or processed for each row of the BB_BASKET table. The output shows that free shipping on baskets 7 and 8 costs Brewbean's $10 because each basket would have been charged $5 for shipping without the discount.

In Figure 6-8, another SQL query uses an aggregate function to determine the overall sum of shipping amounts and the difference. Nested functions are used in this example. First, the `SHIP_CALC_SF` function is used on each row of the table, and then the `SUM` function computes the total of all results the `SHIP_CALC_SF` function produces. Because an aggregate function is used without a `GROUP BY` clause, a single value is returned for each `SUM` calculation.

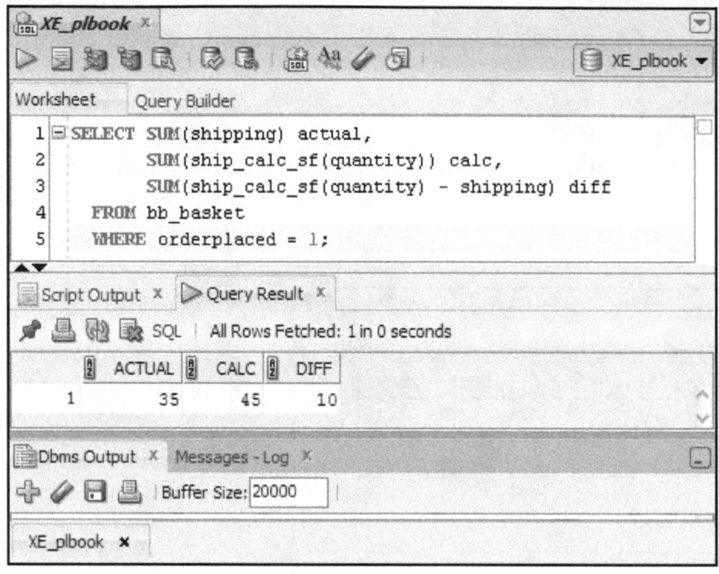

FIGURE 6-8 Using a function in an aggregate query

Building and Testing a Function for the Brewbean's Member Name Display

At the beginning of the chapter, you learned that the Brewbean's application needs formatting for member IDs and names. Follow these steps to create and test a function that meets this need:

1. In SQL Developer, click **File**, **New** from the menu. In the Create a new dialog box, click **Function**, and then click **OK**.
2. Select your current connection.
3. In the Create PL/SQL Function dialog box, enter the name **`MEMFMT1_SP`**.
4. Click **OK** to display a tab with the function name. A basic template of code is filled in automatically, based on your previous input.
5. Enter the following code to create `MEMFMT1_SF`, which accepts three input values and returns a formatted string containing member ID and name information:

```
CREATE OR REPLACE FUNCTION memfmt1_sf
   (p_id IN NUMBER,
    p_first IN VARCHAR2,
    p_last IN VARCHAR2)
  RETURN VARCHAR2
  IS
  lv_mem_txt VARCHAR2(35);
BEGIN
  lv_mem_txt := 'Member '||p_id||' - '||p_first||' '||p_last;
  RETURN lv_mem_txt;
END;
```

6. Click the **Compile** icon at the top of the function's tab to run the statements and create the function. Refresh the Connections pane to confirm that the new function exists.
7. If you get an error on the CREATE FUNCTION statement, review the error messages in the Compiler pane that opens at the bottom. Also, compare what you typed carefully with the code listed in Step 5.
8. Now test the function to make sure it's working correctly. Enter and run the following anonymous block:

```
DECLARE
  lv_name_txt VARCHAR2(50);
  lv_id_num NUMBER(4) := 25;
  lv_first_txt VARCHAR2(15) := 'Scott';
  lv_last_txt VARCHAR2(20) := 'Savid';
BEGIN
  lv_name_txt := memfmt1_sf(lv_id_num, lv_first_txt, lv_last_txt);
  DBMS_OUTPUT.PUT_LINE(lv_name_txt);
END;
```

9. Compare your results with Figure 6-9.

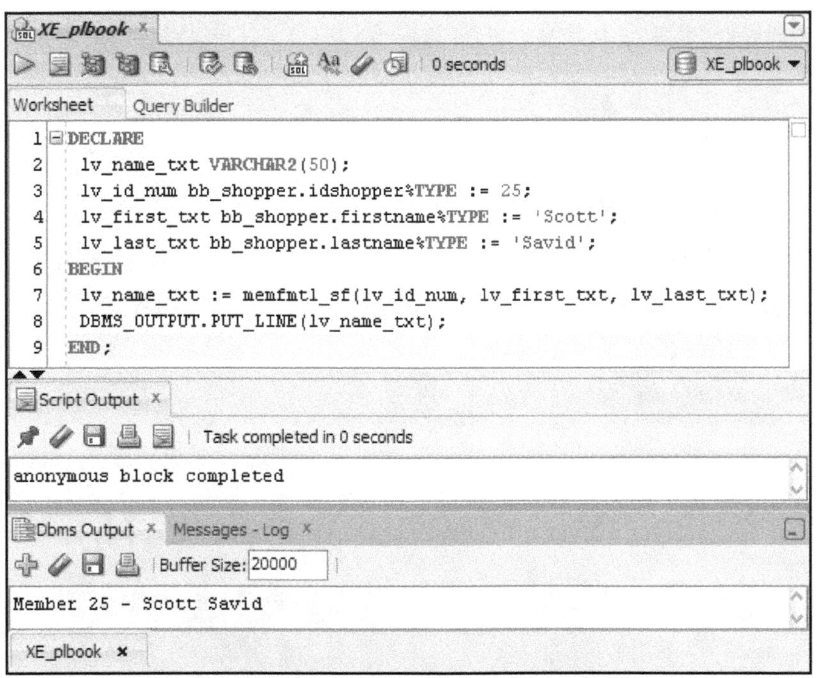

FIGURE 6-9 Testing the MEMFMT1_SF function

Now that you've addressed the need for formatting member IDs and names, continue by using this function in a procedure to complete the member logon process. This exercise helps you understand how procedures and functions are used together. The logon procedure needs to verify the username and password that are entered. If a match is found, the procedure uses the MEMFMT1_SF function to format the member information for display. The procedure returns a flag (to indicate whether logon succeeded), the member ID, and the formatted member name. To create a member logon procedure that uses the MEMFMT1_SF function, follow these steps:

1. In SQL Developer, click **File**, **New** from the menu. In the Create a new dialog box, click **Procedure**, and then click **OK**.
2. Select your current connection.
3. In the Create PL/SQL Procedure dialog box, enter the name **LOGIN_SP**.
4. Click **OK** to display a tab with the procedure name and a basic template of code filled in.

5. Start Notepad, and open the **login06.txt** file in the Chapter06 folder.
6. Copy the CREATE PROCEDURE code in the text file and paste it in SQL Developer to replace the template code.
7. Click the **Compile** icon at the top of the procedure's tab to run the statements and create the procedure. Refresh the Connections pane to confirm that the new procedure exists.
8. Now test this procedure. Enter and run the anonymous block shown in Figure 6-10 to call the procedure and view the values returned from the three DBMS_OUTPUT statements.

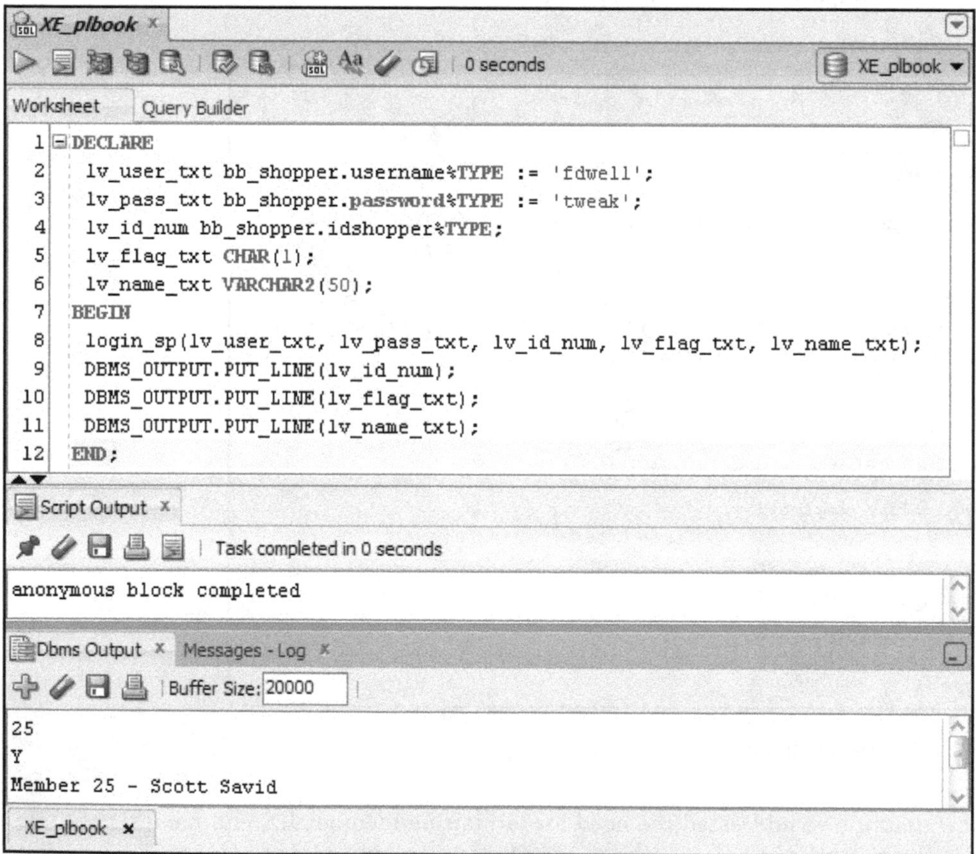

FIGURE 6-10 Displaying values returned from the logon procedure

Now that you have a basic understanding of creating and invoking a function, you can move on to exploring other elements of functions in more detail.

CHALLENGE 6-1

Create a function to return a description for the coffee grind. The input value 3 indicates "Whole Bean," and the value 4 indicates "Ground." If a `NULL` value is provided as input, the function should return `N/A`. First, test the function with an anonymous block. Second, test an SQL statement on the BB_BASKETITEM table, using the OPTION2 column as input.

CHALLENGE 6-2

Create a function to calculate the total pounds of coffee in an order. Keep in mind that the OPTION1 column in the BB_BASKETITEM table indicates the purchase of a half or whole pound. (This column is `NULL` for equipment items.) Also, you need to take the quantity of each item ordered into account. The input value to the function should be a basket ID. First, test the function with basket ID 3, using an anonymous block. Second, test the function in an SQL statement, using the BB_BASKET table, that shows every basket.

USING THE OUT PARAMETER MODE IN A FUNCTION

Did you notice that the functions you have worked with so far have only parameters with an `IN` mode? In Chapter 5, you worked with procedures containing parameters with an `OUT` mode that allowed returning a value from the procedure to the calling environment. Can `OUT` parameters be used in functions? Yes, but in practice, they rarely are for two main reasons. First, developers typically include `OUT` parameters only in procedures because mixing the `RETURN` value with `OUT` parameters in functions tends to be confusing. Second, including an `OUT` parameter in a function means the function can no longer be used in SQL statements.

Coding functions by following the guideline of returning a single value with the `RETURN` statement simplifies using functions. Otherwise, the developer must review the code closely to determine what data is being returned via the `RETURN` statement and what's being returned via parameters. In addition, if a development shop follows the practice of including `OUT` parameters in functions, developers must confirm that no `OUT` parameters are included in a particular function before attempting to use it in an SQL statement. Returning only one value from a function—and doing so with a `RETURN` statement—is considered a better coding practice.

TIP

Don't forget: One of the main reasons `OUT` parameters aren't typically used in a function is that the function doesn't work if it's used in an SQL statement.

Even though avoiding the use of `OUT` parameters in functions is recommended, it's allowed in PL/SQL. Because you might encounter functions coded with `OUT` parameters, you need to be familiar with them. To experiment with the execution of a function including an `OUT` parameter mode, follow these steps:

NOTE

You should be familiar with creating program units now, so from this point on, detailed steps are no longer given.

1. In Notepad, open the **testout06.txt** file in the Chapter06 folder. Use the code to create a function named **TEST_OUT_SF**. Be sure to compile the statement. Notice that the function contains one parameter with an IN OUT mode.
2. Test this function by running the following PL/SQL block. Keep in mind that the function returns two values: one from the RETURN statement and one from the OUT parameter. Confirm that the values 2 and TEST are displayed.

```
DECLARE
  lv_var1_num NUMBER(5) := 1;
  lv_var2_txt VARCHAR2(10);
BEGIN
  lv_var2_txt := test_out_sf(lv_var1_num);
  DBMS_OUTPUT.PUT_LINE( lv_var1_num);
  DBMS_OUTPUT.PUT_LINE( lv_var2_txt);
END;
```

3. Now what happens when you attempt to use this function in an SQL statement? Enter and run the SQL query in Figure 6-11, and review the error message.

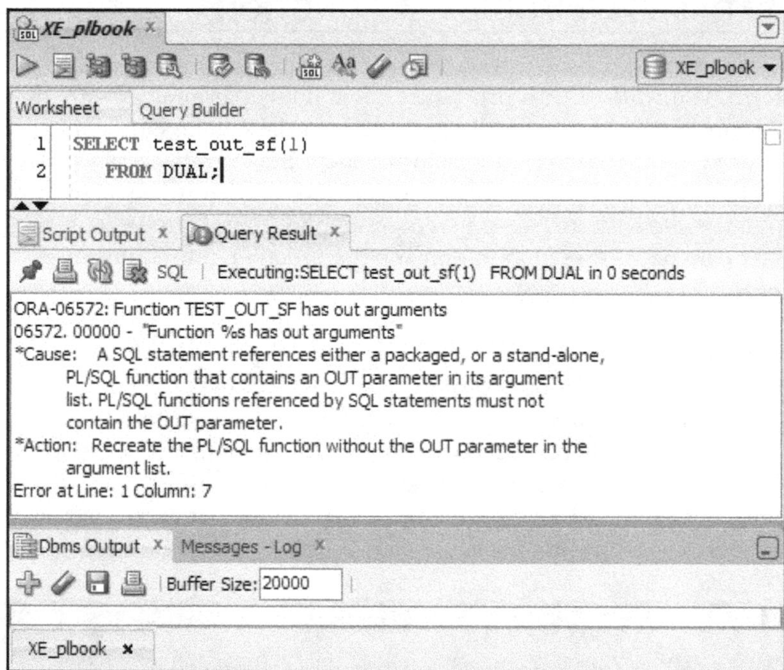

FIGURE 6-11 An SQL query error with a function containing an OUT parameter

The error message states that OUT parameters can't be handled. So even though functions are allowed to include OUT parameters, using these parameters not only leads to confusion, but also prevents you from using functions in SQL statements.

MULTIPLE RETURN STATEMENTS

For simplicity, all the function examples so far contain only a single RETURN statement in the body. However, you can include multiple RETURN statements in the body. Why might you do this? Look at the SHIP_CALC_SF function created earlier (shown in

Figure 6-12). The shipping cost value is saved in the lv_ship_num variable in the IF statement, and then a single RETURN statement references this variable at the end.

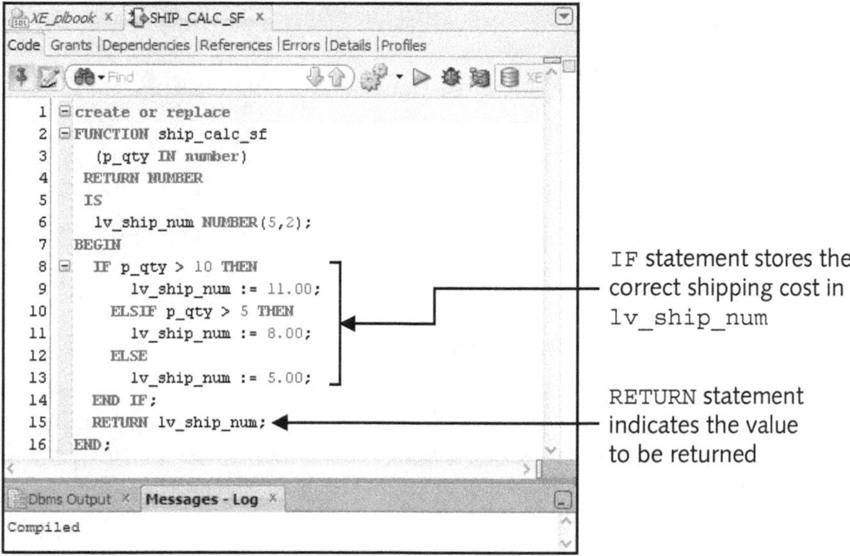

FIGURE 6-12 A function with one RETURN statement

This same function could be written with multiple RETURN statements in the IF statement, as shown in Figure 6-13. You might want to include RETURN statements in the IF statement to avoid having to create a variable for holding the returned value. After an IF clause evaluates to TRUE, the corresponding RETURN statement executes and returns the shipping dollar amount to the calling statement.

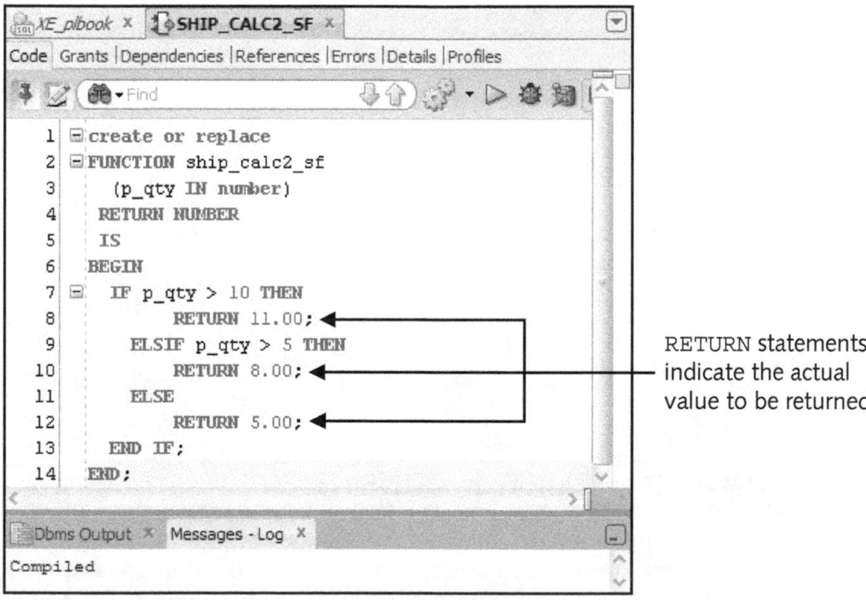

FIGURE 6-13 A function with multiple RETURN statements

TIP

In practice, using a single RETURN statement in a function is considered good form to simplify reviewing code.

CHALLENGE 6-3

Create a function that calculates the discount amount for an order. The discount should be based on a basket's subtotal, and a basket ID is the input to the function. If the subtotal is more than $25, a 5% discount applies; if it's more than $50, a 10% discount applies; and if it's more than $100, a 20% discount applies. Write this block two ways; one block should include multiple RETURN statements. Test with an anonymous block and an SQL statement.

Using a RETURN Statement in a Procedure

A RETURN statement can also be used in a procedure, but it serves a different purpose than it does in a function. In a procedure, it's used to control the flow of execution. It includes no arguments and is followed with a semicolon. When the RETURN statement is executed, the procedure immediately returns execution to the next statement after the procedure call. The values of any OUT parameters at this time are passed back to arguments in the procedure call.

The following code is an example of including a RETURN statement in a procedure that performs a product name change. (Bold code shows what's different from the procedures you're used to seeing.) If a row isn't updated, execution ends because the RETURN statement is issued. At this point, the p_flag parameter returns the value 'N' from the DEFAULT value setting, and no statements after the RETURN statement run.

```
CREATE OR REPLACE PROCEDURE prodname_chg2_sp
  (p_id IN bb_product.idproduct%TYPE,
   p_name IN bb_product.productname%TYPE,
   p_flag CHAR := 'N')
  IS
BEGIN
  UPDATE bb_product
    SET productname = p_name
    WHERE idproduct = p_id;
  IF SQL%ROWCOUNT = 0 THEN
     RETURN;
  END IF;
  COMMIT;
  p_flag := 'Y';
  -- additional statements --
END;
```

ACTUAL AND FORMAL PARAMETER CONSTRAINTS

You might see the terms "formal parameters" and "actual parameters" in discussions of program units. Formal parameters are listed in a program unit. Actual parameters are arguments used when calling a program unit. If an OUT or IN OUT parameter is used in a program unit, the calling statement must provide variables for the arguments (the actual parameters). These variables are necessary because a formal parameter with an OUT mode returns a value that the calling program unit needs to hold.

As you've learned, formal parameters, including the RETURN data type, can't contain any size information. So are there any restrictions on the length of character or numeric parameters? Yes, the actual parameters determine size restrictions. Actual parameters are typically variables that can exist in a program unit or PL/SQL block and are declared with a size. For example, if a PL/SQL variable is declared as VARCHAR(10) and used as an actual parameter to call a procedure or function, the value of the corresponding formal parameter can hold a string only up to 10 characters.

CAUTION

Including size information when declaring a formal parameter causes an error in creating a program unit.

To see how these parameters work, use the MEMFMT1_SF function created earlier to return a string containing a member ID and name. You use an anonymous PL/SQL block to call this function, display the size set on the actual parameter, and determine the size constraint on the formal parameter. Figure 6-14 shows an anonymous block that calls this function. The actual parameter lv_name_txt is set to the length 15, which isn't enough to hold the concatenated string value the function returns.

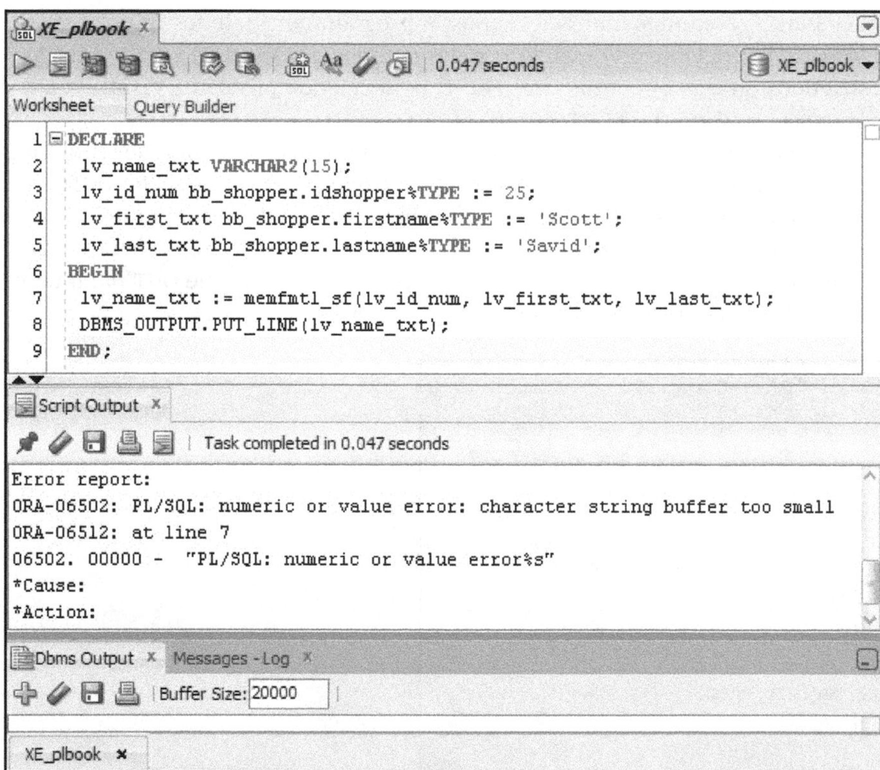

FIGURE 6-14 Testing constraints on parameter size

The error message lists the line where the function is invoked and states that the character string buffer is too small. This occurs because you attempted to retrieve a character value with the length 23 into a formal parameter restricted to 15 characters based on the actual parameter setting. Increase the size of the actual parameter (the lv_name_txt variable) to 50, and test again. The formatted member string should then be displayed correctly.

TIP

Keep in mind that a good way to handle the size issue when declaring variables that hold values from a database table is using the %TYPE attribute to specify the column size. Along these lines, if actual parameters deal with column values returned by a program unit, the %TYPE declaration should still be used to make sure the parameter size is adequate.

Techniques of Passing Parameter Values

PL/SQL uses two techniques for passing values between actual parameters and formal parameters. In the first method, IN parameter values are **passed by reference**, which means a pointer to the value in the actual parameter is created instead of copying the value from the actual parameter to the formal parameter. In the second, OUT and IN OUT parameters are **passed by value**, meaning the value is copied from the actual parameter to the formal parameter. This method is the default behavior.

Passing by reference is generally faster (especially if you're dealing with collections such as tables and VARRAYs that can hold a lot of data) because the copy action doesn't have to take place. Beginning with Oracle 8*i*, you can override passing by value with the NOCOPY compiler hint. A **compiler hint** is a request a programmer includes in code that asks Oracle to modify the default processing in some manner. Oracle acts on the hint as long as any restrictions on this operation are met. If performance problems result, you might want to reconsider using the NOCOPY hint.

Take a look at some examples to see the effect of using the NOCOPY compiler hint on a parameter. Figure 6-15 shows the TEST_NOCOPY_SP procedure, which uses the NOCOPY hint on the p_out parameter. By including this hint immediately after the parameter mode, you're asking the system to pass the actual parameter's value by reference rather than by value (that is, NOCOPY). The procedure assigns the value 'N' to the OUT parameter and raises an error if the IN parameter is equal to 1.

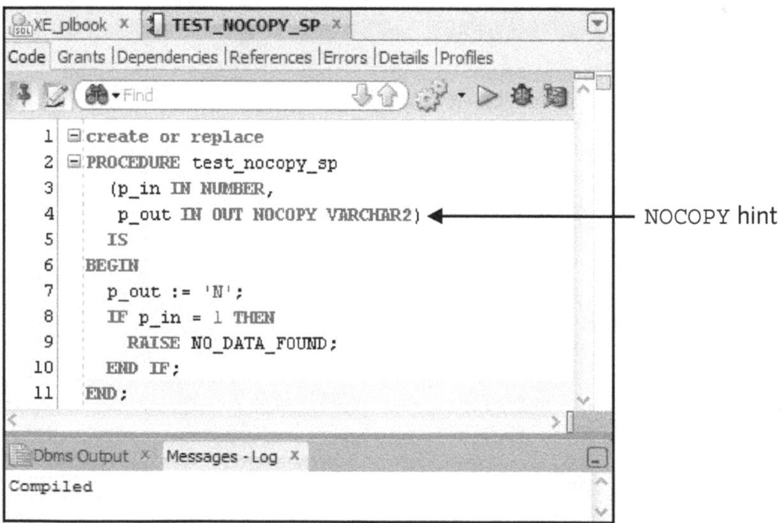

FIGURE 6-15 Using the NOCOPY compiler hint on a parameter

NOTE

The NO_DATA_FOUND error raised in the TEST_NOCOPY_SP procedure has no particular significance in this example. Any error could have been used.

Now try constructing another procedure that calls the TEST_NOCOPY_SP procedure so that you can see the effect of passing values between actual and formal parameters by reference. Figure 6-16 shows the RUN_NOCOPY_SP procedure, which contains the lv_test_txt variable used as the actual parameter for the p_out formal parameter when calling TEST_NOCOPY_SP. It also contains the general exception handler WHEN OTHERS.

XE_plbook | RUN_NOCOPY_SP

Code | Grants | Dependencies | References | Errors | Details | Profiles

```
create or replace
PROCEDURE run_nocopy_sp
 IS
  lv_test_txt VARCHAR2(5);
 BEGIN
  lv_test_txt := 'Y';
  test_nocopy_sp(1,lv_test_txt);
 EXCEPTION
  WHEN OTHERS THEN
    DBMS_OUTPUT.PUT_LINE('Error - var value =  ' || lv_test_txt);
 END;
```

Dbms Output | Messages - Log

```
Compiled
```

FIGURE 6-16 A procedure for testing the NOCOPY hint

To see how the NOCOPY hint works, invoke the RUN_NOCOPY_SP procedure. Figure 6-17 shows the results.

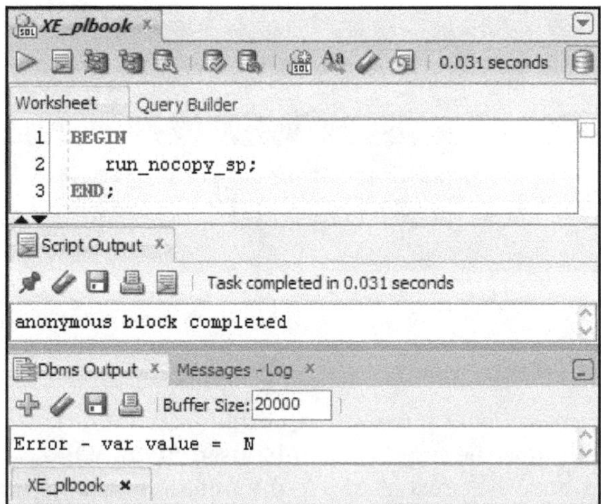

FIGURE 6-17 Invoking the RUN_NOCOPY_SP procedure

The lv_test_txt variable is set to 'Y', and then the TEST_NOCOPY_SP procedure is called with a 1 in the IN parameter to force raising an error. This procedure assigns the value 'N' to the p_out parameter, and then the error is raised. Execution returns to the calling procedure (RUN_NOCOPY_SP), and the exception handler displays a message onscreen showing the current value of lv_test_txt. This variable has the new value 'N', even though the TEST_NOCOPY_SP procedure raises an error. Because the lv_test_txt actual parameter is passed by reference when the formal parameter p_out is altered, the actual parameter (lv_test_txt) is altered because only one value is stored or exists. The formal parameter maintains a pointer to the value only in the actual parameter because the NOCOPY hint is included for this parameter.

If the NOCOPY hint weren't used, the value in lv_test_txt wouldn't have changed because the TEST_NOCOPY_SP procedure raised an error. After an error is raised, values aren't passed or copied between parameters. Remove the NOCOPY hint and run the test again to confirm this operation. Figure 6-18 shows the results of removing the NOCOPY hint. Notice that lv_test_num remains at the value 'Y'.

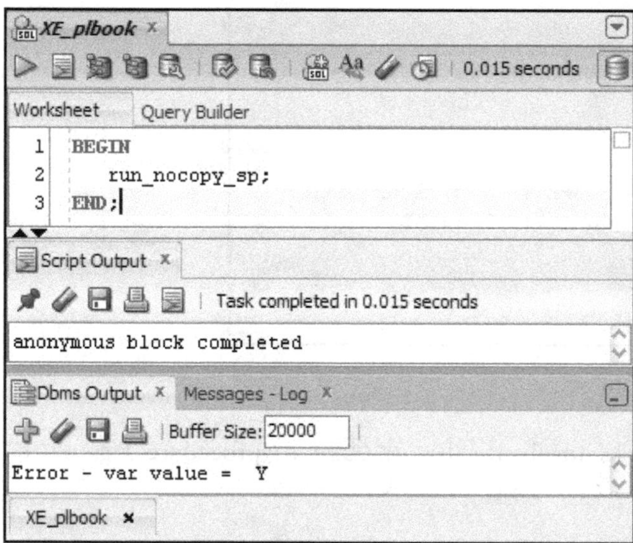

FIGURE 6-18 Removing the NOCOPY hint

> **NOTE**
>
> Compiler hints have rules that must be followed, or Oracle ignores them. For example, one rule for the NOCOPY hint is that the actual parameter can't have a NOT NULL constraint. Restrictions for compiler hints are listed in the Oracle documentation.

FUNCTION PURITY LEVELS

To use user-defined functions in SQL statements, you must follow certain restrictions and requirements. Restrictions are limits on how the function can be used in an SQL statement; requirements are elements that must be present to use the function in an SQL statement. The types of structures and actions affected by a function are described in terms of its purity level. The **purity level** refers to how the function affects database tables and package variables in terms of reading and modifying values. It's also called the "side effects" of a stored program unit.

Before exploring purity levels, you need to be aware of the restrictions on using functions in SQL:

- Functions can't modify any tables in Oracle 8 and earlier versions. Beginning with Oracle 8*i*, a function can't modify a table used in the SQL statement that calls the function; however, it can alter other tables if called from a non-`SELECT` statement.
- If a function is used in a remote or parallel operation, no reading or writing of packaged variables is allowed.
- If a function is used in a `SELECT`, `VALUES`, or `SET` clause, it can write values to packaged variables; otherwise, it isn't allowed.
- Functions can't be used in a `CHECK` constraint or as a default value for a table column.
- If a function calls other subprograms, the subprograms can't break these rules.

In addition to these restrictions, any function you use in an SQL statement—regardless of whether it's created by you or supplied by Oracle—*must* meet the following requirements:

- It must be a stored database object (or in a stored package).
- It can use only `IN` parameters.
- It must be a row function, not a group function.
- Formal parameter data types must use database data types. (No PL/SQL data types, such as `BOOLEAN`, are permitted.)
- Returned value data types must be a database data type.
- It must not issue transaction control statements to end the current transaction before execution.
- It can't issue `ALTER SESSION` or `ALTER SYSTEM` commands.

Four purity levels are available and have acronyms used for identification in coding. Each purity level defines what objects the function, when used in SQL, can legally modify or read. You determine which purity level applies to your programming situation by identifying which restriction applies to the function. Table 6-1 lists the four purity levels.

TABLE 6-1 Function Purity Levels

Level Acronym	Level Name	Level Description
WNDS	Writes No Database State	Function doesn't modify any database tables (no DML).
RNDS	Reads No Database State	Function doesn't read any tables (no `SELECT`).
WNPS	Writes No Package State	Function doesn't modify any packaged variables (which are variables declared in a package specification).
RNPS	Reads No Package State	Function doesn't read any packaged variables.

These purity levels are used in coding to help developers identify the types of actions to expect from a function that's called to prevent unintended consequences. For example, you might call a function that assists in performing a calculation; however, the function also includes DML statements you didn't intend to perform. Using purity levels helps you avoid these situations by declaring functions with purity level information to use in compiling dependent objects (program blocks that call the function). Chapter 7 gives you an overview of how purity level acronyms are included in coding when creating functions in packages as well as changes in handling purity levels that Oracle has recommended starting with Oracle 8*i*.

In the meantime, try an example to see how restrictions affect using your functions in SQL statements:

1. In SQL Developer, enter the following code to create a function named **FCT_TEST1_SF** that performs an update on the BB_TEST1 table:

```
CREATE OR REPLACE FUNCTION fct_test1_sf
  (p_num IN NUMBER)
    RETURN NUMBER
  IS
BEGIN
  UPDATE bb_test1
    SET col1 = p_num;
  RETURN p_num;
END;
```

2. Create a second function named **FCT_TEST2_SF** with the following code. This function performs an update on the BB_TEST2 table:

```
CREATE OR REPLACE FUNCTION fct_test2_sf
  (p_num IN NUMBER)
    RETURN NUMBER
  IS
BEGIN
  UPDATE bb_test2
    SET col1 = p_num;
  RETURN p_num;
END;
```

3. Enter the following `UPDATE` statement and compare your error with Figure 6-19. The error indicates that a function used in an SQL statement can't update the same table being modified by the SQL statement that calls the function. The table is considered to already be mutating (changing) because of the first DML statement.

```
UPDATE bb_test1
  SET col1 = fct_test1_sf(2);
```

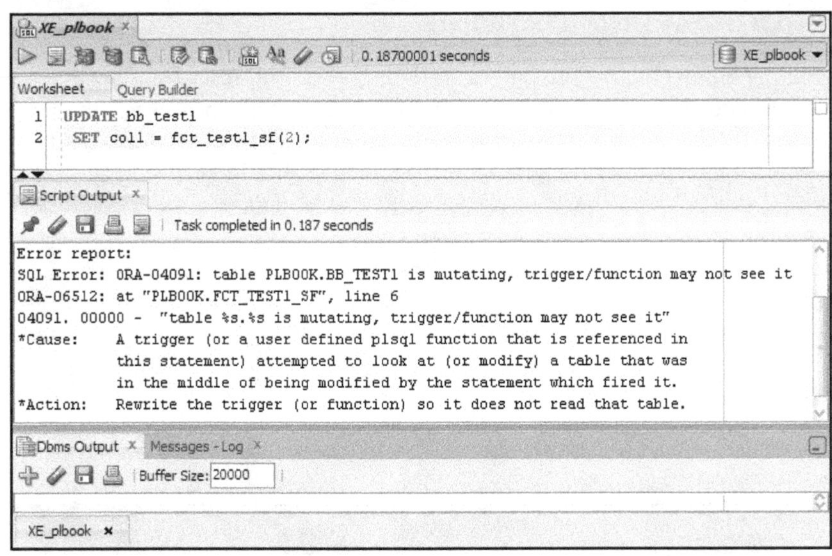

FIGURE 6-19 An error in a function called by an `UPDATE` statement

4. Enter the following `UPDATE` statement, and notice that it runs with no errors. The function is updating a different table (BB_TEST2) from the SQL statement calling the function (BB_TEST1), so it runs just fine.

```
UPDATE bb_test1
  SET col1 = fct_test2_sf(2);
```

5. Enter the following `SELECT` statement, which uses the `FCT_TEST2_SF` function, and compare your error with Figure 6-20. The error indicates that a function called from a `SELECT` statement can't modify table data. As stated in the restrictions list, functions in SQL statements can alter other tables if they're called from a non-`SELECT` statement.

```
SELECT fct_test2_sf(col1)
  FROM bb_test1;
```

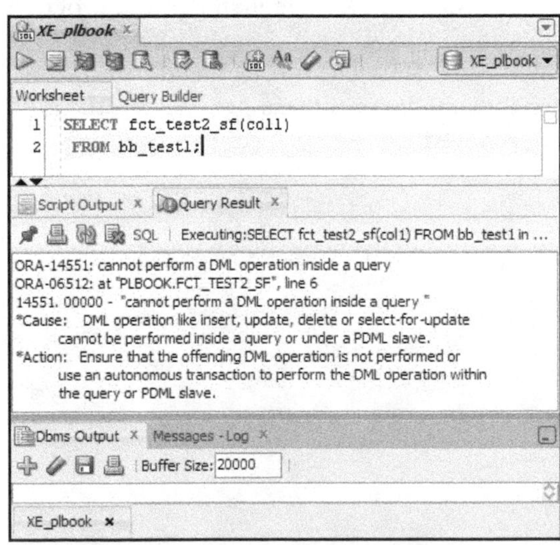

FIGURE 6-20 An error in a function called by a `SELECT` statement

ADDITIONAL PROGRAM UNIT OPTIONS

This chapter and Chapter 5 have addressed the basic construction and use of stored program units. However, additional options can be included as clauses in a program unit's CREATE statement. First, an AUTHID clause is available for both procedures and functions. This clause enables you to designate which privileges should be used for program unit execution: the object owner's or the current user's. This clause is discussed in more detail in Chapter 7.

Second, there are four other options or clauses that apply to functions. They're associated with performance tuning and are beyond the scope of this book; however, every PL/SQL developer needs to be aware of them. As your PL/SQL knowledge advances and you begin to work with large-scale databases, exploring these feature will be helpful. Table 6-2 summarizes these options.

TABLE 6-2 Additional Options for Functions

Option	Description
DETERMINISTIC	Allows the Oracle system to use a saved copy of a function's return value, if it's available.
PARALLEL_ENABLE	Allows using parallel operations when the function is used in a query.
PIPELINED	Instructs the database to return the results of a table function iteratively. A table function creates a result set that's treated like a table in queries. It's typically used for complex, data-heavy operations associated with data-warehousing applications.
RESULT_CACHE	New to Oracle 11g; instructs Oracle to cache function input values and result sets for potential reuse.

DATA DICTIONARY INFORMATION ON PROGRAM UNITS

You can view parameter information quickly by issuing a DESC command on the program unit of interest, as shown in Figure 6-21. Notice that size values are included for the two string IN parameters. Typically, size information isn't declared with parameters; however, because the %TYPE attribute is used to declare the data type in these parameters, the data types of the referenced database columns are retrieved.

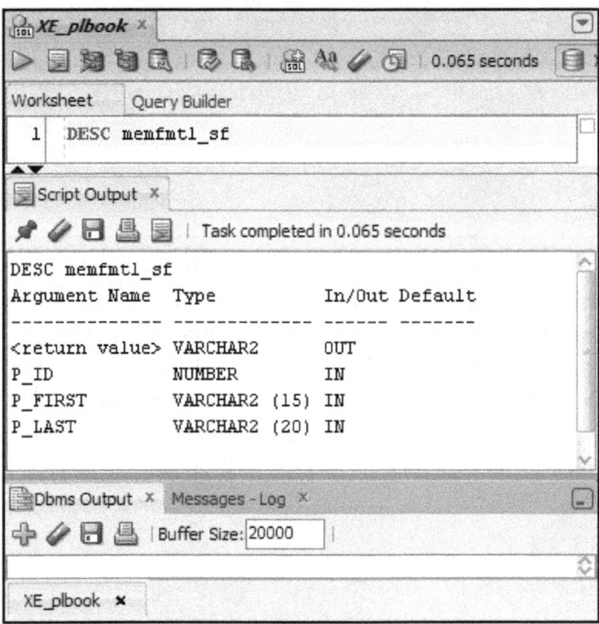

FIGURE 6-21 Using the `DESC` command

In addition, you can reference the data dictionary to determine the code contained in a program unit. This information can be important if you work in a development shop that has limited documentation or few tools available. Use the TEXT column of the `USER_SOURCE` data dictionary view to display the code in the program unit, as shown in Figure 6-22.

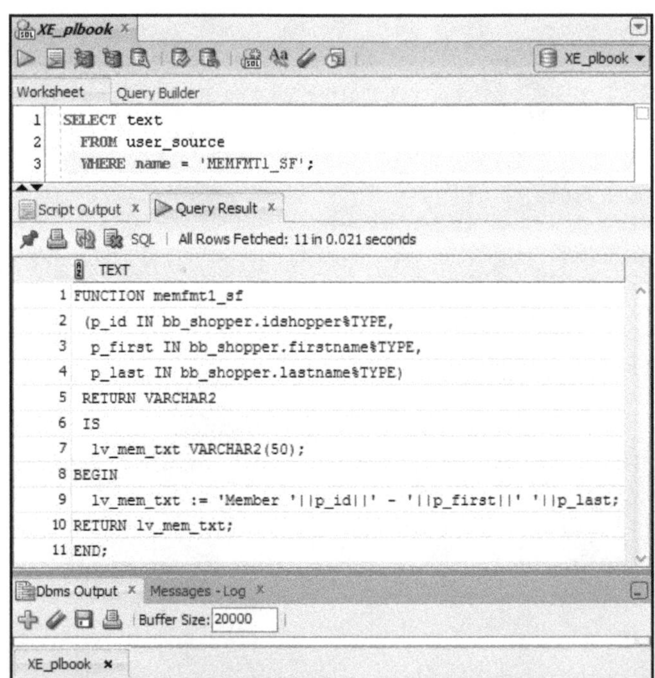

FIGURE 6-22 Using the TEXT column of the `USER_SOURCE` data dictionary view

TIP

Data stored in the data dictionary is uppercase by default. In Figure 6-22, the function name value must be uppercase. If it's not, you need to use a case function to work around this case-sensitivity issue.

DELETING PROGRAM UNITS

At times, you want to eliminate certain procedures and functions, typically when an application or functionality becomes outdated and the program unit is no longer needed. You need to consider program unit dependencies before dropping any objects, however. For example, you have a `LOGIN_SP` procedure that calls the `MEMFMT1_SF` function. If you delete the function, the procedure can no longer compile or run. Program unit dependencies are covered in more detail in Chapter 8.

You delete a program unit with the `DROP` command, which must include the object type and object name, as shown in these examples:

```
DROP PROCEDURE procedure_name;
DROP FUNCTION function_name;
```

Chapter Summary

- A function is another type of program unit, like a procedure; however, a function is part of an expression (not a stand-alone statement), so it can be used in both SQL and PL/SQL statements.
- Oracle has many built-in functions, such as ROUND and TO_CHAR, that can be used in PL/SQL statements. Functions you create are called "user-defined functions."
- Functions use parameters and must return a value. A RETURN statement is included in the header to indicate the return value's data type, and at least one RETURN statement must be included in the function body.
- Even though an OUT parameter is legal in a function, it's rarely used. A function usually returns only a single value via the RETURN statement so that it can be used in SQL statements.
- Multiple RETURN statements can be included in a function; however, only one is executed. In addition, for simplicity, using only a single RETURN statement is considered good form.
- A RETURN statement in a procedure is different, in that it simply controls the flow of statement execution.
- Formal parameters are listed in the program unit. Actual parameters are arguments used when calling a program unit. Formal parameters can't include any size information; actual parameters determine size restrictions.
- Parameter values can be passed by value or by reference. Passing by value (the default behavior) copies the value from the actual parameter to the formal parameter. Passing by reference creates a pointer from the formal parameter to the value in the actual parameter. You can override passing by value with the NOCOPY compiler hint.
- Function purity refers to the rules a function must comply with to be used in SQL statements.
- Performance-tuning options, such as the PARALLEL_ENABLE clause, are available with functions.
- The USER_SOURCE data dictionary view can be used to view the code in a program unit.
- The DROP command is used to delete a program unit.

Review Questions

1. A RETURN statement in a function header performs what task?
    a. It declares the returned value's data type.
    b. It declares the returned value's size and data type.
    c. It moves execution to the body.
    d. A RETURN statement can't be used in a function header.
2. If a function body includes many RETURN statements, which of the following statements is true?
    a. The function can't be used in SQL statements.
    b. An OUT parameter needs to exist for each RETURN.
    c. Only one RETURN statement can execute.
    d. RETURN statements are used only in function headers.

3. How do function and procedure headers differ?
   a. A function can't use `IN OUT` parameters.
   b. No parameters are included in a function.
   c. A function header contains a `RETURN` statement.
   d. A procedure header contains a `RETURN` statement.
4. A formal parameter is ________________.
   a. a parameter in a program unit
   b. a parameter used to call a program unit
   c. a parameter with a constant value
   d. the same as an actual parameter
5. What does a `RETURN` statement in a function body accomplish?
   a. It moves execution to the EXCEPTION section.
   b. It returns a value to the calling statement.
   c. It changes the flow of execution.
   d. `RETURN` statements can't be used in a function body.
6. Are any size restrictions placed on formal parameters?
   a. No.
   b. No, unless a length is included in the formal parameter declaration.
   c. Yes, size constraints are assumed from actual parameters.
   d. Yes, the size must be included in the formal parameter declaration.
7. Passing a parameter value by reference means the value is ________________.
   a. used in an assignment statement
   b. copied to the formal parameter
   c. referenced with a pointer and not copied
   d. used in several parameters
8. Passing a parameter value by value means the value is ________________.
   a. used in an assignment statement
   b. copied to the formal parameter
   c. referenced with a pointer and not copied
   d. used in several parameters
9. Which of the following is a compiler hint used to override the default parameter-passing method?
   a. `ByReference`
   b. `NOCOPY`
   c. `ByValue`
   d. `COPY`
10. A function purity level of WNDS indicates that the function ________________.
    a. reads from database tables
    b. writes to database tables
    c. doesn't read from database tables
    d. doesn't write to database tables

11. Describe the main differences between a function and a procedure.
12. What's the difference between using a RETURN statement in a function and a procedure?
13. Explain the terms "actual parameters" and "formal parameters."
14. What's the difference between passing parameter values by reference and by value?
15. Name two requirements that must be met for a function to be used in an SQL statement.

Advanced Review Questions

1. Based on the following anonymous PL/SQL block, can the program unit named CHECK_SUM be a function?

```
DECLARE
  v_test NUMBER;
BEGIN
  IF v_test > 100 THEN
    check_sum(v_test);
  END IF;
END;
```

   a. Yes.
   b. Yes, but only if the function includes no SQL statements.
   c. Yes, if the v_test variable is initialized.
   d. No.

2. If the CALC_IT function contains an update to the JUNK1 table, can it be used legally in the following PL/SQL block?

```
DECLARE
  v_num NUMBER(1) := 5;
BEGIN
  UPDATE junk2
    SET col1 = calc_it(v_num);
  COMMIT;
END;
```

   a. Yes.
   b. No, a mutating table error is raised.
   c. No, functions can't include DML actions.
   d. No, functions can't be called from SQL statements.

3. If the CALC_IT function contains an update to the JUNK1 table, can it be used as shown in the following SQL statement?

```
SELECT id, calc_it(cost)
  FROM junk2;
```

   a. Yes.
   b. No, a mutating table error is raised.
   c. No, functions called from a query can't include DML actions.
   d. No, functions can't be called from SQL statements.

4. Given the following function, which of the following statements runs successfully?

```
CREATE FUNCTION calc_it
   (p_cost NUMBER)
   RETURN NUMBER
  IS
  v_num NUMBER(8);
BEGIN
   v_num := p_cost*100;
   RETURN v_num;
END;
```

   a. `BEGIN calc_it(55); END;`
   b. `DECLARE lv_num NUMBER; BEGIN calc_it(55, lv_num); END;`
   c. `SELECT calc_it(cost) FROM orders;`
   d. none of the above

5. Which of the following `CREATE FUNCTION` statements produces a compile error?

   a.
```
CREATE OR REPLACE FUNCTION calc_it
   (p_num NUMBER)
  RETURN NUMBER;
  IS
    v_num NUMBER(8);
  BEGIN
    v_num := p_num * 100;
  RETURN v_num;
END;
```

   b.
```
CREATE OR REPLACE FUNCTION calc_it
   (p_num NUMBER(8))
  RETURN NUMBER;
  IS
    v_num NUMBER(8);
  BEGIN
    v_num := p_num * 100;
  RETURN v_num;
END;
```

   c.
```
CREATE OR REPLACE FUNCTION calc_it
  RETURN NUMBER;
  IS
    v_num NUMBER(8);
  BEGIN
    v_num := :p_num * 100;
  RETURN v_num;
END;
```

d.
```
CREATE OR REPLACE FUNCTION calc_it
   (p_num NUMBER)
   RETURN VARCHAR2;
   IS
     v_num VARCHAR2(8);
   BEGIN
     v_num := TO_CHAR(p_num * 100);
   RETURN v_num;
END;
```

Hands-On Assignments Part I

Assignment 6-1: Formatting Numbers as Currency

Many of the Brewbean's application pages and reports generated from the database display dollar amounts. Follow these steps to create a function that formats the number provided as an argument with a dollar sign, commas, and two decimal places:

1. Create a function named **DOLLAR_FMT_SF** with the following code:

```
CREATE OR REPLACE FUNCTION dollar_fmt_sf
   (p_num NUMBER)
    RETURN VARCHAR2
IS
  lv_amt_txt VARCHAR2(20);
BEGIN
  lv_amt_txt := TO_CHAR(p_num,'$99,999.99');
  RETURN lv_amt_txt;
END;
```

2. Test the function by running the following anonymous PL/SQL block. Your results should match Figure 6-23.

```
DECLARE
  lv_amt_num NUMBER(8,2) := 9999.55;
BEGIN
  DBMS_OUTPUT.PUT_LINE(dollar_fmt_sf(lv_amt_num));
END;
```

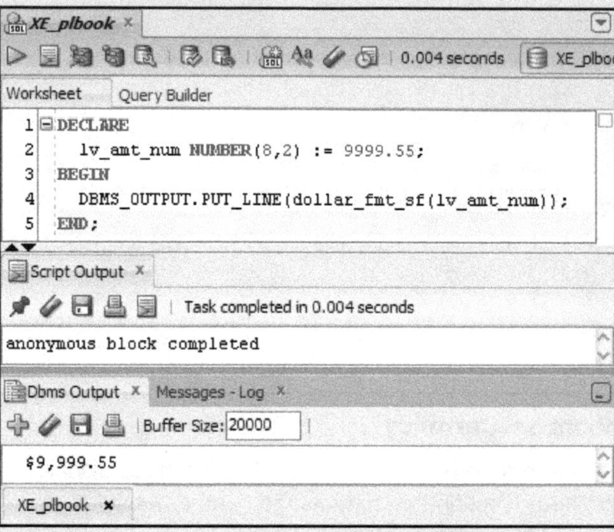

FIGURE 6-23 Testing the dollar-formatting function

3. Test the function with the following SQL statement. Your results should match Figure 6-24.

```
SELECT dollar_fmt_sf(shipping), dollar_fmt_sf(total)
  FROM bb_basket
  WHERE idBasket = 3;
```

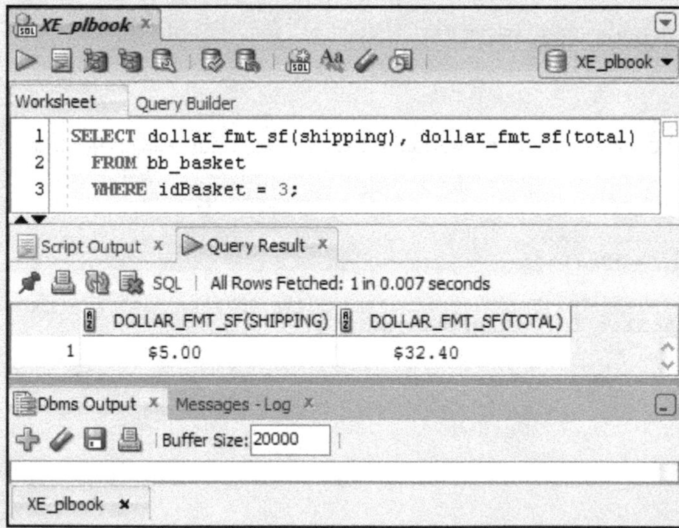

FIGURE 6-24 Testing the dollar-formatting function in a query

Assignment 6-2: Calculating a Shopper's Total Spending

Many of the reports generated from the system calculate the total dollars in a shopper's purchases. Follow these steps to create a function named `TOT_PURCH_SF` that accepts a shopper ID as input and returns the total dollars the shopper has spent with Brewbean's. Use the function in a SELECT statement that shows the shopper ID and total purchases for every shopper in the database.

1. Develop and run a CREATE FUNCTION statement to create the **TOT_PURCH_SF** function. The function code needs a formal parameter for the shopper ID and to sum the TOTAL column of the BB_BASKET table.
2. Develop a SELECT statement, using the BB_SHOPPER table, to produce a list of each shopper in the database and his or her total purchases.

Assignment 6-3: Calculating a Shopper's Total Number of Orders

Another commonly used statistic in reports is the total number of orders a shopper has placed. Follow these steps to create a function named NUM_PURCH_SF that accepts a shopper ID and returns a shopper's total number of orders. Use the function in a SELECT statement to display the number of orders for shopper 23.

1. Develop and run a CREATE FUNCTION statement to create the **NUM_PURCH_SF** function. The function code needs to tally the number of orders (using an Oracle built-in function) by shopper. Keep in mind that the ORDERPLACED column contains a 1 if an order has been placed.
2. Create a SELECT query by using the NUM_PURCH_SF function on the IDSHOPPER column of the BB_SHOPPER table. Be sure to select only shopper 23.

Assignment 6-4: Identifying the Weekday for an Order Date

The day of the week that baskets are created is often analyzed to determine consumer-shopping patterns. Create a function named DAY_ORD_SF that accepts an order date and returns the weekday. Use the function in a SELECT statement to display each basket ID and the weekday the order was created. Write a second SELECT statement, using this function to display the total number of orders for each weekday. (*Hint*: Call the TO_CHAR function to retrieve the weekday from a date.)

1. Develop and run a CREATE FUNCTION statement to create the **DAY_ORD_SF** function. Use the DTCREATED column of the BB_BASKET table as the date the basket is created. Call the TO_CHAR function with the DAY option to retrieve the weekday for a date value.
2. Create a SELECT statement that lists the basket ID and weekday for every basket.
3. Create a SELECT statement, using a GROUP BY clause to list the total number of baskets per weekday. Based on the results, what's the most popular shopping day?

Assignment 6-5: Calculating Days Between Ordering and Shipping

An analyst in the quality assurance office reviews the time elapsed between receiving an order and shipping the order. Any orders that haven't been shipped within a day of the order being placed are investigated. Create a function named **ORD_SHIP_SF** that calculates the number of days between the basket's creation date and the shipping date. The function should return a character string that states OK if the order was shipped within a day or CHECK if it wasn't. If the order hasn't shipped, return the string Not shipped. The IDSTAGE column of the BB_BASKETSTATUS table indicates a shipped item with the value 5, and the DTSTAGE column is the shipping date. The DTORDERED column of the BB_BASKET table is the order date. Review data in the BB_BASKETSTATUS table, and create an anonymous block to test all three outcomes the function should handle.

Assignment 6-6: Adding Descriptions for Order Status Codes

When a shopper returns to the Web site to check an order's status, information from the BB_BASKETSTATUS table is displayed. However, only the status code is available in the BB_BASKETSTATUS table, not the status description. Create a function named **STATUS_DESC_SF** that accepts a stage ID and returns the status description. The descriptions for stage IDs are listed in Table 6-3. Test the function in a `SELECT` statement that retrieves all rows in the BB_BASKETSTATUS table for basket 4 and displays the stage ID and its description.

TABLE 6-3 Basket Stage Descriptions

Stage ID	Description
1	Order submitted
2	Accepted, sent to shipping
3	Back-ordered
4	Cancelled
5	Shipped

Assignment 6-7: Calculating an Order's Tax Amount

Create a function named **TAX_CALC_SF** that accepts a basket ID, calculates the tax amount by using the basket subtotal, and returns the correct tax amount for the order. The tax is determined by the shipping state, which is stored in the BB_BASKET table. The BB_TAX table contains the tax rate for states that require taxes on Internet purchases. If the state isn't listed in the tax table or no shipping state is assigned to the basket, a tax amount of zero should be applied to the order. Use the function in a `SELECT` statement that displays the shipping costs for a basket that has tax applied and a basket with no shipping state.

Assignment 6-8: Identifying Sale Products

When a product is placed on sale, Brewbean's records the sale's start and end dates in columns of the BB_PRODUCT table. A function is needed to provide sales information when a shopper selects an item. If a product is on sale, the function should return the value `ON SALE!`. However, if it isn't on sale, the function should return the value `Great Deal!`. These values are used on the product display page. Create a function named **CK_SALE_SF** that accepts a date and product ID as arguments, checks whether the date falls within the product's sale period, and returns the corresponding string value. Test the function with the product ID 6 and two dates: 10-JUN-12 and 19-JUN-12. Verify your results by reviewing the product sales information.

Hands-On Assignments Part II

Assignment 6-9: Determining the Monthly Payment Amount

Create a function named **DD_MTHPAY_SF** that calculates and returns the monthly payment amount for donor pledges paid on a monthly basis. Input values should be the number of monthly payments and the pledge amount. Use the function in an anonymous PL/SQL block to show its use with the following pledge information: pledge amount = $240 and monthly payments = 12. Also, use the function in an SQL statement that displays information for all donor pledges in the database on a monthly payment plan.

Assignment 6-10: Calculating the Total Project Pledge Amount

Create a function named `DD_PROJTOT_SF` that determines the total pledge amount for a project. Use the function in an SQL statement that lists all projects, displaying project ID, project name, and project pledge total amount. Format the pledge total to display zero if no pledges have been made so far, and have it show a dollar sign, comma, and two decimal places for dollar values.

Assignment 6-11: Identifying Pledge Status

The DoGood Donor organization decided to reduce SQL join activity in its application by eliminating the DD_STATUS table and replacing it with a function that returns a status description based on the status ID value. Create this function and name it `DD_PLSTAT_SF`. Use the function in an SQL statement that displays the pledge ID, pledge date, and pledge status for all pledges. Also, use it in an SQL statement that displays the same values but for only a specified pledge.

Assignment 6-12: Determining a Pledge's First Payment Date

Create a function named `DD_PAYDATE1_SF` that determines the first payment due date for a pledge based on pledge ID. The first payment due date is always the first day of the month after the date the pledge was made, even if a pledge is made on the first of a month. Keep in mind that a pledge made in December should reflect a first payment date with the following year. Use the function in an anonymous block.

Assignment 6-13: Determining a Pledge's Final Payment Date

Create a function named `DD_PAYEND_SF` that determines the final payment date for a pledge based on pledge ID. Use the function created in Assignment 6-12 in this new function to help with the task. If the donation pledge indicates a lump sum payment, the final payment date is the same as the first payment date. Use the function in an anonymous block.

Case Projects

Case 6-1: Updating Basket Data at Order Completion

A number of functions created in this chapter assume that the basket amounts, including shipping, tax, and total, are already posted to the BB_BASKET table. However, the program units for updating these columns when a shopper checks out haven't been developed yet. A procedure is needed to update the following columns in the BB_BASKET table when an order is completed: ORDERPLACED, SUBTOTAL, SHIPPING, TAX, and TOTAL.

Construct three functions to perform the following tasks: calculating the subtotal by using the BB_BASKETITEM table based on basket ID as input, calculating shipping costs based on basket ID as input, and calculating the tax based on basket ID and subtotal as input. Use these functions in a procedure.

A value of 1 entered in the ORDERPLACED column indicates that the shopper has completed the order. The subtotal is determined by totaling the item lines of the BB_BASKETITEM table for the applicable basket number. The shipping cost is based on the number of items in the basket: 1 to 4 = $5, 5 to 9 = $8, and more than 10 = $11.

The tax is based on the rate applied by referencing the SHIPSTATE column of the BB_BASKET table with the STATE column of the BB_TAX table. This rate should be multiplied by the basket subtotal, which should be an `INPUT` parameter to the tax calculation because the subtotal is being calculated in this same procedure. The total tallies all these amounts.

The only INPUT parameter for the procedure is a basket ID. The procedure needs to update the correct row in the BB_BASKET table with all these amounts. To test, first set all column values to NULL for basket 3 with the following UPDATE statement. Then call the procedure for basket 3 and check the INSERT results.

```
UPDATE bb_basket
  SET orderplaced = NULL,
      Subtotal = NULL,
      Tax = NULL,
      Shipping = NULL,
      Total = NULL
    WHERE idBasket = 3;
COMMIT;
```

Case 6-2: Working with More Movies Rentals

More Movies receives numerous requests to check whether movies are in stock. The company needs a function that retrieves movie stock information and formats a clear message to display to users requesting information. The display should resemble the following: “Star Wars is Available: 11 on the shelf.”

Use movie ID as the input value for this function. Assume the MOVIE_QTY column in the MM_MOVIES table indicates the number of movies currently available for checkout.

CHAPTER 7

PL/SQL PACKAGES

LEARNING OBJECTIVES

After completing this chapter, you should be able to understand:

- Creating packages
- Invoking program units in packages
- Including a forward declaration
- Creating one-time-only procedures
- Overloading program units
- Managing restrictions on packaged functions used in SQL
- Using a cursor variable in a package
- Granting execute privileges
- Finding package information with data dictionary views
- Deleting or removing packages

INTRODUCTION

A **package**, which is another type of PL/SQL construct, is a container that can hold multiple program units, such as procedures and functions. You can compare it with an ice tray: The tray represents the package, and the ice cubes represent program units.

Using packages helps programmers organize program units into related groups, establish private program units, share variable values across program units, overload program units, grant user privileges more easily, and improve performance. All these benefits are discussed in this chapter. Packages also make it easier to handle dependencies (covered in Chapter 8).

THE CURRENT CHALLENGE IN THE BREWBEAN'S APPLICATION

The Brewbean's development group needs to solve some new problems with the application. First, the group is accumulating quite a few program units and needs a way to organize and manage them. Second, the group needs to determine how to store values throughout a user session. For example, the manager wants to run daily percentage discount specials, and discount values need to be stored during a shopper's session and applied to the basket subtotal when necessary. Third, a product search page is being developed, and the goal is to allow users to enter a product ID or product name to use in the search. The program unit for conducting the search needs to be able to handle a number or character value and search based on product ID or name. However, the group isn't sure how to achieve this goal because a program unit must use the data type defined for its parameters. Last, the database administrator is concerned with the time it takes to grant users privileges to all the objects and operations needed to run the application and wants to create a mechanism to simplify this process.

Rebuilding the Database

To rebuild the Brewbean's database, follow these steps:

1. Make sure you have the `c7_BBcreate.sql` file in the Chapter07 folder. This file contains the script for creating the database.
2. Start SQL Developer and connect to the Oracle database.
3. Click **File**, **Open** from the menu.
4. Click the **`c7_BBcreate.sql`** file, and then click **Open**. The code in this script is displayed in the Edit pane. Scroll through the SQL statements; they should look familiar.
5. Run the script by clicking the **Run Script** button on the Edit pane toolbar. If necessary, click **OK** in the Select Connection dialog box.
6. Scroll through the Script Output pane at the bottom to review the results of the statements.
7. In the Connections pane on the left, expand the **Tables** node to view the tables that were created. While this node is selected, click the **Refresh** button at the top of the Connections pane to update the list of tables.

CREATING PACKAGES

A package consists of two parts: a specification and a body. The **package specification** declares the package's contents and is referred to as the "package header." A specification is required and must be created before the body. The **package body** contains the full code for all objects in the package, such as procedures and functions.

Declarations in a Package Specification

A package specification can contain declarations for procedures, functions, variables, exceptions, cursors, and types. As you'll recall, a declaration defines a data construct—for example, by specifying a variable, name, and data type. Declarations of procedures and functions contain the program unit's header information (name, parameters, and return data type, if applicable) but not its PL/SQL code block. The full program unit code is in the package body. The package specification serves as a map to what program units and parameters are available in the package. Figure 7-1 shows the syntax for creating a package specification.

```
CREATE [OR REPLACE] PACKAGE package_name
  IS|AS
    declaration section...
 END;

--------------------------------------------------
 Notes  on syntax:
        [ ] - indicates optional portions of the statement
        Key commands - in all uppercase
        User provided - in lowercase
        | - offers an OR option
        . . . - indicates continuation possible
```

FIGURE 7-1 The `CREATE PACKAGE` syntax

To see how this syntax works, try creating a package specification that includes a procedure, a function, and a variable (see Figure 7-2). These package elements are related to the ordering process in the Brewbean's application. The `ORDER_TOTAL_PP` procedure and the `SHIP_CALC_PF` function are used to calculate the order summary amounts when shoppers check out, and the `pv_total_num` variable holds the order total.

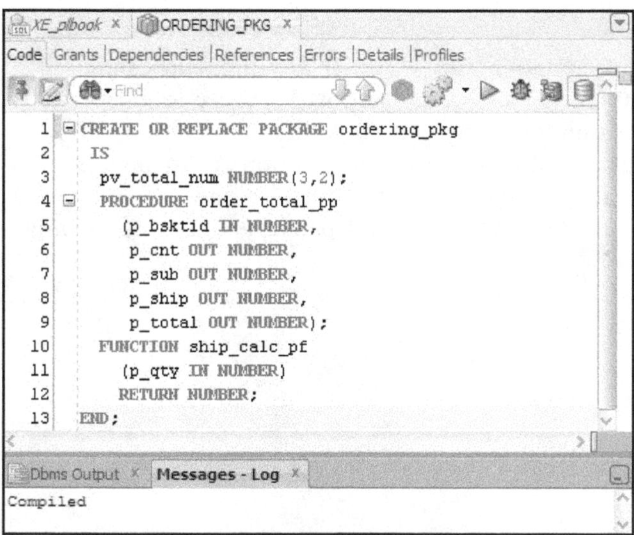
XE_plbook
ORDERING_PKG
Code Grants Dependencies References Errors Details Profiles
Find
CREATE OR REPLACE PACKAGE ordering_pkg
IS
pv_total_num NUMBER(3,2);
PROCEDURE order_total_pp
(p_bsktid IN NUMBER,
p_cnt OUT NUMBER,
p_sub OUT NUMBER,
p_ship OUT NUMBER,
p_total OUT NUMBER);
FUNCTION ship_calc_pf
(p_qty IN NUMBER)
RETURN NUMBER;
END;
Dbms Output
Messages - Log
Compiled

FIGURE 7-2 Creating a package specification for `ORDERING_PKG`

Follow these steps to create the package specification:

1. Start SQL Developer, if necessary. Click **File**, **New** from the menu. In the Create a new dialog box, click **Package**, and then click **OK**. Select your current connection and click **OK**, if necessary. Enter the name **`ORDERING_PKG`**, and click **OK**.
2. Start Notepad, and open the **`ordpkg07.txt`** file in the Chapter07 folder. Copy the code in this file, and paste it in SQL Developer to replace the code template.
3. Compile to create the package specification. Expand the **Packages** node in the Connections pane to see an entry for the new package specification.

NOTE

Packages can be created only as stored program units. A package can't be created in local libraries, as procedures and functions can.

Ordering Items in a Specification

The order of items (such as procedures, functions, and variables) declared in a specification isn't important—unless one declaration item is referenced by another. In this case, the referenced item must be declared first. For example, if you declare a cursor in your package specification that references the `pv_total_num` packaged variable, the variable must be declared before the cursor.

Any mixture of declarations can be used, and no one type of declaration is required in a package specification. For example, a specification might contain only one variable and one cursor. A package specification isn't required to contain a procedure or function, even though including these program units is quite common.

Package Body

A package body is the program unit containing the code for any procedures and functions declared in the specification. It must be created with the same name as the specification to tie the specification and body code together. In addition, all code in the package body's procedure and function header sections must match declarations in the specification exactly. Figure 7-3 points out the package specification and body statements for the `ORDERING_PKG` package you're developing for Brewbean's.

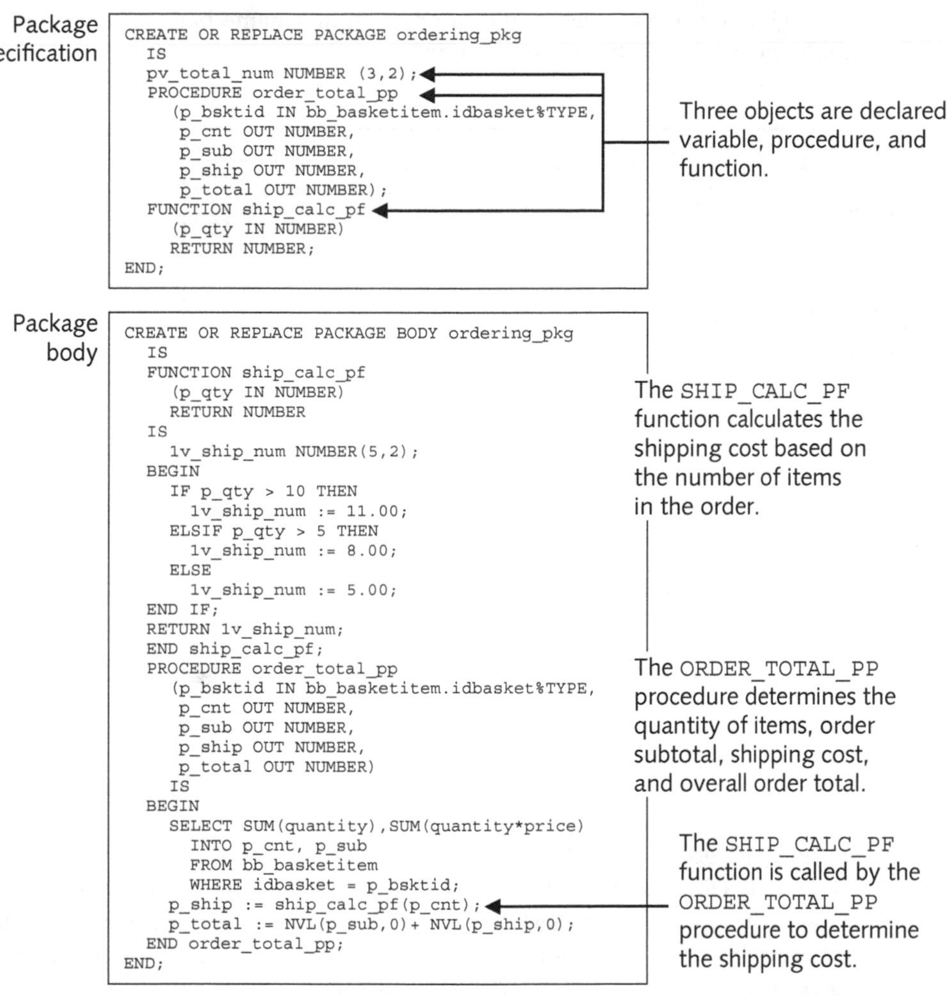

Package specification
CREATE OR REPLACE PACKAGE ordering_pkg
IS
pv_total_num NUMBER (3,2);
PROCEDURE order_total_pp
(p_bsktid IN bb_basketitem.idbasket%TYPE,
p_cnt OUT NUMBER,
p_sub OUT NUMBER,
p_ship OUT NUMBER,
p_total OUT NUMBER);
FUNCTION ship_calc_pf
(p_qty IN NUMBER)
RETURN NUMBER;
END;
Three objects are declared: variable, procedure, and function.
Package body
CREATE OR REPLACE PACKAGE BODY ordering_pkg
IS
FUNCTION ship_calc_pf
(p_qty IN NUMBER)
RETURN NUMBER
IS
lv_ship_num NUMBER(5,2);
BEGIN
IF p_qty > 10 THEN
lv_ship_num := 11.00;
ELSIF p_qty > 5 THEN
lv_ship_num := 8.00;
ELSE
lv_ship_num := 5.00;
END IF;
RETURN lv_ship_num;
END ship_calc_pf;
PROCEDURE order_total_pp
(p_bsktid IN bb_basketitem.idbasket%TYPE,
p_cnt OUT NUMBER,
p_sub OUT NUMBER,
p_ship OUT NUMBER,
p_total OUT NUMBER)
IS
BEGIN
SELECT SUM(quantity),SUM(quantity*price)
INTO p_cnt, p_sub
FROM bb_basketitem
WHERE idbasket = p_bsktid;
p_ship := ship_calc_pf(p_cnt);
p_total := NVL(p_sub,0)+ NVL(p_ship,0);
END order_total_pp;
END;
The SHIP_CALC_PF function calculates the shipping cost based on the number of items in the order.
The ORDER_TOTAL_PP procedure determines the quantity of items, order subtotal, shipping cost, and overall order total.
The SHIP_CALC_PF function is called by the ORDER_TOTAL_PP procedure to determine the shipping cost.

FIGURE 7-3 The package specification and body

> **TIP**
>
> Did you notice that the `END` statements closing the procedure and function statements in the package body reference the program unit's name? Adding the procedure or function name in the `END` statement is optional; however, it's considered a good coding practice because it makes code in the body easier to read by marking which program unit code ends at this point.

The package body can also include declarations of variables, cursors, types, and program units not found in the corresponding specification. Any items declared in the body but not the specification can be used only by other procedures and functions in the same package body. They're considered private items (discussed in "Package Scope" later in this chapter).

Notice in Figure 7-3 that the second `CREATE` statement includes the keyword `BODY`. Follow these steps to create a package body so that you can explore using the package:

1. In SQL Developer, right-click the **`ORDERING_PKG`** node in the Connections pane and click **Create Body** (see Figure 7-4). A code template is displayed on

the right. You don't have to enter a program unit name because it matches the name of the package specification.

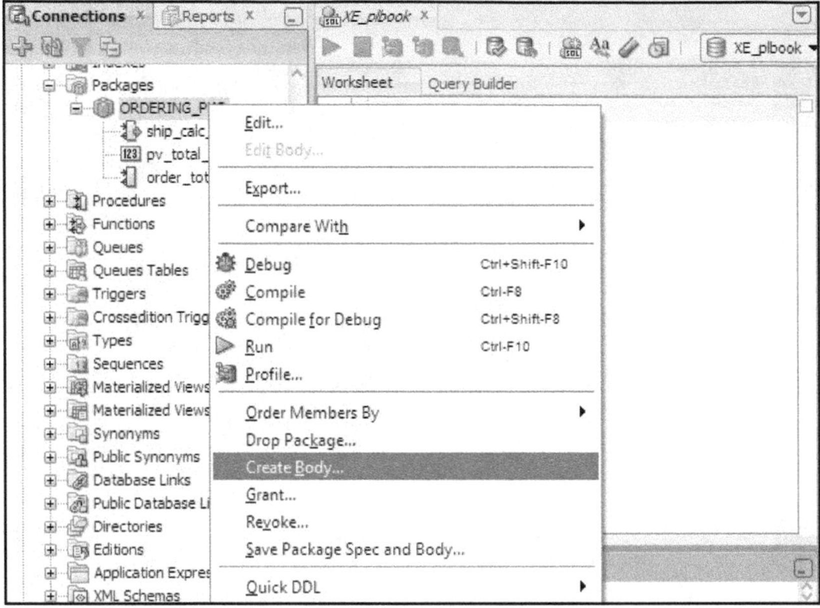

FIGURE 7-4 Selecting the option to create a package body

2. In Notepad, open the **`ordbod07.txt`** file in the Chapter07 folder. Copy the code in this file and paste it in SQL Developer to replace the code template.
3. Compile to create the package body. Refresh the Connections pane, and click to expand the **Packages** node. A node for the new package body is displayed under the `ORDERING_PKG` node (see Figure 7-5).

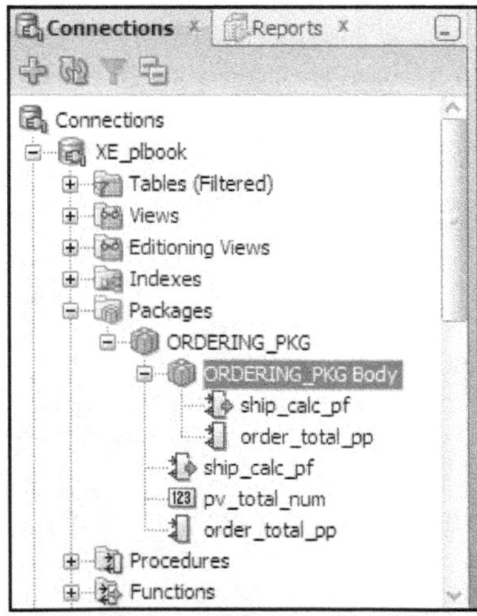

FIGURE 7-5 Package body node displayed in the Connections pane

TIP

To simplify creating packages, developers usually create stand-alone procedures and functions first, and then include all the program unit code in the package. With this method, program units are tested before being included in a package. If this practice is used, stand-alone procedures and functions are normally deleted so that they're not referenced accidentally. In other words, a program unit should exist in only one place in the database.

INVOKING PACKAGE CONSTRUCTS

Next, you test the package you created in the previous section by invoking one of its program units. First, test the `ORDER_TOTAL_PP` procedure, which is used often in the Brewbean's application. To call a package program unit, you reference the package name and program unit name because the program unit is now located in a container or package. Follow these steps to test the `ORDER_TOTAL_PP` procedure:

1. In SQL Developer, enter and run the anonymous block shown in Figure 7-6. The call to the procedure uses the format *`package_name.program_unit_name`*.

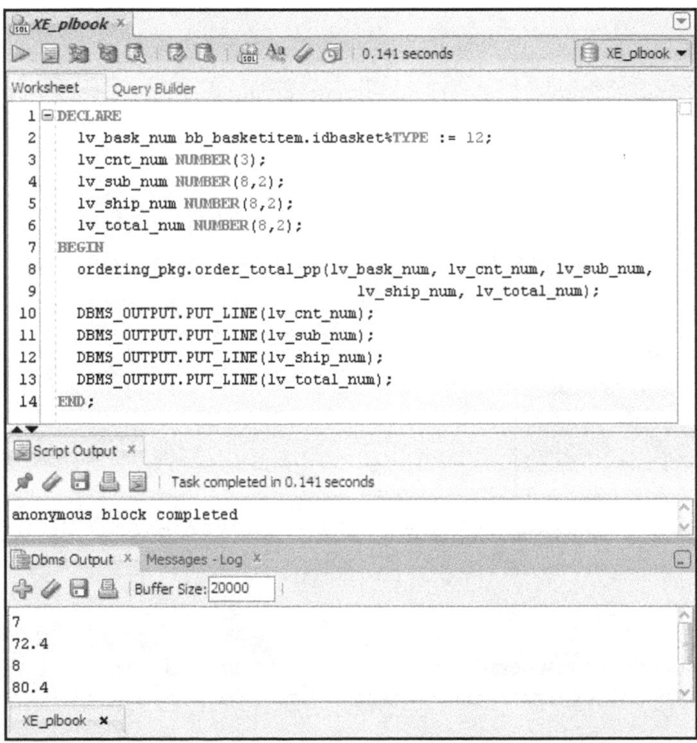

FIGURE 7-6 Checking values to verify the packaged procedure results

2. Compare your results with Figure 7-6 to check whether the packaged procedure is operating correctly. The query displays the order item count, subtotal, shipping cost, and overall total for basket 12.
3. Next, run the following SQL query to verify the results against the database. In addition, by reviewing the `IF` statement in the `SHIP_CALC_PF`, which is called by the `ORDER_TOTAL_PP` procedure, you can confirm that the correct shipping cost of $8 for seven items was calculated.

```
SELECT SUM(quantity),SUM(quantity*price)
  FROM bb_basketitem
  WHERE idbasket = 12;
```


What if you have other procedures outside the `ORDERING_PKG` package that could use the `SHIP_CALC_PF` function? Any procedure or function declared in the package specification can be called from any program unit. Therefore, you could also call the `SHIP_CALC_PF` function from a PL/SQL block outside the package. Follow these steps to test a call to the packaged function `SHIP_CALC_PF` from outside the package via an anonymous block:

1. In SQL Developer, enter and run the anonymous block shown in Figure 7-7. The call to the packaged function passes in the value 7 for the `IN` parameter representing the seven items in the order.

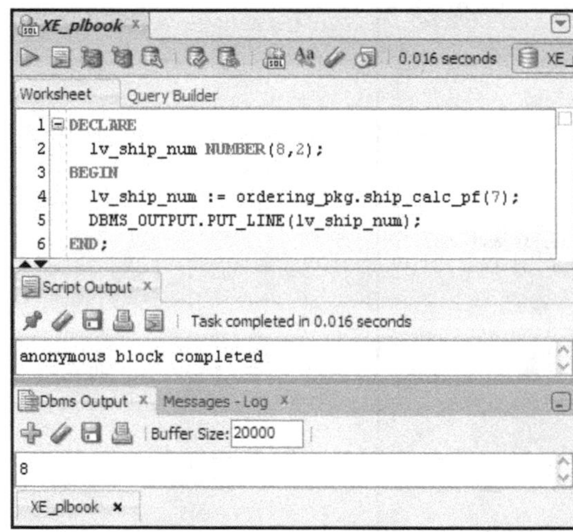

FIGURE 7-7 Testing the packaged function for the shipping calculation

2. Review your results. This Brewbean's packaged function should return a shipping cost of $8 for the seven items ordered.

In this test, you called both a packaged procedure and function. The statements to do this are the same as calling stand-alone program units, except the program unit name must be preceded by the package name and a period, as explained previously. This *package_name.program_unit_name* format instructs the system to find a specific package and then find the program unit in the package with the specified name.

Package Scope

Package scope is the range of visibility for a package element. In this context, "range of visibility" is a shorthand way of describing whether a package item, such as the SHIP_CALC_PF function, can be accessed from outside the package or only from other program units in the same package. Any elements declared in a package specification are considered **public**, which means they can be referenced from outside the package. Elements are considered **private** if they can be called only from other program units in the same package.

Try applying this concept to the package you've been developing for the Brewbean's application. First, you were able to call the SHIP_CALC_PF function from an anonymous block because you declared this function in the package specification, which made it public. However, what would happen if this function declaration weren't included in the package specification? To test public and private package elements, modify the ORDERING_PKG package by removing the SHIP_CALC_PF function declaration from the specification:

1. In SQL Developer, click the **ORDERING_PKG** node to open it for editing.
2. Remove the function declaration from the specification, as shown in Figure 7-8, and compile the package. The red X next to the package body node in the Connections pane indicates that the body should also be compiled because the specification has been changed.

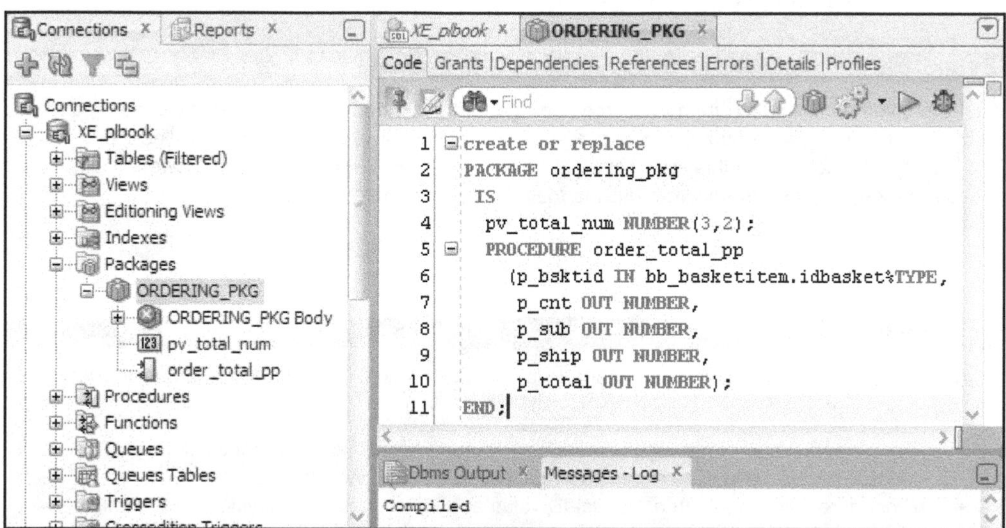

FIGURE 7-8 Creating the ORDERING_PKG package without the SHIP_CALC_PF declaration

3. Open the package body and compile it. Now call the SHIP_CALC_PF function with the anonymous block shown in Figure 7-9. You should get the same error message.

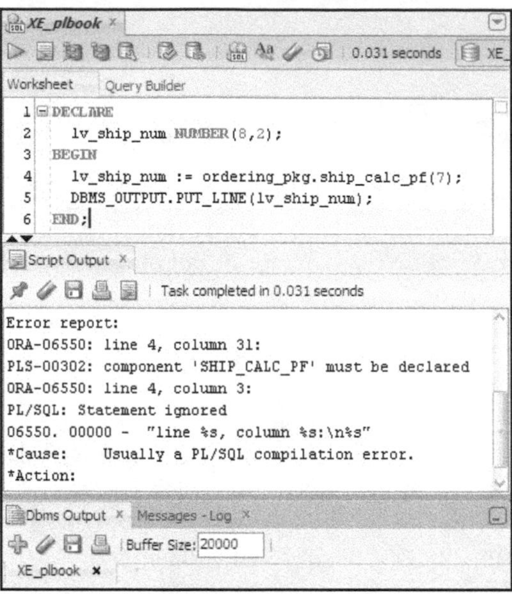

FIGURE 7-9 Error when calling the `SHIP_CALC_PF` function

The function is now considered private because it isn't declared in the package specification. Therefore, it can be called only by other program units in the same package. The call from an anonymous block in the preceding exercise causes the system to check the `ORDERING_PKG` package specification for a program unit named `SHIP_CALC_PF`. Because this function isn't declared, an error is returned.

NOTE

When a program unit is called from the same package body, you don't have to precede the program unit name with the package name. The `ORDER_TOTAL_PP` procedure in the package called the `SHIP_CALC_PF` function with this statement: `p_ship := ship_calc_pf(p_cnt);`. However, any calls to a package's program unit from outside the package must use this notation: *`package_name.program_unit_name`*.

CHALLENGE 7-1

Create a package containing the two program units in the following list. Test the package with a call using the procedure. Name the package `PROD_PKG`.

- *Function*—Accepts a product ID value and returns the product's current stock level. This function should be private to the package. Name the function `STK_PF`.
- *Procedure*—Accepts both a product ID value and the requested quantity. The procedure needs to call the function and then determine whether enough stock is available to fulfill the request. If there's enough stock, update the stock level. If not, display a message to this effect. This procedure should be public. Name the procedure `STKUP_PP`.

Global Constructs in Packages

One advantage of packages is that constructs, such as variables, cursors, types, and exceptions, declared in the specification are **global**. The term "global" indicates two features. First, a global construct can be used by any program unit. Second, the construct's values persist throughout a user session, so they can be referenced (used) in code in different parts of the application during a user session. This capability is valuable because it allows storing and using values throughout an application session, not just in a single program unit. In addition, each user session maintains a separate copy of these constructs that applies only to the session.

For example, the `ORDERING_PKG` specification you created earlier contains the `pv_total_num` variable. Suppose user A logs on to the system at 8:00 a.m. and calls a procedure that sets this packaged variable's value to 0. After this point, whenever user A runs a program unit that references this variable, it returns the value 0. However, at 10:00 a.m., user A runs a procedure that sets the variable's value to 5. Any subsequent references to this variable return the value 5. What happens if user A logs off at lunchtime? When user A returns from lunch and logs back on to the system, a new session is started, and the variable's value is returned to its original setting. In this case, the variable isn't initialized in its declaration, so it contains no value (or is `NULL`) until user A runs a command to set a value for it. Figure 7-10, on the left, illustrates this situation.

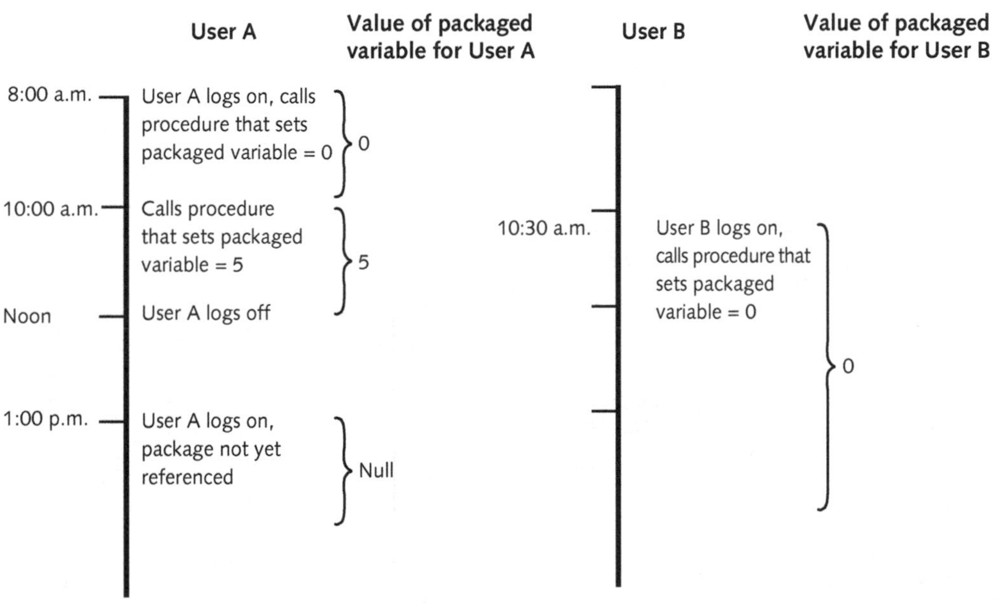

FIGURE 7-10 Initialization issues

What if user B logs on to the same system at 10:30 a.m.? Will user B see the value 5 for the packaged variable? No, the values of these package constructs are global to each user session. In other words, a set of global variables is maintained for each user or session. Therefore, at 10:30 a.m., user A sees the value 5 in the `pv_total_num` packaged variable, and user B sees the value 0 in the same variable.

Testing the Persistence of Packaged Variables

Now try testing the persistence of a packaged variable with the `pv_total_num` variable in the `ORDERING_PKG` package. In this exercise, you use two sessions and compare the packaged variable's value to confirm that its value persists throughout a user session and to verify that a distinct value is stored for each session. Follow these steps:

1. In SQL Developer, edit the **ORDERING_PKG** package specification to initialize the `pv_total_num` variable to 0 with the statement **pv_total_num NUMBER(3,2) := 0;**. Compile both the specification and the body.
2. Test the packaged variable's value with the following statements. The initialized value 0 should be displayed.

```
DECLARE
  lv_pkg_num NUMBER(3);
BEGIN
  lv_pkg_num := ordering_pkg.pv_total_num;
  DBMS_OUTPUT.PUT_LINE(lv_pkg_num);
END;
```

3. Change the packaged variable's value to 5, and test with the following statements. Your result should match Figure 7-11. As shown in the figure, you can continue running additional blocks to read this variable's value, and it should always return the value 5.

```
DECLARE
  lv_pkg_num NUMBER(3) := 5;
BEGIN
  ordering_pkg.pv_total_num := lv_pkg_num;
  DBMS_OUTPUT.PUT_LINE(ordering_pkg.pv_total_num);
END;
```

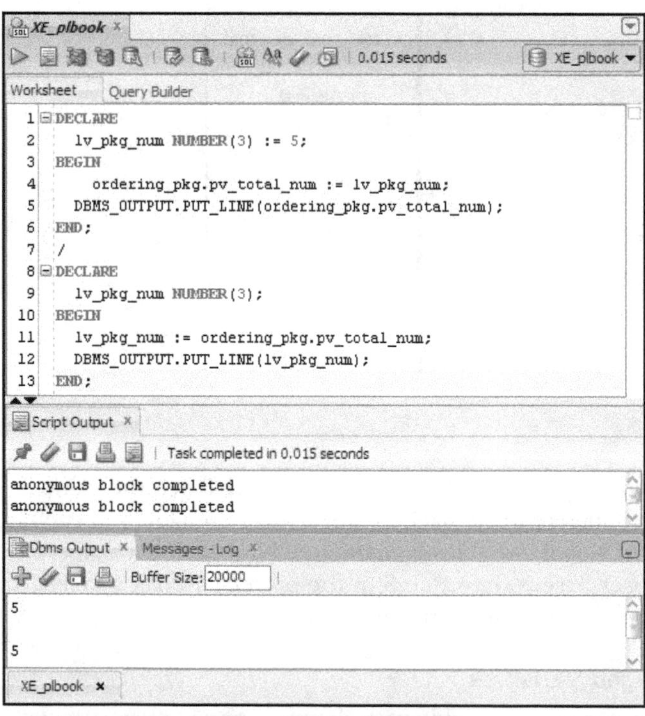

FIGURE 7-11 Setting and testing a packaged variable's value

4. Open a second SQL Developer session. (You can use the same logon as for the first session, or use a different account, if one is available.)
5. Use the following statements to test that the packaged variable's value is 0. The user in the first SQL Developer session currently sees the value 5 in the packaged variable, and the second session user sees the value 0.

```
DECLARE
  lv_pkg_num NUMBER(3);
BEGIN
  lv_pkg_num := ordering_pkg.pv_total_num;
  DBMS_OUTPUT.PUT_LINE(lv_pkg_num);
END;
```


6. In the second session, change the packaged variable's value to 7 with the following statements:

```
DECLARE
  lv_pkg_num NUMBER(3) := 7;
BEGIN
  ordering_pkg.pv_total_num := lv_pkg_num;
  DBMS_OUTPUT.PUT_LINE(ordering_pkg.pv_total_num);
END;
```

7. Verify that the value 7 in the second session persists by reading and displaying the value with the following code:

```
DECLARE
  lv_pkg_num NUMBER(3);
BEGIN
  lv_pkg_num := ordering_pkg.pv_total_num;
  DBMS_OUTPUT.PUT_LINE(lv_pkg_num);
END;
```

8. Move back to the first session, and test the packaged variable's current value with the following statements. The value should remain 5.

```
DECLARE
  lv_pkg_num NUMBER(3);
BEGIN
  lv_pkg_num := ordering_pkg.pv_total_num;
  DBMS_OUTPUT.PUT_LINE(lv_pkg_num);
END;
```

9. Close the second session of SQL Developer.

As this example shows, packaged variables' values persist throughout a user session, and each user has his or her own copy of the packaged variable. This holds true for other types of constructs that can be declared in a package specification: cursors, types, and exceptions.

Package Specifications with No Body

The process of storing and sharing values via packaged variables is often used as a mechanism for holding static data values that are commonly used in programs. For example, say Brewbean's is developing some application pages to support the roasting operation and metric conversions that are commonly needed. Using packaged variables instead of performing a database query can improve processing efficiency. As shown in the following code, you can create a package specification to hold just these conversion factors to reference whenever needed:

```
CREATE OR REPLACE PACKAGE metric_pkg
  IS
  cup_to_liter CONSTANT NUMBER := .24;
  pint_to_liter CONSTANT NUMBER := .47;
  qrt_to_liter CONSTANT NUMBER := .95;
END;
```


A body shouldn't be created for this package because no program units are included in the package. Also, notice that the CONSTANT option is used for each packaged variable that's declared. This option prevents modifying these variables' values.

Improving Processing Efficiency

As you have seen, packages allow sharing values across a user session. This capability not only allows sharing data across procedures and functions during a session, but also provides a way to improve processing efficiency in an application. How? Take a look at the Brewbean's application to see an example.

The Brewbean's manager wants an application that projects increased profits by product type and is based on price increases. In this case, you can use a packaged cursor to retrieve the current product pricing, costs, and sales volumes needed in the analysis. If this data is put in a packaged cursor, it can be reused for each price increase the user generates in a session with only a single SQL query. In other words, no matter how many different pricing schemes the manager tests, only one SQL query is processed to retrieve the data and place it in a cursor. The query results are cached in memory, so they can be reused for each pricing increase that's processed.

Now look at an example of a package with a cursor to understand this concept. The cursor holds the product data needed for the pricing analysis, and the procedure calculates a profit increase based on given percentage price increases for each of the two product types: equipment and coffee. First, review the package creation code in the following example. The package specification includes declarations for a cursor and a procedure. The package body contains code for the procedure that calculates the total sales dollar increase based on given percentage increases for both equipment and coffee products.

```
CREATE OR REPLACE PACKAGE budget_pkg
  IS
  CURSOR pcur_sales IS
    SELECT p.idProduct, p.price, p.type, SUM(bi.quantity) qty
      FROM bb_product p, bb_basketitem bi, bb_basket b
      WHERE p.idProduct = bi.idProduct
      AND b.idBasket = bi.idBasket
      AND b.orderplaced = 1
      GROUP BY p.idProduct, p.price, p.type;
  PROCEDURE project_sales_pp
    (p_pcte IN OUT NUMBER,
     p_pctc IN OUT NUMBER,
     p_incr OUT NUMBER);
END;
```

```
CREATE OR REPLACE PACKAGE BODY budget_pkg
  IS
  PROCEDURE project_sales_pp
    (p_pcte IN OUT NUMBER,
     p_pctc IN OUT NUMBER,
     p_incr OUT NUMBER)
  IS
    equip NUMBER := 0;
    coff NUMBER := 0;
  BEGIN
    FOR rec_sales IN pcur_sales LOOP
    IF rec_sales.type = 'E' THEN
      equip := equip + ((rec_sales.price*p_pcte)*rec_sales.qty);
    ELSIF rec_sales.type = 'C' THEN
      coff := coff + ((rec_sales.price*p_pctc)*rec_sales.qty);
    END IF;
  END LOOP;
    p_incr := equip + coff;
  END;
END;
```

To test the processing time and potential impact of caching data, you need to use a feature that displays execution time. In SQL Developer, enter and run the following statement to turn on the display of elapsed execution time:

```
SET TIMING ON
```

Run the anonymous block in Figure 7-12 to call the packaged procedure. The PL/SQL block initializes two variables, assigning 3% for the equipment price increase and 7% for the coffee price increase. The elapsed time is shown after the block execution. The time that's displayed varies, depending on your Oracle installation.

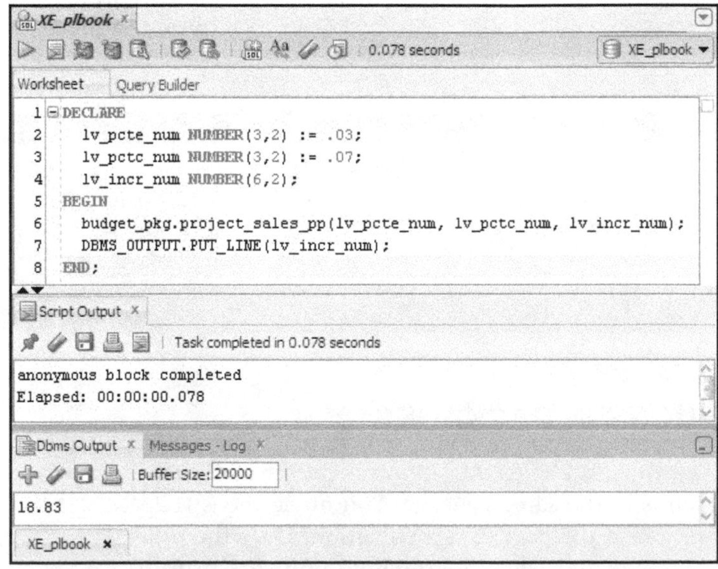

FIGURE 7-12 First call of the packaged procedure

After this first call, the cursor data should be cached and available for faster retrieval. To compare the elapsed times, modify the anonymous block to use a 5% price increase for equipment and a 10% increase for coffee (see Figure 7-13) and run it. Notice in the results that the elapsed time has been reduced.

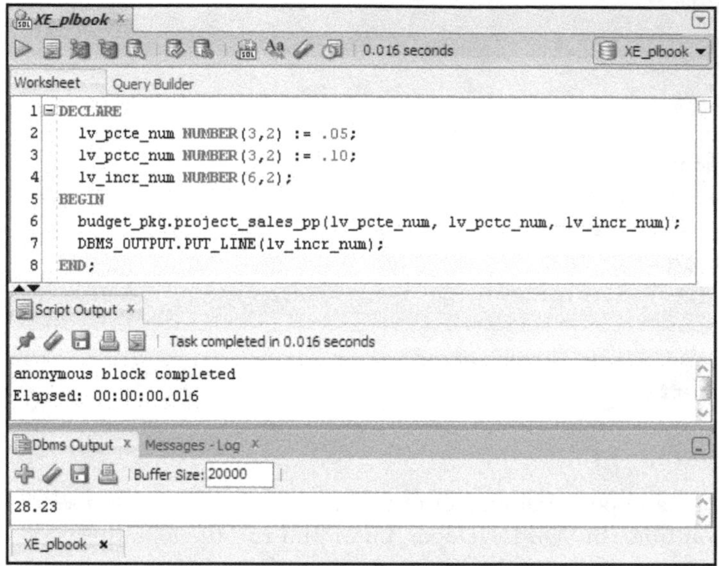

FIGURE 7-13 Second call of the packaged procedure

This example shows that cursor data is stored in cache or memory when the package is first called. After the first call, all other calls are processed much faster because the SQL query doesn't have to be processed again. The reduction in elapsed time might not seem substantial in this example, but in production applications, the database is much larger and there are many users. Improving code efficiency in this way is important because SQL statements and database retrieval tend to require the most processing time.

NOTE

Package code is cached, as is package data, such as variables and cursors; therefore, the elapsed time reduction from the first run to the second run of the `PROJECT_SALES` procedure isn't 100% because the cursor data is cached. A slight savings in time would result from the procedure being cached, too. However, the SQL processing is responsible for the bulk of processing time in this example, so the savings from caching procedures is minimal. Also, keep in mind that elapsed times vary based on software and hardware configurations.

FORWARD DECLARATIONS IN PACKAGES

In the `ORDERING_PKG` package, the `ORDER_TOTAL_PP` procedure called the `SHIP_CALC_PF` function, which is in the same package. You made the `SHIP_CALC_PF` function private by not declaring it in the package specification. Does the order of program units in the package body matter when the program units are private? To find the answer, modify the ORDERING_PKG package by moving the SHIP_CALC_PF function to be the last program unit in the body:

1. In SQL Developer, open the ORDERING_PKG body for editing, and move the **SHIP_CALC_PF** function to be the last program unit declared. (You can also start Notepad, and open the **fwddec07.txt** file in the Chapter07 folder. Copy the code and paste it into SQL Developer.)
2. Compile the body, and note the compiler error message (see Figure 7-14).

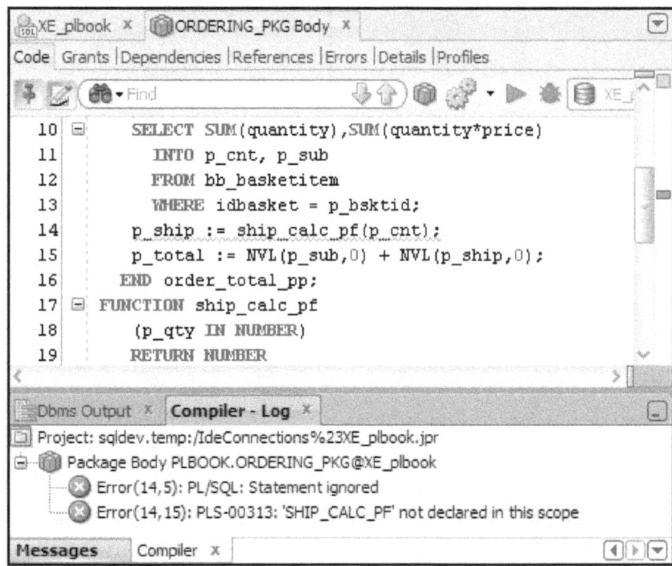

FIGURE 7-14 Compilation error for the package body

What happened? Well, the private function SHIP_CALC_PF has no declaration in the specification, and it's the last item declared in the body. Therefore, an error was raised in the ORDER_TOTAL_PP procedure, which is listed first in the package, because it attempted to call the SHIP_CALC_PF function. As far as the package body is concerned, the function doesn't exist.

You could move the function back to the top of the package body and quit bothering with this compilation error. However, what if you have two program units that are mutually recursive, meaning they call each other? If you have a lot of program units in a package, you might also want to organize them in some order, such as alphabetical or logical groupings, so that they're easier to locate. You might wind up with program units being called before they're declared, however.

You can work around this issue with private program units by using forward declarations in the package body. A **forward declaration** declares a program unit in a package body by placing the header code at the top of the package body's code. Return to the current error in the ORDERING_PKG body and add a forward declaration for the SHIP_CALC_PF function:

1. In SQL Developer, open the package body to edit. The error message from the previous exercise should still be displayed.

2. Add a forward declaration for the function at the top of the package body's code, as shown in Figure 7-15, and compile again. The program unit's header is added to the top of the body to serve as a forward declaration.

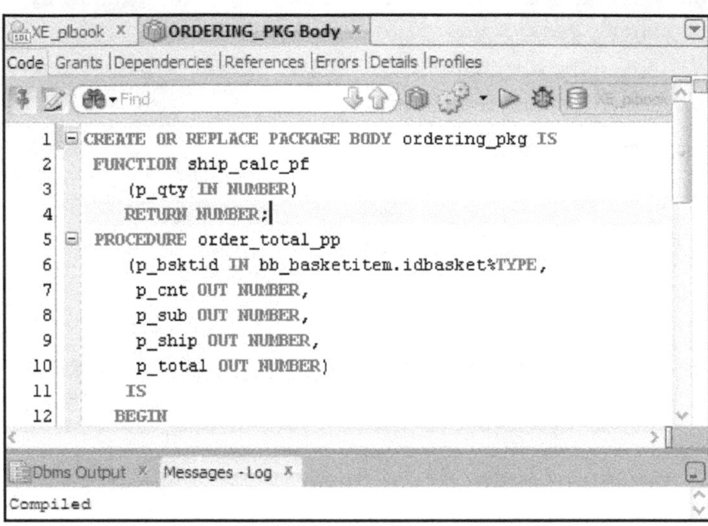
XE_plbook
ORDERING_PKG Body
Code Grants Dependencies References Errors Details Profiles
CREATE OR REPLACE PACKAGE BODY ordering_pkg IS
FUNCTION ship_calc_pf
(p_qty IN NUMBER)
RETURN NUMBER;
PROCEDURE order_total_pp
(p_bsktid IN bb_basketitem.idbasket%TYPE,
p_cnt OUT NUMBER,
p_sub OUT NUMBER,
p_ship OUT NUMBER,
p_total OUT NUMBER)
IS
BEGIN
Dbms Output
Messages - Log
Compiled

FIGURE 7-15 Creating a package body with a forward declaration

The package body containing the forward declaration for the `SHIP_CALC_PF` function compiles successfully because the `ORDER_TOTAL_PP` procedure now recognizes that the function exists in the package.

ONE-TIME-ONLY PROCEDURES

Sometimes assigning a value to a global packaged variable dynamically from the database is useful. For example, Brewbean's wants to allow the Marketing Department to run daily percent specials periodically. These specials reduce order subtotals by a certain percentage (called a "bonus" because it's a bonus for the customer).

To give the Marketing Department access to working with these bonuses, you could develop an application that enables these employees to access and update the bonus percentage in a database table named BB_PROMO. When the `ORDERING_PKG` package is called during the ordering process, you can set a packaged variable to use this bonus percentage in the order total calculation. To do this, you use a **one-time-only procedure**, which is a packaged procedure that runs only once—when the package is first called. Regardless of how many times the package is referenced during a user session, this procedure runs only once—at the first call to the package.

A one-time-only procedure is included in a package body as an anonymous PL/SQL block at the end of the body code. For example, the `CREATE PACKAGE BODY` statement in Figure 7-16 shows the change you need to make to the `ORDERING_PKG` package body to support the Brewbean's bonus process.

Package specification

```
CREATE OR REPLACE PACKAGE ordering_pkg
  IS
  pv_bonus_num NUMBER (3,2);
  pv_total_num NUMBER (3,2) :=0;
  PROCEDURE order_total_pp
    (p_bsktid IN bb_basketitem.idbasket%TYPE,
     p_cnt OUT NUMBER,
     p_sub OUT NUMBER,
     p_ship OUT NUMBER,
     p_total OUT NUMBER);
END;
```

Add the packaged variable pv_bonus_num to the specification

Package body

```
CREATE OR REPLACE PACKAGE BODY ordering_pkg
  IS
  FUNCTION ship_calc_pf
    (p_qty IN NUMBER)
    RETURN NUMBER;
  PROCEDURE order_total_pp
    (p_bsktid IN bb_basketitem.idbasket%TYPE,
     p_cnt OUT NUMBER,
     p_sub OUT NUMBER,
     p_ship OUT NUMBER,
     p_total OUT NUMBER)
    IS
  BEGIN
    SELECT SUM(quantity),SUM(quantity*price)
      INTO p_cnt, p_sub
      FROM bb_basketitem
      WHERE idbasket = p_bsktid;
    p_sub := p_sub - (p_sub*pv_bonus_num);
    p_ship := ship_calc_pf(p_cnt);
    p_total := NVL(p_sub,0) + NVL(p_ship,0);
  END order_total_pp;
  FUNCTION ship_calc_pf
    (p_qty IN NUMBER)
    RETURN NUMBER
  IS
    lv_ship_num NUMBER(5,2);
  BEGIN
    IF p_qty > 10 THEN
      lv_ship_num := 11.00;
     ELSIF p_qty > 5 THEN
      lv_ship_num := 8.00;
     ELSE
      lv_ship_num := 5.00;
    END IF;
  RETURN lv_ship_num;
  END ship_calc_pf;
  BEGIN
  SELECT amount
    INTO pv_bonus_num
    FROM bb_promo
    WHERE idPromo = 'B';
END;
```

Add a calculation to reduce the subtotal by the bonus percentage amount

One-time-only procedure to retrieve the bonus amount from the BB_PROMO table and place it in the pv_bonus_num variable

FIGURE 7-16 Including a one-time-only procedure in a package

A one-time-only procedure starts with the keyword BEGIN at the end of the package body. No END statement is required to close a one-time-only procedure. To see how it works, modify and test the ORDERING_PKG package to include a one-time-only procedure for calculating the bonus amount:

1. In SQL Developer, edit the **ORDERING_PKG** specification and body as shown in Figure 7-16. Be sure to include all three changes: adding a variable, adding a new calculation, and adding the one-time-only procedure.

2. Compile the specification and then the body.
3. Enter the following query to check the current values in the BB_PROMO table. Note that this example applies a 5% bonus.

```
SELECT *
  FROM bb_promo;
```

4. Use the anonymous block shown in Figure 7-17 to call the packaged procedure, and check the results.

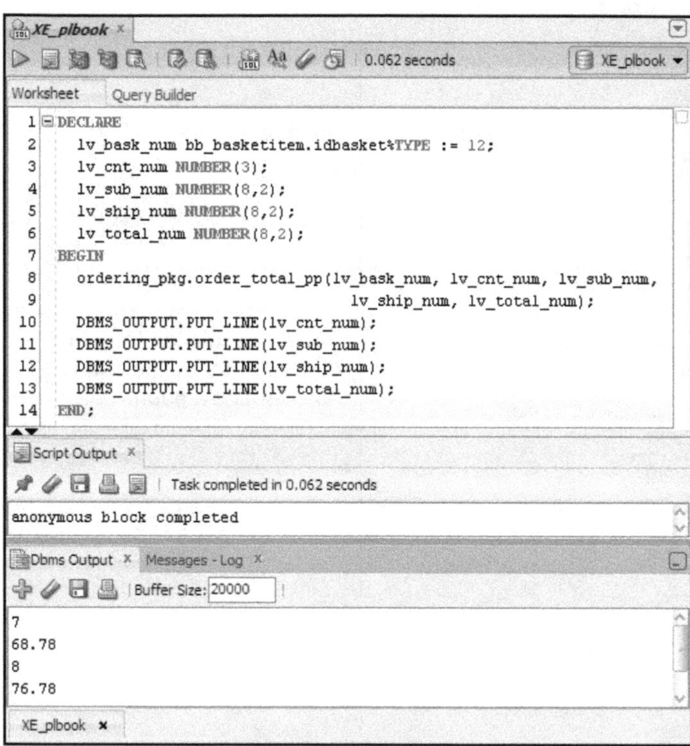

FIGURE 7-17 Testing a one-time-only procedure

5. As always, verify your results by querying the database (see Figure 7-18).

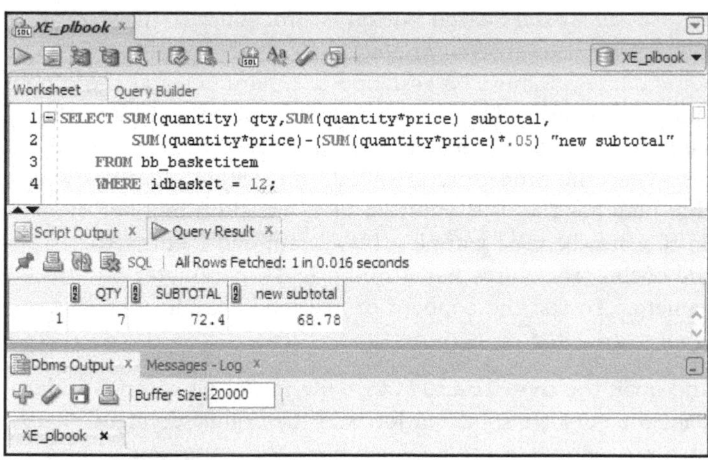

FIGURE 7-18 Verifying the results of a one-time-only procedure

When the ORDER_TOTAL_PP procedure is called, the sequence of events is as follows: The ORDERING_PKG package is loaded, the one-time-only procedure executes and sets the bonus percentage value in the pv_bonus_num packaged variable, and then the ORDER_TOTAL_PP procedure executes and calculates the basket amounts. As the shopper continues to make order changes during the session and the basket totals are updated, the pv_bonus_num packaged variable continues to be referenced to calculate the bonus. The one-time-only procedure doesn't run again during the session, and the bonus value continues to be retrieved from the packaged variable.

NOTE

A one-time-only procedure is also called an "initialization block" of a package body because it's typically used to initialize packaged variables' values for a session.

CHALLENGE 7-2

Modify the package created in Challenge 7-1 to include a one-time-only procedure that populates a public packaged variable with the next shipping date. The company ships every Wednesday. Test the package to confirm that the one-time-only procedure works correctly.

OVERLOADING PROGRAM UNITS IN PACKAGES

In packages, **overloading** is the capability to use the same name for multiple program units in the same package. Why would you want two procedures or functions with the same name? For example, one part of the Brewbean's application is used to look up a product's regular price and sale price. The application page has a text box where the user enters a product ID or name. In this example, you're performing the same action (returning a product's regular and sale prices) no matter what's entered, but in one case, a number (the product ID) is provided as input, and in the other, a string (the product name) is provided as input. When the user clicks the Search button, a procedure should be called that can accept a numeric or character user-entered argument.

How can you do this when a data type must be assigned to a parameter at the time a procedure is created? The solution is overloading—creating two procedures in a package with the same name and having the first contain a numeric parameter and the second contain a character parameter. When the procedure is called, the system identifies which procedure has a parameter that matches the user-entered data, based on number of parameters and data types. In the Brewbean's example, the system can identify the correct procedure because one of the procedures has a numeric `IN` parameter and the other has a character `IN` parameter. To test the concept of overloading, follow these steps to create a new package with an overloaded procedure:

1. Start Notepad, and open the **`overload07.txt`** file in the Chapter07 folder. Review the code for the package specification and the body (see Figure 7-19). Notice that the two procedures in the package have the same name but a different first parameter.

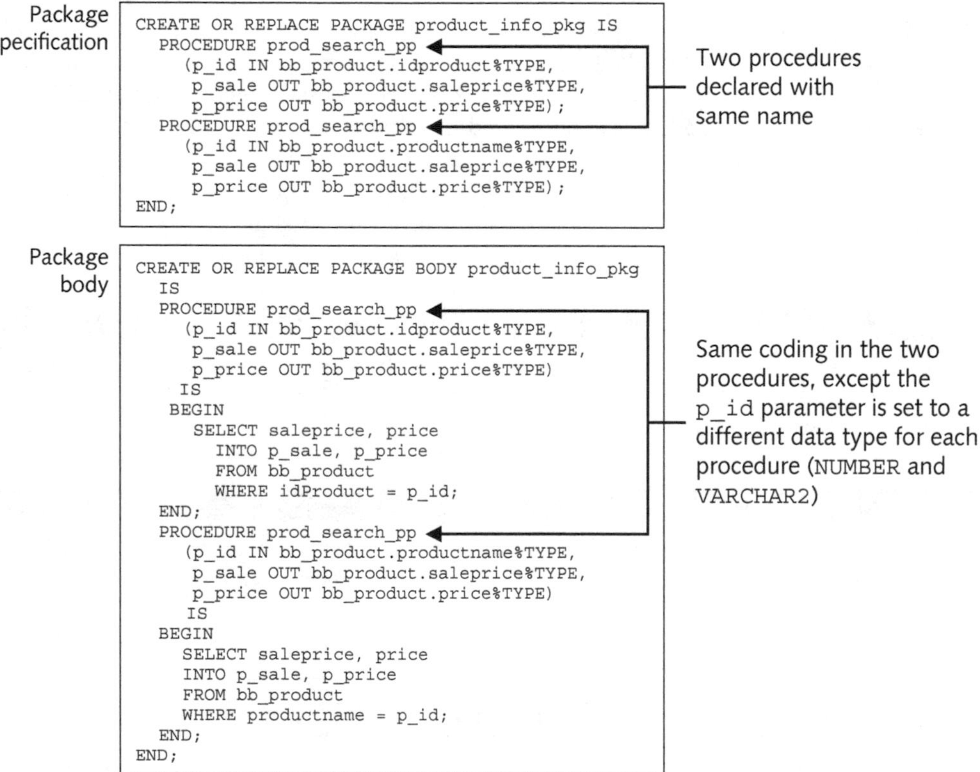

FIGURE 7-19 An overloaded procedure in a package

2. Copy the code in this file, and paste it into SQL Developer to create the package. Next, compile the package.
3. Start your test by calling the packaged procedure with a product ID (number). Use the anonymous block in Figure 7-20 to test the product search based on the ID 6.

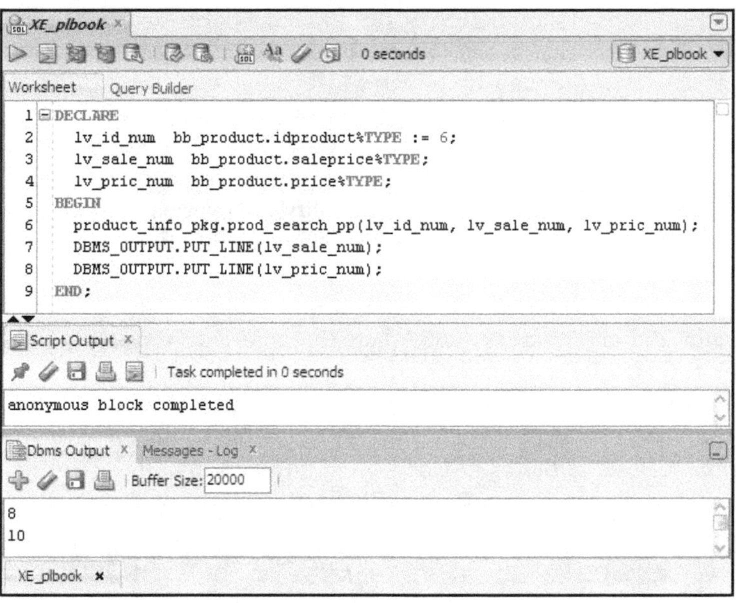

FIGURE 7-20 Calling the overloaded procedure with a product ID

4. Next, call the procedure with a product name. Use the anonymous block shown in Figure 7-21 to test the product search based on the name Guatemala.

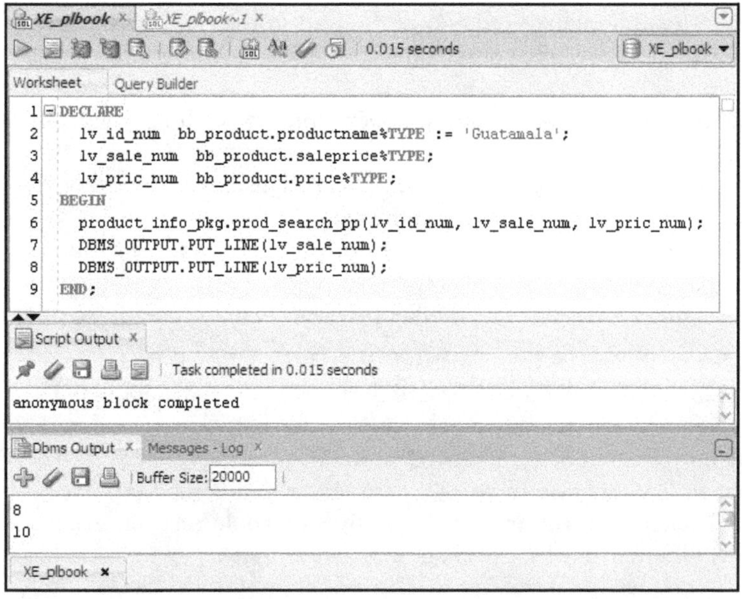

FIGURE 7-21 Calling the overloaded procedure with a product name

For overloading to work, the formal parameters in the procedures or functions must differ in at least one of the following categories: total number of formal parameters, data type family, or listed order. Note that the data types can't just differ; they have to be from different data type families. For example, say you build two procedures with the same name, and one has an `IN` parameter of the data type `CHAR` and the other has an `IN` parameter of the data type `VARCHAR`. Will this overloading work? No, `CHAR` and `VARCHAR` are in the same data type family, so they don't qualify for overloading. In addition, different data types for return values in a function don't qualify functions for overloading.

Listed order is fairly self-explanatory. For example, if both procedures A and B contain two parameters, one character and one numeric, but A lists the character one first and B listed the numeric one first, this difference qualifies the procedures for overloading.

In any case, calling the overloaded program unit is what determines which package program unit is used. The number, data types, and order of arguments in the call are matched to the formal parameter lists of the overloaded program units to determine the correct program unit to run.

CHALLENGE 7-3

Create a package with program units that accept a shopper ID or a username and return the shopper's name and count of baskets. Name the package `SHOPID_PKG`.

MANAGING SQL RESTRICTIONS FOR PACKAGED FUNCTIONS

This list of restrictions on functions used in SQL statements was shown in Chapter 6, but review it again here for this discussion:

- Functions can't modify any tables in Oracle 8*i* and earlier versions. Beginning with Oracle 8*i*, a function can't modify a table used in the SQL statement that calls it; however, it can alter other tables if called from a non-`SELECT` statement.
- If a function is used in a remote or parallel operation, no reading or writing of packaged variables is allowed.
- If a function is used in a `SELECT`, `VALUES`, or `SET` clause, it can write values to packaged variables; otherwise, it's not allowed.
- Functions can't be used in a `CHECK` constraint or as a default value for a table column.
- If a function calls other subprograms, the subprograms can't break these rules.

Are there any differences in managing these restrictions with packaged functions and stand-alone functions? Remember that when you create a program unit, it's compiled, meaning the syntax is checked, referenced objects are verified to make sure they exist, and invocation arguments and parameters are checked to make sure they match. When you create a procedure that uses a function in an SQL statement and compile the procedure, the function is checked to verify that it abides by applicable restrictions. However, compilation works differently with a package's program units.

When compiling objects that call a package's program units, only the package specification or program unit header is used for verification. For example, if you create a procedure that uses a packaged function in an SQL statement, when the procedure is compiled, only the function header information is reviewed to see whether it exists and has the correct parameters. However, because only the header information is used, the PL/SQL compiler doesn't see the entire block of code for the function and can't determine whether the restrictions on functions in SQL statements are being followed. You wouldn't discover restriction violation issues until runtime, when an error is produced if the restrictions haven't been followed in the function.

On the other hand, needing only the header to compile an object referencing a package program unit gives developers an advantage. After a package specification has been created, other program units can be created by calling any program unit in the package, even if the package body doesn't exist yet. The PL/SQL compiler checks the package specification only to determine whether the parameters in the call match the parameters in the specification for the function.

Why Developers Indicate Purity Levels

To enable the compiler to verify that a packaged function being called is conforming to SQL restrictions, developers can use the `PRAGMA RESTRICT_REFERENCES` compiler instruction to indicate the function's purity level. Purity levels, introduced in Chapter 6, define what type of data structures a function reads or modifies. If the purity level is declared in the package specification, the PL/SQL compiler can use this information to determine whether the function meets all the calling program unit's restrictions. In addition, when the package body is created, the PL/SQL compiler can determine whether the function code adheres to the purity level the function was declared with in the specification. In other words, you can discover errors at compile time rather than runtime. For convenience, Table 7-1 repeats the purity level restrictions described in Chapter 6.

TABLE 7-1 Purity Levels for Packaged Functions

Level Acronym	Level Name	Level Description
`WNDS`	Writes No Database State	Function doesn't modify any database tables (no DML).
`RNDS`	Reads No Database State	Function doesn't read any tables (no `SELECT`).
`WNPS`	Writes No Package State	Function doesn't modify any packaged variables (which are variables declared in a package specification).
`RNPS`	Reads No Package State	Function doesn't read any packaged variables.

The `PRAGMA RESTRICT_REFERENCES` directive specifies each purity level that applies to a packaged function. Being able to discover problems at compile time is helpful; in addition, using this directive offers some performance advantages because the purity level is verified at compile time rather than runtime. When the object using the packaged function is compiled, its compliance with restrictions is verified. In addition, when the complete package body, including the entire function code, is compiled, this code is checked to verify that it matches the purity levels declared in the specification. All verification is done during compilation, so it doesn't have to take place while the application is running.

NOTE

The PRAGMA RESTRICT_REFERENCES compiler directive is required in versions before Oracle 8*i*. Starting with Oracle 8*i*, this directive is optional because the compile-time restrictions were relaxed for more flexible support of stored programs written in other languages, such as Java. In versions 8*i* and later, the DETERMINISTIC and PARALLEL_ENABLE options can be used to convey function purity and help with performance tuning. These two options convey that all four purity levels apply and are included in the function header, as shown in the following code:

```
FUNCTION ship_calc_pf
  (p_qty IN NUMBER)
  RETURN NUMBER
  PARALLEL_ENABLE;
```

The DETERMINISTIC and PARALLEL_ENABLE options are typically used as optimization hints and are implemented as part of a performance-tuning strategy, which is beyond the scope of this book.

PRAGMA RESTRICT_REFERENCES in Action

The PRAGMA RESTRICT_REFERENCES directive should be included in the package specification to clarify the purity levels that apply to the function. The following code is an example of a package specification that includes a function header. In the PRAGMA RESTRICT_REFERENCES statement, the first argument defines the function it applies to; the remaining arguments specify the purity levels that apply to the function:

```
CREATE OR REPLACE PACKAGE pack_purity_pkg IS
  FUNCTION tax_calc_pf
    (p_amt IN NUMBER)
  RETURN NUMBER;
PRAGMA RESTRICT_REFERENCES(tax_calc_pf,WNDS,WNPS);
END;
```

In this example, the WNDS and WNPS purity levels are indicated, which means the function doesn't contain any DML statements and doesn't modify any packaged variables. This information leads you to assume that the function does include reads on database tables and packaged variables because the RNDS and RNPS purity levels aren't listed. Note that the PRAGMA statement must follow the function declaration in the package specification.

Default Purity Levels for Packaged Functions

You can also set a default purity level for packaged functions by using PRAGMA RESTRICT_REFERENCES for Oracle 8*i* and later. The default purity level applies to all functions in the package specification that don't have their own PRAGMA RESTRICT_REFERENCES statement. In the following code, notice that the word DEFAULT (shown in bold) is used instead of a specific function name:

```
PRAGMA RESTRICT_REFERENCES(DEFAULT,WNDS,WNPS);
```

Functions Written in External Languages

Functions written in other languages, such as Java, can also be called from Oracle programs. Even though the PL/SQL compiler can't confirm the purity of an externally written function, you can still use PRAGMA RESTRICT_REFERENCES to help in compilation. In this case, you use the TRUST option with the PRAGMA RESTRICT_REFERENCES statement to allow the calling program unit to compile successfully. It instructs the compiler to trust that the purity levels indicated are indeed followed in the function code. In the following example, notice that the TRUST keyword is listed as the last argument:

```
CREATE OR REPLACE PACKAGE java_pkg
  AS
  FUNCTION phone_fmt_pf
    (p_phone IN VARCHAR2)
  RETURN VARCHAR2
    IS
    LANGUAGE JAVA
    NAME 'External.phone (char[]) return char[]';
    PRAGMA RESTRICT_REFERENCES (phone_fmt_pf, WNDS, TRUST);
END;
```


USING A REF CURSOR PARAMETER IN PACKAGES

Chapter 4 introduced cursor variables, and you take another look at them now to see how to declare a REF CURSOR data type in a package specification. A data type declared in a package specification with a TYPE statement can be referenced by multiple program units. Figure 7-22 shows a package containing a procedure that uses REF CURSOR as a parameter data type. Notice that the TYPE statement in the package specification creates a public REF CURSOR data type. It's used as a parameter data type in the procedure contained in the package.

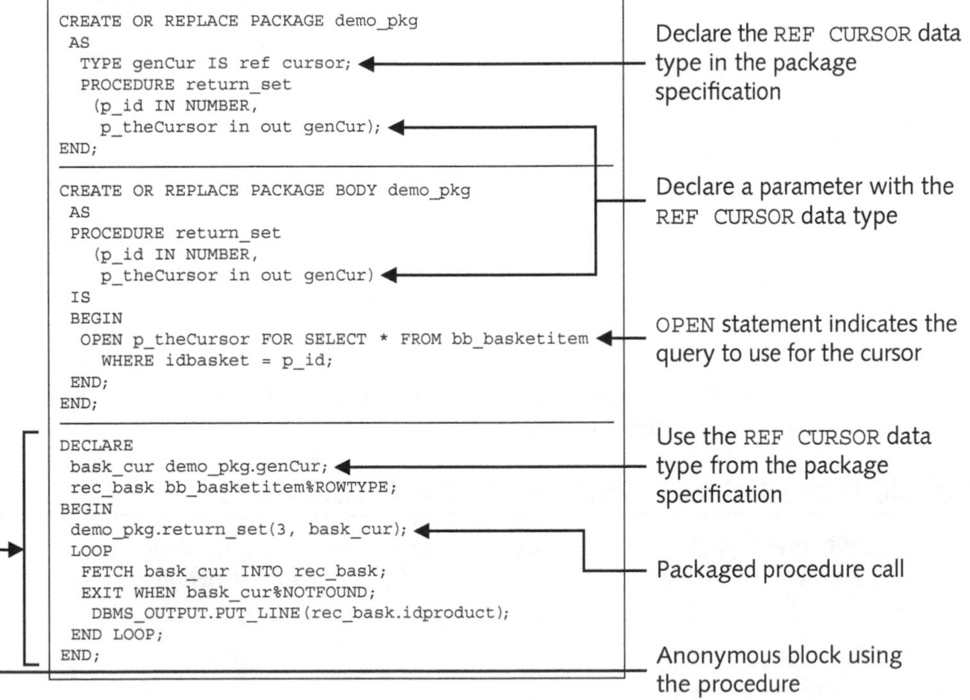

FIGURE 7-22 Declaring a public REF CURSOR data type

The procedure's executable section uses an OPEN statement to indicate the query used to populate the REF CURSOR parameter. The anonymous block at the bottom of Figure 7-22 calls the packaged procedure to retrieve and display items in basket 3. The procedure also uses the public REF CURSOR data type declared in the package for a local cursor variable to hold the results from the procedure's OUT parameter cursor.

This example shows using a REF CURSOR as a parameter data type. Keep in mind that a package can contain many program units. Any program units requiring a cursor can use the REF CURSOR data type declared in the package specification.

GRANTING EXECUTE PRIVILEGES FOR PROGRAM UNITS AND PACKAGES

Another advantage of using program units and packages is that they make granting privileges to application users easier. Users need rights or privileges for each object (tables, sequences, and so on) they access and each type of action (such as INSERT and DELETE) they perform. If your application has multiple objects and actions, granting these rights can be time consuming.

Fortunately, if you grant the execute privilege to a user for a program unit or package, the user is allowed to use the program unit owner's privileges by default while running the program unit. The package's owner, of course, already has all the privileges needed to run the code. Using this method is called **definer rights**; the user assumes the program unit owner's rights only while that program unit is processing. The user can use these rights *only* during execution of the program unit, which adds another level of security because the user is never granted direct access to objects.

Definer rights might not work in all situations, however. If you want the user's own privileges in effect when a program unit is processed, you must override the default definer rights. To do this, use the AUTHID CURRENT_USER clause in the program unit header, which forces use of the user's own privileges instead of the owner's privileges; using this method is called **invoker rights**.

The following package specification shows how to include the AUTHID clause (indicated in bold) so that it applies to the entire package:

```
CREATE OR REPLACE PACKAGE pack_purity_pkg
AUTHID CURRENT_USER IS
 FUNCTION tax_calc_pf
  (p_amt IN NUMBER)
  RETURN NUMBER;
END;
```

You can also do this with separate program units by including the AUTHID clause as the last item in the a program unit's header.

DATA DICTIONARY INFORMATION FOR PACKAGES

As you saw in Chapter 6 with program units, you can use the USER_SOURCE data dictionary view to view a package's source code. The following query displays the source code for PRODUCT_INFO_PKG, including both specification and body.

```
SELECT text
  FROM user_source
  WHERE name = 'PRODUCT_INFO_PKG';
```

The USER_OBJECTS data dictionary view is also useful to identify what packages exist on the system, as shown in Figure 7-23. A separate entry is listed for both the specification and body. The STATUS column identifies whether the program unit is compiled successfully by indicating VALID. An INVALID value indicates unsuccessful compilation or changes to a related object, such as the specification. In this case, the program unit should be compiled again.

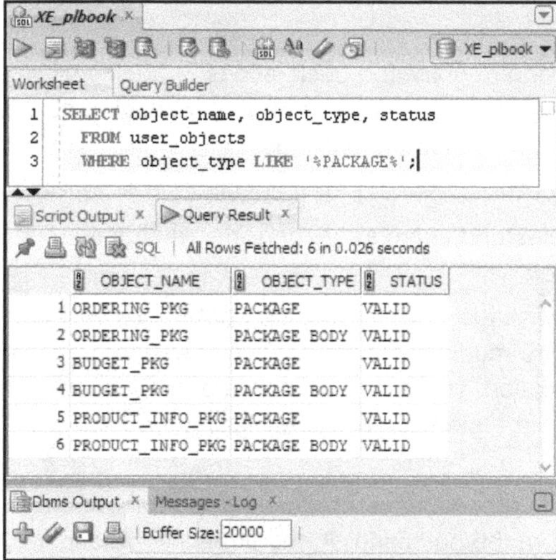

FIGURE 7-23 Listing package objects with the USER_OBJECTS view

TIP

Recall that all data stored in the data dictionary is in uppercase, so the WHERE clause conditions need to be uppercase, or you must use the UPPER function to make this query work correctly.

DELETING PACKAGES

At times, you want to eliminate procedures and functions, and you can use a DROP command for this purpose in the same way you delete any object in a database. The DROP command must include the object type and object name.

The following code shows examples of DROP commands. The first example removes the package specification and body. The second example removes only the package body.

```
DROP PACKAGE package_name;
DROP PACKAGE BODY package_name;
```

TIP

As mentioned previously, developers usually create separate program units, test them, and then place them in packages. Deleting these stand-alone program units after placing them in a package is a good practice. Otherwise, it's easy to call the stand-alone program unit mistakenly instead of the package program unit. By keeping only one copy of any program unit on the system, you can ensure that only one is used and updated.

Chapter Summary

- A package is a program construct that can contain multiple program units and other constructs, such as variables and cursors. Packages offer performance benefits and new capabilities, such as overloading and global constructs.
- A package specification contains declarations for all constructs to be used in the package and is called the "package header." You can have a package specification without a body. Everything declared in the specification is considered public and can be referenced from outside the package.
- A package body contains the code for any program units and declarations of additional constructs, such as variables. Anything in the body that isn't declared in the specification is considered private or can't be referenced from outside the package.
- The package scope is the range of visibility (public or private) for a construct in a package.
- Values of package constructs, such as variables and cursors, are considered global because they persist throughout a user session.
- Any program unit referenced from the same package must be declared before it's called. If you can't do this because two program units are mutually recursive or you need to organize program units in a specific order for easier location, you can use a forward declaration. A forward declaration declares a program unit in a package body by placing the header code at the top of the package body's code.
- When a package is first called, a one-time-only procedure can be used to perform such tasks as initializing global variables' values from the database. A one-time-only procedure runs only once, when the package is first referenced.
- Overloading is a package feature that allows creating multiple program units with the same name so that a program unit can accept different parameter settings. In this way, calls to the program unit can be flexible in handling different data types. The parameters of overloaded program units must differ in total number of parameters, data type family, or listed order.
- Additional restrictions called purity levels apply to functions used in SQL statements. Because package specifications insulate the PL/SQL compiler from the function code, the `PRAGMA RESTRICT_REFERENCES` directive is used in the function declaration to indicate what purity levels the function code adheres to.
- A `REF CURSOR` is a data type. A variable with this data type can be populated with different queries at runtime and used to pass results between program units.
- The `USER_SOURCE` view gives you access to a package's source code. The `USER_OBJECTS` data dictionary view is also useful to identify what packages exist on the system. A separate entry is listed for both the specification and body.
- You use the `DROP` command to remove a package. You can remove the package body without removing the package specification by adding the package body's name in the `DROP` command, as in `DROP PACKAGE BODY` *`package_name`*`;`.

Review Questions

1. A procedure that's included in a package body but not declared in the specification is considered which of the following?
   a. illegal
   b. private

c. public

d. restricted

2. A function named `CALC` in the `TAX_INFO` package accepts one numeric value. Which of the following is a legal call of this function?

   a. `calc(12);`

   b. `calc.tax_info(12)`

   c. `tax_info.calc(12,10)`

   d. `tax_info.calc(12);`

3. A procedure named `PROC_A` in the `PACK_A` package calls a procedure named `PROC_B` in the same package. Which of the following is a valid call of `PROC_B` from `PROC_A`? Assume `PROC_B` accepts one value and returns two. (Choose all that apply.)

   a. `proc_b(var1,var2,var3);`

   b. `proc_b(var1);`

   c. `pack_a.proc_b();`

   d. `pack_a.proc_b(var1,var2,var3);`

4. If a package specification includes the following code, which of the following declarations is a valid overloading declaration? (Choose all that apply.)

   a.
   ```
   PROCEDURE test_it (p_one IN NUMBER,
     p_two OUT CHAR,
     p_three OUT NUMBER);
   ```

   b.
   ```
   PROCEDURE test_it (p_one IN DECIMAL,
     p_two OUT CHAR,
     p_three OUT NUMBER);
   ```

   c.
   ```
   PROCEDURE test_it (p_one IN NUMBER,
     p_two OUT VARCHAR2,
     p_three OUT NUMBER);
   ```

   d.
   ```
   PROCEDURE test_it (p_one IN NUMBER,
     p_two OUT CHAR);
   ```

   e.
   ```
   PROCEDURE test_it (p_one IN NUMBER,
     p_two OUT NUMBER,
     p_three OUT NUMBER);
   ```

5. Which of the following conditions allows overloading for parameters in two package program units with the same name? (Choose all that apply.)

   a. different data types

   b. different number of parameters

   c. different names

   d. different data type family

6. If invoker rights are in effect when a user runs a program unit, what privileges are being used?

   a. the user's

   b. the program unit owner's

   c. the program unit schema owner's

   d. the system's default privileges

7. What Oracle directive indicates a function's purity level in a package specification?
   a. PRAGMA RESTRICT_FUNCTION
   b. PRAGMA RESTRICT_SQL
   c. PRAGMA RESTRICT_REFERENCES
   d. PRAGMA REFERENCES_RESTRICT
8. Which of the following data dictionary views enables you to review the code in a package?
   a. CODE
   b. SOURCE
   c. USER_CODE
   d. USER_SOURCE

9. Which of the following is *not* an advantage of packages?
   a. They allow ignoring function restrictions in SQL statements.
   b. They allow global variables in a session.
   c. They allow logical grouping of multiple program units.
   d. They allow program units to be private.
10. Where is a one-time-only procedure placed in a package?
    a. at the top of the specification
    b. at the bottom of the specification
    c. at the top of the body
    d. at the bottom of the body
11. What resources can you use to identify all packages created on the system and the source code they contain?
12. How does persistence of value for global constructs contribute to processing efficiency?
13. Explain the concept of overloading and why it's used.
14. Why might you have a package specification without a body?
15. Explain what a private package construct is.

Advanced Review Questions

1. Which of the following statements is true about this package specification?

```
CREATE OR REPLACE PACKAGE sales_process
  IS
    FUNCTION calc_tax
      (p_bask IN NUMBER)
      RETURN NUMBER;
  PRAGMA RESTRICT_REFERENCES(calc_tax,WNDS,WNPS);
END;
```

   a. The CALC_TAX function is private.
   b. A package body isn't needed for this specification.
   c. The CALC_TAX function doesn't write to a database or package construct.
   d. The PRAGMA statement raises an error.

2. Given the following package specification, how many private or local functions does the package contain?

```
CREATE OR REPLACE PACKAGE sales_process
  IS
  PROCEDURE sale_sum
    (p_bask IN NUMBER,
     p_total OUT NUMBER,
     p_sub OUT NUMBER);
END;
```

   a. 1
   b. 2
   c. none
   d. can't be determined

3. To declare a set of public constants, the variable declarations in the package specification must do which of the following?
   a. include the `CONSTANT` option
   b. include the `CONSTANT` option and initialize the variable values
   c. match the variables declared in the body
   d. retrieve the correct data from the database

4. Which of the following data dictionary views can you use to view the code in a package?
   a. USER_OBJECTS
   b. USER_PACKAGE_TEXT
   c. USER_SOURCE
   d. USER_TEXT

5. What code items in the package specification and body must match? (Choose all that apply.)
   a. declared variables
   b. parameter lists of public program units
   c. package names
   d. parameter lists of private program units

Hands-On Assignments Part I

Assignment 7-1: Creating a Package

Follow the steps to create a package containing a procedure and a function pertaining to basket information. (*Note*: The first time you compile the package body doesn't give you practice with compilation error messages.)

1. Start Notepad, and open the **`Assignment07-01.txt`** file in the Chapter07 folder.
2. Review the package code, and then copy it.
3. In SQL Developer, paste the copied code to build the package.
4. Review the compilation errors and identify the related coding error.
5. Edit the package to correct the error and compile the package.

Assignment 7-2: Using Program Units in a Package

In this assignment, you use program units in a package created to store basket information. The package contains a function that returns the recipient's name and a procedure that retrieves the shopper ID and order date for a basket.

1. In SQL Developer, create the **`ORDER_INFO_PKG`** package, using the **`Assignment07-02.txt`** file in the Chapter07 folder. Review the code to become familiar with the two program units in the package.
2. Create an anonymous block that calls both the packaged procedure and function with basket ID **12** to test these program units. Use `DBMS_OUTPUT` statements to display values returned from the program units to verify the data.
3. Also, test the packaged function by using it in a `SELECT` clause on the BB_BASKET table. Use a `WHERE` clause to select only the basket 12 row.

Assignment 7-3: Creating a Package with Private Program Units

In this assignment, you modify a package to make program units private. The Brewbean's programming group decided that the `SHIP_NAME_PF` function in the `ORDER_INFO_PKG` package should be used only from inside the package. Follow these steps to make this modification:

1. In Notepad, open the **`Assignment07-03.txt`** file in the Chapter07 folder, and review the package code.
2. Modify the package code to add to the **`BASKET_INFO_PP`** procedure so that it also returns the name an order is shipped by using the `SHIP_NAME_PF` function. Make the necessary changes to make the `SHIP_NAME_PF` function private.
3. Create the package by using the modified code.
4. Create and run an anonymous block that calls the `BASKET_INFO_PP` procedure and displays the shopper ID, order date, and shipped-to name to check the values returned. Use `DBMS_OUTPUT` statements to display the values.

Assignment 7-4: Using Packaged Variables

In this assignment, you create a package that uses packaged variables to assist in the user logon process. When a returning shopper logs on, the username and password entered need to be verified against the database. In addition, two values need to be stored in packaged variables for reference during the user session: the shopper ID and the first three digits of the shopper's zip code (used for regional advertisements displayed on the site).

1. Create a function that accepts a username and password as arguments and verifies these values against the database for a match. If a match is found, return the value **`Y`**. Set the value of the variable holding the return value to **`N`**. Include a **`NO_DATA_FOUND`** exception handler to display a message that the logon values are invalid.
2. Use an anonymous block to test the procedure, using the username **`gma1`** and the password **`goofy`**.
3. Now place the function in a package, and add code to create and populate the packaged variables specified earlier. Name the package **`LOGIN_PKG`**.
4. Use an anonymous block to test the packaged procedure, using the username **`gma1`** and the password **`goofy`** to verify that the procedure works correctly.

5. Use DBMS_OUTPUT statements in an anonymous block to display the values stored in the packaged variables.

Assignment 7-5: Overloading Packaged Procedures

In this assignment, you create packaged procedures to retrieve shopper information. Brewbean's is adding an application page where customer service agents can retrieve shopper information by using shopper ID or last name. Create a package named **SHOP_QUERY_PKG** containing overloaded procedures to perform these lookups. They should return the shopper's name, city, state, phone number, and e-mail address. Test the package twice. First, call the procedure with shopper ID **23**, and then call it with the last name **Ratman**. Both test values refer to the same shopper, so they should return the same shopper information.

Assignment 7-6: Creating a Package with Only a Specification

In this assignment, you create a package consisting of only a specification. The Brewbean's lead programmer has noticed that only a few states require Internet sales tax, and the rates don't change often. Create a package named **TAX_RATE_PKG** to hold the following tax rates in packaged variables for reference: pv_tax_nc = .035, pv_tax_tx = .05, and pv_tax_tn = .02. Code the variables to prevent the rates from being modified. Use an anonymous block with DBMS_OUTPUT statements to display the value of each packaged variable.

Assignment 7-7: Using a Cursor in a Package

In this assignment, you work with the sales tax computation because the Brewbean's lead programmer expects the rates and states applying the tax to undergo some changes. The tax rates are currently stored in packaged variables but need to be more dynamic to handle the expected changes. The lead programmer has asked you to develop a package that holds the tax rates by state in a packaged cursor. The BB_TAX table is updated as needed to reflect which states are applying sales tax and at what rates. This package should contain a function that can receive a two-character state abbreviation (the shopper's state) as an argument, and it must be able to find a match in the cursor and return the correct tax rate. Use an anonymous block to test the function with the state value **NC**.

Assignment 7-8: Using a One-Time-Only Procedure in a Package

The Brewbean's application currently contains a package used in the shopper logon process. However, one of the developers wants to be able to reference the time users log on to determine when the session should be timed out and entries rolled back. Modify the LOGIN_PKG package (in the **Assignment07-08.txt** file in the Chapter07 folder). Use a one-time-only procedure to populate a packaged variable with the date and time of user logons. Use an anonymous block to verify that the one-time-only procedure works and populates the packaged variable.

Hands-On Assignments Part II

Assignment 7-9: Creating a Package for Pledges

Create a package named **PLEDGE_PKG** that includes two functions for determining dates of pledge payments. Use or create the functions described in Chapter 6 for Assignments 6-12 and 6-13, using the names **DD_PAYDATE1_PF** and **DD_PAYEND_PF** for these packaged functions. Test both functions with a specific pledge ID, using an anonymous block. Then test both functions in a single query showing all pledges and associated payment dates.

Assignment 7-10: Adding a Pledge Display Procedure to the Package

Modify the package created in Assignment 7-9 as follows:

- Add a procedure named `DD_PLIST_PP` that displays the donor name and all associated pledges (including pledge ID, first payment due date, and last payment due date). A donor ID is the input value for the procedure.
- Make the procedure public and the two functions private.

Test the procedure with an anonymous block.

Assignment 7-11: Adding a Payment Retrieval Procedure to the Package

Modify the package created in Assignment 7-10 as follows:

- Add a new procedure named `DD_PAYS_PP` that retrieves donor pledge payment information and returns all the required data via a single parameter.
- A donor ID is the input for the procedure.
- The procedure should retrieve the donor's last name and each pledge payment made so far (including payment amount and payment date).
- Make the procedure public.

Test the procedure with an anonymous block. The procedure call must handle the data being returned by means of a single parameter in the procedure. For each pledge payment, make sure the pledge ID, donor's last name, pledge payment amount, and pledge payment date are displayed.

Case Projects

Case 7-1: Reviewing Brewbean's Order Checkout Package

In Chapter 6, you created a procedure and functions to handle updating basket columns during the shopper checkout process. Create a package named `SHOP_PROCESS_PKG` that contains all the program units created in Chapter 6. Modify the `BASK_CALC_PP` procedure so that the subtotal, tax, shipping, and total amounts are placed in packaged variables rather than the database so that the application can display a purchase confirmation page for shoppers. Test this procedure with basket **3**.

The lead programmer has requested that all package program units be in alphabetical order to make them easy to locate. Use forward declarations, if needed, to allow alphabetizing program units.

Case 7-2: Working with More Movies Program Unit Packaging

In the Chapter 5 More Movies case project, you created two procedures to support checking out and checking in rented movies. In Chapter 6, you created a function for making inquiries about movie availability. Create a package named `MM_RENTALS_PKG` to contain all these program units, and make all the program units public. Test the `MOVIE_INFO` function with the movie IDs **6** and **7**.

CHAPTER 8

DEPENDENCIES, PRIVILEGES, AND COMPILATION

LEARNING OBJECTIVES

After completing this chapter, you should be able to understand:

- Direct and indirect dependencies
- Data dictionary information on dependencies
- Using the dependency tree utility
- The unique nature of package dependencies
- Remote object dependency actions
- Avoiding recompilation errors
- Granting program unit privileges
- PL/SQL compiler parameters and features

INTRODUCTION

In this chapter, you learn about **program unit dependencies**, which are the interrelationships of objects as they relate to procedures, functions, and packages. Understanding program unit dependencies helps you prevent complications caused by object references.

Relationships or dependencies determine the validity of any program unit. A modification to a database object the program unit references causes the status of the program unit to change to `INVALID`. This status change simply instructs Oracle to recompile the program unit before the next execution. Why? A referenced object modification can affect whether the program unit executes successfully. For example, if the `ORDER_TOTAL_SP` procedure reads particular columns from a table, what happens when the table is modified and one of these columns is dropped? Is the procedure still valid? If the table dependencies can be identified, can any execution errors be corrected before a runtime error? In this chapter, you discover the answers to these questions and more as you explore the nature of dependencies and the information and tools needed to manage them.

This chapter also introduces PL/SQL compiler options, which can help improve your coding and your application's performance. You get an overview of compiler parameters, compile-time warnings, and conditional compilation.

THE CURRENT CHALLENGE IN THE BREWBEAN'S APPLICATION

The Brewbean's manager has been reviewing user feedback on application performance and wants to take steps to make the application run more efficiently. Also, users have encountered some unexpected errors lately when using the Brewbean's application. The programmers noticed that many of these errors were related to recent modifications to the database and program units. The lead programmer determined that both types of modifications involve object dependencies and has recommended that the development group learn more about database dependencies and their effects. The group has gathered for a brief workshop to explore dependency issues.

Rebuilding the Database

To rebuild the Brewbean's database, follow these steps:

1. Make sure you have the `c8_BBcreate.sql` file in the Chapter08 folder. This file contains the script for creating the database.
2. Start SQL Developer and connect to the Oracle database.
3. Click **File**, **Open** from the menu.
4. Click the **`c8_BBcreate.sql`** file, and then click **Open**. The code in this script is displayed in the Edit pane. Scroll through the SQL statements; they should look familiar.
5. Run the script by clicking the **Run Script** button on the Edit pane toolbar. If necessary, click **OK** in the Select Connection dialog box.
6. Scroll through the Script Output pane at the bottom to review the results of the statements.
7. In the Connections pane on the left, expand the **Tables** node to view the tables that were created. While this node is selected, click the **Refresh** button at the top of the Connections pane to update the list of tables.

LOCAL DEPENDENCY ACTIVITY

First, take a look at a procedure and its dependencies. The ORDER_TOTAL_SP procedure is used in the Brewbean's ordering application to calculate order totals, including item subtotal, shipping cost, and overall total. As shown in Figure 8-1, this procedure references two database objects: a table and another procedure.

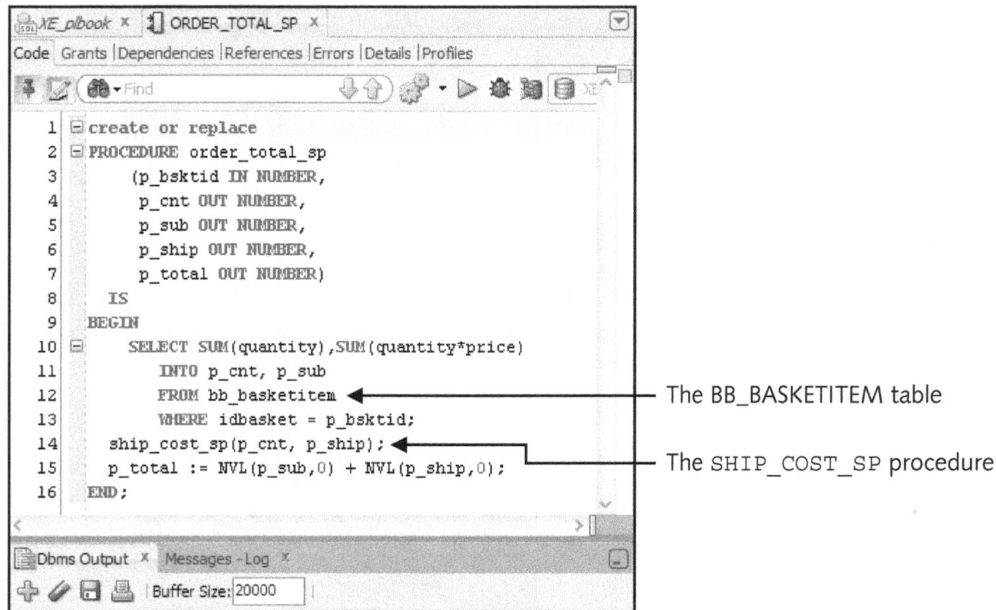

FIGURE 8-1 The ORDER_TOTAL_SP procedure

Both the BB_BASKETITEM table and the SHIP_COST_SP procedure are considered the referenced objects, and the ORDER_TOTAL_SP procedure is considered the dependent object. If you modify one of the referenced objects, the status of the dependent object (the ORDER_TOTAL_SP procedure) is flagged as INVALID, meaning this program unit needs to be recompiled. You can check a database object's status with the USER_OBJECTS data dictionary view. To check the current status of procedures in the Brewbean's application, follow these steps:

1. Start SQL Developer, if necessary.
2. Type the query in Figure 8-2 to review the status of all procedures in your schema. Having additional procedures listed isn't a problem. Depending on experiments you've tried in previous chapters, you might have created other procedures. You should at least find all the ones listed in Figure 8-2.

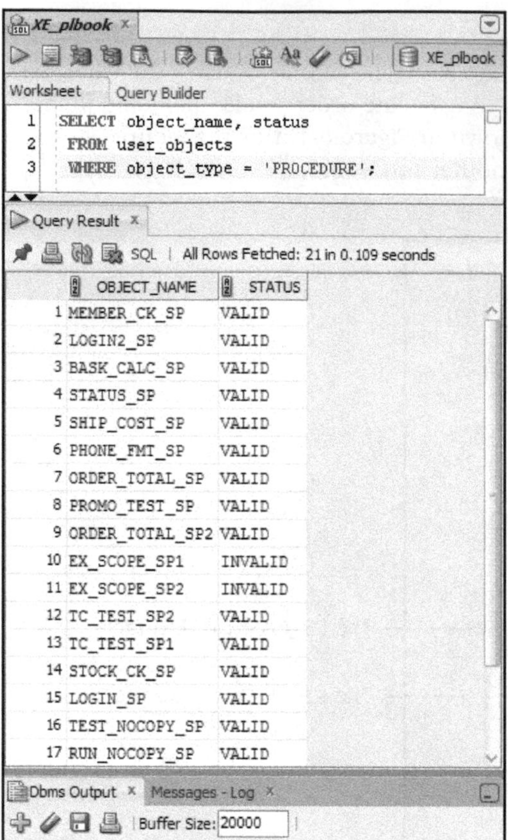

FIGURE 8-2 Querying the status of all procedures

The results show all procedures in your schema and their current status. After you save or compile a procedure successfully, the status is marked as `VALID`. The STATUS column's value changes to `INVALID` automatically if one of the procedures' referenced objects is modified. For example, the `ORDER_TOTAL_SP` procedure contains a query on the BB_BASKETITEM table. If you modify the table, the `ORDER_TOTAL_SP` procedure then has the status `INVALID` until it's recompiled. Oracle has methods for recompiling a procedure to return it to the status `VALID`, including manual and automatic database actions.

To confirm a program unit's status, make a modification and review its effect on the status:

1. Review the query results in Figure 8-2, which confirmed that the status of the `ORDER_TOTAL_SP` and `SHIP_COST_SP` procedures is currently `VALID`.
2. Modify the BB_BASKETITEM table by running the `ALTER TABLE` command shown in Figure 8-3. This command resizes the QUANTITY column.

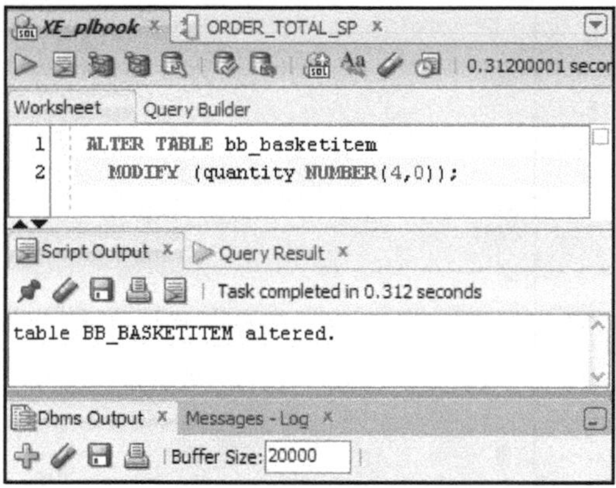

FIGURE 8-3 Modifying the column size

3. Enter the query of the USER_OBJECTS view shown in Figure 8-4 to check the status of ORDER_TOTAL_SP. Note that its status is now INVALID because one of the referenced objects, the BB_BASKETITEM table, has been changed.

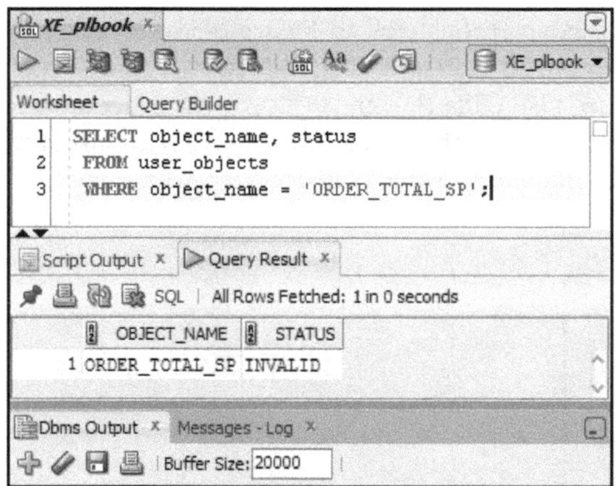

FIGURE 8-4 Checking the ORDER_TOTAL_SP procedure's status

4. The INVALID status indicates that the program unit must be recompiled before it's run again. You can recompile a procedure manually in two ways: using the CREATE OR REPLACE statement to rebuild the procedure (which completes a compile action) or using the ALTER COMPILE command to instruct Oracle to compile a specific object. In this example, the command is ALTER PROCEDURE ORDER_TOTAL_SP COMPILE;, which is the same command issued when you click the Compile button in the program unit pane.
5. To recompile the ORDER_TOTAL_SP procedure, open the procedure and click the **Compile** button *or* run the ALTER COMPILE command given in Step 4. Figure 8-5 shows the results of recompiling this procedure.

```
XE_plbook × ORDER_TOTAL_SP ×
Code Grants Dependencies References Errors Details Profiles

create or replace
PROCEDURE order_total_sp
    (p_bsktid IN NUMBER,
     p_cnt OUT NUMBER,
     p_sub OUT NUMBER,
     p_ship OUT NUMBER,
     p_total OUT NUMBER)
  IS
BEGIN
    SELECT SUM(quantity),SUM(quantity*price)
      INTO p_cnt, p_sub
      FROM bb_basketitem
      WHERE idbasket = p_bsktid;
  ship_cost_sp(p_cnt, p_ship);
  p_total := NVL(p_sub,0) + NVL(p_ship,0);
END;

Dbms Output × Messages - Log ×
Compiled
```

FIGURE 8-5 Recompiling the `ORDER_TOTAL_SP` procedure

6. Query the `USER_OBJECTS` view again (refer back to Figure 8-4) to confirm that the `ORDER_TOTAL_SP` procedure's status is now `VALID`.
7. The `ORDER_TOTAL_SP` procedure also calls the `SHIP_COST_SP` procedure, which creates another dependency. Open the **`SHIP_COST_SP`** procedure and modify to add a third parameter named **`p_junk`** (see Figure 8-6). Be sure to compile the procedure.

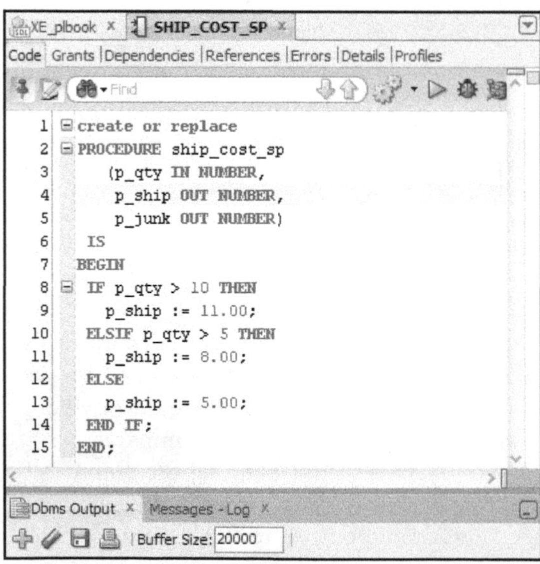

FIGURE 8-6 Modifying the `SHIP_COST_SP` procedure

8. Query the `USER_OBJECTS` view again and confirm that the `ORDER_TOTAL_SP` procedure's status is `INVALID` again.

9. Open the **ORDER_TOTAL_SP** procedure and click the **Compile** button. Why do you get the compilation errors shown in Figure 8-7? One error indicates that the number of arguments in the procedure call is incorrect. The call includes only two parameters, but the SHIP_COST_SP procedure now contains three parameters. If you didn't understand dependencies and neglected to test the ORDER_TOTAL_SP procedure after modifying the SHIP_COST_SP procedure, you would cause a runtime error.

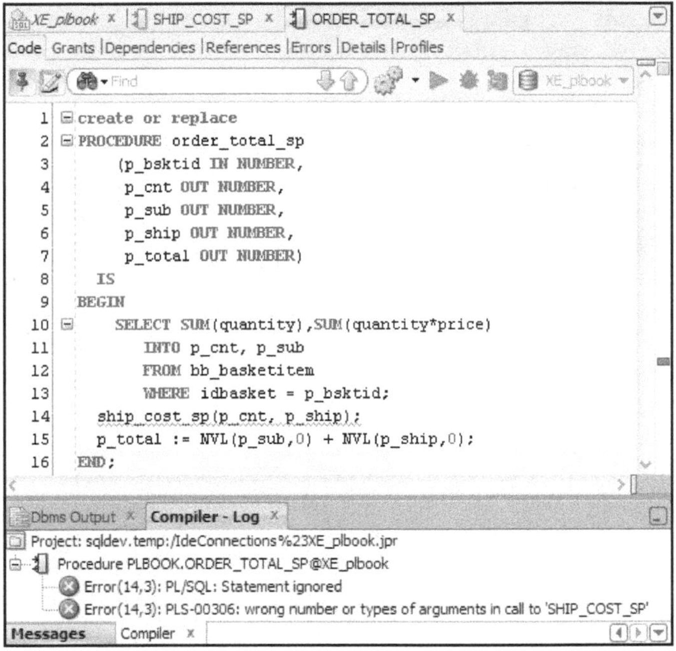

FIGURE 8-7 Compilation error caused by a parameter mismatch

10. Remove the **p_junk** parameter from the SHIP_COST_SP procedure, and compile it again.

This exercise shows the effect of modifying a referenced object on the status of a program unit dependent on that object. As you learned, you can recompile invalid program units manually by issuing the ALTER COMPILE command or re-creating the program unit. However, what happens if you don't take either action and a program unit with the status INVALID is called during runtime? The Oracle system automatically compiles the invalid program unit the next time it's called. This automatic recompilation applies only to local objects or dependent objects in the same database. If dependent objects are located in remote databases, the behavior is different. (**Remote databases** are connections to other Oracle database servers.)

There are a couple of drawbacks to letting Oracle handle this recompilation automatically:

- First, the compile operation occurs while an application is running, and this compile time adds to the time users wait for processing.
- Second, if the referenced object is changed in such a way that the recompile isn't successful, users get a runtime error on this program unit.

In the preceding exercise, if you had changed the number of parameters in the SHIP_COST_SP procedure, the ORDER_TOTAL_SP procedure wouldn't recompile successfully. For the ORDER_TOTAL_SP procedure to work correctly, you need to modify it. Using the manual recompile methods gives you a way to test modifications to make sure the dependent object isn't affected adversely by the changes.

IDENTIFYING DIRECT AND INDIRECT DEPENDENCIES

A **direct dependency** occurs when one database object, such as the ORDER_TOTAL_SP procedure, references other objects specifically, such as the BB_BASKETITEM table and the SHIP_COST_SP procedure. In this example, you can review the procedure code and identify the referenced objects fairly easily. However, what if one of the object names referenced is actually a public synonym for an object? You might not be able to tell what schema houses this object. Recall that when you create objects in a database, by default they're stored in your own schema. However, if you're granted the necessary rights, you can call database objects from other schemas.

For example, say a table named BB_BASKETITEM is created in the DBA1 schema and assigned the public synonym ITEMS for developers to reference in their program units. Without the public synonym, a reference to this table is made as DBA1.BB_BASKETITEM to instruct the system to go to the DBA1 schema and look for the BB_BASKETITEM table. However, a reference using the public synonym is made simply as ITEMS, which doesn't clearly indicate the schema or object name.

In addition, a program unit might contain a number of **indirect dependencies**, which involve references to database objects that reference other database objects, making the chain of dependencies harder to track. For example, a procedure can reference a database view, which then references a database table. The procedure has a direct dependency on the view and an indirect dependency on the table through this view. If the underlying table is modified, the procedure status changes to INVALID because of the indirect dependency. Therefore, indirect dependencies are just as important to consider as direct dependencies. The next two sections explore methods for identifying object dependencies.

Data Dictionary Views for Dependencies

The USER_DEPENDENCIES data dictionary view is helpful for giving you information on direct object dependencies. If you run a DESCRIBE command on this view, you find the columns listed in Table 8-1.

TABLE 8-1 Columns in the USER_DEPENDENCIES Data Dictionary View

Column Name	Description
NAME	Object name
TYPE	Object type
REFERENCED_OWNER	Schema name of the referenced object
REFERENCED_NAME	Name of the referenced object
REFERENCED_TYPE	Type of the referenced object
REFERENCED_LINK_NAME	Name of the database link if one is used to access the referenced object
SCHEMAID	Internal ID assigned to the schema
DEPENDENCY_TYPE	All objects show the value HARD except dependencies created by using a REF data type in Oracle's object technology features

You can list the dependency information for the ORDER_TOTAL_SP procedure by using a query of the USER_DEPENDENCIES view (see Figure 8-8). The output shows four items the ORDER_TOTAL_SP procedure is dependent on. The first two objects are related to common Oracle-supplied packages that are included to allow running PL/SQL code and program units. The last two objects are from your schema: a table and a procedure.

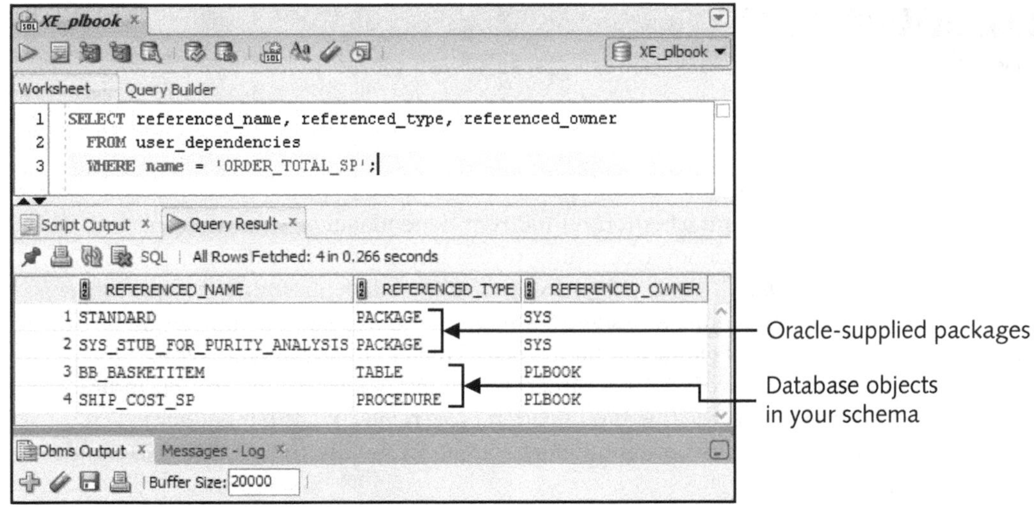

FIGURE 8-8 Querying the USER_DEPENDENCIES view for a specific object

Another way to use this data dictionary view is to list all objects that are dependent on a particular object—in other words, search based on the REFERENCED_NAME column. This method can answer the question "Now that the SHIP_COST_SP procedure has been changed, which objects are dependent on it?" Figure 8-9 shows a query of the USER_DEPENDENCIES view to answer this question.

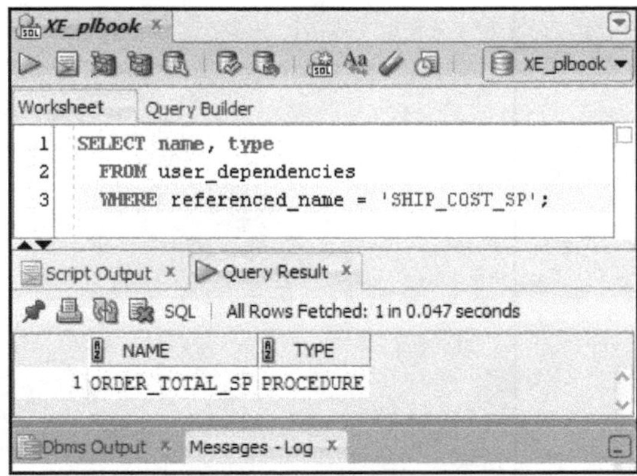

FIGURE 8-9 Querying the USER_DEPENDENCIES view for a referenced object

If you have object dependencies across schemas, you can view the owner of each object in addition to the data listed in Figure 8-9. Another data dictionary view, DBA_DEPENDENCIES, contains the same columns as USER_DEPENDENCIES and adds an OWNER column.

NOTE

By default, the `DBA_DEPENDENCIES` view is accessible only to users with administrative privileges. To list data in this view, you must log on to Oracle with a DBA account (such as the default SYSTEM user) and grant privileges to other users.

CHALLENGE 8-1

List all objects that are dependent on the `MEMFMT1_SF` function and the BB_SHOPPER table.

The Dependency Tree Utility

Data dictionary views lack information on indirect dependencies, so in this section, you learn how to use the dependency tree utility to track indirect dependencies. First, you need to modify the `ORDER_TOTAL_SP` procedure to introduce an indirect dependency, and then modify this procedure to issue a `SELECT` statement from a *view* of the BB_BASKETITEM table instead of the table itself. This change results in the `ORDER_TOTAL_SP` procedure having a direct dependency on the view and an indirect dependency on the table. After this modification, you review what dependency information is available in the data dictionary views. To modify the `ORDER_TOTAL_SP` procedure, follow these steps:

1. In SQL Developer, open the **`ORDER_TOTAL_SP`** procedure and modify the `FROM` clause in the query to use the `BB_BASKETITEM_VU` view (see Figure 8-10). Compile the procedure.

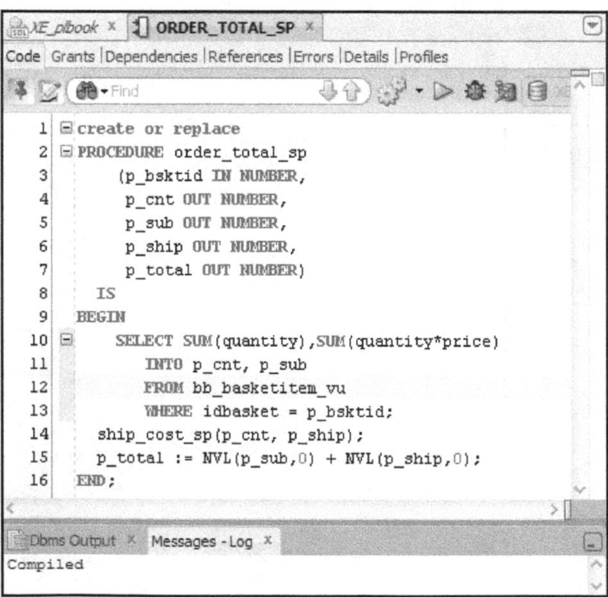

FIGURE 8-10 Modifying the `ORDER_TOTAL_SP` procedure to use a view

2. Run the query in Figure 8-11 to list all objects the `ORDER_TOTAL_SP` procedure references. Notice that the BB_BASKETITEM table isn't included in the list because it's an indirect dependency.

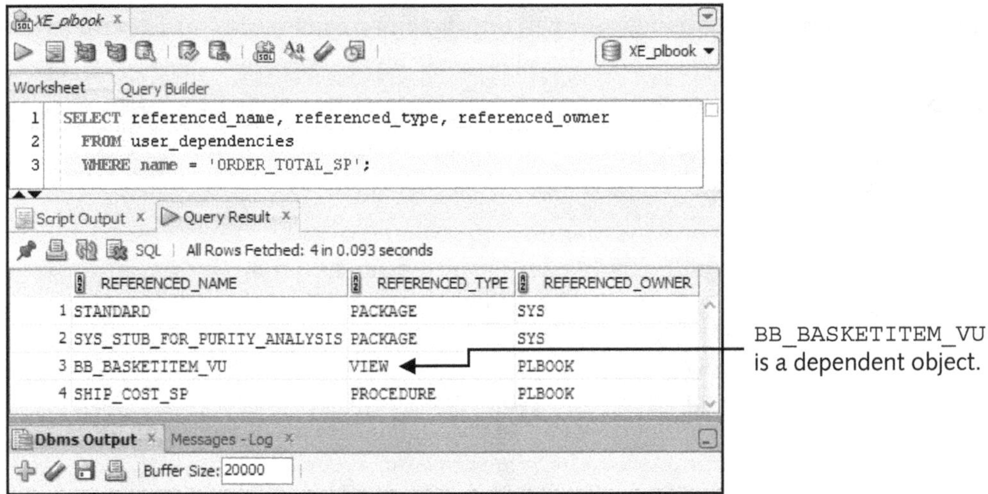

FIGURE 8-11 A query of the `USER_DEPENDENCIES` view confirming that indirect dependencies aren't listed

3. Run a second query to list all objects that are dependent on the BB_BASKETITEM table (see Figure 8-12). The `ORDER_TOTAL_SP` procedure isn't included in this list because it's indirectly dependent on the BB_BASKETITEM table via the `BB_BASKETITEM_VU` view.

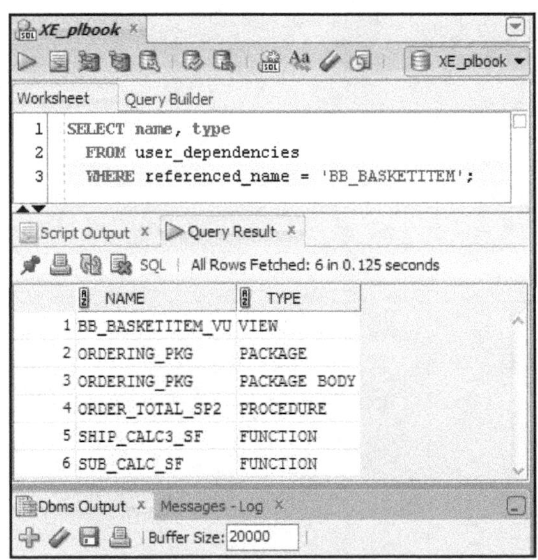

FIGURE 8-12 A second query of the `USER_DEPENDENCIES` view confirming that indirect dependencies aren't listed

Because data dictionary views make identifying all dependencies a little cumbersome, Oracle provides a utility to make this process easier. The **dependency tree utility** creates a "map" showing both direct and indirect dependencies in the database. For this utility to work, you must run a script that builds the necessary views, tables, sequences, and procedures. You can find this script in the Oracle home directory where the database is installed; the `\rdbms\admin` subdirectory of this directory contains the `utldtree.sql` file. A copy of this script is included in the Chapter 8 student data files.

TIP

To become familiar with objects the `utldtree.sql` script creates, open the file and review the statements. Helpful comments are included to explain parts of the script.

Some statements (such as the `DROP` commands) fail the first time you run the `utldtree.sql` script. Some errors are caused by the script containing `DROP` statements for objects you have created (in case you have run the script previously). In addition, which `CREATE` statements succeed depends on whether you're logged in with a database administrator account. Different objects are created for administrator and non-administrator users, so don't worry if some `CREATE` statements produce errors. The following steps help you determine whether the script ran successfully.

This script needs to be run only once to create the needed objects. It creates a `DEPTREE_FILL` procedure that can fill a table with data on an object's dependencies. You can then use the views this script creates to display a listing of dependencies. To create the necessary objects, follow these steps:

1. In SQL Developer, open the **`utldtree.sql`** script in the Chapter08 folder.
2. Click the **Run Script** button on the toolbar.
3. Review the messages, which should match the following listing for the first run. These errors are expected. Confirm that five objects were created (shown in bold in this listing): sequence, table, procedure, and two views.

```
Error starting at line 43 in command:
drop sequence deptree_seq
Error report:
SQL Error: ORA-02289: sequence does not exist
02289. 00000 -  "sequence does not exist"
*Cause:    The specified sequence does not exist, or the user does
           not have the required privilege to perform this operation.
*Action:   Make sure the sequence name is correct, and that you have
           the right to perform the desired operation on this sequence.
sequence DEPTREE_SEQ created.

Error starting at line 47 in command:
drop table deptree_temptab
Error report:
SQL Error: ORA-00942: table or view does not exist
00942. 00000 -  "table or view does not exist"
*Cause:
*Action:
table DEPTREE_TEMPTAB created.
PROCEDURE deptree_fill compiled
```

```
Error starting at line 81 in command:
drop view deptree
Error report:
SQL Error: ORA-00942: table or view does not exist
00942. 00000 -  "table or view does not exist"
*Cause:
*Action:
> REM This view will succeed if current user is sys. This view shows
> REM which shared cursors depend on the given object. If the current
> REM user is not sys, then this view get an error, either about lack
> REM of privileges or about the nonexistence of table x$kglxs.

Error starting at line 92 in command:
create view sys.deptree
  (nested_level, type, schema, name, seq#)
as
  select d.nest_level, o.object_type, o.owner, o.object_name, d.seq#
  from deptree_temptab d, dba_objects o
  where d.object_id = o.object_id (+)
union all
  select d.nest_level+1, 'CURSOR', '<shared>', '"'||c.kglnaobj||'"',
d.seq#+.5
  from deptree_temptab d, x$kgldp k, x$kglob g, obj$ o, user$ u, x$kglob c,
      x$kglxs a
    where d.object_id = o.obj#
    and o.name = g.kglnaobj
    and o.owner# = u.user#
    and u.name = g.kglnaown
    and g.kglhdadr = k.kglrfhdl
    and k.kglhdadr = a.kglhdadr  /* make sure it is not a transitive */
    and k.kgldepno = a.kglxsdep  /* reference, but a direct one */
    and k.kglhdadr = c.kglhdadr
    and c.kglhdnsp = 0 /* a cursor */
Error at Command Line:96 Column:7
Error report:
SQL Error: ORA-00942: table or view does not exist
00942. 00000 -  "table or view does not exist"
*Cause:
*Action:
> REM This view will succeed if current user is not sys. This view
> REM does *not* show which shared cursors depend on the given object.
> REM If the current user is sys, then this view will get an error
> REM indicating that the view already exists (since prior view create
> REM will have succeeded).
view DEPTREE created.
```

```
Error starting at line 130 in command:
drop view ideptree
Error report:
SQL Error: ORA-00942: table or view does not exist
00942. 00000 -  "table or view does not exist"
*Cause:
*Action:
view IDEPTREE created.
```

Next, try using the `utldtree` utility to review all dependencies of the BB_BASKETITEM table:

1. Run the **DEPTREE_FILL** procedure, as shown in Figure 8-13, to populate the DEPTREE_TEMPTAB table with dependency data for the BB_BASKETITEM table. The `DEPTREE_FILL` procedure has three parameters: object type, object schema, and object name.

NOTE

This command assumes you're using the `PLBOOK` schema. Replace `PLBOOK` with your schema name, if needed.

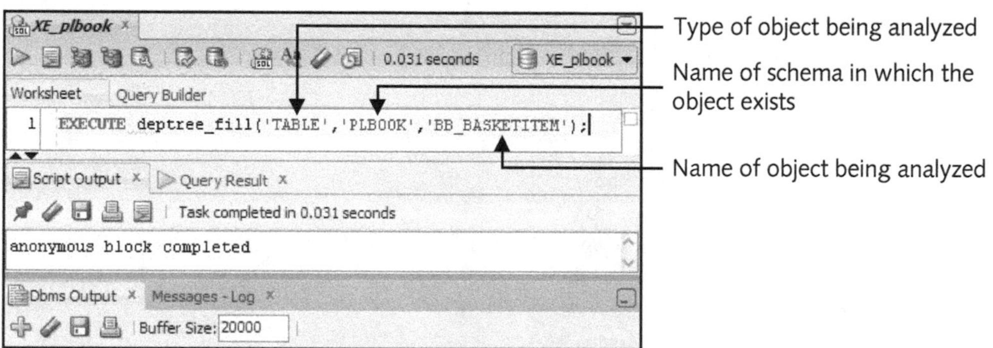

FIGURE 8-13 Running the `DEPTREE_FILL` procedure

2. You have two choices in listing dependency information. First, use the `DEPTREE` view to list the dependencies with a numeric level scheme. Run the query, as shown in Figure 8-14. The number in the NESTED_LEVEL column represents the relation to the object being analyzed.

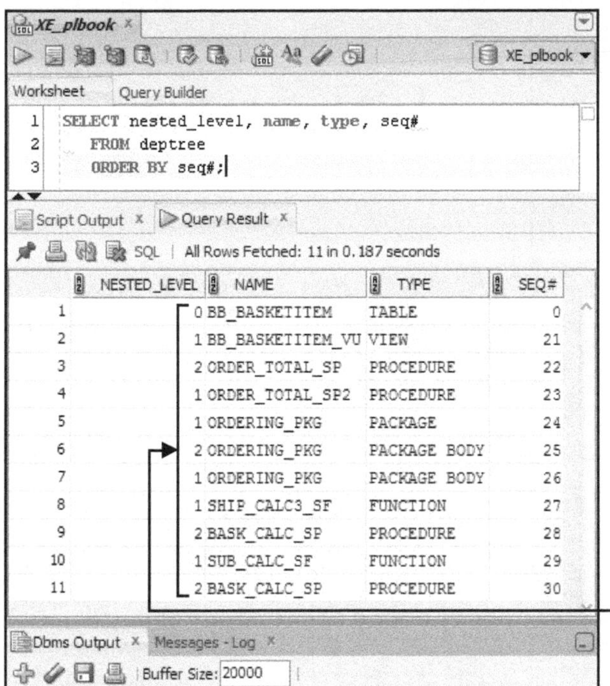

FIGURE 8-14 Listing all dependencies with the `DEPTREE` view

3. Using the `seq#` sort in the `ORDER BY` clause ensures that dependencies are listed in a logical order so that you can identify the path of direct and indirect dependencies. (*Note*: The SEQ# column output might differ.) Your output might vary from the figure, depending on the exercises you have done in this book. However, the `ORDER_TOTAL_SP` procedure is directly related to the `BB_BASKETITEM_VU` view, which is directly related to the BB_BASKETITEM table. In other words, the `ORDER_TOTAL_SP` procedure is indirectly dependent on the BB_BASKETITEM table via the `BB_BASKETITEM_VU` view.
4. Another view, `IDEPTREE`, displays the same dependency information in an indented format; the “I” means “indented.” Run a **`SELECT`** statement on this view (see Figure 8-15). This view indicates the dependency paths with indentations. No indent is used on the line with the object being analyzed. A single indent means a direct dependency, and a double indent means an indirect dependency.

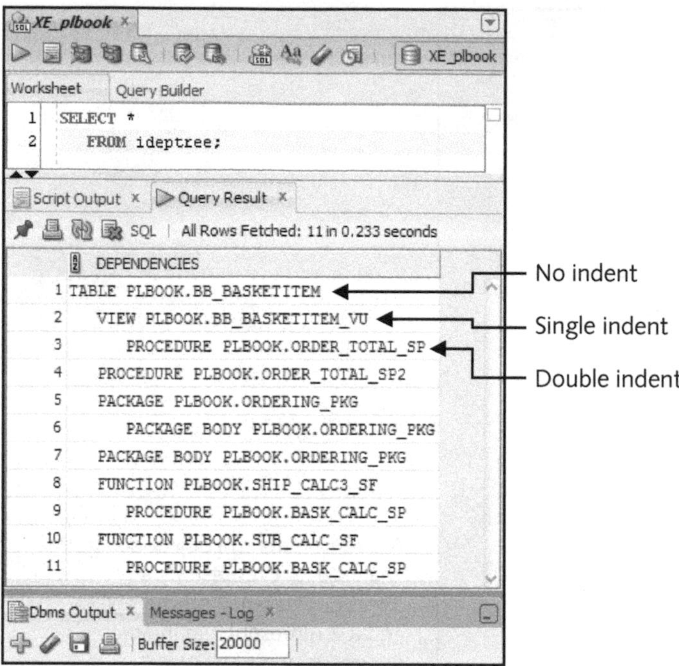

FIGURE 8-15 Listing all dependencies with the `IDEPTREE` view

CAUTION

In some versions of Oracle Express, a clause has been left out of the `CREATE IDEPTREE VIEW` statement in the `utldtree.sql` script. This statement should include the sorting clause `ORDER BY seq#`. The script in the data files contains this clause.

As you've seen, the `USER_DEPENDENCIES` view is quite helpful in identifying direct dependencies; however, the dependency tree utility gives you a broader picture of all dependencies, both direct and indirect, and the path of dependencies through database objects.

CHALLENGE 8-2

Use the dependency tree utility to identify all direct and indirect dependencies of the `MEMFMT1_SF` function and the BB_SHOPPER table.

PACKAGE DEPENDENCIES

One of the advantages of packages is improved handling of dependencies, a result of the package structure separating the program unit code (the body) from the program unit header (the specification). If you modify code in the package body, the status of dependent objects isn't changed to `INVALID`, as with stand-alone program units. Only modifications to the package specification (program unit header) result in changing dependent objects' status to `INVALID`. For this reason, you don't have to do as much recompiling as you would if all the program units were stand-alone.

Take a look at how package dependencies work in the Brewbean's application. The ORDER_INFO_PKG package you use to test package dependencies contains a public procedure and a private function. A stand-alone procedure, PKG_DEPTEST_SP, calls the procedure in the ORDER_INFO_PKG package, so it's dependent on the package. Figure 8-16 shows the package and procedure code and the dependency between these two objects.

ORDER_INFO_PKG package

```
CREATE OR REPLACE PACKAGE order_info_pkg
  IS
  PROCEDURE basket_info_pp
  (p_basket IN NUMBER,
   p_shop OUT NUMBER,
   p_date OUT DATE,
   p_name OUT VARCHAR2);
END;

CREATE OR REPLACE PACKAGE BODY order_info_pkg IS
FUNCTION ship_name_pf
  (p_basket IN NUMBER)
  RETURN VARCHAR2
  IS
    lv_name_txt VARCHAR2(25);
BEGIN
  SELECT shipfirstname||' '||shiplastname
    INTO lv_name_txt
    FROM bb_basket
    WHERE idBasket = p_basket;
  RETURN lv_name_txt;
EXCEPTION
  WHEN NO_DATA_FOUND THEN
    DBMS_OUTPUT.PUT_LINE('Invalid basket ID');
END ship_name_pf;
PROCEDURE basket_info_pp
  (p_basket IN NUMBER,
   p_shop OUT NUMBER,
   p_date OUT DATE,
   p_name OUT VARCHAR2)
  IS
BEGIN
  SELECT idshopper, dtordered
    INTO p_shop, p_date
    FROM bb_basket
    WHERE idbasket = p_basket;
  p_name := ship_name_pf(p_basket);
EXCEPTION
  WHEN NO_DATA_FOUND THEN
    DBMS_OUTPUT.PUT_LINE('Invalid basket ID');
  END basket_info_pp;
END;
```

PKG_DEPTEST_SP procedure

```
CREATE OR REPLACE PROCEDURE pkg_deptest_sp
  (p_bask NUMBER)
  IS
  lv_shop_num NUMBER(4);
  lv_bask_dat DATE;
  lv_name_txt VARCHAR2(25);
BEGIN
  order_info_pkg.basket_info_pp(p_bask,
    lv_shop_num, lv_bask_dat, lv_name_txt);
  DBMS_OUTPUT.PUT_LINE(lv_shop_num);
  DBMS_OUTPUT.PUT_LINE(lv_bask_dat);
  DBMS_OUTPUT.PUT_LINE(lv_name_txt);
END;
```

The PKG_DEPTEST_SP procedure calls the BASKET_INFO_PP packaged procedure, so PKG_DEPTEST_SP is dependent on the ORDER_INFO_PKG package.

FIGURE 8-16 Dependency of the PKG_DEPTEST_SP procedure

To work with package dependencies, follow these steps:

1. In SQL Developer, create the **PKG_DEPTEST_SP** procedure shown on the right side of Figure 8-16. Enter the query in Figure 8-17 to confirm that the procedure's status is VALID.

```
SELECT status
 FROM user_objects
 WHERE object_name = 'PKG_DEPTEST_SP';
```

STATUS
1 VALID

FIGURE 8-17 Checking the status of the PKG_DEPTEST_SP procedure

2. Next, you modify the package body to determine the effect on the dependent procedure. Brewbean's wants to list shoppers' names with an asterisk if the basket contains multiple items. Open the **ORDER_INFO_PKG** body and modify the **BASKET_INFO_PP** procedure as shown in Figure 8-18.

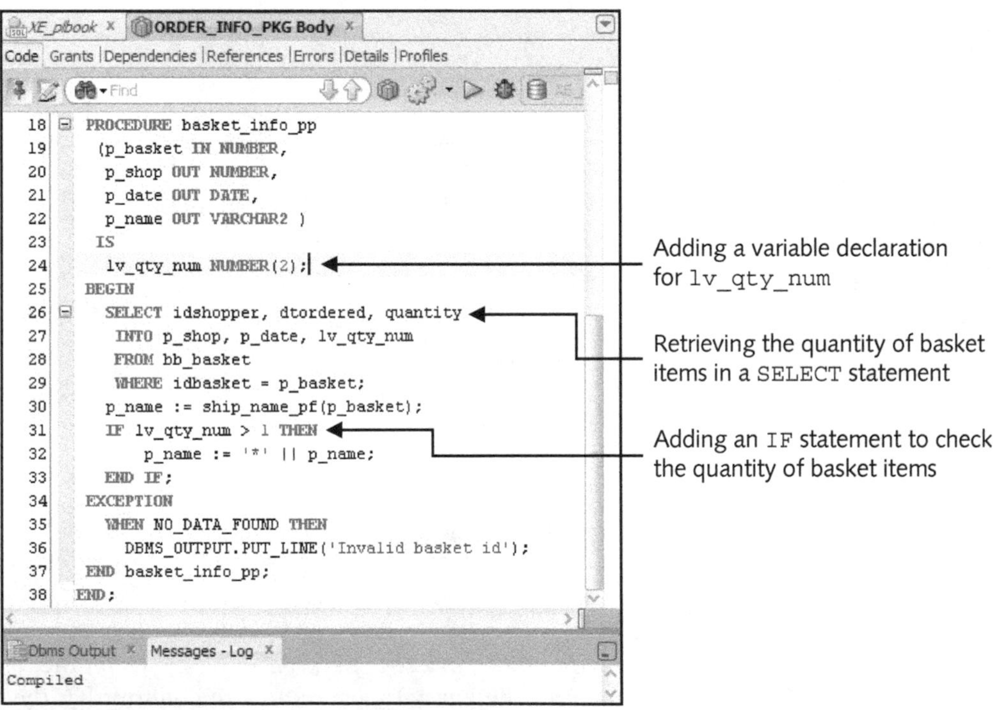

FIGURE 8-18 Modifying the package body

3. Check the status of the dependent object, the PKG_DEPTEST_SP procedure, to see whether the modifications affected the dependent object's status. Enter the query in Figure 8-17 again to confirm that the procedure's status is still VALID.

4. Now test a modification of the package specification. Brewbean's has decided that the asterisk indicating multiple items in an order should be displayed as a separate value from the procedure instead of being attached to a shopper's name. Open the **ORDER_INFO_PKG** package specification. Modify it by adding a parameter to the BASKET_INFO_PP procedure header (see Figure 8-19), and compile.

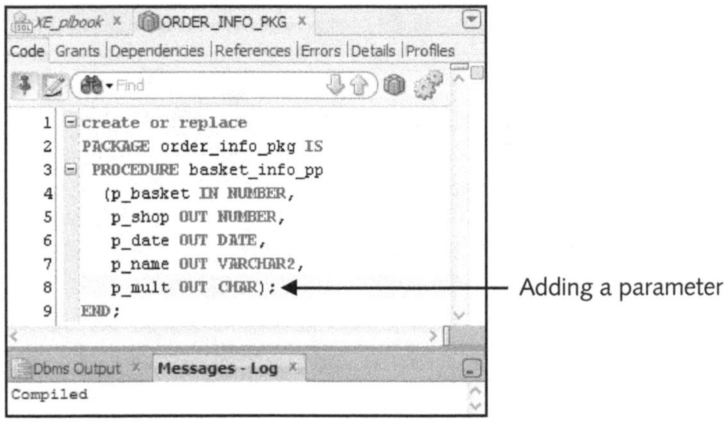

FIGURE 8-19 Modifying the package specification

NOTE

Of course, adding a parameter means you also need to modify this procedure's code in the package body. However, you can skip doing so now because the change isn't necessary for this example.

5. Now you can check the status of the dependent object, the PKG_DEPTEST_SP procedure, to see whether the modifications affected the dependent object's status. Enter the query shown in Figure 8-20 to confirm that the procedure status is now INVALID.

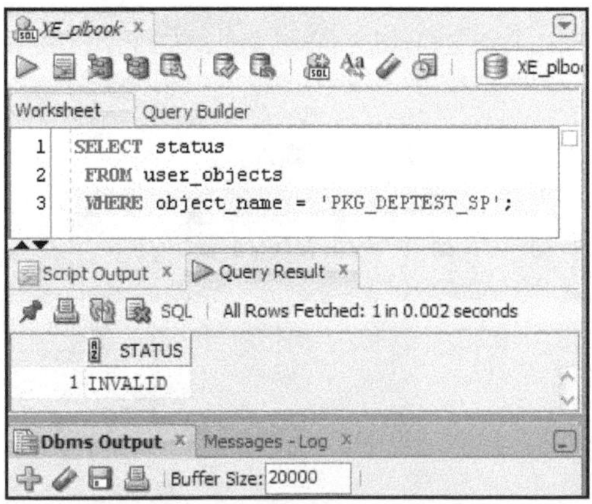

FIGURE 8-20 Checking the procedure's status again

This exercise shows the benefit of packages in handling object dependencies: Only modifications to program unit headers require recompiling dependent objects. As you know, any changes to a procedure's parameters require modifying any associated procedure calls because arguments in the call must match parameters in the program unit. With this separation of the specification and body, developers can create code with calls to package program units before they've finished writing the package code. This feature is quite useful for large development projects because all you need to create dependent objects is the package specification.

REMOTE OBJECT DEPENDENCIES

Remote database connections are used to link to another database and use or call objects in that database. Object dependencies are handled slightly differently when remote database dependencies are involved because the data dictionary doesn't track remote dependencies. Therefore, if an object in one database is changed, any remote program units using or depending on that object aren't immediately changed to an `INVALID` status. Oracle made this decision because this operation could result in longer processing times and raise other problems if remote databases aren't available at the time of modifications. Remote dependencies are checked at runtime instead of instantly, as with local database objects. This runtime check causes a failure during a dependent object's first run if the referenced object has been altered.

To work with remote dependencies in the Brewbean's application, follow these steps:

1. In SQL Developer, you need to create a database link so that the system treats a call to an object as a remote connection. To add this link, type and run the command shown in Figure 8-21. The `USING` clause must include a connection string based on your TNS-defined connection; the default in Oracle Express is XE, and in Oracle Standard or Enterprise, it's ORCL.

NOTE

TNS (transparent network substrate) is Oracle's networking architecture; it uses a configuration file, `tnsnames.ora`, to define database addresses for establishing connections.

NOTE

A **database link** is simply a pointer that instructs Oracle to look for the referenced object in a database instance other than the current connection. (Remember that when you log in to Oracle, you connect to a specific database instance.)

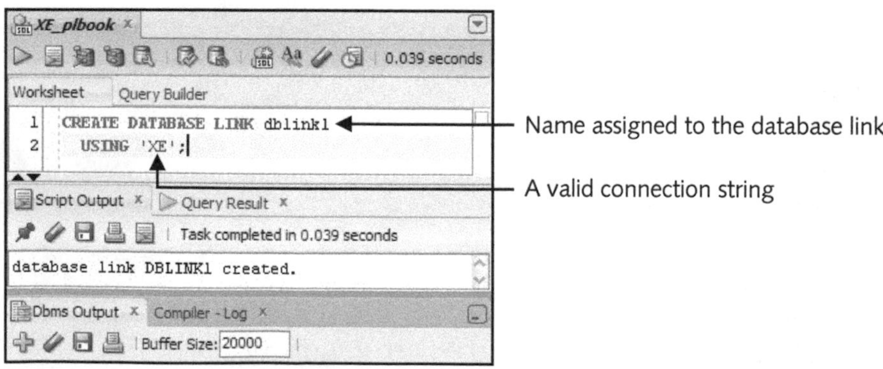

FIGURE 8-21 Creating a database link

2. In this exercise, you use the `SHIP_COST_SP` procedure as the referenced object and the `ORDER_TOTAL_SP` procedure, which calls `SHIP_COST_SP`, as the dependent object. You need to modify the call to `SHIP_COST_SP` to use the database link and simulate a remote connection. Modify the **`ORDER_TOTAL_SP`** procedure by making the changes in Figure 8-22, and compile the procedure.

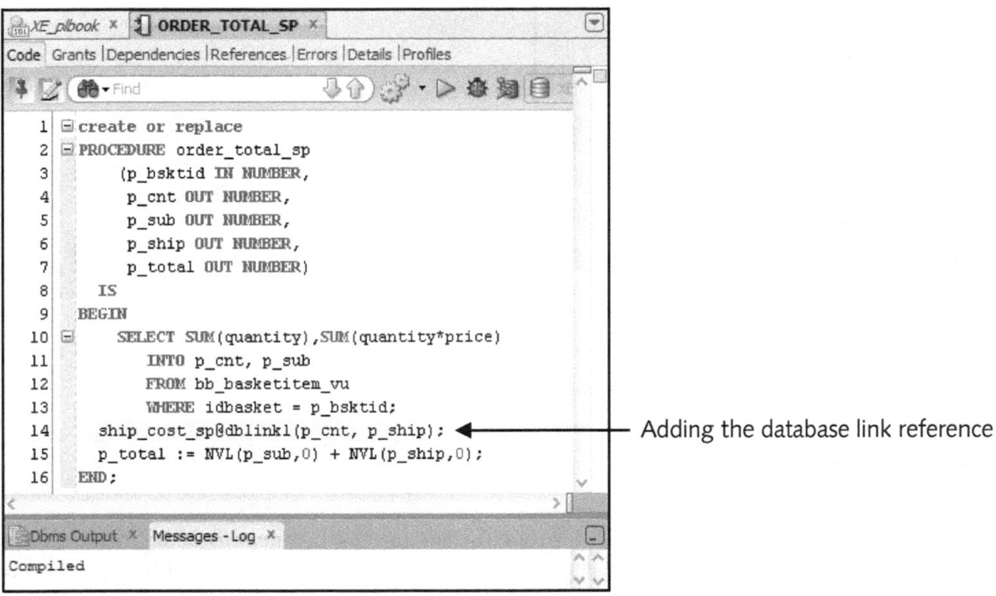

FIGURE 8-22 Modifying the `SHIP_COST_SP` procedure to use the database link

3. Query the **`USER_OBJECTS`** data dictionary view to confirm that the status of both procedures is `VALID`, as shown in Figure 8-23.

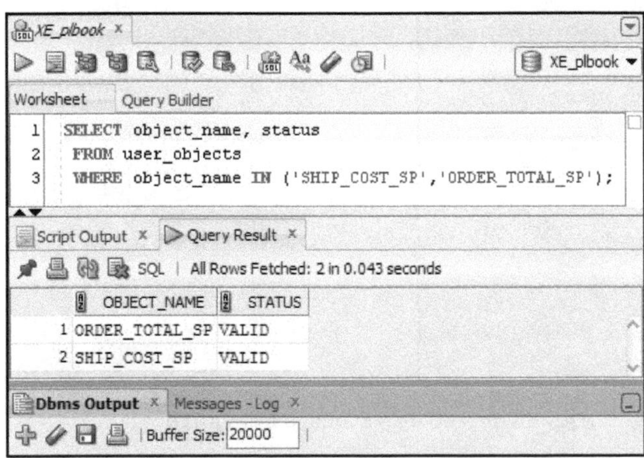

FIGURE 8-23 Checking the status of both procedures

4. Next, you change this referenced object to test the effect on the dependent object's status. Modify the **SHIP_COST_SP** procedure by making the shipping cost change indicated in Figure 8-24, and compile the procedure.

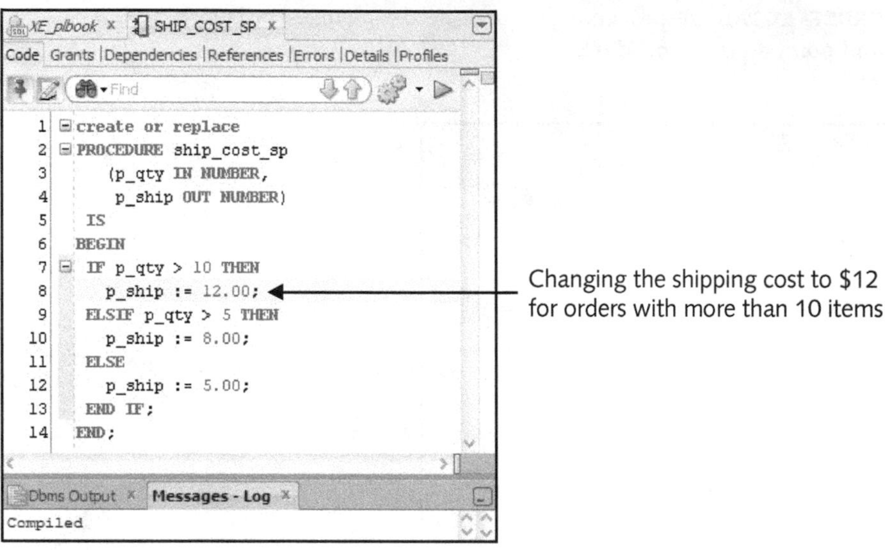

FIGURE 8-24 Modifying the `SHIP_COST_SP` procedure

5. Check the status of the two procedures again (see Figure 8-25). Notice that the dependent object, the `ORDER_TOTAL_SP` procedure, is still `VALID`. If this procedure didn't use the database link to call the `SHIP_COST_SP` procedure, it would have an `INVALID` status; however, it's treated as a remote connection, so it's not updated immediately.

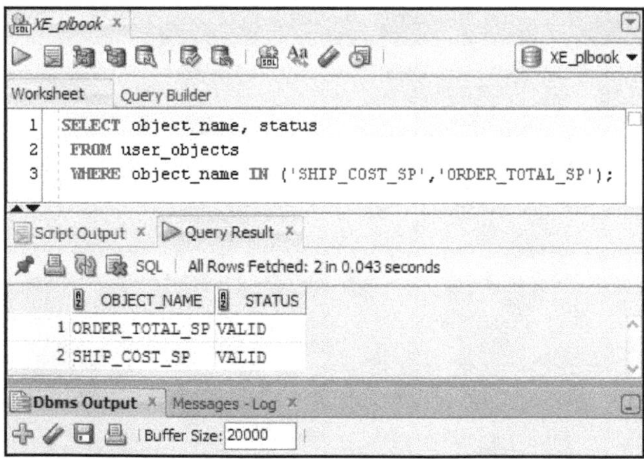

FIGURE 8-25 Verifying that the `ORDER_TOTAL_SP` procedure's status is still `VALID`

6. Run the **ORDER_TOTAL** procedure, as shown in Figure 8-26. What happens? The `ORDER_TOTAL_SP` procedure's dependency on `SHIP_COST_SP` is checked at runtime because a remote connection is used. The first run after modifying the

referenced object fails because Oracle recognizes that a change has been made and ORDER_TOTAL_SP needs to be recompiled. Notice that one of the error messages shows that the timestamp of SHIP_COST has been changed.

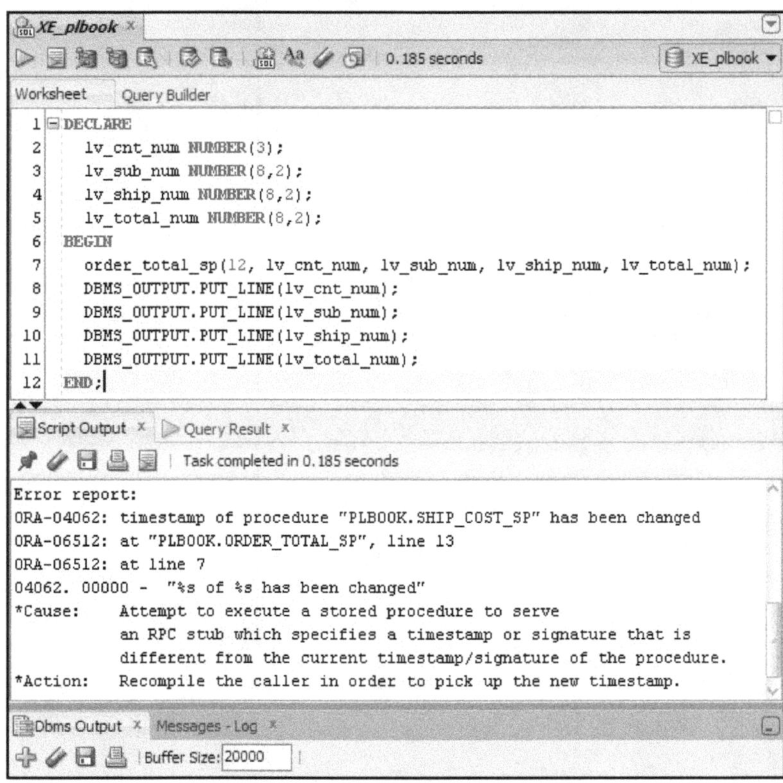
```
DECLARE
  lv_cnt_num NUMBER(3);
  lv_sub_num NUMBER(8,2);
  lv_ship_num NUMBER(8,2);
  lv_total_num NUMBER(8,2);
BEGIN
  order_total_sp(12, lv_cnt_num, lv_sub_num, lv_ship_num, lv_total_num);
  DBMS_OUTPUT.PUT_LINE(lv_cnt_num);
  DBMS_OUTPUT.PUT_LINE(lv_sub_num);
  DBMS_OUTPUT.PUT_LINE(lv_ship_num);
  DBMS_OUTPUT.PUT_LINE(lv_total_num);
END;
```

```
Error report:
ORA-04062: timestamp of procedure "PLBOOK.SHIP_COST_SP" has been changed
ORA-06512: at "PLBOOK.ORDER_TOTAL_SP", line 13
ORA-06512: at line 7
04062. 00000 -  "%s of %s has been changed"
*Cause:    Attempt to execute a stored procedure to serve
           an RPC stub which specifies a timestamp or signature that is
           different from the current timestamp/signature of the procedure.
*Action:   Recompile the caller in order to pick up the new timestamp.
```

FIGURE 8-26 First run of a dependent procedure after the referenced object is modified

7. Check the current status of both procedures (see Figure 8-27). The ORDER_TOTAL_SP procedure's status is now INVALID.

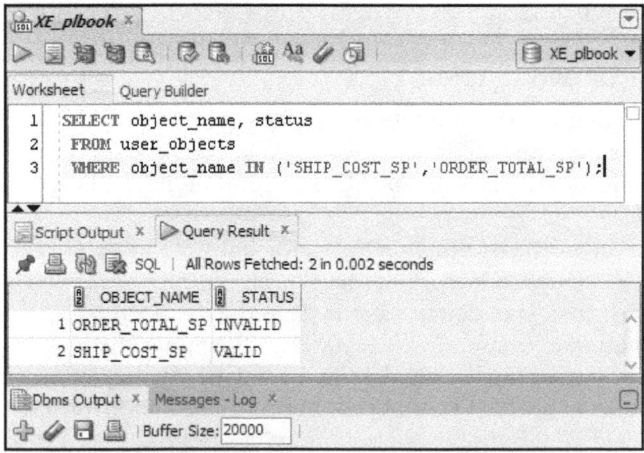
```
SELECT object_name, status
 FROM user_objects
 WHERE object_name IN ('SHIP_COST_SP','ORDER_TOTAL_SP');
```

	OBJECT_NAME	STATUS
1	ORDER_TOTAL_SP	INVALID
2	SHIP_COST_SP	VALID

FIGURE 8-27 Verifying that the ORDER_TOTAL_SP procedure status is now INVALID

8. Run the **ORDER_TOTAL_SP** procedure again (see Figure 8-28). This second run recompiles ORDER_TOTAL_SP automatically, and the procedure runs successfully.

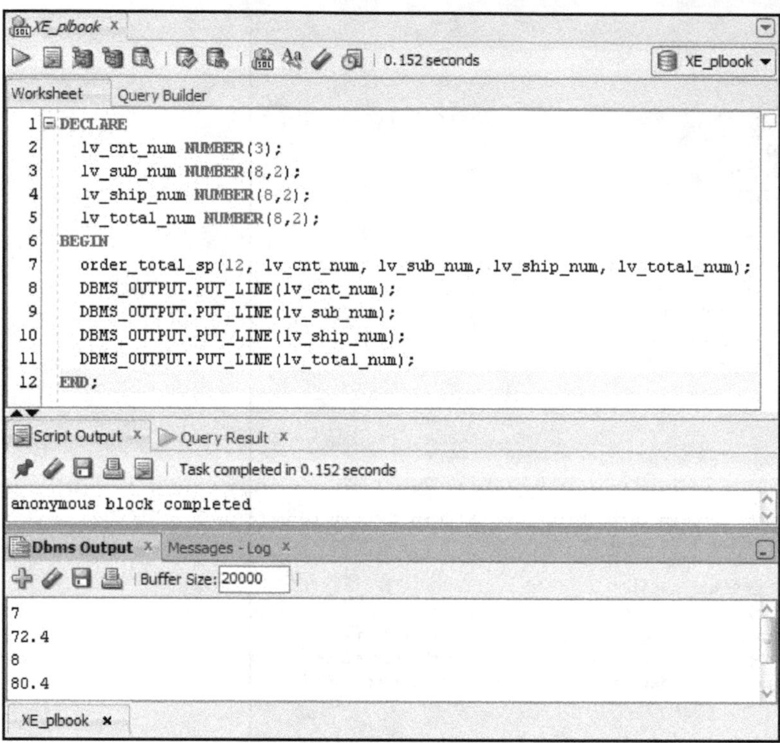

FIGURE 8-28 The second run of ORDER_TOTAL_SP is successful

The preceding exercise shows that you must pay extra attention to working with remote database connections because they're less forgiving with modifications and dependencies. The first run doesn't recompile dependent objects automatically; instead, it raises an error. To prevent a runtime error, the ALTER COMPILE command should be used to recompile any remote dependencies.

Models for Checking Remote Dependencies

Oracle offers two models for determining whether remote dependent objects should be flagged as INVALID at runtime: timestamp and signature. Oracle calls this process "invalidation" because dependent objects are marked INVALID at runtime depending on a comparison of object attributes.

The **timestamp model** compares objects' last modification date and time to determine whether invalidation has occurred. If the dependent object has an older timestamp than the referenced object when it's called, the dependent object is flagged as INVALID and needs to be recompiled. The data dictionary maintains a TIMESTAMP column that's included in the USER_OBJECTS view. Returning to the remote dependency example in the previous section, calling the dependent procedure ORDER_TOTAL_SP raised an error after the referenced procedure was modified. Figure 8-29 shows a query of the USER_OBJECTS view, which displays timestamp information for both procedures.

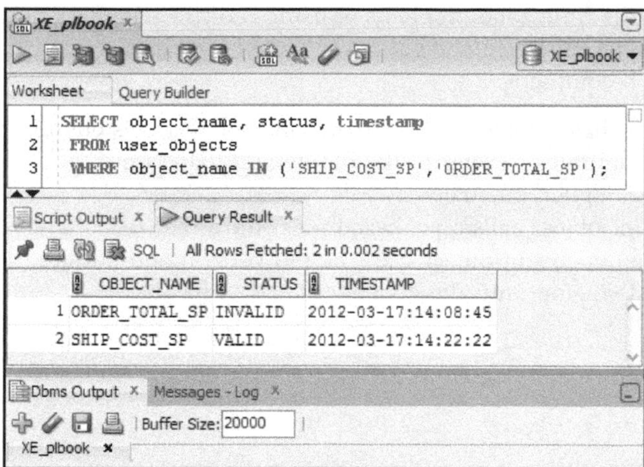

FIGURE 8-29 Displaying timestamp information

NOTE

The timestamp for SHIP_COST_SP is more recent than the timestamp for ORDER_TOTAL_SP. Therefore, ORDER_TOTAL_SP is flagged as INVALID and is recompiled on the second run because a remote database link is involved.

The timestamp model is the default method, but it does have a couple of issues to consider. First, if the databases are in different time zones, the timestamp model doesn't reflect this information and might cause unnecessary recompilation. Second, this method is also used if the dependent procedure is a client-side procedure, and the referenced object is on the server. If the client-side procedure is part of an Oracle Forms application, the source code might not be available in the runtime environment, so it can't be recompiled.

The **signature model** compares the mode, data type, and order of parameters and the RETURN data type (for functions) when a remote object call is used to determine invalidation. When a procedure is compiled, it stores the signature of any referenced objects. When the procedure runs, it compares the signature information stored about the referenced object with the actual parameters in the referenced object. If anything has changed in the parameters, the dependent object is flagged as INVALID and needs to be recompiled. Because the signature model isn't the default method, it must be set in the system by using one of the methods in Table 8-2.

TABLE 8-2 Setting the Signature Mode

Setting or Command	What the Setting Affects
REMOTE_DEPENDENCIES_MODE=SIGNATURE; (Set this parameter in the database initialization file, typically init.ora.)	All user sessions since the database startup
ALTER SYSTEM SET REMOTE_DEPENDENCIES_MODE = SIGNATURE;	All user sessions after the command is issued
ALTER SESSION SET REMOTE_DEPENDENCIES_MODE = SIGNATURE;	The user session that issued the command

The signature model can solve the time zone problems of using the timestamp model; however, in the following situations, parameter modifications aren't viewed as a signature modification, so they don't prompt recompiling:

- First, if an IN parameter has a default value setting and this value is changed, the dependent object continues to refer to the old default value until the dependent object is recompiled manually.
- Second, if the dependent object calls a packaged procedure that has a new overloaded version, the dependent object uses the old version and doesn't see the new overloaded version until the dependent object has been recompiled manually.

In both cases, the dependent object isn't flagged as INVALID, so it doesn't indicate that recompiling is needed.

TIPS TO PREVENT RECOMPILATION ERRORS

All applications need maintenance and modifications periodically, so as a developer, you should strive to write code that's as flexible as possible to reduce maintenance and possible recompilation errors. The Oracle documentation suggests several techniques for coding program units to prevent errors associated with program changes:

- Use the %TYPE and %ROWTYPE attributes in variable declarations. These declarations instruct the system to assign the variable data type based on the underlying table column's data type at runtime. If changes are made to tables, such as column length or data type, program units using these columns in variables or parameters don't have to be edited. Keep in mind that this method doesn't prevent other logic errors that can be raised by data type modifications. For example, if you change a variable data type from NUMBER to VARCHAR2 and the program unit code uses a numeric function, such as ROUND, on this variable, an error is raised.
- Use SELECT * instead of a named column list when querying data from the database. If the table changes, as with a column drop, the query won't fail if it's using this notation. There's some debate among Oracle users about whether the benefit of this technique is greater than the downside. The program unit might be retrieving far more data than is needed, which adds to the processing time.
- Use a column list in INSERT statements so that changes to a table, such as dropping and adding columns, don't necessarily raise an error. If a column list isn't used, the INSERT statement expects data to match the physical order of columns and requires a value for each column, which raises an error for any table column deletions or additions.

GRANTING PROGRAM UNIT PRIVILEGES

As you know from your SQL experience, users must have privileges granted, typically by the DBA, to access any object in the database. For example, if the user scott needs query and modification rights on the BB_BASKET table, the DBA must issue the following GRANT command:

```
GRANT SELECT, INSERT, UPDATE ON bb_basket TO scott;
```

The first items in a GRANT command are the privileges being granted, which are SELECT, INSERT, and UPDATE in this example. The ON clause specifies an object, if applicable, and the TO clause indicates which user or role should have these privileges.

The same form of the GRANT command is used to assign privileges for program units. Table 8-3 lists privileges related to procedures, functions, and packages. The term "program units" in this table equates to all these objects. The keyword PROCEDURE is used when granting privileges to represent all program unit objects.

TABLE 8-3 Program Unit Privileges

System Privilege	Explanation
CREATE PROCEDURE	Allows users to create, modify, and drop program units in their own schemas
CREATE ANY PROCEDURE	Allows users to create program units in any schema; doesn't allow modifying or dropping the program units
ALTER ANY PROCEDURE	Allows users to modify program units in any schema
DROP ANY PROCEDURE	Allows users to drop program units in any schema
EXECUTE ON *program_unit_name*	Allows users to run a specific program unit
EXECUTE ANY PROCEDURE	Allows users to run program units in any schema

Again, there's no CREATE FUNCTION or CREATE PACKAGE privilege because the CREATE PROCEDURE privilege encompasses all program unit types. Also, the EXECUTE privilege can't be granted for package elements; it must be granted for the entire package. All privileges can be canceled with the REVOKE command. The following commands are some examples of granting privileges to the user plbook:

```
GRANT CREATE PROCEDURE TO plbook;
GRANT ALTER ANY PROCEDURE TO plbook;
GRANT EXECUTE ON basc_calc_sp TO plbook;
```

TIP

Remember that privileges can also be granted to roles (including the PUBLIC role) to address a group of users, not just specific users.

The data dictionary has a variety of views containing information on user privileges. Table 8-4 lists details of important data dictionary views for privileges.

TABLE 8-4 Data Dictionary Views for Privileges

View Name	Description	Column Information
SESSION_PRIVS	Shows all privileges of the current schema, direct and indirect	PRIVILEGE (name of the privilege granted)
SESSION_ROLES	Shows all roles granted to the current schema	ROLE (name of the role granted)
USER_SYS_PRIVS	Shows only direct privileges of the current schema	USERNAME (recipient of the privilege), PRIVILEGE (name of the privilege granted), and ADMIN_OPTION (Yes or No to indicate whether privileges were granted with WITH ADMIN OPTION)
USER_ROLE_PRIVS	Shows only direct roles granted to the current schema	USERNAME (recipient of the privilege), GRANTED_ROLE (name of the role granted), ADMIN_OPTION (Yes or No to indicate whether privileges were granted with WITH ADMIN OPTION), DEFAULT_ROLE (Yes if it's the user's default role; otherwise, No), OS_GRANTED (Yes if the OS manages the roles; otherwise, No)

Figure 8-30 shows a query of the SESSION_PRIVS view to list the current user's privileges. Notice this user doesn't have some of the privileges you do to perform the tasks in this book, such as CREATE VIEW and CREATE DATABASE LINK.

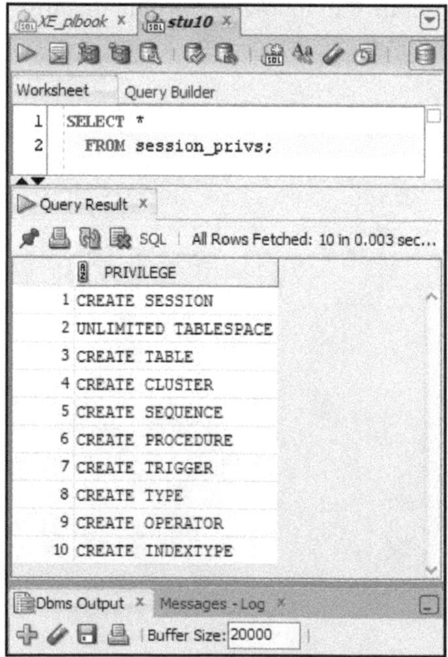

FIGURE 8-30 Querying the SESSION_PRIVS view

PL/SQL COMPILATION

The PL/SQL compiler offers several options (parameters) that affect how program units are compiled. These parameters can help you discover coding problems, improve runtime performance, and develop more flexible code. This section explores PL/SQL compiler parameters, compile-time warnings, and conditional compilation.

Compiler Parameters

Developers should be familiar with compiler parameter settings on their systems because these settings affect code optimization techniques and determine whether features such as warning messages and conditional compilation are available. Table 8-5 lists the compiler parameters available in Oracle 11*g*.

TABLE 8-5 PL/SQL Compiler Parameters

Parameter	Description
PLSQL_OPTIMIZE_LEVEL	The optimizer is on by default and attempts to apply optimization techniques to code behind the scenes. Three levels are available (0, 1, 2), with 2 being the default and most aggressive optimizing level.
PLSQL_WARNINGS	Enables the PL/SQL compiler to report warning messages. Warnings can help developers avoid coding problems and improve performance.
PLSQL_CCFLAGS	Allows using object-level flags in conditional compilation, which makes it possible to produce different results based on a flag value at compile time.
PLSQL_CODE_TYPE	Determines whether the PL/SQL unit is compiled in the INTERPRETED or NATIVE mode. The PLSQL_OPTIMIZE_LEVEL parameter must be set to 2 for NATIVE mode compilation to occur.
PLSCOPE_SETTINGS	Controls the collection of source code identifier data, which the PL/Scope tool uses to track identifier use through data dictionary views.
NLS_LENGTH_SEMANTICS	Determines whether byte or character semantics are applied to CHAR and VARCHAR2 columns.

NOTE

Additional parameters exist in Oracle 11*g*, but they have been deprecated as of version 11.1.

The next sections introduce compile-time warnings and conditional compilation; however, as a PL/SQL developer, you need to be aware of all these settings when you compile program units. You can verify the settings for a program unit by querying the USER_PLSQL_OBJECT_SETTINGS data dictionary view. Run the query in Figure 8-31 to verify the compiler parameter settings for the SHIP_COST_SP procedure. You can also check the value of most of these parameters for your current session with the SHOW PARAMETERS PLSQL command.

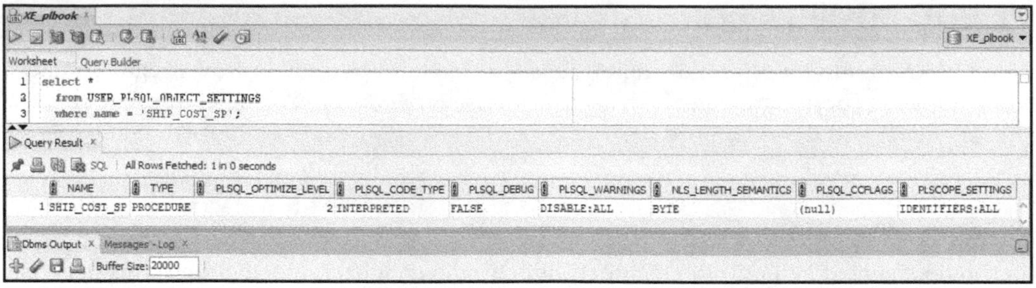

```
select *
  from USER_PLSQL_OBJECT_SETTINGS
  where name = 'SHIP_COST_SP';
```

	NAME	TYPE	PLSQL_OPTIMIZE_LEVEL	PLSQL_CODE_TYPE	PLSQL_DEBUG	PLSQL_WARNINGS	NLS_LENGTH_SEMANTICS	PLSQL_CCFLAGS	PLSCOPE_SETTINGS
1	SHIP_COST_SP	PROCEDURE	2	INTERPRETED	FALSE	DISABLE:ALL	BYTE	(null)	IDENTIFIERS:ALL

FIGURE 8-31 Verifying PL/SQL compiler parameters for a specific object

Parameter settings can be changed in a session by using an `ALTER SESSION` command. The following example enables PL/SQL warnings:

```
ALTER SESSION SET PLSQL_WARNINGS= 'ENABLE:ALL';
```

Settings for compiler parameters are stored with each program unit's metadata and can be reused when recompiling is necessary. When you issue an `ALTER COMPILE` statement on a program unit, use the `REUSE SETTINGS` clause to preserve existing compiler parameter settings. Otherwise, the parameter setting for the current session is applied to the program unit. The following example shows including the `REUSE` clause when recompiling:

```
ALTER PROCEDURE ship_cost_sp COMPILE
  REUSE SETTINGS;
```

Also, be aware that if you use the `CREATE OR REPLACE` statement to rebuild a program unit, the compiler parameter settings for the current session are applied.

PL/SQL Compiler Warnings

Even if code compiles successfully, it might still have problems, such as unreachable code (code that's never performed based on the program logic) and performance degradation caused by implicit variable type conversion. Compiler warnings can help you discover these types of problems at compile time. There are three classifications of warnings, described in the following list, and each can be enabled or disabled:

- *Informational*—Identifies potential coding problems, such as unreachable code
- *Performance*—Identifies coding that could degrade performance, such as data type mismatches
- *Severe*—Identifies problems that could lead to unexpected behavior, such as using keywords that could result in name resolution issues

Take a look at an example of each classification of warnings to become familiar with how they work. To make sure warnings are enabled, issue the `ALTER SESSION` command in Figure 8-32.

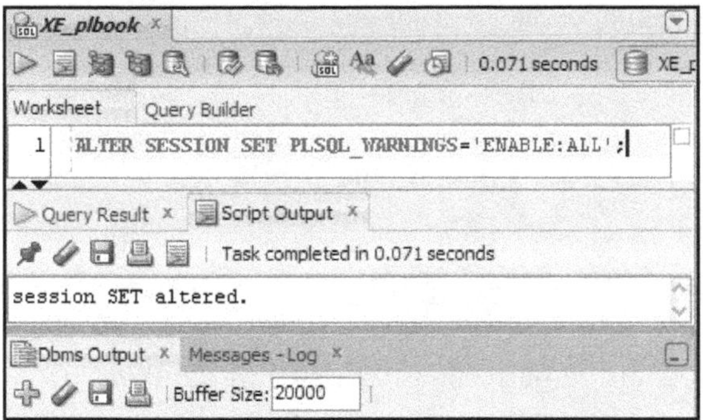

FIGURE 8-32 Enabling all PL/SQL compiler warnings

NOTE

A warning classification can be enabled or disabled by using a setting such as `ENABLE:SEVERE`, which has a comma-separated list to address multiple classifications, if needed.

As you review these warning messages, note that each message has an associated warning message number in the format PLW-#####. Warning messages use the following number ranges:

- *Severe*—5000–5999
- *Informational*—6000–6249
- *Performance*—7000–7249

Review the code in the procedure shown in Figure 8-33. The `IF` statement contains a logic problem: The first `IF` clause checks for a value less than 500, and the next `IF` clause checks for a value less than 300. The processing never reaches the second `IF` clause because a value less than 300 already finds a true condition in the first `IF` clause.

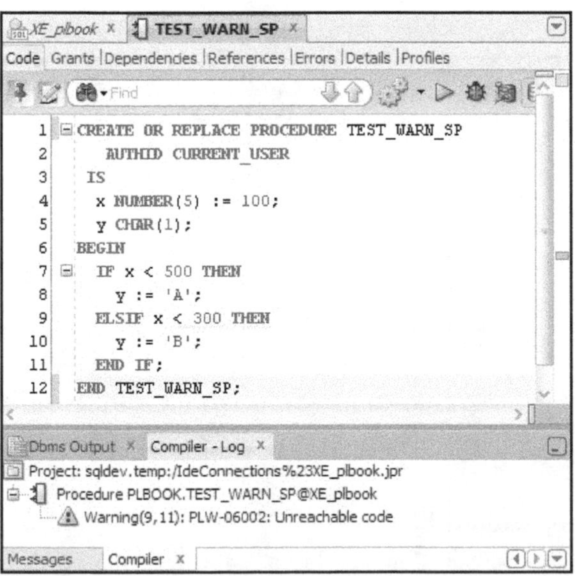

FIGURE 8-33 Informational warning for unreachable code

When you compile the procedure, a warning about unreachable code is given for line 9. Keep in mind that the procedure does compile and can be used; it has the status VALID. These warnings are given to help developers by highlighting potential problems.

To see what a performance warning looks like, try testing a procedure that initiates an implicit data type conversion by Oracle. First, create a table to use for the test with the following statement.

```
CREATE TABLE bb_warn
  (col1 VARCHAR2(5));
```

Next, modify the TEST_WARN_SP procedure to perform an INSERT in the table, as shown in Figure 8-34. Notice that this INSERT uses a numeric value; however, the column has a character data type.

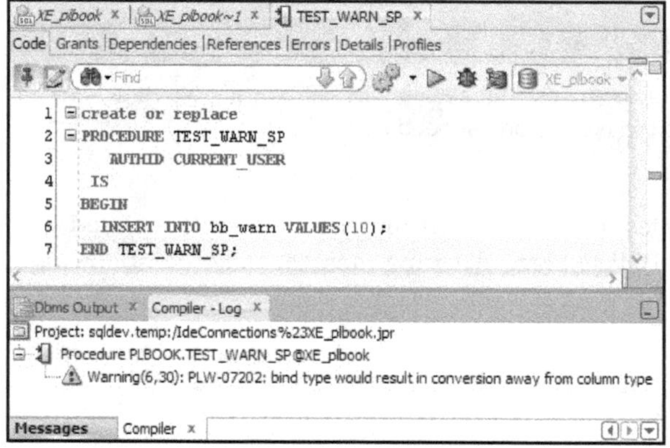

FIGURE 8-34 Performance warning for a data type conversion

To test severe warnings, modify the TEST_WARN_SP procedure to include a function named ROUND. Keep in mind that an Oracle-supplied function named ROUND is already available, so creating a function with the same name generates the warning shown in Figure 8-35.

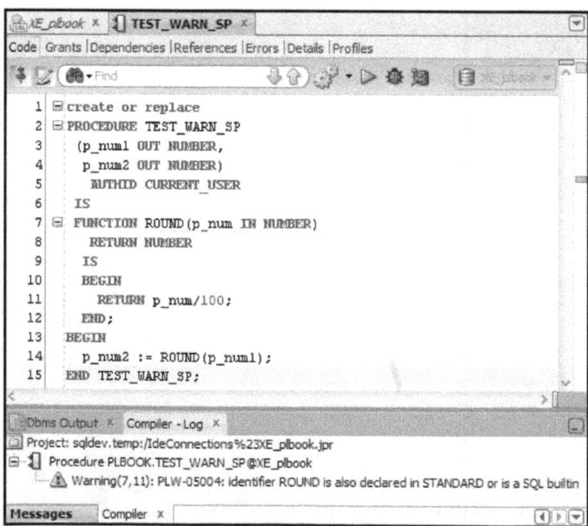

FIGURE 8-35 Severe warning for reusing an existing object name

Conditional Compilation

Conditional compilation enables developers to tailor PL/SQL program unit code based on compiler directives (instructions). Tailoring code can include specifying unique code in a program unit depending on conditions at compile time or raising an error at compilation based on a condition. A benefit of conditional compilation is being able to create code that can be used in a variety of Oracle versions but still take advantage of version-specific features. For example, you have a procedure to be deployed in several Oracle versions, and you want to make sure the Oracle 11*g* result-caching feature is used when the procedure is deployed in an Oracle 11*g* installation. To do this, you can use a selection directive to create an `IF THEN` structure for compilation. Figure 8-36 shows an example of including the `RESULT_CACHE` hint based on the database version used to compile the procedure. The `IF` selection directive uses the `$` prefix to indicate a compiler directive.

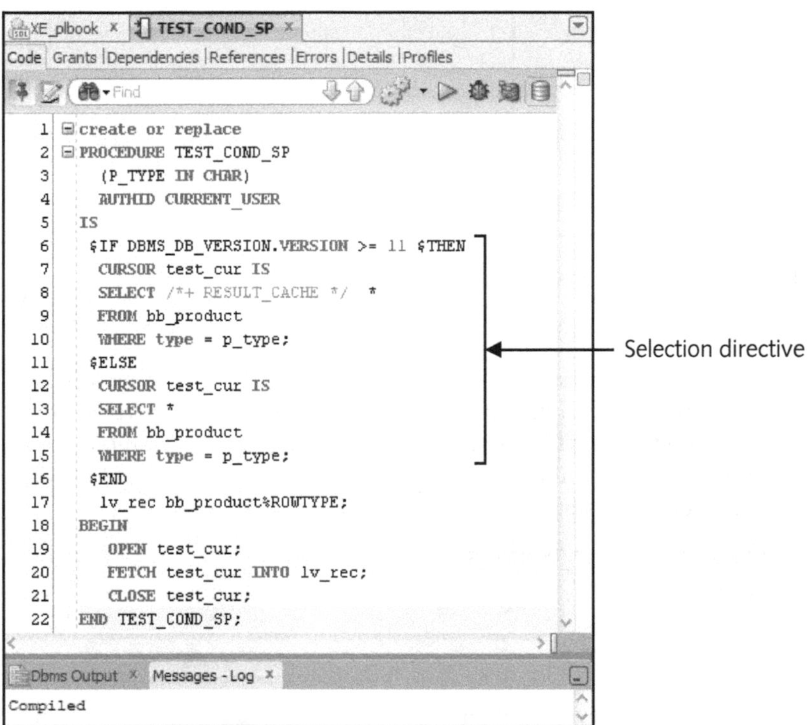

FIGURE 8-36 Conditional compilation with a selection directive

The `DBMS_PREPROCESSOR` package can be used to confirm the resulting code for compilation after evaluating any compilation conditions. The following command lists the resulting source code for the `TEST_COND_SP` procedure:

```
BEGIN
  DBMS_PREPROCESSOR.PRINT_POST_PROCESSED_SOURCE('PROCEDURE','PLBOOK',
    'TEST_COND_SP');
END;
```

The results are shown in Figure 8-37, which was run in Oracle 11.2. The output verifies that only the code conditionally marked for use with Oracle 11 or later is maintained for the compiled program unit.

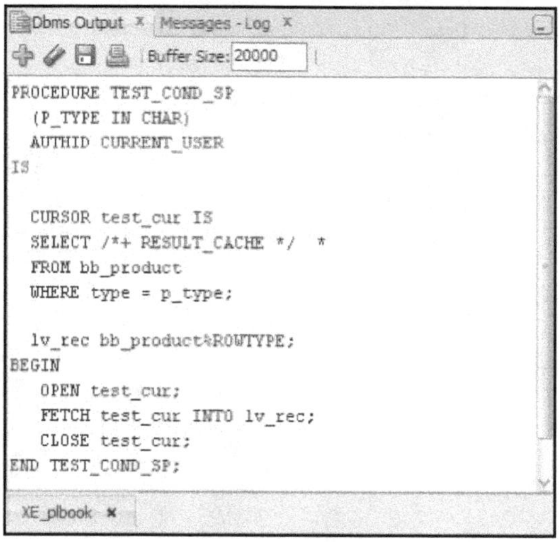

```
Dbms Output × | Messages - Log ×
Buffer Size: 20000
PROCEDURE TEST_COND_SP
  (P_TYPE IN CHAR)
  AUTHID CURRENT_USER
IS

  CURSOR test_cur IS
  SELECT /*+ RESULT_CACHE */  *
  FROM bb_product
  WHERE type = p_type;

  lv_rec bb_product%ROWTYPE;
BEGIN
   OPEN test_cur;
   FETCH test_cur INTO lv_rec;
   CLOSE test_cur;
END TEST_COND_SP;
XE_plbook ×
```

FIGURE 8-37 Verifying conditional compilation results

You can set an object-level compilation flag with the `PLSQL_CCFLAGS` compilation parameter. This parameter can be helpful in distinguishing code in different environments, such as development versus production. The code for the following procedure references a `TESTIT` compiler flag by using the `$$` prefix. This flag's value at compile time (`TRUE` or `FALSE`) determines the procedure's result.

```
CREATE OR REPLACE PROCEDURE TEST_COND2_SP
  AUTHID CURRENT_USER
  IS
BEGIN
  $IF $$TESTIT $THEN
    DBMS_OUTPUT.PUT_LINE('TESTIT is TRUE');
  $ELSE
    DBMS_OUTPUT.PUT_LINE('TESTIT is FALSE');
  $END
END TEST_COND2_SP;
```

To clarify how these flag values work, Figure 8-38 shows a series of statements to verify the effect of using the PLSQL_CCFLAGS parameter and changing the flag value. The first run of the procedure shows that the selection directive's ELSE clause is processed because the TESTIT flag hasn't been set or used for the program unit compilation yet. The ALTER SESSION command creates the flag and sets the value to TRUE. Then the procedure is compiled and run again. The last run shows that the TESTIT flag has the value TRUE, based on the procedure output.

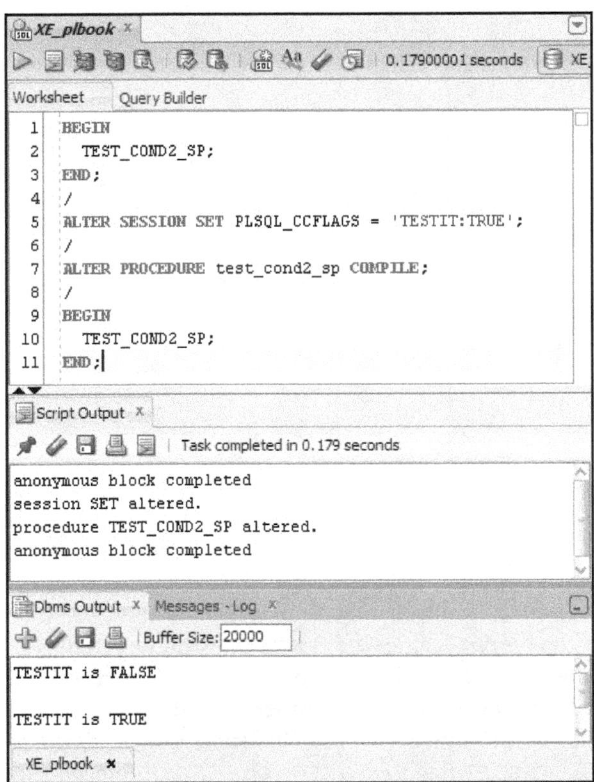

FIGURE 8-38 Testing a compilation flag

The previous examples have shown that the current session's compilation parameters are applied to any program units compiled in the session. However, this behavior can be overridden at compile time with the REUSE SETTINGS option. Figure 8-39 returns to the TEST_COND2_SP procedure to show how it works. Even though the TESTIT flag is set to FALSE in the session, the REUSE SETTINGS option in the COMPILE command forces the procedure to retain the compilation parameter settings from the earlier compile action. Therefore, for this object, the compilation flag still has the value TRUE.

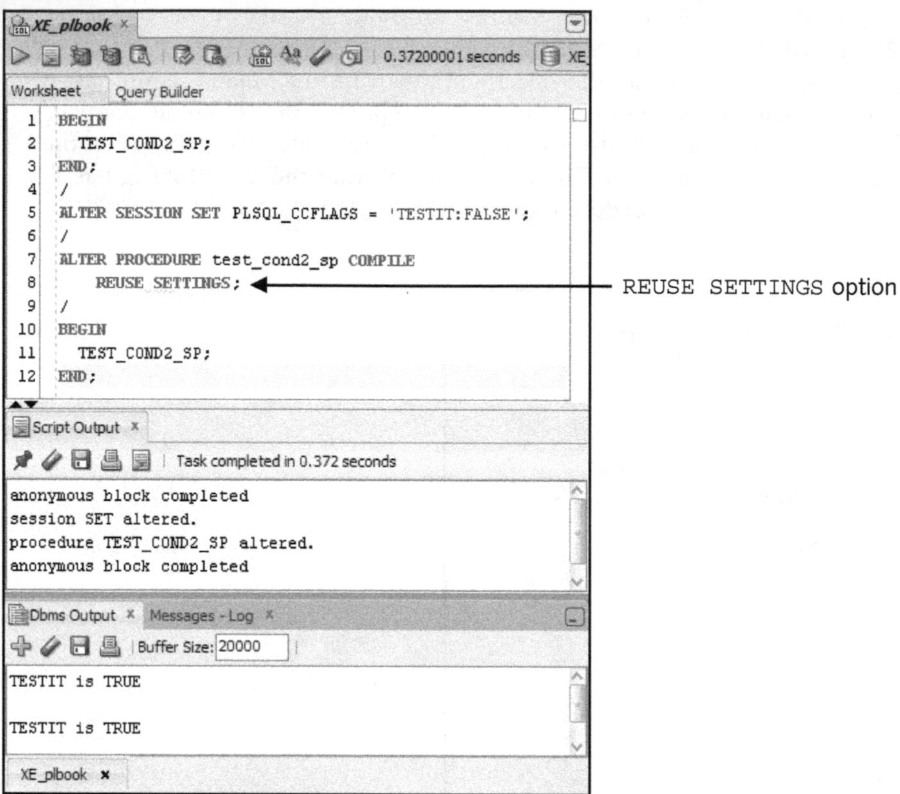

FIGURE 8-39 Compiling with the REUSE SETTINGS option

You might not want a program unit to compile successfully based on some condition. In this situation, an error directive can be used in conditional compilation to force unsuccessful compilation and even associate a custom error number with it, if needed. The following procedure code includes an $ERROR directive that instructs Oracle to raise an error at compilation if the value of the TESTIT flag isn't TRUE. The $$ERR references the error number in the PLSQL_CCFLAGS parameter settings.

```
CREATE OR REPLACE PROCEDURE TEST_COND3_SP
  AUTHID CURRENT_USER
  IS
BEGIN
  $IF $$TESTIT $THEN
    DBMS_OUTPUT.PUT_LINE('TESTIT is TRUE');
  $ELSE
    $ERROR 'Not correct installation:' || $$ERR $END
  $END
END TEST_COND3_SP;
```

To test the error directive, run the following ALTER SESSION command to set the PLSQL_CCFLAGS parameter values:

```
ALTER SESSION SET PLSQL_CCFLAGS = 'TESTIT:FALSE,ERR:84566';
```

Now if a compile action is attempted on the procedure, a compilation error is raised (see Figure 8-40). The error message in the compile log includes the error number set in the `PLSQL_CCFLAGS` parameter.

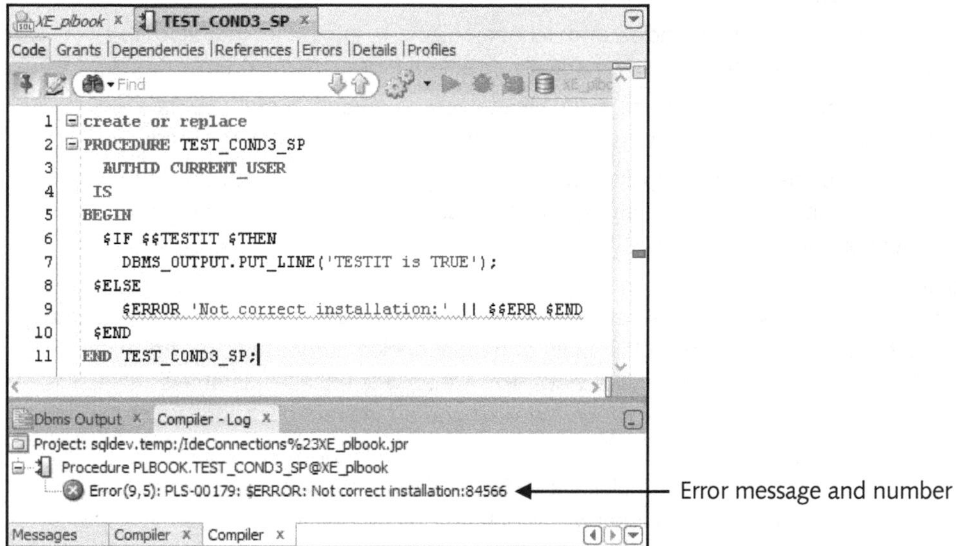

FIGURE 8-40 Compilation error raised by an error directive

Chapter Summary

- When a program unit refers to other database objects, it's considered dependent on that object. If the referenced object is modified, the dependent object's status changes to INVALID, indicating it must be recompiled.
- With local database dependencies or database objects in the same database, the dependent object can be compiled manually or automatically the next time it runs.
- You can recompile a program unit manually in two ways: using a CREATE OR REPLACE statement to rebuild the program unit or using the ALTER COMPILE command.
- Certain changes call for recompiling dependent program units manually instead of raising an error at runtime, such as modifying a table structure when you have program units that are dependent on that table.
- A direct dependency occurs when one database object references other objects specifically. An indirect dependency involves references to database objects that reference other database objects, making the chain of dependencies harder to track. For example, a procedure can reference a database view, which then references a database table. The procedure has a direct dependency on the view and an indirect dependency on the table through this view.
- The USER_DEPENDENCIES data dictionary view is helpful for giving you information on direct object dependencies. To identify indirect dependencies, however, you use the dependency tree utility, which displays all dependencies in numeric order or an indented format. To use this utility, you must run the utldtree.sql file to create necessary objects, such as the DEPTREE_FILL procedure.
- If you modify code in a package body, the status of dependent objects isn't changed to INVALID, as with stand-alone program units. Only modifications to the package specification result in changing dependent objects' status to INVALID. For this reason, you don't have to do as much recompiling as you would if all the program units were stand-alone.
- Remote dependencies are checked at runtime instead of instantly, as with local database objects. This runtime check causes a failure during a dependent object's first run if the referenced object has been altered, unless the dependent object is recompiled manually.
- You can check remote dependencies with two models. The timestamp model, the default method, compares objects' last modification date and time to determine whether invalidation has occurred. The signature model compares the mode, data type, and order of parameters and the RETURN data type (for functions) when a remote object call is used to determine invalidation.
- To minimize recompilation errors, Oracle recommends using the %TYPE and %ROWTYPE attributes in variable declarations, using SELECT * instead of a named column list when querying data from the database, and using a column list in INSERT statements.
- To run a program unit, users must be granted the EXECUTE privilege. This privilege can't be granted for package elements; it must be granted for the entire package.
- Several compiler parameters are available in PL/SQL that affect how program units are compiled. For example, enabling the PLSQL_WARNINGS parameter displays warning messages that help you discover coding problems at compile time.
- Conditional compilation enables developers to tailor PL/SQL program unit code based on compiler directives (instructions). A benefit of this feature is being able to create code that can be used in a variety of Oracle versions but still take advantage of version-specific features.

Review Questions

1. Which data dictionary view can be used to check a program unit's status?
   a. USER_DEPENDENCIES
   b. USER_OBJECTS
   c. USER_ERRORS
   d. USER_STATUS
2. Procedure A includes a call to function A. If the code in function A is modified, the status of procedure A is ________________.
   a. ON
   b. OFF
   c. INVALID
   d. VALID
3. A program unit with an INVALID status can be recompiled by doing which of the following? (Choose all that apply.)
   a. using the ALTER COMPILE command
   b. using the RECOMPILE command
   c. running it
   d. all of the above
4. A query on the USER_DEPENDENCIES view for an object displays all the ________________ associated dependencies.
   a. formal
   b. direct
   c. indirect
   d. informal
5. The dependency tree utility enables you to view which of the following dependencies? (Choose all that apply.)
   a. indirect
   b. direct
   c. valid
   d. invalid
6. To review the dependencies of an object with the dependency tree utility, the ________________ procedure must be run first.
   a. LOAD_DEPTREE
   b. FILL_DEPTREE
   c. DEPTREE_LOAD
   d. DEPTREE_FILL

7. The IDEPTREE view created by the dependency tree utility displays dependencies in which of the following formats?
   a. numbered level
   b. indented
   c. matrix
   d. tabular
8. In Figure 8-41, the BASK_CALC_SP procedure has which of the following dependencies on the BB_BASKETITEM table?

```
NESTED_LEVEL NAME                           TYPE                    SEQ#
------------ ------------------------------ ------------------ ----------
           0 BB_BASKETITEM                  TABLE                       0
           1 SUB_CALC_SF                    FUNCTION                    9
           2 BASK_CALC_SP                   PROCEDURE                  10
           1 BB_BASKETITEM_VU               VIEW                       11
           2 ORDER_TOTAL_SP                 PROCEDURE                  12
           1 ORDER_TOTAL_SP2                PROCEDURE                  13
           1 SHIP_CALC3_SF                  FUNCTION                   14
           2 BASK_CALC_SP                   PROCEDURE                  15
```

FIGURE 8-41 The DEPTREE view listing

   a. direct
   b. indirect
   c. no dependency
   d. can't be determined
9. In Figure 8-42, the BB_BASKETITEM_VU view has which of the following dependencies on the BB_BASKETITEM table?

```
----------------------------------------------
TABLE SCOTT.BB_BASKETITEM
   FUNCTION SCOTT.SUB_CALC_SF
      PROCEDURE SCOTT.BASK_CALC_SP
   VIEW SCOTT.BB_BASKETITEM_VU
      PROCEDURE SCOTT.ORDER_TOTAL_SP
   PROCEDURE SCOTT.ORDER_TOTAL_SP2
   FUNCTION SCOTT.SHIP_CALC3_SF
      PROCEDURE SCOTT.BASK_CALC_SP

8 rows selected.

SQL>
```

FIGURE 8-42 Determining dependency type

   a. direct
   b. indirect
   c. no dependency
   d. can't be determined
10. A database link is used to create ________________ database connections.
   a. direct
   b. indirect
   c. remote
   d. A database link doesn't exist.

11. If you have object dependencies on remote databases with one server in Virginia and the other in California, which invalidation model should *not* be used?
    a. tracking
    b. timestamp
    c. signature
    d. check
12. Currently, procedure A has a `VALID` status. Procedure A calls function B, which is in a package. A programmer just added an `IF` statement to the code in function B. Now the status value of procedure A is which of the following?
    a. `INVALID`
    b. `VALID`
    c. `CHECK`
    d. can't be determined
13. Procedure A calls function C. If a parameter is added to function C, which of the following is true about procedure A?
    a. It can recompile successfully.
    b. It doesn't recompile successfully.
    c. It doesn't need to be recompiled.
    d. It isn't affected.
14. The signature model of checking remote dependencies compares which of the following?
    a. time of last compile
    b. object status
    c. parameter names
    d. type and order of parameters
15. Oracle recommends which of the following to reduce program unit recompilation errors after database modifications? (Choose all that apply.)
    a. using `%TYPE` variable declarations
    b. using numeric variables if possible
    c. using a column list in `INSERT` statements
    d. Recompilation errors can't be avoided.
16. Explain how dependencies in packaged program units are handled differently from those in stand-alone program units.
17. Review the dependency listing in Figure 8-42 again. List all objects that are indirectly dependent on the BB_BASKETITEM table.
18. Why should developers be concerned with dependencies?
19. Explain the different handling of local and remote dependencies.
20. If you're about to modify an object, what's the best way to view its direct and indirect dependencies? What steps should you take to make this feature available?

Advanced Review Questions

1. You have a stored procedure named CALC_COST, which was created in the SCOTT schema. Which of the following statements issued in the SCOTT schema allow the user TESTER to run the procedure?
   a. GRANT PROCEDURE calc_cost TO TESTER;
   b. GRANT EXECUTE ON calc_cost TO TESTER;
   c. GRANT EXECUTE calc_cost TO TESTER;
   d. none of the above
2. Which of the following data dictionary views contains information on the status of program units?
   a. USER_TABLES
   b. USER_SOURCE
   c. USER_STATUS
   d. USER_OBJECTS
3. Given the following CREATE PROCEDURE and ALTER TABLE statements, what happens if the next statement you issue calls the LOAD_HOURS procedure?

```
CREATE PROCEDURE load_hours
  (p_id IN NUMBER,
   p_hours IN NUMBER)
  IS
BEGIN
  INSERT INTO work_track (e_id, hours)
    VALUES (p_id, p_hours);
  END;
ALTER TABLE work_track ADD job_id NUMBER(5);
```

   a. The execution raises an error because the ALTER TABLE statement made the procedure status INVALID.
   b. The system attempts to recompile the procedure automatically.
   c. The procedure runs with no compilation action.
   d. The procedure fails because of the table modification.
4. Which data dictionary view contains information on all your privileges, direct and indirect?
   a. SESSION_PRIVS
   b. USER_SYS_PRIVS
   c. SESSION_ROLES
   d. USER_ROLE_PRIVS
5. You create a package specification that has the status VALID, and you issue a CREATE OR REPLACE statement to modify the package body. This statement produces errors, and the package body has the status INVALID. Now what's the status of the package specification?
   a. INVALID
   b. VALID
   c. NULL
   d. can't be determined

Hands-On Assignments Part I

Assignment 8-1: Reviewing Dependency Information in the Data Dictionary

Two data dictionary views store information on dependencies: USER_OBJECTS and USER_DEPENDENCIES. Take a closer look at these views to examine the information in them:

1. In SQL Developer, issue a DESCRIBE command on the USER_OBJECTS view and review the available columns. Which columns are particularly relevant to dependencies? The STATUS column indicates whether the object is VALID or INVALID. The TIMESTAMP column is used in remote connections to determine invalidation.
2. Query the USER_OBJECTS view, selecting the OBJECT_NAME, STATUS, and TIMESTAMP columns for all procedures. Recall that you can use a WHERE clause to look for object types of PROCEDURE to list only procedure information.
3. Now issue a DESCRIBE command on the USER_DEPENDENCIES view to review the available columns. If you query this table for the name of a specific object, a list of all the objects it references is displayed. However, if you query for a specific referenced name, you see a list of objects that are dependent on this particular object.
4. Say you intend to make a modification to the BB_BASKET table and need to identify all dependent program units to finish recompiling. Run the following query to list all objects that are dependent on the BB_BASKET table:

```
SELECT name, type
  FROM user_dependencies
  WHERE referenced_name = 'BB_BASKET';
```


Assignment 8-2: Testing Dependencies on Stand-Alone Program Units

In this assignment, you verify the effect of object modifications on the status of dependent objects. You work with a procedure and a function.

1. In a text editor, open the **assignment08-02.txt** file in the Chapter08 folder. This file contains statements to create the STATUS_CHECK_SP procedure and the STATUS_DESC_SF function. Review the code, and notice that the procedure includes a call to the function. Use the code in this file to create the two program units in SQL Developer.
2. Enter and run the following query to verify that the status of both objects is VALID:

```
SELECT object_name, status
  FROM user_objects
  WHERE object_name IN
  ('STATUS_CHECK_SP','STATUS_DESC_SF');
```

3. The STATUS_DESC_SF function adds a description of the numeric value for the IDSTAGE column. The company needs to add another order status stage for situations in which credit card approval fails. In SQL Developer, modify the function by adding the following ELSIF clause, and compile it. (Don't compile or run the function again.)

```
ELSIF p_stage = 6 THEN
  lv_stage_txt := 'Credit Card Not Approved';
```

4. Does the modification in Step 3 affect the STATUS_CHECK_SP procedure's status? Verify by repeating the query in Step 2. The procedure is dependent on the function, so it's now INVALID and must be recompiled.

5. Call the procedure for basket 13, as shown in the following code:

```
DECLARE
   lv_stage_num NUMBER(2);
   lv_desc_txt VARCHAR2(30);
BEGIN
   status_check_sp(13,lv_stage_num,lv_desc_txt);
END;
```

6. Repeat the query in Step 2 to verify the STATUS_CHECK_SP procedure's status. The procedure now shows the status VALID as a result of automatic recompiling when the procedure was called.

Assignment 8-3: Testing Dependencies on Packaged Program Units

In this assignment, you verify the effect of object modifications on the status of dependent objects. You work with a procedure and a packaged function.

1. In a text editor, open the **assignment08-03.txt** file in the Chapter08 folder. This file contains statements to create the STATUS_CHECK_SP procedure and the LOOKUP_PKG package. Review the code, and note that the procedure includes a call to the packaged function STATUS_DESC_PF. Use the code in this file to create the procedure and package in SQL Developer.
2. Use the following query to verify the procedure's status:

```
SELECT status
  FROM user_objects
  WHERE object_name = 'STATUS_CHECK_SP';
```

3. The function adds a description of the numeric value for the IDSTAGE column. The company needs to add another order status stage for situations in which credit card approval fails. In SQL Developer, edit the function by adding the following ELSIF clause to the packaged function:

```
ELSIF p_stage = 6 THEN
  lv_stage_txt := 'Credit Card Not Approved';
```

4. Does the modification in Step 3 affect the STATUS_CHECK_SP procedure's status? Verify that it's still VALID by repeating the query in Step 2. The procedure is dependent on the function; however, if the referenced program unit is in a package, only changes to the package specification result in the dependent object's status changing to INVALID.

Assignment 8-4: Testing Remote Object Dependencies

As you learned, program unit calls that use a database link to another database are called remote dependencies and act differently with program unit invalidation, as you see in the following steps:

1. Create a database link named **dblink2**. If you have a second Oracle database running, use a valid connection string for that database. Otherwise, use a connection string for the database you're connected to.
2. In a text editor, open the **assignment08-04.txt** file in the Chapter08 folder. This file contains statements to create the STATUS_CHECK_SP procedure and the STATUS_DESC_SF function. The procedure uses a database link when calling the function, which is treated as a remote database connection. (*Note*: If your database link connects to

another database, be sure to create the function on that database.) Use the code in this file to create the two program units in SQL Developer.

3. Check the procedure's status with a query of a data dictionary view.
4. The function adds a description of the numeric value for the IDSTAGE column. The company needs to add another order status stage for situations in which credit card approval fails. Return to the text file and add the following `ELSIF` clause to the packaged function:

```
ELSIF p_stage = 6 THEN
  lv_stage_txt := 'Credit Card Not Approved';
```

5. Copy the package code and paste it in SQL Developer to rebuild with the modifications. Does the modification in Step 4 affect the `STATUS_CHECK_SP` procedure's status? Verify that it's still `VALID`. The procedure is dependent on the function; however, because it's a remote dependency, the status isn't checked at the time the referenced object is modified.
6. Try calling the procedure, and verify its status again.
7. Call the procedure a second time. What happens?

Assignment 8-5: Identifying Dependencies

At this point, you have created a variety of database objects in your schema. Use an Oracle tool to identify all the direct and indirect dependencies on the BB_BASKET table, and produce dependency lists in two different formats. Identify each object as a direct or an indirect dependency, and describe the path of dependency for each indirectly dependent object.

Assignment 8-6: Reviewing the `utldtree.sql` Script

In Windows, search for the `utldtree.sql` file. It should be in the database directory under the `rdbms\admin` subdirectory. Open the file in a text editor and review the script. List all the objects that are created (name and type), and write a brief description of how each object is used for tracking dependencies.

Assignment 8-7: Avoiding Recompilation Errors

All applications undergo modifications, and as a developer, you should strive to produce code that helps minimize maintenance. Describe two coding techniques that help prevent recompilation errors after referenced objects have been modified, and explain briefly how these techniques help prevent recompilation errors.

Assignment 8-8: Defining Types of Dependencies

In this chapter, you learned about direct, indirect, and remote dependencies. Define these dependency types, and explain how they differ in program unit invalidation and recompilation.

Hands-On Assignments Part II

Assignment 8-9: Using Compilation Parameters

Open and compile the **`DDCKBAL_SP`** procedure. Run a command to display all compiler parameter settings for the procedure; the results should reflect the settings for your current Oracle session. Next, run a command to make sure only informational PL/SQL compiler warnings are enabled in the session. Recompile the procedure again, and display all compiler parameter settings after your change to the warnings parameter.

Assignment 8-10: Using Conditional Compilation

Create a procedure named **DD_COMP1_SP** that compiles to contain a single DBMS_OUTPUT statement based on a compilation flag value. If the compilation flag value is TRUE, this value should be displayed. If the compilation flag value is FALSE, this value should be displayed. Name the compilation flag **ASSIGN**. Create and run the procedure for both compiler flag values. In addition, run a command that displays the compile source code for the procedure when the compiler flag value is TRUE.

Case Projects

Case 8-1: Performing Brewbean's Application Maintenance

To prevent users from getting unexpected application errors, the Brewbean's head programmer wants you to automate the process of recompiling any program units that have an INVALID status. This procedure will be run nightly to recompile any program units that didn't get recompiled after modifications were made. This procedure could reference the USER_OBJECTS view to determine which program units have an INVALID status.

Case 8-2: Working with the More Movies Rental Application

In previous chapters, you have created procedures, functions, and packages to support the rental process. As application modifications are made in the future, you need to be able to identify all object dependencies to test your changes. Use the data dictionary view and/or the dependency tree utility to display a list of dependencies for all the More Movies database objects in the format shown in the following chart. The dependency type should be listed as direct or indirect.

Object Name	Dependent Object	Dependency Type

CHAPTER 9

DATABASE TRIGGERS

LEARNING OBJECTIVES

After completing this chapter, you should be able to understand:

- Database triggers and syntax
- How to create and test a DML trigger
- How to create and test an INSTEAD OF trigger
- Applying other triggers
- Identifying when triggers should be used
- Using compound triggers
- Setting the firing order of triggers
- Using the ALTER TRIGGER statement
- Deleting a trigger
- Using data dictionary information relevant to triggers

INTRODUCTION

A database trigger is a block of PL/SQL code that runs automatically when a particular database event occurs. It's quite different from the procedures and functions you have built in previous chapters. Procedures and functions are called specifically by name to run. A database trigger is fired by an event, such as a DML statement: INSERT, UPDATE, and DELETE. It doesn't matter to a DML trigger where the DML action was generated from, whether it's from an application or an SQL command entered in SQL Developer. Any time the DML action is executed, the trigger fires automatically.

This chapter explores the creation and potential uses of database triggers. First, you learn the structure of database triggers, concentrating on the often used DML event triggers. After understanding the fundamentals of triggers, you explore triggers based on system events and DDL statements as well as compound triggers. In addition, you learn how to use triggers, make use of relevant data dictionary views, and modify existing triggers.

THE CURRENT CHALLENGE IN THE BREWBEAN'S APPLICATION

The Brewbean's coffee-ordering application is coming along; you have already addressed order-processing issues, such as shipping cost calculations. However, the owner described the product inventory process to the application development group today, and you have been given the task of developing PL/SQL blocks to handle updating the product inventory when a sale is completed.

The in-stock level of products needs to be updated in real time so that customers can be informed at the time of ordering whether an item is out of stock. After shoppers have selected all their items and viewed the basket listing, shown in Figure 9-1, they click the Check Out link to see the order confirmation page. This page asks shoppers to enter credit card, name, address, and contact information; part of this information is shown in Figure 9-2. After the Submit button is clicked, the order is confirmed, and the inventory data in the BB_PRODUCT table needs to be updated.

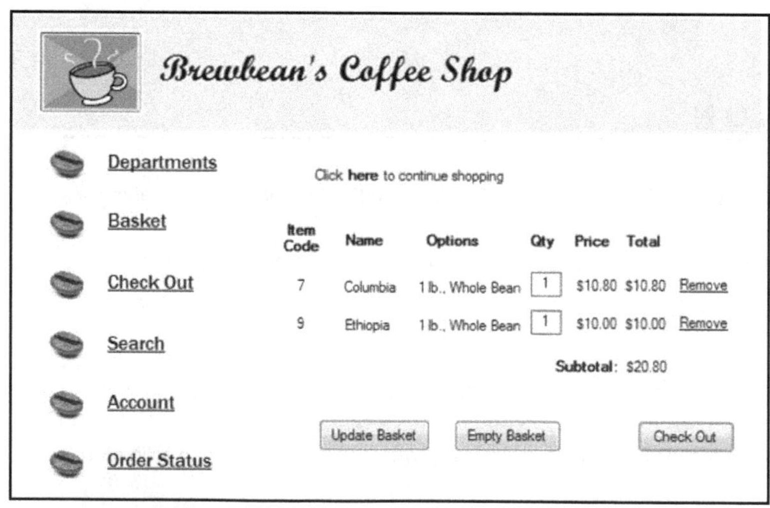

FIGURE 9-1 Brewbean's basket

State: Virginia
Zip Code: 23322
Email: jshop@cen.com

Enter your credit card information:
Enter name on card: Joe Shopper
Card number: 999999999999
Card type: Visa Expire: January 2015
Submit

FIGURE 9-2 Brewbean's order confirmation page

The BB_PRODUCT table has three columns involving inventory: STOCK holds the current number of items available, ORDERED holds the current number on request or to be purchased to replenish stock, and REORDER holds the number at which the stock should be replenished. The BB_PRODUCT_REQUEST table holds information on each stock replenishment request.

Brewbean's uses the term "request" instead of "order" because it roasts and packages all its own coffee products. Only the equipment items must be purchased from wholesalers. In addition, coffee stock and replenishment amounts are in terms of whole pounds. Therefore, if a customer purchases a half-pound of coffee, indicated by the OPTION1 column in the BB_BASKETITEM table, the stock level must be reduced by only .5.

Brewbean's has a similar application process in the in-store ordering system for walk-in customers. Therefore, regardless of whether the order is processed by the in-store application or the Web site application, the product inventory needs to be updated at the time of sale. For this setup, a database trigger is a suitable mechanism for performing this task because the sales confirmation can take place in different applications.

Rebuilding the Database

To rebuild the Brewbean's database, follow these steps:

1. Make sure you have the `c9_BBcreate.sql` file in the Chapter09 folder. This file contains the script for creating the database.
2. Start SQL Developer and connect to the Oracle database.
3. Click **File**, **Open** from the menu.
4. Click the **`c9_BBcreate.sql`** file, and then click **Open**. The code in this script is displayed in the Edit pane. Scroll through the SQL statements; they should look familiar.
5. Run the script by clicking the **Run Script** button on the Edit pane toolbar. If necessary, click **OK** in the Select Connection dialog box.
6. Scroll through the Script Output pane at the bottom to review the results of the statements.
7. In the Connections pane on the left, expand the **Tables** node to view the tables that were created. While this node is selected, click the **Refresh** button at the top of the Connections pane to update the list of tables.

INTRODUCTION TO DATABASE TRIGGERS

A **database trigger** is a block of PL/SQL code that runs automatically when a particular database event occurs. The event can be a DML action, such as `INSERT`, `UPDATE`, and `DELETE`, or an Oracle system action, such as a user logging on. The trigger contains a PL/SQL block with a header that specifies which event this trigger is associated with in the database. For example, if the trigger is associated with an `UPDATE` statement on the BB_BASKET table, the trigger code runs or fires automatically whenever an `UPDATE` statement on the BB_BASKET table is processed—regardless of its source.

It doesn't matter whether Brewbean's Web site application or in-store application issues the `UPDATE`; in either case, the trigger fires. Even if you log on to the database with SQL Developer and enter an `UPDATE` for the BB_BASKET table, the trigger still fires. A database trigger is tied to a database table or view, and Oracle fires it automatically (called "implicitly" in Oracle documentation) when the table or view is affected by the associated DML action. This behavior is quite a change from procedures and functions that are called by name (or "explicitly" in documentation) in program code.

Database Trigger Syntax and Options

Take a look at the basic syntax of a `CREATE TRIGGER` statement, shown in Figure 9-3. Notice that the clauses related to trigger timing and events are labeled.

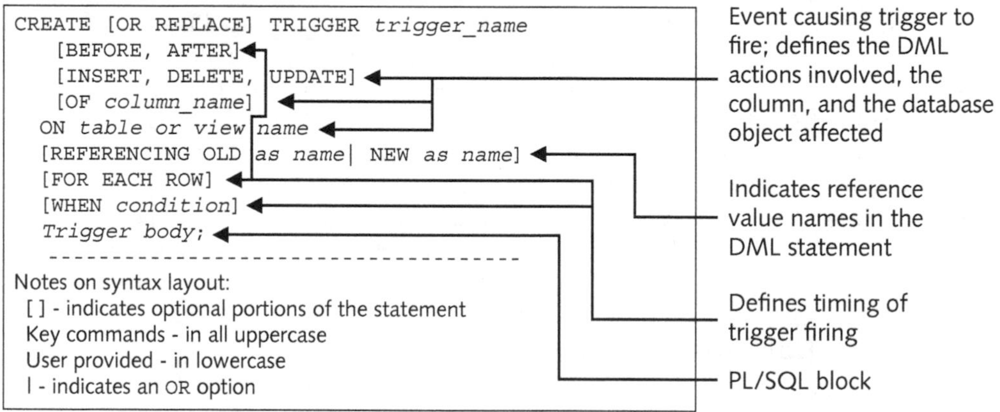

FIGURE 9-3 A `CREATE TRIGGER` statement

As shown, the code must indicate what events cause the trigger to fire (`INSERT`, `DELETE`, or `UPDATE`) and whether the firing occurs before or after the event. Additional options indicate whether to fire the trigger only one time for the DML action or for each row the DML action affects. In addition, you can include a condition that's checked when the event occurs and causes the trigger to fire only when the condition is true.

The trigger body is a PL/SQL block containing the actions that take place when the trigger fires. Other important features of triggers include conditional predicates and correlation identifiers, discussed later in this chapter. Many options are available in each area of the `CREATE TRIGGER` statement; before exploring these options, however, take a look at a code example in the next section.

Database Trigger Code Example

Understanding a database trigger is easier when you have an actual code example. The following code creates a trigger named `PRODUCT_INVENTORY_TRG` that's been developed to solve the inventory-updating problem in the Brewbean's application. Line numbers are listed for easier reference. This example familiarizes you with the `CREATE TRIGGER` statement and is the basis for discussion in subsequent sections. Don't worry about understanding or running this code yet; the following sections explain its parts.

```
1  CREATE OR REPLACE TRIGGER product_inventory_trg
2    AFTER UPDATE OF orderplaced ON bb_basket
3    FOR EACH ROW
4    WHEN (OLD.orderplaced <> 1 AND NEW.orderplaced = 1)
5  DECLARE
6    CURSOR basketitem_cur IS
7    SELECT idproduct, quantity, option1
8      FROM bb_basketitem
9      WHERE idbasket = :NEW.idbasket;
10     lv_chg_num NUMBER(3,1);
11 BEGIN
12   FOR basketitem_rec IN basketitem_cur LOOP
13     IF basketitem_rec.option1 = 1 THEN
14       lv_chg_num := (.5 * basketitem_rec.quantity);
15     ELSE
16       lv_chg_num := basketitem_rec.quantity;
17     END IF;
18   UPDATE bb_product
19   SET stock = stock - lv_chg_num
20     WHERE idproduct = basketitem_rec.idproduct;
21   END LOOP;
22 END;
```


TIP

To help you follow along in the next sections, you might want to print the `c9invent.sql` text file in the Chapter09 folder of your student data files. You can make notes on this printout as you read the following sections.

Trigger Timing and Correlation Identifiers

Trigger correlation and timing features are so intertwined that they're discussed together in this section. A trigger's timing involves several factors, including firing before or after the associated DML action, firing only once for the entire DML action or for each row the DML action affects, and firing only if a particular condition is true.

First, the timing must be indicated as `BEFORE` or `AFTER`. Line 2 of the trigger code includes the `AFTER` keyword, indicating that the trigger body's code should run after the DML statement that fired the trigger is finished. In this case, you want the trigger code to run only after the BB_BASKET table has been updated, and this update meets the `WHEN` clause requirements of setting the ORDERPLACED column to 1 and confirming that the order has been completed.

After you know the order has been completed, you need to make the inventory changes. If you used `BEFORE` instead of `AFTER`, the inventory would be updated before the order was confirmed. What if a problem, such as credit card approval failing, occurs when the order information is confirmed? You would end up with an inaccurate stock level in the BB_PRODUCT table because the order wasn't completed, but you updated the inventory as though it *were* completed.

Another factor in trigger timing is whether to run the trigger code for every row the DML action affects or run it just one time. A **row-level trigger** means the trigger is fired for each row the DML statement affects, and a **statement-level trigger** means the trigger is fired only once for the DML action, regardless of the number of rows affected. The `FOR EACH ROW` clause on Line 3 establishes this trigger as a row-level trigger. Simply omitting this clause creates a statement-level trigger. The `BEFORE` and `AFTER` options combine with row- or statement-level options to produce a trigger-firing sequence, shown in Figure 9-4, for a `DELETE` statement that affects two rows. Keep in mind that you can construct multiple triggers on one table, so a DML action on that table can fire off more than one trigger.

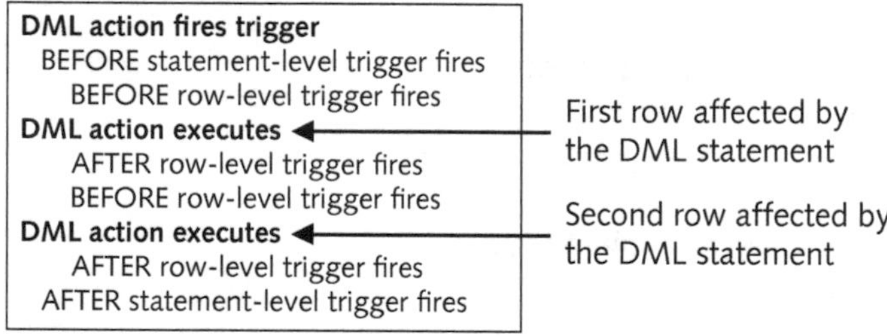

FIGURE 9-4 A trigger-firing sequence

TIP

If you have multiple triggers on a table, there's no guarantee of their firing order. A `BEFORE` statement-level trigger fires before a `BEFORE` row-level trigger; however, if you have two statement-level triggers, the order in which they fire is random.

Row-level timing is applicable only for `UPDATE` and `DELETE` events because these DML statements can affect more than one row. An `INSERT` can affect only one row at a time, so it can't be used with a row-level trigger. Because the Brewbean's application completes only one order at a time, a statement-level trigger should be all that's needed. A trigger's default timing is statement level, so you don't need to add any code for this timing. However, Line 3 of the `PRODUCT_INVENTORY_TRG` trigger is `FOR EACH ROW`, which specifies a row-level trigger. This timing has been selected so that `WHEN` clause features can be used. In addition, you need correlation identifiers in the inventory trigger, and they're available only with row-level triggers.

Line 4 of the `PRODUCT_INVENTORY_TRG` trigger contains a `WHEN` clause, which enables you to include a condition so that the trigger fires only if the condition is true. For example, you want the inventory update to occur only when the order is being confirmed. Your code needs to check whether the `UPDATE` on the BB_BASKET table changes the ORDERPLACED column from 0 to 1 to indicate that the order has been placed.

Of course, other update actions can occur on the BB_BASKET table, but you want to perform this inventory update only with the first order confirmation. What do the OLD and NEW in the WHEN clause mean? They're **correlation identifiers**, or qualifiers, which are special PL/SQL bind variables that refer to values associated with the DML action that fires a trigger. Correlation identifiers make it possible for you to refer to and use the DML action's row data values.

As an example of their usefulness in the inventory trigger, notice that you can check the ORDERPLACED column to see that a 0 represents the old (original) value for the row being updated and a 1 represents the new value. An UPDATE involves an existing row with original values and a new row with the updated values. If an UPDATE fires a trigger, the Oracle server actually holds both the old and new values in these bind variables that can be referenced. As Line 4 shows, the notation is the correlation identifier name (OLD or NEW), a period, and then the column name: OLD.orderplaced or NEW.orderplaced.

As shown in Table 9-1, not all DML actions can use both OLD and NEW identifiers. Only an UPDATE statement has both an original row and a new row, so both identifiers are available.

TABLE 9-1 Correlation Identifier Availability

DML Action	OLD Identifier	NEW Identifier
INSERT	Not available	Contains INSERT values
UPDATE	Contains original row's values	Contains new values for any columns that are updated and original values for any columns that aren't updated
DELETE	Contains original row's values	Not available (indicates any references that retrieve a NULL value)

NOTE

The REFERENCING clause shown previously in Figure 9-3 can be used to change the OLD and NEW identifiers to other names of your choice. However, the OLD and NEW names are so logical that most PL/SQL developers continue using them.

Remember these three critical pieces of information for a trigger's WHEN clause:

- A WHEN clause can be used only in row-level triggers.
- The values checked in the WHEN clause must reference correlation identifiers.
- The condition must be enclosed in parentheses.

Trigger Events

The trigger event information defines which DML statements on which table cause the trigger to fire. The first item to specify is the DML event, such as INSERT, UPDATE, or DELETE. You can include any or all of them. For example, take a look at Line 2 in the PRODUCT_INVENTORY_TRG example:

```
AFTER UPDATE OF orderplaced ON bb_basket
```

The only DML event that can cause this trigger to fire is an UPDATE. The OF clause after the UPDATE keyword is optional. It can be used only with the UPDATE event and allows specifying a column name. In this example, the trigger fires only if the UPDATE affects the ORDERPLACED column. If the UPDATE statement's SET clause doesn't affect the ORDERPLACED column, this trigger doesn't fire. For example, review the following UPDATE statements. The first example causes the trigger to fire because it affects the ORDERPLACED column; the second example doesn't cause the trigger to fire.

```
DML event example 1:  UPDATE bb_basket
                      SET orderplaced = 1
                      WHERE idbasket = 15;
DML event example 2:  UPDATE bb_basket
                      SET tax = 3.64
                      WHERE idbasket = 15;
```


If you want the trigger to fire for an UPDATE or DELETE action, you list these events as shown:

```
AFTER DELETE OR UPDATE OF orderplaced ON bb_basket
```

The ON clause indicates which table is being affected by DML events. The PRODUCT_INVENTORY_TRG trigger fires when the UPDATE is issued on the BB_BASKET table, which contains the ORDERPLACED column. Unlike procedures and functions, a database trigger is tied to the table named in the ON clause. When a DML action occurs on this table, Oracle first checks through all triggers associated with this table and determines whether any should fire.

Trigger Body

The trigger body is a PL/SQL block. A trigger header isn't followed by the IS keyword, as in procedures and functions, so the DECLARE keyword must be used if you need to declare any variables in the trigger body code.

In this example, DECLARE is used to declare a cursor for updating the inventory. The block retrieves the items ordered from the BB_BASKETITEM table into a cursor so that each product's stock amount can be updated. To retrieve the correct rows for the basket being ordered, you need to reference the idbasket value from the UPDATE statement that fires this trigger by using correlation identifiers. The following lines show the cursor declaration in the trigger:

```
CURSOR basketitem_cur IS
  SELECT idproduct, quantity, option1
    FROM bb_basketitem
    WHERE idbasket = :NEW.idbasket;
```

The WHERE clause references the idbasket value from the UPDATE statement by using the :NEW.idbasket notation. A colon precedes the correlation identifier because this code is in the trigger body. In this example, it doesn't matter if you reference the NEW or OLD idbasket value; both hold the same value because the UPDATE statement didn't modify this column. The OPTION1 column value is retrieved because it indicates whether the order quantity of coffee is a half-pound or whole pound. If it's a half-pound, the quantity is multiplied by .5 to determine the change in inventory amount because the coffee inventory is in terms of whole pounds.

TIP

A common point of confusion is when to precede a correlation identifier with a colon. In Line 4's WHEN clause that you examined earlier, no preceding colon is used to check OLD.orderplaced and NEW.orderplaced. However, as you see in the WHERE clause of the cursor declaration, a preceding colon must be used with correlation identifiers in the trigger body's code.

The trigger body's executable section uses a CURSOR FOR loop to allow looping through all products ordered and updating the product's stock value in the BB_PRODUCT table. An IF clause is included in this loop to check whether the coffee's order quantity is a half-pound. If it is, an adjustment is made to the quantity to update the stock amount. The trigger issues DML UPDATE statements on the BB_PRODUCT table to modify the stock amount. Take a look at Figure 9-5's flow of database activity for this trigger. An UPDATE statement on the BB_BASKET table causes the trigger to fire, the trigger retrieves the products ordered by querying the BB_BASKETITEM table, and UPDATEs are issued on the BB_PRODUCT table to modify the products' stock amounts.

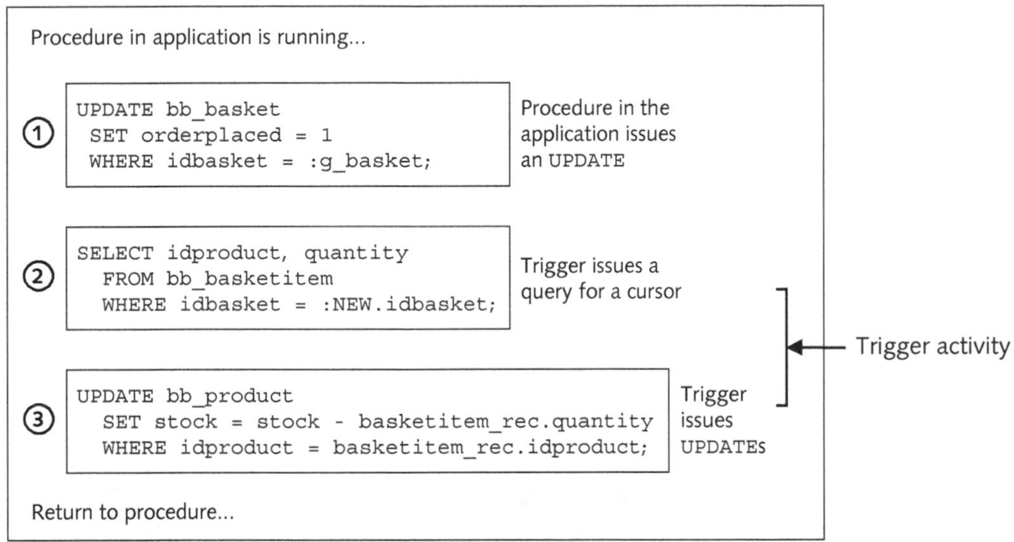

FIGURE 9-5 The flow of database activity for the PRODUCT_INVENTORY_TRG trigger

In the example, the PL/SQL block code is entered right in the trigger body. However, you can also use a CALL statement to invoke a stored subprogram (procedure or function) or a wrapper for a C or Java routine. What if you already have a procedure named UPDATE_STOCK_SP containing the code you want to use in the trigger body? You can use the following CALL statement. If the procedure requires parameters, they're included, too, just as you would normally call the procedure. The OLD and NEW values can also be used to supply parameter values.

```
CREATE OR REPLACE TRIGGER product_inventory_trg
  AFTER UPDATE OF orderplaced ON bb_basket
  FOR EACH ROW
  WHEN (OLD.orderplaced <> 1 AND NEW.orderplaced = 1)
  CALL update_stock_sp(:NEW.idbasket)
```

Conditional Predicates

What if you want to perform different actions in the trigger based on the DML statement that's issued? **Conditional predicates** are clauses you can use in a trigger to handle different database-triggering events in a single trigger. They consist of an `IF` statement to establish the condition and a predicate, which is a verb specifying the DML action. Remember that you can list multiple DML events in a trigger, so you could use a statement such as the following to have a `DELETE` or an `UPDATE` action on the BB_BASKET table cause the trigger to fire:

```
AFTER DELETE OR UPDATE ON bb_basket
```

To see how conditional predicates work, simplify the inventory trigger example for a moment. The following code reduces the product stock level if an `UPDATE` occurs but increases the stock level if the order is deleted or canceled. It also assumes all coffee orders are for whole pounds. Notice the `IF` clauses in Lines 10 and 17:


```
1  CREATE OR REPLACE TRIGGER product_inventory_trg
2    AFTER DELETE OR UPDATE ON bb_basket
3    FOR EACH ROW
4  DECLARE
5    CURSOR basketitem_cur IS
6    SELECT idproduct, quantity
7      FROM bb_basketitem
8      WHERE idbasket = :NEW.idbasket;
9  BEGIN
10 IF UPDATING THEN
11   FOR basketitem_rec IN basketitem_cur LOOP
12   UPDATE bb_product
13     SET stock = stock - basketitem_rec.quantity
14     WHERE idproduct = basketitem_rec.idproduct;
15   END LOOP;
16 END IF;
17 IF DELETING THEN
18   FOR basketitem_rec IN basketitem_cur LOOP
19   UPDATE bb_product
20     SET stock = stock + basketitem_rec.quantity
21     WHERE idproduct = basketitem_rec.idproduct;
22   END LOOP;
23 END IF;
22 END;
```

The predicates `INSERTING`, `DELETING`, and `UPDATING` indicate certain actions based on an event. The `UPDATING` conditional predicate can also specify a column. For example, if you want to perform an action only if the `UPDATE` modifies the ORDERPLACED column, you could use the following code:

```
IF UPDATING ('orderplaced') THEN
```

TIP

You should specify the column in the `UPDATING` predicate if the trigger fires, regardless of which columns are updated. In this case, you can specify a column to indicate different actions, depending on the column updated. However, if you've already used the `UPDATE OF` syntax to indicate that the trigger should fire only after an update of a particular column, specifying a column in the `UPDATING` predicate is redundant.

CREATING AND TESTING A DML TRIGGER

Now that you have a basic understanding of trigger code, create the `PRODUCT_INVENTORY_TRG` trigger that's been discussed in this chapter:

1. In SQL Developer, click **File**, **New** from the menu. In the Create a new dialog box, click **Trigger**, and then click **OK**.
2. Select your current connection.
3. In the Create Trigger dialog box, enter the trigger name. In the Table Name list box, click **BB_BASKET**, and select the DML action and timing option shown in Figure 9-6. You can set up all trigger header information in this dialog box, including the columns to use with an `UPDATE` trigger. In this exercise, however, you do just the minimum setup because the text file has all the code you need.

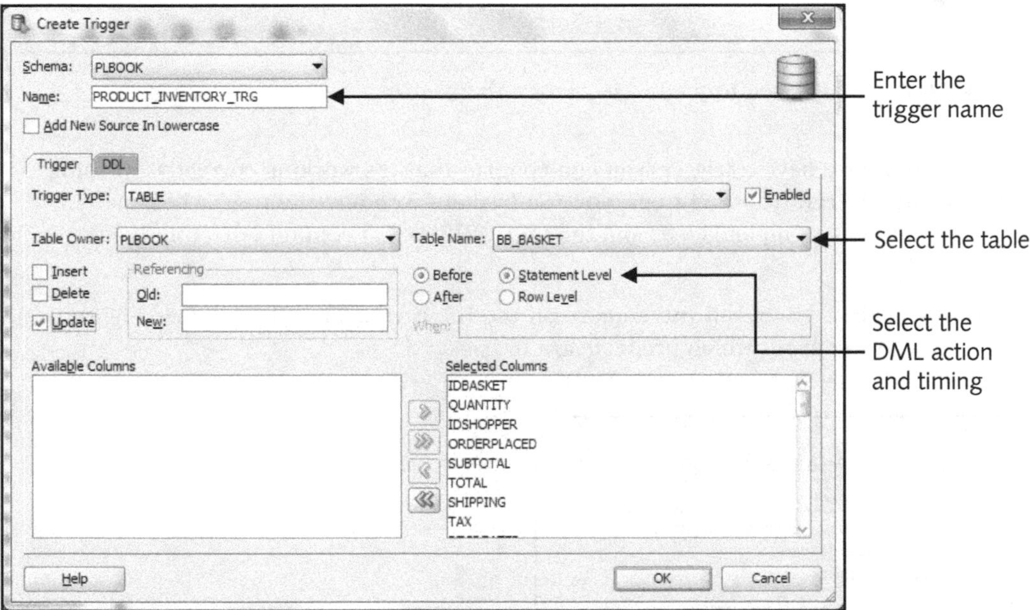

FIGURE 9-6 Creating a trigger

4. Click **OK**, and a basic template of code is displayed.
5. In Notepad, open the **`c9invent.txt`** file in the Chapter09 folder. Copy this code to SQL Developer to replace the code in the Trigger pane.
6. Compile the code to create the trigger. In the Connections pane on the left, you should see the trigger under the Triggers node (see Figure 9-7). You might need to refresh this pane to see it.

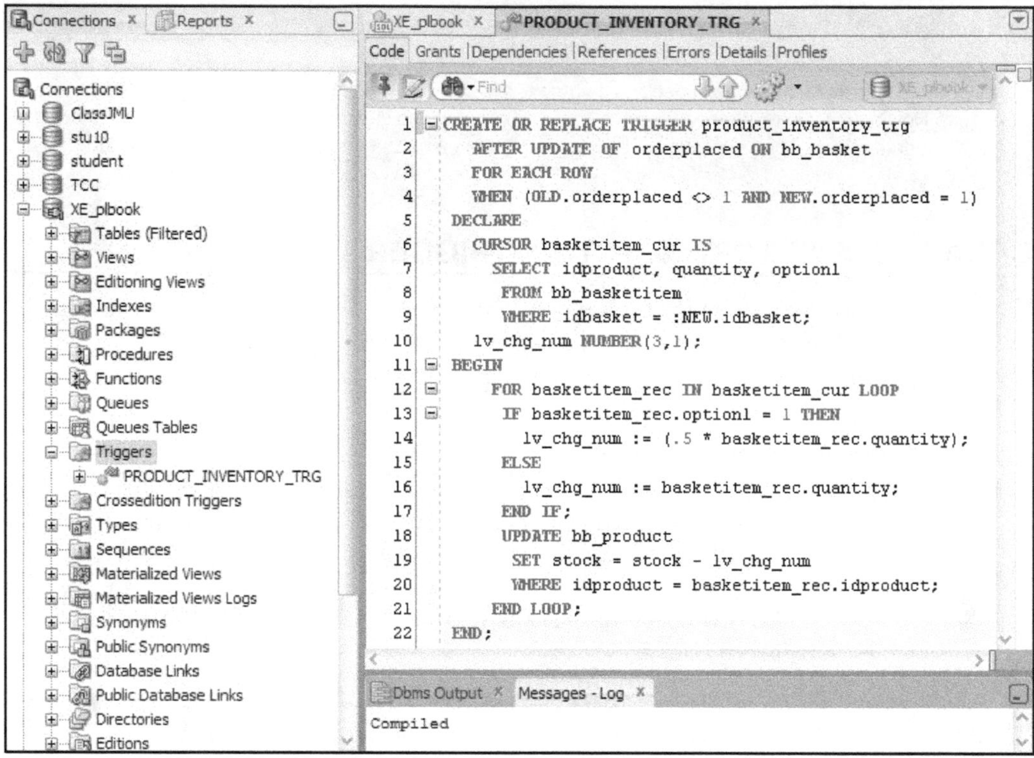

FIGURE 9-7 Creating the PRODUCT_INVENTORY_TRG trigger

Now that you have a trigger, you can confirm that it's working correctly by doing some testing. In the following steps, you use basket 15 to test the trigger because this order hasn't been completed yet, and the ORDERPLACED column currently holds the value 0:

1. First, enter and run a query on the BB_BASKETITEM table (see Figure 9-8) to confirm which products are in basket 15.

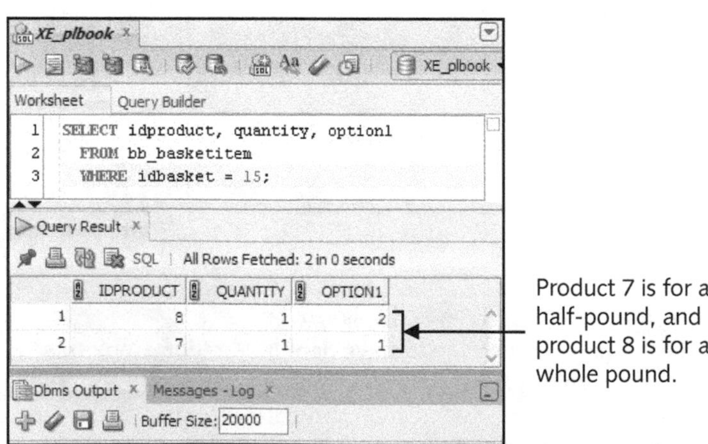
Product 7 is for a half-pound, and product 8 is for a whole pound.

FIGURE 9-8 Querying the database to view a basket's product list

2. Enter the query shown in Figure 9-9 to verify the current stock amounts for the two products to determine whether the correct modifications are being made.

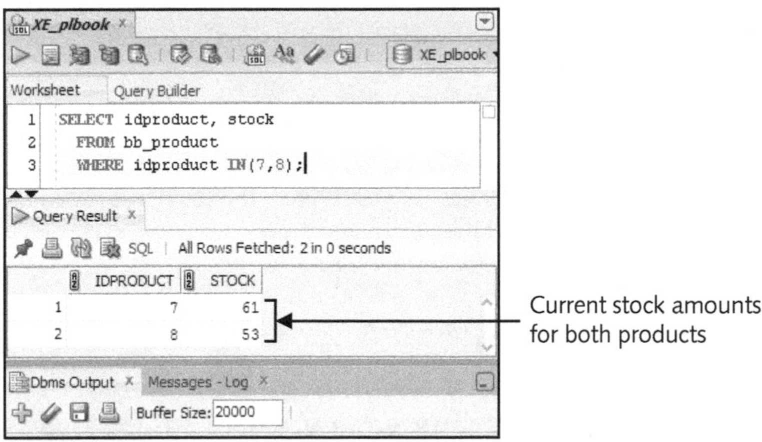

FIGURE 9-9 Querying the database to confirm the stock amounts

3. Now that you know what should happen when the trigger fires, issue the `UPDATE` statement in Figure 9-10 to change the ORDERPLACED column's value from 0 to 1 to indicate that the order has been placed. Also, issue a `COMMIT` statement to save the transaction because you're using DML actions.

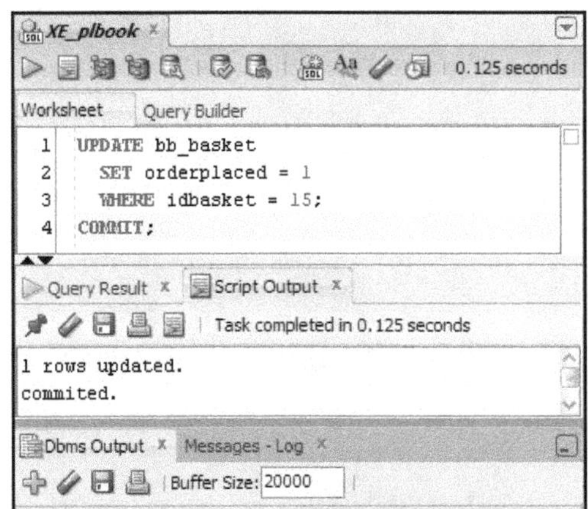

FIGURE 9-10 Issuing an `UPDATE` to fire the trigger

4. Next, query the BB_PRODUCT table, as shown in Figure 9-11, to verify that the trigger fired and performed the expected modification to each product's stock value.

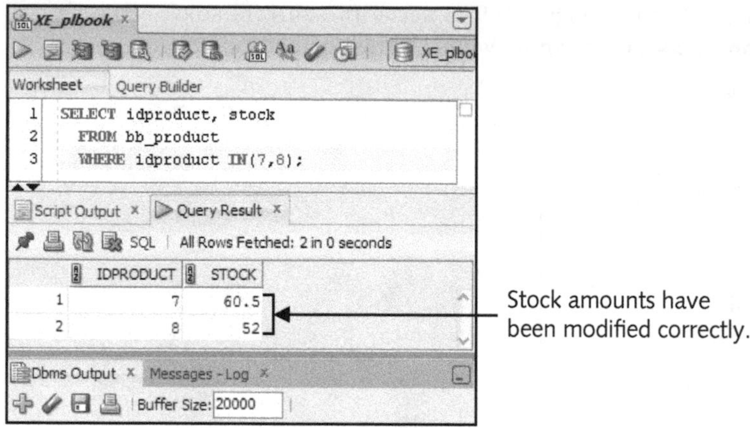

FIGURE 9-11 Querying the BB_PRODUCT table to check the new stock values

CHALLENGE 9-1

Assume a QUANTITY column in the BB_BASKET table is used to track the total items in a basket (BB_BASKETITEM). The QUANTITY value can be used to determine shipping costs and potential discounts. A basket's quantity should include the total number of items in it. Each item added to the basket indicates a quantity; for example, if an item with the quantity 2 is added to the basket, the value 2 should be added to the total quantity of items for the basket. Create a trigger named `BB_QTY_TRG` that handles modifying a basket's quantity value as items are added, removed, or changed. Show statements that test the trigger for adding and removing an item.

CREATING AND TESTING AN `INSTEAD OF` TRIGGER

An **`INSTEAD OF` trigger** is a PL/SQL block that runs in place of a DML action on a database view. Typically, it's used to allow modifying data through a view that can't be modified. As you learned in your SQL studies, a view containing any of the following usually can't be modified:

- Joins
- Set operators
- Aggregate functions
- `GROUP BY`, `CONNECT BY`, and `START WITH` clauses
- `DISTINCT` operators

You might want to use a view that can't be modified in DML statements to simplify data modifications affecting more than one table. You might also need to process DML actions via a view but want to affect each table in the view differently. For example, suppose Brewbean's develops an application page where store employees enter shipping information for orders (see Figure 9-12).

FIGURE 9-12 Brewbean's shipping information page

The SHIPFLAG column needs to be updated in the BB_BASKET table, and the DTSTAGE, SHIPPER, SHIPPINGNUM, and NOTES columns need to be updated in the BB_BASKETSTATUS table. When an order is approved and sent to shipping, a new row is inserted in the BB_BASKETSTATUS table with the `idstage` value 3 to hold the order's shipping information. A view including columns from the BB_BASKET and BB_BASKETSTATUS tables was created in the database creation script for this book and looks like the following:

```
CREATE OR REPLACE VIEW bb_ship_vu
AS SELECT b.idbasket, b.shipflag, bs.idstage, bs.dtstage, bs.notes,
  bs.shipper, bs.shippingnum
  FROM bb_basket b, bb_basketstatus bs
  WHERE b.idBasket = bs.idBasket;
```

This view doesn't include the primary key column IDSTATUS in the BB_BASKETSTATUS table. What happens if you attempt an `UPDATE` with this view? As Figure 9-13 shows, the error message refers to a "non-key-preserved table."

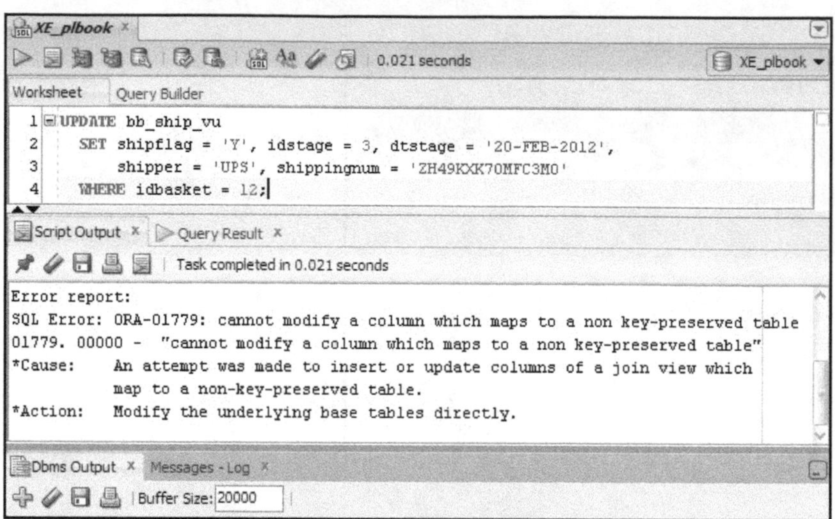

FIGURE 9-13 An `UPDATE` action via a view containing a join

A **key-preserved table** is one that's involved in a join, and the original table's keys are included in the keys of the resulting join. In this case, the primary key column IDSTATUS isn't included in the view, yet you're attempting to insert a new row in the BB_BASKETSTATUS table, which would require a value for this column. Before you create the trigger, review the `INSTEAD OF` trigger code needed to update the shipping data (see Figure 9-14). The keywords `INSTEAD OF` are used, and the `UPDATE` in this trigger runs instead of the `UPDATE` on the `BB_SHIP_VU` view that fires this trigger.

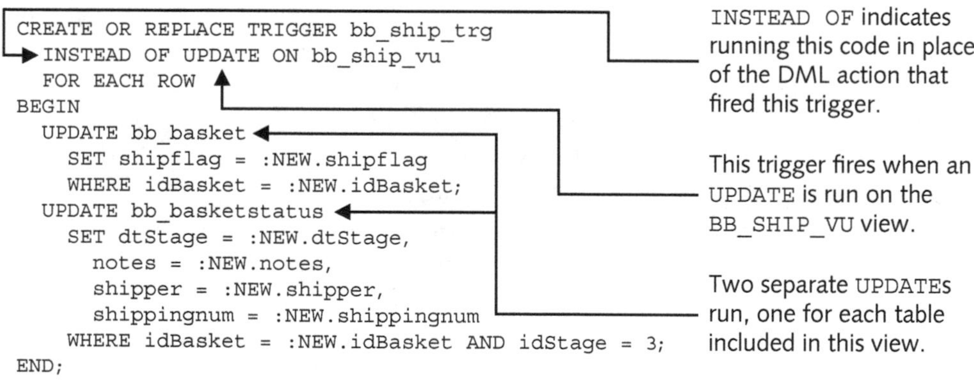

CREATE OR REPLACE TRIGGER bb_ship_trg
INSTEAD OF UPDATE ON bb_ship_vu
FOR EACH ROW
BEGIN
UPDATE bb_basket
SET shipflag = :NEW.shipflag
WHERE idBasket = :NEW.idBasket;
UPDATE bb_basketstatus
SET dtStage = :NEW.dtStage,
notes = :NEW.notes,
shipper = :NEW.shipper,
shippingnum = :NEW.shippingnum
WHERE idBasket = :NEW.idBasket AND idStage = 3;
END;
INSTEAD OF indicates running this code in place of the DML action that fired this trigger.
This trigger fires when an UPDATE is run on the BB_SHIP_VU view.
Two separate UPDATEs run, one for each table included in this view.

FIGURE 9-14 The `INSTEAD OF` trigger code

To support the Brewbean's shipping information page, create this `INSTEAD OF` trigger:

1. In SQL Developer, click **File**, **New** from the menu. In the Create a new dialog box, click **Trigger**, and then click **OK**.
2. Select your current connection.

3. In the Create Trigger dialog box, enter the trigger name **BB_SHIP_TRG**. In the Trigger Type list box, click **VIEW**. In the View Name list box, click **BB_SHIP_VU**, and for the DML action, click the **Update** option button. Click **OK**.
4. In Notepad, open the **c9ship.txt** file in the Chapter09 folder. Copy this code to SQL Developer, and use it to create the trigger.

Now you have an INSTEAD OF trigger on the BB_SHIP_VU view. To test it, you issue an UPDATE on the view you attempted earlier. Follow these steps:

1. In SQL Developer, enter the UPDATE statement shown in Figure 9-15.

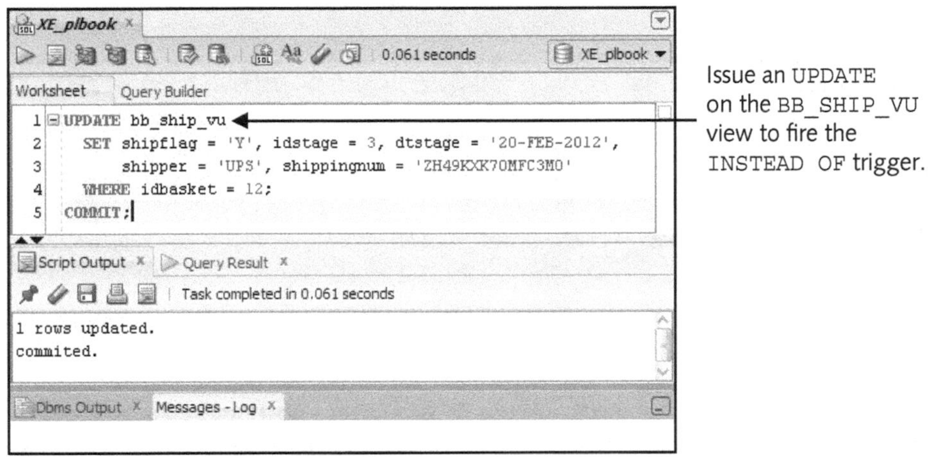

FIGURE 9-15 Issuing an UPDATE on the BB_SHIP_VU view

2. Next, query the BB_BASKET table, as shown in Figure 9-16, to verify that shipflag has been set to Y for basket 12.

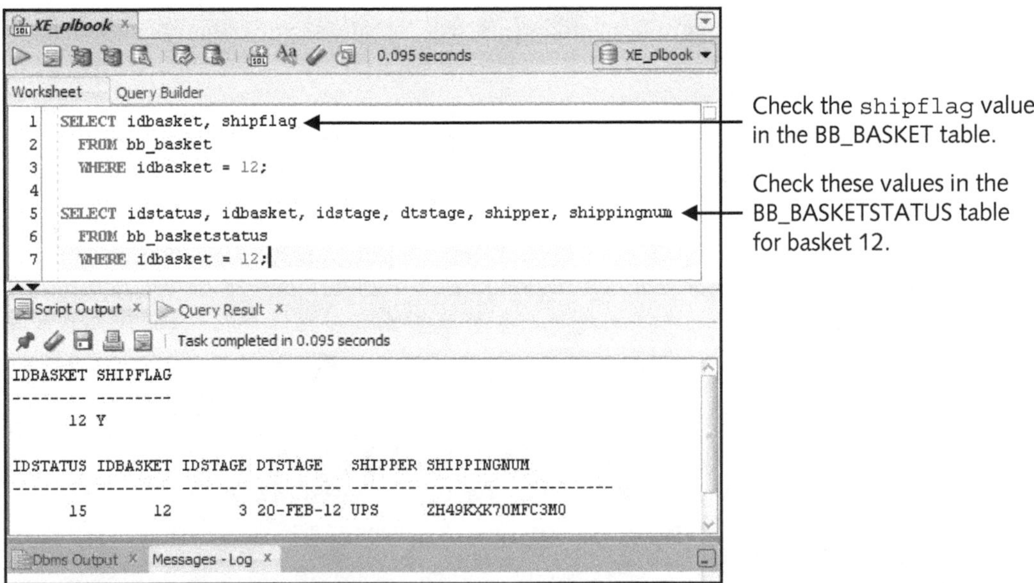

FIGURE 9-16 Checking the results of the trigger firing

3. Finally, query the BB_BASKETSTATUS table, as shown in Figure 9-16, to verify that the DTSTAGE, SHIPPER, and SHIPPINGNUM columns have been updated for basket 12.

The goal of an INSTEAD OF trigger is to replace a DML statement issued on a view. It not only simplifies code by using views, but also allows a variety of actions to occur, if needed.

NOTE

The INSTEAD OF trigger body needs to perform any checking included in the view as a CHECK option. The CHECK option for views isn't enforced when inserts or updates to the view are done with INSTEAD OF triggers.

CHALLENGE 9-2

Review the CREATE VIEW and INSERT statements in the chall_vu.txt file in the Chapter09 folder. This view is used on a page in the Brewbean's application that allows an employee to add a new product with a selected option (such as "whole pound"). Create the view and then attempt to issue the INSERT statement. Notice that the INSERT statement raises an error. Create an INSTEAD OF trigger to perform the necessary INSERTs. It must include both the BB_PRODUCT and BB_PRODUCTOPTION tables. Test the trigger with the INSERT statement supplied in the file.

ADDITIONAL TRIGGERS

Triggers can address more than just DML events. In addition to DML and INSTEAD OF triggers, you can create system, user logon, and DDL statement triggers. All these database triggers are considered to fall into two general categories of triggers: system and user event. **System triggers** are fired by database events, such as startup and shutdown, and server error messages. **User event triggers** are fired by users performing database actions, such as logons and logoffs, and issuing DML or DDL statements.

System events that can be used in triggers include STARTUP, SHUTDOWN, and SERVERERROR. A system trigger's syntax, shown in the following example, is similar to other triggers in timing factors and listing events. The ON clause indicates that the trigger is a database-level or schema-level trigger instead of a specific table or view, as used in DML triggers.

```
CREATE [OR REPLACE] TRIGGER trigger_name [BEFORE, AFTER]
[list of database system events] [ON DATABASE | ON SCHEMA]
  trigger body;
```

To see an example, here's the code for a trigger that captures failed logon attempt information, which is a typical security-auditing task:

```
CREATE OR REPLACE TRIGGER bb_logonfail_trg
  AFTER SERVERERROR ON DATABASE
BEGIN
  IF (IS_SERVERERROR (1017)) THEN
    INSERT INTO bb_audit_logon (userid, logdate)
      VALUES(SYS_CONTEXT('USERENV', 'OS_USER'), SYSDATE);
  ELSE
    NULL;  --could address additional server errors
  END IF;
END;
```

CAUTION

If you try to build this trigger in your Oracle installation, you might run into two limitations. First, if you're on a shared Oracle system, you might not have privileges to create a database-level trigger. In this case, simply change the `ON DATABASE` option to `ON SCHEMA` so that you can create and test the trigger. Second, you might need to increase the USERID column's size in the BB_AUDIT_LOGON table to accommodate larger usernames on your system.

Notice that the trigger fires on `AFTER SEVERERROR ON DATABASE` and uses an `IF` statement to determine what to do based on the specific error that occurs. Server error 1017 is raised at a failed logon attempt. Also, the `SYS_CONTEXT` function is used to identify the user attempting to log on; it refers to the user's operating system username because an Oracle username isn't established for a failed logon attempt. To test the trigger after it's created, you can disconnect from the database in SQL Developer and connect again by using an incorrect password to raise an error, as shown in Figure 9-17.

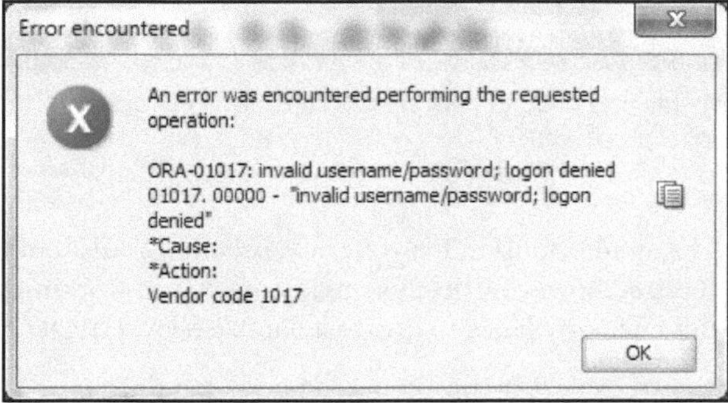

FIGURE 9-17 A system trigger for a failed logon

To verify that the trigger fired correctly, log on successfully and query the BB_AUDIT_LOGON table, as shown in Figure 9-18.

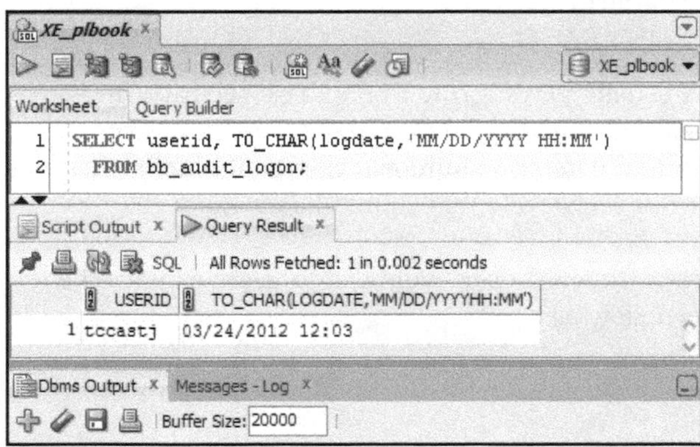

FIGURE 9-18 The system trigger recorded a failed logon

Because this trigger uses the `ON DATABASE` option rather than the `ON SCHEMA` option, it fires when anyone attempts to log on to the database, regardless of the schema. Notice that the logon event's timing is `AFTER`. There are some common-sense limitations on which timings work with which events. For example, the system couldn't entertain a BEFORE logon trigger because it can't anticipate this event—unless, of course, the next version of Oracle software builds in psychic powers! In addition, the STARTUP and SHUTDOWN events must be used in a database-level trigger.

Now take a look at the user event of a successful logon rather than a failed logon attempt. Another typical audit file contains data on who accessed the database and when. If you modify the previous trigger to track successful logon actions, the event is changed to LOGON and the trigger body needs to perform only an INSERT action to record the logon action, as shown in the following code:

```
CREATE OR REPLACE TRIGGER bb_logon_trg
  AFTER LOGON ON DATABASE
BEGIN
  INSERT INTO bb_audit_logon (userid, logdate)
    VALUES (USER, SYSDATE);
END;
```


NOTE

In practice, successful and unsuccessful logon attempts need to be identified separately. For these exercises, the data inserts use the same table for simplicity.

Now try creating this trigger to track logon information for your own schema. You should change the ON DATABASE option to ON SCHEMA, however, because many of you are working on a shared database system and might not have privileges to create a database-level trigger.

1. In SQL Developer, create the trigger with the preceding code for the BB_LOGON_TRG trigger. However, be sure to use the ON SCHEMA option rather than ON DATABASE option.
2. In the Connections pane, disconnect from the database, and then reconnect.
3. Verify that the trigger fired by querying the BB_AUDIT_LOGON table, using the TO_CHAR function to display the date and time. A row should be displayed indicating that you just logged on.

System triggers typically fall under the responsibility of a database administrator (DBA) rather than a developer. A DBA usually plays a role in database security, and system triggers assist in tracking database access. In addition, a DBA might want to perform system maintenance tasks before a database shutdown that could be handled via a BEFORE SHUTDOWN system trigger. However, developers should be aware of the capabilities of system triggers.

As mentioned, DDL actions can be considered user events, so triggers can also be fired for DDL statements, including the following:

- CREATE
- ALTER
- DROP
- GRANT
- REVOKE
- RENAME
- TRUNCATE
- ANALYZE

- AUDIT
- NOAUDIT
- COMMENT
- ASSOCIATE STATISTICS
- DISASSOCIATE STATISTICS

Follow these steps to create a DDL trigger that records information when a CREATE action or an ALTER action occurs on your schema objects:

1. In SQL Developer, create a table to log DDL actions by using the code in the **c9DDLtabl.sql** file in the Chapter09 folder. Note the columns included in the table.
2. Create the trigger, as shown in Figure 9-19.

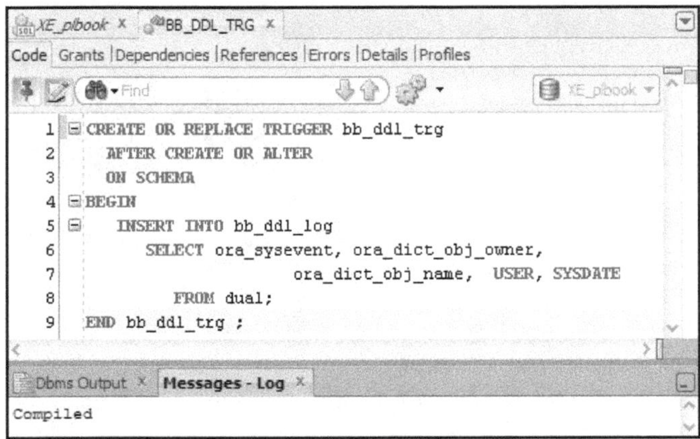

FIGURE 9-19 Creating a DDL trigger

3. Issue the following command:

```
ALTER TABLE bb_audit_logon
  MODIFY (userid VARCHAR2(27));
```

4. Query the BB_DDL_LOG table, as shown in Figure 9-20, to confirm that the ALTER TABLE action has been logged, including the type of action, the object affected, the user, and when the action took place.

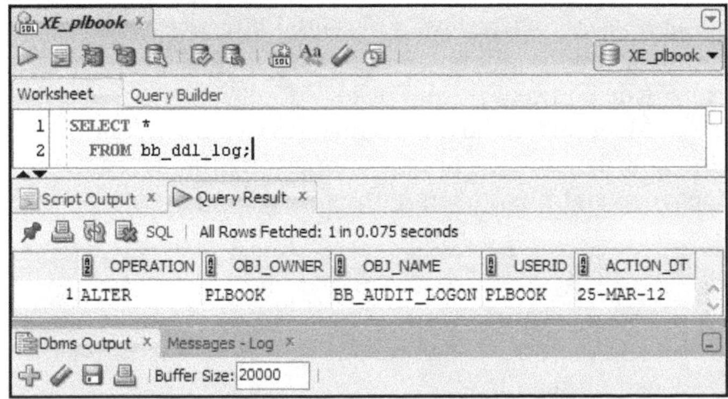

FIGURE 9-20 Verifying that the DDL trigger fired

USING TRIGGERS TO ADDRESS PROCESSING NEEDS

Now that you understand the types of triggers and their basic operation, you might wonder about common uses of triggers. As Table 9-2 shows, a variety of tasks are well suited for triggers.

TABLE 9-2 Possible Trigger Uses

Task	How a Trigger Can Be Applied
Auditing	Log files of database activity are widely used; for example, they can be used to track modifications to confidential data, such as employee payroll records. A trigger could be used to write the original and new values of employee salary updates to an audit table. With this table, a record of the original values and the new assigned values is available to answer any questions about changes.
Data integrity	Simple data validity checks can be done with `CHECK` constraints. However, more complex `CHECK` constraints that require comparison with a live data value from the database can be done with triggers. A trigger could be used to ensure that any changes to a product's regular price don't allow a decrease from the current price, for example. This trigger can compare new and old price values.
Referential integrity	Foreign key constraints are used to enforce relationships between tables. If a parent key value, such as a department number, is modified, a foreign key error occurs if products are still assigned to that department. Triggers give you a way to prevent this error and perform a cascade update action. You see an example of this use after this table.
Derived data	You might have columns that hold values derived from using other columns in a calculation. For example, say Brewbean's has a product sales summary table storing the total quantity and dollar sales by product. If this table needs to be updated in real time, a trigger could be used. Every time a new sale is recorded, the trigger fires and adds the new sales amounts to the totals in the sales summary table.
Security	You can perform additional checks on database access, such as a simple check on the time of user logons. Some companies use a trigger to determine whether a logon is attempted on a weekend; if so, access is denied. In this case, the company identifies any weekend access as suspicious. (Don't you wish all companies were like this?)

Now look at an example of using triggers to reinforce referential integrity. At times, Brewbean's changes department numbers and wants to be sure that products assigned to a department are changed accordingly. Currently, because there's a foreign key constraint on department values between the product and department tables, any department number changes require adding the new department number, modifying the department number on each associated product row, and then deleting the original department row. This process is tedious, so the head developer has asked you to create a trigger that simplifies changing department numbers. Follow these steps to create a referential integrity trigger:

1. In SQL Developer, try to run the `UPDATE` statement shown in Figure 9-21 to verify the foreign key constraint error.

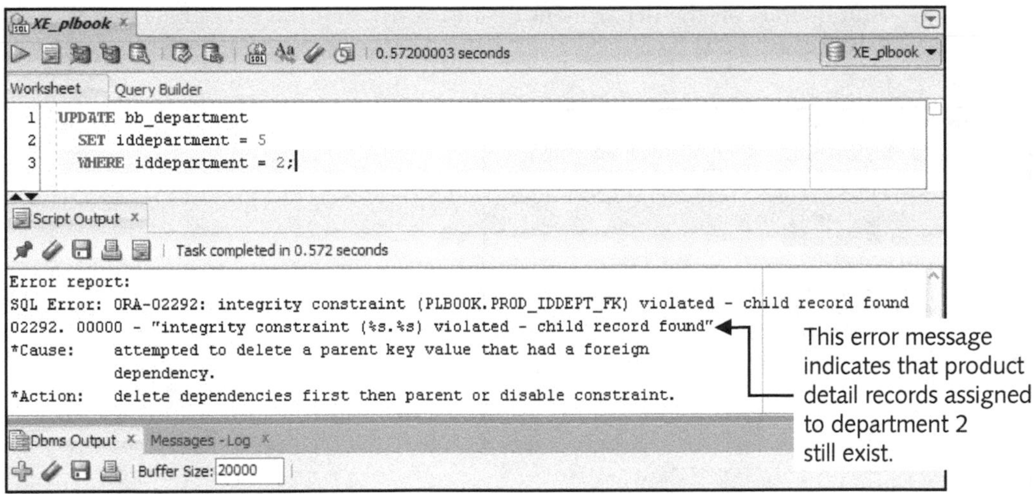

FIGURE 9-21 Verifying a foreign key constraint issue

2. Review the trigger code shown in Figure 9-22. The trigger fires before the `UPDATE` and uses the `:NEW` and `:OLD` references to identify the rows in the BB_PRODUCT table that need to be updated for the department change. When you're finished, use this code to create the trigger.

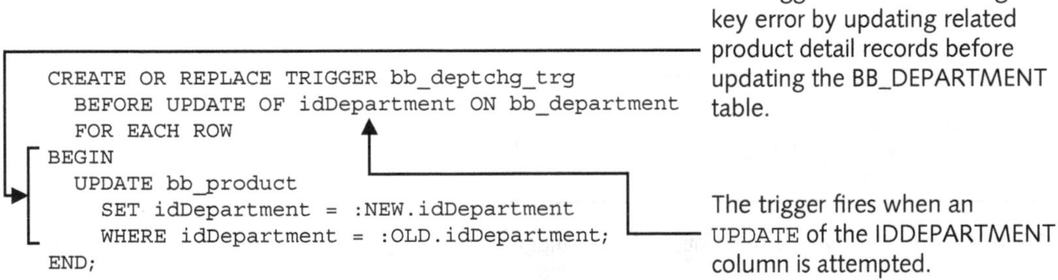

CREATE OR REPLACE TRIGGER bb_deptchg_trg
BEFORE UPDATE OF idDepartment ON bb_department
FOR EACH ROW
BEGIN
UPDATE bb_product
SET idDepartment = :NEW.idDepartment
WHERE idDepartment = :OLD.idDepartment;
END;
The trigger avoids the foreign key error by updating related product detail records before updating the BB_DEPARTMENT table.
The trigger fires when an UPDATE of the IDDEPARTMENT column is attempted.

FIGURE 9-22 A trigger to prevent a foreign key error

3. Run the `UPDATE` statement you used in Step 1 to see whether the error has been addressed (see Figure 9-23).

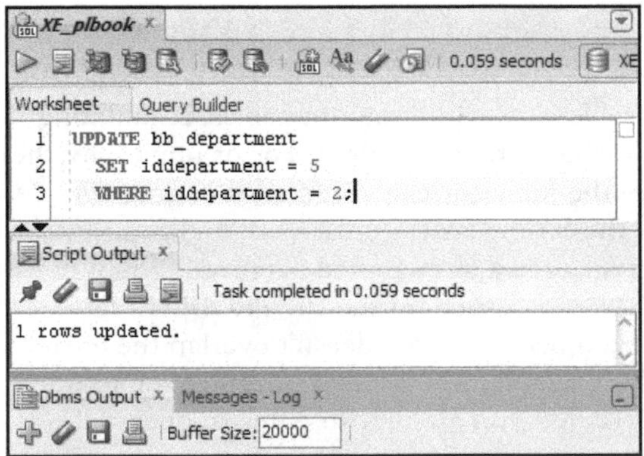

FIGURE 9-23 Addressing an `UPDATE` error

4. Run queries on the department data to verify that the data changes (see Figure 9-24).

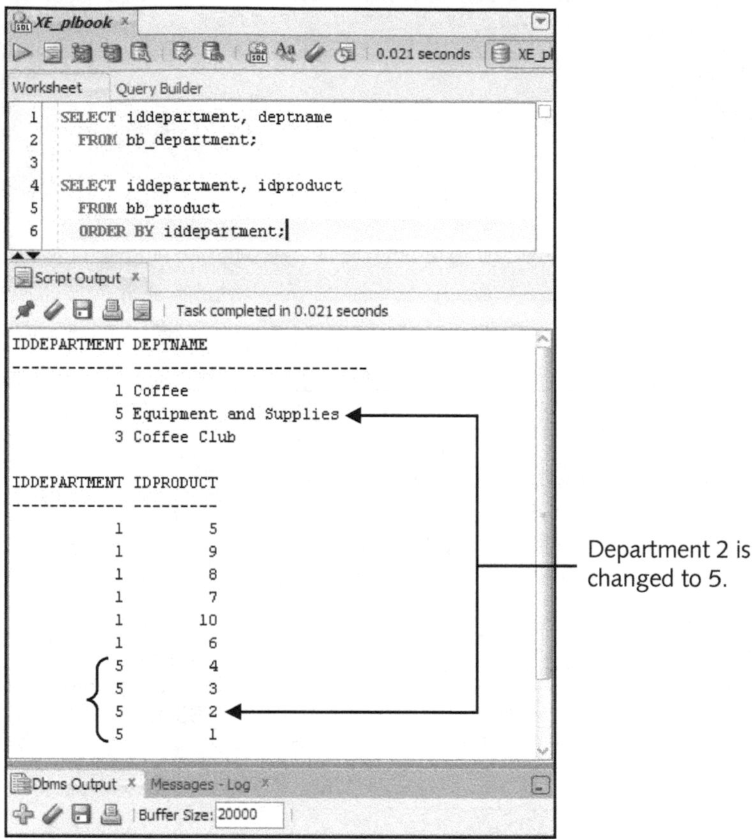

FIGURE 9-24 Verifying a referential integrity trigger

5. Be sure to do a rollback to undo these changes. Verify that the data is returned to the original state of `iddepartment 2` with the same queries you used to check the data changes.

COMPOUND TRIGGERS

Probably one of the most common trigger problems is with mutating tables. A **mutating table** is one that's modified by a DML action when a trigger is fired. For example, say the Brewbean's application includes pages where the manager can enter sales periods for products. The BB_PRODUCT table contains the SALESTART, SALEEND, and SALEPRICE columns that indicate when a product's current or last sales period occurred. When new sales period information is entered with an `UPDATE` issued on the BB_PRODUCT table, you need a trigger to check that the sales period being entered doesn't overlap the current sales period information for that product. For example, if a product's current information indicates a sale running from 6/1/12 to 6/15/12 and you attempt to enter the new sales period 6/10/12 to 6/20/12, you would want to stop the transaction because you already have a special running for that product on 6/10/12.

What does this trigger need to do to check the current sales period? You need to query the BB_PRODUCT table to retrieve the current SALESTART and SALEEND dates for comparison. This is where the trouble begins. The row-level trigger is fired by an `UPDATE` issued on the BB_PRODUCT table, so the trigger considers the BB_PRODUCT table to be a mutating table; in other words, the table modification process has already started. However, you want to issue a query on this same table.

To understand this process, review the trigger code in Figure 9-25. This trigger fires when an `UPDATE` statement is attempted on a product's sales period and checks whether the new sales period overlaps an existing sales period. If so, the trigger raises an error.

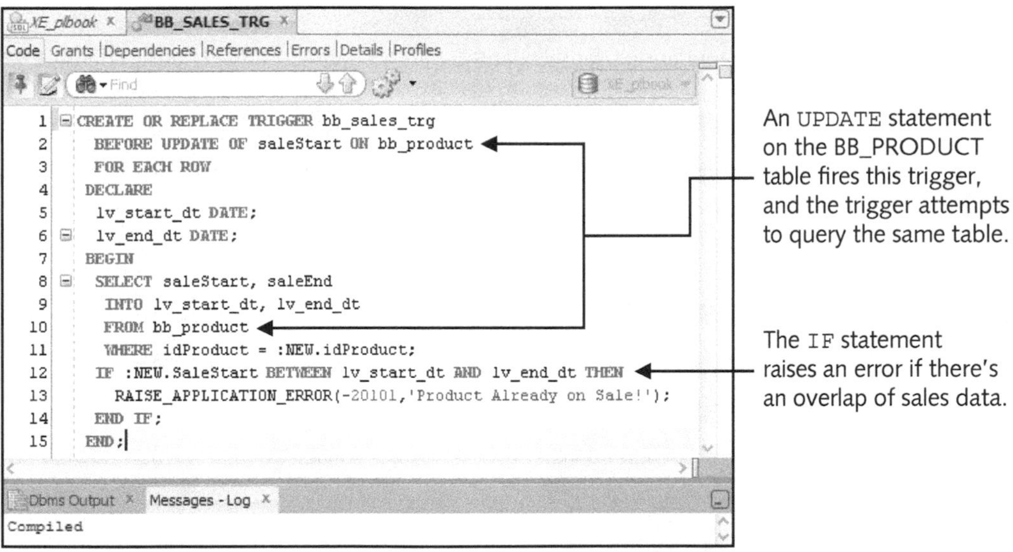

FIGURE 9-25 A trigger to test the mutating table problem

The query in Figure 9-26 confirms that a sales period currently exists for product 6. Now take a look at the attempted `UPDATE` in Figure 9-27. Because the system was currently in the middle of an update on the BB_PRODUCT table when the trigger fired and the trigger attempted to query the same table, the mutating table error was raised. This problem is specific to row-level triggers only because a statement-level trigger occurs in its entirety before or after the triggering DML statement.

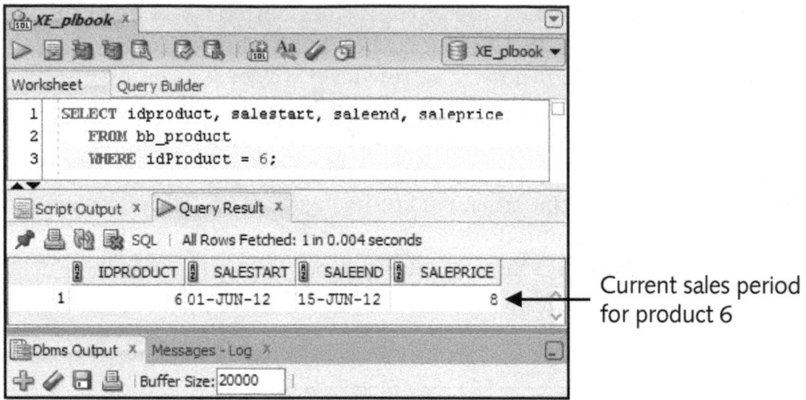

FIGURE 9-26 Current sales information for product 6

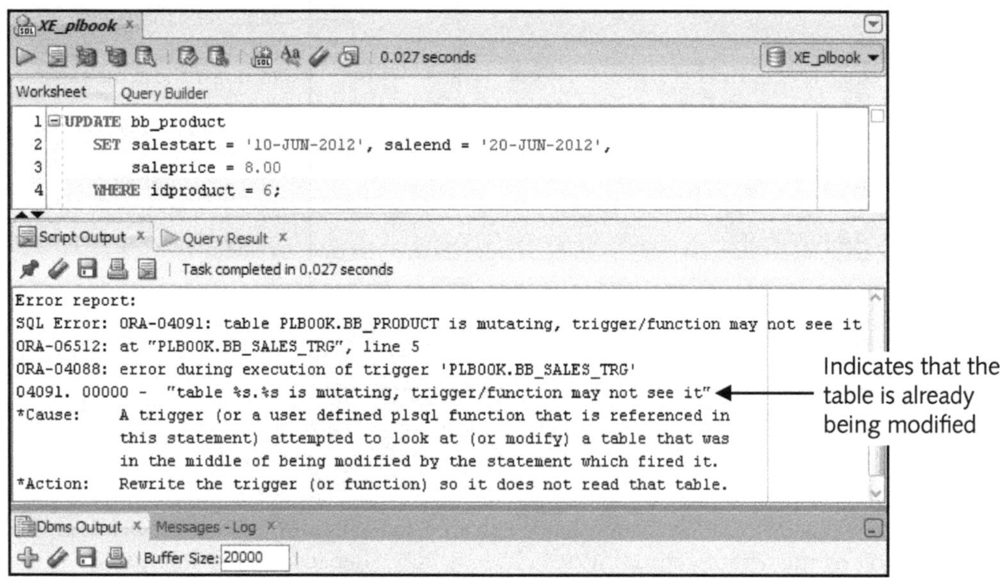

FIGURE 9-27 A DML action resulting in a mutating table error

So is there a way to work around this problem? In the past, this problem was solved by using a combination of statement-level and row-level triggers along with packaged variables as a workaround to a mutating table error. However, Oracle 11g introduced compound triggers, which allow combining all four triggering events into a single trigger object. BEFORE and AFTER statement-level and row-level actions can't be housed together in only one trigger, but these actions can share variable values. The trigger in Figure 9-28 is a compound trigger that could be used to solve the problem of the mutating sales period table. It includes statement-level and row-level activity and establishes a shared table of records variable that holds existing sales period data.

```
CREATE OR REPLACE TRIGGER bb_sales_trg
  FOR UPDATE OF salestart ON bb_product
  COMPOUND TRIGGER
    CURSOR sdates_cur IS
      SELECT idproduct, salestart, saleend
      FROM bb_product;
    TYPE slist_typ IS TABLE OF sdates_cur%ROWTYPE
      INDEX BY BINARY_INTEGER;
    sdates_tbl slist_typ;
    int NUMBER(2) := 0;
BEFORE STATEMENT IS
  BEGIN
  FOR rec IN sdates_cur LOOP
    int := int + 1;
    sdates_tbl(int).idproduct := rec.idproduct;
    sdates_tbl(int).salestart := rec.salestart;
    sdates_tbl(int).saleend := rec.saleend;
  END LOOP;
END BEFORE STATEMENT;
BEFORE EACH ROW IS
  lv_start_dt DATE;
  lv_end_dt DATE;
BEGIN
  FOR i IN 1..sdates_tbl.COUNT LOOP
    IF sdates_tbl(i).idproduct = :NEW.idProduct THEN
      lv_start_dt := sdates_tbl(i).salestart;
      lv_end_dt := sdates_tbl(i).saleend;
      EXIT;
    END IF;
  END LOOP;
  IF :NEW.SaleStart BETWEEN lv_start_dt AND lv_end_dt THEN
    RAISE_APPLICATION_ERROR(-20101,'Product Already on Sale!');
  END IF;
  END BEFORE EACH ROW;
END;
```

Compound trigger clause

Shared declaration area

Statement-level trigger

Row-level trigger

FIGURE 9-28 A compound trigger

After this compound trigger is created, a product sales period UPDATE statement is processed and is stopped if there's an overlapping sales period, as shown in Figure 9-29.

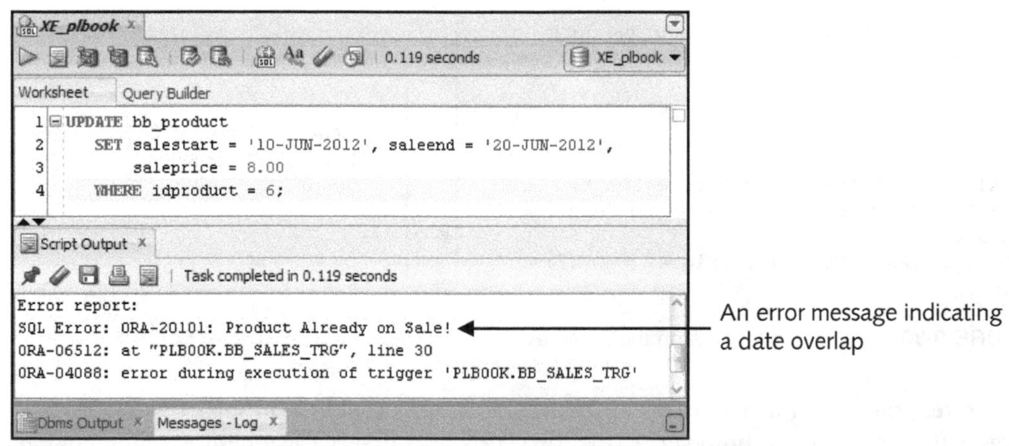

FIGURE 9-29 A compound trigger raises an error for overlapping sales dates

Here are two final notes on the mutating table problem:

- First, a table in an INSERT statement that fires a row-level trigger affecting the same table isn't considered a mutating table unless the INSERT includes a subquery.
- Second, there are restrictions on constraining tables. A **constraining table** is referenced via a foreign key constraint on the table a trigger is modifying. These tables might need to be queried by the trigger to enforce the referential integrity constraint. Therefore, the trigger body can't read or modify a constraining table's primary, unique, or foreign key columns.

Another important limitation is that triggers can't issue the transaction control statements COMMIT, ROLLBACK, and SAVEPOINT. If you do include a transaction control statement, the trigger compiles fine but then produces a runtime error when it's fired. This limitation includes any subprogram code a trigger calls, with the exception of a subprogram declared as an autonomous transaction.

Two other limitations deal with handling specific data types. No LONG or LONG RAW variables can be declared in triggers, and the NEW and OLD identifiers can't refer to these types of columns. In addition, LOB and OBJECT columns can be referenced in a trigger but can't be modified.

NOTE

LOB data types are used to store large objects, such as large text items or binary objects (for example, images). OBJECT data types are user-defined structures associated with object-oriented design.

TRIGGER-FIRING ORDER

In the past, one complication with having multiple DML triggers at the same level (statement or row) on the same object was that the order in which triggers fired couldn't be guaranteed. Oracle 11g introduced the trigger options FOLLOWS and PRECEDES to control the firing order of DML triggers. To see how they work, review the two triggers created in Figure 9-30. Both triggers are fired on the same event and are statement level. They simply display a row of output to indicate which trigger fired.

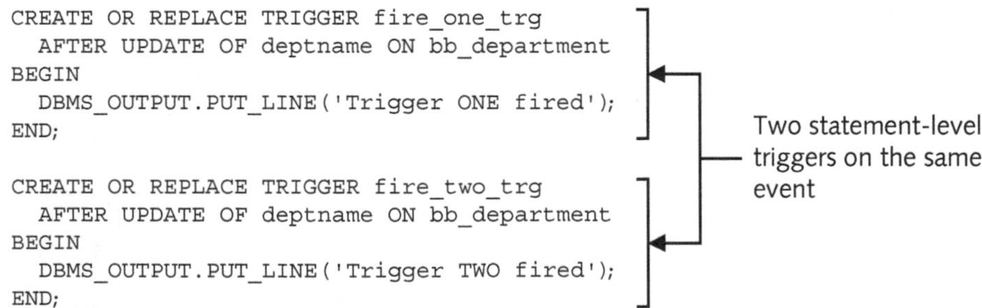

CREATE OR REPLACE TRIGGER fire_one_trg
  AFTER UPDATE OF deptname ON bb_department
BEGIN
  DBMS_OUTPUT.PUT_LINE('Trigger ONE fired');
END;
CREATE OR REPLACE TRIGGER fire_two_trg
  AFTER UPDATE OF deptname ON bb_department
BEGIN
  DBMS_OUTPUT.PUT_LINE('Trigger TWO fired');
END;
Two statement-level triggers on the same event

FIGURE 9-30 Using two triggers on the same event

To test the actual firing order, an UPDATE is issued, as shown in Figure 9-31. Both triggers fire; in this case, however, FIRE_TWO_TRG fires first. (A ROLLBACK statement can be used to undo the UPDATE changes.)

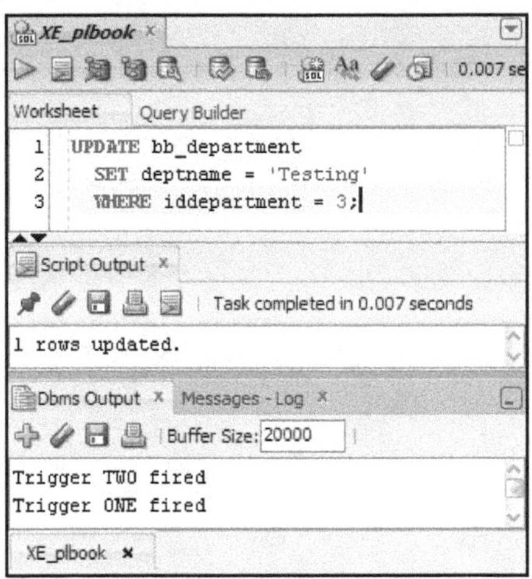

FIGURE 9-31 Confirming the trigger-firing order

The new FOLLOWS option is added to the FIRE_TWO_TRG trigger (see Figure 9-32) to force this trigger to fire after the FIRE_ONE_TRG trigger.

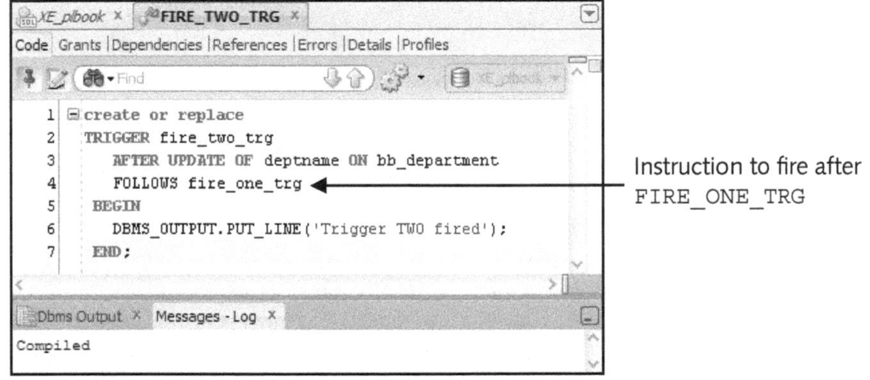

FIGURE 9-32 Adding the FOLLOWS option

The UPDATE statement is run again to test the firing order, and the FIRE_ONE_TRG trigger fires first (see Figure 9-33).

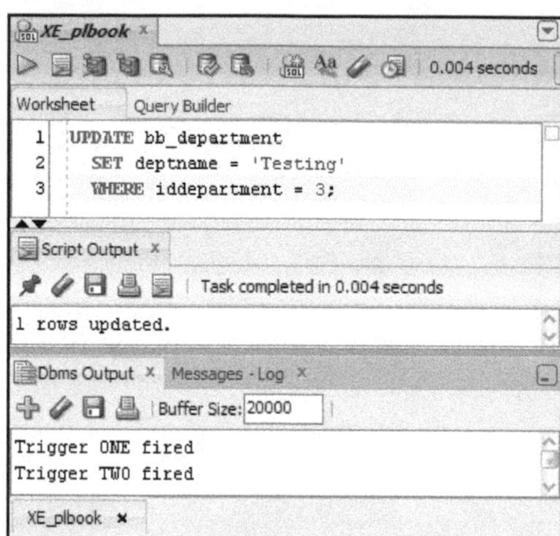

FIGURE 9-33 Confirming the new trigger-firing order

THE ALTER TRIGGER STATEMENT

The ALTER TRIGGER statement is used to recompile, enable, or disable a trigger. If a trigger body references a database object that's modified, the trigger's status is set to INVALID and must be recompiled. The following statement recompiles a trigger named SALES_TRG:

```
ALTER TRIGGER sales_trg COMPILE;
```

Another use of the ALTER TRIGGER statement is disabling and enabling a trigger. Disabling a trigger puts it on hold. It remains stored in the database, but it doesn't fire. Why would you disable a trigger? Sometimes you need to import a large amount of data into your database. If you know the data is already clean (that is, complies with all your business rules), you can save a lot of processing time by disabling triggers—and constraints, for that matter! Keep in mind that each row that's inserted is checked by every applicable constraint and fires off associated triggers. Inserting 500,000 rows, for example, takes a lot of processing. To disable or enable a specific trigger, use the following statement:

```
ALTER TRIGGER trigger_name DISABLE | ENABLE;
```

TIP

You should identify all the triggers you have created so far and disable them to avoid any confusion when building and testing triggers in the future.

If you want to enable or disable all triggers associated with a table, you can use the ALTER TABLE statement:

```
ALTER TABLE table_name DISABLE | ENABLE ALL TRIGGERS;
```

By default, when a trigger is created, it's enabled. As a developer, you might not want the trigger to be active as soon as you create it. Oracle 11g offers the DISABLED option for the CREATE TRIGGER statement so that the trigger is created in a disabled state. This option is part of the trigger header in the following example:

```
CREATE OR REPLACE TRIGGER fire_two_trg
  AFTER UPDATE OF deptname ON bb_department
  DISABLED
BEGIN
  DBMS_OUTPUT.PUT_LINE('Trigger TWO fired');
END;
```

DELETING A TRIGGER

As with all database objects, you can use the DROP statement to delete a trigger from the database, as shown in this example:

```
DROP TRIGGER trigger_name;
```

There's a striking difference in how dropping associated database objects affects triggers and program units. As you've learned, a program unit can use database objects but isn't tied to or associated with a specific object. DML triggers, however, are tied to a table or view. If a table that a procedure used is dropped, the procedure remains in the system but is marked with the status INVALID. However, if you drop a table or view that a DML trigger is built on, the trigger is dropped, too.

DATA DICTIONARY INFORMATION FOR TRIGGERS

You can query many of the same data dictionary views you use with program units to retrieve information on triggers, such as USER_OBJECTS, USER_DEPENDENCIES, and USER_ERRORS. However, the source code for triggers isn't in the USER_SOURCE view used for program units. For triggers, you use the USER_TRIGGERS data dictionary view, which maintains details on all triggers. Table 9-3 describes some columns in this view.

TABLE 9-3 Columns in the USER_TRIGGERS View

Column Name	Description
TRIGGER_NAME	Assigned name
TRIGGER_TYPE	Timing (such as BEFORE) and whether the trigger is row level or statement level
TRIGGERING_EVENT	Applicable DML, DDL, or system events
TABLE_NAME	Table or view name the trigger is associated with
BASE_OBJECT_TYPE	Type of object associated with the trigger: table, view, schema, or database
WHEN_CLAUSE	Code for a WHEN clause (if applicable)
STATUS	Enabled or disabled
DESCRIPTION	Summary of type and event information
TRIGGER_BODY	PL/SQL block in the trigger

A simple query retrieving the DESCRIPTION and TRIGGER_BODY columns, as shown in Figure 9-34, produces a helpful listing of details for a trigger. Scroll to the right to see the trigger body code in the output.

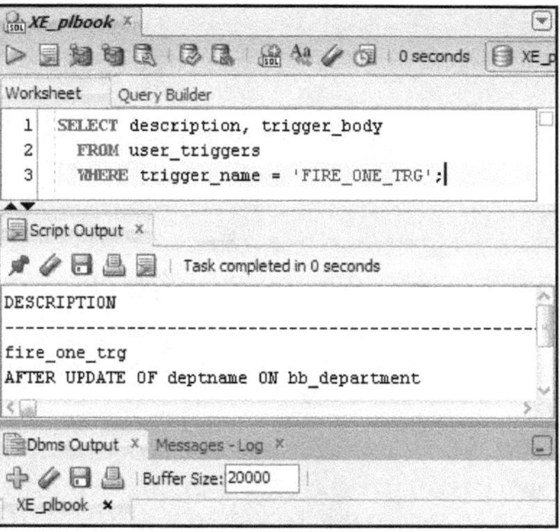

FIGURE 9-34 Querying `USER_TRIGGERS`

Keep in mind that you can always use the `USER_OBJECTS` data dictionary view to see a list of objects of a specific type. For example, the query in Figure 9-35 displays a list of all triggers in your schema.

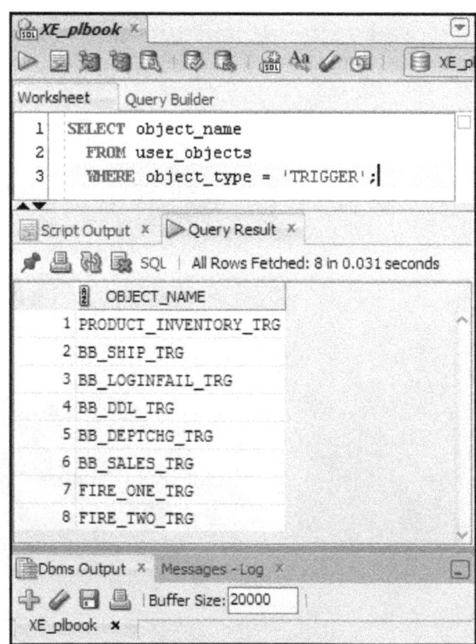

FIGURE 9-35 Querying for a list of all triggers

Chapter Summary

- A database trigger is a block of PL/SQL code that runs automatically when a particular database event occurs, such as a DML statement: INSERT, UPDATE, or DELETE.
- The CREATE TRIGGER statement must indicate what events cause the trigger to fire and whether the firing occurs before or after the event (by using the BEFORE or AFTER keyword).
- A row-level trigger is fired for each row the DML statement affects, and a statement-level trigger is fired only once for the DML action, regardless of the number of rows affected.
- The CREATE TRIGGER statement includes an optional WHEN clause that can check a condition to determine whether the trigger should fire.
- The correlation identifiers OLD and NEW are special PL/SQL bind variables that refer to the original and new values associated with the DML action that fires a trigger.
- Conditional predicates are clauses you can use in a trigger to handle different database-triggering events in a single trigger. They consist of an IF statement to establish the condition and a predicate, which is a verb specifying the DML action: INSERTING, UPDATING, or DELETING.
- An INSTEAD OF trigger is a PL/SQL block that runs in place of a DML action on a database view. Typically, it's used to allow modifying data through a view that can't be modified.
- System triggers are fired by database events, such as startup and shutdown, and server error messages. User event triggers are fired by users performing database actions, such as logons and logoffs, and issuing DML or DDL statements.
- Triggers can be used for a variety of purposes, including auditing, security measures, and checks for data integrity and referential integrity.
- A mutating table is one that's modified by a DML action when a trigger is fired. It causes an error if a trigger tries to reference the same table involved in the DML event that fires the trigger. This error can be corrected with compound triggers, which allow combining all four triggering events into a single trigger object.
- You can use the FOLLOWS and PRECEDES options to control the firing order of DML triggers.
- The ALTER TRIGGER statement is used to recompile, enable, or disable a trigger. If a trigger body references a database object that's modified, the trigger's status is set to INVALID and must be recompiled.
- To remove a trigger from the system, use the DROP statement. Because DML triggers are tied to a table or view, if you drop an object that a DML trigger is built on, the trigger is dropped, too.
- The USER_TRIGGERS data dictionary view contains trigger header information and source code.

Review Questions

1. Which of the following is a type of trigger? (Choose all that apply.)
   a. system
   b. transaction
   c. user event
   d. INSTEAD OF
2. If a trigger needs to fire when an UPDATE is issued on the CK_DATE column of the BB_JUNK table and needs to perform an INSERT on another table only if the UPDATE that fires the trigger succeeds, which event is needed in this trigger?
   a. BEFORE UPDATE ON bb_junk
   b. AFTER UPDATE ON bb_junk
   c. BEFORE UPDATE OF ck_date ON bb_junk
   d. AFTER UPDATE OF ck_date ON bb_junk

3. An INSTEAD OF trigger can be attached to which of the following database objects?
   a. view
   b. table
   c. sequence
   d. trigger
4. A mutating table error can occur only with which type of trigger?
   a. statement level
   b. row level
   c. system level
   d. none of the above
5. Which statement do you use to disable a trigger?
   a. ALTER TABLE
   b. MODIFY TRIGGER
   c. ALTER TRIGGER
   d. None of the above; the trigger must be dropped to be disabled.
6. What data dictionary view contains a trigger's source code?
   a. USER_OBJECTS
   b. USER_TRIGGERS
   c. USER_SOURCE
   d. USER_TRIGGER_CODE
7. Which events are available in a DML trigger? (Choose all that apply.)
   a. INSERT
   b. UPDATE
   c. DELETE
   d. SELECT

8. Conditional predicates enable triggers to do which of the following?
   a. identify different actions for different events
   b. refer to original and new values in an `UPDATE` statement
   c. add a `WHEN` clause to the trigger
   d. add a condition that must be met before the trigger fires
9. Correlation identifiers enable triggers to do which of the following?
   a. identify different actions for different events
   b. refer to original and new values in an `UPDATE` statement
   c. add a `WHEN` clause to the trigger
   d. add a condition that must be met before the trigger fires
10. What clause can be used to change the names of correlation identifiers?
    a. `INSTEAD OF`
    b. `REFERENCING`
    c. `WHEN`
    d. None of the above; these names can't be changed.
11. System triggers fire on ________________. (Choose all that apply.)
    a. database events, such as `STARTUP`
    b. DDL statements, such as `ALTER TABLE`
    c. DML statements, such as `UPDATE`
    d. transaction control statements, such as `COMMIT`
12. How is a trigger different from a procedure?
    a. A trigger doesn't need to be called by name.
    b. A trigger needs to be called by name.
    c. A trigger contains a PL/SQL block.
    d. A trigger can refer to packaged variables.
13. An `AFTER UPDATE` trigger can be attached to which of the following?
    a. table
    b. view
    c. procedure
    d. DDL event
14. Which correlation identifier contains values in an `INSERT` trigger?
    a. `OLD`
    b. `NEW`
    c. `REFERENCE`
    d. none of the above
15. Explain the mutating table problem with database triggers.
16. Describe two typical uses of triggers.
17. What are the fundamental differences between a program unit (procedure and function) and a database trigger?

18. Explain why the NEW correlation identifier contains no values when associated with a DELETE event.
19. What is a compound trigger?

Advanced Review Questions

1. If the following statement runs, what happens to existing triggers for this table?

```
DROP TABLE bb_junk;
```

   a. The triggers are disabled.
   b. The triggers are dropped.
   c. The triggers aren't affected.
   d. The triggers' status is marked as INVALID.

2. When an UPDATE statement is issued on the BB_JUNK table, which of the following triggers fires first?

```
CREATE TRIGGER trig_1
  BEFORE UPDATE OF ck_date ON item_sale
FOR EACH ROW
BEGIN
  CALL proc_1
END;
CREATE TRIGGER trig_2
  BEFORE UPDATE OF ck_date ON item_sale
BEGIN
  CALL proc_2
END;
```

   a. TRIG_1
   b. TRIG_2
   c. PROC_2
   d. can't be determined

3. With this trigger header, which of the following statements deletes the trigger from the database?

```
CREATE TRIGGER trig_1
  BEFORE DELETE ON item_sale
```

   a. ALTER TABLE item_sale DELETE ALL TRIGGERS;
   b. ALTER TABLE item_sale DROP ALL TRIGGERS;
   c. DROP TRIGGER trig_1;
   d. DELETE TRIGGER trig_1;

4. A row-level trigger is the only type of trigger that can include which of the following?
   a. a WHEN clause
   b. conditional predicates
   c. correlation identifiers
   d. an OF column clause

5. If a trigger is fired from an `INSERT` statement, which of the following situations raises a mutating table error if the trigger includes a DML action on the same table used in the `INSERT` statement?
    a. The table is in the middle of being modified.
    b. The trigger is a statement-level trigger.
    c. The trigger is a row-level trigger.
    d. The trigger is a row-level trigger, and the `INSERT` includes a subquery.

Hands-On Assignments Part I

Assignment 9-1: Creating a Trigger to Handle Product Restocking

Brewbean's has a couple of columns in the product table to assist in inventory tracking. The REORDER column contains the stock level at which the product should be reordered. If the stock falls to this level, Brewbean's wants the application to insert a row in the BB_PRODUCT_REQUEST table automatically to alert the ordering clerk that additional inventory is needed. Brewbean's currently uses the reorder level amount as the quantity that should be ordered. This task can be handled by using a trigger.

1. Take out some scrap paper and a pencil. Think about the tasks the triggers needs to perform, including checking whether the new stock level falls below the reorder point. If so, check whether the product is already on order by viewing the product request table; if not, enter a new product request. Try to write the trigger code on paper. Even though you learn a lot by reviewing code, you improve your skills faster when you create the code on your own.
2. Open the **`c9reorder.txt`** file in the Chapter09 folder. Review this trigger code, and determine how it compares with your code.
3. In SQL Developer, create the trigger with the provided code.
4. Test the trigger with product ID **4**. First, run the query shown in Figure 9-36 to verify the current stock data for this product. Notice that a sale of one more item should initiate a reorder.

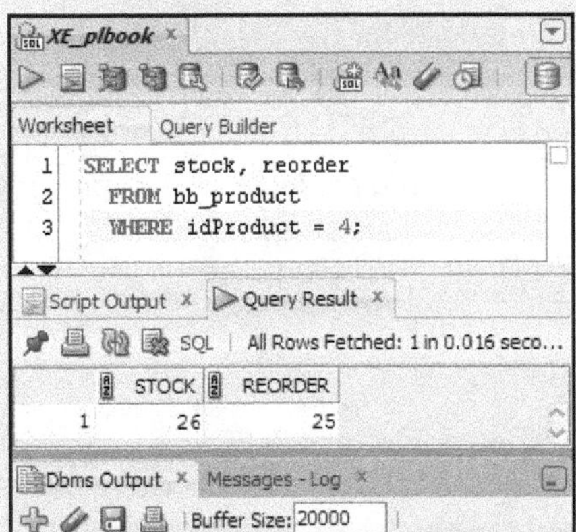

FIGURE 9-36 Checking stock data

5. Run the UPDATE statement shown in Figure 9-37. It should cause the trigger to fire. Notice the query to check whether the trigger fired and whether a product stock request was inserted in the BB_PRODUCT_REQUEST table.

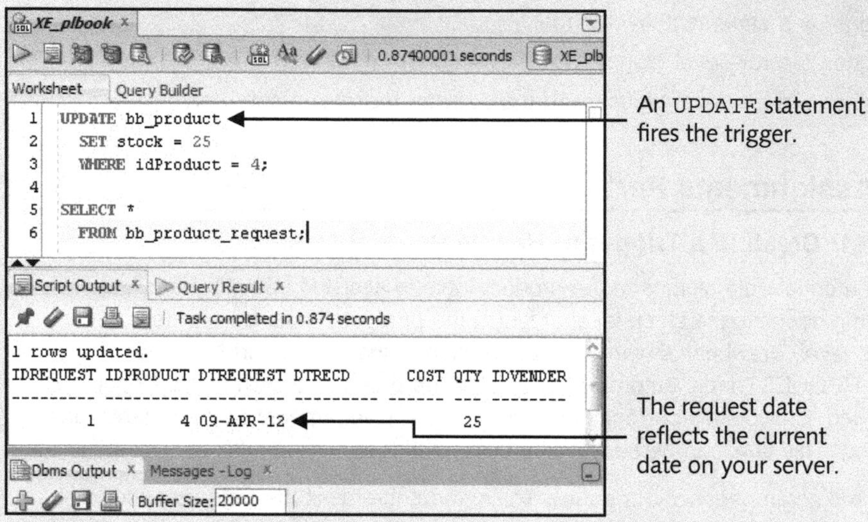

FIGURE 9-37 Updating the stock level for product 4

6. Issue a ROLLBACK statement to undo these DML actions to restore data to its original state for use in later assignments.
7. Run the following statement to disable this trigger so that it doesn't affect other projects:

```
ALTER TRIGGER bb_reorder_trg DISABLE;
```

Assignment 9-2: Updating Stock Information When a Product Request Is Filled

Brewbean's has a BB_PRODUCT_REQUEST table where requests to refill stock levels are inserted automatically via a trigger. After the stock level falls below the reorder level, this trigger fires and enters a request in the table. This procedure works great; however, when store clerks record that the product request has been filled by updating the table's DTRECD and COST columns, they want the stock level in the product table to be updated. Create a trigger named **BB_REQFILL_TRG** to handle this task, using the following steps as a guideline:

1. In SQL Developer, run the following INSERT statement to create a product request you can use in this assignment:

```
INSERT INTO bb_product_request (idRequest, idProduct, dtRequest, qty)
  VALUES (3, 5, SYSDATE, 45);
COMMIT;
```

2. Create the trigger (BB_REQFILL_TRG) so that it fires when a received date is entered in the BB_PRODUCT_REQUEST table. This trigger needs to modify the STOCK column in the BB_PRODUCT table to reflect the increased inventory.
3. Now test the trigger. First, query the stock and reorder data for product **5**, as shown in Figure 9-38.

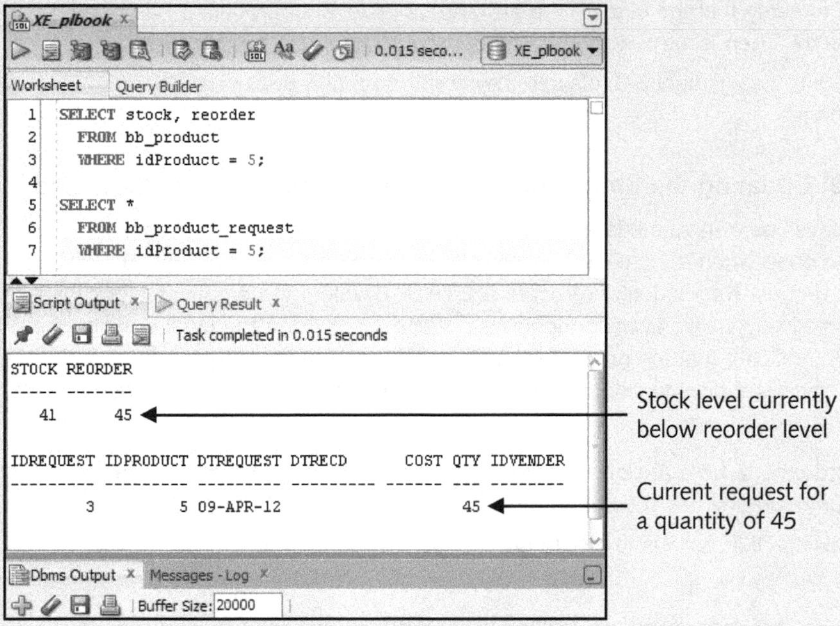

FIGURE 9-38 Querying the data for product 5 stock and reorder amount

4. Now update the product request to record it as fulfilled by using the `UPDATE` statement shown in Figure 9-39.

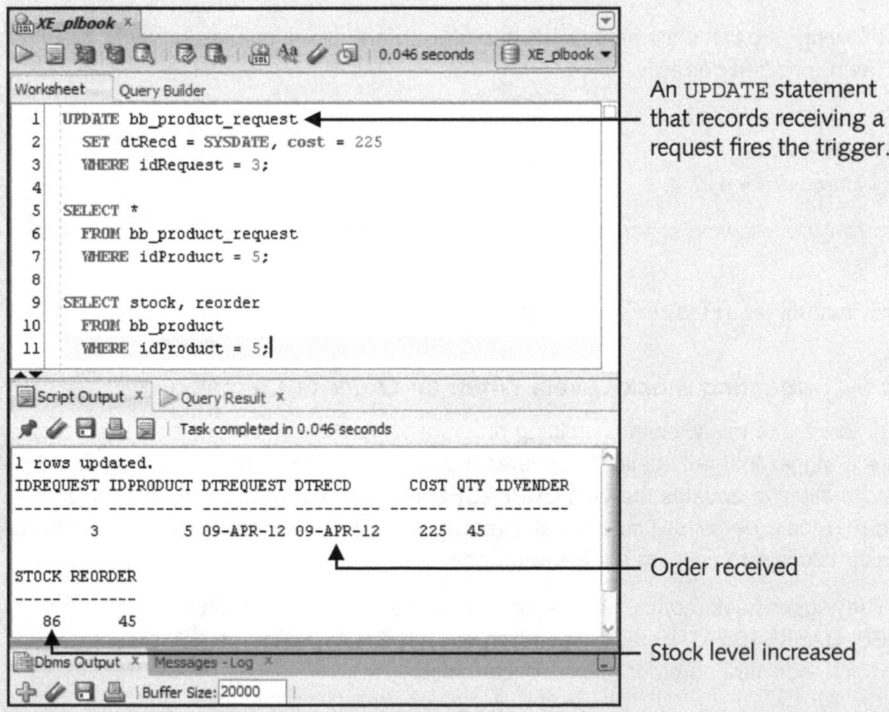

FIGURE 9-39 Updating the product request

5. Issue queries to verify that the trigger fired and the stock level of product 5 has been modified correctly. Then issue a ROLLBACK statement to undo the modifications.
6. If you aren't doing Assignment 9-3, disable the trigger so that it doesn't affect other assignments.

Assignment 9-3: Updating the Stock Level If a Product Fulfillment Is Canceled

The Brewbean's developers have made progress on the inventory-handling processes; however, they hit a snag when a store clerk incorrectly recorded a product request as fulfilled. When the product request was updated to record a DTRECD value, the product's stock level was updated automatically via an existing trigger, BB_REQFILL_TRG. If the clerk empties the DTRECD column to indicate that the product request hasn't been filled, the product's stock level needs to be corrected or reduced, too. Modify the **BB_REQFILL_TRG** trigger to solve this problem.

1. Modify the trigger code from Assignment 9-2 as needed. Add code to check whether the DTRECD column already has a date in it and is now being set to NULL.
2. Issue the following DML actions to create and update rows that you can use to test the trigger:

```
INSERT INTO bb_product_request (idRequest, idProduct, dtRequest, qty,
  dtRecd, cost)
  VALUES (4, 5, SYSDATE, 45, '15-JUN-2012',225);
UPDATE bb_product
  SET stock = 86
  WHERE idProduct = 5;
COMMIT;
```

3. Run the following UPDATE statement to test the trigger, and issue queries to verify that the data has been modified correctly.

```
UPDATE bb_product_request
  SET dtRecd = NULL
  WHERE idRequest = 4;
```

4. Be sure to run the following statement to disable this trigger so that it doesn't affect other assignments:

```
ALTER TRIGGER bb_reqfill_trg DISABLE;
```

Assignment 9-4: Updating Stock Levels When an Order Is Canceled

At times, customers make mistakes in submitting orders and call to cancel an order. Brewbean's wants to create a trigger that automatically updates the stock level of all products associated with a canceled order and updates the ORDERPLACED column of the BB_BASKET table to zero, reflecting that the order wasn't completed. Create a trigger named **BB_ORDCANCEL_TRG** to perform this task, taking into account the following points:

- The trigger needs to fire when a new status record is added to the BB_BASKETSTATUS table and when the IDSTAGE column is set to 4, which indicates an order has been canceled.

- Each basket can contain multiple items in the BB_BASKETITEM table, so a `CURSOR FOR` loop might be a suitable mechanism for updating each item's stock level.
- Keep in mind that coffee can be ordered in half or whole pounds.
- Use basket 6, which contains two items, for testing.

1. Run this `INSERT` statement to test the trigger:

```
INSERT INTO bb_basketstatus (idStatus, idBasket, idStage, dtStage)
  VALUES (bb_status_seq.NEXTVAL, 6, 4, SYSDATE);
```

2. Issue queries to confirm that the trigger has modified the basket's order status and product stock levels correctly.
3. Be sure to run the following statement to disable this trigger so that it doesn't affect other assignments:

```
ALTER TRIGGER bb_ordcancel_trg DISABLE;
```


Assignment 9-5: Processing Discounts

Brewbean's is offering a new discount for return shoppers: Every fifth completed order gets a 10% discount. The count of orders for a shopper is placed in a packaged variable named `pv_disc_num` during the ordering process. This count needs to be tested at checkout to determine whether a discount should be applied. Create a trigger named **BB_DISCOUNT_TRG** so that when an order is confirmed (the ORDERPLACED value is changed from 0 to 1), the `pv_disc_num` packaged variable is checked. If it's equal to 5, set a second variable named `pv_disc_txt` to `Y`. This variable is used in calculating the order summary so that a discount is applied, if necessary.

Create a package specification named **DISC_PKG** containing the necessary packaged variables. Use an anonymous block to initialize the packaged variables to use for testing the trigger. Test the trigger with the following `UPDATE` statement:

```
UPDATE bb_basket
  SET orderplaced = 1
  WHERE idBasket = 13;
```

If you need to test the trigger multiple times, simply reset the ORDERPLACED column to 0 for basket 13 and then run the `UPDATE` again. Also, disable this trigger when you're finished so that it doesn't affect other assignments.

Assignment 9-6: Using Triggers to Maintain Referential Integrity

At times, Brewbean's has changed the ID numbers for existing products. In the past, developers had to add a new product row with the new ID to the BB_PRODUCT table, modify all the corresponding BB_BASKETITEM and BB_PRODUCTOPTION table rows, and then delete the original product row. Can a trigger be developed to avoid all these steps and handle the update of the BB_BASKETITEM and BB_PRODUCTOPTION table rows automatically for a change in product ID? If so, create the trigger and test it by issuing an `UPDATE` statement that changes the IDPRODUCT 7 to **22**. Do a rollback to return the data to its original state, and disable the new trigger after you have finished this assignment.

Assignment 9-7: Updating Summary Data Tables

The Brewbean's owner uses several summary sales data tables every day to monitor business activity. The BB_SALES_SUM table holds the product ID, total sales in dollars, and total quantity sold for each product. A trigger is needed so that every time an order is confirmed or the ORDERPLACED column is updated to 1, the BB_SALES_SUM table is updated accordingly. Create a trigger named **BB_SALESUM_TRG** that performs this task. Before testing, reset the ORDERPLACED column to 0 for basket 3, as shown in the following code, and use this basket to test the trigger:

```
UPDATE bb_basket
  SET orderplaced = 0
  WHERE idBasket = 3;
```


Notice that the BB_SALES_SUM table already contains some data. Test the trigger with the following UPDATE statement, and confirm that the trigger is working correctly:

```
UPDATE bb_basket
  SET orderplaced = 1
  WHERE idBasket = 3;
```

Do a rollback and disable the trigger when you're finished so that it doesn't affect other assignments.

Assignment 9-8: Maintaining an Audit Trail of Product Table Changes

The accuracy of product table data is critical, and the Brewbean's owner wants to have an audit file containing information on all DML activity on the BB_PRODUCT table. This information should include the ID of the user performing the DML action, the date, the original values of the changed row, and the new values. This audit table needs to track specific columns of concern, including PRODUCTNAME, PRICE, SALESTART, SALEEND, and SALEPRICE. Create a table named **BB_PRODCHG_AUDIT** to hold the relevant data, and then create a trigger named **BB_AUDIT_TRG** that fires an update to this table whenever a specified column in the BB_PRODUCT table changes.

TIP

Multiple columns can be listed in a trigger's OF clause by separating them with commas.

Be sure to issue the following command. If you created the SALES_DATE_TRG trigger in the chapter, it conflicts with this assignment.

```
ALTER TRIGGER sales_date_trg DISABLE;
```

Use the following UPDATE statement to test the trigger:

```
UPDATE bb_product
  SET salestart = '05-MAY-2012',
    saleend = '12-MAY-2012'
    saleprice = 9
  WHERE idProduct = 10;
```

When you're finished, do a rollback and disable the trigger so that it doesn't affect other assignments.

Hands-On Assignments Part II

Assignment 9-9: Tracking Pledge Payment Activity

The DoGood Donor organization wants to track all pledge payment activity. Each time a pledge payment is added, changed, or removed, the following information should be captured in a separate table: username (logon), current date, action taken (`INSERT`, `UPDATE`, or `DELETE`), and the `idpay` value for the payment record. Create a table named **DD_PAYTRACK** to hold this information. Include a primary key column to be populated by a sequence, and create a new sequence named **`DD_PTRACK_SEQ`** for the primary key column. Create a single trigger for recording the requested information to track pledge payment activity, and test the trigger.

Assignment 9-10: Identifying First Pledges

The DD_PLEDGE table contains the FIRSTPLEDGE column that indicates whether a pledge is the donor's first pledge. The DoGood Donor organization wants this identification to be automated. Create a trigger that adds the corresponding data to the FIRSTPLEDGE column when a new pledge is added, and test the trigger.

Case Projects

Case 9-1: Mapping the Flow of Database Triggers

After you learn how to create triggers, you realize that one statement can end up firing off a number of triggers. Not only can you have multiple triggers attached to a single table, but also a trigger can perform DML operations that might affect other tables and fire off other triggers. To prevent this problem, you might be able to combine triggers to make your code clearer and easier to maintain. For example, if you have one trigger for an `INSERT` statement on the BB_PRODUCT table and another for an `UPDATE` statement on the BB_PRODUCT table, you might want to combine them into one trigger and use conditional predicates. In addition, triggers that run DML statements that could fire off additional triggers could lead to a mutating table error. However, this error might not be apparent unless you identify the flow of trigger processing and associated objects.

Review the `CREATE TRIGGER` statements in the **`c9case1.txt`** file in the Chapter09 folder. Prepare a flowchart illustrating which triggers will fire and the firing sequence if a user logs on and issues the following code:

```
UPDATE bb_product
  SET stock = 50
  WHERE idProduct = 3;
```

Case 9-2: Processing Inventory for More Movies

The More Movies company needs to make sure the quantity of each movie is updated for each rental recorded and returned. The MM_MOVIE table contains the MOVIE_QTY column that reflects the current number of copies in stock for a movie. Create triggers that update the MOVIE_QTY column for rentals (named **MM_RENT_TRG**) and returns (named **MM_RETURN_TRG**). Test your triggers with the following DML actions, which add a rental and update it to reflect that it has been returned. Issue queries to confirm that the triggers fired and worked correctly.

```
INSERT INTO mm_rental (rental_id, member_id, movie_id,
  payment_methods_id)
  VALUES (13, 10, 6, 2);
UPDATE mm_rental
  SET checkin_date = SYSDATE
  WHERE rental_id = 13;
```

CHAPTER **10**

ORACLE-SUPPLIED PACKAGES, DYNAMIC SQL, AND HIDING SOURCE CODE

LEARNING OBJECTIVES

After completing this chapter, you should be able to understand:

- Generating output via packages
- Including large objects in the Oracle database
- Using communication packages
- Using important built-in packages
- Exploring dynamic SQL and PL/SQL
- Hiding PL/SQL source code

INTRODUCTION

Oracle includes built-in features to address many common operations. PL/SQL users should be familiar with Oracle-supplied or built-in packages, which are complete packages that extend the functionality of PL/SQL. Each Oracle-supplied package comes with parameters, just like the packages you construct. Reviewing the scripts that create each package is helpful; you can find them in the rdbms\admin directory of the Oracle 11*g* database software. You can open these scripts with a text editor; they contain comments documenting the code. This chapter introduces a handful of frequently used packages. A few are covered in some detail to give you a good foundation in how to analyze and use built-ins. These packages are discussed in the following categories: output, large objects, communication, miscellaneous, and dynamic SQL.

THE CURRENT CHALLENGE IN THE BREWBEAN'S APPLICATION

The Brewbean's lead programmer has compiled a list of the most important functionality needs to address for the Web application. This list includes a communication mechanism for submitting and verifying credit card information, real-time messages to notify personnel when product inventory falls below the restocking level, automatic creation of e-mails to confirm customer purchases, the capability to read external text files to import product information from vendors, the capability to integrate product images into the database to be displayed on the Web site, and automatic submission of programs that can be scheduled to run during low-usage hours.

In talking with colleagues at other companies, Brewbean's programmers determined that many of these functions are available with Oracle's built-in capabilities. First, the lead programmer narrowed down a list of Oracle-supplied packages to explore. Table 10-1 lists information on each package covered in this chapter. Notice that all built-in package names begin with the prefix `DBMS_` or `UTL_`.

TABLE 10-1 Built-in Packages

Chapter Section	Built-in Package Name	Description	Script Filename
"Generating Output"	`DBMS_OUTPUT`	Displays data onscreen	`dbmsotpt.sql`
"Generating Output"	`UTL_FILE`	Reads and writes data to external files	`utlfile.sql`
"Large Objects"	`DBMS_LOB`	Creates and manipulates LOBs in the database	`dbmslob.sql`
"Communication Capabilities"	`DBMS_ALERT`	Handles notification of database events	`dbmsalrt.sql`
"Communication Capabilities"	`UTL_MAIL`	Enables e-mail features	`utlmail.sql`
"Communication Capabilities"	`UTL_HTTP`	Enables HTML retrieval	`utlhttp.sql`
"Additional Packages"	`DBMS_DDL`	Provides access to DDL statements not allowed directly in PL/SQL	`dbmsdesc.sql`
"Dynamic SQL and PL/SQL"	`DBMS_SQL`	Constructs and parses statements at runtime	`dbmssql.sql`

Rebuilding the Database

To rebuild the Brewbean's database, follow these steps:

1. Make sure you have the `c10_BBcreate.sql` file in the Chapter10 folder. This file contains the script for creating the database.
2. Start SQL Developer and connect to the Oracle database.
3. Click **File**, **Open** from the menu.
4. Click the **`c10_BBcreate.sql`** file, and then click **Open**. The code in this script is displayed in the Edit pane. Scroll through the SQL statements; they should look familiar.

5. Run the script by clicking the **Run Script** button on the Edit pane toolbar. If necessary, click **OK** in the Select Connection dialog box.
6. Scroll through the Script Output pane at the bottom to review the results of the statements.
7. In the Connections pane on the left, expand the **Tables** node to view the tables that were created. While this node is selected, click the **Refresh** button at the top of the Connections pane to update the list of tables.

NOTE

Keep in mind that errors on DROP commands simply indicate that the objects didn't exist previously.

GENERATING OUTPUT

Built-in packages offer a variety of methods to create output in a PL/SQL block. This section covers two basic, widely used packages: DBMS_OUTPUT and UTL_FILE. DBMS_OUTPUT is used for displaying data onscreen, and UTL_FILE is used for reading from and writing to external files.

The DBMS_OUTPUT Package

The DBMS_OUTPUT package is used to display messages onscreen from a stored program unit or an anonymous block. You have used this package's PUT_LINE procedure quite a bit already to display and check values in PL/SQL blocks while constructing code for the Brewbean's application. As a matter of fact, debugging is a popular use of this package.

When a stored program is running, any DBMS_OUTPUT lines are placed in an output buffer, which dumps its contents to the screen when the program has finished running. These output lines are displayed only after execution is finished; they can't be displayed in real time. However, numerous DBMS_OUTPUT statements can be used in a block, which is quite helpful for checking values at different points in the execution. Table 10-2 lists procedures in this package.

TABLE 10-2 DBMS_OUTPUT Procedures

Procedure Name	Description
ENABLE	Permits message display
DISABLE	Blocks message display
PUT	Places information in the buffer
PUT_LINE	Places information in the buffer followed by an end-of-line marker
NEW_LINE	Places an end-of-line marker in the buffer
GET_LINE	Retrieves a line from the buffer
GET_LINES	Retrieves an array of lines from the buffer

This package is enabled by default, so you need to run the ENABLE procedure only if a DISABLE procedure has been run previously. This procedure has only one parameter for the buffer size, which is set in bytes. The default value is 20000, so you don't need to set any values to run the ENABLE procedure. The maximum buffer size is 1 MB. The DISABLE procedure, of course, does the opposite—disables all procedures in the package except ENABLE. DISABLE has no parameters.

The PUT and PUT_LINE procedures place information in the buffer for display. These procedures accept one value that can be the data type VARCHAR2, NUMBER, or DATE. If needed, you can use concatenation or data type–conversion functions to create a single value from several different values. The major difference between the two procedures is that PUT_LINE adds a new line marker in the buffer; PUT continues placing information on the same line in the buffer. Try using PUT and PUT_LINE in the following steps:

1. Start SQL Developer, if necessary.
2. To make sure DBMS_OUTPUT display is enabled in your SQL Developer session so that the output buffer can be displayed, enter the following anonymous block:

```
BEGIN
  DBMS_OUTPUT.PUT('This');
  DBMS_OUTPUT.PUT(' is a ');
  DBMS_OUTPUT.PUT('test');
  DBMS_OUTPUT.PUT_LINE('This is test 2');
  DBMS_OUTPUT.PUT('Working?');
END;
```

3. Compare the display with Figure 10-1.

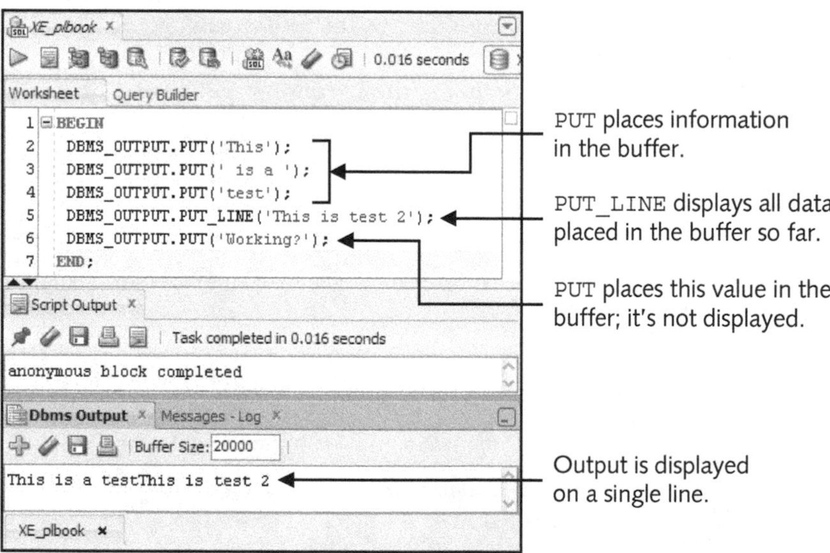

FIGURE 10-1 Using the PUT and PUT_LINE procedures

4. Add the following code line in two places: after the third DBMS_OUTPUT.PUT statement (before the DBMS_OUTPUT.PUT_LINE statement in line 5 in Figure 10-1) and as the last line in the block (see Figure 10-2).

   DBMS_OUTPUT.NEW_LINE;

5. Run the block, and compare the display with Figure 10-2. Notice that the NEW_LINE procedure forces the display of lines in the buffer.

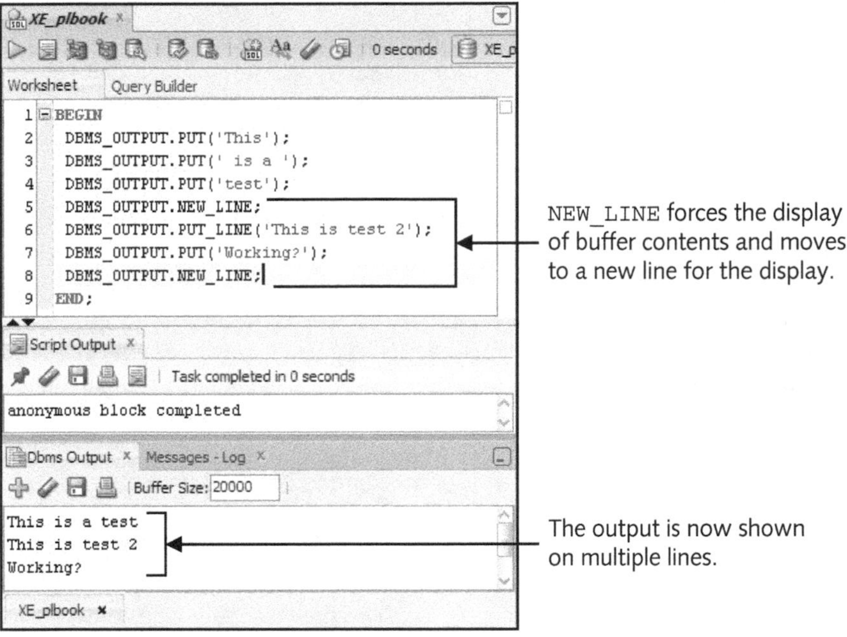

FIGURE 10-2 Using the NEW_LINE procedure

The GET_LINE and GET_LINES procedures retrieve values from the buffer, but this task isn't necessary in SQL Developer because the buffer display is handled automatically. However, other application development environments, such as Java, require using these procedures to retrieve buffer information. You can also use these procedures to extract information that another program unit placed in the buffer. The GET_LINE procedure has two OUT parameters, as the following header shows:

```
DBMS_OUTPUT.GET_LINE
  (line     OUT  VARCHAR2,
   status   OUT  INTEGER);
```

The line parameter holds the line retrieved from the buffer, which can be up to 255 bytes. The status parameter contains a 0 if the procedure runs successfully and a 1 if it doesn't. If there are no lines in the buffer to retrieve, the status 1 is returned.

The GET_LINES procedure retrieves multiple lines from the output buffer. This procedure has one OUT and one IN OUT parameter, as shown in the following header:

```
DBMS_OUTPUT.GET_LINES
  (lines      OUT     CHARARR,
   numlines   IN OUT  INTEGER);
```

> **NOTE**
>
> The CHARARR data type is a table of VARCHAR2(255).

The lines parameter holds the returned lines; the maximum length of each line is 255 bytes. The numlines parameter accepts a numeric value that specifies the number of lines to retrieve and returns the number of lines actually retrieved. For example, you can supply the value 40 for the numlines parameter, but there are only 35 lines in the buffer, so these lines are retrieved and 35 is returned in the numlines parameter.

Brewbean's is considering using the DBMS_OUTPUT package and the PUT and GET_LINES procedures to log debugging information. Exception handlers include DBMS_OUTPUT.PUT_LINE statements to place information in a buffer and then call a procedure that reads the buffer and inserts messages in a log table. Try this task in the following steps:

1. Start SQL Developer, if necessary. Make sure DBMS_OUTPUT display is enabled in your SQL Developer session so that the output buffer is available.
2. Open the **buffer10.txt** file in the Chapter10 folder. Review the code for creating the two procedures shown in Figure 10-3. The BSK_QUERY_SP procedure attempts to retrieve data for a specific basket. If no data is retrieved, information is written to the output buffer. The EXCEPT_LOG_SP procedure inserts the buffer information in a table. Create the two procedures in SQL Developer.

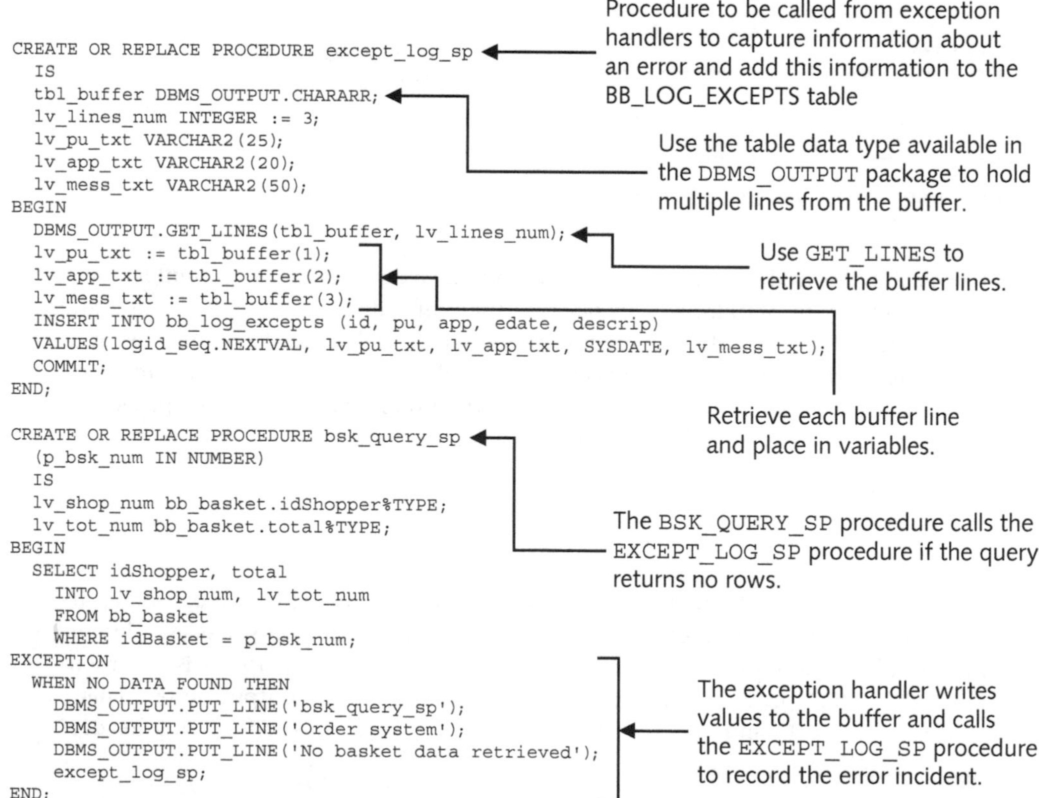

```
CREATE OR REPLACE PROCEDURE except_log_sp
  IS
  tbl_buffer DBMS_OUTPUT.CHARARR;
  lv_lines_num INTEGER := 3;
  lv_pu_txt VARCHAR2(25);
  lv_app_txt VARCHAR2(20);
  lv_mess_txt VARCHAR2(50);
BEGIN
  DBMS_OUTPUT.GET_LINES(tbl_buffer, lv_lines_num);
  lv_pu_txt := tbl_buffer(1);
  lv_app_txt := tbl_buffer(2);
  lv_mess_txt := tbl_buffer(3);
  INSERT INTO bb_log_excepts (id, pu, app, edate, descrip)
  VALUES(logid_seq.NEXTVAL, lv_pu_txt, lv_app_txt, SYSDATE, lv_mess_txt);
  COMMIT;
END;

CREATE OR REPLACE PROCEDURE bsk_query_sp
  (p_bsk_num IN NUMBER)
  IS
  lv_shop_num bb_basket.idShopper%TYPE;
  lv_tot_num bb_basket.total%TYPE;
BEGIN
  SELECT idShopper, total
    INTO lv_shop_num, lv_tot_num
    FROM bb_basket
    WHERE idBasket = p_bsk_num;
EXCEPTION
  WHEN NO_DATA_FOUND THEN
    DBMS_OUTPUT.PUT_LINE('bsk_query_sp');
    DBMS_OUTPUT.PUT_LINE('Order system');
    DBMS_OUTPUT.PUT_LINE('No basket data retrieved');
    except_log_sp;
END;
```

Procedure to be called from exception handlers to capture information about an error and add this information to the BB_LOG_EXCEPTS table
Use the table data type available in the DBMS_OUTPUT package to hold multiple lines from the buffer.
Use GET_LINES to retrieve the buffer lines.
Retrieve each buffer line and place in variables.
The BSK_QUERY_SP procedure calls the EXCEPT_LOG_SP procedure if the query returns no rows.
The exception handler writes values to the buffer and calls the EXCEPT_LOG_SP procedure to record the error incident.

FIGURE 10-3 Procedures to test DBMS_OUTPUT.GET_LINES

3. Test the procedures by entering the following statement. Basket 88 doesn't exist and raises the NO_DATA_FOUND error. You won't see an error message because the BSK_QUERY_SP procedure contains an exception handler.

```
BEGIN
  bsk_query_sp(88);
END;
```

4. Query the BB_LOG_EXCEPTS table to determine whether the values were inserted (see Figure 10-4).

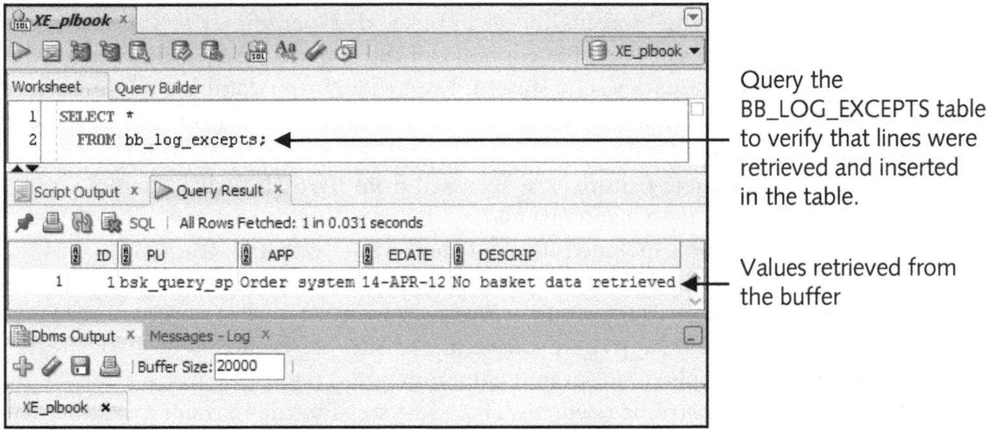

FIGURE 10-4 Testing the buffer procedures

In this example, the DBMS_OUTPUT.GET_LINES procedure is used to capture values from multiple lines of the buffer. You don't see any values displayed from the DBMS_OUTPUT.PUT_LINE statements because the GET_LINES procedure retrieves and then clears the buffer.

The UTL_FILE Package

The UTL_FILE package allows access to files stored on an operating system that are accessible from the database server, so you can read from and write to external files. This function is useful if another party provides data in the form of a text file. For example, say Brewbean's decides to add a large selection of teas from one vendor, who can provide a text file containing product information, such as name and description. Using the UTL_FILE features can automate adding these items to the product inventory table. In addition, the Brewbean's manager might want to use data exported from the database in analysis software, such as a spreadsheet program. Table 10-3 lists some programs in the UTL_FILE package that you use to test reading from and writing to a text file.

TABLE 10-3 A Partial List of UTL_FILE Programs

Program Unit Name	Description
FOPEN	Opens a file to write to or read from
PUT_LINE	Writes a line to a file
GET_LINE	Reads a line from a file
FCLOSE	Closes a file

The UTL_FILE package also contains a FILE_TYPE data type used to declare a file variable. It's used with the FOPEN function, which needs three IN parameter values: file location, filename, and open mode (r for read, w for write, and a for append). This function returns an identifier for the file that should be stored in a variable declared with the FILE_TYPE data type. This variable is then referenced in other statements to refer to this file.

The PUT_LINE procedure needs IN parameter values to identify the file and text that's written to the file. The GET_LINE procedure needs an IN parameter value to identify the file and an OUT parameter to hold the line data that's read. The FCLOSE procedure needs only one IN parameter, which identifies the file.

Before using the UTL_FILE features, you need to specify access to the corresponding directories in the init.ora file by using the utl_file_dir parameter or the CREATE DIRECTORY command. The init.ora file contains all the settings and parameters for the database and is read when the database is started. Even though the database administrator typically handles the init.ora file, developers should be familiar with this file because it contains environment settings, such as the utl_file_dir parameter, that determine whether and how certain Oracle features are accessed from PL/SQL code. A sample init.ora file is included in the Chapter10 folder; you can open it in a text editor. The utl_file_dir parameter isn't included in the default init.ora file; it's added as needed for specific installations. In the following exercise, you use the CREATE DIRECTORY command to make sure you have directory access.

Before you try to use the UTL_FILE package, make sure it's available in your Oracle installation. Many Oracle-supplied output and communication packages aren't available by default, so the system administrator needs to take a few steps to make them available. For the UTL_FILE package, the system administrator must grant execution privileges for users who need to access it. If you're on your own installation of Oracle, start the Run SQL command-line program (from the Oracle menu in Windows). You need to log in as the SYS administrative user and then issue a GRANT command (see Figure 10-5).

```
SQL*Plus: Release 11.2.0.2.0 Production on Sat Apr 14 10:45:51 2012

Copyright (c) 1982, 2010, Oracle.  All rights reserved.

SQL> connect sys/oracle as sysdba
Connected.
SQL> GRANT EXECUTE ON UTL_FILE TO PUBLIC;

Grant succeeded.

SQL> _
```

FIGURE 10-5 Making the UTL_FILE package available

In the following steps, you use UTL_FILE to write a line to an external file and then read that file from PL/SQL code:

1. Start SQL Developer, if necessary. If you're running Oracle on your machine, create a directory on your computer named **c:\oraclass**. If you're connected to an Oracle server, your instructor will provide the directory information.
2. Issue the following command to create an Oracle directory object for referencing the c:\oraclass directory:

   ```
   CREATE DIRECTORY ora_files AS 'c:\oraclass';
   ```

3. Click **File**, **Open** from the menu. Navigate to and click the **filew10.sql** file in the Chapter10 folder, and then click **Open**. Review and run this code (see Figure 10-6).

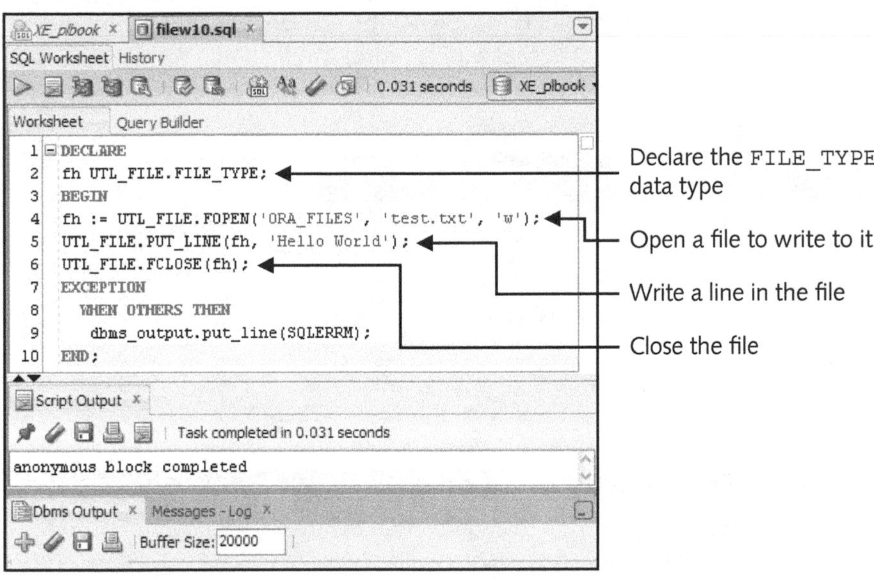

FIGURE 10-6 A procedure using `UTL_FILE` to write to a text file

4. In a text editor, open the **`text.txt`** file in the c:\oraclass directory and verify that the line "Hello World" has been written to this file.
5. To read from this file, click **File**, **Open** from the menu. Navigate to and click the **`filer10.sql`** file in the Chapter10 folder, and then click **Open**. Review and run this code (see Figure 10-7).

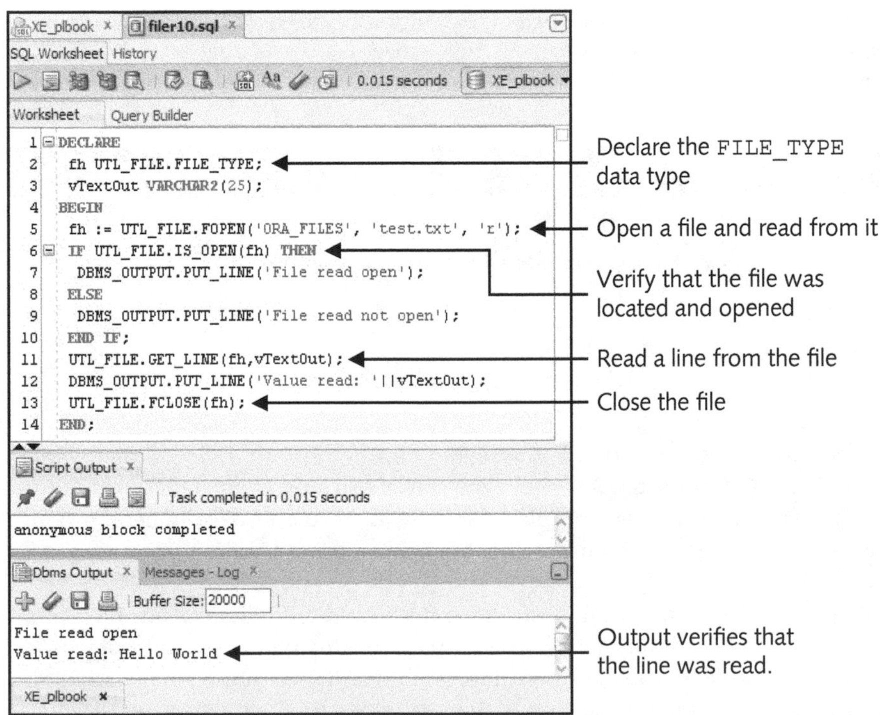

FIGURE 10-7 A procedure using `UTL_FILE` to read from a text file

In addition to reading from and writing to files, you should review other useful file management procedures in the UTL_FILE package, listed in Table 10-4.

TABLE 10-4 New Procedures in the UTL_FILE Package

Program Unit Name	Description
FREMOVE	Deletes a file
FRENAME	Renames a file
FCOPY	Copies all or part of a file to another file
FGETATTR	Retrieves file attributes, such as size

CHALLENGE 10-1

The Brewbean's manager wants to prepare some presentation materials and needs data files to finish the analyses. Create a comma-delimited file named cust_sales.txt containing these data elements for each customer: shopper ID, average number of items in each order, average sales dollars per order, and total dollars spent. (In comma-delimited files, commas are placed between each value in a line.)

LARGE OBJECTS

As media technology progressed, the types and size of data used in a database began to expand. As a result, Oracle 8 introduced features for storing and manipulating large text data, graphic, and streaming video files. These types of data are referred to as **large objects (LOBs)** and take on different forms, such as those listed in Table 10-5.

TABLE 10-5 LOB Types

LOB Type	Description
BLOB	Binary large object, such as a photo file
CLOB	Character large object, such as text documentation
BFILE	Binary large object, such as a streaming video or movie file
NCLOB	Fixed-width character data for storing character data in other languages

An LOB is actually a column in the database and can hold up to 4 GB of data, which well surpasses the 2 GB limit of the LONG data type. After learning about LOB capabilities, the technical staff members at Brewbean's plan to use it to store an image of each product in the database. In this way, product images can be displayed easily when customers are shopping on the Web site.

One advantage of LOBs is that a table can have multiple LOB columns but only one LONG column. A table's LOB column actually contains a locator pointing to the object. BLOB, CLOB, and NCLOB objects can be stored internally (in the database) and are typically stored in a separate tablespace from database tables to allow optimizing each tablespace's attributes for the type of data being stored. (A tablespace is similar to a partition of a physical disk.) However, a BFILE object must be stored outside the Oracle database as a file on the server.

The DBMS_LOB Package

The DBMS_LOB package includes features that enable you to handle LOBs in program code. Programs in this package can be grouped into mutators and observers. Mutators are programs that add, change, or remove LOBs, and observers are programs that read an LOB or information about an LOB. Like other types of data, LOBs can be inserted and retrieved by SQL DML and query statements. However, keep in mind that images can be viewed only in an environment that manages displaying graphical images, such as Oracle Forms. Even though you can manipulate LOBs in SQL Developer, you can't display them because it can't handle graphical displays. Table 10-6 lists some useful programs in the DBMS_LOB package to give you an idea of what tasks you can handle with it.

TABLE 10-6 DBMS_LOB Programs

Program Unit Name	Description
LOADFROMFILE	Loads a binary file in an internal LOB
WRITE	Writes data to an LOB
READ	Reads data from an LOB
ERASE	Deletes LOB data

Using DBMS_LOB to Manipulate Images

Because Brewbean's wants to add product images for shoppers, you need to add a BLOB column to the BB_PRODUCT table for storing these images. The DBMS_LOB package can then be used to load images in the database columns. Follow these steps:

1. Start SQL Developer, if necessary. Use the following statement to add a BLOB column to the BB_PRODUCT table:

```
ALTER TABLE bb_product
  ADD pimage BLOB;
```

2. Use the following statement to initialize the BLOB column. The EMPTY_BLOB function prepares the column to hold image locator information.

```
UPDATE bb_product
  SET pimage = empty_blob();
```

3. Copy the **fpress.gif** image file in the Chapter10 folder to the c:\oraclass folder created earlier for the Oracle directory object ORA_FILES. If you're using another directory, copy the image file to that directory.
4. Next, you create a procedure to load the image file in the BLOB column. Open the **blob.txt** file in the Chapter10 folder, and use its code to create the **INSERT_IMAGE_SP** procedure in SQL Developer. Review the code shown in Figure 10-8.

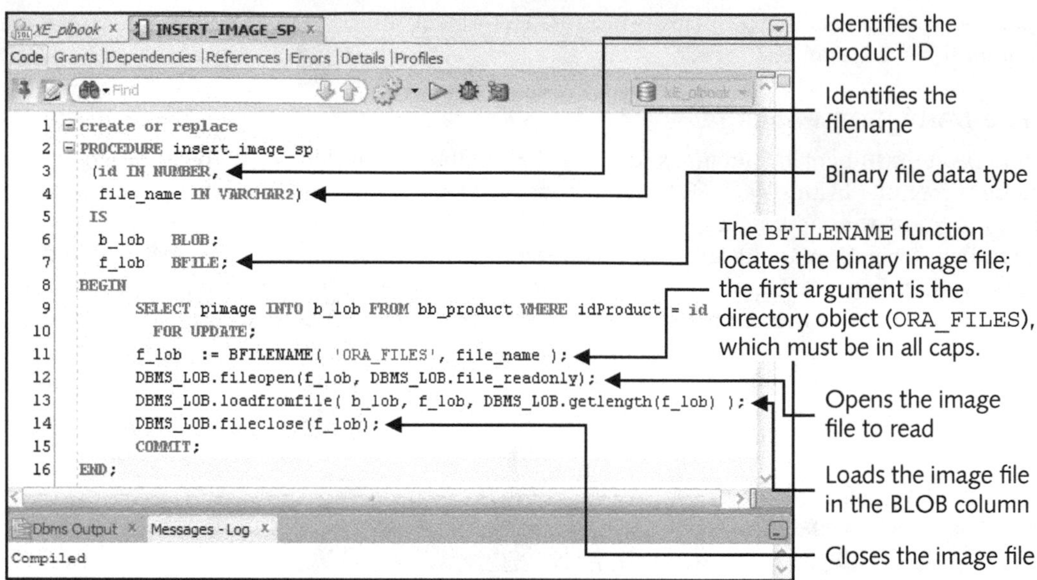

FIGURE 10-8 A procedure using `DBMS_LOB` to load image files

5. Use the following code to load the `fpress.gif` image file for product 3:

```
BEGIN
  insert_image_sp(3,'fpress.gif');
END;
```

6. To verify that the file has been loaded, use the query shown in Figure 10-9. The `GETLENGTH` function is used to confirm that the image was loaded because SQL Developer can't display the image directly.

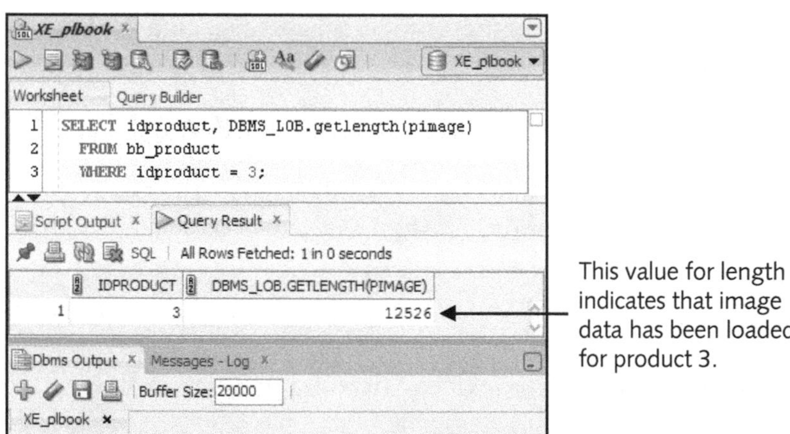

FIGURE 10-9 Listing the BLOB column's length

Now that Brewbean's has product images stored in the database, you can query the BLOB column for display when you're developing application pages, just as you would with any other column. Figure 10-10 shows the Brewbean's product page containing the French press image you just loaded.

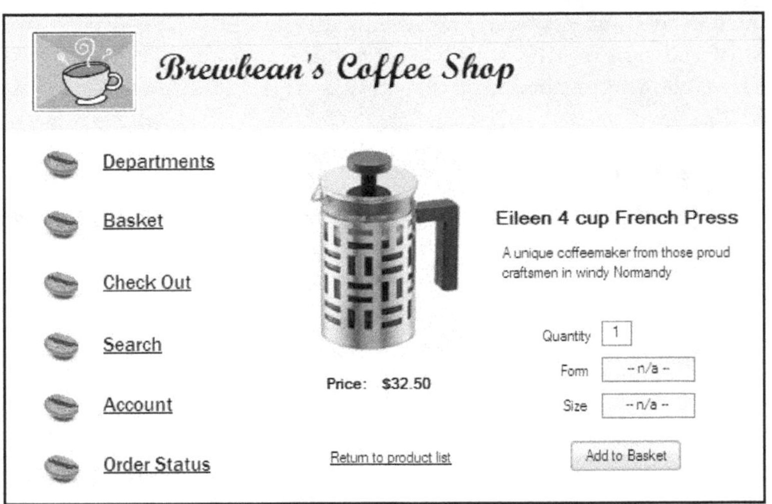

FIGURE 10-10 Brewbean's product page

COMMUNICATION CAPABILITIES

Communication technology plays an increasingly critical role as applications rely more on real-time data. For example, online auctions depend on messaging capabilities to supply updated bid information to participants. In addition, online merchants depend on generating order confirmation e-mails automatically to send to customers. The following sections cover built-in packages dealing with communications.

The `DBMS_ALERT` Package

The `DBMS_ALERT` package is used to send notifications of database events to interested users when an event occurs. For example, if you monitor an online auction, you might want to see a new high bid when it's placed. Instead of having the system poll data continuously to check for changes, an alert can be generated in a database trigger. The application for allowing users to participate in the bid would register to get alerts. Alerts are transaction based and sent only if the transaction is committed.

The Brewbean's developers plan to use the `DBMS_ALERT` package to send alerts when product stock levels fall below the reorder point. (You set up these alerts in Hands-On Assignment 10-2.) Note that granting `EXECUTE` privileges to general users and a package synonym aren't done automatically in the package that's created during installation.

The basic mechanics of the alert process include registering an alert name, setting up when an alert should signal, and registering certain users to get the alert. The `REGISTER`, `SIGNAL`, and `WAITONE` procedures of the `DBMS_ALERT` package can handle these tasks.

Take a look at some examples of setting up an alert. First, the following code uses the `REGISTER` procedure to set up an alert name. This procedure has only one `IN` parameter, which is a `VARCHAR2` data type, for the alert name:

```
DBMS_ALERT.REGISTER('new_bid');
```

Next, you need to set up firing a signal for this alert. Normally, it would be in an `AFTER INSERT` or `UPDATE` database trigger to capture the data change. The `SIGNAL` procedure has two `IN` parameters of the `VARCHAR2` data type. The first parameter is the alert name, which must match one that has been identified with the REGISTER procedure. The second parameter is the message to send with the alert, such as a new bid in the online auction example. The following statement is placed in a trigger and references the alert name created earlier:

```
DBMS_ALERT.SIGNAL('new_bid', TO_CHAR(:new.bid));
```

Finally, the last step is registering users to get this alert. The WAITONE procedure used for this task has the following header containing four parameters:

```
DBMS_ALERT.WAITONE
   (name       IN    VARCHAR2,
    message    OUT   VARCHAR2,
    status     OUT   INTEGER,
    timeout    IN    NUMBER DEFAULT MAXWAIT);
```


The name parameter references a specific alert name—new_bid, in this example. The message parameter returns the message placed in the alert signal. The status parameter returns a 0 when an alert is received and a 1 if it times out. The timeout parameter determines how long the session waits (in seconds) for an alert signal before returning a timeout status. To indicate wanting to receive new bid messages, the user application needs to issue a statement, as shown in the following code:

```
DBMS_ALERT.WAITONE('new_bid', v_msg, v_status, 600);
```

The v_msg and v_status variables need to be declared in this block because they receive the information returned by the WAITONE procedure's OUT parameters. The DBMS_ALERT package contains several more procedures, such as the REMOVE procedure used to delete alerts from the system. If you need to update viewed information periodically, you should explore this package because it's more efficient than polling data constantly to determine when a change has occurred.

The UTL_MAIL Package

Sending e-mails from PL/SQL code has been simplified with the UTL_MAIL package (introduced in Oracle 10*g*). Sending automatic e-mail notices from the database system is quite useful in many situations. Brewbean's, of course, is going to use this package to send e-mail order confirmations to customers automatically. Other examples of using this package include the following:

- Sending customers notifications when airline ticket prices on a specified route have changed
- Sending customers notifications when a stock price reaches a particular price
- Notifying employees when inventory levels of items fall below the reorder point

The UTL_MAIL package isn't installed with the database by default because of the requirement to enable e-mail server communication. Therefore, the database administrator must take a couple of steps to prepare the Oracle server to use UTL_MAIL features. First, the package is loaded by running these two scripts:

```
@$ORACLE_HOME/rdbms/admin/utlmail.sql
@$ORACLE_HOME/rdbms/admin/prvtmail.plb
```

To run these scripts, you must be logged in as the SYS user and use the Run SQL command-line tool described previously for UTL_FILE. In addition, the smtp_out_server parameter must be set to identify the SMTP server. **Simple Mail Transfer Protocol (SMTP)** is the protocol for sending e-mail across networks and the Internet. The SYS user sets this parameter with the following command:

```
ALTER SYSTEM SET smtp_out_server='smtp.domain.com';
```

For example, if the SMTP server host is `mail.tcc.edu`, using port 25, the `smtp_out_server` parameter is set as follows:

```
ALTER SYSTEM SET smtp_out_server='mail.tcc.edu:25';
```

Starting with Oracle 11*g* Release 2, there's one more requirement to make some communication packages usable. The system administrator must create an access control list (ACL), using two procedures in the `DBMS_NETWORK_ACL_ADMIN` package. The first procedure, `CREATE_ACL`, establishes an ACL identifying users or roles and the access privilege to assign, as shown in the following code:


```
BEGIN
  DBMS_NETWORK_ACL_ADMIN.CREATE_ACL
    (acl         => 'e-mail.xml',
     description => 'Permissions for e-mail server use',
     principal   => 'PLBOOK',
     is_grant    => TRUE,
     privilege   => 'connect');
  COMMIT;
END;
```

The second procedure, `ASSIGN_ACL`, is used to add a network host or an access point, such as an e-mail server, to the ACL:

```
BEGIN
  DBMS_NETWORK_ACL_ADMIN.ASSIGN_ACL
    (acl         => 'e-mail.xml',
     host        => 'mail.tcc.edu',
     lower_port  => 25);
  COMMIT;
END;
```

After the server setup is finished, sending e-mails from PL/SQL code is easy. The `UTL_MAIL` package's `SEND` procedure is used to create an e-mail with familiar components, such as a "send to" address, "copy to" address, blind copy address, subject, and message. The following anonymous PL/SQL block shows an example of constructing and sending an e-mail:

```
BEGIN
  UTL_MAIL.SEND(sender => 'sendit@tcc.edu',
                recipients => 'JoeShopper@gmail.com',
                cc => 'person3@domain.com',
                bcc => 'myboss@domain.com',
                subject => 'UTL_MAIL Test',
                message => 'If you get this message, it worked!');
END;
```

Keep in mind that the values you supply for each parameter can be values or variables existing in the PL/SQL block. You can perform additional tasks, such as attaching files, with this package. For full details, see the Oracle documentation.

The UTL_HTTP Package

The UTL_HTTP package enables you to make Hypertext Transfer Protocol (HTTP) calls from PL/SQL programs. This package can be used to analyze Web sites' HTML source code to perform tasks such as tracking competitors' pricing, gathering cost information for raw materials, and collecting relevant business news for a particular industry. For example, Brewbean's might want to monitor leading online coffee companies to compare product prices.

Two functions, REQUEST and REQUEST_PIECES, retrieve HTML source code from a specified URL. The REQUEST function retrieves only the first 2000 bytes of data from the specified Web page. However, the REQUEST_PIECES function returns the entire page, regardless of size, in 2000-byte segments. This is done by storing each segment in a PL/SQL table variable of the HTML_PIECES data type; this variable and data type are included in the UTL_HTTP package. Typically, the REQUEST_PIECES function is used to prevent truncating or omitting information on the Web page.

The following exercise shows how Brewbean's can use the UTL_FILE package to track coffee press prices of a leading online competitor, *www.peets.com*. The HTML source code that's returned by UTL_HTTP functions is written to a file for viewing. Follow these steps:

1. Start a Web browser, and enter the URL **http://www.peets.com/shop/essentials_presspot.asp** to view a page listing available coffee presses.

NOTE

The *www.peets.com* site is an actual online coffee retailer at the time of this writing. If this site no longer exists, you need to substitute another one.

2. Start SQL Developer, if necessary. If you didn't create the Oracle directory object earlier, enter the following command to establish the directory:

```
CREATE DIRECTORY ora_files AS 'c:\oraclass';
```

NOTE

Users must be granted the correct privileges to create directories.

3. Open the **http10.txt** file in the Chapter10 folder, and use its code to create the **READ_HTTP_SP** procedure in SQL Developer.
4. Run the procedure by using the following block:

```
BEGIN
   read_http_sp('http://www.peets.com/shop/essentials_presspot.asp');
END;
```

5. Open the **c:\oraclass\test_http.htm** file in a text editor. You'll see the HTML source code for the page you viewed previously in the Web browser.

NOTE

A copy of the file produced at the time of this writing is included in the Chapter10 folder: `test_http.htm`.

Because this example retrieves all source code from the specified Web page, code could be added to search the retrieved HTML source code and extract only the needed data, such as products' item numbers or prices, in this example. The block shown in Figure 10-11 uses the `INSTR` and `SUBSTR` functions to search the page's contents and retrieve the list of items.

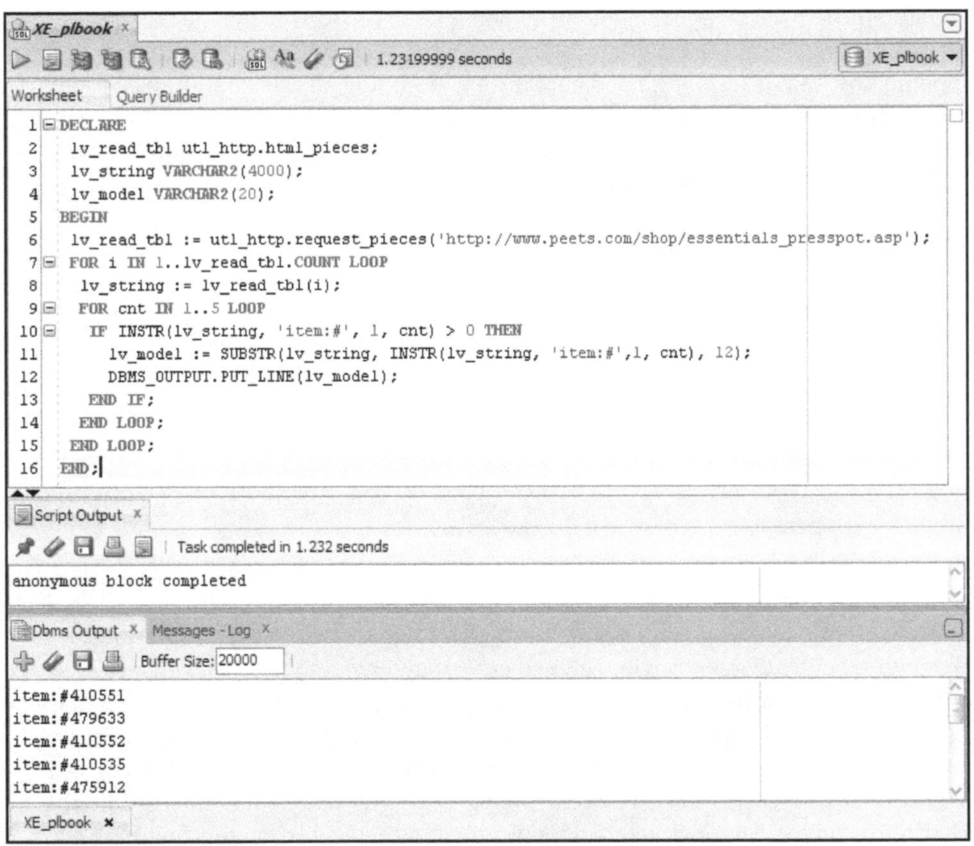
XE_plbook
1.23199999 seconds
XE_plbook
Worksheet
Query Builder
DECLARE
lv_read_tbl utl_http.html_pieces;
lv_string VARCHAR2(4000);
lv_model VARCHAR2(20);
BEGIN
lv_read_tbl := utl_http.request_pieces('http://www.peets.com/shop/essentials_presspot.asp');
FOR i IN 1..lv_read_tbl.COUNT LOOP
lv_string := lv_read_tbl(i);
FOR cnt IN 1..5 LOOP
IF INSTR(lv_string, 'item:#', 1, cnt) > 0 THEN
lv_model := SUBSTR(lv_string, INSTR(lv_string, 'item:#',1, cnt), 12);
DBMS_OUTPUT.PUT_LINE(lv_model);
END IF;
END LOOP;
END LOOP;
END;
Script Output
Task completed in 1.232 seconds
anonymous block completed
Dbms Output
Messages - Log
Buffer Size: 20000
item:#410551
item:#479633
item:#410552
item:#410535
item:#475912
XE_plbook

FIGURE 10-11 Searching for specific content on a Web page

NOTE

You might need to use additional options if you're connected to the Internet through a firewall or want to access Web pages via HTTPS. Refer to "Oracle 11*g* Supplied PL/SQL Packages and Types Reference" on the OTN site for more information.

ADDITIONAL PACKAGES

Developers soon find a plethora of useful built-in packages on the Oracle server. This section covers another widely used package, DBMS_DDL, that gives you access to DDL statements that can't be included directly in PL/SQL code. This section also offers information on exploring additional Oracle-supplied packages.

The DBMS_DDL Package

The DBMS_DDL package gives you access to two DDL procedures that can't be used directly in a PL/SQL block: ALTER_COMPILE and ANALYZE_OBJECT. ALTER_COMPILE allows compiling program units, and ANALYZE_OBJECT creates statistics for database objects that can be used to enhance performance.

The developers at Brewbean's want to explore using this package to create a procedure for compiling any INVALID objects and another for analyzing all tables. If they can handle these tasks with procedures, these jobs can be placed in the job queue and scheduled to run routinely during off hours. The following sections describe these procedures and explain how the DBMS_DDL package allows including them in PL/SQL code.

The ALTER_COMPILE Procedure

Object modifications can change dependent objects' status to INVALID, and these objects need to be recompiled before running them again. For example, if you change a table and a procedure references this table, the procedure is marked as INVALID. You can use the ALTER_COMPILE procedure to compile database objects via code. This procedure's header shows that it contains three IN parameters. (Remember that if no mode is indicated, the default is IN.)

```
DBMS_DDL.ALTER_COMPILE
  (type    VARCHAR2,
   schema VARCHAR2,
   name    VARCHAR2);
```

The type parameter value can be one of the following: PROCEDURE, FUNCTION, TRIGGER, PACKAGE, PACKAGE BODY, or PACKAGE SPECIFICATION. Entering just PACKAGE compiles both the specification and body. The schema parameter is the object's owner, and name is the object name. The schema and name parameter values are case sensitive. By default, these values are stored in the database in uppercase characters, so they should be uppercase in this statement. However, if you use double quotes to enter object names in mixed-case characters, this parameter value must match that case exactly. All these parameters have character data types, so any literal values must be enclosed by single quotes.

To compile a program, you must own the object or be granted the ALTER ANY PROCEDURE privilege to compile an object in another schema. If a NULL value is supplied for the schema parameter, the user's schema is used. When the compile action begins, other objects that the object depends on are checked for an INVALID status. If any object is INVALID, it's recompiled before recompiling the targeted object.

Although the COMPILE command can be entered in SQL Developer, being able to use the COMPILE action in a PL/SQL block is important because it allows you to create procedures that can be placed in the job queue. Depending on what's needed, developers typically create a procedure that makes it easy to recompile all invalid objects or invalid objects of a specific type. In this situation, the ALL_OBJECTS data dictionary view could be used to retrieve all objects with the status INVALID. These object names could be retrieved in a cursor that can be processed through a loop by using the ALTER_COMPILE procedure. This capability is quite valuable because you don't have to track dependencies while you finish modifications. To verify successful compilation, the procedure can scan the STATUS and LAST_DDL_TIME columns in the USER_OBJECTS view. Table 10-7 lists typical exceptions raised by the ALTER_COMPILE procedure.

TABLE 10-7 ALTER_COMPILE Exceptions

Oracle Error Number	Description
ORA-20000	The object doesn't exist or you have insufficient privileges for this object.
ORA-20001	Attempted to compile remote object; only local database objects can be compiled.
ORA-20002	Not a valid object type value.

The ANALYZE_OBJECT Procedure

The ANALYZE_OBJECT tasks are typically part of the DBA's duties, but a developer needs to be aware of the options for performance-tuning tasks. This procedure computes statistics, such as a range of values, on database objects, typically tables and indexes. Generating these statistics can have an influence on program performance, as the procedure can affect how Oracle processes statements by determining which optimizer is used. The Oracle cost-based Optimizer attempts to determine the best path of execution by using these statistics. If there are no statistics for an object, the rule-based Optimizer is used.

Take a look at the ANALYZE_OBJECT procedure's header:

```
DBMS_DDL.ANALYZE_OBJECT
  (type               VARCHAR2,
   schema             VARCHAR2,
   name               VARCHAR2,
   method             VARCHAR2,
   estimate_rows      NUMBER     DEFAULT NULL,
   estimate_percent   NUMBER     DEFAULT NULL,
   method_opt         VARCHAR2   DEFAULT NULL,
   partname           VARCHAR2   DEFAULT NULL);
```

Table 10-8 describes the available parameters.

TABLE 10-8 Parameters of the ANALYZE_OBJECT Procedure

Parameter Name	Description
type	Value must be TABLE, INDEX, or CLUSTER
schema	Owner of object to analyze; case sensitive and NULL default to current schema
name	Object name; case sensitive
method	Value must be ESTIMATE, COMPUTE, or DELETE; if it's ESTIMATE, one of the next two parameters must have a non-zero value
estimate_rows	Number of rows to be used
estimate_percent	Percent of rows to be used
method_opt	Indicates which database structure associated with the object is analyzed: FOR TABLE, FOR ALL INDEXES, or FOR ALL INDEXED COLUMNS
partname	If using partitions, allows specifying a partition

The method parameter value is the most important in determining how statistics for an object are calculated. The COMPUTE method uses the object's entire contents, but the ESTIMATE method uses only the number or percent of rows specified in the other parameters. In both cases, statistics are stored in the data dictionary. The DELETE method simply erases an object's existing statistics in the data dictionary. To verify successful analysis, check the LAST_ANALYZED column in the USER_OBJECTS view, which stores the date of the last analysis. Table 10-9 lists typical exceptions raised by the ANALYZE_OBJECT procedure.

TABLE 10-9 ANALYZE_OBJECT Exceptions

Oracle Error Number	Description
ORA-20000	The object doesn't exist, or you have insufficient privileges for this object.
ORA-20001	Not a valid object type value.

Exploring Additional Oracle-Supplied Packages

This chapter is far from an exhaustive coverage of Oracle built-in packages; it's intended just to introduce you to these packages. As you delve into PL/SQL programming, discovering what's available is worthwhile so that you can take advantage of built-in packages' capabilities and review their code to get ideas for coding techniques. Table 10-10 describes more packages you might find useful. Again, the Oracle database documentation on the OTN Web site has a full listing and description of built-in packages.

TABLE 10-10 Other Built-In Packages

Package Name	Description
DBMS_CRYPTO	Encrypts and decrypts stored data
DBMS_JAVA	Controls the behavior of the Java Virtual Machine used to run Java stored procedures
DBMS_JOB	Manages jobs in the Oracle job queue
DBMS_METADATA	Retrieves information about database objects
DBMS_RANDOM	Generates random numbers
DBMS_SESSION	Allows access to session options directly from PL/SQL
DBMS_UTILITY	Contains a miscellaneous group of programs, ranging from procedure management capabilities to reporting error information
DBMS_XMLGEN	Converts data from an SQL query to XML
UTL_INADDR	Retrieves a Web site's hostname or IP address
UTL_SMTP	Allows e-mail communication
UTL_TCP	Supports TCP/IP communication

These packages with parameters are the same as those you can construct. When the database is installed, the `catproc.sql` script calls each script for creating these built-ins. Reviewing these scripts is helpful; you can find them in the rdbms\admin directory of the Oracle database software. Each script contains comments documenting the code; these comments give you a feel for what's going on in the package and can give you ideas to use in your own code. In addition, the OTN Web site includes a manual on Oracle-supplied packages. For each package, this documentation shows the package header, explains the parameters, describes all its programs, and sometimes includes an example of how it's used.

DYNAMIC SQL AND PL/SQL

So far, the extent of SQL statements being dynamic has been limited to supplying values in `WHERE` and `HAVING` clauses. You can use conditions in these clauses to have a statement affect different rows each time the code runs. However, you have had to supply all other parts of a statement, such as a table name, in the code at compile time.

Fortunately, **dynamic SQL** and PL/SQL enable you to construct and parse statements at runtime rather than compile time. **Parsing** means checking statement syntax. With dynamic SQL, you can perform the following tasks:

- Create utilities that enable users to create or drop objects, such as tables and indexes.
- Create an ad-hoc query interface where users can specify information such as table columns and sort ordering.
- Create a mechanism that enables users to select data manipulations that are actually called procedures. The front end could allow users to select a functionality and enter the necessary data values.

Before Oracle 8*i*, the only mechanism for using dynamic code in PL/SQL blocks was the `DBMS_SQL` package. In Oracle 8*i*, a feature called native Dynamic SQL was introduced to simplify the process of building dynamic code. Covering both types of dynamic SQL generation is worthwhile, however, because a lot of deployed code uses `DBMS_SQL`.

Because of the early binding of SQL statements, only DML and query statements can be included directly in PL/SQL blocks, and these statements are flexible only in the sense of supplying values at runtime. For example, you can use a procedure's parameter to provide `WHERE` clause values at runtime. However, what if you need to make the code more flexible, such as allowing users to specify column names at runtime so that they can choose the column where criteria are set for a query?

Say Brewbean's is developing a product lookup page where users can specify a lookup based on product ID, name, or description. The column name must be entered at runtime because you don't know ahead of time which column users will use to set criteria. To do this, you need to use the dynamic SQL features available with the Oracle server.

To understand dynamic SQL better, compare some procedures. First, the `DYN_TEST1_SP` procedure shows how parameters are used to supply values in an SQL statement at runtime. Figure 10-12 shows the code for this procedure, and Figure 10-13 shows the results of running this procedure, which is successful in returning product information based on the parameter value (`p_value`) supplied for the product ID.

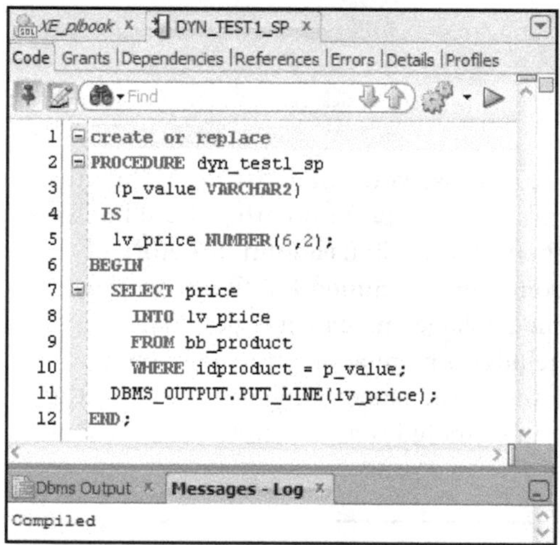

FIGURE 10-12 Testing the dynamic nature of SQL in PL/SQL

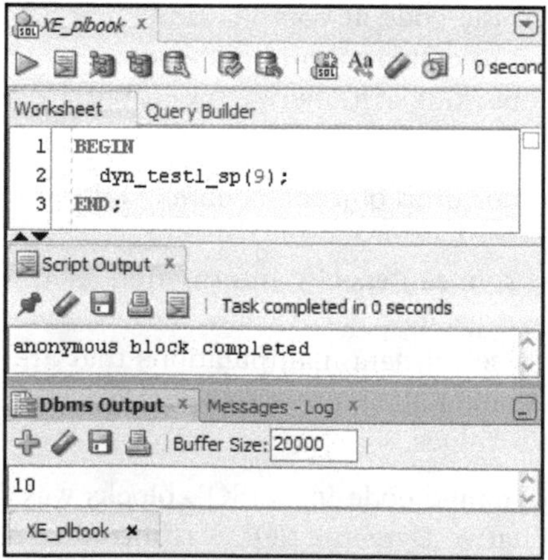

FIGURE 10-13 Results of the `WHERE` clause value test

However, what if you try to expand SQL's dynamic nature by supplying both a column name and value at runtime? The DYN_TEST2_SP procedure attempts this task, as shown in Figure 10-14. This block allows setting criteria in the WHERE clause, including the column name and value, at runtime.

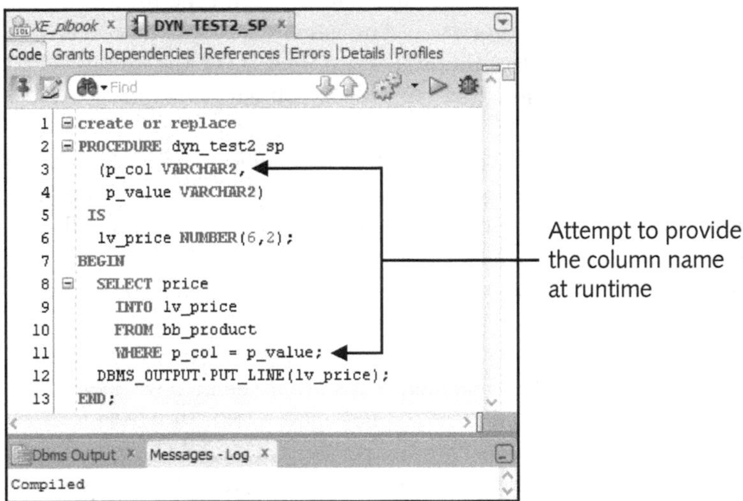

FIGURE 10-14 Expanding the dynamic nature of SQL

Notice that an error is raised when the DYN_TEST2_SP procedure runs (see Figure 10-15). Attempting to use a parameter to provide an identifier, such as a column name or table name, in an SQL statement in PL/SQL raises an error. Using a DDL statement, such as ALTER TABLE or CREATE TABLE, in PL/SQL also produces an error.

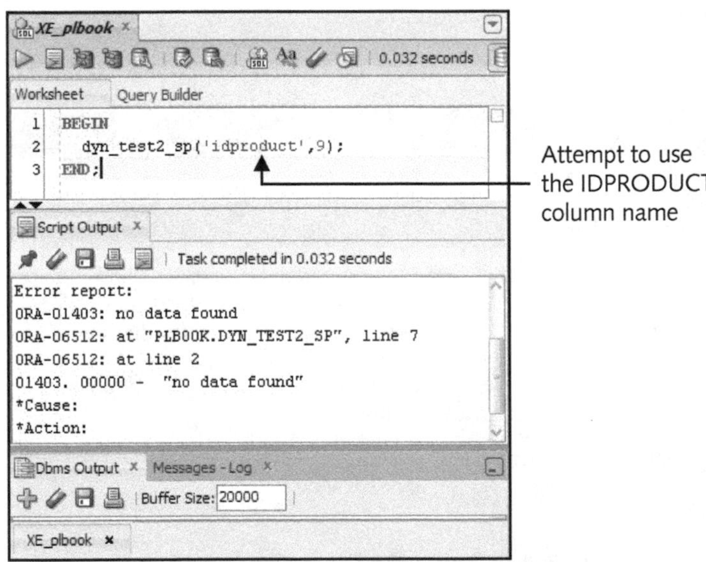

FIGURE 10-15 Error in providing a column name at runtime

Two features of dynamic SQL give you workarounds for these situations. The DBMS_SQL package, introduced in Oracle 7, allows using more dynamic SQL code in PL/SQL. In Oracle 8*i*, native dynamic SQL was introduced to simplify coding dynamic

SQL and to improve the code's performance. The following sections introduce both features and discuss which one is more suitable in different circumstances.

The DBMS_SQL Package

The process flow of DBMS_SQL procedures is slightly different for each type of SQL statement; these types include DML, DDL, and queries. The general process involves establishing a cursor to contain and manipulate the SQL statement. Like the cursor handling you've already seen, each process must be handled specifically, including opening, parsing, running, and closing.

One distinctive aspect of the DBMS_SQL package is using placeholders as a mechanism for supplying values to an SQL statement. This package allows using parameters directly as identifiers, such as column names and table names. However, parameters can still provide values to check criteria, such as values supplied in a WHERE clause. Therefore, placeholders are used to distinguish parameter values used as criteria from parameters that provide identifiers, such as column names.

When the SQL statement is built in the PL/SQL block, placeholders with colon prefixes mark where values are supplied at runtime. These placeholders are associated with a PL/SQL variable, typically a parameter, by using the DBMS_SQL package's BIND_VARIABLE procedure. These placeholders are referred to as "bind variables." The following sections explain how to use each type of SQL statement with the DBMS_SQL package.

DML Statements with DBMS_SQL

First, take a look at the steps to perform a DML statement via the DBMS_SQL package. In this case, Brewbean's needs a procedure to support an application page where users can set a new product price. The new price can be a sales price or the regular product price, as indicated by the user; therefore, the block needs to allow supplying a column name—PRICE or SALEPRICE—at runtime. Table 10-11 lists the steps and packaged program units that need to be used for a dynamic DML statement.

TABLE 10-11 Steps to Perform DML Statements

Step	Program Unit	Description	Parameters
1	OPEN_CURSOR	Establishes a cursor or work area for the statement to handle	N/A
2	PARSE	Checks the statement's syntax	Cursor, statement to parse, and version behavior (*Note*: Using NATIVE for the version behavior indicates that the statement should be processed based on the database version the program is running on.)
3	BIND_VARIABLE	Associates placeholders in the statement with PL/SQL variables	Cursor, placeholder name, and value to be assigned
4	EXECUTE	Runs the statement and returns the number of rows affected	Cursor
5	CLOSE_CURSOR	Frees resources allocated to the cursor	Cursor

The following procedure performs the price-setting task via the DBMS_SQL package. The procedure code includes comments to highlight the steps in managing a DML statement via dynamic SQL:

```
CREATE OR REPLACE PROCEDURE dyn_dml_sp
  (p_col VARCHAR2,
   p_price NUMBER,
   p_id NUMBER)
  IS
  lv_cursor INTEGER;
  lv_update VARCHAR2(150);
  lv_rows NUMBER(1);
BEGIN
  --Open cursor
  lv_cursor := DBMS_SQL.OPEN_CURSOR;
  --Create DML statement
  lv_update := 'UPDATE bb_product
                SET ' || p_col || ' = :ph_price
                WHERE idProduct= :ph_id';
  --Parse the statement
  DBMS_SQL.PARSE(lv_cursor, lv_update, DBMS_SQL.NATIVE);
  --Associate parameters with placeholders in the statement
  DBMS_SQL.BIND_VARIABLE(lv_cursor, ':ph_price', p_price);
  DBMS_SQL.BIND_VARIABLE(lv_cursor, ':ph_id', p_id);
  --Run the DML statement
  lv_rows := DBMS_SQL.EXECUTE(lv_cursor);
  --Close the cursor
  DBMS_SQL.CLOSE_CURSOR(lv_cursor);
  --Save changes
  COMMIT;
  --Check how many rows are affected
  DBMS_OUTPUT.PUT_LINE(lv_rows);
END;
```

When constructing the DML statement that's stored in the lv_update variable, everything (including the placeholder) is enclosed in single quotes as a text string except the p_col parameter, which supplies the identifier value (the column name). Figure 10-16 shows two runs of this procedure. First, product 3's regular price is modified. Second, its sale price is modified.

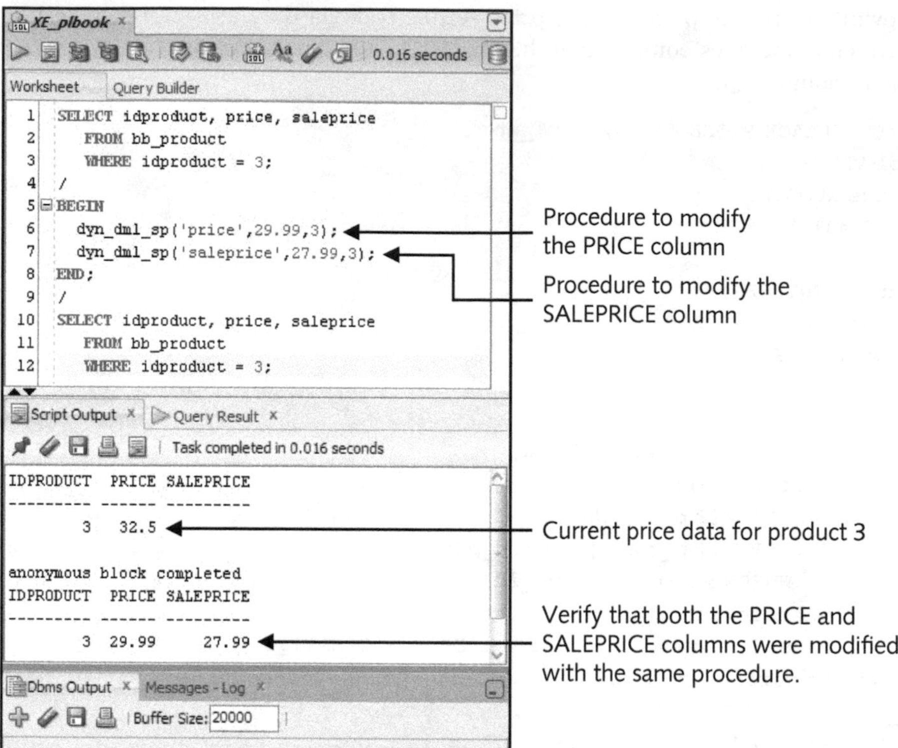

FIGURE 10-16 Performing DML statements with column names provided at runtime

In the application page for the price change (see Figure 10-17), users can specify in a drop-down list which column should be modified. An input box is used to enter the price value.

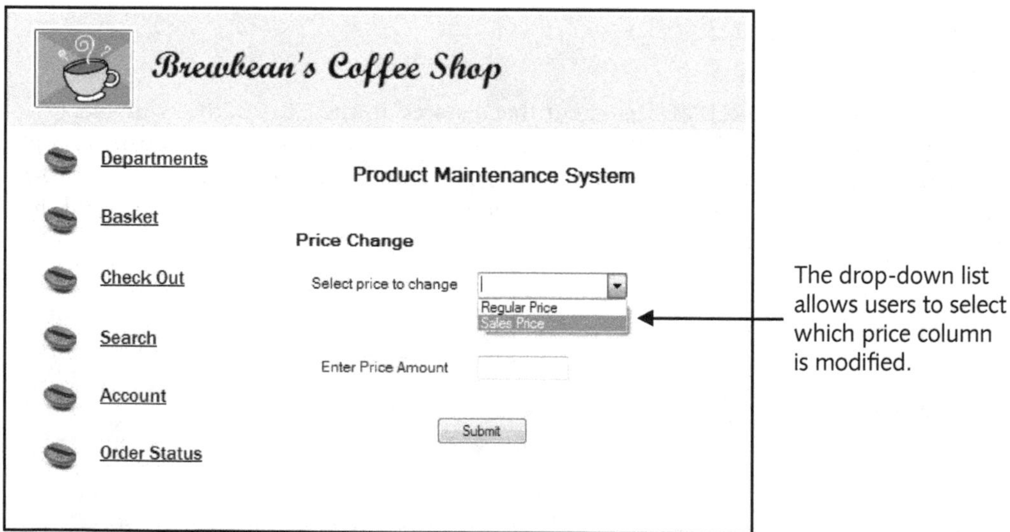

FIGURE 10-17 Brewbean's price change page

DDL Statements with DBMS_SQL

The DBMS_SQL package not only allows including DDL statements, such as CREATE, ALTER, and DROP, but also allows these statements to operate dynamically (supplying column and table names at runtime). Using DDL statements dynamically gives you a way to build application pages that simplify database modifications. This capability could be invaluable to Brewbean's because the company doesn't need a full-time DBA to manage its Oracle database. Instead, Brewbean's developers want the flexibility of making database modifications, such as adding new columns, on their own. Table 10-12 describes the DBMS_SQL steps for creating dynamic DDL statements.

TABLE 10-12 Steps to Perform DDL Statements

Step	Program Unit	Description	Parameters
1	OPEN_CURSOR	Establishes a cursor or work area for the statement to handle	N/A
2	PARSE	Checks the DDL statement's syntax and runs the statement	Cursor, statement to parse, and version behavior
3	CLOSE_CURSOR	Frees resources allocated to the cursor	Cursor

An EXECUTE step isn't needed with DDL statements because the PARSE step runs the statement automatically after successful parsing. The following procedure supports an application page that allows Brewbean's employees to add a column to any table:

```
CREATE OR REPLACE PROCEDURE dyn_ddl_sp
  (p_table IN VARCHAR2,
   p_col IN VARCHAR2,
   p_type IN VARCHAR2)
  IS
  lv_cursor INTEGER;
  lv_add VARCHAR2(100);
BEGIN
  --Open the cursor
  lv_cursor := DBMS_SQL.OPEN_CURSOR;
  --Build the DDL statement
  lv_add := 'ALTER TABLE '|| p_table || ' ADD ('|| p_col || ' '
                         || p_type || ')';
  --Parse and run the statement
  DBMS_SQL.PARSE(lv_cursor, lv_add, DBMS_SQL.NATIVE);
  --Close the cursor
  DBMS_SQL.CLOSE_CURSOR(lv_cursor);
END;
```

Notice that parameters are used to supply values for the table name, column name, and the data type. The Brewbean's manager decided to assign an employee as the leader of each product line. To do so, the manager needs to add a column to the BB_DEPARTMENT table to store the employee name for each department. Follow these steps to use dynamic DDL via the DBMS_SQL package:

1. Start SQL Developer, if necessary. Use the contents of the **ddl10.txt** file from the Chapter10 folder to create the **DYN_DDL_SP** procedure.
2. Add a column to the BB_DEPARTMENT table by entering the following procedure call:

```
BEGIN
  dyn_ddl_sp('bb_department','leader', 'VARCHAR2(20)');
END;
```

3. Confirm the new column's addition, shown in Figure 10-18.

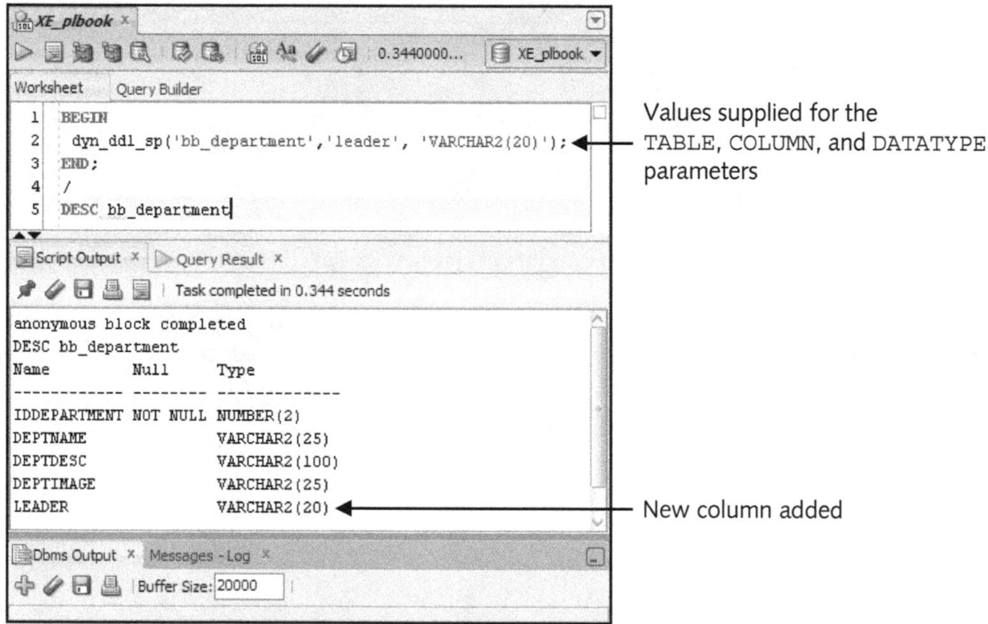

FIGURE 10-18 Performing DDL statements with table and column values supplied at runtime

Queries with DBMS_SQL

Dynamic SQL is often used to provide flexible, easy-to-use query capabilities for end users who need to perform data analysis and reporting. Even users with little or no SQL skills can perform a variety of data queries. As mentioned, dynamic SQL also makes it possible to supply query criteria at runtime.

Say the Brewbean's application needs more flexibility in the product lookup page so that users can enter a product ID or name for lookups. To support this page, you can build a procedure with dynamic SQL. First, Table 10-13 lists the steps for processing a query with the DBMS_SQL package. Because you're now retrieving data, the DEFINE_COLUMN and COLUMN_VALUE program units are used to associate a PL/SQL variable with each column value returned in the query. Also, the FETCH_ROWS program unit is used to retrieve the returned data.

TABLE 10-13 Steps to Perform Queries

Step	Program Unit	Description	Parameters
1	OPEN_CURSOR	Establishes a cursor or work area for the statement to handle	N/A
2	PARSE	Checks the statement's syntax	Cursor, statement to parse, and version behavior
3	BIND_VARIABLE	Associates placeholders in the statement with PL/SQL variables	Cursor, placeholder name, and value to assign
4	DEFINE_COLUMN	Identifies the type and length of PL/SQL variables that hold the column values selected when fetched	Cursor, column position in query, associated PL/SQL variable, and size (*Note*: Size is needed only for columns of type VARCHAR2, CHAR, and RAW.)
5	EXECUTE	Runs the statement and returns the number of rows affected	Cursor
6	FETCH_ROWS	Retrieves the data returned by the query	Cursor
7	COLUMN_VALUE	Returns the values fetched to the indicated variables	Cursor, column position in query, and associated PL/SQL variable
8	CLOSE_CURSOR	Frees resources allocated to the cursor	Cursor

First, review the following code with comments for the query task, and then you can run the procedure. The DEFINE_COLUMN program unit is now used to associate a data type with each value the query returns by matching a declared PL/SQL variable with each column that's queried. In addition, FETCH_ROWS and COLUMN_VALUE are used to retrieve query results from the cursor and pass the returned values to PL/SQL variables.

```
CREATE OR REPLACE PROCEDURE dyn_query1_sp
  (p_col IN VARCHAR2, p_value IN VARCHAR2)
  IS
  lv_query LONG;
  lv_status INTEGER;
  lv_cursor INTEGER;
  lv_col1 NUMBER(2);
  lv_col2 VARCHAR2(25);
  lv_col3 NUMBER(6,2);
  lv_col4 NUMBER(5,1);
BEGIN
  --Open the cursor
  lv_cursor := DBMS_SQL.OPEN_CURSOR;
  --Build the query
  lv_query := 'SELECT idProduct, productname, price, stock
               FROM bb_product
               WHERE '|| p_col ||' = :ph_value) ';
  --Parse the statement
  DBMS_SQL.PARSE(lv_cursor, lv_query, DBMS_SQL.NATIVE);
  --Identify data types for each item selected
```

```
  DBMS_SQL.DEFINE_COLUMN(lv_cursor, 1, lv_col1);
  DBMS_SQL.DEFINE_COLUMN(lv_cursor, 2, lv_col2, 25);
  DBMS_SQL.DEFINE_COLUMN(lv_cursor, 3, lv_col3);
  DBMS_SQL.DEFINE_COLUMN(lv_cursor, 4, lv_col4);
  --Associate placeholder with a parameter
  DBMS_SQL.BIND_VARIABLE(lv_cursor, ':ph_value', p_value);
  --Run the query
  lv_status := DBMS_SQL.EXECUTE(lv_cursor);
 --Fetch row returned and place in PL/SQL variables
  IF (DBMS_SQL.FETCH_ROWS(lv_cursor) > 0) THEN
    DBMS_SQL.COLUMN_VALUE(lv_cursor, 1, lv_col1);
    DBMS_SQL.COLUMN_VALUE(lv_cursor, 2, lv_col2);
    DBMS_SQL.COLUMN_VALUE(lv_cursor, 3, lv_col3);
    DBMS_SQL.COLUMN_VALUE(lv_cursor, 4, lv_col4);
    DBMS_OUTPUT.PUT_LINE(lv_col1||' '||lv_col2||' '
                         ||lv_col3||' '||lv_col4);
  END IF;
  --Close the cursor
  DBMS_SQL.CLOSE_CURSOR(lv_cursor);
END;
```


Create and run the following procedure to test the query activity based on a product ID and then based on a product name. Follow these steps:

1. Start SQL Developer, if necessary. Use the contents of the **query10.txt** file in the Chapter10 folder to create the **DYN_QUERY1_SP** procedure.
2. Test the procedure with a query based on a product ID by entering the first procedure call, shown in Figure 10-19.
3. Now test the procedure with a query based on a product name by entering the second procedure call, shown in Figure 10-19.

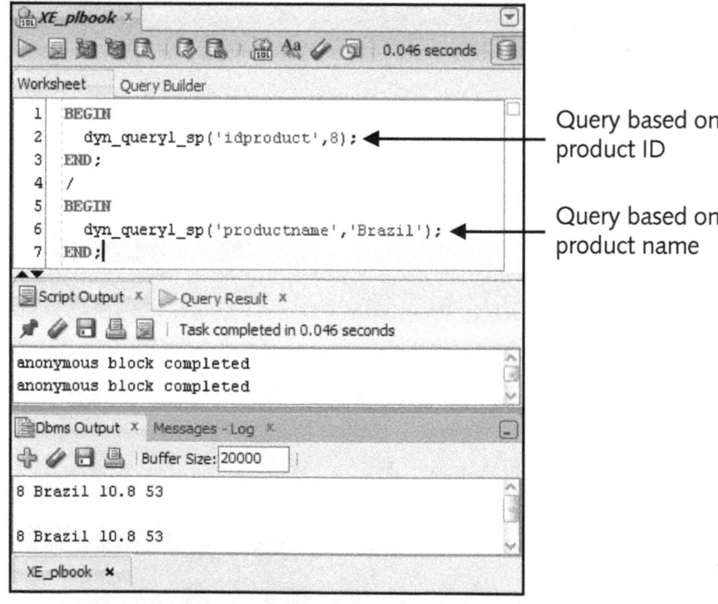

FIGURE 10-19 Dynamic query results

Even though this query is more dynamic than could be achieved in a PL/SQL block, it's just a fraction of the full dynamic potential. In this procedure, for example, you could have used parameters to supply the table name at runtime, too, and the procedure could query columns from any table based on a chosen criterion.

The procedure now handles only one row returned from the query. What if you want users to be able to identify more than one criterion and return more than one row of data? This feature could be useful for Brewbean's to offer users a product search, which can be based on product description, price, availability, and so forth, or whatever features users need. The DBMS_SQL package is particularly suited for handling array-type processing to simplify this task, as shown in the following exercise:

1. Start SQL Developer, if necessary. Create a data type by using the following TYPE command. (The ARRAY type is an associative array structure that allows array-like processing in this procedure.)

```
CREATE TYPE array IS TABLE OF VARCHAR2(100);
```


2. Open the **query10b.txt** file in the Chapter10 folder. Examine the code and the comments included to clarify the code. Notice that a FOR loop is used to construct a query with multiple criteria. Use the code to create the **DYN_QUERY2_SP** procedure.
3. Call the procedure by using the following anonymous block, which provides two search criteria: one for the description to include the term "nut" and another for the stock level to be above 25. The results are shown in Figure 10-20.

```
BEGIN
  dyn_query2_sp(array('description','stock'),
                array('LIKE','>'),
                array('%nut%','25'));
END;
```

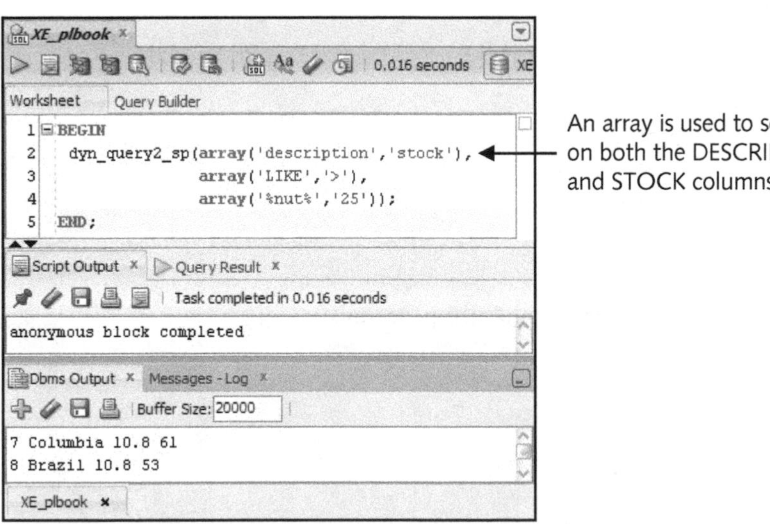

FIGURE 10-20 Using array-like processing in DBMS_SQL queries

Native Dynamic SQL

Native dynamic SQL, introduced with Oracle 8*i*, gives you a declarative method for performing dynamic SQL. Native dynamic SQL statements are much simpler to code than DBMS_SQL statements and process more efficiently because native dynamic SQL support is built into the PL/SQL interpreter. Native dynamic SQL has two methods for performing queries: the EXECUTE IMMEDIATE statement for single-row queries and the OPEN FOR statement for multiple-row queries. The following sections describe these statements and then examine the differences between the DBMS_SQL package and native dynamic SQL.

Using EXECUTE IMMEDIATE

The EXECUTE IMMEDIATE statement contains four clauses with the following syntax:

```
EXECUTE IMMEDIATE 'SQL statement'
  [INTO (var1, var2, ... |  record]
  [USING [IN | OUT | IN OUT] bindvar1, bindvar2, ...]
  [RETURNING | RETURN INTO outvar1, outvar2, ...];
```

The SQL statement is built as a text string by using parameters and placeholders, as you did with the DBMS_SQL package. The INTO clause, used with queries, indicates which PL/SQL variables should hold the values returned from the SELECT statement. The USING clause associates placeholders in the SQL statement with PL/SQL variables or parameters. The RETURNING clause associates values with OUT parameters or a RETURN clause in a function.

To compare coding DBMS_SQL with native dynamic SQL, redo the DML statement and query you already did with the DBMS_SQL package. First, redo the product price UPDATE statement, shown in following code. Notice how compact the code is compared with the DBMS_SQL code:

```
CREATE OR REPLACE PROCEDURE dyn_dml2_sp
  (p_col VARCHAR2,
   p_price NUMBER,
   p_id NUMBER)
  IS
BEGIN
  EXECUTE IMMEDIATE 'UPDATE bb_product
    SET ' || p_col || ' = :ph_price
    WHERE idProduct = :ph_id'
    USING p_price, p_id;
END;
```

Figure 10-21 shows running the DYN_DML2_SP procedure.

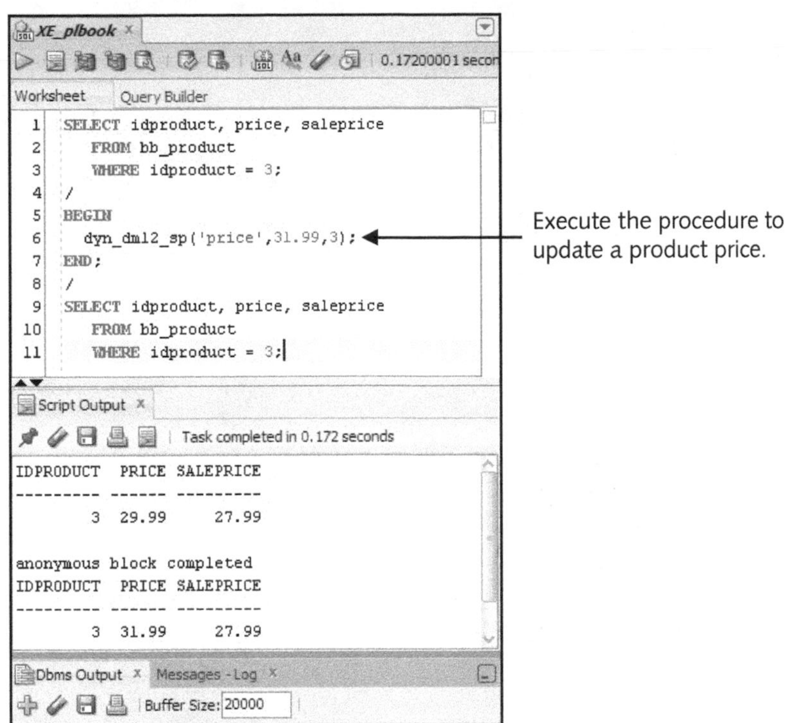

FIGURE 10-21 Executing a DML statement with native dynamic SQL

You can also redo the product search query done previously with the DBMS_SQL package. The following code uses EXECUTE IMMEDIATE to do a product lookup based on the product ID or name. Review the code, paying attention to the comments describing the activities:

```
CREATE OR REPLACE PROCEDURE dyn_query3_sp
   (p_col IN VARCHAR2,
    p_value IN VARCHAR2)
   IS
     lv_query VARCHAR2(200);
     lv_id bb_product.idProduct%TYPE;
     lv_name bb_product.productname%TYPE;
     lv_price bb_product.price%TYPE;
     lv_stock bb_product.stock%TYPE;
BEGIN
   --Use a variable to hold the query construction to
   -- make it more readable
   lv_query := 'SELECT idProduct, productname, price, stock
                  FROM bb_product
                  WHERE UPPER(' || p_col || ') =
                    UPPER(:ph_value)';
   --Run the dynamic query supplying variables to hold return
   -- values in the INTO clause and associate the parameter
   -- with the placeholder in the USING clause
```

```
    EXECUTE IMMEDIATE lv_query
      INTO lv_id, lv_name, lv_price, lv_stock
      USING p_value;
    DBMS_OUTPUT.PUT_LINE(lv_id||' '||lv_name||' '
                          ||lv_price||' '||lv_stock);
  END;
```

Figure 10-22 shows calling this procedure with searches for both a product ID and a product name.

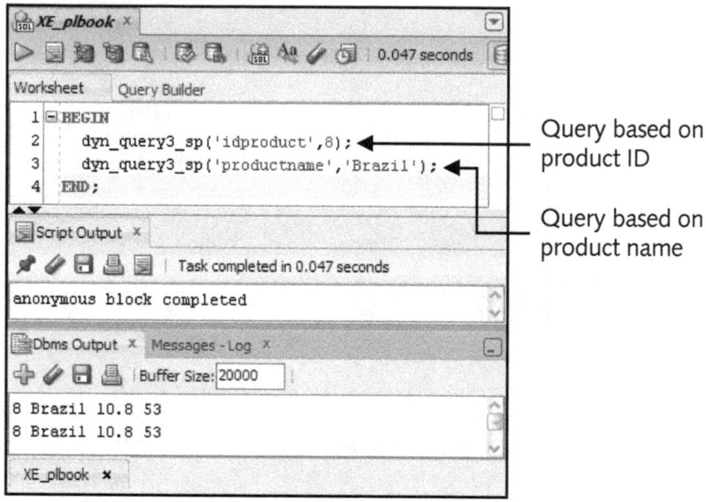

FIGURE 10-22 Using native dynamic SQL to query data

Using `OPEN FOR`

Now take a look at the `OPEN FOR` native Dynamic SQL statement for performing multiple-row queries. A `REF CURSOR` (a pointer to a cursor or SQL work area) is used to reference values the query returns. The package in the following code contains a `TYPE` statement to create a `REF CURSOR` type and one procedure, which enables users to select rows from the BB_PRODUCT table based on a single criterion to include whatever column and value they want.

```
CREATE OR REPLACE PACKAGE dyn_pkg
  AS
  TYPE refcur_type IS REF CURSOR;
  PROCEDURE dyn_query4_sp
    (p_col IN VARCHAR2,
     p_value IN VARCHAR2,
     p_cursor IN OUT refcur_type);
END;

CREATE OR REPLACE PACKAGE BODY dyn_pkg
  AS
  PROCEDURE dyn_query4_sp
    (p_col IN VARCHAR2,
     p_value IN VARCHAR2,
     p_cursor IN OUT refcur_type)
```

```
  IS
    lv_query VARCHAR2(200);
    lv_bind VARCHAR2(20);
BEGIN
  --Build query
  lv_query := 'SELECT idProduct, productname, price, stock
               FROM bb_product
               WHERE UPPER(' || p_col || ') LIKE
UPPER(:ph_value)';
  --Use a variable to add wildcard characters to the value
  lv_bind := '%'|| p_value || '%';
  --Open the cursor with the query and associate a variable
  -- with the placeholder
  OPEN p_cursor FOR lv_query USING lv_bind;
  END;
END;
```


Figure 10-23 shows the DYN_QUERY4_SP procedure checking for any product containing the term "nut" in the DESCRIPTION column.

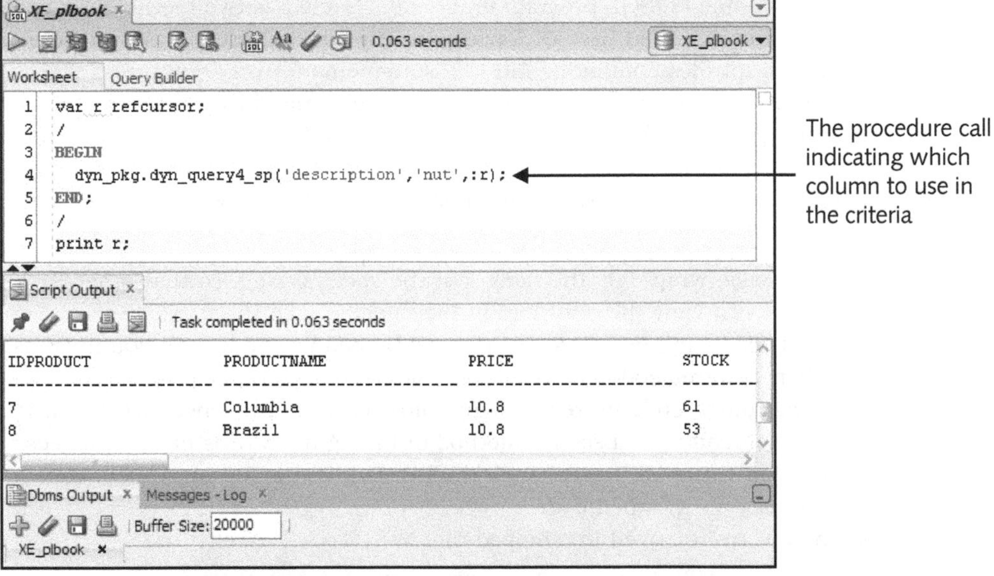

FIGURE 10-23 Using the OPEN FOR native dynamic SQL statement

TIP

The var statement shown in Figure 10-23 creates a variable in the SQL Developer environment that's used to simplify displaying the cursor contents. A cursor loop could also be used with DBMS_OUTPUT statements to produce the display.

DBMS_SQL Versus Native Dynamic SQL

Native dynamic SQL hasn't completely replaced the DBMS_SQL package's functions for processing dynamic SQL. Native dynamic SQL is simpler to code and processes more efficiently, so it should be used, if possible. However, not all situations can be handled with native dynamic SQL; in these cases, the DBMS_SQL package must be used. The following are guidelines for when using native dynamic SQL is best:

- The number and types of columns to be used are known.
- The number and type of bind variables are known.
- You want to perform DDL statements.
- You're running the statement only once or twice.

EXECUTE IMMEDIATE can't reuse parsed statements, so using the DBMS_SQL package improves performance if a statement is to be used repeatedly, which is often a problem in multiuser environments. In addition, the array-like processing in the DBMS_SQL package can make working with many rows easier.

HIDING SOURCE CODE

Developers are often concerned with protecting their source code from other users, such as customers purchasing their applications. Oracle uses the terms "obfuscating" and "wrapping" to refer to hiding PL/SQL program unit code. Oracle has two methods for code wrapping: the wrap utility and the DBMS_DDL package. The wrap utility is a command-line operation to process script files containing CREATE statements for program units. The DBMS_DDL package can wrap a single program unit that's generated dynamically. If you wrap a program unit's source code with either method, the code can't be read by using data dictionary views, such as USER_SOURCE.

Before looking at examples of these two methods, review the following tips on wrapped code:

- For a package, wrap only the body, not the specification, so that other developers can view the information they need to use the package.
- Wrapped code can't be edited. To edit a wrapped program unit, you must use the original source code.
- Wrapping source code protects it from most users but not necessarily all. It isn't recommended as a secure method of hiding passwords or table names.
- Substitution variables created with the DEFINE command in PL/SQL code can't be used in wrapped code.
- Comments are removed in wrapped files.

The wrap utility accepts an input file containing a script of SQL and PL/SQL commands. Users can't read the CREATE statements for program units, but the PL/SQL compiler can. To see how this utility works, take a look at wrapping a script file named test_sql that contains one CREATE PROCEDURE statement. This file is in the Chapter10 folder and is copied to the c:\oraclass directory for this example. You run the wrap utility from the command line, as shown in Figure 10-24. This command contains an infile location and an optional outfile location.

```
C:\Program Files\Support Tools>wrap iname=c:\oraclass\test.sql oname=c:\oraclass
\test.plb

PL/SQL Wrapper: Release 11.2.0.1.0- Production on Sat Apr 14 08:29:44 2012

Copyright (c) 1993, 2009, Oracle.  All rights reserved.

Processing c:\oraclass\test.sql to c:\oraclass\test.plb

C:\Program Files\Support Tools>
```

FIGURE 10-24 Starting the wrap utility

You can open the resulting wrapped file, `test.plb`, in a text editor to verify that it's been obsfucated (see Figure 10-25). The file is also in the Chapter10 folder for reference.


```
CREATE OR REPLACE PROCEDURE prodname_chg_sp wrapped
a000000
b2
abcd
abcd
abcd
abcd
abcd
abcd
abcd
abcd
abcd
abcd
abcd
abcd
abcd
abcd
abcd
7
d1 df
1KPejxuvCtY1D5HNw0pL5x95wKcwg0xK2Z7hf3TpTP7VwvOO2ywW0eguUFaSDutm
4hhXUf0y
ULVb2mOFj8Uf/76hz7jsfESsCHOrQcHGKg+
5xOSIRN2XF2BwmfIBLHYbpMRfYmKG+uvoVI8D
zXRzQnncGuwe4MCWjs0xp3V6n/fJAt7z0o44K0ZMBUzuCGdD2ZpznogBOIOIasye
whYfDwOG
32g=

/
```

FIGURE 10-25 A wrapped script file's contents

The `DBMS_DDL` package contains the `CREATE_WRAPPED` procedure for creating and wrapping a dynamically generated program unit. Figure 10-26 shows the block that creates a procedure dynamically; the procedure name is determined at runtime.

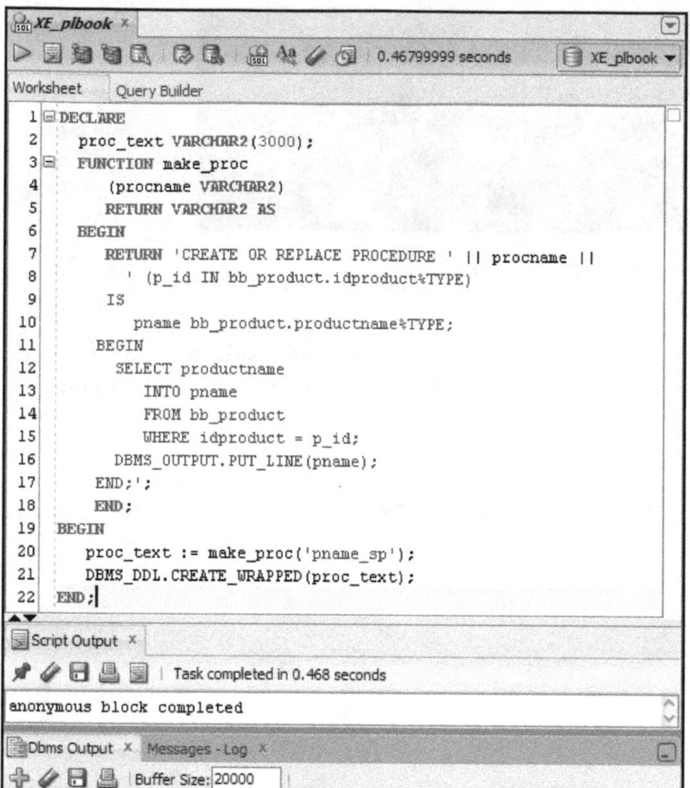

FIGURE 10-26 Wrapping a procedure that's created dynamically

Querying the source code from the data dictionary verifies that the procedure exists and is wrapped (see Figure 10-27). Even though the procedure is wrapped, a call to it runs successfully; in terms of execution, it seems no different from a procedure that isn't wrapped.

NOTE

Database triggers can't be wrapped. Oracle suggests placing the required logic in a procedure and calling the procedure from the trigger.

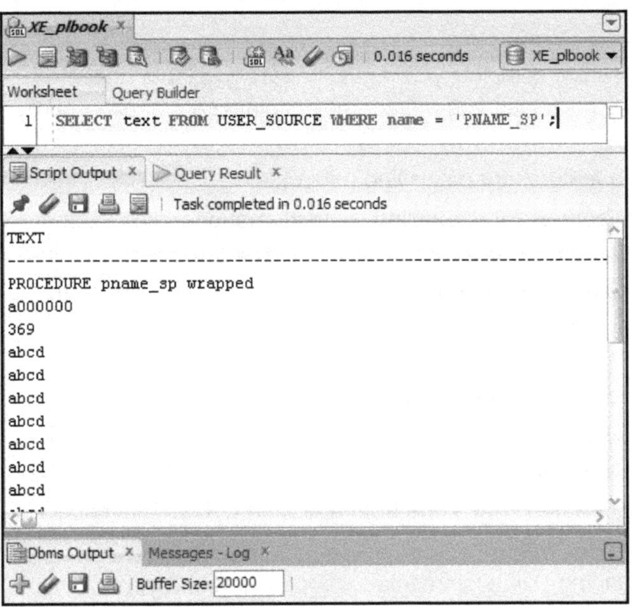

FIGURE 10-27 Querying `USER_SOURCE` to verify that a procedure has been wrapped

Chapter Summary

- Oracle built-in or supplied packages are complete packages that are available after installing the Oracle database. Like packages you create, they contain sets of procedures and functions.
- The `DBMS_OUTPUT` package offers features for displaying data onscreen.
- The `UTL_FILE` package contains features for interacting with external operating system files, such as opening a file, writing to a file, reading a file, and deleting a file.
- The `DBMS_LOB` package is used to manage large objects, such as a `BLOB` or `CLOB`, in the database. The package programs allow inserting a LOB into and retrieving it from the database.
- The `DBMS_ALERT` package is used to generate notifications of database events to users.
- E-mails can be sent via PL/SQL with the `UTL_MAIL` package. Before Oracle 10*g*, the `UTL_SMTP` package was used to generate and send e-mails from PL/SQL code.
- The `UTL_HTTP` package allows retrieving HTML code from specified URLs. This capability is used to scan information from Web pages.
- The `DBMS_DDL` package allows running DDL statements to recompile and analyze database objects from PL/SQL code.
- Dynamic SQL allows supplying identifiers, such as table names and column names, at runtime and enables you to include DDL statements in PL/SQL code. It can be implemented with the `DBMS_SQL` package or by using native dynamic SQL.
- With `DBMS_SQL`, all processing is handled manually, including opening the cursor, parsing, executing the statement, and closing the cursor. Placeholders are used to provide values in SQL statements, and multiple-row queries are managed with `FETCH_ROWS`. It's most suitable when the number of columns or bind variables used in the statement isn't known until runtime.
- Native dynamic SQL is easier to code and processes statements more efficiently; however, it can't handle all the tasks that `DBMS_SQL` can. It uses the `EXECUTE IMMEDIATE` and `OPEN FOR` statements.
- Oracle has two methods for hiding code: the wrap utility and the `DBMS_DDL` package. The wrap utility is a command-line tool that processes script files containing `CREATE` statements for program units. The `DBMS_DDL` package can wrap a single program unit that's generated dynamically.

Review Questions

1. Oracle built-in packages ________________.
    a. need to be created with special scripts by each user
    b. are ready for use when the database is installed
    c. can be purchased separately
    d. are the only recommended package code

2. If your application needs to send notifications to users when a data change (such as a higher bid in an auction) occurs, which built-in package would be most helpful?
   a. `DBMS_NOTICE`
   b. `DBMS_EMAIL`
   c. `DBMS_ALERT`
   d. `DBMS_DDL`
3. The `DBMS_DDL` package allows performing which of the following actions in PL/SQL code? (Choose all that apply.)
   a. recompiling a database object
   b. communicating between sessions
   c. computing statistics for a database object
   d. marking a database object as `INVALID`

4. A `BLOB` is an Oracle data type that holds which of the following?
   a. up to 4 GB of character data
   b. a video file
   c. a graphics image
   d. foreign-language elements
5. Which package is most helpful in automatically sending e-mails from an application?
   a. `DBMS_OUTPUT`
   b. `DBMS_SMTP`
   c. `DBMS_JOB`
   d. `UTL_MAIL`
6. If an application needs to write data to an external file, which package is the most helpful?
   a. `UTL_FILE`
   b. `DBMS_FILE`
   c. `UTL_OUT`
   d. `DBMS_WRITE`
7. Why do you have more flexibility with runtime values in SQL statements when using dynamic SQL?
   a. Identifier values, such as table and column names, can be supplied at runtime.
   b. The `WHERE` clause can affect different rows based on runtime input.
   c. Users can write their own SQL statements.
   d. It allows using parameters that supply values in the SQL statement.
8. Which SQL statement can be included in a PL/SQL block only in dynamic SQL?
   a. `INSERT`
   b. `UPDATE`
   c. `DELETE`
   d. `CREATE TABLE`

9. You can implement dynamic SQL with which of the following? (Choose all that apply.)
   a. `EXECUTE IMMEDIATE`
   b. `DBMS_EXECUTE`
   c. `DBMS_SQL`
   d. `DYNAMIC EXECUTE`
10. In which of the following situations is using native dynamic SQL more suitable than using the `DBMS_SQL` package?
    a. You're performing DDL operations.
    b. The statement is going to run repeatedly.
    c. The number of columns isn't known until runtime.
    d. The column data types aren't known until runtime.

11. What does "wrapping" PL/SQL program unit code mean?
12. How is an Oracle built-in package different from packages you construct?
13. Describe an Oracle-supplied package not covered in this chapter and explain briefly how it might be useful.
14. How would dynamic SQL help in creating a database query system to be used by all Brewbean's employees?
15. Explain when using native dynamic SQL is more suitable than using the `DBMS_SQL` package.

Advanced Review Questions

1. `DBMS_ALERT` actions are transaction-based, which means the action is ______________.
   a. independent of the transaction
   b. completed only when a `COMMIT` statement is issued
   c. a DML statement
   d. unpredictable
2. In the following `CREATE` statement, which items represent placeholder names? (Choose all that apply.)

```
CREATE OR REPLACE PROCEDURE update_prod
  (p_one VARCHAR2,
   p_two NUMBER,
   p_three NUMBER)
  IS
  lv_a INTEGER;
  lv_b VARCHAR2(150);
  lv_c NUMBER(1);
BEGIN
  lv_a := DBMS_SQL.OPEN_CURSOR;
  lv_b := 'UPDATE product
         SET ' || p_one || ' = :price
           WHERE idProd = :id';
  DBMS_SQL.PARSE(lv_a, lv_b, DBMS_SQL.NATIVE);
  DBMS_SQL.BIND_VARIABLE(lv_a, ':price', p_two);
```

```
   DBMS_SQL.BIND_VARIABLE(lv_a, ':id', p_three);
   lv_c := DBMS_SQL.EXECUTE(lv_a);
   DBMS_SQL.CLOSE_CURSOR(lv_a);
   COMMIT;
   DBMS_OUTPUT.PUT_LINE(lv_c);
END;
```

a. `p_col`
b. `price`
c. `idProduct`
d. `id`

3. In Question 2's code, which variable contains a cursor reference?
   a. `lv_a`
   b. `lv_b`
   c. `lv_c`
   d. `p_three`
4. In Question 2's code, what value should be supplied for the `p_one` parameter?
   a. table name
   b. column name
   c. column value
   d. placeholder
5. In the following `EXECUTE IMMEDIATE` statement (assume it's included as part of a complete block), what do `two` and `three` represent?

```
EXECUTE IMMEDIATE 'UPDATE product
   SET ' || one || ' = :price
      WHERE idProd = :id'
      USING two, three;
```

   a. placeholders
   b. parameters
   c. columns
   d. data types

Hands-On Assignments

Assignment 10-1: Using the DBMS_ALERT Package

Brewbean's wants to add an alert in the product management page to advise the manager of a product stock level falling below the reorder point. The alert simply needs to state which product needs reordering.

1. Start SQL Developer, if necessary.
2. Create a database trigger on the BB_PRODUCT table, using the `DBMS_ALERT` package to send an alert when the stock value falls below the reorder value. Name the alert **`reorder`** and have it contain a message stating that a product needs to be reordered. Include the product number in the message.

3. If an error is raised because you don't have permission to use the DBMS_ALERT package, you need to log on as SYSDBA and enter the following command to grant the necessary permissions. (This code assumes you're the user PLBOOK.)

```
GRANT EXECUTE ON DBMS_ALERT TO PLBOOK;
```

4. Start a second session of SQL Developer as **SYSTEM MANAGER**.
5. Type and run the following block to register the alert:

```
BEGIN
  DBMS_ALERT.REGISTER('reorder');
END;
```

6. Type and run the following block to initiate the wait for an alert:

```
DECLARE
  lv_msg_txt VARCHAR2(25);
  lv_status_num NUMBER(1);
BEGIN
  DBMS_ALERT.WAITONE('reorder', lv_msg_txt, lv_status_num, 120);
  DBMS_OUTPUT.PUT_LINE('Alert: '|| lv_msg_txt);
  DBMS_OUTPUT.PUT_LINE('Status: '|| lv_status_num);
END;
```


7. The preceding code sets a wait period of two minutes. Return to the first SQL Developer session. Type and run the following code to cause the alert to fire:

```
UPDATE bb_product
  SET stock = stock - 2
   WHERE idproduct = 4;
COMMIT;
```

8. Return to the second SQL Developer session. The alert message should be displayed.

Assignment 10-2: Using the DBMS_DDL Package

Because Brewbean's is in the middle of constructing its application and making several database modifications, the developers are going to build a procedure to recompile all invalid objects automatically.

1. Start SQL Developer, if necessary.
2. Type and run the following code:

```
SELECT object_name, status
  FROM user_objects
  WHERE object_type = 'PROCEDURE';
```

3. If you see the BB_JOBTEST procedure listed with a VALID status onscreen, skip to Step 7. If this procedure doesn't exist, proceed with Step 4.
4. Open the **assignment02.txt** file in the Chapter10 folder, and use its code to create the **BB_JOBTEST** procedure.

5. Type and run the following code:

```
SELECT object_name, status
  FROM user_objects
  WHERE object_type = 'PROCEDURE';
```

6. Verify that the query results list `BB_JOBTEST` with a `VALID` status, which tells you the procedure exists.
7. Type and run the following statement to modify the BB_JOBQ table. Because the `BB_JOBTEST` procedure uses this table, the procedure changes to the status `INVALID`, indicating the need for recompiling.

```
ALTER TABLE bb_jobq
  MODIFY (msg VARCHAR2(30));
```

8. Type and run the following query to confirm the status `INVALID`:

```
SELECT object_name, status
  FROM user_objects
  WHERE object_type = 'PROCEDURE';
```

9. Create an anonymous block, using `DBMS_DDL.ALTER_COMPILE` to compile all `INVALID` objects. To simplify this process, retrieve all the `INVALID` objects in a cursor. Run the anonymous block.
10. Type and run the following query to confirm that these objects' status is now `VALID`:

```
SELECT object_name, status
  FROM user_objects
  WHERE object_type = 'PROCEDURE';
```


Assignment 10-3: Using the UTL_FILE Package to Read and Insert Data

Brewbean's has struck a deal with a new tea product supplier, who has sent a test file showing how files containing product names and descriptions will be submitted. Create a PL/SQL block, using the `UTL_FILE` package, to read from the file and insert data in the BB_PRODUCT table.

NOTE

A directory object named `ORA_FILES` should already be on the Oracle server, and the `tea.txt` file should be in this directory.

1. Start Windows Explorer. Open the **tea.txt** file in the Chapter10 folder. Check the file's contents to confirm that it contains product names and descriptions, and review the data's format.
2. Start SQL Developer, if necessary.
3. Create an anonymous block that reads each line in the `tea.txt` file and inserts the values in the BB_PRODUCT table. Use the `UTL_FILE` reading feature in a loop to read each line from the text file.
4. Run the block to perform the `INSERT` statements.

5. Type and run the following code. The results should display the three tea products from the `tea.txt` file.

```
SELECT productname, description
  FROM bb_product;
```

Assignment 10-4: Using the UTL_FILE Package to Export Data Columns

The Brewbean's manager wants to have a file extracted from the database containing product information for inventory and cash flow analysis. The manager uses this file in spreadsheet software on a laptop computer. Using the `UTL_FILE` package, create a PL/SQL block that places data columns in a comma-delimited text file named **prod_ext.txt** in the c:\oraclass directory. The extracted file should contain one line per product and the following columns of the BB_PRODUCT table: IDPRODUCT, PRODUCTNAME, PRICE, TYPE, STOCK, ORDERED, and REORDER.

Assignment 10-5: Sending E-mail with UTL_SMTP

NOTE

This assignment requires e-mail addresses that are suitable for your environment. In addition, the system `smtp_out` parameter must be set to an accessible SMTP server, and an access control list (ACL) must be created.

The Brewbean's manager decided he wants to get e-mail notifications when product stock levels fall below the reorder point. Create the **BB_STKALERT_TRG** trigger on the BB_PRODUCT table to perform this task. The e-mail body should state the product ID and name. Use the following `UPDATE` statement to set up a product to test:

```
UPDATE bb_product
  SET stock = 26
  WHERE idProduct = 4;
COMMIT;
```

Test the trigger with this code:

```
UPDATE bb_product
  SET stock = stock - 2
   WHERE idproduct = 4;
COMMIT;
```

When you finish the assignment, disable the trigger so that it doesn't affect other assignments.

Assignment 10-6: Using DBMS_OUTPUT

Using the `DBMS_OUTPUT` package, create and run a PL/SQL block that displays lines for each product in the BB_PRODUCT table. If the stock level for a product is above the reorder point, only a single line should be displayed that looks like the following code:

```
Product 5 - Sumatra does NOT need ordering
```

If the stock level is below the reorder point, lines such as the following should be displayed:

```
Product 5 - Sumatra needs ordering!
  Stock = 24 , reorder point = 25
```

Before running the block, issue the following statements to make sure product 4's stock level is below the reorder point:

```
UPDATE bb_product
  SET stock = 24
  WHERE idProduct = 4;
COMMIT;
```

Assignment 10-7: Using the `DBMS_SQL` Package

Brewbean's employees want an application page where they can query the CUSTOMER table for ID and last name based on one criterion on any customer information column. To perform this task, you create a procedure by using `DBMS_SQL` to set up a dynamic query. Name the procedure **`DYN_CUST_SP`** and verify that the procedure works by issuing two queries: one with the state **NC** and one with the e-mail value **ratboy@msn.net**. Keep in mind that any column can be used as a criterion, which could result in the query returning more than one row. For example, two customers might have the same last name. Therefore, this procedure needs to be able to handle multiple rows being returned.

1. Start SQL Developer, if necessary.
2. Open the **`assignment07.txt`** file in the Chapter10 folder, and use its code to create the **`DYN_CUST_SP`** procedure.
3. Next, you need to run the procedure with the two test cases. First, use the STATE column criteria, and run an anonymous block that includes the statement **`dyn_cust_sp ('state', 'NC');`**.
4. Now check the customer e-mail address by using an anonymous block that includes the statement **`dyn_cust_sp('e-mail', 'ratboy@msn.net');`**.

Assignment 10-8: Using Native Dynamic SQL to Add Columns

The Brewbean's manager wants an application page that makes it easy for employees to add columns to the database. Create a procedure that accepts input and uses native dynamic SQL to perform this task. Test the procedure by adding a column named MEMBER to the BB_SHOPPER table with the data type `CHAR(1)`.

1. Start SQL Developer, if necessary.
2. Open the **`assignment08.txt`** file in the Chapter10 folder. Review the uncompleted procedure code, and then finish the `EXECUTE IMMEDIATE` statement to allow column additions.
3. Create the procedure in SQL Developer.
4. Run the procedure by using the following block to add the MEMBER column:

```
BEGIN
  dyn_addcol_sp('member','bb_shopper','CHAR(1)');
END;
```

5. Type **`DESC bb_shopper`** and press **Enter** to list the table structure and confirm the addition of the MEMBER column.

Assignment 10-9: Using Native Dynamic SQL for Product Searches

Brewbean's wants to allow customers to do product search by selecting a product name or description, and then typing a search term. Using native dynamic SQL, create a procedure named **SEARCH_SP** that returns the product name, description, and price based on users' search criteria. This procedure needs to handle multiple rows being returned.

Assignment 10-10: Understanding Business Intelligence

Business intelligence (BI) is a term used to describe providing more database power for users. Describe briefly what it means in applications, including the terms "data mining," "data marts," "OLAP," and "executive dashboards." What role might dynamic SQL play in BI? Describe BI products that Oracle offers.

Assignment 10-11: Using the Wrap Utility

In this assignment, you show how to use the Oracle wrap utility to obfuscate the `BB_JOBTEST` procedure's source code. Create an `.sql` file (`job.sql`) using the script file for the procedure (available in `assignment02.txt` in the Chapter10 folder of the data files). Use the wrap utility on the `job.sql` file to hide the script's source code. Check the file the utility produces.

Case Project

Case 10-1: Working with More Movies

The More Movies inventory clerk has requested a text file containing a line for each time all copies of a movie are checked out. The clerk wants to use this information in a software program for inventory analysis. Each line in the file should contain the date, movie ID, and movie stock quantity. To do this, code needs to be created in a database trigger. Keep in mind that this file should maintain a continuous record, so each new line should be *appended* to the file. Name the file **checkout.txt** and save it in the C:\oraclass directory.

TIP

To append to a file, research the `UTL_FILE.FOPEN` procedure's `OPEN MODE` parameter on the OTN Web site.

Test the trigger by using the following `UPDATE` statements. Using two is necessary to be sure data is appended in the file.

```
UPDATE mm_movie
  SET movie_qty = 0
  WHERE movie_id = 7;

UPDATE mm_movie
  SET movie_qty = 0
  WHERE movie_id = 8;
```

TABLES FOR THE BREWBEAN'S DATABASE

INTRODUCTION

This appendix shows the structure and original data contents of each table in Chapter 1's database ERD. Columns containing no initial data are excluded from the data listing where space is limited. In addition, some column names are truncated in data listings because the column's display width is determined by the actual data's width. Column widths haven't been increased because of space limitations in this book. Keep in mind that structure and data changes will occur as you work through the book.

TABLE A-1 Structure of BB_SHOPPER

NAME	NULL?	TYPE
IDSHOPPER	NOT NULL	NUMBER(4)
FIRSTNAME		VARCHAR2(15)
LASTNAME		VARCHAR2(20)
ADDRESS		VARCHAR2(40)
CITY		VARCHAR2(20)
STATE		CHAR(2)
ZIPCODE		VARCHAR2(15)
PHONE		VARCHAR2(10)
FAX		VARCHAR2(10)
EMAIL		VARCHAR2(25)
USERNAME		VARCHAR2(8)
PASSWORD		VARCHAR2(8)
COOKIE		NUMBER(4)
DTENTERED		DATE
PROVINCE		VARCHAR2(15)
COUNTRY		VARCHAR2(15)
PROMO		CHAR(1)

TABLE A-2 Data in BB_SHOPPER

IDSHOPPER	FIRSTNAM	LASTNAM	ADDRESS	CITY	STAT	ZIPCOD	PHONE	FAX
21	John	Carter	21 Front St.	Raleigh	NC	54822	9014317701	
22	Margaret	Somner	287 Walnut Drive	Cheasapeake	VA	23321	7574216559	
23	Kenny	Ratman	1 Fun Lane	South Park	NC	54674	9015680902	
24	Camryn	Sonnie	40162 Talamore	South Riding	VA	20152	7035556868	
25	Scott	Savid	11 Pine Grove	Hickory	VA	22954	7578221010	
26	Monica	Cast	112 W. 4th	Greensburg	VA	27754	7573217384	
27	Pete	Parker	1 Queens	New York	NY	67233	1013217384	

TABLE A-2 Data in BB_SHOPPER (*continued*)

EMAIL	USERNAME	PASSWORD	COOKIE	DTENTERED	PROVINCE	COUNTRY	PRO
Crackjack@aol.com	Crackj	flyby	1	13-JAN-12		USA	
MargS@infi.net	MaryS	pupper	1	03-FEB-12		USA	
ratboy@msn.net	rat55	kile	0	26-JAN-12		USA	
kids2@xis.net	kids2	steel	1	19-MAR-12		USA	
scott1@odu.edu	fdwell	tweak	1	19-FEB-12		USA	
gma@earth.net	gma1	goofy	1	09-FEB-12		USA	
spider@web.net			0	14-FEB-12		USA	

TABLE A-3 Structure of BB_BASKET

NAME	NULL?	TYPE
IDBASKET	NOT NULL	NUMBER(5)
QUANTITY		NUMBER(2)
IDSHOPPER		NUMBER(4)
ORDERPLACED		NUMBER(1)
SUBTOTAL		NUMBER(7,2)
TOTAL		NUMBER(7,2)
SHIPPING		NUMBER(5,2)
TAX		NUMBER(5,2)
DTCREATED		DATE
PROMO		NUMBER(2)
SHIPFIRSTNAME		VARCHAR2(10)
SHIPLASTNAME		VARCHAR2(20)
SHIPADDRESS		VARCHAR2(40)
SHIPCITY		VARCHAR2(20)
SHIPSTATE		VARCHAR2(2)
SHIPZIPCODE		VARCHAR2(15)
SHIPPHONE		VARCHAR2(10)
SHIPFAX		VARCHAR2(10)
SHIPEMAIL		VARCHAR2(25)
BILLFIRSTNAME		VARCHAR2(10)
BILLLASTNAME		VARCHAR2(20)
BILLADDRESS		VARCHAR2(40)
BILLCITY		VARCHAR2(20)
BILLSTATE		VARCHAR2(2)
BILLZIPCODE		VARCHAR2(15)
BILLPHONE		VARCHAR2(10)
BILLFAX		VARCHAR2(10)
BILLEMAIL		VARCHAR2(25)
DTORDERED		DATE
SHIPPROVINCE		VARCHAR2(20)

TABLE A-3 Structure of BB_BASKET (*continued*)

NAME	NULL?	TYPE
SHIPCOUNTRY		VARCHAR2(20)
BILLPROVINCE		VARCHAR2(20)
BILLCOUNTRY		VARCHAR2(20)
CARDTYPE		CHAR(1)
CARDNUMBER		VARCHAR2(20)
EXPMONTH		CHAR(2)
EXPYEAR		CHAR(4)
CARDNAME		VARCHAR2(25)
SHIPBILL		CHAR(1)
SHIPFLAG		CHAR(1)

TABLE A-4 Data in BB_BASKET

IDBASKET	QUANTITY	IDSHOPPER	ORDERPLACED	SUBTOTAL	TOTAL	SHIPPING
3	3	21	1	26.6	32.4	5
4	1	21	1	28.5	34.36	5
5	4	22	1	41.6	48.47	5
6	3	22	1	149.99	161.74	5
7	2	23	1	21.6	27.25	5
8	2	23	1	21.6	27.25	5
9	2	23	1	21.6	27.25	5
10	3	24	1	38.9	45.65	5
11	1	24	1	10	15.45	5
12	7	25	0	72.4	83.66	8
13	2	26	0	20	0	0
14	0	26	0	0	0	0
15	2	27	0	16.2	21.69	5
16	2	27	0	16.2	21.69	5

TABLE A-4 Data in BB_BASKET (*continued*)

TAX	DTCREATED	PROMO	DTORDERED	SHI	SHI
.8	23-JAN-12	0	23-JAN-12	N	N
.86	12-FEB-12	0	12-FEB-12	N	N
1.87	19-FEB-12	0	19-FEB-12	N	N
6.75	01-MAR-12	0	01-MAR-12	N	N
.65	26-JAN-12	0	26-JAN-12	N	N
.65	16-FEB-12	0	16-FEB-12	N	N
.65	02-MAR-12	0	02-MAR-12	N	N
1.75	07-FEB-12	0	12-FEB-12	N	N
.45	27-FEB-12	0	27-FEB-12	N	N
3.26	19-FEB-12	0		N	N
0	09-FEB-12	0		N	N
0	10-FEB-12	0		N	N
.49	14-FEB-12	0	03-MAR-12	N	N
.49	24-FEB-12	0	03-MAR-12	N	N

TABLE A-5 Structure of BB_BASKETITEM

NAME	NULL?	TYPE
IDBASKETITEM	NOT NULL	NUMBER(2)
IDPRODUCT		NUMBER(2)
PRICE		NUMBER(6,2)
QUANTITY		NUMBER(2)
IDBASKET		NUMBER(5)
OPTION1		NUMBER(2)
OPTION2		NUMBER(2)

TABLE A-6 Data in BB_BASKETITEM

IDBASKETITEM	IDPRODUCT	PRICE	QUANTITY	IDBASKET	OPTION1	OPTION2
15	6	5	1	3	1	4
16	8	10.8	2	3	2	4
17	4	28.5	1	4		
18	7	10.8	1	5	2	3
19	8	10.8	1	5	2	3
20	9	10	1	5	2	3
21	10	10	1	5	2	3
22	10	10	2	6	2	4
23	2	129.99	1	6		
24	7	10.8	1	7	2	3
25	8	10.8	1	7	2	3
26	7	10.8	1	8	2	3
27	8	10.8	1	8	2	3
28	7	10.8	1	9	2	3
29	8	10.8	1	9	2	3
30	6	5	1	10	1	3
31	8	5.4	1	10	1	3
32	4	28.5	1	10		
33	9	10	1	11	2	3
34	8	10.8	2	12	2	3
35	9	10	2	12	2	3
36	6	10	2	12	2	3

TABLE A-6 Data in BB_BASKETITEM (*continued*)

IDBASKETITEM	IDPRODUCT	PRICE	QUANTITY	IDBASKET	OPTION1	OPTION2
37	7	10.8	1	12	2	3
38	9	10	2	13	2	3
40	8	10.8	1	15	2	3
41	7	5.4	1	15	1	3
42	8	10.8	1	16	2	3
43	7	5.4	1	16	1	3

TABLE A-7 Structure of BB_PRODUCT

NAME	NULL?	TYPE
IDPRODUCT	NOT NULL	NUMBER(2)
PRODUCTNAME		VARCHAR2(25)
DESCRIPTION		VARCHAR2(100)
PRODUCTIMAGE		VARCHAR2(25)
PRICE		NUMBER(6,2)
SALESTART		DATE
SALEEND		DATE
SALEPRICE		NUMBER(6,2)
ACTIVE		NUMBER(1)
FEATURED		NUMBER(1)
FEATURESTART		DATE
FEATUREEND		DATE
TYPE		CHAR(1)
IDDEPARTMENT		NUMBER(2)
STOCK		NUMBER(5,1)
ORDERED		NUMBER(3)
REORDER		NUMBER(3)

TABLE A-8 Data in BB_PRODUCT

IDPRODUCT	PRODUCTNAME	DESCRIPTION	PRODUCTIMAGE	PRICE	SALESTART	SALEEND
1	CapressoBar Model #351	A fully programmable pump espresso machine and 10-cup coffeemaker complete with GoldTone filter.	capresso.gif	99.99		
2	Capresso Ultima	Coffee and espresso and cappuccino machine. Brews from one espresso to two six-ounce cups of coffee.	capresso2.gif	129.99		
3	Eileen 4-cup French Press	A unique coffeemaker from those proud craftsmen in windy Normandy.	frepress.gif	32.5		
4	Coffee Grinder	Avoid blade grinders! This mill grinder allows you to choose a fine grind to a coarse grind.	grind.gif	28.5		
5	Sumatra	Spicy and intense with herbal aroma.	sumatra.jpg	10.5		
6	Guatamala	Heavy body, spicy twist, aromatic and smoky flavor.	Guatamala.jpg	10	01-JUN-12	15-JUN-12
7	Columbia	Dry, nutty flavor and smoothness.	columbia.jpg	10.8		
8	Brazil	Well-balanced mellow flavor, a medium body with hints of cocoa and a mild, nutlike aftertaste.	brazil.jpg	10.8		
9	Ethiopia	Distinctive berry-like flavor and aroma; reminds many of a fruity, memorable wine.	ethiopia.jpg	10		
10	Espresso	Dense, caramel-like sweetness with a soft acidity. Roasted somewhat darker than traditional Italian.	espresso.jpg	10		

TABLE A-8 Data in BB_PRODUCT (*continued*)

SALEPRICE	ACTIVE	TYP	IDDEPARTMENT	STOCK	ORDERED	REORDER
	1	E	2	23	0	12
	1	E	2	15	0	9
	1	E	2	30	0	15
	1	E	2	26	0	25
	1	C	1	41	0	45
	1	C	1	42	0	35
8	1	C	1	61	0	35
	1	C	1	53	0	35
	1	C	1	54	0	35
	1	C	1	50	50	50

TABLE A-9 Structure of BB_PRODUCTOPTION

NAME	NULL?	TYPE
IDPRODUCTOPTION	NOT NULL	NUMBER(3)
IDOPTION		NUMBER(2)
IDPRODUCT		NUMBER(2)

TABLE A-10 Data in BB_PRODUCTOPTION

IDPRODUCTOPTION	IDOPTION	IDPRODUCT
1	1	5
2	2	5
3	3	5
4	4	5
5	1	6
6	2	6
7	3	6
8	4	6
9	1	7
10	2	7
11	3	7
12	4	7
13	1	8
14	2	8
15	3	8
16	4	8
17	1	9
18	2	9
19	3	9
20	4	9
21	1	10
22	2	10
23	3	10
24	4	10

TABLE A-11 Structure of BB_PRODUCTOPTIONDETAIL

NAME	NULL?	TYPE
IDOPTION	NOT NULL	NUMBER(2)
OPTIONNAME		VARCHAR2(25)
IDOPTIONCATEGORY		NUMBER(2)

TABLE A-12 Data in BB_PRODUCTOPTIONDETAIL

IDOPTION	OPTIONNAME	IDOPTIONCATEGORY
1	1/2 lb.	1
2	1 lb.	1
3	Whole Bean	2
4	Regular Grind	2

TABLE A-13 Structure of BB_PRODUCTOPTIONCATEGORY

NAME	NULL?	TYPE
IDOPTIONCATEGORY	NOT NULL	NUMBER(2)
CATEGORYNAME		VARCHAR2(25)

TABLE A-14 Data in BB_PRODUCTOPTIONCATEGORY

IDOPTIONCATEGORY	CATEGORYNAME
1	Size
2	Form

TABLE A-15 Structure of BB_DEPARTMENT

NAME	NULL?	TYPE
IDDEPARTMENT	NOT NULL	NUMBER(2)
DEPTNAME		VARCHAR2(25)
DEPTDESC		VARCHAR2(100)
DEPTIMAGE		VARCHAR2(25)

TABLE A-16 Data in BB_DEPARTMENT

IDDEPARTMENT	DEPTNAME	DEPTDESC	DEPTIMAGE
1	Coffee	Many types of coffee beans	coffee.gif
2	Equipment and Supplies	Coffee makers to coffee filters available	machines.gif
3	Coffee Club	What are the benefits of our club membership?	club.gif

TABLE A-17 Structure of BB_BASKETSTATUS

NAME	NULL?	TYPE
IDSTATUS	NOT NULL	NUMBER(5)
IDBASKET		NUMBER(5)
IDSTAGE		NUMBER(1)
DTSTAGE		DATE
NOTES		VARCHAR2(50)
SHIPPER		VARCHAR2(5)
SHIPPINGNUM		VARCHAR2(20)

TABLE A-18 Data in BB_BASKETSTATUS

IDSTATUS	IDBASKET	IDSTAGE	DTSTAGE	NOTES	SHIPPER	SHIPPINGNUM
1	3	1	24-JAN-12			
2	3	5	25-JAN-12	Customer called to confirm shipment	UPS	ZW845584GD89H569
3	4	1	13-FEB-12			
4	4	5	14-FEB-12			
15	12	3				

TABLE A-19 Structure of BB_TAX

NAME	NULL?	TYPE
IDSTATE	NOT NULL	NUMBER(2)
STATE		CHAR(2)
TAXRATE		NUMBER(4,3)

TABLE A-20 Data in BB_TAX

IDSTATE	STATE	TAXRATE
1	VA	.045
2	NC	.03
3	SC	.06

TABLE A-21 Structure of BB_SHIPPING

NAME	NULL?	TYPE
IDRANGE	NOT NULL	NUMBER(2)
LOW		NUMBER(3)
HIGH		NUMBER(3)
FEE		NUMBER(6,2)

TABLE A-22 Data in BB_SHIPPING

IDRANGE	LOW	HIGH	FEE
1	1	5	5
2	6	10	8
3	11	99	11

APPENDIX **B**

ORACLE INSTALLATION AND USING ORACLE SQL DEVELOPER

INTRODUCTION

Oracle Database 11*g* and SQL Developer are used throughout this book, and you need them to perform tasks in chapters, including hands-on assignments. Check with your instructor first to determine what access has been set up and is recommended at your location. You might not have to perform an installation on your own equipment, or you might be given specific instructions for an installation.

The first part of this appendix outlines the installation process for Oracle Database 11*g* Release 2 for Microsoft Windows (32-bit) Enterprise or Standard Edition and Oracle Database 11*g* Express Edition. The Enterprise and Standard editions are included on the DVD accompanying this book. The Express Edition requires fewer resources than the Enterprise Edition and can be downloaded free from Oracle. If you plan to continue with more advanced Oracle classes and study database administration, the Enterprise or Standard edition might be more helpful than the Express Edition. However, review the hardware and software requirements for each edition. The Enterprise Edition demands more resources and is typically installed on a server machine. The Express Edition is suitable for a desktop or laptop installation; however, it does have some processing limitations, such as a maximum of one CPU and 1 GB RAM. These limitations won't affect your ability to complete the coursework in this book, but more advanced classes might require switching to a different Oracle edition.

The second part of this appendix is a basic introduction to Oracle SQL Developer, which is used in this book for creating and testing program units. Its capabilities include browsing database objects, creating and modifying objects, querying and exporting data, and editing, testing, and debugging program units. One feature that's particularly helpful in developing program units is automatic color-coding of programming statements. This feature simplifies reading code and finding syntax problems. The program unit execution features simplify testing by generating a test block automatically to run the program unit.

To explore all the features in this tool, refer to the Oracle SQL Developer section of the OTN Web site, which offers documentation, technical information, and tutorials.

ORACLE DATABASE INSTALLATION

This section gives you an overview of installations for two Oracle versions: Oracle Database 11*g* Release 2 for Microsoft Windows (32-bit), which is included on this book's DVD, and Oracle Database 11*g* Express Edition, which is downloaded from the OTN Web site.

NOTE

If you're prompted to log on to OTN and haven't created an account yet, you need to create one. An OTN account is free and allows you to access all the free resources on this site.

The following steps are for installing Oracle Database 11*g* Release 2:

1. Review the installation guide on the OTN Web site. You should always verify the hardware and software requirements for an Oracle installation. The Database Quick installation guide is at *http://docs.oracle.com/cd/E11882_01/install.112/e24281/toc.htm*. Make sure your computer meets the following minimum requirements:
    - Hardware: 1 GB RAM, 2 GB virtual memory, and 5.35 GB free disk space
    - Software: Windows Server 2003, XP Professional, Vista (Business, Enterprise, or Ultimate), Server 2008 (Server Core option not supported), or Windows 7 (Professional, Enterprise, or Ultimate)

2. Insert the DVD supplied with this book.
3. In the root directory, double-click the **`Setup.exe`** file to start the installation. The software performs some environment checks, which takes a few minutes.
4. When the installation begins, a series of windows prompt you to make selections. First, you're asked to enter contact information so that you can be informed of security updates (see Figure B-1). You can enter an e-mail address, but you don't have to supply any contact information to do the installation. Click **Next**.

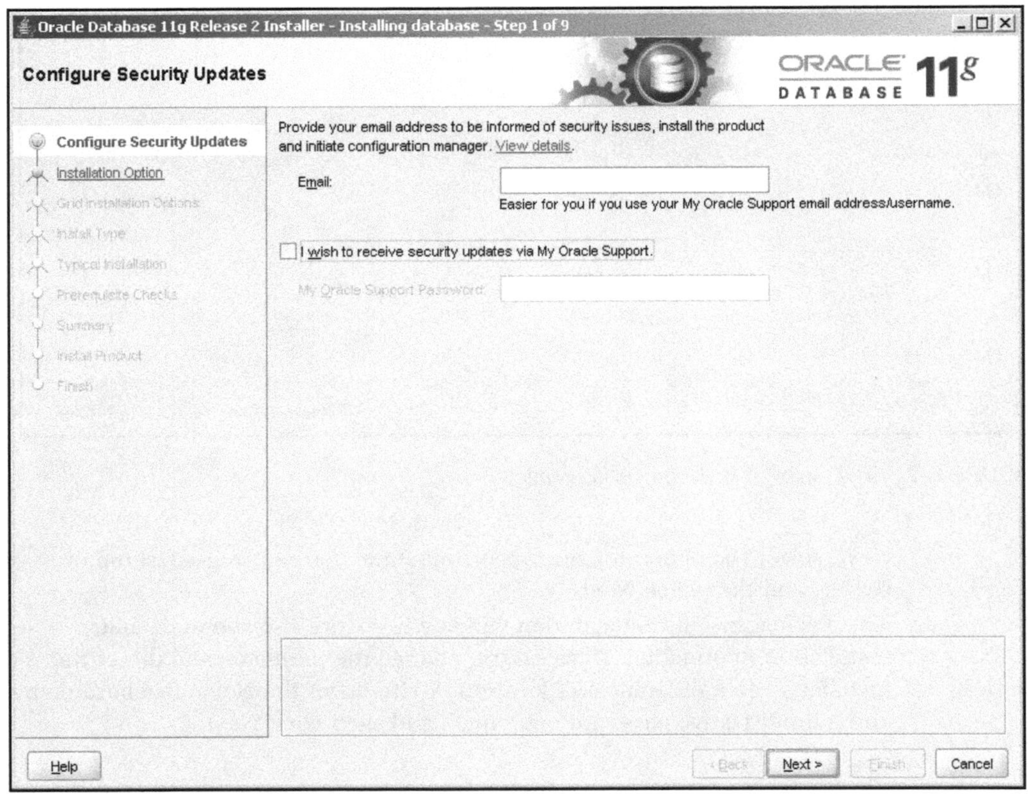

FIGURE B-1 Entering contact information

5. In the Select Installation Option window, click the **Create and configure a database** option button (see Figure B-2), and then click **Next**.

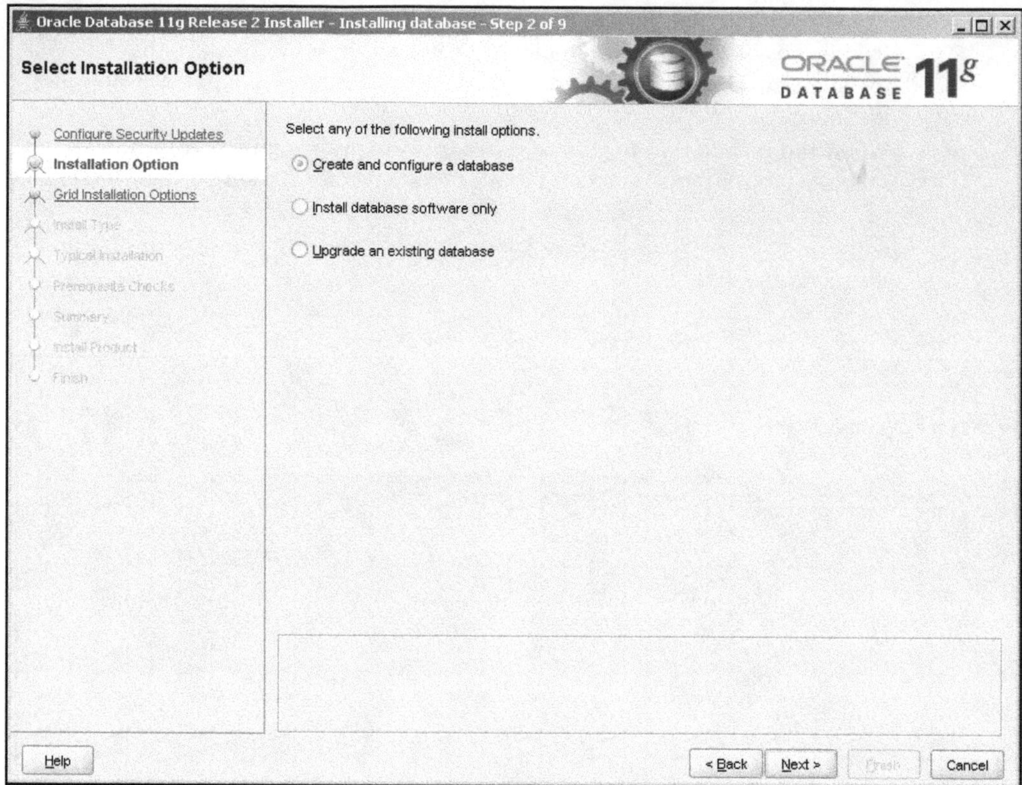

FIGURE B-2 The Select Installation Option window

6. Next, select the option for the type of machine you're using—desktop or server, and then click **Next**.
7. The Typical Install Configuration window in Figure B-3 shows default installation information. If necessary, change the pathnames to direct the installation to a different disk location. Write down the global database name and administrative password you enter, and then click **Next**.

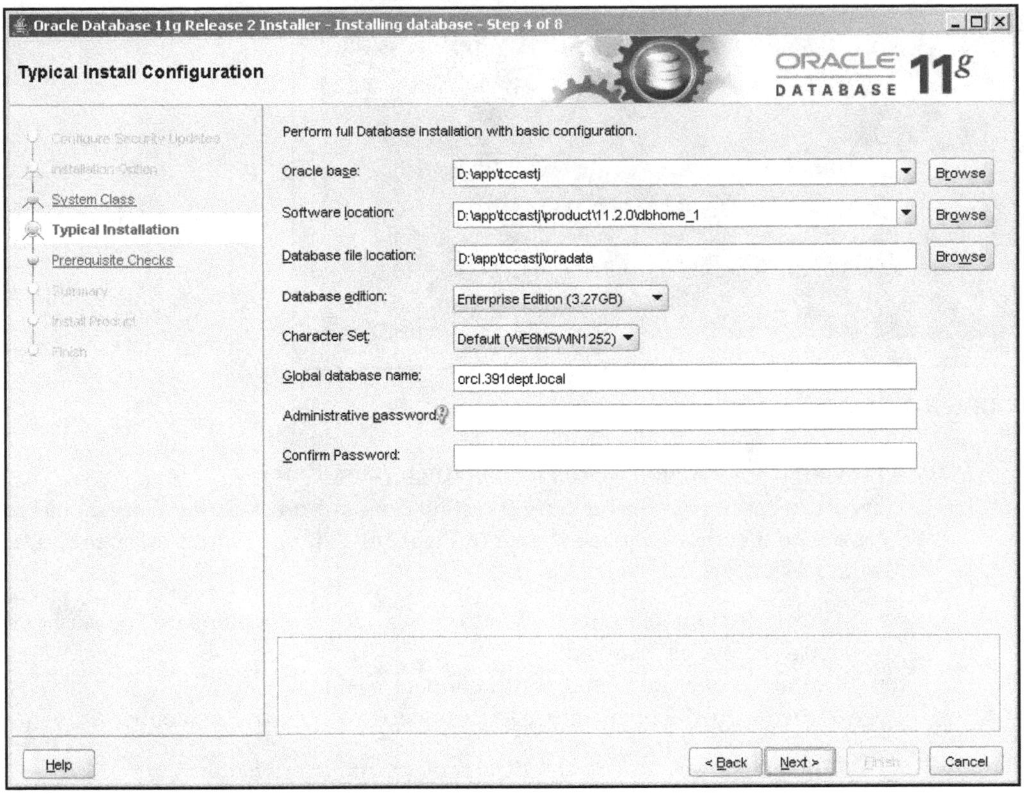

FIGURE B-3 The Typical Install Configuration window

TIP

Make sure you remember the global database name and password you set for the Oracle administrative login. The password is used for the SYSTEM and SYS administrative database accounts.

8. Click **Finish** to complete the installation.
9. When the installation is finished, you can check it by logging in with the command-line tool Oracle supplies. In Windows, click **Start**, **Oracle**, and then click **Application Development and SQL Plus**. Start SQL*Plus. Figure B-4 shows the command prompt window that opens.

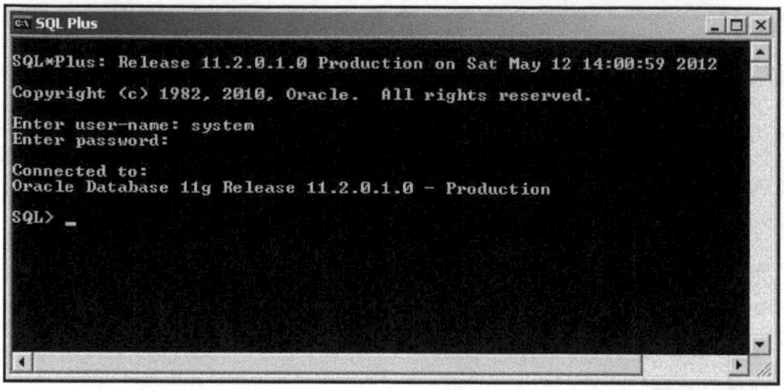

```
SQL Plus
SQL*Plus: Release 11.2.0.1.0 Production on Sat May 12 14:00:59 2012

Copyright (c) 1982, 2010, Oracle.  All rights reserved.

Enter user-name: system
Enter password:

Connected to:
Oracle Database 11g Release 11.2.0.1.0 - Production

SQL> _
```

FIGURE B-4 Starting SQL*Plus

10. Type **system** and your username, and then press **Enter**.
11. Type the password you set during installation and press **Enter**. You should get the connection message shown in Figure B-4. If you get an error message, do the following:
    - Check the Oracle items in Windows Services and make sure the service's status shows as "Started."
    - Restart your system and try to connect again.
    - Write down the error message and check with your instructor.
12. To disconnect, type **exit** at the SQL prompt and press **Enter**.

TIP

In most Oracle installations, Oracle services start automatically by default when the machine is started. If you're working on a multipurpose machine, you might want to change this setting to Manual in Windows Services and start the Oracle database only when it's needed. This setting also prevents any slowdown in system startup and application processing as you work on other tasks.

The following steps are for installing Oracle Database 11g Express Edition:

1. Review the installation guide on the OTN Web site. You should always verify the hardware and software requirements for an Oracle installation. The Database Quick installation guide is at *http://docs.oracle.com/cd/E11882_01/install.112/e24281/toc.htm*. Make sure your computer meets the following minimum requirements:
    - Hardware: 512 MB RAM and 1.5 GB free disk space
    - Software: Windows Server 2003, XP Professional, Server 2008 (Server Core option not supported), or Windows 7 (Professional, Enterprise, or Ultimate)

NOTE

You need to run this installation as an administrative user.

2. Start a Web browser, if necessary. Go to **www.oracle.com/technetwork/products/express-edition/downloads/index.html** and download the Oracle Express Edition for Windows. Accept the license agreement and then select the correct download file for your Windows version.

3. After the download is finished, unzip the file.
4. Move to the root folder and double-click the **Setup.exe** file to start the installation.
5. In the welcome window, click **Next**.
6. In the Choose Destination Location window, click the **Oracle Database 11g Express Edition** check box, if necessary (see Figure B-5). If you want to change the installation location, click the **Browse** button, navigate to and click a location, and then click **Next**.

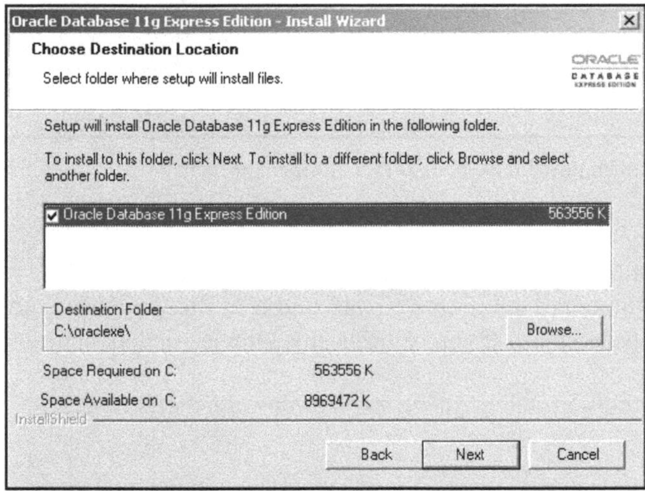

FIGURE B-5 Selecting an installation location

7. Next, enter your administrative password. (*Note*: Write down this password; you need it to manage the database.) This password is assigned to both the SYSTEM and SYS users.
8. Click **Next** to continue and finish the installation.
9. When the installation is finished, you can check it by logging in with the command-line tool Oracle supplies. In Windows, click **Start**, **Oracle Express**, and then click **Run SQL Command Line**. The command prompt window in Figure B-6 opens and displays an SQL> prompt to indicate that you're connected.

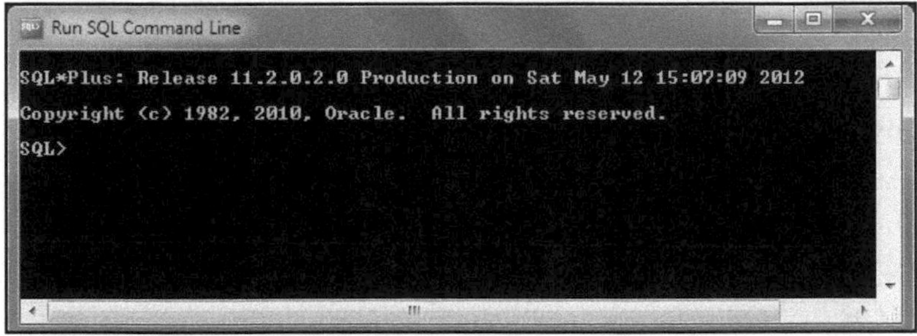

FIGURE B-6 Connecting to SQL*Plus

10. If you get an error message, do the following:
    - Check the Oracle items in Windows Services and make sure the service's status shows as "Started." You can also use the Stop and Start Database options in the Windows Start menu under Oracle Express.

- Restart your system and try to connect again.
- Write down the error message and check with your instructor.

11. To disconnect, type **exit** at the SQL prompt and press **Enter**.

TIP

As noted previously, most Oracle services start automatically by default when the machine is started. If you're working on a multipurpose machine, you might want to change this setting to Manual in Windows Services and start the Oracle database only when it's needed.

SQL DEVELOPER

The following sections explain installing and using SQL Developer.

Installation

SQL Developer is installed by default with the Oracle Database 11*g* Release 2 for Microsoft Windows Enterprise and Standard editions. You can find it in the Windows Start menu under Oracle Application Development. If you're using this Oracle version, skip to the next section.

If you're using Oracle Express Edition, follow these steps to download and install SQL Developer:

1. Start a Web browser, if necessary, and go to **www.oracle.com/technetwork/developer-tools/sql-developer/downloads/index.html**.
2. Accept the license agreement and select the correct download for your Oracle version: Oracle SQL Developer for 32-bit Windows. (This zip file includes the JDK1.6.0_11. Version 3.1.06 was used in writing this book.)
3. After the download is finished, unzip the file, which contains an `.exe` file for starting SQL Developer. In the sqldeveloper folder, double-click the **`sqldeveloper.exe`** file to start SQL Developer.

TIP

You might want to create a desktop shortcut for this `.exe` file.

Establishing a Database Connection

To access database objects, such as tables, you must establish a database connection first. Follow these steps:

1. Start Oracle SQL Developer. As Figure B-7 shows, the Connections pane is on the left. The first time you start SQL Developer, no connections are listed. You have to create connections and save them for later use.

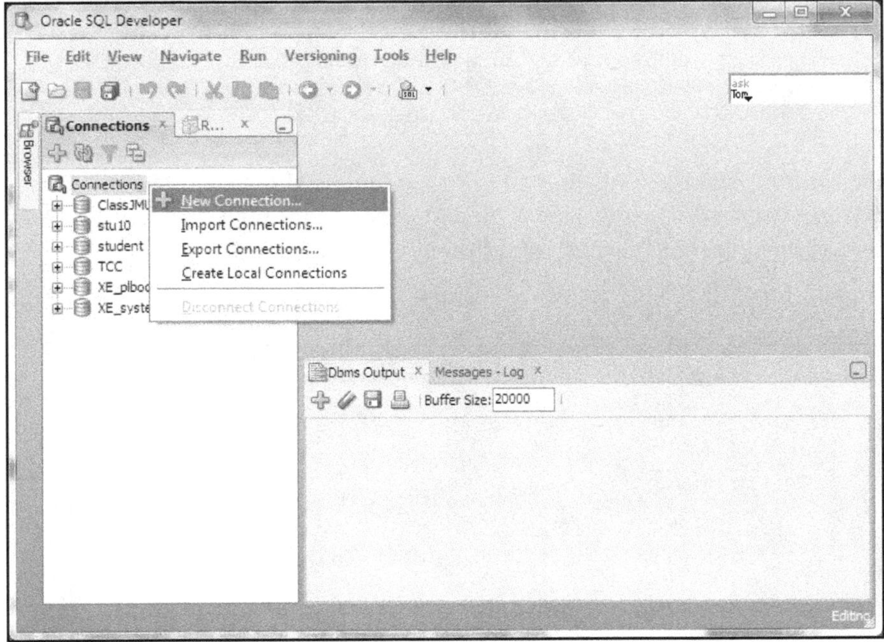

FIGURE B-7 The Connections pane in SQL Developer

2. Right-click the **Connections** node and click **New Connection**.
3. The New/Select Database Connection dialog box shown in Figure B-8 opens. The Basic connection type is selected by default. To establish the connection, enter the information shown in Figure B-8 but modify it as needed for your database. You can enter any connection name you like. Enter **system** for the username, and enter your administrative password. The default SID is orcl for the Enterprise Edition and xe for the Express Edition. If you're connecting to a provided Oracle server, your instructor will give you the required username and connection information.

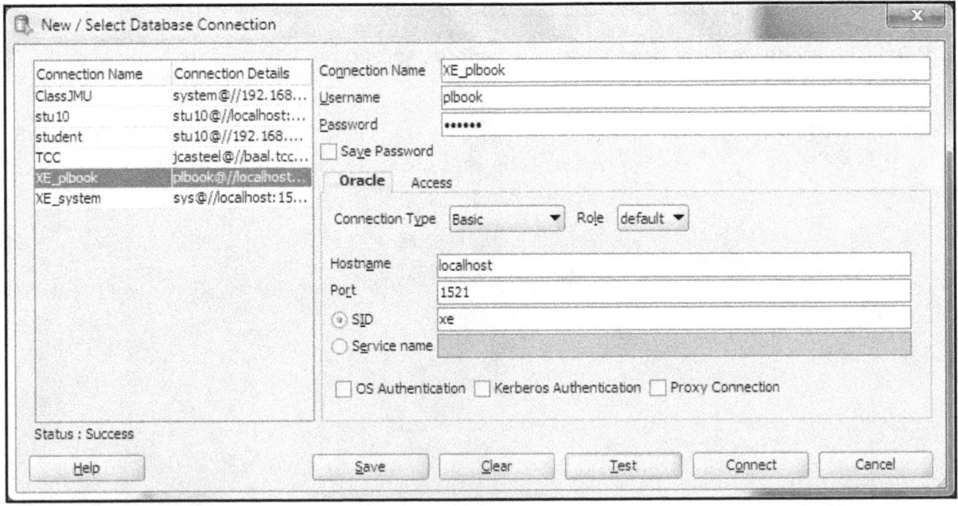

FIGURE B-8 Supplying connection information

NOTE

You can select other connection types, such as an Oracle TNS connection. The SQL Developer documentation has more information on these options.

After the connection has been made, you see the window shown in Figure B-9. Database objects are listed in the left pane. You can expand any node, such as Tables, to see a listing of objects in that category and find more details, such as columns in a table.

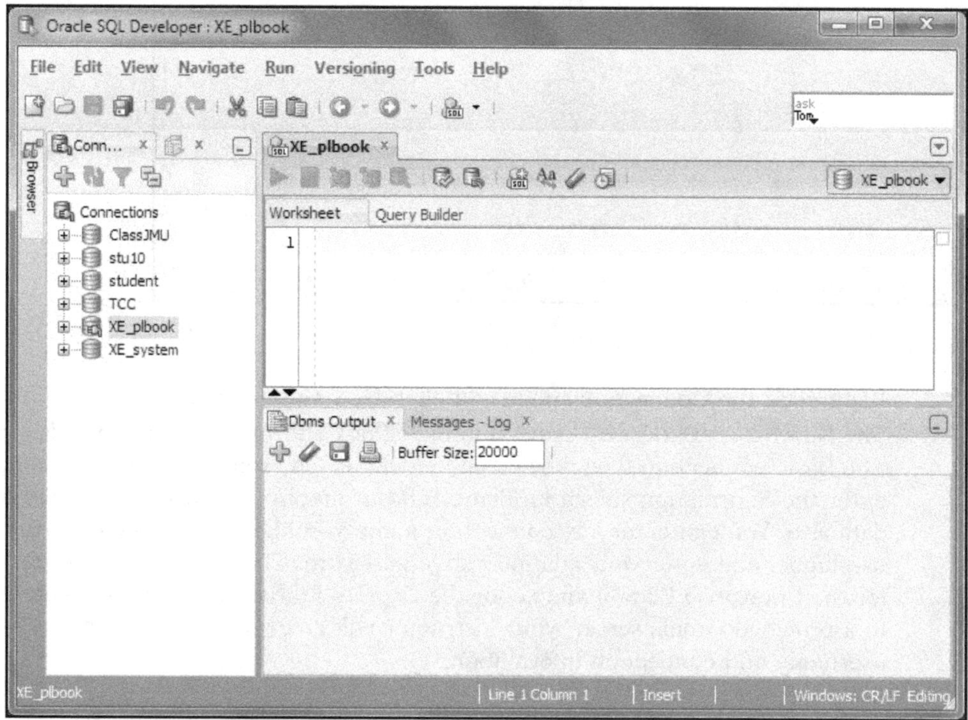

FIGURE B-9 The window after a connection has been established

When you select an object under a node, tabs in the right pane give you information on the object. As Figure B-10 shows, these tabs include data contents, indexes, and constraints for a table.

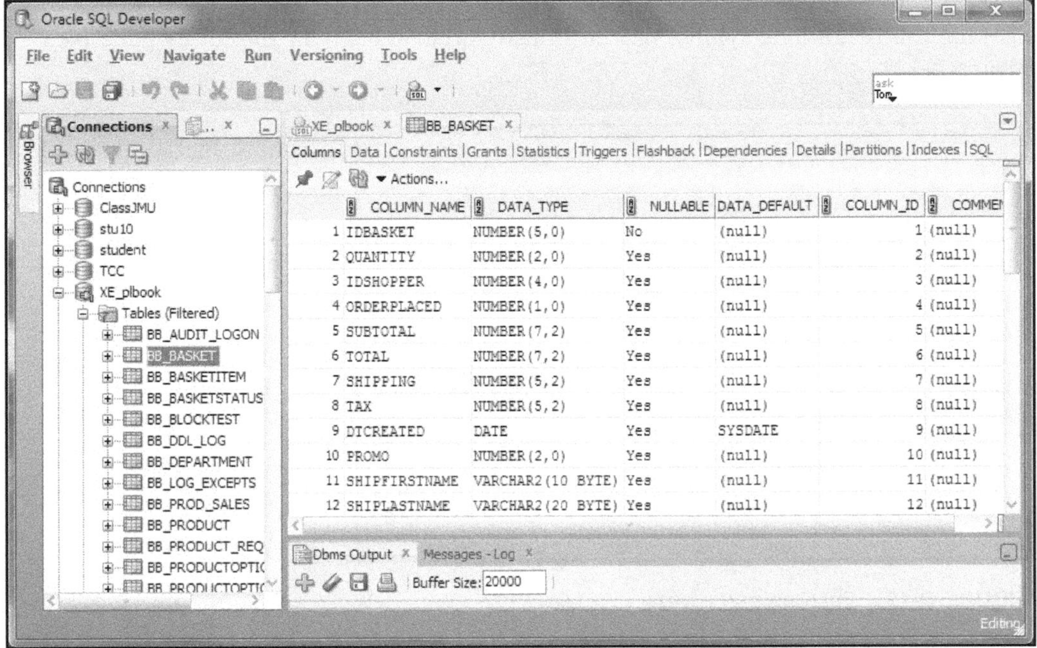

FIGURE B-10 Database object information

Executing Statements

The statement area is where you enter SQL statements or PL/SQL blocks. Figure B-11 shows entering an SQL statement. You click the Run button to run the statement and display output in the lower pane.

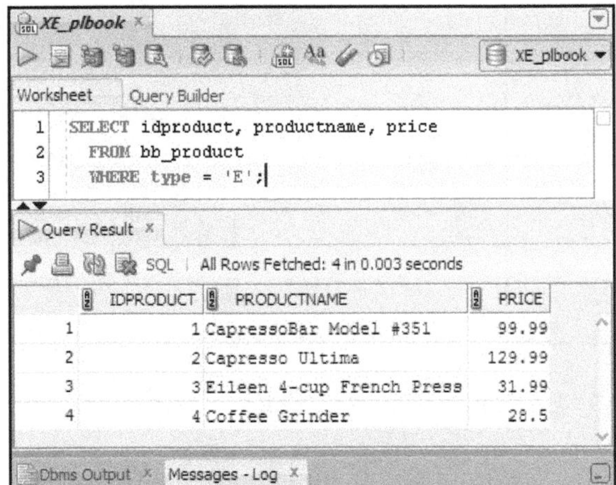

FIGURE B-11 Running an SQL statement

If you right-click the Output pane, you get the option to send the results to an external file, which is a quick way to export data for others to use in programs such as Microsoft Excel. In this same pane, you can enter PL/SQL blocks to run. If you use

DBMS_OUTPUT statements to display results, you need to enable this display by clicking the green plus symbol on the Dbms Output toolbar in the lower pane (see Figure B-12).

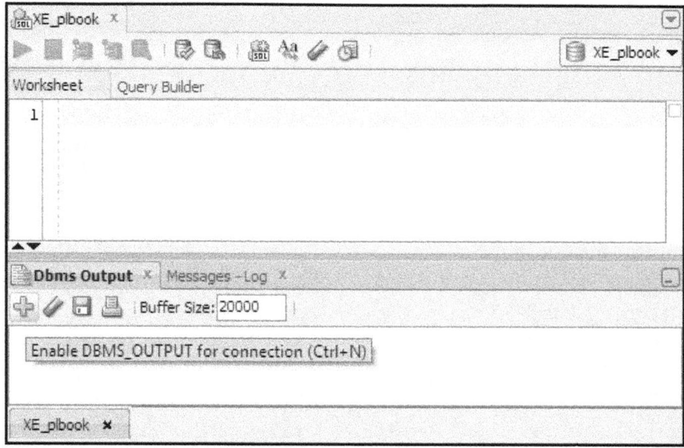

FIGURE B-12 Enabling DBMS_OUTPUT display

Figure B-13 shows entering a PL/SQL block. When you click the Run Script button, the output indicates a successful compilation or lists compilation errors. The DBMS_OUTPUT lines are displayed in the lower pane.

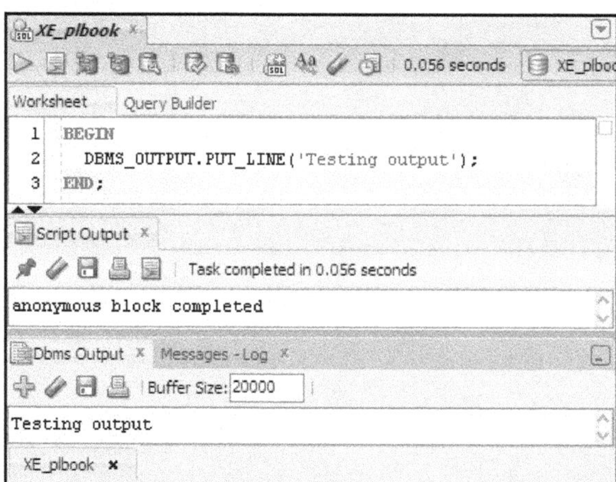

FIGURE B-13 Entering a PL/SQL statement

To create a new program unit, click File, New from the menu to open the Create a new dialog box shown in Figure B-14. After you select what type of object you want to create and click OK, a basic code template for this object is displayed in SQL Developer to give you a starting point for coding your program unit.

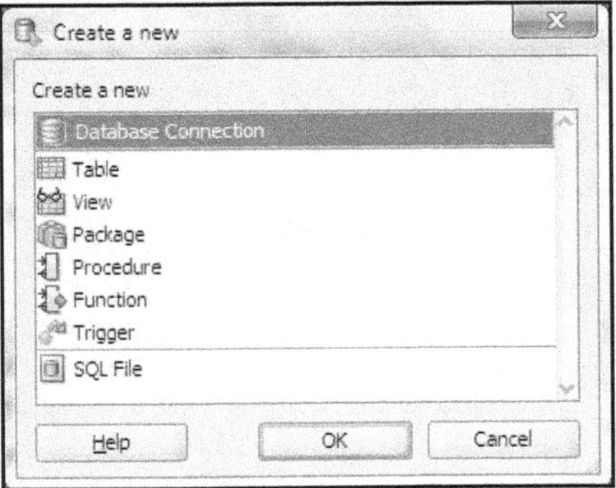

FIGURE B-14 Creating a program unit

To review and modify an existing program unit, expand a node in the Connections pane, such as Procedures, and then select the program unit (see Figure B-15). The program unit's code is displayed on the right in color-coded format. All PL/SQL keywords are shown in blue, for example. To modify a program unit, you can edit the code and click the Compile button.

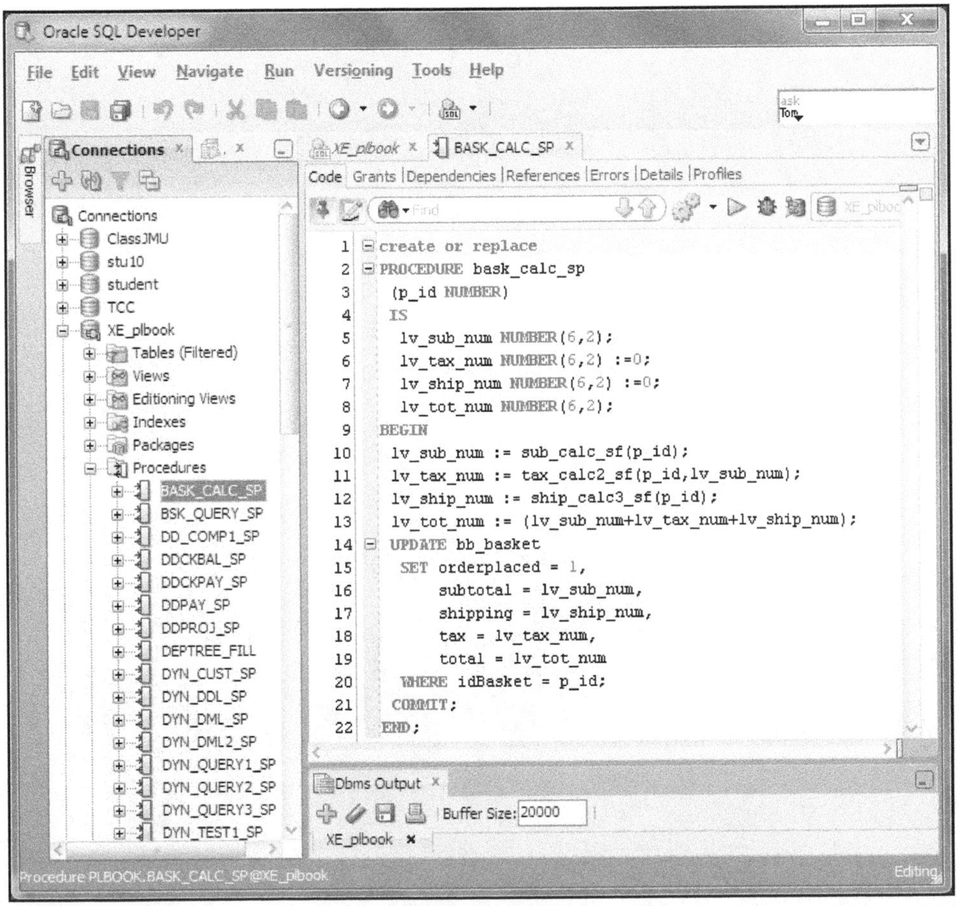

```
create or replace
PROCEDURE bask_calc_sp
 (p_id NUMBER)
 IS
  lv_sub_num NUMBER(6,2);
  lv_tax_num NUMBER(6,2) :=0;
  lv_ship_num NUMBER(6,2) :=0;
  lv_tot_num NUMBER(6,2);
BEGIN
 lv_sub_num := sub_calc_sf(p_id);
 lv_tax_num := tax_calc2_sf(p_id,lv_sub_num);
 lv_ship_num := ship_calc3_sf(p_id);
 lv_tot_num := (lv_sub_num+lv_tax_num+lv_ship_num);
 UPDATE bb_basket
  SET orderplaced = 1,
      subtotal = lv_sub_num,
      shipping = lv_ship_num,
      tax = lv_tax_num,
      total = lv_tot_num
  WHERE idBasket = p_id;
 COMMIT;
END;
```

FIGURE B-15 Selecting a program unit in the Connections pane

SUMMARY

This appendix has shown you how to get started with installing Oracle and using Oracle SQL Developer. Refer to documentation on the OTN Web site for more detailed information on installation and to learn more about SQL Developer. This tool offers more advanced features for PL/SQL development, including setting breakpoints during program unit debugging and viewing information during program execution, such as variable values.

GLOSSARY

actual parameters Values from an application that are passed to parameters when calling a program unit.

anchored data type A data type that's provided for database column values by using the `%TYPE` attribute in the variable declaration.

anonymous blocks Code blocks that aren't stored to be reused and, as far as the Oracle server is concerned, no longer exist after they run.

associative array A structure that can handle many rows of data but only one field; it's a set of key-value pairs in which each key uniquely identifies a value in the array. Also called a "PL/SQL table" or an "index-by table" in earlier Oracle versions.

autonomous transactions Transactions created in another transaction called a "parent transaction"; they can be treated independently of the parent transaction.

basic loop A looping structure that uses the `LOOP` and `END LOOP` markers to begin and end the loop code, which includes any statements to be repeated.

`CASE` expression An expression that evaluates conditions and returns a value in an assignment statement.

collection A composite data type that can store an ordered group of elements of the same type, with each element having a unique subscript or index; similar to arrays used in other languages.

compiler hint A request a programmer includes in code that asks Oracle to modify the default processing in some manner.

conditional predicates Clauses used in a trigger to handle different database-triggering events in a single trigger.

constraining table A table referenced via a foreign key constraint on the table a trigger is modifying.

control structures Statements used to control the flow of logic processing in programs. They make it possible to use conditional logic that determines which statements should run, how many times statements should run, and what the overall sequence of events should be.

correlation identifiers Special PL/SQL bind variables that refer to values associated with the DML action that fires a trigger. *See also* database trigger.

cursor A mechanism that represents a work area or section of memory where an SQL statement is processed in the Oracle server. It's a powerful method for handling multiple rows of data retrieved with an SQL query.

cursor variables References or pointers to a work area where a query can be processed; they make it possible to pass the results of queries more efficiently. *See also* cursor.

database link A pointer that instructs Oracle to look for a referenced object in a database instance other than the current connection.

database trigger A block of PL/SQL code that runs automatically when a particular database event occurs.

debugging The process of identifying errors in program code so that they can be removed.

definer rights A method of granting execute privileges for a package; the user assumes the program unit owner's rights *only* while that program unit is processing.

dependency tree utility An Oracle tool that creates a "map" showing both direct and indirect dependencies in the database. *See also* direct dependency *and* indirect dependencies.

direct dependency A relationship that occurs when one database object references other objects specifically. *See also* program unit dependencies.

dynamic SQL A variation of SQL that allows constructing and parsing statements at runtime.

event An action occurring in a program; can range from a user action, such as clicking a button, to a table UPDATE statement that calls a database trigger automatically.

exception handler A mechanism for trapping an error that occurs in processing. Its code handles the error in a user-friendly manner and allows the application to continue.

exception propagation The process of searching for an exception handler that matches an error. An exception raised in the executable section searches for a handler in this section first; if it doesn't find one, it moves to the enclosing block's EXCEPTION section to continue the search for a handler. *See also* exception handler.

explicit cursors Cursors declared and manipulated in PL/SQL code for handling rows returned by a SELECT statement. *See also* cursor.

FOR loop A loop that indicates how many times to iterate by including a range in the opening LOOP clause.

formal parameters Parameters listed in a procedure's declaration.

forward declaration A statement that declares a program unit in a package body by placing the header code at the top of the package body's code. *See also* package.

function A program unit that performs a task, can receive input values, and returns values to the calling environment. A function is part of an expression and can't serve as an entire statement.

global A characteristic of package constructs; means they can be used by any program unit and their values persist throughout a user session, so they can be referenced in code in different parts of the application during a session. *See also* package.

GOTO statement A statement that's sometimes called a "jumping control" because it instructs a program to "jump to" a specific area of the code. It can branch program logic so that only certain portions of code are processed (based on a condition). This technique should be used sparingly because it interrupts the flow of execution.

implicit cursors Cursors declared automatically for all DML and SELECT statements issued in a PL/SQL block. *See also* cursor.

indirect dependencies Relationships that involve references to database objects that reference other database objects, making the chain of dependencies harder to track. *See also* program unit dependencies.

infinite loop A loop that's never instructed to stop, so it continues looping indefinitely; causes program processing to stop at this point.

INSTEAD OF trigger A PL/SQL block that runs in place of a DML action on a database view.

invoker rights A method of granting execute privileges for a package; adding the AUTHID CURRENT_USER clause in the program unit's header forces use of the user's own privileges instead of the owner's privileges.

key-preserved table A table involved in a join; the original table's keys are included in the keys of the resulting join.

large objects (LOBs) Data types such as graphics and streaming video files; can hold up to 4 GB of data.

looping constructs Control structures that make it possible to repeat processing a block of code. *See also* control structures.

mode An indicator assigned to a parameter that specifies which way the value supplied for the parameter flows: into the program unit, out of the program unit, or both.

mutating table A table that's modified by a DML action when a trigger is fired.

named association A way of passing arguments used in a procedure call. The special symbol => is used to assign a value for each parameter by name in the calling statement.

named program unit A block of PL/SQL code that's named so that it can be saved (stored) and reused.

one-time-only procedure A packaged procedure that runs only once, when the package is first called.

overloading The capability to use the same name for multiple program units in the same package.

package A type of PL/SQL construct; a container that can hold multiple program units, such as procedures and functions.

package body The program unit containing the full code for all objects declared in the package specification. *See also* package.

package scope The range of visibility for a construct in a package. *See also* package.

package specification The required part of a package that declares the contents; referred to as the "package header." *See also* package.

parameters Mechanisms for sending values into and out of a program unit.

parsing The process of checking statement syntax.

passed by reference A technique for passing values between actual parameters and formal parameters; a pointer to the value in the actual parameter is created instead of copying the value from the actual parameter to the formal parameter. *See also* actual parameters *and* formal parameters.

passed by value A technique for passing values between actual parameters and formal parameters; the value is copied from the actual parameter to the formal parameter. *See also* actual parameters *and* formal parameters.

positional method A way of passing arguments used in a procedure call. When a procedure is called, values are listed in the order in which parameters are declared in the procedure.

`PRAGMA` statement A compiler directive that specifies using additional information that's supplied when compiling and running the block.

predefined exceptions Names associated with common Oracle errors.

private The scope for package elements that can be called only from other program units in the same package. *See also* package scope.

procedural language A language programmers use to code a logical sequence of steps for making decisions and instructing a computer to perform tasks.

program A set of instructions requesting the computer to perform specific actions; sometimes used to support a system or an application.

program unit dependencies The interrelationships of objects as they relate to procedures, functions, and packages.

programming language A language that converts users' actions into instructions a computer can understand.

public The scope for elements declared in a package specification, meaning they can be referenced from outside the package. *See also* package scope.

purity level A way to describe how a function affects database tables and package variables in terms of reading and modifying values.

record A composite data type that can store and handle multiple values or fields (each having its own name and data type) as one unit; similar to the structure of a row in a database table.

remote database connections Connections that link to another database and use or call objects in it.

remote databases Connections to other Oracle database servers.

row-level trigger A trigger that's fired for each row the DML statement affects. *See also* database trigger.

scalar variables Variables that can hold a single value. *See also* variables.

searched `CASE` statement A method for checking conditions; it doesn't use a selector but checks conditions placed in `WHEN` clauses separately that must evaluate to a Boolean value of `TRUE` or `FALSE`.

signature model A method of checking remote dependencies; compares the mode, data type, and order of parameters to determine whether invalidation has occurred.

Simple Mail Transfer Protocol (SMTP) The protocol used to send e-mail across networks and the Internet.

statement-level trigger A trigger that's fired only once for a DML action, regardless of the number of rows affected. *See also* database trigger.

stored program units PL/SQL modules that are saved in the database; they can be shared and used by many applications. *See also* named program unit.

subprogram *See* named program unit.

system triggers Triggers that are fired by database events, such as startup and shutdown, and server error messages.

table attributes Functions that can be used with table variables and give you more capability to manipulate table values. *See also* associative array.

table methods *See* table attributes.

table of records A type of collection similar to a record data type except that it can handle more than one record or row of data. *See also* collection.

timestamp model A method of checking remote dependencies; compares objects' last modification date and time to determine whether invalidation has occurred.

undefined exception An unnamed Oracle error; you must declare an exception and associate an Oracle error number with it.

user-defined exception An exception that a developer raises in a block to enforce a business rule.

user event triggers Triggers that are fired by users performing database actions, such as logons and logoffs, and issuing DML or DDL statements.

variables Named memory areas that hold values so that they can be retrieved and manipulated in programs.

variable scope Specifies the area of a block that can identify a particular variable.

`WHILE` loop A loop that includes a condition to check at the top of the loop in the `LOOP` clause. The condition is checked in each iteration of the loop.

INDEX

A

B

C

D

E

F

G

H

I

J

K

L

M

N

O

Q

R

S

T

W

X

Z

CPSIA information can be obtained
at www.ICGtesting.com
Printed in the USA
FFHW012355200519
52583445-58046FF